Teacher Companion

CW01460757

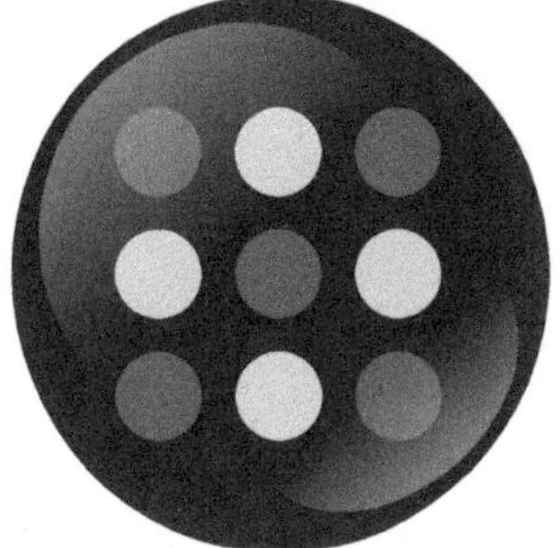

MyMaths
for Key Stage 3

2C

Powered by MyMaths.co.uk

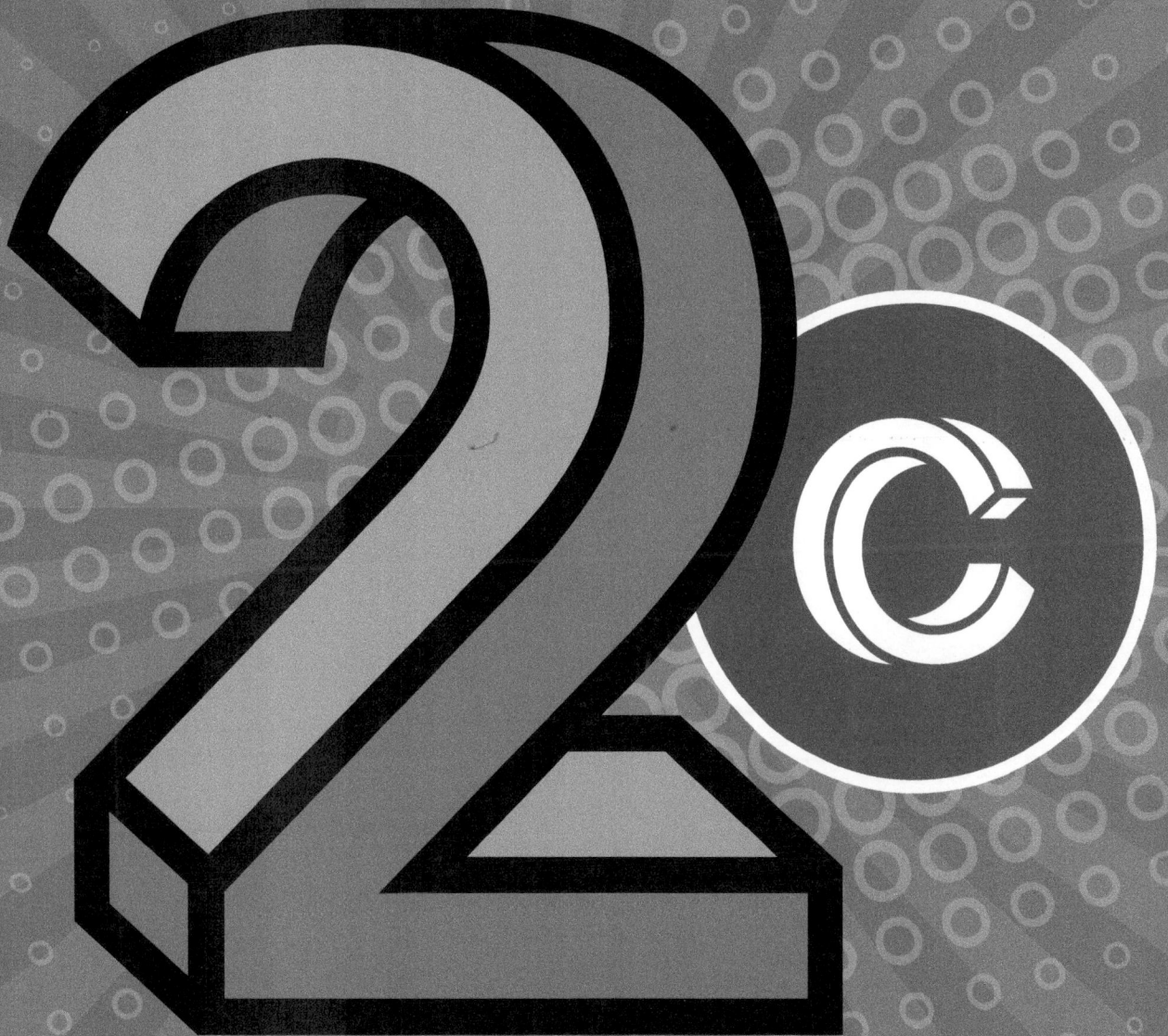

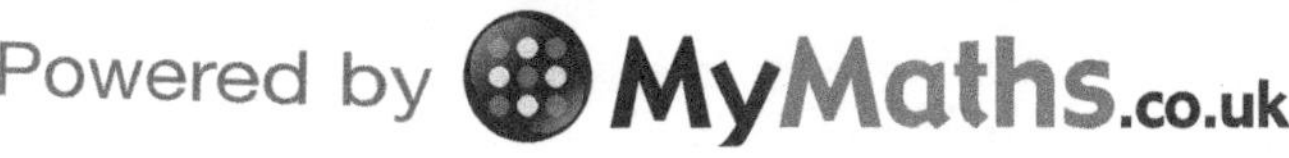

OXFORD UNIVERSITY PRESS

Great Clarendon Street, Oxford, OX2 6DP, United Kingdom

Oxford University Press is a department of the University of Oxford. It furthers the University's objective of excellence in research, scholarship, and education by publishing worldwide. Oxford is a registered trade mark of Oxford University Press in the UK and in certain other countries.

First published in 2014

British Library Cataloguing in Publication Data
Data available

978-0-19-830461-6

10 9

Paper used in the production of this book is a natural, recyclable product made from wood grown in sustainable forests. The manufacturing process conforms to the environmental regulations of the country of origin.

Printed in Great Britain by CPI Group (UK) Ltd., Croydon CR0 4YY

Acknowledgements

The editors would like to thank John Atkins, Katie Wood and Ian Bettison for their excellent work on this book.

Contents

About this book

This Teacher Companion is part of the MyMaths for Key Stage 3 series which has been specially written for the new National Curriculum for Key Stage 3 Mathematics in England. It accompanies Student Book **2C** and is designed to help you have the greatest impact on the learning experience of higher ability students in the middle of their Key Stage 3 studies.

The author team collectively brings a wealth of classroom experience to the Teacher Companion making it easy for you to plan and deliver lessons with confidence.

The structure of this book closely follows the content of the student book so that it is easy to find the information and resources you need. These include for each

Lesson: objectives; a list of resources – including MyMaths 4-digit codes; a starter, teaching notes, plenary and alternative approach; simplification and extension ideas; an exercise commentary and full answers; the key ideas and checkpoint questions to test them; and a summary of the key literacy issues.

Chapter: National Curriculum objectives; any assumed prior knowledge; notes supporting the Student Book introduction and starter problem; the associated MyMaths and InvisiPen resources – including those offering extra support to weaker students; questions to test understanding; and how the material is developed and used.

The accompanying CD-ROM makes all the lesson plans available as Word files, so that you can customise them to suit your students' needs. Also on the CD are full sets of answers for Homework Book **2C**.

The integrated solution

This teacher guide is part of a set of resources designed to support you and your students with a fully integrated package of resources.

MyMaths

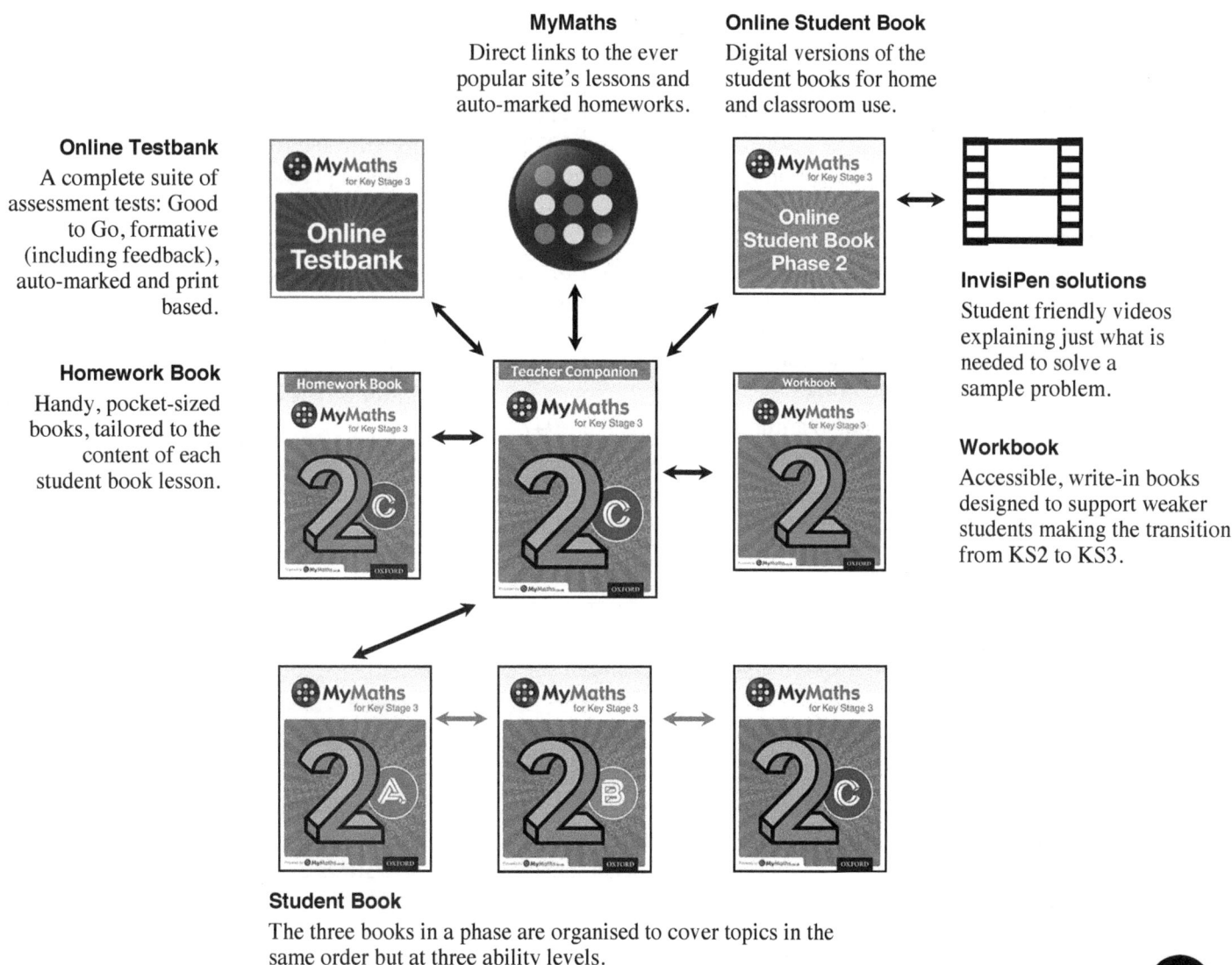

Direct links to the ever popular site's lessons and auto-marked homeworks.

Online Student Book

Digital versions of the student books for home and classroom use.

Online Testbank

A complete suite of assessment tests: Good to Go, formative (including feedback), auto-marked and print based.

Homework Book

Handy, pocket-sized books, tailored to the content of each student book lesson.

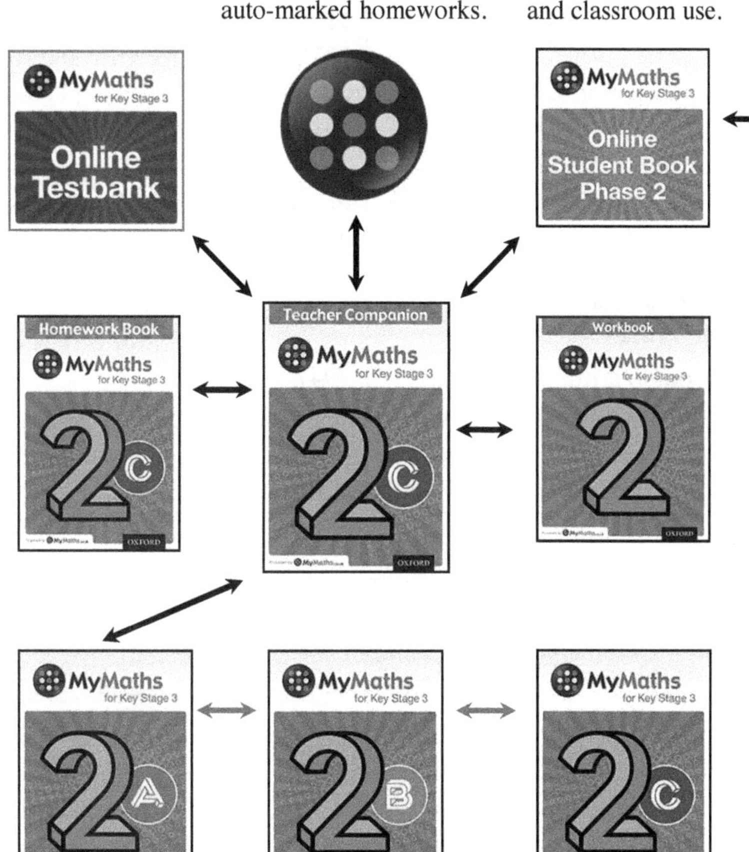

InvisiPen solutions

Student friendly videos explaining just what is needed to solve a sample problem.

Workbook

Accessible, write-in books designed to support weaker students making the transition from KS2 to KS3.

Student Book

The three books in a phase are organised to cover topics in the same order but at three ability levels.

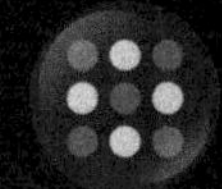

1 Whole numbers and decimals

Learning outcomes		
N1	Understand and use place value for decimals, measures and integers of any size	(L6)
N3	Use the concepts and vocabulary of prime numbers, factors (or divisors), multiples, common factors, common multiples, highest common factor, lowest common multiple, prime factorisation, including using product notation and the unique factorisation property	(L6)
N5	Use conventional notation for the priority of operations, including brackets, powers, roots and reciprocals	(L6)
N7	Use integer powers and associated real roots (square, cube and higher), recognise powers of 2, 3, 4, 5 and distinguish between exact representations of roots and their decimal approximations	(L6)
N13	Round numbers and measures to an appropriate degree of accuracy (for example, to a number of decimal places or significant figures)	(L6)

Introduction

The chapter starts by revising factors and multiples, including divisibility tests. Prime factor decomposition and finding LCMs and HCFs are then covered along with square and cube roots before a section on indices. Rounding and estimation is covered before finally square and cube roots found either by calculator or trial-and-improvement.

The introduction discusses sending sensitive information, such as credit card details, over the internet where there is a risk that it can be intercepted. The first step is to convert any message into a number, say using ASCII codes. The number is then encrypted to turn it into apparent gibberish that can only be decrypted using a secret key. The difficulty is in giving enough information to encrypt a message without making it obvious how to decrypt the message.

One solution called public key encryption is RSA, named after Rivest, Shamir and Adleman. This involves sending, via the internet, two numbers, e and N, to allow a message to be encrypted. The trick is that the decryption requires N to be factored into two primes. N is typically 100 digits long and factorising such large numbers is ferociously difficult making the encryption practically unbreakable if you don't already know the two primes.

The technical details involve modulo arithmetic and Fermat's little theorem. A discussion is available here

http://www.claymath.org/publications/posters/primes-go-forever

Prior knowledge

Students should already know how to...

- Identify factors and multiples
- Use place value with integers and decimals
- Use a calculator for simple sums

Starter problem

The starter problem leads naturally to discussing factorisation and prime numbers. In testing n for primality, $\sqrt{n}$ provides a cut-off on numbers to test.

All primes (after 2 and 3) fall into the pattern $6n + 1$ or $6n - 1$ (or $6n + 5$). These are the numbers that remain in the sieve of Eratosthenes after striking out multiples of 2 and 3. (Numbers of the form $6n$, $6n + 2$, $6n + 3$ and $6n + 4$ have obvious factors of 2 or 3.)

The formula $n^2 - n + 41$, was proposed by Euler in 1772. It works for all values of n from 1 to 40. (Thought of as a finite quadratic sequence the differences between the primes generated, 41, 43, 47, 53, 61..., are 2, 4, 6, 8, ...)

Primes of the form $2^n - 1$, where n must itself be prime, are named after the French friar Marin Mersenne who studied them in the seventeenth century. The formula works for $n = 2, 3, 5, 7, 13, 17, 19$ and 31 but not for, say, $n = 11$ when it gives $2047 = 23 \times 89$.

The current largest prime is a Mersenne prime $M_{57\,885\,161} = 2^{57\,885\,161} - 1 = 5.81887266... \times 10^{17\,425\,170}$. How many digits does it have? (17 425 170)

Resources

MyMaths

Decimal places	1001	Factors and primes	1032	Indices 1	1033
LCM	1034	Multiples	1035	HCF	1044
Squares and cubes	1053	Trial and improvement	1057	Error intervals	1968

Online assessment

Chapter test	2C-1
Formative test	2C-1
Summative test	2C-1

InvisiPen solutions

Rounding	112	Estimating and approx	135
HCF and LCM	172	Primes and prime factors	173
Prime factor decomposition	174	Powers and roots	181
Indices	184	Indices	221

Topic scheme

Teaching time = 7 lessons/3 weeks

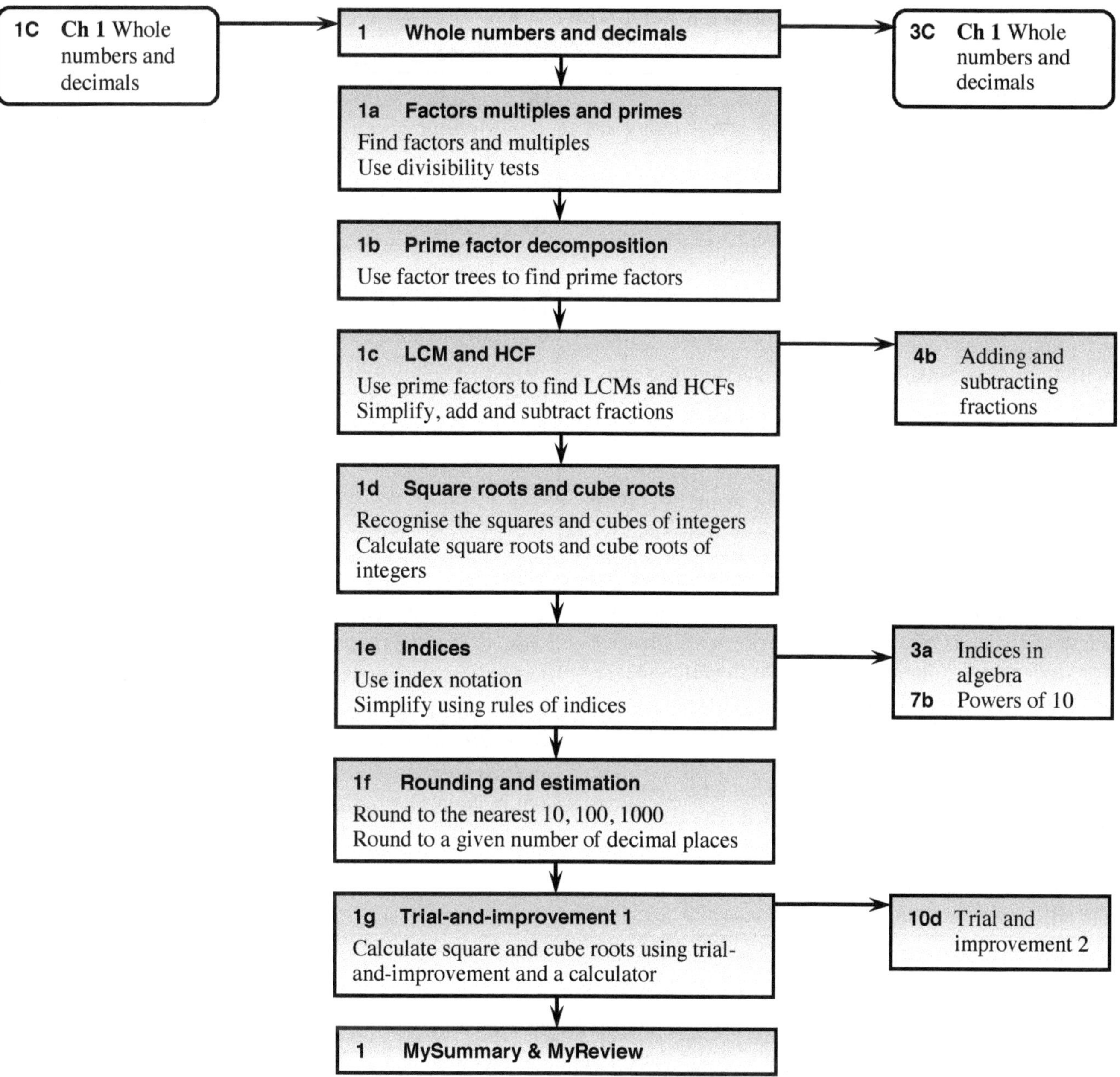

1C Ch 1 Whole numbers and decimals
1 Whole numbers and decimals
3C Ch 1 Whole numbers and decimals
1a Factors multiples and primes
Find factors and multiples
Use divisibility tests
1b Prime factor decomposition
Use factor trees to find prime factors
1c LCM and HCF
Use prime factors to find LCMs and HCFs
Simplify, add and subtract fractions
4b Adding and subtracting fractions
1d Square roots and cube roots
Recognise the squares and cubes of integers
Calculate square roots and cube roots of integers
1e Indices
Use index notation
Simplify using rules of indices
3a Indices in algebra
7b Powers of 10
1f Rounding and estimation
Round to the nearest 10, 100, 1000
Round to a given number of decimal places
1g Trial-and-improvement 1
Calculate square and cube roots using trial-and-improvement and a calculator
10d Trial and improvement 2
1 MySummary & MyReview

Differentiation

Student book 2A 2 – 23

Negative numbers
Multiples and factors
Common factors
Prime numbers
Ordering decimal numbers
Rounding
Square numbers
Square numbers and square roots

Student book 2B 2 – 23

Integers and decimals
Multiplying and dividing integers
Multiples and factors
Prime numbers
LCM and HCF
Squares and cubes
Square roots
Cube roots

Student book 2C 2 – 21

Factors, multiples and primes
Prime factor decomposition
LCM and HCF
Square roots and cube roots
Indices
Rounding and estimation
Trial-and-improvement 1

1a Factors multiples and primes

Objectives

- Use factors and primes (L5)
- Extend mental methods of calculation, working with factors (L5)

Key ideas

1 Divisibility tests can be used to find factors

Resources

Factors and primes (1032)
Multiples (1035)

List of integers: 10 000 to 10 050
Examples of each divisibility test

Simplification

Provide students with an example of each divisibility test to help with applying them for question **1**.

Use a strict approach to listing the factors in one line, with large gaps, smallest and largest at opposite ends. This will help students not to miss any factors. Ask: How do you know when you can stop searching for factors? Use 36 as an example. Is 6 is the last one to check? Why is this? Explore what is meant by square root.

Extension

How long would it take to write out the largest known prime number if you did not have to work it out, just copy it? Students could use a calculator or estimate without a calculator. Use the example in the student book of 12 978 189 digits. Between 2 and 4 months. How can students estimate the speed that they can write down digits?

Literacy

A quick check of understanding of 'factor', 'sum of digits' and 'divisibility' (which may be a little harder for students to explain) would be worthwhile. So would a discussion of the difference between 'to divide a number exactly', 'to divide into a number exactly' and 'to be divided exactly by a number', the first of which is a non-standard and somewhat ambiguous phrasing that is probably best avoided.

Note the different phrasing for the divisibility rules for 3 and 9; again, discussion might clarify both the specific rules and the general concepts.

Links

Bring in some dictionaries for the class to use. The word *divisibility* has five i's, the word *indivisibilities* has seven. Ask the class to find other words with at least four i's. Some examples include *infinitesimal* (4), *impossibilities* (5), *invisibility* (5) and *indistinguishability* (6). The dictionary will probably not include *supercalifragilisticexpialidocious* (7)!

Alternative approach

For divisibility by 11 (which appears in question **3**), with three-digit numbers, the test would be whether the middle digit is the sum of the two other digits. This is a rule that can probably be fairly easily both spotted, and established by reasoning, by students, rather than simply given to them. They may then like to consider trying to extend this divisibility rule for 11 for larger numbers, again as in question **3**, and perhaps be helped towards an identification of the word missing ('sign' between 'alternating' and 'sum') from the divisibility rule given.

Similarly, the reason for the divisibility rule for 4 (that each 100 is divisible by 4) could be extended to simplify the divisibility rule given for 8 (since each 1000 is divisible by 8, only the last three digits need be considered).

Note that many modern calculators will give the prime factorisation of a number.

Checkpoint

1 All of these numbers have only 4 factors. What are they?

a 1203 **b** 6193 **c** 6839 **d** 15 815

(**a** 1, 3, 401, 1203 **b** 1, 11, 563, 6193 **c** 1, 7, 977, 6839 **d** 1, 5, 3163, 15 815)

Starter

Ask students to write down questions where the answer is -1.2. Score 1 point for an addition question, 2 points for a subtraction question, 3 for a multiplication or division question.

Teaching notes

Ask the students how they can tell if a number divides exactly by 2, 5 or 10. Do students know any ways of telling if a number divides by other numbers? Introduce the divisibility tests and try one of them. Which do students think is the most complex?

Define the term **factor**. Show how listing a number's factors in pairs quickly helps complete the set of all factors. How will you know when you have them all? Listing factors in ascending order from two different ends is very helpful.

Which of these statements define prime numbers?

- an odd number but not 3, 9, 15, 21, etc.
- a number with exactly two factors
- a number whose factors are only 1 and itself.

Perform a divisibility test on 157 (prime); why don't you have to check beyond 12?

Plenary

Could the knowledge about primes gained from question **8** help in answering question **6**? All the numbers turn out to be multiples of 6 ± 1, so does this mean they are all prime? Challenge students to give an example where a multiple of 6 ± 1 is not prime. (25 is the lowest number).

Exercise commentary

Question 1 – Draw attention to the way in which a new pair of factors can be produced by doubling one factor and by halving the other, and so on.

Question 2 – Question can be answered orally.

Question 3 – Use the divisibility tests to check each potential factor, as far as possible. Challenge students about alternative ways to check a factor, short division or subtracting known multiples of the factor.

Question 4 – List factors in pairs. A calculator could be used since these are time consuming.

Question 5 – A calculator could be used. Students may suggest 221 is prime because none of listed divisibility tests work, but $221 = 13 \times 17$.

Question 6 – Provide students with a printed grid of integers 10 000 to 10 050 and encourage elimination of multiples of 2, 3, 5, etc. (as in the sieve of Eratosthenes). For those left, use a calculator to check for factors from a list of primes up to 100.

Question 7 – Centred hexagonal numbers, $3n(n-1)+1$. Make sure students look at how the sum is built up, not just the total. They appear to be primes, but the 8th term is 169 (13^2).

Question 8 – The sieve of Eratosthenes implies all primes are in fact a multiple of 6 ± 1, apart from 2 and 3.

Answers

1 **a** $1 \times 18, 2 \times 9, 3 \times 6$
b $1 \times 20, 2 \times 10, 4 \times 5$
c $1 \times 30, 2 \times 15, 3 \times 10, 5 \times 6$
d $1 \times 35, 5 \times 7$

2 **a** 3, 6, 9, 12, 15 **b** 5, 10, 15, 20, 25
c 7, 14, 21, 28, 35 **d** 8, 16, 24, 32, 40
e 11, 22, 33, 44, 55 **f** 15, 30, 45, 60, 75

3 **a** Yes $385 \div 5 = 77$
b No $746 \div 3 = 248$ r 2
c No $164 \div 7 = 23$ r 3
d Yes $3234 \div 11 = 294$
e No $458 \div 12 = 38$ r 2
f Yes $2010 \div 15 = 134$
g Yes $1926 \div 18 = 107$
h Yes $2712 \div 24 = 113$

4 **a** 1, 2, 4, 5, 10, 20, 23, 46, 92, 115, 230, 460
b 1, 2, 3, 4, 6, 8, 9, 12, 16, 18, 24, 27, 32, 36, 48, 54, 72, 96, 108, 144, 216, 288, 432, 864
c 1, 5, 25, 125, 625
d 1, 2, 3, 4, 6, 7, 11, 12, 14, 21, 22, 28, 33, 42, 44, 66, 77, 84, 132, 154, 231, 308, 462, 924
e 1, 2, 4, 8, 16, 32, 64, 128, 256, 512, 1024
f 1, 5, 7, 25, 35, 49, 175, 245, 1225

5 **a** Yes
b No $161 \div 7 = 23$
c No $221 \div 13 = 17$
d Yes
e No $301 \div 7 = 43$
f Yes

6 10 007, 10 009, 10 037, 10 039

7 **a** 1, 7, 19, 37
b 61, 91
c All prime numbers except 1.
d $T(n) = 3n^2 - 3n + 1$ generates more prime numbers: $T(7) = 127, T(8) = 169 = 13^2, T(9) = 217 = 7 \times 31, T(10) = 271, \ldots$

8 **a** $6n + 1$: $7, 13, 19, 25 = 5 \times 5, 31, 37, 43, 49 = 7 \times 7, \ldots$
b $6n - 1$: $5, 11, 17, 23, 29, 35 = 5 \times 7, 41, 47, \ldots$
All primes, other that 2 and 3, fall into one of these two sequences.
c $n^2 - n + 41$: $41, 43, 47, 53, 61, 71, \ldots$
Found by Euler; first fails for $n = 41$ (gives 41^2)
d $2^n - 1$: $M_2 = 3, M_3 = 7, M_5 = 31, M_7 = 127, M_{13} = 8191, M_{19} = 524\,287, M_{31} = 2\,147\,483\,647, \ldots$

1b Prime factor decomposition

Objectives

- Find the prime factor decomposition of a number (L5)
- Use the prime factor decomposition of a number (L6)
- Use index notation for integer powers (L5)

Key ideas

1 Numbers can be written as a product of their prime factors

2 This version of a number can be used to find the complete list of its factors

Resources

HCF (1044)

Simplification

When finding prime factor decompositions, encourage students to check that the numbers at the ends of the branches are in the prime number list. Give the list of primes from 2 to 11.

Extension

What is the prime factor decomposition of 1 trillion? Hint that you could first try 10, then 100, then 1000 etc. What about a googol (10^{100}) and a googolplex (10^{google})?

Literacy

Is the first statement true?

The term decomposition, as in breaking down, should be discussed. So should the combination of prime number with factor, to produce the idea of prime factors.

Ask students if they can see any point in the 'two' in the sentence between the first and second examples.

Links

A message broadcast by the Arecibo radio telescope in 1974 consisted of 1679 0s and 1s, or bits. An alien trying to decipher the message would need to identify the prime factors of 1679, arrange the characters in a 23 × 73 rectangle and replace each 0 by a blank space and each 1 by a solid space. The deciphered message forms a picture showing the integers from 1–10, the chemical make-up of DNA, a stick man, a diagram of the solar system and an image of the telescope. There is a picture of the deciphered message at http://en.wikipedia.org/wiki/Arecibo_message

Alternative approach

When using repeated division, continue until 1 is reached. The list of factors is then all in the same place on the left. This is also helpful later when finding HCFs and LCMs.

The number of factors can be given by the product of the various numbers of each prime factor there can be; for example, with $140 = 2^2 \times 5 \times 7$, there can be 0, 1, or 2 twos (so, three different numbers of them), 0 or 1 fives (so, two different numbers of them), and 0 or 1 sevens (so, two different numbers of them). Hence, $3 \times 2 \times 2 =$ 12 factors in all. This can be a useful check that no factors have been omitted, in addition to the pairing of factors.

Note that we are not interested in negative numbers here, only the decomposition of the absolute values. However, students could be asked where the negative would go, if we were dealing with the decomposition of a negative. And then, of course, they might be encouraged to realise that there could be many negatives in the decomposition … and how they can be considered as being paired … and then of how there will need to be an odd number of negatives, if decomposing a negative, and an even number, if decomposing a positive.

Note that many modern calculators will give the prime factorisation of a number. This could be helpful here, but needs to be used with intelligence.

Checkpoint

1 Write each of these numbers as the product of its prime factors.

a 118 800 ($2^4 \times 3^3 \times 5^2 \times 11$)

b 659 736 ($2^3 \times 3^2 \times 7^2 \times 11 \times 17$)

Starter

Throw three dice and ask students to make one number between 1 and 15 inclusive using all three scores and any operation(s). Throw again; students make another number between 1 and 15. Repeat until all the numbers have been made by a student.

Teaching notes

Challenge students to find the prime factors of a number. How can the number be made by multiplying these prime factors? Can every integer be written as the product (multiplication) of prime factors? Not -1, 0, 1.

Look at two methods for finding the product of prime factors. A factor tree and repeated division. Which method is easier? Does it depend on the number you are starting with? Ask students for a strategy to break down large numbers quickly. Ask why this method might be called prime factor decomposition. Decompose means breaking down into pieces.

Ask how having the product of prime factors can help in the finding of all the factors of a number. In the example in the student book of 140, how can you list the combinations of prime factors in an organised way to ensure no factor is missed?

Plenary

Look at the number sequence 2, 6, 30, 210. Challenge students to find the next two numbers in the sequence; no calculators allowed (2310, 30 030). After a few minutes give students the hint that they should try to write each term as the product of its prime factors. (2, 2×3, $2 \times 3 \times 5$, $2 \times 3 \times 5 \times 7$). How many terms would you need to find before you had a value over one billion? Encourage students to use estimates, for example, $30\,000 \times 20 \times 20 \times 20 \times 30$ when multiplying by 17, 19, 23 and 29 (ten terms).

Exercise commentary

Question 1 – Students may need reminding about index notation.

Question 2 – Challenge students to work in pairs. One student to use repeated division, the other to use the factor tree. Which process works best?

Question 3 – Encourage use of a calculator to check for the error. Ask students if they would have decomposed the number differently.

Question 4 – Ask students to derive a method of listing all the factors from prime factors.

Question 5 – The rule is add one to each index and find the product.

Question 6 – Don't allow students to use calculators, to encourage greater thought of what solution could be.

Question 7 – There are only 13 possible solutions.

Answers

1 **a** 60 **b** 28 **c** 90 **d** 700
e 220 **f** 252 **g** 104 **h** 1764
i 4200 **j** 880

2 **a** 2×3^2 **b** $2 \times 3 \times 7$
c $2^4 \times 5$ **d** 2×3^3
e 2^7 **f** $2^2 \times 3 \times 5 \times 7$
g $2^3 \times 5^2$ **h** $5^2 \times 7$
i $2^3 \times 3^2 \times 5$ **j** $2^5 \times 3 \times 5$
k $2^6 \times 3^2$ **l** $2^3 \times 3^3 \times 5$
m $2^3 \times 3^2 \times 5 \times 7$ **n** $2^4 \times 3^4$
o $3^4 \times 5^2$

3 **a** $9 \times 13 = 117$ not 126
$55 \times 49 = 2695$ not 2646
b $12\,600 = 2^3 \times 3^2 \times 5^2 \times 7$
$26\,460 = 2^2 \times 3^3 \times 5 \times 7^2$
c Students' answers

4 **a** 1, 2, 4, 5, 8, 10, 16, 20, 40, 80
b 1, 2, 3, 4, 5, 6, 9, 10, 12, 15, 18, 20, 30, 36, 45, 60, 90, 180
c 1, 2, 3, 5, 6, 9, 10, 15, 18, 25, 30, 45, 50, 75, 90, 150, 225, 450
d 1, 2, 3, 5, 6, 10, 11, 15, 22, 30, 33, 55, 66, 110, 165, 330
e 1, 2, 3, 5, 6, 7, 10, 14, 15, 21, 30, 35, 42, 49, 70, 98, 105, 147, 210, 245, 294, 490, 735, 1470
f 1, 2, 4, 5, 8, 10, 20, 25, 40, 50, 100, 125, 200, 250, 500, 1000

5 **a** 3 **b** 4 **c** 5 **d** 3
e 4 **f** 5 **g** 9 **h** 12

6 **a** $2 \times 3 \times 5 = 30$, $2^2 \times 3 \times 5 = 60$, $2 \times 3^2 \times 5 = 90$, $2^3 \times 3 \times 5 = 120$, $2 \times 3 \times 5^2 = 150$
Multiples of $2 \times 3 \times 5 = 30$
b $204 = 2^2 \times 3 \times 17$ **c** $210 = 2 \times 3 \times 5 \times 7$

7

$3 \times 5 \times 7$	$= 105$	5^3	$= 125$
$3^3 \times 5$	$= 135$	3×7^2	$= 147$
$3^3 \times 7$	$= 189$	$3^2 \times 5^2$	$= 225$
5×7^2	$= 245$	$3^2 \times 5 \times 7$	$= 315$
7^3	$= 343$	3×5^3	$= 375$
$3^4 \times 5$	$= 405$	$3^2 \times 7^2$	$= 441$
$3 \times 5^2 \times 7$	$= 525$	$3^4 \times 7$	$= 567$
$5^2 \times 7$	$= 175$	3^5	$= 243$

1c LCM and HCF

Objectives	
• Use highest common factors and lowest common multiples	(L6)
• Use efficient methods to add and subtract fractions	(L6)

Key ideas	Resources
1 Prime factorisation can be used to find HCFs and LCMs **2** HCFs can be used to simplify, and LCMs to add or subtract, fractions	LCM (1034) HCF (1044) List of products of prime factors for integers up to 100.

Simplification	Extension
The questions can be very time consuming; students could be provided with a list of prime factor decompositions up to 100 to help with many of the questions.	Explore the ways in which HCF and LCM can be used with decimals. Students should begin by looking at how a decimal might be decomposed using a factor tree. Do the same rules apply for decimals and integers? Encourage students to set a challenge for a partner.

Literacy	Links
The terms HCF and LCM often cause confusion. To help avoid this confusion between the two terms, remind students that HCFs, since they are factors, are smallish, and LCMs, since they are multiples, are largish; and the idea of 'common' may need to be reviewed also.	Venn diagrams were invented by John Venn in around 1880. He was a fellow and lecturer in moral sciences at Cambridge University. A stained glass window at Gonville and Caius College, Cambridge commemorates him. For more information see, http://en.wikipedia.org/wiki/John_venn

Alternative approach

One advantage of the method shown is that it delivers the prime factors in the desired order … provided that division is by prime numbers, in order. If this approach is not a problem, then the method can be improved by working on both numbers simultaneously. For example:

```
2) 36   60
2) 18   30
3)  9   15
    3    5
```

The HCF is then the product of the prime factors on the left, the LCM is this with the inclusion of the factors at the bottom (which will not automatically be prime factorised, so that a little warning is due here – but this approach may avoid unnecessary work, as a countervailing consideration), and the factors (with the same caveat) of each original number can be easily read from the HCF with the appropriate inclusion from the bottom.

This can further help to avoid any confusion between HCF and LCM.

Calculators, used intelligently, can be immensely useful here: they will give prime factorisations, and simplified answers to fraction calculations. For a question such as question **3** part **a**, entering 108 ÷ 144 to obtain $\frac{3}{4}$ is a good step to answering the question. (HCF = 108 ÷ 3 or 144 ÷ 4; LCM = 108 × 4 or 144 × 3)

Checkpoint

1 Find the HCF and LCM of these pairs of numbers.

a 1350 and 3000 (HCF = 150, LCM = 27 000)

b 2156 and 5082 (HCF = 154, LCM = 71 148)

Starter

Ask students questions involving prime numbers less than 30. For example,

Two prime numbers with a difference of 9? (2, 11)

Three prime numbers with a total of 45? (5, 17, 23)

Teaching notes

Explain what is meant by factor and HCF. Use small number examples to illustrate that the HCF is the product of the common prime factors. Show how a Venn diagram can illustrate this more clearly. Explain what is meant by a multiple and LCM. Use small examples and ask if the Venn diagram can also prove useful for LCMs.

When two numbers are drawn in a Venn diagram using their prime factors, you could think of the overlapping circles like a person's face. If you spike up their hair and stick out their tongue, what numbers will you be using? The LCM and HCF.

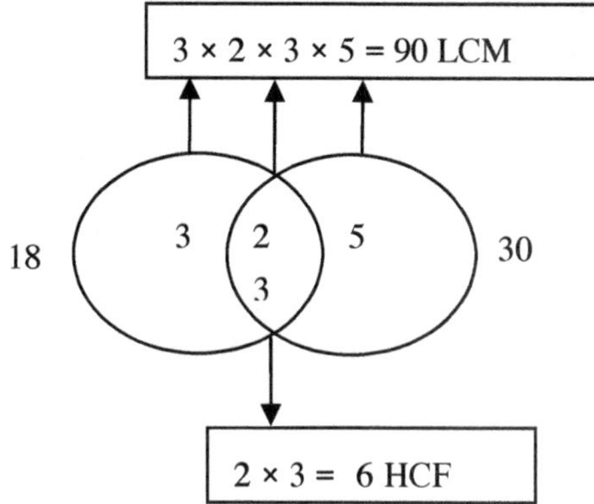

Give simple examples of simplifying and adding fractions. How can HCFs and LCMs help with these types of questions? What happens when the HCF and LCM are not used when working with fractions? Ask students what method they think computers use to deal with fractions? Why?

Plenary

The LCM of any two consecutive integers above zero is the product of the two numbers. Is this statement 'always true', 'sometimes true', 'never true'? Encourage students to investigate in a systematic way. If they find that this is true for all the examples they try, does this prove that the statement is always true?

Exercise commentary

Question 1 – For these smaller numbers, writing 2 lists of factors and then finding HCF is as efficient method. Part **d** may trip up students. All these questions are well suited to using mini whiteboards.

Question 2 – Finding LCM is more difficult than HCF. It is much easier to use prime factors except for part **a**.

Question 3 – Encourage use of Venn diagrams, as a visual approach will benefit some learners.

Question 4 – Encourage students to use the HCF, although in practice it is likely to be faster to use repeated cancelling.

Question 5 – Use of prime factors does make finding lowest common denominators easier.

Question 6 – Allow students time to attempt questions. Most will try trial-and-improvement. Then lead students to how they can use Venn diagrams to find common factors other than the highest.

Question 7 – Does the answer have to be a whole number of orbits? Would taking out a factor of 7 make the question much simpler? Would it still give the same answer? Does it make any difference if the orbits are not all in the same direction?

Question 8 – Encourage a systematic approach. Suggest students find the smallest answers first (don't forget 20 and 20 as a possibility to consider), then steadily larger numbers. Are there a finite (how many?) or an infinite number of solutions?

Answers

1 **a** 5 **b** 5 **c** 24 **d** 19
e 3 **f** 8

2 **a** 30 **b** 350 **c** 340 **d** 980
e 210 **f** 200

3 **a** HCF = 36, LCM = 432
b HCF = 40, LCM = 2520
c HCF = 55, LCM = 4620
d HCF = 63, LCM = 5733
e HCF = 12, LCM = 4320
f HCF = 180, LCM = 5040
g HCF = 7, LCM = 2520
h HCF = 15, LCM = 450

4 **a** $\frac{2}{3}$ **b** $\frac{5}{9}$ **c** $\frac{3}{4}$ **d** $\frac{3}{5}$
e $\frac{5}{8}$

5 **a** $\frac{7}{30}$ **b** $\frac{53}{60}$ **c** $\frac{47}{100}$ **d** $\frac{161}{200}$

6 **a** Top = 15 Bottom left = 20 Bottom right = 25
b Top = 36 Bottom left = 27 Bottom right = 45

7 **a** 588 weeks
b 21, 14 and 12 orbits respectively

8 **a** $n \times 20$ and $m \times 20$ where the HCF of n and m is 1
b 2, 25; $100 = 2^2 \times 5^2$, two numbers must have no common factors

1d Square roots and cube roots

Objectives

- Use the function keys (on a calculator) for powers and roots (L6)
- Use ICT to estimate square roots and cube roots (L6)

Key ideas

1. Square roots and cube roots can be found with calculators
2. Exact square roots and cube roots can be found with the help of prime factorisation

Resources

Squares and cubes (1053)
Trial and improvement (1057)

Simplification

Ensure students are not confusing doubling with squaring. At the start of the exercise encourage students to check answers by repeated multiplication.

Extension

A large cube is made from many smaller cubes. How many smaller cubes are on each face if the large cube contains 4913 smaller cubes? (Answer $17^2 = 289$).

Literacy

Check the concepts of square root and cube root, but do not insist on a clear definition. Use examples to illustrate how a positive number has a positive cube root, and a negative number has a negative cube root. Ask if a negative number can have a square root.

Links

Bring in some sheets of A3, A4 and A5 paper and other ISO sizes if available. Ask the class to measure the paper and calculate the ratio of the length to the width for each size. The ratio is $\sqrt{2}$: 1 or 1.4142 : 1 in all cases. Now fold a sheet of A4 in half and compare with a sheet of A5 (same size). ISO paper sizes are designed so that A0 has an area of one square metre but with a length to width ratio of $\sqrt{2}$: 1. When a sheet of A0 is cut in half, it makes two smaller sheets size A1, each with a length to width ratio of $\sqrt{2}$: 1. There is a chart illustrating ISO paper sizes at http://en.wikipedia.org/wiki/Image:A_size_illustration.svg

Alternative approach

Note that, because the √ symbol, on its own, is used exclusively for the positive root, there is only one solution to an expression such as $x = \sqrt{9}$ ($x = 3$), whereas there are two solutions to $x^2 = 9$: $x = \pm 3$.

Do note that appropriate degrees of accuracy are most intelligently given as a number of significant figures, rather than a number of decimal places.

Remember that calculators can carry out prime factorisation; even if the working needs to be shown, the help of a calculator can be valuable. But do encourage students to save time by learning some common square numbers.

For trial-and-improvement, always first equate to zero. It is then far simpler to see whether a result is positive or negative, or when a positive and a negative bracket the solution, or which of two values (one positive, one negative) is closer to zero, in order to allow an intelligent choice for the next step.

Checkpoint

1. Neither $\sqrt{2}$ nor $\sqrt{8}$ is a whole number. Investigate why you get a whole number when you multiply these two numbers together. Can you find any other numbers this works for?

(Any numbers whose product is a square number, e.g. $\sqrt{3}$ and $\sqrt{12}$.)

Starter

Write the following numbers on the board: 30, 125, 75, 16, 48. Ask students

Which numbers are factors of 5000? (Only 125)
What is the lowest common multiple of the 5 numbers? (6000)
What is the largest square number that is a factor of 5000? (2500), etc.

Teaching notes

Ask students what is meant by *square* and *cube*. Include negative examples. Ask what is meant by *square root*. Why is there a positive and negative square root? What other types of roots might there be? Conclude that *cube roots* work in a similar way to square roots.

Investigate these functions on a calculator. Note that almost all scientific calculators have a cube function, but slightly fewer have a cube root function. Other calculators have a cube root key, but not a cube key. Some students may need to be helped to use their calculators here.

Ask students to work out 'the square of -4' using the correct function on the calculator. Most students will probably obtain -16, although some calculators insert brackets around the negative value automatically. How can we ensure that the calculator correctly squares -4? Insert brackets around the negative number.

Explore the link between area/length/perimeter and square roots. Imagine a square field, the side length is 5 m, the perimeter is 20 m, the area is 25 m^2. Ask students if any two of these measurements can be found by knowing the third.

Plenary

Discuss methods for finding square roots without a calculator. One method for finding an approximation to a square root is as follows. Suppose $x \sim n^2$ is a close approximation, that is $\sqrt{x} \approx n$, then a better approximation is:

$$\sqrt{x} \approx n - \frac{(n-x)}{2n}$$

Try finding $\sqrt{15}$ starting from $n^2 = 4^2 = 16$.

$$\sqrt{15} \approx 4 - \frac{(16-15)}{2\times 4} = 4 - \frac{1}{8} = 3\frac{7}{8}$$

How good is the estimate? Check using a calculator.

Exercise commentary

Question 1 – Encourage students to use the proper functions on their calculators rather than repeated multiplication. Emphasise the need to use brackets when squaring negative numbers, as scientific calculators adhere strictly to BIDMAS.

Question 2 – Students will need scientific calculators, which will have a [$^3\sqrt{}$] key.

Question 3 – Use the number 36 to help explain how the method works.

Question 4 – Introduce by comparing the product of two consecutive numbers with its square root.

Question 5 – On modern scientific calculators the number will have to be retyped not using the 'ANS' key to illustrate point.

Question 6 – Encourage a tabular approach and the writing down of the trials. Why do you need to test to 2 dp when only looking for the solution to 1 dp?

Answers

1 **a** 144 **b** 361 **c** 625 **d** 343
e 2197 **f** 64 **g** 1000 **h** 12.25
i 8000 **j** 74.088 **k** 1771.561 **l** -125

2 **a** 8.4 **b** 11.0 **c** 4.1 **d** 7.4
e 14.1 **f** Non-real **g** -4.5 **h** -5.3

3 **a** 15 **b** 18 **c** 24 **d** 6
e 8 **f** 36 **g** -5 **h** -7

4 **a** 94, 95 **b** 56, 57, 58
c 8.4 cm

5 $\sqrt{10}$ is irrational and 3.16227766 is just a decimal approximation.

6 **a** 4.5, 9.7, 17.3 **b** 4.6, 2.2, 11.7

1e Indices

Objectives	
• Recognise the equivalence of 0.1, 1/10 and 10^{-1}	(L5)
• Know and use the index laws for multiplication and division of positive integer powers	(L6)

Key ideas	Resources
1 Indices give a way of writing large and small numbers **2** They can also be used for multiplications and divisions	Indices 1 (1033) Multi-link cubes

Simplification	Extension
Students without a scientific calculator will find the need to use repeated multiplication for questions **1** to **5**. Leaving out question **1e**, **1h**, **1i**. To improve understanding of the 4 rule for indices, show students how it is related to simplifying fractions.	There is a special button on a scientific calculator that can help solve problems like question **8**. It is the 'log' button. See if students can see how to use it to find 'x'. For example, part **a** $3^x = 81$. Already found $x = 4$ by trial-and-improvement. How can 'log' help? Log 81 = 1.9084….. log 3 = 0.4771…. How can the answer '4' be made from these?

Literacy	Links
Be clear about indices being the plural of index, and also about what is meant by 'the big number'. Introduce the term 'reciprocate' for negative powers, speak of reciprocals.	The traditional nursery rhyme below is a riddle that can be investigated using indices. As I was going to St. Ives (1) I met a man with 7 wives Each wife had 7 sacks Each sack had 7 cats Each cat had 7 kits Kits, cats, sacks, wives How many were going to St. Ives? $(1 + 1 + 7 + 7^2 + 7^3 + 7^4 = 2802)$ Of course the answer to the riddle is actually 1 as everyone else is on their way back!

Alternative approach

Encourage students to know some powers, especially of 2, 3 and 5. For a start, two that are memorable are $2^6 = 64$ (the 6s match) and $2^{10} = 1024$. (The 10s match and, if it helps, what does 6 + 4 from 64 equal? And what does 6 × 4 from 64 equal?) These put them in easy reach (by halving or doubling) of most of the other higher powers of 2 that will turn up.

Checkpoint

1 3 to the power 10 is 59 049. 3 to the power 8 is 6561.
What is 59 049 ÷ 6561? (3^2 or 9)

Starter

Ask students questions involving square numbers up to 144. For example,

Two square numbers that have a difference of 27? (36, 9)
Three square numbers that have a total of 101? (1, 36, 64)
Two square numbers with a product of 441? (9, 49)
Sum of first five square numbers? (55)

Teaching notes

Ask students why we need indices. Establish that they are a useful shorthand for repeated multiplication and a neat way of writing large numbers, for example, 100 trillion (US) is 10^{14}. Introduce the use of the power button, giving its different appearance on various calculators.

Investigate the patterns in the powers of 10 sequence in the student book. What is the meaning of the zero and negative powers? Challenge students to produce a similar list using a different base; include zero and negative powers.

Sometimes we don't want to calculate an answer exactly, but would rather write it as a power. For example, $3^2 \times 3^3 = 243$, but 3^5 gives the same answer and is easier to work out. Ask students how this can be done – adding the indices. Establish that you are multiplying 3s, but the number of 3s that are being multiplied is 3 + 2 so 5. Note, avoid saying 'the number of times you are multiplying 3 is 5', since the meaning of *times* is ambiguous. Illustrate as
$3^3 \times 3^2 = 3 \times 3 \times 3 \quad \times \quad 3 \times 3 = 3^5$

Construct a similar example for division and show that the indices subtract because you are cancelling a common factor from the numerator and denominator.

Plenary

If you put 1 penny on the first square of a chess board and then 2p on the next, 4p on the next, etc., how much money would you put on the last square? Allow students to exhaust themselves (with or without a calculator) before suggesting the use of indices to express the solution. (2^{63}p, about ten million trillion pence, or £14 million for everyone on Earth!)

What is this exactly in pounds? (£2^{61}/25).

Exercise commentary

Question 1 – Introduce the power button on a scientific calculator. Allow time for a discussion on negative indices, and possibility for students to investigate this further. Resist the temptation of explaining them too quickly.

Question 2 – Challenge students to explain why you add and subtract the indices.

Question 3 – Emphasise that the same base is needed to use the indices rules. Encourage students to check that this is true. For example, $5^2 \times 2^3 = 25 \times 8 = 200$ but $\neq 10^5$.

Question 4 – This is the first question with a number without an index.

Question 5 – Note the value of two of the indices is equal.

Questions 6 and **7** – Remind students that indices are repeated multiplication.

Question 8 – Encourage students to use the power button and not repeated multiplication. Part **h** involving a negative power may invoke further discussion.

Question 9 – Allow students to make errors in the 125 cube, but improve their solution by looking at the 27 and 64 cube problems and trying to spot a pattern in the results. Multi-link cubes could be useful in helping to visualise the problem.

Answers

1 **a** 125 **b** 64 **c** 27 **d** 1
e 1 **f** 100 000 **g** 2 **h** 1
i $\frac{1}{10}$ **j** 1331 **k** $\frac{1}{512}$ **l** $\frac{1}{6}$

2 **a** 4^5 **b** 3^6 **c** 5^7 **d** 4^7
e 2^8 **f** 6^9 **g** 4^3 **h** 3^4
i 5^2 **j** 4^2 **k** 2 **l** 6^2

3 **a** 200 **b** 36 **c** 48 **d** 15.1875
e 2^{-1} **f** 3

4 **a** 3^7 **b** 4^6 **c** 10^9 **d** 2^6
e 4^3 **f** 10^{-2} **g** 5^5 **h** 1

5 $3^5 < 2^8 = 4^4 < 11^3$ (243 < 256 < 1331)

6 Multiply 256 by 2 × 2 = 1024

7 **a** 1024 **b** 16 384

8 **a** 4 **b** 5 **c** 6 **d** 2
e 5 **f** 4 **g** 8 **h** -1
i 2

9 **a** 54 **b** 0 red 27, 2 red 36, 3 red 8
c 0 red $(n-2)^3$, 1 red $6(n-2)^2$, 2 red $12(n-2)$, 3 red 8, total n^3

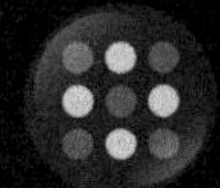

1f Rounding and estimation

Objectives	
• Round positive numbers to any given power of ten	(L5)
• Round decimals to the nearest whole number or to one or two decimal places	(L5)
• Use rounding to make estimates	(L6)

Key ideas	Resources
1 Measurements and calculations often need to be rounded to sensible degrees of precision **2** Rounded values can be used for estimations	Decimal places (1001) Error intervals (1968) Number lines marked with thousands, hundreds etc. Internet access

Simplification	Extension
Help students to visualise the numbers by referring to their place on a number line. Use prepared lines marked with thousands, hundreds, etc.	Investigate the measurements of various famous heights. For example, Mount Everest, Statue of Liberty, Burj Khalifa (world's tallest building). What degree of accuracy is used in the sources you find? The answers for these examples are 8848 m, 46 m or 93 m (depending on how it is measured), 828 m. Encourage the use of more than one source.

Literacy	Links
Students should understand that rounding is writing a number as a near approximation. Consider what level of accuracy is appropriate for different real-life situations. Discuss the terms rounding and estimating with students, and discuss the difference between guessing and estimating.	In parliamentary elections in Germany in 1992, a rounding error caused the wrong results to be announced. Under German law, a party cannot have any seats in Parliament unless it has 5.0% or more of the vote. The Green Party appeared to have exactly 5.0%, until it was discovered that the computer that printed out the results only used one place after the decimal point and had rounded the vote up to 5.0%. The Green Party only had 4.97% of the vote and the results had to be changed.

Alternative approach

Following a modelling and discussion of the principles of rounding pairs of students can be given a list of results, say from the last olympics, or of current sporting records, (times, distances and weights) which they then record as values correct to the nearest integer, one decicmal place and/or two decimal places. Make sure that the aspect of correctness is addressed by comparing what happens if a previouslu rounded up value is further approximated.

Checkpoint

1 A room measures 5.84 m by 4.40 m to the nearest cm. Calculate the area in m^2 to 2 decimal places. ($25.70\ m^2$)

Starter

I am even but not square.

I am a multiple of 3.

I am greater than the number of days in November.

I am less than the product of 2^3 and 3^2.

I have 8 factors. (54)

Can be extended by asking students to make up their own puzzles.

Teaching notes

Many measurements can't be given exactly, so they are rounded. For example, your height maybe given as 167 cm, but this is only accurate to the nearest cm. In this case what must your height be between? Establish that it is between 166.5 cm and 167.5 cm. This can be illustrated on a number line. Many students will want to use 167.4 or 167.49 cm as the upper limit. Discuss why this is not possible and why the accepted method is to use 167.5 cm.

If a number has not yet been rounded, there are different methods of rounding that can be used. Look at examples that round off to the nearest 10, 100, etc. Include examples of decimal values.

Alternatively, a number can be rounded off to a specific number of decimal places. Include awkward examples like 3.049604 rounded to 3 decimal places.

An alternative way of asking to round to 3 dp is to round to the nearest 0.001 or nearest thousandth.

Plenary

When finding the maximum possible value of a rounded number, some measurements are treated differently. Discuss the difference between discrete and continuous measures. For example, the attendance at a sporting event is 4000 and the length of a rope is 4000 cm. Both measures have been rounded to the nearest thousand. (4499 people and 4500 m) What other examples can students think of that need to be treated differently?

Exercise commentary

Question 1 – Highlight numbers like part **f** and part **i**, which are the same when rounded to the nearest 10 or the nearest 100.

Question 2 – Part **g** rounds to zero. Discuss with students whether this is useful. Elicit increasing accuracy so value is not zero. Use this to introduce significant figures, although this is thoroughly covered next year.

Question 3 – Be prepared for discussion on upper limits, that there is no real difference between 0.5 and $0.4\dot{9}$. At this level it is not necessary to insist on 0.5.

Question 4 – Since students are asked to estimate and not calculate, students should use sensible rounded values. 'Estimate, to the nearest metre' must mean 'Estimate, and then give your answer rounded to the nearest metre'; this will not, always, be accurate to the nearest metre, and students should be able to see this.

Question 5 – Ask students for some guidelines when buying a carpet. E.g. always round up and never down.

Answers

1

	i	ii	iii
a	12 000	12 100	12 090
b	2000	2400	2400
c	1000	900	890
d	8000	8500	8500
e	23 000	23 500	23 460
f	1000	700	700
g	3000	3000	2990
h	1 436 000	1 436 400	1 436 380
i	10 000	10 000	10 000
j	7000	7500	7470
k	5000	4700	4750
l	107 000	106 800	106 840
m	3 107 000	3 106 800	3 106 840
n	56 000	55 600	55 560
o	455 000	454 500	454 550

2

	i	ii	iii	iv
a	5	5.0	5.05	5.047
b	3	3.5	3.45	3.454
c	18	17.5	17.52	17.517
d	3	3.0	3.05	3.049
e	13	13.0	13.01	13.009
f	130	130.3	130.25	130.254
g	0	0.0	0.03	0.030
h	8	7.9	7.90	7.901

3 **i** length 3.75 mm width 1.255 mm
ii length 3.85 mm width 1.265 mm
(or 3.8499… mm) (or 1.26499… mm)

4 **a** Students' answers, for example,
$(73 \times 1.48) + (81 \times 1.35) = 217.39 = 217$ m
b Students' answers, for example,
i $430\,000 \div 25 = 17\,200$ lengths
ii $17\,200 \times 50 = 860\,000$ s $= 14\,333$ min $= 239$ hours

5 Students' answers, but essentially that Kevin has rounded his measurements so $3.4 \times 2.3 = 7.82$ m^2, which makes his piece look big enough; but when we take the max possible size of Kevin's room it is $3.45 \times 2.35 = 8.1075$ m^2, which means his piece, is too small.

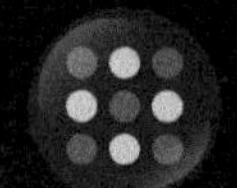

1g Trial-and-improvement 1

Objectives	
• Use ICT to estimate square roots and cube roots (L6)	
Key ideas	**Resources**
1 Improved values of roots can be found by a trial-and-improvement process	Trial and improvement (1057)
Simplification	**Extension**
Use pre-prepared grids for the trial-and-improvement questions. Include some initial calculations.	Solve $10x^2 + 11x - 7 = 0$. Find x to 1 dp. Use trial-and-improvement. Tell students that there is more than one answer. (0.5 and -1.6).
Literacy	**Links**
It might be necessary to explain why we now say trial-and-improvement, rather than trial-and-error, even though this is easier to say.	The world record for mental calculation is held by Alexis Lemaire. In December 2007 he found the 13th root of a 200-digit number in 70.2 seconds without using a calculator, pen or paper. The solution has 16 digits. Lemaire already held one world record as in 2004 he found the 13th root of a 100-digit number in just 3.625 seconds.

Alternative approach

For trial-and-improvement, always first equate to zero. It is then far simpler to see whether a result is positive or negative, or when a positive and a negative bracket the solution, or which of two values (one positive, one negative) is closer to zero, in order to allow an intelligent choice for the next step.

It is essential that students are discouraged from going too far in one step; insist that they improve the accuracy of their bounds one significant figure at a time, or they can become very confused, even if equating to zero (much more, if not).

It is also essential that all steps are shown – this is a matter of process, much more than a matter of result.

The other meaning of root, as in the solution to an equation, may arise here.

Checkpoint

1 A number plus its square is equal to 50. What is that number correct to 2 dp? (6.59)

Starter

Draw a 4 × 4 table on the board.

Label the columns: 9, -4, 18, 11. Label the rows: 3, 7, 14, -5.

Ask students to fill in the table with the products (no calculators). For example, the top row in the table would read 27, -12, 54, 33.

Are there any short cuts? Hint: 18 is double 9 and 14 is double 7.

Can be differentiated by the choice of numbers.

Teaching notes

Solve $x^2 = 71.4026$ by trial-and-improvement correct to 1 dp.

x	8	8.5	8.4	8.45
x^2	64	72.25	70.56	71.4025
High/low	low	high	low	low

$8.5^2 = 72.25$ too high.
$72.25 - 71.4026 =$ **0.8474** away from the required value.

$8.4^2 = 70.56$ too low.
$71.4026 - 70.56 =$ **0.8426** away from the required value.

So $x = 8.4$ gives a closer answer to $x^2 = 71.4026$ than $x = 8.5$; can we conclude that $x = 8.4$ to 1 dp? We must make sure by looking half way between 8.4 and 8.5. That is, $8.45^2 = 71.4025$ too low.

So value of x lies just above 8.45 and so the answer is 8.5 to 1dp.

Conclusion, don't just use 1 decimal place; you need to go to the next decimal place to be sure of the answer.

Explore the square root and cube root functions of calculators. Note that some students may not have a dedicated cube root button and will have to use the power root function.

Plenary

What is the drawback of a trial-and-improvement method? Discuss the method of bisection for finding accurate square roots of numbers. That is using half the interval each time. Is this a quicker method? Is this a more difficult method to use?

Exercise commentary

Questions 1 and **2** – Encourage students to set out their working in a clear tabular form.

Question 3 – Some students may confuse cube root with division by 3. Consolidate understanding of cube root by using some simpler examples. For example, 2 cubed means $2 \times 2 \times 2 = 8$.

Question 4 – Ask the students to investigate the power of iteration compared with trial-and-improvement. How many iterations does it take to agree with the calculator screen? This depends on initial value.

Try adapting the method to find $\sqrt{2}$. Can you do better than the result on the Babylonian table in the 'Did you know?' feature?

Answers

1 **a** Students' answers; Yes **b** 8.660
2 **a** 5.48 **b** 8.37 **c** 12.04 **d** 13.42
e 15.81 **f** 24.49
3 **a** 3.4 **b** 5.8 **c** 4.1 **d** 2.4
e 12.6 **f** 17.1
4 **a** 7.745967742, 7.745966692, 7.745966692
b The same! **c** 17.32050808
d Students' answers
e Check students' equations

Key outcomes	Quick check
Use divisibility tests to find factors and identify primes.	Two of the following seven numbers are prime. Use divisibility tests to find the prime numbers. 2723, 2731, 2745, 2753, 2762, 2781, 2783 (2731 and 2753)
Find and use the HCF and LCM of two numbers using prime factors.	Use prime factors to find the HCF and LCM of 1260 and 1512. (HCF = 252, LCM = 7 560)
Find square roots and cube roots.	Calculate $\sqrt[3]{74088} \div \sqrt{28224}$ (0.25)
Use, multiply and divide numbers written in index form.	Evaluate the following: $\frac{7^4 \times 7^5}{7^3 \times 7^6}$ (7^1 or 7)
Round numbers to a given power of 10 and use rounding to make estimates.	A piece of cloth measures 196 cm by 83 cm. By rounding to the nearest 10 cm, give the approximate area of the cloth. (16 000 cm^2 or 1.6 m^2)
Use trial-and-improvement to find square and cube roots.	The cube of a number plus that number equals 40. Use trial-and-improvement to find that number to 2 decimal places. (3.32)

MyMaths extra support

Lesson/online homework			Description
Estimating introduction	1002	L4	Using rounding to estimate answers to simple calculations
Rounding decimals	1004	L5	Rounding numbers to the nearest whole number and to one decimal place
Ordering decimals	1072	L4	Putting decimals into size order

MyReview

1 MySummary

Check out

You should now be able to ...

	Test it ➡ Questions
✓ Use divisibility tests to find factors and identify primes.	1, 2
✓ Find and use the HCF and LCM of two numbers using prime factors.	3 - 5
✓ Find square roots and cube roots.	6, 7
✓ Use, multiply and divide numbers written in index form.	8
✓ Round numbers to a given power of 10 and use rounding to make estimates.	9, 10
✓ Use trial-and-improvement to find square and cube roots.	11

Language	Meaning	Example
Prime number	A number divisible by itself and 1	2, 3, 5, 7, 11, 13 ...
Factor	A quantity that divides another given quantity without a remainder	2 and 3 are factors of 6, because $2 \times 3 = 6$
Multiple	The product of any quantity and an integer	3, 6, 9, 12 are multiples of 3
Prime factor decomposition	Writing a number as a product of prime factors	$2000 = 2^4 \times 5^3$
Factor tree	A method for finding the prime factors of a number	See p 6
Highest Common Factor (HCF)	The largest number that divides each of a given set of numbers exactly	For 12 and 18 the HCF is 6 and the LCM is 36
Lowest Common Multiple (LCM)	The smallest number that each of a given set of numbers divides into exactly	
Square root	A square root is a number that when multiplied by itself is equal to a given number.	$\sqrt{25} = 5$ because $5 \times 5 = 5^2 = 25$
Cube root	A cube root is a number that when multiplied by itself three times is equal to a given number.	$\sqrt[3]{27} = 3$ because $3 \times 3 \times 3 = 3^3 = 27$
Indices	A compact way of writing a repeated product	$5^3 = 5 \times 5 \times 5$

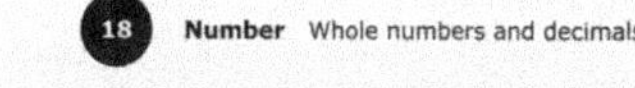
18 **Number** Whole numbers and decimals

1 MyReview

1. Use divisibility tests to answer these questions. Explain your answer.
   - **a** Is 8 a factor of 508?
   - **b** Is 6822 divisible by 6?
   - **c** Is 617 a multiple of 3?
   - **d** Is 127 a prime number?
2. Write each of these numbers as a product of its prime factors. Use index notation in your answers.
   - **a** 297 **b** 2450
3. Find the highest common factor of each pair of numbers.
   - **a** 27 and 117
   - **b** 385 and 144
4. Find the lowest common multiple of each pair of numbers.
   - **a** 35 and 77
   - **b** 126 and 588
5. Work these out. Leave each answer as a fraction in its simplest form.
   - **a** $\frac{5}{6} + \frac{8}{9}$ **b** $\frac{11}{12} - \frac{7}{15}$
6. Find these using a calculator. Give your answer to 2dp where possible.
   - **a** $\sqrt{250}$ **b** $\sqrt{-225}$
   - **c** $\sqrt[3]{500}$ **d** $\sqrt[3]{-160}$
7. Find these without using a calculator.
   - **a** 11^2 **b** $\sqrt{169}$
   - **c** 8^3 **d** $\sqrt[3]{-64}$
8. Evaluate these expressions. Leave each answer in index form where possible.
   - **a** $4^6 \times 4$ **b** $5^0 \times 5^7$
   - **c** $12^6 \div 12^4$ **d** $6^2 \div 3^2$
   - **e** $3^4 - 3^2$ **f** $2^7 \times 2^5 \div 2^{10}$
9. Round 160.0952 to the nearest
   - **a** whole number **b** 1dp
   - **c** 2dp **d** 3dp.
10. A table is measured to be 95cm long to the nearest cm. What is the
    - **a** shortest
    - **b** longest length the table could actually be?
11. Use trial and improvement to find $\sqrt[3]{20}$ to 1dp. Show your working clearly.

What next?

Score		
0 – 4		Your knowledge of this topic is still developing. To improve look at Formative test: 2C-1; MyMaths: 1032 – 1035, 1044, 1045, 1053 and 1057
5 – 9		You are gaining a secure knowledge of this topic. To improve look at InvisiPen: 112, 135, 172, 173, 174, 181, 184 and 221
10 – 11		You have mastered this topic. Well done, you are ready to progress!

MyMaths.co.uk

Question commentary

Question 1 – Encourage students to explain their reasoning clearly.

Question 2 – Challenge students not to use a calculator.

Questions 3 and **4** – Students should write out each number as a product of its prime factors.

Question 5 – Students should use knowledge of LCM to find a common denominator of 18 in part **a** and 60 in part **b**.

Questions 6 and **7 –** Students need to be aware that negative numbers do not have square roots but do have cube roots.

Question 8 – Students may need to be reminded that $5^0 = 1$. Some students may try to apply index rule for division to the subtraction in part **e**.

Questions 9 and **10** – Part **9c** may catch students out, use a number line to demonstrate correct answer.

Question 11 – Encourage students to show working in tabular form.

Answers

1	**a**	No	**b**	Yes	**c**	No	**d**	Yes
2	**a**	$3^3 \times 11$	**b**	$2 \times 5^2 \times 7^2$				
3	**a**	9	**b**	1				
4	**a**	385	**b**	1764				
5	**a**	$\frac{31}{18}$	**b**	$\frac{9}{20}$				
6	**a**	15.81	**b**	Not possible				
	c	7.94	**d**	-5.43				
7	**a**	121	**b**	13				
	c	512	**d**	-4				
8	**a**	4^7	**b**	5^7	**c**	12^2	**d**	4
	e	72	**f**	2^2				
9	**a**	160	**b**	160.1	**c**	160.10	**d**	160.095
10	**a**	94.5 cm	**b**	95.5 cm				
11	2.7							

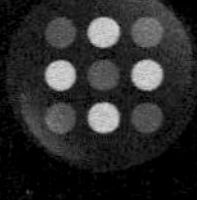

1 MyPractice

1a

1 Write all the factors of these numbers.

a 200 **b** 288 **c** 289 **d** 300 **e** 440 **f** 256
g 500 **h** 639 **i** 777 **j** 999 **k** 1000 **l** 2304

2 Use the divisibility tests to say which of these numbers are prime.
In each case explain your answer.

a 401 **b** 413 **c** 419 **d** 437 **e** 451 **f** 479

1b

3 Write each of these numbers as the product of its prime factors.

a 22 **b** 46 **c** 84 **d** 58 **e** 132 **f** 104
g 185 **h** 425 **i** 205 **j** 181 **k** 366 **l** 309
m 489 **n** 585 **o** 1089 **p** 2529 **q** 1305 **r** 3025

4 Use prime factors to list all the factors of these numbers.

a 60 **b** 96 **c** 110 **d** 165 **e** 430 **f** 600
g 950 **h** 1225 **i** 2116 **j** 1764 **k** 3136 **l** 3969

1c

5 Find the HCF and LCM of

a 100 and 120 **b** 144 and 192 **c** 210 and 240 **d** 336 and 378
e 315 and 495 **f** 616 and 728 **g** 40, 56 and 72 **h** 48, 80 and 176

6 Cancel down each of these fractions into its simplest form.

You can use the HCF.

a $\frac{35}{49}$ **b** $\frac{100}{120}$ **c** $\frac{144}{192}$ **d** $\frac{210}{240}$ **e** $\frac{105}{175}$
f $\frac{234}{273}$ **g** $\frac{210}{378}$ **h** $\frac{96}{528}$ **i** $\frac{477}{583}$ **j** $\frac{198}{858}$

1d

7 Find these using a calculator. Give your answers to 1 dp.

a $\sqrt{11}$ **b** $\sqrt{111}$ **c** $\sqrt[3]{111}$ **d** $\sqrt[3]{-111}$ **e** $\sqrt{-9}$ **f** $\sqrt[3]{91}$

8 **a** Three consecutive numbers are multiplied together to give -1716.
What are the three numbers?

b Two consecutive numbers are multiplied together to give 1806.
Find the two possible pairs of consecutive numbers.

9 Find these without a calculator.

a $\sqrt{256}$ **b** $\sqrt{441}$ **c** $\sqrt{729}$
d $\sqrt[3]{1728}$ **e** $\sqrt[3]{3375}$ **f** $\sqrt{2025}$

1e

10 Use your calculator to find the power x in these questions.

a $3^x = 2187$ **b** $2^x = 512$ **c** $4^x = 65536$ **d** $5^x = 15625$
e $10^x = 1$ **f** $7^x = 16807$ **g** $4^x = 1$ **h** $6^x = 7776$
i $2^x = 16$ **j** $2^x = 0.5$

11 Simplify each of these, leaving your answer as a single power of the number.

a $2^3 \times 2^4$ **b** $7^4 \times 7^8$ **c** $4^3 \times 4^9$ **d** $3^5 \times 3^0$ **e** $6^5 \times 6^5$
f $2^5 \div 2^3$ **g** $2^7 \div 2^7$ **h** $4^5 \div 4^4$ **i** $3^6 \div 3$ **j** $10^5 \div 10^6$

12 Calculate these, leaving your answer in index form where possible.

a $3^4 \times 4^3$ **b** $2^3 + 4^2$ **c** $5^3 - 2^4$ **d** $4^5 \div 2^2$ **e** $3^2 \times 3^2$

13 Simplify each of these, leaving your answer as a single power of the number.

a $5^3 \times 5^3 \times 5^3$ **b** $3^5 \times 3^5 \times 3^5$ **c** $10^4 \times 10^4 \times 10^4$
d $(2^4)^3$ **e** $(5^3)^3$ **f** $8^9 \div 8^9$
g $\frac{3^4 \times 3^3}{3^2}$ **h** $\frac{2^2 \times 2^4 \times 2^6}{2^8}$ **i** $10^3 \div 10^3$

1f

14 Round each of these numbers to the nearest

i whole number **ii** 1 dp **iii** 2 dp **iv** 3 dp.

a 6.1583 **b** 4.5648 **c** 18.6262 **d** 4.15494 **e** 16.00468
f 3.90909 **g** 9.99999 **h** 87.65432 **i** 0.000707 **j** 0.282828...

15 Work out an estimate for each of these problems.
Show all the steps of your working out.

a The average height of a man in Scotland is 1.78 m. There are 662954 people living in Glasgow, of whom 49% are men. Estimate the combined height of all the men in Glasgow.
Give your answer to the nearest kilometre.

b Giuseppe runs the marathon which is 42.195 km in length.
He covers each kilometre in 3 mins 48 secs.
Estimate the time it will take Giuseppe to complete the race.
Give your answer to the nearest minute.

1g

16 Use a trial and improvement method to find the square root of each of these numbers to 2 dp.

a $\sqrt{45}$ **b** $\sqrt{13}$ **c** $\sqrt{361}$ **d** $\sqrt{876}$ **e** $\sqrt{2640}$

Use the square root key on your calculator to check your answers.

17 Use a trial and improvement method to find the cube root of each of these numbers to 1 decimal place.

a $\sqrt[3]{95}$ **b** $\sqrt[3]{300}$ **c** $\sqrt[3]{10}$ **d** $\sqrt[3]{999}$ **e** $\sqrt[3]{87654}$

20 **Number** Whole numbers and decimals

MyMaths.co.uk 21

Question commentary

Question 1 – Encourage students to write factors in pairs. Part **l** is a challenge, as there are 27 factors.

Question 2 – Ask students to explain why testing up to 20 is sufficient.

Question 4 – Students must adopt a systematic approach. For example 3136 has 23 factors.

Question 7 – Students need to be aware that negative numbers do not have square roots but they do have cube roots.

Question 9 – Suggest students find these by using prime factors.

Question 11 – Students may need reminding that $3 = 3^1$ and $3^0 = 1$

Question 12 – Note that part **d** can be left in index form, although students may not immediately recognise this.

Question 13 – Note that questions in the form $(x^a)^b$ have not been taught explicitly but students should be able to deduce answer.

Questions 16 and **17** – Encourage students to set out working in tabular form. Check working to spot those students who have reached for the calculator prematurely.

Answers

1 **a** 1, 2, 4, 5, 8, 10, 20, 25, 40, 50, 100, 200
b 1, 2, 3, 4, 6, 8, 9, 12, 16, 18, 24, 32, 36, 48, 72, 96, 144, 288
c 1, 17, 289
d 1, 2, 3, 4, 5, 6, 10, 12, 15, 20, 25, 30, 50, 60, 75, 100, 150, 300
e 1, 2, 4, 5, 8, 10, 11, 20, 22, 40, 44, 55, 88, 110, 220, 440
f 1, 2, 4, 8, 16, 32, 64, 128, 256
g 1, 2, 4, 5, 10, 20, 25, 50, 100, 125, 250, 500
h 1, 3, 9, 71, 213, 639
i 1, 3, 7, 21, 37, 111, 259, 777
j 1, 3, 9, 27, 37, 111, 333, 999
k 1, 2, 4, 5, 8, 10, 20, 25, 40, 50, 100, 125, 200, 250, 500, 1000
l 1, 2, 3, 4, 6, 8, 9, 12, 16, 18, 24, 32, 36, 48, 64, 72, 96, 128, 144, 192, 256, 288, 384, 576, 768, 1152, 2304

2 **a** Yes **b** No, $413 \div 7 = 59$
c Yes **d** No, $437 \div 19 = 23$
e No, $451 \div 11 = 41$ **f** Yes

3 **a** 2×11 **b** 2×23 **c** $2^2 \times 3 \times 7$
d 2×29 **e** $2^2 \times 3 \times 11$ **f** $2^3 \times 13$
g 5×37 **h** $5^2 \times 17$ **i** 5×41
j Prime **k** $2 \times 3 \times 61$ **l** 3×103
m 3×163 **n** $3^2 \times 5 \times 13$ **o** $3^2 \times 11^2$
p $3^2 \times 281$ **q** $3^2 \times 5 \times 29$ **r** $5^2 \times 11^2$

4 **a** $2^2 \times 3 \times 5$: 1, 2, 3, 4, 5, 6, 10, 12, 15, 20, 30, 60
b $2^5 \times 3$: 1, 2, 3, 4, 6, 8, 12, 16, 24, 32, 48, 96
c $2 \times 5 \times 11$: 1, 2, 5, 10, 11, 22, 55, 110
d $3 \times 5 \times 11$: 1, 3, 5, 11, 15, 33, 55, 165
e $2 \times 5 \times 43$: 1, 2, 5, 10, 43, 86, 215, 430
f $2^3 \times 3 \times 5^2$: 1, 2, 3, 4, 5, 6, 8, 10, 12, 15, 20, 24, 25 30, 40, 50, 60, 75, 100, 120, 150, 200, 300, 600
g $2 \times 5^2 \times 19$: 1, 2, 5, 10, 19, 25, 38, 50, 95, 190, 475, 950
h $5^2 \times 7^2$: 1, 5, 7, 25, 35, 49, 175, 245, 1225
i $2^2 \times 23^2$: 1, 2, 4, 23, 46, 92, 529, 1058, 2116
j $2^2 \times 3^2 \times 7^2$: 1, 2, 3, 4, 6, 7, 9, 12, 14, 18, 21, 28, 36, 42, 49, 63, 84, 98, 126, 147, 196, 252, 294, 441, 588, 882, 1764
k $2^6 \times 7^2$: 1, 2, 4, 7, 8, 14, 16, 28, 32, 49, 56, 64, 98, 112, 196, 224, 392, 448, 784, 1568, 3136
l $3^4 \times 7^2$: 1, 3, 7, 9, 21, 27, 49, 63, 81, 147, 189, 441, 567, 1323, 3969

5 **a** HCF = 20, LCM = 600
b HCF = 48, LCM = 576
c HCF = 30, LCM = 1680
d HCF = 42, LCM = 3024
e HCF = 45, LCM = 3465
f HCF = 56, LCM = 8008
g HCF = 8, LCM = 2520
h HCF = 16, LCM = 2640

6 **a** $\frac{5}{7}$ **b** $\frac{5}{6}$ **c** $\frac{3}{4}$ **d** $\frac{7}{8}$
e $\frac{3}{5}$ **f** $\frac{6}{7}$ **g** $\frac{5}{9}$ **h** $\frac{2}{11}$
i $\frac{9}{11}$ **j** $\frac{3}{13}$

7 **a** 3.3 **b** 10.5 **c** 4.8
d -4.8 **e** Not possible **f** 4.5

8 **a** -11, -12, -13 **b** 42, 43 and -42, -43

9 **a** 16 **b** 21 **c** 27 **d** 12
e 15 **f** 45

10 **a** 7 **b** 9 **c** 8 **d** 6
e 0 **f** 5 **g** 0 **h** 5
i 4 **j** -1

11 **a** 2^7 **b** 7^{12} **c** 4^{12} **d** 3^5
e 6^{10} **f** 2^2 **g** 2^0 **h** 4
i 3^5 **j** 10^{-1}

12 **a** 5184 **b** 24 **c** 109
d $256 = 4^4 = 2^8$ **e** 3^4

13 **a** 5^9 **b** 3^{15} **c** 10^{12} **d** 2^{12}
e 5^9 **f** 8^0 **g** 3^5 **h** 2^4
i 10^0

14

	i	ii	iii	iv
a	6	6.2	6.16	6.158
b	5	4.6	4.56	4.565
c	19	18.6	18.63	18.626
d	4	4.2	4.15	4.155
e	16	16.0	16.00	16.005
f	4	3.9	3.91	3.909
g	10	10.0	10.00	10.000
h	88	87.7	87.65	87.654
i	0	0.0	0.00	0.001
j	0	0.3	0.28	0.283

15 **a** 578 km **b** 160 minutes

16 **a** 6.71 **b** 3.61 **c** 19.00 **d** 29.60 **e** 51.38

17 **a** 4.6 **b** 6.7 **c** 2.2 **d** 10.0 **e** 44.4

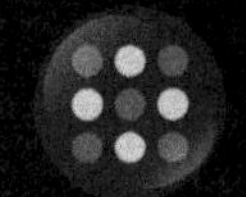

2 Measures, perimeter and area

Learning outcomes	
N12 Use standard units of mass, length, time, money and other measures, including with decimal quantities	(L5)
G1 Derive and apply formulae to calculate and solve problems involving: perimeter and area of triangles, parallelograms, trapezia, volume of cuboids (including cubes) and other prisms (including cylinders)	(L6)
G2 Calculate and solve problems involving: perimeters of 2D shapes (including circles), areas of circles and composite shapes	(L6)

Introduction

The chapter starts by looking at metric and imperial units of measure. Estimating the size of measurements is also included. The main focus is on mensuration: finding the area and perimeter of rectangles (including composite shapes) and then the area of triangles, parallelograms and trapeziums. The final two sections introduce the concepts of circumference and area of a circle.

The introduction discusses how the ancient Egyptians used geometry and measure to solve practical problems. Other ancient civilisations such as the Babylonians and the Greeks also used measure to solve problems. Eratosthenes even managed to calculate a fairly accurate value for the circumference of the earth using a basic understanding of geometry and measure.

Another Greek mathematician Euclid is considered to be the father of geometry and he wrote 13 books that together are known as 'Elements' where he outlined many different geometrical proofs using a very simple basis of 5 *axioms*. He worked in ancient Egypt in around 300 BC and although very little is known about his life, he is referred to by many other ancient scholars and original fragments of his work still exist today.

A good biography of Eratosthenes can be found at http://www-groups.dcs.st-and.ac.uk/~history/Biographies/Eratosthenes.html

A good biography of Euclid can also be found at http://www-history.mcs.st-and.ac.uk/Mathematicians/Euclid.html

Prior knowledge

Students should already know how to…

- Multiply and divide numbers, including decimals given to 1 decimal place
- Find areas and perimeters of rectangles

Starter problem

The starter problem actually requires students to have completed the work on circumference and area of a circle (sections **2e** and **2f**). Knowledge that a tangent to a circle and its radius are at 90° might also be useful.

In working out the perimeter of the band, students might notice that the band touches each circle for one third of its circumference and so the total of touching band is equal to one complete circumference. The three lengths of band that do not touch the circles are actually equal to two times the radius each so we need to add on six times the radius in total.

$2 \times \pi \times 10 + 6 \times 10 = 20\pi + 60 \approx 122.8$ cm

The area is more difficult to find. We have to break the enclosed area down into three components: three one third circles on each corner, three rectangles down each side (vertices at the centre of each circle and where the tangents meet the circles) and an equilateral triangle in the middle (vertices at the centre of each circle). The three one third circles add up to a complete circle area. Calculating the area of the triangle without knowledge of trigonometry is not possible so this might be given to the students: 173.2 cm^2.

$\pi \times 10^2 + 10 \times 20 \times 3 + 173.2 \approx 1087$ cm^2

Resources

MyMaths

Metric conversion	1061	Area of circles	1083	Areas of rectangles	1084
Circumference of a circle	1088	Area of a parallelogram	1108	Perimeter	1110
Area of a trapezium	1128	Area of a triangle	1129	Imperial measures	1191

Online assessment

Chapter test	2C–2
Formative test	2C–2
Summative test	2C–2

InvisiPen solutions

Perimeter and area of a triangle			314
Area of a parallelogram and a trapezium			315
Metric measure	332	Imperial measure	333
Circumference of a circle	351	Area of a circle	352

Topic scheme

Teaching time = 6 lessons/2 weeks

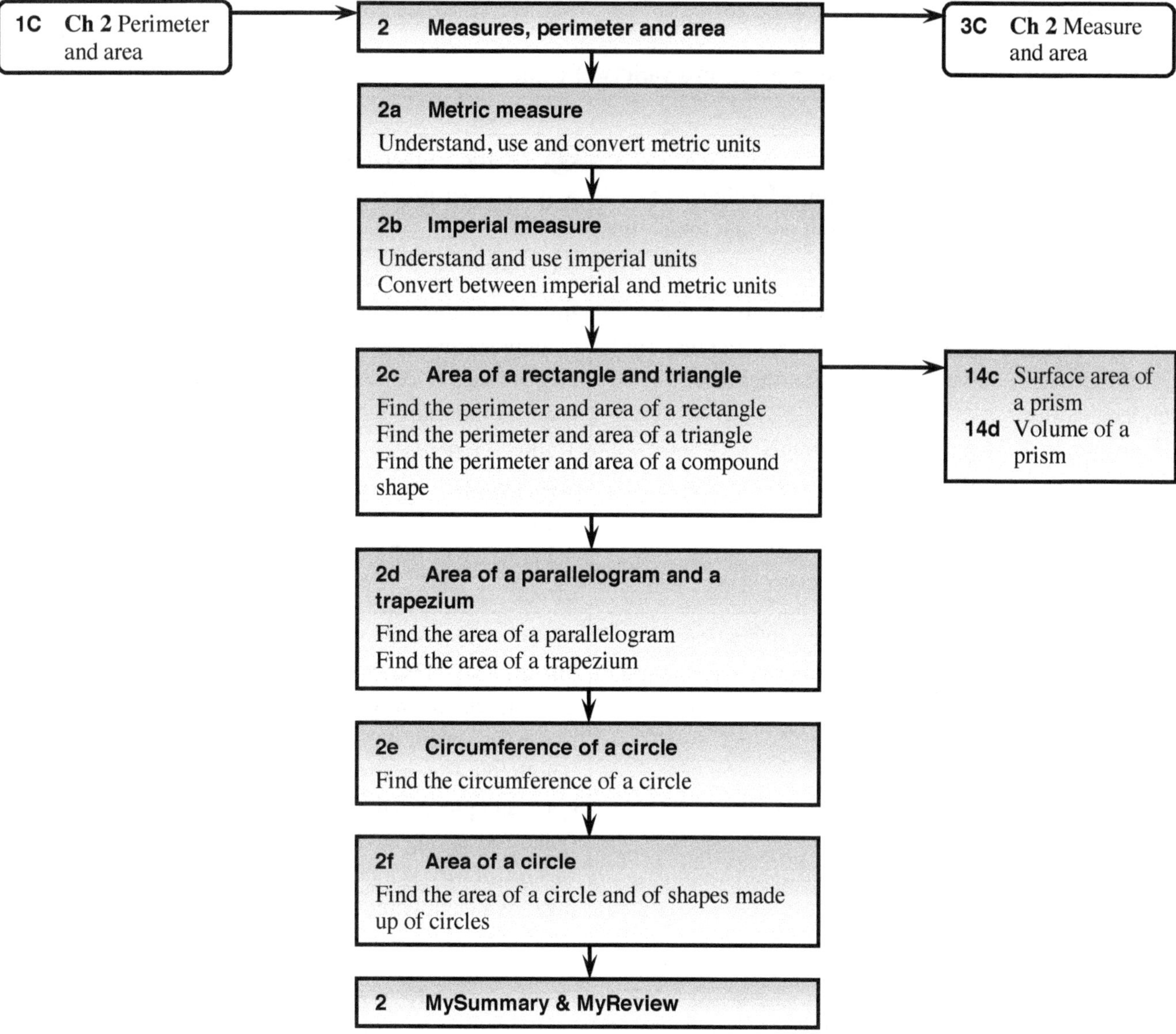

1C Ch 2 Perimeter and area
2 Measures, perimeter and area
3C Ch 2 Measure and area
2a Metric measure
Understand, use and convert metric units
2b Imperial measure
Understand and use imperial units
Convert between imperial and metric units
2c Area of a rectangle and triangle
Find the perimeter and area of a rectangle
Find the perimeter and area of a triangle
Find the perimeter and area of a compound shape
14c Surface area of a prism
14d Volume of a prism
2d Area of a parallelogram and a trapezium
Find the area of a parallelogram
Find the area of a trapezium
2e Circumference of a circle
Find the circumference of a circle
2f Area of a circle
Find the area of a circle and of shapes made up of circles
2 MySummary & MyReview

Differentiation

Student book 2A 24 – 43	Student book 2B 24 – 39	Student book 2C 22 – 39
Metric measure	Metric measure	Metric measure
Metric and money conversions	Imperial measure	Imperial measure
Other units of measure	Perimeter and area of a rectangle	Area of a rectangle and a triangle
Reading scales	Area of a triangle	Area of a parallelogram and a trapezium
Perimeter and area	Area of a parallelogram and a trapezium	Circumference of a circle
Area of a rectangle		Area of a circle
Shapes made from rectangles		

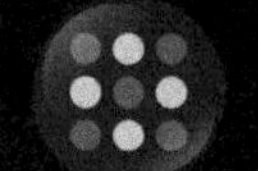

2a Metric measure

Objectives

- Choose and use units of measurement to measure, estimate, calculate and solve problems in a range of contexts (L5)
- Convert one metric unit to another (L5)
- Solve problems involving measurements in a variety of contexts (L5)

Key ideas

1 The naming of metric units
2 Amounts can be expressed in any of a choice of units, and can be converted from one unit to another

Resources

Metric conversion (1061)

250 ml and 1 litre bottles, filled

Simplification

Students who find it difficult to appreciate the varying values of measures depending on place value may find it useful to use equivalence to help further their understanding.
For example, 0.2 kg = how many grams?
Begin with 1 kg = 1000 g.
Divide by 10 → 0.1 kg = 100 g.

Extension

Investigate the use of prefixes in measurements. What examples can pupils find? For example, megaton bomb or gigabytes of computer memory. Some commonly used prefixes are:

kilo	10^3	thousands	milli	10^{-3}	thousandths
Mega	10^6	millions	micro	10^{-6}	millionths
Giga	10^9	billions	nano	10^{-9}	billionths
Terra	10^{12}	trillions	pico	10^{-12}	trillionths

Literacy

Some words may need a little more explanation.

The understanding of mass, in particular, may need to be checked, and the distinction between this and weight discussed a little.

Links

Measurement of length was originally based on the human body. The ancient Egyptians used a unit called a cubit, which was the length of an arm from the elbow to the fingertips. As everybody's arm was a different length, the Egyptians developed the standard Royal cubit and preserved this length as a black granite rod. Other measuring sticks were made the same length as this rod. There is a picture of a cubit rod at http://www.globalegyptianmuseum.org/detail.aspx?id=4424

Alternative approach

The term metric should be explored a little, and also perhaps the definition and historical context of the metre as a unit of measurement based on the Earth rather than the human body. (Explore the connection between the metre, the French Revolution and the distance of 10 million metres from North Pole to Equator.) All other metric units follow from the metre. For example, the kilogram is the mass of a cubic decimetre of water, again based on a natural substance rather than anything to do with a person.

Could a more convenient unit have been found? (For example, if there had been 100 million metres from Pole to Pole, the metre would have measured approximately a hand span, about the right length for a ruler.)

Checkpoint

1 How many 750 g bags of flour can be fitted into a 7.5 tonne lorry? (10 000)

Starter

Write 10.72 on the board.

Ask students what answer you will get if you multiply the number by 10^3, 10^2, 10^4.

Repeat with different start numbers.

Can be extended by using division.

Teaching notes

Ask students to suggest a number of different measures, which are metric and which are imperial? Are any measurements neither? (Time) Students could fill in a list of metric measures. How many were known?

When converting between measures, place value can speed up the process. Examine what each digit represents in a measurement. For example, 2.304 km in metres. An analogy could be made with pounds and pence.

An alternative approach is to use multiplication and division by a power of ten. Look at the examples in the student book, challenge students to explain how to tell which of multiplication or division is needed.

Some students may rely on the answer being of the correct order of magnitude. Encourage students to consider if the answer is sensible.

Estimation of the mass of everyday objects can be difficult. For small objects students can be encouraged to relate mass to water. Pass round a litre bottle and equate this to 1 kg or 1000 g. For larger objects the mass of a student is helpful. Average for a year 8 student is around 40 to 50 kg.

Plenary

Match the English coins to their corresponding approximate masses in grams, listed here is ascending order.

3.3, 3.6, 5.0, 6.5, 7.1, 8.0, 9.5, 12.0
(5p, 1p, 20p, 10p, 2p, 50p, £1, £2 respectively)

Slot machines use a coin's weight to help identify it.

Exercise commentary

Question 1 – This question could be a good way to promote class debate. Homework could be set for pupils to investigate how close their estimates are.

Questions 2 – 8 – Ask students what each digit represents, emphasise the importance of place value.

Question 9 – Encourage students to sketch a hectare to help find the side lengths.

Question 10 – Encourage students to give an estimate at the outset. Could also lead to a discussion on how accurately a person's height can be measured.

Answers

1 **a** 300 000 to 3 000 000 litres
b 30 to 120 cm **c** 500 cm^2
d 1 to 50 litres **e** 30 to 80 kg
f 4 000 to 11 000 km **g** 80 to 700 m
h ≈ 50 g **i** ≈ 100 cm^2
j 200 ml or 20 cl

2 **a** 176 cm **b** 1760 mm

3 50 000 m

4 **a** 400 mm **b** 200 g **c** 25 000 m^2
d 8500 m **e** 650 cl **f** 0.5 l
g 6.3 t **h** 80 cm **i** 14 100 kg
j 13.8 ha **k** 10 cl **l** 500 000 cm
m 1 kg

5 **a** 8375 g **b** 8.375 kg

6 4770 m

7 The shampoo in the smaller bottle is cheaper.
4×250 ml = 1 litre
4×99p = £3.96 whereas 1 litre bottle costs £3.99
So, four small bottles cost less than one large bottle.

8 30 teaspoons

9 100 m by 100 m

10 1 cm = 100 sheets
Typically 150 cm = 15 000 sheets

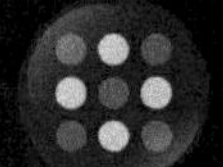

2b Imperial measure

Objectives

- Know rough metric equivalents of imperial measures in common use, such as miles, pounds (lb) and pints (L5)
- Read and interpret scales on a range of measuring instruments (L5)

Key ideas

1. The naming of imperial units
2. Amounts can be expressed in a choice of units, and can be converted from one unit to another
3. Amounts can also be converted approximately between metric and imperial

Resources

Imperial measures (1191)

Packet of biscuits

Simplification

Students who find it difficult to decide whether multiplication or division is appropriate may find it easier to use a proportional method. For example, change 70 miles into km.

$$1 \text{ mile} \approx 1.6 \text{ km}$$
$$\times 70 \downarrow \qquad \times 70 \downarrow$$
$$70 \text{ miles} \approx 112 \text{ km}$$

Extension

Most drivers used to measure a car's economy by stating the number of miles to the gallon that could be achieved. Today many people still continue to use this, but in the future people may well state the number of km to the litre. How would you covert miles/gallon to km/litre? Multiply by approximately 0.35 (0.354006…) Students could construct their own examples of a car's economy.

Literacy

Time could be spent on others of the many units that have been in use until relatively recently … and those that are still in use, such as the chain (a tenth of a furlong, which is an eighth of a mile), the distance between the wickets in cricket. Many schools will still have an actual chain somewhere on the premises, for measuring this.

Note that imperial measures could fairly be seen and termed as British. Discuss why.

Links

The United States has its own system of weights and measures which is largely similar to the imperial system. Yards, feet, inches and pounds are all in everyday use; however, the US pint and gallon are both smaller than the imperial pint and gallon. For more information see
http://home.clara.net/brianp/usa.html
or
http://en.wikipedia.org/wiki/Imperial_units

Alternative approach

How might someone reliably use a measure for fuel consumption of either miles per gallon, or km per litres, when fuel is sold in litres and distances are measured in miles? (Students might have interesting information about the metering facilities of modern vehicles.) Would a measurement of miles per litre be natural and sensible here? (Opinions may vary.)

This would hardly be unique in its mixed units. For example, boarding for flooring is manufactured in sheets 2.4 m by 4 foot. We are not going to rebuild all our houses, so the sheets must fit the standard 16 inch separation of floor joists. Ask students to say how these dimensions do this.

There is one exact matching of metric to imperial, ever since the inch was redefined as exactly 2.54 cm. (It used to be a little over that.) A mile is accordingly 1609.344 m, exactly.

The advice that we should drink two litres of water a day is a very commonly quoted guideline. The original reports agreed that we need about two litres a day, and then also said that most or all of this can be derived from food eaten. Discuss recent advice on daily fluid consumption. Is the recommendation the same for men and women? What factors might influence someone's required daily intake of water? What is the imperial equivalent of two litres? How does this measure equate to an average sized glass?

Checkpoint

1. The national speed limit in Canada is 100 km per hour. What is this speed in miles per hr? (62.5 mph)

Starter

Write the following measurements on the board:

0.01 g, 0.1 g, 0.1 kg, 1 g, 1 kg, 1t, 10 mg, 10 g, 100 mg, 100 g, 1000 mg, 1000 g, 1000 kg, 10 000 mg.

Ask students to find the equivalent pairs.

This can be extended by asking students to make their own equivalent pairs for capacity or length.

Teaching notes

Some rhymes may be useful here:

- A litre of water's a pint and three quarters.
- Two and a quarter pounds of jam are round about a kilogram.
- A meter measures three foot three; it's longer than a yard you see.

An unusual way to remember that 5 miles ≈ 8 km is as follows.

- Find a student in the class who lives about 5 miles from school, this is best done using an online map for the whole class to see.
- Send that student outside the classroom and ask them to act out something that they do at home. For example, watching TV, cutting the grass.
- Give every member of the remaining class a biscuit and ask them to scratch 'km' onto their biscuit.
- Explain that the whole class is now going to 'walk' five miles to the student's house. Take the class to where the student is pretending to be at home.
- When you get there ask the students what have they done so far. They answer, 'Walked 5 miles!'
- Now ask them all to eat their biscuits. Ask again what they have done so far. Establish that they have all 'Walked 5 miles and ate (8) km'.

Plenary

Using a list of measure conversions with blanks, ask students to fill in as many gaps as they can based on the lesson. Ask students if they have any particular ways of recalling the measures now. Many students may be able to draw on outside experiences, for example, the kitchen, athletics, fishing, where they may be using metric and imperial measures.

Exercise commentary

Questions 2–4 – Encourage students to memorise the conversions. Tell them you will have a little test at the end of the lesson.

Question 4 – Challenge the students to give one metric answer and one imperial.

Question 5 – Petrol used to be sold in gallons. The fuel consumption rate for cars is still given as miles per gallon. A harder conversion would be to convert 35 miles per gallon into km per litre. This is the measurement used in Europe.

Question 7 – Students may have a preference as to which they use. 1 mile ≈ 1.6 km, 1 km ≈ 0.625 mile, 5 miles ≈ 8 km ?

Question 8 – Encourage the use of an estimate, for example, 2 × 350 = 700 litres. Use 1 litre ≈ 2 pints.

Question 9 – Conduct a class poll before they answer the question. Once it is established that they are in fact the same length, ask why it is that BC appears shorter.

Question 10 – This question assumes that American fluid ounces and imperial fluid ounces are equal. They are only approximately equal, so if a student were to look up how many litres are in an American gallon, they would find a different result.

Answers

1 **a** inch **b** kilogram **c** litre **d** mile
e metre

2 **a** 3.6 litres **b** 9.9 lb **c** 45 litres **d** 112 km
e 90 cm **f** 99 lb **g** 1500 ml **h** 150 cm
i 135 g **j** 62.5 miles

3 **a** 12 inches **b** 7 pints **c** 7.5 miles **d** 0.5 pints
e 9 gallons **f** 47 kg **g** 15 oz **h** 9.6 inches
i 22 feet **j** 50 inches

4 **a** 11 t, 11 000 kg; 11.5 t, 11 500 kg
b 8.6 cm, 86 mm; 9.2 cm, 92 mm
c 2.25 inches, 0.1875 ft; 2.6 inches, 0.2167 ft
d 0.4 litre, 400 ml, 40 cl; 0.7 litre, 700 ml, 70 cl
e 0.8 kg, 800 g; 1.4 kg, 1400 g, 1 kg 400 g
f 0.25 gallons, 2 pints;
0.5 gallons, 4 pints

5 **a** 13 200 inches, 1920 inches
b 33 000 cm, 4800 cm
c 330 m, 48 m

6 £5.58

7 5 miles per hour

8 1217 pints

9 **a** Same length in reality
b AB = 3 cm BC = 3 cm
c AB = 1.2 inches BC = 1.2 inches

10 ≈ 3.8 litres

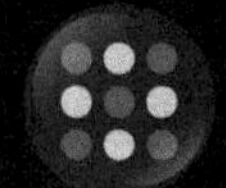

2c Area of a rectangle and a triangle

Objectives	
• Calculate the area and perimeter of shapes made from rectangles	(L5)
• Derive and use the formula for the area of a triangle	(L6)

Key ideas	Resources
1 Formula for the area of a rectangle **2** Formula for the area of a triangle	Area of rectangles (1084) Perimeter (1110) Area of a triangle (1129) Square grid paper

Simplification	Extension
Students could use pre-printed copies of questions, some of which are draw full size on cm square grids. Students should feel free to annotate the drawings.	A regular hexagon has a perimeter of 60 cm. Why is it difficult to find the area? Give the hint that six congruent equilateral triangles make a regular hexagon. Encourage students to sketch the shape and discover what lengths they can. The problem is that, although two lengths are known, they are not perpendicular. Encourage a student to explain to others what information can be found and what information is still missing.

Literacy	Links
It is important that an effort is made to clarify the idea of the units as square cm, square km, and so on, and not cm square, and so on. The use of cm^2 as the symbol for square cm is confusing, and it should be made clear that it is a single symbol. The ^{2} can be seen as an indication of dimensions, area being 2-dimensional. A sketch of, say, a 5cm square might help; clearly, 5 cm square (or squared, but saying square makes the point well) is 25 square cm, or cm^2.	An area of 10 000 m^2 is called a hectare and is often used to measure land areas. Measure or estimate the size of the classroom. What fraction is this of a hectare? Estimate how many hectares the school field or other local open space covers. The O_2 complex in Greenwich has a ground area of over 80 000m^2. How many hectares is this? There is information on the O_2 at http://en.wikipedia.org/wiki/The_O2

Alternative approach

Talking of the area as being a number of squares (and then, bits that add up to squares or bits of squares) seems to be a natural and therefore comprehensible and memorable way of conveying the idea.

Note that for diagrams such as that in the first example, there is no need to find any missing lengths in order to find the perimeter; cutting off corners in the way shown – however many, as long as no indenting (as in question **1** part **c**) takes place and the cuts are all parallel to the sides and the overall dimensions stay the same, as shown – does not change the perimeter, which is therefore still twice length plus width. Students could be encouraged to see this. In the example, 2 × 19. Similarly for question **1** parts **a** and **b**.

For the method shown of finding area, only one of the missing lengths is needed. Will either do? Students should be able to see that this is so. Both missing lengths will be needed if subtracting the missing piece from the whole rectangle (in the example, 10 × 9 – 3 × 5) – which may be a method that appeals to some students.

In the second example, encourage students to spot that there is no need to work out the area of any triangle, since a pair of triangles will make a rectangle.

For question **6**, ask students what shape has the greatest area for a given perimeter (in this context, length of rope). A circle should be agreed. Then, what kind of rectangle is most like a circle? A square should be acceptably obvious, especially if extremely non-symmetric, thin, rectangles, with nearly zero area, are considered, to encourage the idea of the importance of symmetry here.

Checkpoint	
1 What is the height of a triangle with a base of 8 cm and an area of 20 cm^2?	(5 cm)

Starter

Draw lines on the board.

Ask students to estimate the length of the lines in cm.

Ask how much this would be in inches.

Use a scoring system for the estimations, for example, within 10% score 3 points, within 20% score 1 point. Bonus points for correct metric to imperial conversion.

Teaching notes

What is meant by area? Do not accept answers that just relate to 'the space inside'. Draw a rectangle with dimensions 3 by 4. The area is 12. But 12 what? Establish that area is just '*the number of squares inside a shape*'. Once the individual squares are drawn in place ask why do we multiply the two side lengths of the rectangle together? Invite answers that explain the way that multiplication totals up the rows by the columns, that is, a quick way to add up all the squares.

What strategies could be used with compound shapes? Sketch a few examples made from rectangles. Is there more than one way to subdivide a shape? Does it matter how you cut the shape up?

Cut your original rectangle in half through the diagonal. What is the area of the resulting triangle? Establish that this area is exactly half of the rectangle around it. How can the area of any triangle be found? Look at the way in which a rectangle around the triangle always gives twice the area of the triangle. Introduce the formula area

$$= \frac{1}{2} \text{ base} \times \text{perpendicular height}$$

Plenary

Can the students write a formula for the side length given the area and one of the side lengths? Will the formula be different for a rectangle and a right-angled triangle? What about a square?

Exercise commentary

Question 1 – Cutting up the shapes is likely to be the best approach. Some students may prefer to draw a bounding rectangle and subtract to find the area. Some students will incorrectly find the perimeter unless they label every edge.

Questions 1–4 – Remind students to always use correct units for area.

Question 3 – Prepare from card two large identical triangles. Cut one down its perpendicular heights. Use this as an illustration to emphasise to students calculations for area must involve multiplying two perpendicular lengths.

Question 4 – Students may initially try to count squares. Elicit a more accurate method of subtracting triangles.

Question 5 – What are the advantages/disadvantages of a trial and improvement method? Encourage students to check their final solution.

Question 6 – A spreadsheet could be used to show the maximum area is a square.

Answers

1 **a** 20 cm, 18 cm^2 **b** 40 cm, 72 cm^2
c 30 cm, 26 cm^2

2 **a** 18 cm^2 **b** 18.75 m^2 **c** 90 cm^2 **d** 4 m^2

3 **a** $w = 3$ cm **b** $w = 7.5$ mm
c $b = 8$ cm **d** $h = 7.2$ m
e $x = 6$ cm **f** $s = 2$ m

4 **a** 17 square units **b** 12 square units
c 12.5 square units **d** 9 square units

5 $h = 9$ cm

6 56.25 m^2

2d Area of a parallelogram and a trapezium

Objectives	
• Derive and use the formulae for the area of a parallelogram and trapezium (L6)	
Key ideas	**Resources**
1 Formula for the area of a parallelogram **2** Formula for the area of a trapezium	Area of a parallelogram (1108) Area of a trapezium (1128)
Simplification	**Extension**
Provide students with a printout of the exercise and encourage them to label the base, perpendicular height, etc. before performing the calculations. Check that the student has correctly identified the required measurements before they begin using the formulae.	Challenge students to provide a formula for the area of a kite. Do you need to know all the side lengths or the diagonal lengths or a mixture? Formulae is (width × height) / 2 where the width and height are the lengths of the two diagonals. Students might adopt the method of a bounding rectangle or subdivide into smaller triangles.
Literacy	**Links**
Check the understanding of the students of what a parallelogram and a trapezium are – perhaps review their properties.	The Trapezium cluster is a bright cluster of stars in the constellation of Orion discovered by Galileo in 1617. The four brightest stars form the shape of a trapezium. There is more information about the Trapezium cluster at http://en.wikipedia.org/wiki/Trapezium_cluster and at http://www.astropix.com/HTML/B_WINTER/TRAPEZ.HTM

Alternative approach

There is a need for an initial step of showing that the area of a parallelogram is the same as that of a rectangle, base × perpendicular height. This can be quite easily and convincingly demonstrated by taking a pile of books, agreeing that the spines make a rectangle, and then pushing the pile sideways (shearing, if a word is wanted) to create a parallelogram … which clearly has the same area as the rectangle. The slant height, or slope length, can be made longer and longer. Is this relevant, or is it only the perpendicular height that matters?

Then, note that the parallelogram consists of two congruent triangles, so that the formula for the area of the triangle must be half this; this will work nicely for triangles with one of their base angles obtuse, extending the work of the last spread.

The formula for the area of a trapezium can be found in a variety of ways, and students could be encouraged to make their own suggestions. For example, divide into two triangles, and add their areas. Or, to follow from the division of a parallelogram into two triangles, move the dividing line to create two congruent trapeziums instead, and then label each base (the two parallel sides can quite helpfully each be seen as a base) as $a + b$. The area of the parallelogram is clear, and each trapezium is half of this.

For question **3**, the simplest approach is to reconfigure the shape as a rectangle by drawing a horizontal line through the gable, halfway up from the eaves level to the ridge level. Check students can then see that two triangles from the apex have effectively been moved onto the eaves, so that the height of the rectangle is … 17 m. When the area is simply 17×20 m^2. This method is worth remembering.

Checkpoint

1 What is the area of a parallelogram with a base of 8 cm, a sloping side of 5 cm and a perpendicular height of 4 cm? (32 cm^2)

Starter

Give the area and base of triangles and ask students for the heights, for example,

Area = 18 cm^2 and base = 3 cm (12 cm)
Area = 24 cm^2 and base = 6 cm (8 cm)
Area = 25 cm^2 and base = 10 cm (5 cm)

This can be extended by using numbers that will generate decimal heights.

Teaching notes

Remind students that area represents the number of squares inside a shape. Look at a parallelogram, base = 4, perpendicular height = 3. Why is it awkward to find the exact area? Show how the triangle at one end of the parallelogram can be moved to the other end to form a rectangle. What is the area of the rectangle? 4 × 3 = 12. Draw a general parallelogram and establish the formula for the area:
Area = base × perpendicular height

Draw a trapezium and ask students for suggestions for methods for finding the area. These may include breaking up the shape into two triangles and a rectangle. Why will this not work? Show how two identical trapeziums can fit together to form a parallelogram. How can the area of the parallelogram be found? Establish that the trapezium is just half of the area of the parallelogram. How is the base of the parallelogram made? From the sum of the two parallel sides of the trapezium. Establish the formula: Area =

$$\frac{\text{sum of parallel sides} \times \text{perpendicular height}}{2}$$

This rhyme may aid remembering the formula '*Half the sum of the parallel sides, times the distance between them, that's how you calculate, the area of a trap-eee-zium*' sung to the tune of 'half a pound of tuppenny rice'.

Plenary

Can a formula be constructed to find the area of a wall like the one in question **3**? Imagine that the width and overall height are always the same (x) and the shorter side height is different (y). You can split the area as a rectangle and a triangle or as two identical trapeziums.

$$\text{Area} = xy + \frac{x(x-y)}{2} \quad \text{or} = \frac{x(x+y)}{2}$$

Exercise commentary

All the questions can be done without a calculator, but one could prove useful in checking the answers for question **3**.

Question 1 – Prepare from card two large identical triangles and two large identical trapeziums to be able to show students visually why the formulae for the areas of parallelograms and trapeziums work.

Question 4 – Students should check their answer using their formulae for area.

Question 5 – Ask students to first calculate the compound area as a rectangle and triangle and then as two trapeziums and check whether they get the same result.

Question 6 – At first a trial-and-improvement method would be suitable. Examination of the formula with the area and height substituted in should lead to a discussion about the value of $a + b$ (=10). If you only allow integers then there are only four possible solutions. How many solutions are there all together?

Answers

1 **a** 432 cm^2 **b** 360 cm^2 **c** 6 m^2 **d** 36 cm^2
e 2.5 m^2 **f** 8 mm^2

2 **a** 50 cm^2 **b** 20 mm^2 **c** 55.44 m^2
d 11 400 cm^2, 1.14 m^2

3 **a** 140 cm^2 **b** 199.5 cm^2 **c** 44.16 m^2

4

	i	**ii**
a	h = 2.5 cm	h = 6 m
b	w = 4.75 cm	l = 5 mm
c	y = 22 mm	x = 14 cm

5 **a** 340 m^2 **b** 68 litres of paint

6 Find values of a and b, with $a < b$, such that $a + b = 10$,
For example, a = 1 cm, b = 9 cm

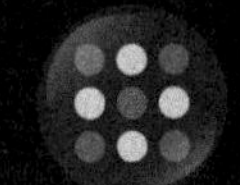

2e Circumference of a circle

Objectives

- Know the definition of a circle and the names of its parts (L5)
- Know and use the formula for the circumference of a circle (L6)

Key ideas

1 The naming of parts of a circle

2 $C = \pi D = 2\pi r$

Resources

Circumference of a circle (1088)

Pi to 100 dp

Simplification

Provide students with a table to help record their working. For example

Pi (3.14)	Diameter	Circumference (remember the units)
3.14	3 cm	3.14 × 3 = 9.42 cm

Extension

One way to calculate the value of pi is to use the Gregory-Leibnitz series. Calculate $\frac{4}{1}$ to get your first approximation, then calculate $\frac{4}{1}-\frac{4}{3}$ to get a better approximation. Next calculate $\frac{4}{1}-\frac{4}{3}+\frac{4}{5}$ to get a third and improved approximation. How far can you approximate pi to?

$\pi = \frac{4}{1}-\frac{4}{3}+\frac{4}{5}-\frac{4}{7}+\frac{4}{9}-\frac{4}{11}$ (convergence is very slow).

If this went on forever, would it give you the 'correct' value of pi? (Yes)

Literacy

See what other circle terms students know, such as semicircle, sector, segment, and so on. Share with the class whatever terms are recalled.

Links

Stone circles can be found across the British Isles with the most famous example at Stonehenge in Wiltshire. The circles vary in size and are not always completely circular but they all date from about 3000 BC to 1500 BC. Their exact purpose is unknown but there are often burial mounds nearby. There is a map showing all the stone circles in the UK at http://www.megalith.ukf.net/bigmap.htm

Alternative approach

The exact value of pi can only be written with a symbol, such as π; as a decimal, it cannot be written exactly, only with as many hundreds, thousands or millions of digits as we care to manage.

The value on the calculator will be far more accurate than we ever need, and is easier to use that any keyed-in decimal value, so it is definitely preferable to, say, 3.14, even though some rounding of answers will be necessary – and rounding is necessary with 3.14, in any case. So use the calculator key.

When measuring, as in question **2**, only a couple of figures of accuracy can be given in the answer, at best; when given values, as in question **3** onwards, that are only given to a couple of figures, then again only a couple of figures can be given in the answer, at best. But still, it is good practice to use the calculator key.

Checkpoint

1 Calculate to 1 dp the circumference of a circle with a radius of 4.5 cm. (28.3 cm)

Starter

Write a list of areas on the board, for example, 88, 12, 20, 36, 132, 54, 28, 24, 96, 45, 18, 49 cm^2.

Ask students to draw a 3 × 3 grid and enter nine areas from the list. Give information such as:

The base of a triangle is 3 cm, the height is 8 cm.
The base of a parallelogram is 14 cm, the height is 3.5 cm.

The winner is the first student to cross out all their areas.

Teaching notes

Introduce the parts of a circle: radius, diameter, circumference and arc. What abbreviations do students think mathematicians use for the first three?

There is a connection between the diameter and the circumference of a circle, the same connection for every circle. Give a set of examples and ask students to use a calculator to try to find the connection. (Note that the circumferences have been rounded to 1 dp.)

Diameter (cm)	10	5	1	3
Circumference (cm)	31.4	15.7	3.1	9.4

Agree the answer is multiplication by about 3.1 to 3.2; it is not possible to get an exact answer.

Introduce students to the symbol for pi and examine its value to 9 dp. State the equation for finding the circumference: $C = \pi d$. The alternative formula involving radius could also be looked at.

Give examples of circumference calculations for a given diameter/radius, using $\pi = 3.14$. Emphasise the structure of the calculation.

- Write formula
- Substitute in values
- Work out the answer

Plenary

Who in the class can memorise pi to the greatest number of decimal places? Display the value to 100 places.

Exercise commentary

Question 1 – Students may need reminding how to convert a fraction into a decimal using a calculator. Take every opportunity to reinforce the fact that the fraction line is also a dividing line.

Question 2 – When measuring the radius and diameter, one can be worked out from the other. If the centre dot were absent, which one can be measured more accurately? (Diameter)

Question 4 – Encourage students to (i) write the formula, (ii) substitute in values, (iii) work out the answer. Note that the units vary.

Question 5 – An annotated diagram will help to connect the side length of the square with the diameter of the circle. Drawing a chord across a quadrant of the circle/diagonal of the square may help to answer part **c**.

Question 5 – Discuss whether smaller or bigger objects would give a more accurate value. Collect all the class results for diameter and circumference onto a spreadsheet and calculate a class average for π. Compare it with the actual value.

Answers

1 **d** 3.142

2 **a** $r = 0.6$ cm $d = 1.25$ cm $C = 3.93$ cm^2
b $r = 0.85$ cm $d = 1.7$ cm $C = 5.34$ cm^2
c $r = 0.4$ cm $d = 0.8$cm $C = 2.51$ cm^2

3 **a** 21.98 cm **b** 50.24 m
c 62.8 cm **d** 15.7 m

4 **a** 37.68 cm **b** 13.19 mm
c 3.93 m **d** 219.8 mm

5 **a** 40 cm **b** 31.4 cm
c The distance around the outside of the square is more than the distance around the circle.

6 Students' measurements and calculations; π

7

	i	ii
a	6.0 cm	3.0 cm
b	15.6 mm	7.8 mm
c	17.2 m	8.6 m
d	26.9 m	13.5 m

Objectives	
• Know the definition of a circle and the names of its parts	(L5)
• Know and use the formula for the area of a circle	(L6)

Key ideas

1 More naming of parts of a circle
2 $A = \pi r^2$

Resources

Area of circles (1083)

Simplification

Provide students with a table to help record their working. For example,

Pi (π)	Radius	Circumference (remember the units)
π	3 cm	$\pi \times 3^2 = 28.3$ cm^2

Extension

How can the circumference of a circle be calculated if only the area is known? Investigate.

Literacy

Check words as before, to see what else is recalled. Ask, what is the longest chord called? What is a segment that is also a sector? (A semicircle.)

Links

Since 1988, Pi Day has been celebrated around the world on 14th March, which coincidentally was also Einstein's birthday. In the US the date is written 3/14. On Pi Day, people eat pies and pizzas and march around circular spaces. There is more information at
http://www.piday.org/
and at
http://news.bbc.co.uk/2/hi/uk_news/magazine/7296224.stm

Alternative approach

It can be quite memorable for students to take part in a class discussion from which the formula for the area of a circle emerges. Students will agree that there will have to be two dimensions multiplied, in order to find an area, and that, since there is only one measure for a circle, the radius, it will have to be $r \times r$ … and that, since the shape is a circle, π will also have to be involved.

Show students one of the reasons that the old BODMAS rule was replaced with BIDMAS was precisely for this formula: in what order should calculations be made, if not keying the entire calculation into the calculator?

Remind students to use the π key on the calculator, rather than keying in some other less accurate value, and then to give a sensible answer.

Checkpoint

1 Calculate the area of a circle with a diameter of 13.6 cm. (145.3 cm^2)

Starter

Write the following measurements on the board:

Circumference: 60 cm, 176 cm, 113 cm, 88 cm, 22 cm, 25 cm
Radius: 14 cm, 4 cm, 18 cm
Diameter: 56 cm, 19 cm, 7 cm

Ask students to find the equivalent pairs.

Can be extended by changing some of the units.

Teaching notes

Introduce the parts of a circle: chord, segment and sector.

There is a connection between the radius and the area of a circle, the same connection for every circle. Give a set of examples and ask students to use a calculator to try to find the connection. (Note that the areas have been rounded to 1 dp.) You could hint that the value of radius^2 needs to be used. For example,

Radius (cm)	10	5	1	3
Area (cm^2)	314.2	78.5	3.1	28.3

Agree the answer is multiplication by π and radius^2. State the equation for finding the area: $A = \pi r^2$. Give examples of area calculations for a given radius/diameter, using $\pi = 3.14$. Emphasise the structure of the calculation.

- Write formula
- Substitute in values
- Work out the answer

Point out the common error in calculating the area: multiplying π and r and then squaring that answer rather than just squaring the value of r.

The 'Did you know?' shows the obverse of a Field's medal – the mathematician's 'Nobel prize'.

Plenary

A rhyme may help remember the formulae for area and circumference. It can include two diagrams or hand actions.

If a ring round the moon you see, use the formula πd.

If the hole needs to be repaired, use the formula πr^2.

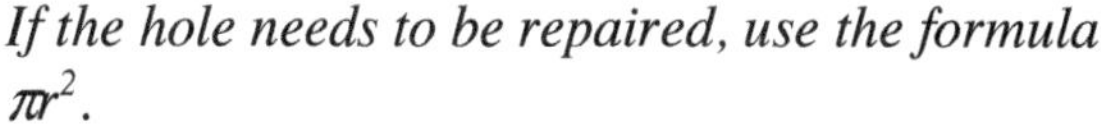

An alternative plenary could ask the following question: is the perimeter of a semicircle half the perimeter of the whole circle? Investigate.

Exercise commentary

Students should be familiar with the π key on scientific calculators.

Question 1 – Encourage students to square the radius and then multiply by π.

Question 2 – Encourage students to sketch the whole circle. This may help reduce the confusion over the radius and diameter measure. Finding the area of the whole circle first is a good procedure.

Question 4 – Some students will find it difficult to see the diameter as being equal to the width of the window. Ask students to label the length of every side they can.

Question 6 – Refer back to question **4** to help illustrate. Ask what happens if the radius is tripled, or quadrupled, or increased by 50%.

Answers

1 **a** 50.24 m^2 **b** 113.04 cm^2
c 1256 cm^2 **d** 153.86 cm^2
e 200.96 cm^2 **f** 706.5 m^2
g 415.27 mm^2 **h** 1017.36 m^2
i 379.94 cm^2 **j** 20096 cm^2
k 17662.5 mm^2 **l** 6358.5 m^2
m 145.19 cm^2 **n** 459.73 mm^2
o 7.79 m^2

2 **a** 39.25 cm^2 **b** 100.48 cm^2
c 7.065 cm^2

3 **a** 86 cm^2 **b** 86 cm^2

4 5481.25 cm^2

5 **a** 235.5 cm^2 **b** 117.75 cm^2
c 157 cm^2

6 The area of the circle is 4 times larger.

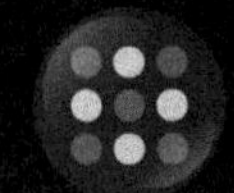

2 Measures, perimeter and area – MySummary

Key outcomes	Quick check
Use appropriate metric units to measure length, mass, capacity and area.	A pharmaceutical company makes a medicine. This medecine needs to have 15 mg of the active ingredient per 25 cl of liquid. Convert this to kg per cubic metre. ($1m^3$ = 1000 litres) (60 kg)
Convert between metric units and metric and imperial units.	Convert 46 miles per gallon into km per litre. (16 km/litre)
Read and interpret scales on a range of measuring instruments.	A pair of very accurate scientific scales has 4 small dashes between 10 mg and 20 mg. How much is each dash worth in grams? (0.002 mg)
Calculate the area of a rectangle and a triangle.	A shape is made from a square and an isosceles triangle above the square. The height of the triangle is half the height of the square. The height of the square is 8 cm. What is the total area of the shape? (80 cm^2)
Calculate the area of a parallelogram and trapezium.	Draw a diagram of two identical parallelograms put together to make a trapezium. Use this diagram to show the formula for the area of a trapezium.
Know the names of parts of a circle.	Draw a diagram of a circle and label the radius, diameter, circumference, and an arc, a chord, a segment and a sector.
Calculate the circumference and area of a circle.	A £2 coin has a diameter of 28 mm. Calculate the circumference and area of the coin to the nearest whole number. (88 mm, 2463 mm^2)

MyMaths extra support

Lesson/online homework			Description
Units of length	1101	L4	Estimating and using standard units of length

MyReview

2 MySummary

Check out

You should now be able to ...

	Test it ➡ Questions
✓ Use appropriate metric units to measure length, mass, capacity and area.	1
✓ Convert between metric units and metric and Imperial units.	2, 3
✓ Read and interpret scales on a range of measuring instruments	4
✓ Calculate the area of a rectangle and a triangle.	5 – 8
✓ Calculate the area of a parallelogram and trapezium.	9, 10
✓ Know the names of parts of a circle.	11
✓ Calculate the circumference and area of a circle.	11

Language	Meaning	Example
Metric measurement	An international system of measurement based on the decimal system	m = metre, kg = kilogram ℓ = litre
Imperial measurement	System of measurement used in the US, Liberia and Myanmar as well as occasionally in the UK	yd = yard, lb = pound pt = pint
Perimeter	The sum of all the sides of a two-dimensional shape	The perimeter of a square = 4 × length of its side
Circumference	The perimeter of a circle	π × diameter
Arc	Part of the circumference	arc
Radius	The distance from the centre of the circle to the circumference	$r = \frac{\text{diameter}}{2}$
Diameter	The diameter is the distance across the circle through the centre	$D = 2r$

2 MyReview

1 Write an appropriate metric unit for each measurement.
- a The amount of water in a bucket.
- b The length of a pair of sunglasses.
- c The distance from London to Newcastle.

2 a Convert 2.5 km into cm.
- b Convert 3000 g into tonnes.

3 a Convert 4.5 kg into pounds.
- b Convert 3 pints into millilitres

4 Write down the readings on this scale.

ml 200 400 a b c d e

5 Calculate the area of this rectangle.

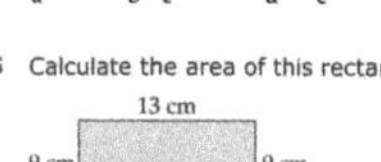

6 The area of this rectangle is 35 m². What is its perimeter?

7 m

7 Calculate the area of this triangle.

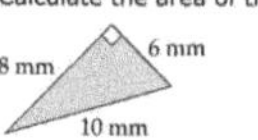

8 Calculate the area of this shape which has been made using two rectangles.

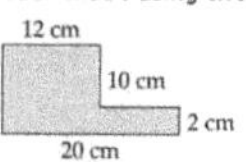

9 A parallelogram has a base of length 13 cm and an area of 104 cm². What is the height of the parallelogram?

10

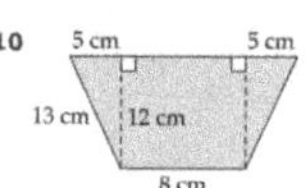

- a What is this shape called?
- b Calculate the area of the shape.

11

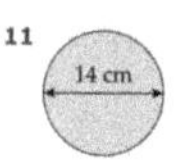

For this circle, calculate
- a its area
- b its circumference.

What next?

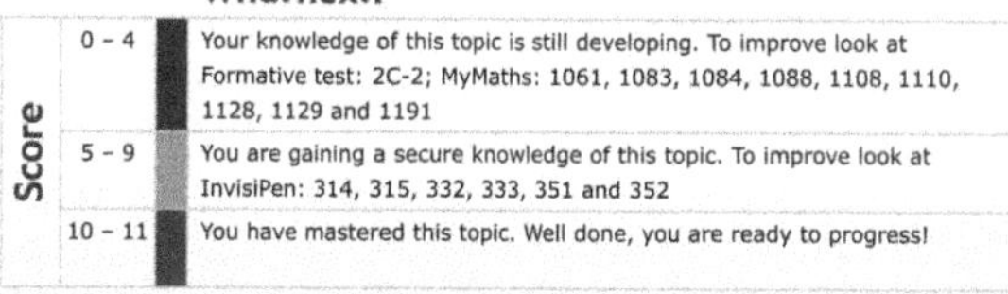

Score	
0 – 4	Your knowledge of this topic is still developing. To improve look at Formative test: 2C-2; MyMaths: 1061, 1083, 1084, 1088, 1108, 1110, 1128, 1129 and 1191
5 – 9	You are gaining a secure knowledge of this topic. To improve look at InvisiPen: 314, 315, 332, 333, 351 and 352
10 – 11	You have mastered this topic. Well done, you are ready to progress!

36 **Geometry** Measures, perimeter and area

MyMaths.co.uk 37

Question commentary

Question 1 – Students need to understand the meaning of the term 'metric'.

Questions 2 and **3** – Encourage students to recall conversions without having to look them up.

Questions 5 – 11 – Emphasise that correct units must always be stated.

Question 8 – Students can split the shape into 20 × 2 and 10 × 12 rectangles or 12 × 12 and 8 × 2.

Question 10 – The formula for the area of a trapezium does not necessarily need to be memorized but students need to know how to apply it and be able to identify trapeziums.

Question 11 – Encourage students to use the π button on their calculator. If non-scientific calculator, allow them to use $\pi = 3.14$.

Answers

1 **a** l **b** cm **c** km

2 **a** 250 000 cm **b** 0.003 tonnes

3 **a** 9.9 lb **b** 1800 ml

4 **a** 100 ml **b** 250 ml **c** 300 ml **d** 460 ml **e** 540 ml

5 117 cm²

6 24 m

7 24 mm²

8 160 cm²

9 8 cm

10 **a** (isosceles) trapezium **b** 156 cm²

11 **a** 153.86 cm² **b** 43.96 cm

2 MyPractice

2a

1 Calculate the number of 10 cm lengths of string that can be cut from a 5 m ball of string.

2 Convert these measurements to the units indicated in brackets.

a 8.5 ℓ (mℓ) **b** 456 mm (cm) **c** 8.5 ha (m^2) **d** 25 cl (mℓ) **e** 4.2 t (kg)

2b

3 Convert these measurements to the units indicated in brackets.

a 27.5 kg (lbs) **b** 120 cm (inches) **c** 135 g (oz)

d 750 ml (pints) **e** 850 miles (km)

4 Write down each reading on the scales.
Give an answer for each arrow.

a **b** **c**

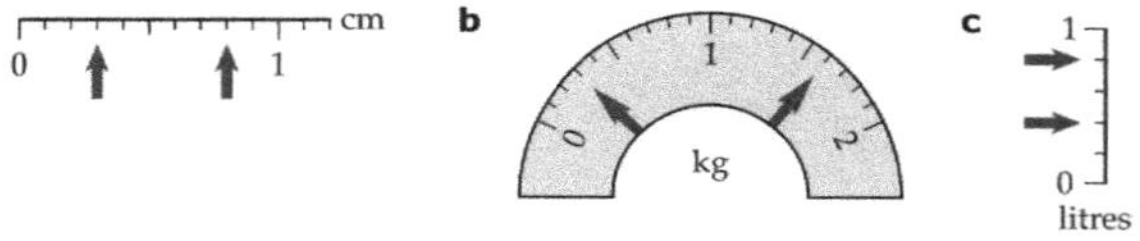

2c

5 Six identical rectangles are arranged in the shape of a large rectangle.
Calculate the area of one of the rectangles.

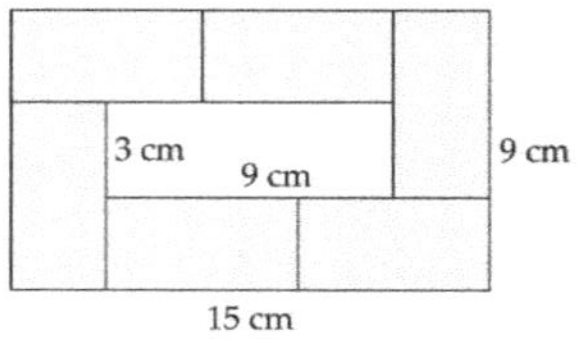

6 The area of each of these triangles is 40 cm^2.
Calculate the unknown values.

a **b** **c** **d**

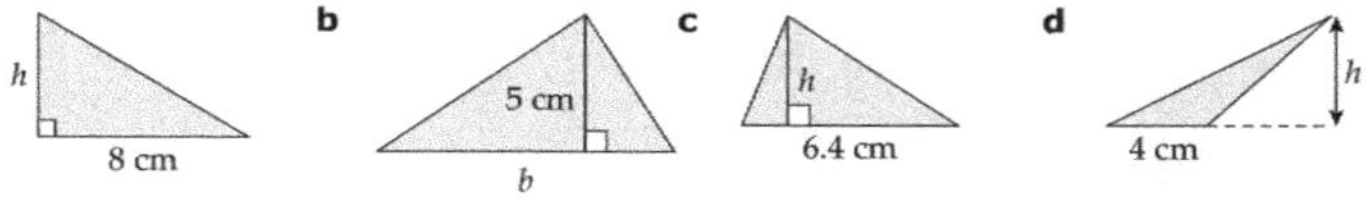

2d

7 Calculate the areas of the parallelogram and trapezia.

a **b** **c**

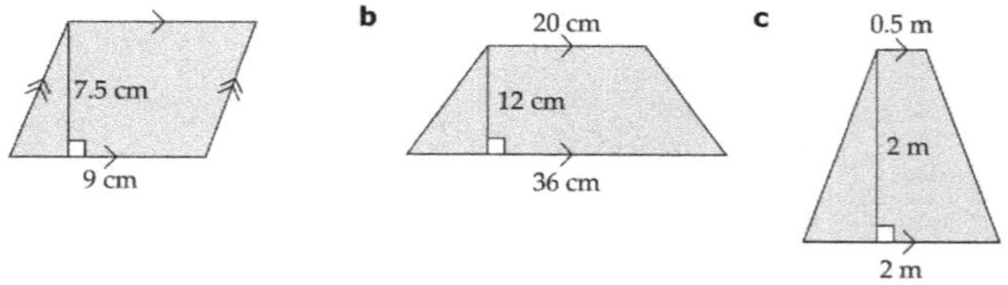

2d

8 The area of the parallelogram and the trapezium are the same.
Calculate the value of h.

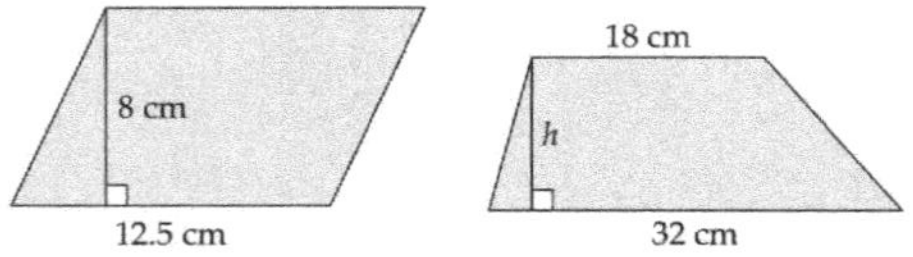

2e

Use π = 3.14 for the remaining questions on this page.

9 A penny-farthing was a type of bike used in the 19th century.
The diameter of the large wheel is 120 cm and is 3 times larger than the diameter of the small wheel.
Calculate

a the diameter of the small wheel

b the circumference of the small wheel

c the circumference of the large wheel.

The large wheel turns one complete revolution.

d How many times will the small wheel turn?

10 Six equilateral triangles of side 6 cm are arranged to form a hexagon.
A circle is drawn passing through the vertices of the hexagon.
Calculate the circumference of the circle.

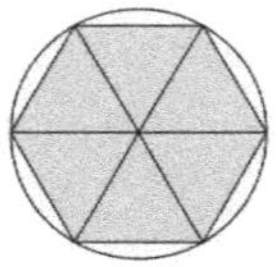

2f

11 A circular pond has a radius of 5 metres.
Calculate the surface area of the water.

12 The 'No entry' sign consists of a white rectangle on a red circle of radius 30 cm.
The rectangle has dimensions of 50 cm by 11.5 cm.
Calculate the red area of the sign.

13 Calculate the shaded areas.

a **b**

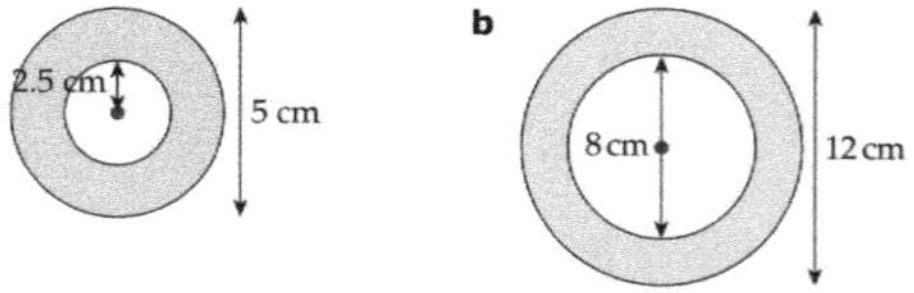

Question commentary

Questions 1–4 – Encourage students to learn metric and imperial units and also approximate conversions between metric and imperial.

Questions 5–13 – Stress to students the importance of using and stating correct units every time.

Questions 7 and **8** – Although students are not expected to know the formula for the area of a trapezium, encourage students to be able to justify why the formula works by recognizing that two conjoined identical trapeziums make a parallelogram.

Questions 9–13 – Allow students to use the π button on their calculator and then give answers to 2 dp.

Question 10 – Students can also be asked to calculate the area of the yellow region.

Answers

1 50 lengths

2 **a** 8500 ml **b** 45.6 cm
c 85 000 m^2 **d** 250 ml
e 4200 kg

3 **a** 60.5 lb **b** 48 inches **c** 4.5 oz **d** 1.25 pints
e 1360 km

4 **a** 0.3 cm, 3 mm; 0.8 cm, 8 mm
b 0.3 kg, 300 g; 1.6 kg, 1600 g, 1 kg 600 g
c 0.4 litre, 400 ml, 40 cl; 0.8 litre, 800 ml, 80 cl

5 18 cm^2

6 **a** $h = 10$ cm **b** $b = 16$ cm
c $h = 12.5$ cm **d** $h = 20$ cm

7 **a** 67.5 cm^2 **b** 336 cm^2
c 2.5 m^2

8 $h = 4$ cm

9 **a** 40 cm **b** 125.6 cm **c** 376.8 cm **d** 3 times

10 37.68 cm

11 78.5 m^2

12 2251 cm^2

13 **a** 14.72 cm^2 **b** 62.8 cm^2

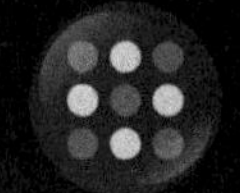

3 Expressions and formulae

Learning outcomes

A1 Use and interpret algebraic notation, including:
- ab in place of $a \times b$
- a^2 in place of $a \times a$, a^3 in place of $a \times a \times a$, a^2b in place of $a \times a \times b$
- a/b in place of $a \div b$
- $3y$ in place of $y + y + y$ and $3 \times y$
- coefficients written as fractions rather than as decimals
- brackets (L6)

A2 Substitute numerical values into formulae and expressions, including scientific formulae (L6)

A3 Understand and use the concepts and vocabulary of expressions, equations, inequalities, terms and factors (L6)

A4 Simplify and manipulate algebraic expressions to maintain equivalence by:
- collecting like terms
- multiplying a single term over a bracket
- taking out common factors (L6)

A5 Understand and use standard mathematical formulae; rearrange formulae to change the subject (L6)

A6 Model situations or procedures by translating them into algebraic expressions or formulae and by using graphs (L6)

Introduction

The chapter starts by looking at index notation and index laws. Collecting like terms, expanding a single bracket and simple factorisation are covered followed by evaluating and rearranging simple formulae. Writing expressions and simplifying algebraic fractions are covered in the final two spreads.

The introduction discusses the Voyager 1 space probe. Its primary goal was to investigate Jupiter and Saturn and their moons before heading into the outer solar system and beyond. It has been sending back information for over 36 years and is currently almost 20 billion kilometres away. It takes a signal over 19 hours to reach us at that distance. Voyager 1 has a sister probe, Voyager 2, actually launched 16 days earlier, which also visited Neptune and Uranus.

Algebra is the language mathematicians use to write down general statements that can apply to one or more numbers. An equation for an unknown is a familiar example. Likewise, formulae tell you what one thing equals given the value of another arbitrary quantity.

Prior knowledge

Students should already know how to…
- Use basic algebraic notation
- Work with indices, HCF and LCM
- Extract information from a written description
- Calculate perimeters and areas of simple shapes

Starter problem

The starter problem is an investigation into polygons on dotty paper. While this investigation is designed to be open-ended, students may need guidance in working out the areas of their polygons. Students should also be guided to work systematically.

This is essentially an interesting investigation into what is called 'Pick's Theorem' where the area of the shape enclosed, generally, is found by working out the number of dots contained inside (i) and the number of dots on the edge of the shape (b). Pick's formula for the area of the shape is given by:

$$A = i + b/2 - 1$$

Resources

MyMaths

Indices 1	1033	Factorising linear	1155	Rules and formulae	1158
Simplifying 2	1178	Simplifying 1	1179	Substitution 2	1186
Substitution 1	1187	Single brackets	1247	Indices 2	1951

Online assessment

Chapter test	2C–3
Formative test	2C–3
Summative test	2C–3

InvisiPen solutions

Add/subtract fractions	145	Prime factor decomposition	174
Indices	184	Negative/fractional indices	185
Collecting like terms	212	Multiplying/dividing terms	213
Expanding brackets	214	Laws of indices	221
Factorising single brackets	222	Algebraic fractions	223
Formulae	251	Changing the subject	256

Topic scheme

Teaching time = 9 lessons/3 weeks

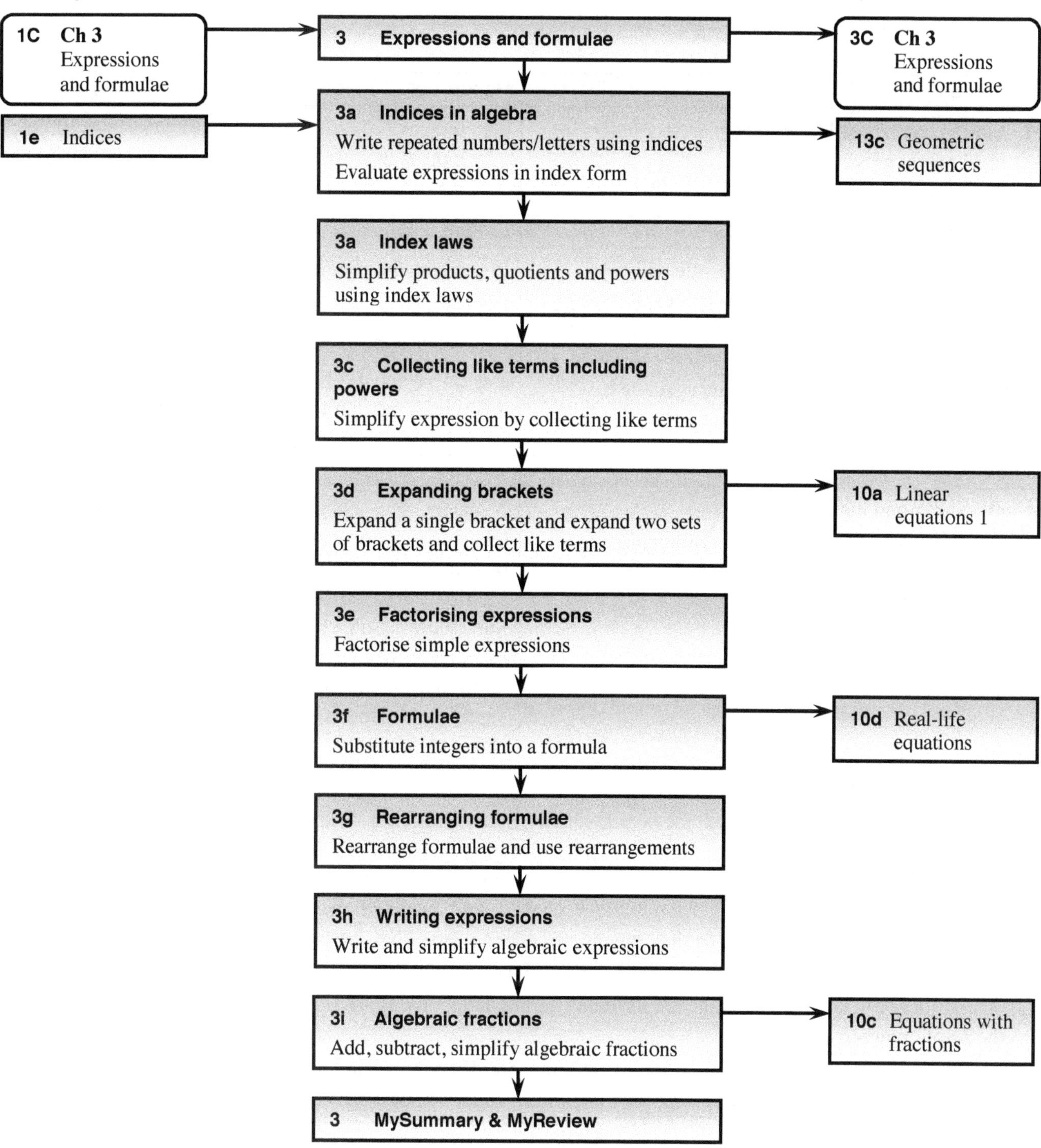

1C Ch 3
Expressions and formulae
1e Indices
3 Expressions and formulae
3a Indices in algebra
Write repeated numbers/letters using indices
Evaluate expressions in index form
3a Index laws
Simplify products, quotients and powers using index laws
3c Collecting like terms including powers
Simplify expression by collecting like terms
3d Expanding brackets
Expand a single bracket and expand two sets of brackets and collect like terms
3e Factorising expressions
Factorise simple expressions
3f Formulae
Substitute integers into a formula
3g Rearranging formulae
Rearrange formulae and use rearrangements
3h Writing expressions
Write and simplify algebraic expressions
3i Algebraic fractions
Add, subtract, simplify algebraic fractions
3 MySummary & MyReview
3C Ch 3
Expressions and formulae
13c Geometric sequences
10a Linear equations 1
10d Real-life equations
10c Equations with fractions

Differentiation

Student book 2A 44 – 63	Student book 2B 40 – 57	Student book 2C 40 – 63
Using symbols	Simplifying and substituting	Indices in algebra
Substitution	Indices	Index laws
Simplifying expressions	Like terms	Collecting like terms including powers
Expanding brackets	Expanding brackets	Expanding brackets
Simplifying harder expressions	Substitution into formulae	Factorising expressions
Formulae	Writing a formula	Formulae
Writing a formula		Rearranging formulae
		Writing expressions
		Algebraic fractions

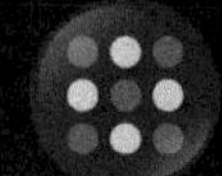

3a Indices in algebra

Objectives	
• Use index notation for integer powers (L6) • Use index notation with negative powers (L7) • Substitute numbers into expressions and formulae (L6)	
Key ideas	**Resources**
1 Indices can be used for numbers and for letters in algebraic expressions. **2** Indices can be negative	Indices 1 (1033) Indices 2 (1951)
Simplification	**Extension**
Constant reminder of the BIDMAS rule will help students. Also encourage the writing of expressions in full and discuss why this is not going to be efficient in the future. Allow students to pass over the negative indices if necessary. Will be covered again next academic year.	Investigate the pattern $64^3, 64^2, 64^1, 64^0$. What link can you see? Can you use this pattern to predict the value of $64^{\frac{1}{2}}$ and $64^{\frac{1}{3}}$ (8 and 4)? Encourage students to be creative in their ideas, but don't necessarily lead on to formal discussion of roots.
Literacy	**Links**
Clarify index and indices. Demonstrate the idea of reciprocal, with integers, unitary fractions, and vulgar fractions. Maybe with mixed numbers also.	A mnemonic is a memory aid that uses words and letters to jog the memory. The order of operations can be recalled using BIDMAS. (Brackets, Indices, Multiplication and Division, Addition and Subtraction). Some well-known mnemonics are *Richard of York Gives Battle In Vain* (colours of the rainbow), and the rhyme *Thirty Days hath September*... How many other mnemonics can the class remember?

Alternative approach

Begin a list, perhaps a vertical list on the board, with any number offered – but perhaps only a single digit. Or begin with a square number offered. Show in index form, and as a simple number. Write increasing powers above, agreeing that to move up the list involves multiplying by the number given. Then, elucidate that moving back down will involve dividing by that number, each step. And then continue downwards, to the zeroth power and beyond. Discuss various ways of showing the negative powers. They are fractions, so they can be written in a variety of other ways, besides in index form. The term reciprocal can be brought in again here.

Then consider how this would change if a different starting number was used. And what would not change, such as the zeroth power.

Emphasise that indices are not numbers in any familiar way, although we are using the familiar symbols, but are representing a quite different idea. This is why negative powers do not mean negative values – only negative base numbers can lead to negative values.

Then, emphasise how the negative part of an index can be regarded quite distinctly from the numerical bit; the reciprocation, and the raising to a power, are separate operations, and can be carried out in either order.

Checkpoint

1 Write these expressions as a single power of p.
a $p^3 \times p^5$ **b** $p^5 \div p^2$ **c** $p^3 \times p^{-3}$ (**a** p^8 **b** p^3 **c** p^0 or 1)

Starter

I am greater than 3^3 and…
I am less than 4^3 and…
I am a multiple of 7 and…
I have exactly 3 factors. (49)

Can be extended by asking students which clue could have been omitted and asking them to make up their own puzzles.

Teaching notes

Look at how indices can be used to abbreviate repeated multiplication. An example of prime factor decomposition could be used.

What is the meaning of a power of zero or a negative power? Look at the sequence of results for the powers of 2 from 2 cubed downwards.

$$\begin{array}{ccccccccccccc} & \div 2 & & \div 2 & & \div 2 & & \div 2 & & \div 2 & & \div 2 & \\ 2^3 & \rightarrow & 2^2 & \rightarrow & 2^1 & \rightarrow & 2^0 & \rightarrow & 2^{-1} & \rightarrow & 2^{-2} & \rightarrow & 2^{-3} \\ =8 & & =4 & & =2 & & =? & & =? & & =? & & =? \end{array}$$

Following the pattern means that $2^0 = 1$. What will other number to the power of zero produce? What about the negative powers? Establish that the negative part of the power is causing the number to 'turn upside down' known as the *reciprocal*. What role is the number playing? Establish that this works in the same way as an ordinary power. Include fractional examples of negative integer powers.

Remind students of the BIDMAS rule and look at examples of substituting values into algebraic expressions. Include negative values raised to a power.

Plenary

Explore other examples of the type in question **3**. What misconceptions can students come up with?

Exercise commentary

Question 1 – Use of mini whiteboards for practice is advantageous. Allow students to recognise that negative numbers raised to an even power are positive, and to a negative power are negative.

Question 2 – Again use mini whiteboards for consolidation.

Question 3 – After students attempt this question, encourage them to check their results by choosing a value to substitute. Advise students that 0, 1, 2 are not always the best values to choose, but they should still choose simple numbers.

Questions 4 and **5** – Care will need to be taken with a^3, a^{-2} and $(x^4 - y^2)^2$. On scientific calculators brackets must be used when raising negative numbers to a power. Remind students that scientific calculators follow BIDMAS strictly.

Question 6 – Students should leave parts **c** and **d** as mixed numbers, as are recurring decimals. Show students that entering $16 \times r^3 \div 3$ is the most efficient use of the calculator. Some students will prefer to use the fraction button, but make sure they don't leave r^3 in the denominator.

Question 8 – Encourage students to write out these in full to help appreciate what is being calculated. For example,
$(2^2)^3 = 2^2 \times 2^2 \times 2^2 = 2 \times 2 \times 2 \times 2 \times 2 \times 2 = 2^6$.

What incorrect answer might a student put?

Answers

1 **a** 9 **b** 64 **c** 100 000 **d** 1
e 0 **f** 1 **g** -1 **h** 81

2 **a** $\frac{1}{16}$ **b** $\frac{1}{36}$ **c** $\frac{1}{125}$ **d** 1
e 32 **f** 27 **g** $\frac{81}{16}$ **h** $\frac{81}{16}$

3 **a** True **b** False, $x^3 = x \times x \times x$
c True **d** True
e True **f** False, $y - 4 = -4 + y$
g True **h** False, $(3b)^2 = 9b^2$
i False, $-n \times -n = (-n)^2 = n^2$
j True

4 $a^3 = -27 < 4a = -12 < a^{-2} = \frac{1}{9} < a^0 = 1 < 2a^2 = 18 < (2a)^2 = 36$

5 **a** 128 **b** -125 **c** 40 **d** 64
e 31 **f** 21 **g** -20 **h** 81
i $\frac{16}{25}$ **j** 400

6 **a** 144 cubic units **b** 1152 cubic units
c $42\frac{2}{3}$ cubic units **d** $341\frac{1}{3}$ cubic units

7 **a** 2^6 **b** 3^9 **c** x^{12} **d** y^2

8 **a** 2^6 **b** 3^8 **c** 4^{15}

Rule is $(2^m)^n = 2^{m \times n}$

Objectives	
• Use index notation for integer powers and simple instances of the index laws (L7)	
Key ideas	**Resources**
1 When multiplying numbers in index form (with the same base number), add indices **2** When dividing numbers in index form (with the same base number), subtract indices **3** When raising a number in index form to a power, multiply the index by the power	Indices 1 (1033) Indices 2 (1951)
Simplification	**Extension**
Although time consuming, encourage students to write out questions like question **3** in full, at least initially. This may help to re-enforce why the rules of indices operate in the way they do. Students must not be allowed to just apply the rules and make no attempt to understand why they work.	What is $(-1)^{20}$ and $(-1)^{25}$? What can you deduce about -1 to the power of any positive whole number? What about -1 to the power of a negative whole number? And what of -1 to the zeroth power? Then, what of the powers of other negative base numbers?
Literacy	**Links**
Are these laws, or just rules? (Any views are to be welcomed.) Check the term base number, and warn that it will sometimes be referred to as the base.	In 1965, Gordon Moore, the cofounder of the computer company Intel, made a prediction that the number of transistors that manufacturers could fit onto a silicon chip would double every two years. This means that every two years, computers become twice as powerful and computing costs go down. A graph of Moore's law is at http://en.wikipedia.org/wiki/Image:Moores_law.svg

Alternative approach

Again, indices behave like familiar numbers, but a little differently. When we are multiplying the numbers written in index form, then the indices are only added; but when we are raising a number written in index form to a power, the indices are multiplied. These laws can be made clearer for students if work is set out in full.

Deducing the rules (or laws) together will be a valuable investment of time.

Emphasise that in expressions, such as that in part **c** of the last example, the numbers and the letters can be dealt with entirely separately, in turn. Numbers will be multiplied and so on in the usual way, but numbers or letters with indices will have to be treated differently … according to the rules we have deduced.

Checkpoint

1 Simplify $2a^5b^3c \times 3a^{-2}b^3c^4 \times (2a^3)^2 \times a^2b^{-1}c^{-5}$ $(24a^{11}b^5)$

Starter

Ask students to draw a 3 × 3 grid and enter 9 numbers that are square numbers (up to 144), cube numbers (up to 125) or triangular numbers (up to 55).

Give possible numbers, for example, 6^2, second cube number, fourth triangular number, etc.

Winner is the first student to cross out all their numbers.

Teaching notes

Why are powers useful in mathematics? Discuss the way in which they show repeated multiplication. How are negative numbers raised to a power? Stress the importance of brackets because of the BIDMAS rule. Remind students of the power function on their calculators, covered in the previous spread.

How can indices be simplified? Look at questions like those in the second example from the student book. In the case of multiplication, establish that the indices are not multiplied. Show this by writing out the meaning of the calculation. Use a similar explanation for division.

What happens to powers of different bases? For example, $3^4 \times 2^5 \times 3^2 \times 2$.

What happens when a number is already raised to a power and then is powered again? Can this be simplified? For example, $(5^3)^4$. Expand the question and establish the solution. Is there a convenient rule that can be used?

Summarise the rules for indices.

Plenary

Discuss the power to a power rule for question **5**. At this stage it is probably unnecessary to look at the rule formally. Discuss the type of errors students might make when tacking questions like this, for example, $(3t^5)^2 = 6t^{10}$ (wrong!).

Exercise commentary

Mini whiteboards are again helpful to consolidate index laws.

Question 1 – Students could check their answers by evaluating them on a calculator, once in non-simplified form and then using the power, if desired.

Question 3 – Students may be tempted to multiply the indices. Expect them to be able to justify why indices should be added.

Question 5 – Encourage students to first write out the question in expanded form. Allow students to discover the rule for themselves.

Question 6 – No calculator. Some students might need to be reminded of the number of sides on a heptagon, or possibly a decagon. Ask students to find the number of sides on a polygon that has 49 985 000 diagonals. A calculator would be needed. (10 000, a myriagon)

Question 7 – When finding the missing term, encourage students to check their solution using the rules from the exercise. Part **d** involves subtracting a negative number. Students may need reminding of subtracting negative numbers.

Answers

1	**a** 2^3	**b** 5^5	**c** 8^6	**d** x^4
	e k^2	**f** $(-3)^4$	**g** $4^3 \times 7^2$	**h** $a^5 \times b^3$
2	**a** 16	**b** 32	**c** 81	**d** 1 000 000
	e 125	**f** 1	**g** -8	**h** 1
3	**a** 3^6	**b** 6^8	**c** 2^{11}	**d** 9^8
	e x^9	**f** y^{10}	**g** p^9	**h** q^{16}
4	**a** 5^5	**b** 10^2	**c** 7^9	**d** 1
	e x^7	**f** y		
5	**a** 4^{15}	**b** 10^{18}	**c** a^{24}	**d** $64k^{18}$
	e $81t^{20}$	**f** $-8b^9$	**g** b^{10}	**h** $15\,625a^{12}$
6	**a** 5	**b** 2	**c** 14	**d** 35
7	**a** 8^4	**b** 3^7	**c** 5	**d** x^{-2}
	e y^2	**f** k^4	**g** 2, 2	**h** 2, 6
8	**a** 4^1	**b** 2		
	c i 3	**ii** 4	**iii** 9	**iv** 12
	d 3			

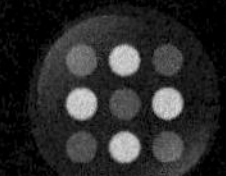

3c Collecting like terms including powers

Objectives	
• Simplify or transform linear expressions by collecting like terms	(L6)
• Simplify simple algebraic fractions to produce linear expressions	(L8)

Key ideas	Resources
1 Like terms in an expression can be collected and combined **2** Terms can be multiplied or divided one letter at a time	Simplifying 1 (1178) Simplifying 2 (1179)

Simplification	Extension
Ask students to try to explain in words what they think an expression means. Encourage a checking approach using a simple value for substitution into the question and simplified expression.	Ask students to create their own examples of expressions that can be simplified to a given term. Their examples should include multiplication, division and indices.

Literacy	Links
A little counting of terms in expressions may be useful to clarify meaning. Note that mathematicians use the word 'like' here in the way that in everyday usage we would normally use 'alike'; we mean similar, in a particular way.	People who collect and study postage stamps are called philatelists. Some philatelists collect stamps from a particular country while others collect stamps showing a particular theme such as trains, birds or insects. All postage stamps show the country of issue except those from Great Britain which carry an image of the head of the ruling monarch. There are collections of stamps showing insects at http://www.bugsonstamps.com/country_master.htm and of birds at http://www.bird-stamps.org/

Alternative approach

Ask what sign goes with which term, and what is the sign at the start of the expression? Emphasise that signs stay with the term they precede. Is it strange that no expression here begins with a negative sign? Can students guess why?

Similarly, why do we prefer terms to be written in alphabetical order? Does the practice actually help to make life a little easier?

Again, is there a good reason for writing numbers before letters? A poorly written $w3$ or similar here should make the point; $3w$ is not ambiguous in the same way. A reference to the bad writing of mathematicians, or of maths teachers, and hence the need for wise setting out practices, generally goes down well.

Zoo algebra (or fruit algebra, but this is less fun) can be useful here. Three antelopes and two baboons cannot be added, whereas three antelopes and two antelopes can be. The visual nature of this can be helpful to some students, and can be good to appeal to, for example when there is only one baboon – simplifying an expression such as $2b + 3b + b$ should be a checkpoint. Students generally have little problem with the extension to negatives, or indeed to such things as the square root of an elephant squared, if they have not already decided to take little notice of this approach; either way, no harm is done.

Checkpoint

1 Simplify $5a^2 + 3a^2b - 3a^2 + 2ab^2 - 4a^2b + 3b^2a$ $(2a^2 - a^2b + 5ab^2)$

Starter

Each letter of the alphabet represents a number:

$a = 1, b = 2, c = 3, d = 4, e = 5$, etc.

Challenge students to decode the following message

$(3e - 2)$ $(t - s)$ $(2j)$ $\left(\frac{p}{b}\right)$ $(dg - i)$ (c^2) $(3f + a^2)$ $\left(\frac{r}{c}\right)$ $(3g)$ $(d^2 - b)$

Can be extended by asking students to code their own message.

Teaching notes

Look at examples of adding and subtracting algebraic terms. Include terms like x, y, x^2, constants, xy, yx. Some students may need reminding that x^2 means $x \times x$. Why can some terms be put together when others can't?

Look at examples of multiplying algebraic terms. Can the order of the multiplication be rearranged? For example, is $3ab \times 2a$ the same as $3 \times 2 \times a \times a \times b$? Use numerical examples to justify that multiplication can be done in any order, for example, $3 \times 4 \times 4 \times 3$. Establish the common procedure of dealing with the numbers followed by the letters.

Look at examples of algebraic division. Insist on the expressions being written one over the other. Include examples similar to those in question **4**. Show how terms can be cancelled. Compare this with the method for simplifying vulgar fractions.

Plenary

Look at question **5** again. How could you express the volume of a cuboid that is twice as high as it is wide and twice as long as it is high? Encourage a sketch and the possible use of numerical values before introducing algebra. (width = x, volume = $8x^3$)

Exercise commentary

Question 1 – The last fraction may cause some discussion. It can be written in an alternative way, but is it simpler? Compare with $2(y + 4)$ and $2y + 8$ or $1\frac{1}{3}$ and $\frac{4}{5}$. Is this simplification or just an alternative way to express the answer?

Question 2 – For part **g**, ask, when letters are written in a different order, do they still make the same value? Use any numerical example to reinforce this concept, reminding in passing that we are dealing with multiplication here.

Question 3 – Reinforce the idea that multiplication can be achieved in any order; conventionally, the numbers are multiplied before the letters, for example, $2ab \times 2ab = 2 \times 2 \times a \times a \times b \times b$.

Question 4 – Look at this question in a number of different ways. **i** Each separate term in the numerator is divided by the denominator. **ii** A common term in the numerator will cancel with the same common term in the denominator. **iii** The numerator and denominator can both be divided by a common term. Each of these approaches suits different parts of this question. Explore them all.

Question 5 – Students may need reminding of the concept of volumes of cuboids by multiplication. A sketch of a cuboid 2 by 3 by 4 split into unit cubes will help reinforce this.

Question 6 – Ensure students use the simplification skills they have been practicing in the exercise. Some students may need to be reminded of the terms 'sum' and 'product'.

Answers

1

Can be simplified	Cannot be simplified
$p^2 + p^2 = 2p^2$ $3g \times 8h = 24gh$ $6m - 3m + n = 3m + n$ $\frac{14b}{7} = 2b$ $ab + 3ba = 4ab$	$4x + 1$ $5a^2 - 2a$ $\frac{2k + k^2}{2}$

2 **a** $3x$ **b** $12m$ **c** $7t$ **d** a^2
e $3p^2 + 9p$ **f** $7k + 3 - 5k^2$
g $5ab + 6bc - 1$ **h** $g^3 + 5p^2 - 2p$
i $x^2 + 2x + 3$

3 $4 \times a \times a$ pairs with $4a^2$
$4a \times 2$ pairs with $8a$
$2a \times 4b$ pairs with $8ab$
$2ab \times 2ba$ pairs with $4a^2b^2$

4 **a** $\frac{x}{3}$ **b** $4a$ **c** q **d** 4
e $5g$ **f** $5b$ **g** $5p^2$ **h** $3n$
i $a + 2$ **j** $3 - k$

5 **a** $8a^3$ **b** $30p^2q$

6 **a**

$3a + b + b^2$
$2a + b$ | $a + b^2$
$a + 2b$ | $a - b$ | $b + b^2$

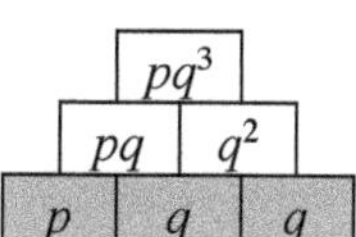

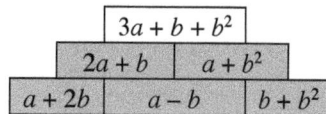

b Students' answers

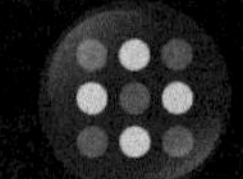

3d Expanding brackets

Objectives	
• Multiply a single term over a bracket	(L?)
• Derive a formula	(L?)

Key ideas	Resources
1 Products with factors in brackets can be expanded to give sums of terms 2 Expanded expressions can then be simplified	Simplifying 1 (1179) Single brackets (1247) Books and magazines

Simplification	Extension
Use arrows to reinforce the fact that the term in front of the brackets is multiplying each term inside the brackets. Highlight that negative signs make dealing with brackets more challenging. Build confidence with the positive multipliers first.	Expand and simplify $-(-3 - 4x) - (-2 - 4x)(-5)$. Ask, what makes this very challenging? Ask, what is each bracket being multiplied by? $(-16x - 7)$. Encourage various methods of tackling this expression.

Literacy	Links
The names of square brackets (brackets) and curly brackets (braces) could also be mentioned, as could the term parenthetical, for an aside or similar comment. Note that brackets need to come in pairs, so that 'inside the bracket' or 'outside the bracket' is a bit of nonsense, as is 'expand the bracket'. But it is cumbersome to keep saying 'pair of brackets', or indeed 'pairs of brackets', far less 'the expression inside the pair of brackets', and we are, at times, using the term 'bracket' to mean 'the expression inside the brackets'. Take care when explaining what is happening here, and be prepared to use phrases such as 'the expression inside the pair of brackets' in order to ensure clarity. Introducing the term 'binomial' for an expression with two terms may maintain clarity whilst reducing the explanation needed.	Bring in some written text (books, magazines) for the class to use. Ask the students to find examples of the use of brackets in the text. Round brackets (also known as *parentheses*) are often used for explanations or to add to the information already given. They can also be used for translations and abbreviations. What is the purpose of the brackets in the examples?

Alternative approach

Point out how expanding brackets in this way rewrites a product, of a number or letter and a factor in brackets, as an expression that is a sum of terms. Students might be able to guess what the opposite process, rewriting a sum as a product, is called.

If using zoo algebra, the observation that different powers of a letter are different kinds of animal will work nicely.

Regarding the 'Did you know?' box, the offering by spreadsheets of various examples may be worth mentioning.

Checkpoint

1 Expand and simplify this expression: $5(2x + 3) + 3(3x - 1) - 4(2x - 3)$ $(11x + 24)$

Starter

Draw a 4 × 4 table on the board. Label the columns 2^4 2^{-3} 2^3 3^{-2}. Label the rows 2^2 2^{-2} 3^5 3^2.

Ask students to fill in the table with the products, for example, the top row in the table would read $2^6, 2^{-1}, 2^5, 2^2 \times 3^{-2}$.

Can be differentiated by the choice of powers.

Teaching notes

What does multiplying a bracket by a number represent? For example, $3(x + 4)$. Explain that this is just repeated addition $x + 4 + x + 4 + x + 4$. What does this simplify to and how could the answer be found without the need to write out all the working? Establish that the term outside the bracket multiplies **every** term inside the bracket.

Include examples that like those used in questions **1** and **3**. Students may need reminding of the rules for multiplying with negatives.

For examples like those in questions **3** and **6**, encourage students to tackle the expansion of brackets in one line rather than split up the work into two separate parts. This is likely to reduce mistakes, especially when dealing with a negative multiplier.

Plenary

In the expressions $(3x + 4) + (7x - 2)$ and $4 - (3x + 1)$ what number are the brackets being multiplied by? Establish that 1 and -1 are being used. Expand and simplify. Why aren't the '1s' written in? Are there other examples of the number '1' not being written in? x rather than x^1.

Exercise commentary

Question 1 – Students may need reminding of the rule for multiplying two negatives.

Question 2 – Encourage students to set out workings down the page, lining up the equals signs. Highlight situations where there is a negative multiplied by a negative. These are often missed.

Question 3 – Does it matter which way round the expressions are written?

For example, $5(3x - 4)$ or $(3x - 4)5$?

Question 4 – The term 'surface area' may need explanation. Some students might like to make use of a net and write in the areas.

Question 5 – This could be done with Question 2, or used as a check that the work in Question 2 has been assimilated.

Question 6 – Encourage students to check their solutions by multiplying out the brackets. In these examples, is there only one solution? Can students make up an algebraic expression that can be put into brackets in more than one way?

Answers

1 **a** $3x + 12$ **b** $8f - 4$
c $t^2 + 9t$ **d** $mn - 7m$
e $10p - pq$ **f** $3a^2 + 3ab$
g $-32 + 16y$ **h** $-x^2 + 10x$

2 **a** $7x + 23$ **b** $11p + 19$
c $21a - 6$ **d** $t + 6$
e $2k + 17$ **f** $y - 8$
g $2m + 19$ **h** $4n$

3 **a** $6(k - 1) = 6k - 6$ **b** $k(k + 5) = k^2 + 5k$
c $5(3x - 4) = 15x - 20$ **d** $p(2p + q) = 2p^2 + pq$

4 $6p^2 + 4p$

5 $x(x + 1) + 2(x - 5)$ pairs with $x(x + 5) - 2(x + 5)$
$2x(x - 2) + 3(2 - x)$ pairs with $5x(x + 1) - 3x(x + 4) + 6$
$3(x + 2) - 2x(2 - x)$ is the odd one out.

6 **a** x **b** 4 **c** 2 **d** k and 3
e 3 and 5 **f** 5 and $3a$

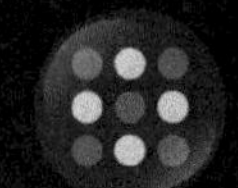

3e Factorising expressions

Objectives	
• Simplify or transform algebraic expressions by taking out single-term common factors	(L7)
• Construct and solve linear equations with integer coefficients (with and without brackets, negative signs anywhere in the equation, positive or negative solution)	(L6)

Key ideas	Resources
1 An expression that is a sum of terms may sometimes be rewritten as a product of the HCF of the terms and of a factor in brackets	Factorising linear (1155) Dictionaries

Simplification	Extension
Show how the expressions can be split into their prime and algebraic factors. What common groups can be seen in each term? For example, $6xy - 18x = 2 \times 3 \times x \times y - 2 \times 3 \times 3 \times x$; we can then see that $2 \times 3 \times x$ is common to both terms.	A cuboid has a length 2 m shorter than its width, but a height twice as high as its width. Write a fully factorised expression for its volume. Allow students to make their own choices of how to label their cuboid. [width = x, volume = $2x^2(x - 2)$]

Literacy	Links
Ensure complete familiarity with the terms factorising, simplifying. Emphasise that factorising is the opposite of expanding.	Bring in some dictionaries for the class to use. The word *bracket* can have several meanings and can be used as a noun or a verb. What do the meanings have in common? (Perhaps the idea of grouping or holding together – but terms such as *bracket fungus* show how language can develop, with new meanings that gradually become more distant from the original.)

Alternative approach

If the last spread was explained as a rewriting of a product as a sum, then the explanation of this spread as the rewriting of a sum as a product should seem a fairly natural development. Students could be asked why the two topics are tackled in this order … is this second topic a bit harder?

Perhaps begin with binomial expressions such as those in question **2**, and see whether students can write the factorised forms. There is almost no need (the exception being part **b**) to consider HCFs until part **j** – only common factors, so this aspect should not be dwelt on here.

Then, proceed with question **1**, again simply asking for common factors and not emphasising the idea that HCFs are, in principle, required.

Checkpoint

1 Factorise these expressions fully.

a $12x^2 - 18x$ $(6x(2x - 3))$

b $24p^2q + 16pq^2$ $(8pq(3p + 2q))$

Starter

$a = 2, b = 3, c = 5$

Ask students for expressions that have a value of 24 For example, $3(b + c), c^2 + a - b$.

Encourage students to think of interesting expressions!

Can be extended by changing the target number or values of a, b and c.

Teaching notes

Students may need reminding about HCF, possibly covered previously in spread **1c**. Include algebraic examples.

Look at the expansion of a simple expression in brackets, for example, $3(x + 4) = 3x + 12$. Is it possible to work backwards? Look at $3x$ and 12. What factors do they both share? Show how this leads to the 'common factor' being put outside the bracket. What must the common factor be multiplied by to produce the correct result?

Look at examples where there is more than one common factor. Does this mean that there is more than one way to factorise? How can you tell which common factor to use? By using the highest common factor you are 'fully factorising'.

Include examples where the HCF is actually one of the terms, for example, $3x + 9xy$.

What error might students make here? Putting the HCF of $3x$ outside the bracket does not mean it has been 'removed', it still needs to make $3x$ when expanded, so what multiplication is needed? $3x(? + 3y)$.

Plenary

Look at question **4** again. Do the students think they might make similar mistakes? If so, which ones?

Exercise commentary

Question 1 – Best orally or with mini whiteboards. Use words like 'what is the biggest thing that is in each term?', but note that the 'biggest' is hardly needed. On the other hand, do insist that the letters are included – point out to students that the factor required can be a number, or letter, or both.

Question 2 – Ask students to write their own 'expand a single bracket' question, and to write the answer on the reverse. These answers can then be used as a bank of factorising questions, with the answers on the reverse, which can be used to consolidate.

Question 3 – Can students' answers for part **a** be factorised? Is there any other part of this question that can be factorised?

Question 4 – Encourage students to try to explain what it is that Maggie thought she was doing correctly.

Question 5 – What can both sides be divided by once the left hand side is factorised fully? When forming an example for a partner, look at the way in which the original question was made to be able to factorise.

Question 6 – Students may be unsure which way round to subtract in order to find the difference. Encourage both ways around to be tried. The result $2x + 16$ or $-2x - 16$ is not immediately obvious as an even value. Allow informal approaches to proving it's even, not necessarily through factorisation.

Answers

1 **a** 2 **b** 3 **c** 6 **d** 5
e 3 **f** 4 **g** $6p$ **h** $2t$

2 **a** $3(x + 2)$ **b** $4(a - 3)$
c $3(4b - 5)$ **d** $5(2k + 3)$
e $2(8 - 3p)$ **f** $7(1 - t)$
g $m(n + 2)$ **h** $2(4a - b)$
i $5pq + 2$ **j** $6x(y - 3)$

3 **a** Mum's age $= 4(a - 3)$
b $4a - 12 = 4(a - 3)$
c 44

4 **a** Factor should be $3x$ **b** Factor should be $2a$
c Factor should be $8k$
d Second term in bracket is $15t \div 3t = 5$
e Need to leave a 1 as the first term
f Second term in bracket is $10x^2 \div 5x = 2x$

5 $x = 3$
$x = (32 - 20) \div 4 = 32 \div 4 - 5$

6 **a** $5(x + 2)$ **b** $3(x - 2)$
c $5(x + 2) - 3(x - 2) = 2x + 16$
$= 2(x + 8)$ which is always even

3f Formulae 1

Objectives	
• Use formulae from mathematics and other subjects	(L7)
• Derive a formula	(L6)

Key ideas	Resources
1 The value of the subject of a formula can be found if values are substituted for the other variables 2 Formulae can be written for described situations	Rules and formulae (1158) Substitution 2 (1186) Substitution 1 (1187)

Simplification	Extension
Ask students to explain what is being asked for in the formulae. What operations are being done and in what order. Make use of the BIDMAS rule. Encourage the formal approach of writing down the question, substituting in values and calculating the answer in stages.	The formula in question **1c** is used for finding the temperature in degrees Fahrenheit when the temperature in degrees centigrade is given. Can the formula be written in reverse? $C = \frac{5(F-32)}{9}$ An arrow diagram/function machine may help to reinforce the inverse processes required.

Literacy	Links
Discuss the words formula, formulas, formulae, at least enough to reassure and avoid later confusion. There are a lot more terms here, to be used carefully and checked and explained frequently; slowly at first is probably necessary. 'Derive' and 'deduce' could here be replaced by 'create' or just 'write'. Ask students, are we making these formulae or finding them?	The amount of energy (calorific value) contained in domestic gas depends on its composition. To make sure that everybody pays the same price for their energy, companies test the gas and publish the calorific value for each area. This is then used in a formula to convert the volume of gas used as measured by the gas meter to the amount of energy used by a household. There is more information at http://www.nationalgrid.com/uk/Gas/Data/misc/reports/description/

Alternative approach

Explain that the = in a formula is one of the many lazy misuses of this symbol; we commonly use simpler words (such as minus when we mean negative) for ease, we use simple symbols (such as -1) for a wide variety of uses, and we use some simpler symbols (such as =, in different contexts and situations) for convenience.

Is a formula an equation, where we can find the only value on the left of the =? Or is it really more like a recipe for an equation, where we can put in (substitute) different values for all the letters (that's why they are variables) on the right of the =, to make a different equation each time, and then solve that to find the value of the subject of the formula, on the left of the =, that goes with these particular values?

And then examples will show that what is wanted is not really that complicated.

And then, if appropriate, students could be asked whether it might be possible to substitute values for all variables except for one … on the right, that wasn't the subject of the formula. Or would they prefer to rearrange the formula so that the unknown value was on the left of the =?

Checkpoint

1 The equation $s = ut + ½at^2$ is a formula used in speed and distance calculations.
Calculate the distance (s) when the initial speed (u) is 3 m/s, acceleration (a) is 4 m/s^2 after 4 seconds. (s = 44m)

Starter

If A costs 2p, B costs 4p, C costs 6p etc. How much is your name worth?

Are you more expensive than the person beside you?

Which of your school subjects is worth the most?

What topic in maths is worth 92p? (Algebra)

Teaching notes

Remind students of the BIDMAS rule. Give examples of substitution into formulae. Include examples that involve fractions and powers. Include examples similar to those in question **1**.

Is there a difference between the way in which $-p^2$ and $-p \times -p$ would be calculated? Show how the BIDMAS rule, specifically indices before subtraction, means that the two expressions are not the same.

Examine some of the formulae used in physics for measuring speed/distance/time/acceleration.

$v = u + at$ $\qquad v^2 = u^2 + 2as$

$s = ut + \frac{1}{2}at^2$

$s = \dfrac{t(v-u)}{2}$ $\qquad s = vt - \frac{1}{2}at^2$

Experiment with both non-calculator and calculator methods of evaluation.

How are negative numbers and fractions to be correctly put into a calculator? Note that there is a wide variation in how calculators deal with these more complex operations. Encourage good practice when dealing with negatives and fractions. The negative function [-] or [+/-] should be used instead of the subtraction button. Fractions and negative numbers should be put into brackets if they are raised to a power. Some calculators automatically do this, others do not.

Plenary

The formula for the time (in seconds) it takes for a person on a swing to go forwards then backwards to the same point is given by $T \approx 2\sqrt{L}$. What might L stand for? (Length of the chain in metres) What measurements do not matter in this formula? Mass of the person; is this a surprise? Work out the time for various sensible lengths of chain. An improved formula is $T = 2\pi\sqrt{\frac{L}{9.81}}$. How close are the answers you just calculated when you use this formula?

Exercise commentary

This exercise could be achieved with or without a calculator depending on the required focus.

Question 1 – Students may need support with fractional coefficients.

Question 2 – Challenge students to write the formula so that it converts into kilometres from miles instead. They may have learned this conversion as $k = 1.6m$.

Question 3 – Using the first 100 numbers, pair off the first and last, the second and second last, etc. and show why the formula works. Link this to the story about Gauss.

Question 4 – It is helpful to show this question graphically.

Question 5 – If students can't see why it works ask them to consider the four corners. Ask if there is anything in the formula that might link to the number of corners.

Question 6 – A hint could be given by drawing a square, a car, the sun and a rocket blasting off. Internet searches could be used for the formulae; how could divide, squared and ½ be entered?

Answers

1 **a** 28 **b** 48 **c** 86 **d** 25

2 Route B (14 km < 16 km)

3 **a** 15 **b** 5050

4 **a** **i** $C = 20h + 35$
where C = total cost and h = hours worked
ii $C = 15h + 50$
where C = total cost and h = hours worked
b **i** Mike (75 < 80) **ii** Phil (125 < 135)
c 3

5 **a** The $4l$ part gives the number of red squares that touch the inside square edge to edge. The + 4 part adds on the four red squares in the corners.
b 44

6 **a** Perimeter of a square
b Speed given distance and time
c Temp in °F given °C
d Distance travelled given constant acceleration, initial velocity and time

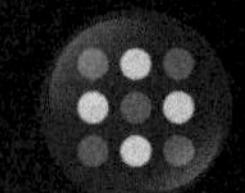

3g Rearranging formulae

Objectives	
• In simple cases, change (a formula's) subject	(L7)

Key ideas	Resources
1 A formula can be rearranged to make a different variable the subject of the formula	
Simplification	**Extension**
Keep asking students, what is stopping the subject from being on its own? How can we 'get rid' of this?	How can x be made the subject in $3x + xy = p$? Allow students to try various methods before suggesting factorisation. Can students make up similar examples of these types? Encourage students to test their partners.
Literacy	**Links**
When dealing with inverse functions, be very clear that the inverse steps need to be carried out in the reverse order to the original construction. Like unwrapping a parcel in the pass-the-parcel game; each layer of complication needs to be undone in reverse order, to reveal the variable, we seek to make the subject, on its own.	Albert Einstein's famous formula $E = mc^2$ says that mass can be converted into energy. The amount of energy contained in a piece of matter can be found by multiplying the mass m by the square of the speed of light, c. This means that there is enough energy in a grain of sand to boil 10 million kettles.

Alternative approach

Here's where we try changing the subject of the formula, as a prelude to solving the newly rearranged formula to find the value of a variable that was on the right of the =. Do students remember, or can they say anyway, the alternative of substituting values and then working out the unknown value? Which method did they prefer?

It might be good to explain why the rearranging approach is preferred. Partly because this give a new formula, that can then be used for any value. Partly because the new expression can then, with values substituted, be entered into a calculator to give the answer with only one use of the = or enter key. Partly because of what this shows about this approach, in terms of its elegance … an important idea in maths. If it looks good, it probably is. On the whole, it is best to do the hard work at the start to make things easier in the long run.

In the second example, the 77 could be substituted first, and the value of C then found. But the same steps of work will be needed, only with numbers instead of letters, and there will be more chances of miscalculation because of this. To rearrange the formula first, and then to insert the values and maybe just key the calculation into the calculator once and obtain the value wanted, is safer and, with a little practice, easier. At least for students for whom this level of work is appropriate.

Checkpoint

1 Rearrange these formulae to make x the subject.

a $y = 3x - 1$ $(x = (y + 1)/3)$

b $y = 4(x - 2)$ $(x = \frac{1}{4}y + 2)$

c $ax - y = b - y$ $(x = b/a)$

Starter

Write the following on the board and ask students which are always **T**rue, **S**ometimes true, always **F**alse:

$x^2 = (-x^2)$ (**S**, only if $x = 0$)

$2(x - 3) = 2x - 3$ (**F**)

$x - y = y - x$ (**S**, only if $x = y$)

$x^2 > x$ (**S**, not true if $0 \le x \le 1$)

$3(2x + 4) = 2(3x + 6)$ (**F**)

Ask students to justify their answers using substitution.

Teaching notes

Look back at the methods of solving linear equations. By performing an operation on each side of the equations, the equation can be solved. The x is finally made to be 'on its own'. In one way we could say we are *rearranging* the equation to make x the *subject*.

Look at an example of a simple formula. What is the subject at the moment? How can it be rearranged to make one of the other letters the subject? Can the methods used for solving linear equations be used to rearrange formulae? Use examples that require operations of $+, -, \times, \div$.

How can formulae that have brackets be rearranged? If appropriate, draw on the work covered in spread **3d**.

Is there more than one way to rearrange formulae? Will the final answer be the same? Look at such an example and examine two possible ways of expressing the solution.

Plenary

Can the formulae from the plenary in spread **3f** be rearranged to make L the subject? Particularly discuss the problem with the square root.

Exercise commentary

Writing down the formula to be rearranged, showing working on both sides and working down the page is a clear and useful procedure. A few parts could be attempted with mini whiteboards.

Questions 1–3 – Emphasise balance method; any operation carried out on one side of the equation must be done on the other.

Question 2 – In parts **g** and **h** show students they can divide by multiple variables at the same time.

Question 3 – In part **h** allow students to expand the bracket, but show them it is more efficient if you do not.

Question 6 – Making w the subject is considerably harder, as it involves factorising. Suggest students solve this by substituting values first. You may wish to show using factorising to rearrange formulae as an extension, especially is factorising has been covered in recent lessons.

Question 7 – Make the point that negative x's cause problems in equations and formulae, it is best to 'get rid of them' as soon as possible. How do you get rid of $-x$? Create examples where the negative x term can't be got rid of immediately. For example, $3(y - 2x) = p$.

Answers

1 **a** $x = a - b$ **b** $x = y + t$
c $x = q + r - p$ **d** $x = p - y - z$
e $x = 3y$ **f** $x = m^2 + n$
g $x = c - ab$ **h** $x = pq$

2 **a** $y = \frac{z}{x}$ **b** $y = \frac{q + r}{p}$
c $y = \frac{a + c}{b}$ **d** $y = \frac{a - r}{x}$
e $y = \frac{p - 2m}{n}$ **f** $y = \frac{f}{d}$
g $y = \frac{p}{xz}$ **h** $y = \frac{m + n}{kl}$

3 **a** $x = P - y - z$ **b** $l = \frac{P}{4}$
c $l = \frac{A}{w}$ **d** $b = \frac{P - 2a}{2}$
e $r = \frac{C}{2\pi}$ **f** $m = \frac{y - c}{x}$
g $t = \frac{v - u}{a}$ **h** $a = 2m - b$

4 **a** Twice the length of one of the equal sides, a, plus the base, b.
b $b = P - 2a$ **c** 9

5 **a** Perimeter, P, is equal to twice the length, l, plus twice the width, w.
b $w = \frac{P - 2l}{2}$ **c** 5
d $P = 8a$ where width $= a$

6 **a** $w = \frac{S - 2hl}{2l + 2h}$ $w = 2$
b $l = 5$
c Surface area of the cuboid is the sum of the surface areas of the sides,
$w \times l + w \times h + l \times h + l \times w + h \times l + h \times w = 2lw + 2lh + 2hw$

7 **a** **i** $x = a - b$ **ii** $x = \frac{p - r}{q}$
b Students' answers
c **i** $x = \frac{a}{b}$ **ii** $x = \frac{r}{p + q}$
d Students' answers

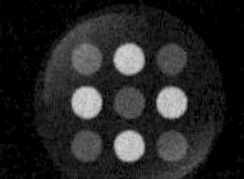

3h Writing expressions

Objectives	
• Simplify or transform linear expressions by collecting like terms	(L6)
• Multiply a single term over a bracket	(L6)

Key ideas	Resources
1 Expressions can be created from diagrams or information presented in other ways **2** Like terms in an expression can be collected and combined	Simplifying 1 (1179) Simplifying 2 (1178) Single brackets (1247)

Simplification	Extension
Encourage students to circle the like terms and join them, perhaps using colours for questions **1** and **2**.	Set questions similar to question **4** involving compound shapes including right-angled triangles. Find possible values of the unknowns if the area is given.

Literacy	Links
The idea of the *difference* being what one adds to one thing to make another, as an alternative to seeing it as the result of a subtraction, may need explaining with a little algebraic manipulation. The various terms for dimensions may need to be discussed here: length, width, depth, height, breadth, and so on. Does it matter which way around they are? Must the length be greater than the width? What if we have an algebraic expression, and we do not know which is which? What if it depends on the values we put into the expression, so that either dimension could be the greater?	The city of Milton Keynes in the UK is laid out in a grid system with ten horizontal roads (Ways) at 1 km intervals and eleven vertical roads (Streets), also at 1 km intervals. Milton Keynes was designed as a new town and construction began in 1967. The roads are numbered with H or V numbers for horizontal or vertical, for example, H6 Childs Way. There is more information about the Milton Keynes grid system at http://www.road-to-nowhere.co.uk/features/milton_keynes.html

Alternative approach

In the first example, students could simply be asked what needs to be added, or what the missing bit must be; instead of adopting the formal approach of subtraction.

In the second example, students may prefer to double each expression given before adding. Again, the process shown is useful for students to see, but not the only approach, and an alternative formula for perimeter is permitted. Which method do students find easiest?

Again in the third example, the entire area is 200, and the bit not wanted is $10k$. Hence the answer of $200 - 10k$ can be arrived at without the formalised approach shown. However, the approach shown in the student book should be fully understood.

Encourage students to always seek the easiest method for each question, but be able to manage harder methods when unavoidable.

Checkpoint

1 Find the area and perimeter of a rectangle that measures $3x - 2y$ by $2x$.

(perimeter = $10x - 4y$; area = $6x^2 - 4xy$)

Starter

Ask students to calculate 100 using the digits 1 to 9 and any operation(s). For example, $123 - 4 - 5 - 6 - 7 + 8 - 9 = 100$.

Students score a point for each different calculation. Bonus points if the digits are kept in numerical order as in the example!

Teaching notes

Recapitulate work covered in spreads **3c** and **3d**. Give examples of addition and subtraction of terms including two variables. Ask students to fill in the missing terms to make a simplification complete. For example, $3x + ? - 5 = 7x - 8$. Include examples that involve adding and subtracting negatives.

Give examples of multiplication of terms including two variables and squared terms.

Look at the use of brackets in practical contexts, for example, for expressing the area of a shape.

Look at examples of the expansion of a single bracket, include calculations that involve negatives and squaring terms.

Look at an example of the area of a triangle. This will allow exploration of division in algebra. Can the expression be simplified?

Look back at the expressions discussed. Can any of them be factorised?

Plenary

How can the magic square in question **2** be used to create a non-algebraic magic square? Substitute values for a and b. How can the magic square be adapted to create another magic square? Add or subtract the same terms to each square.

Exercise commentary

Question 1 – Encourage students to choose routes that involve both positive and negative terms. Ask how the problem would change if total distance walked was being calculated.

Question 2 – Ask students to substitute values for a and b to make their own magic square. As an extension ask if they can come up with their own magic square template, using algebra.

Question 3 – Most students are likely to see what else is needed to make the whole length of the rectangle. Encourage students to check their solution by summing.

Question 4 – Encourage students to sketch the rectangles and fill in missing lengths where necessary. In part **a**, students may need help when multiplying $2x$ by $3x$. In part **b**, different methods may lead to apparently different answers, for a useful discussion. Encourage students to use the simplest method they can think of.

Question 5 – Some students may think it possible to collect the terms in y^2 and y. Make up a value for y and show that this does not work. Encourage students to make a guess as to the simplification of $(x + 1)(x + 4)$ before trying a diagram approach.

Answers

1 **a** Three possible routes which all simplify to $4a + 3b$
b All expressions simplify to $4a + 3b$

2 Each row, column and diagonal sums to $3a + 3b$

3 **a** $3k + 2$ **b** $3t + 6$

4 **a** **i** $3x(2x - 5)$ **ii** $6x^2 - 15x$
b **i** $q(p - 8)$ **ii** $pq - 8q$
c **i** $3(10 - 2k)$ **ii** $30 - 6k$

5 **a** $(y + 3)(y + 2) = y^2 + 3y + 2y + 6 = y^2 + 5y + 6$
b $(x + 1)(x + 4) = x^2 + 1x + 4x + 4 = x^2 + 5x + 4$

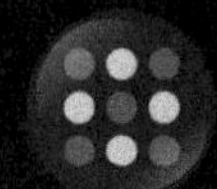

3i Algebraic fractions

Objectives

- Add simple algebraic fractions (L?)

Key ideas

1 As with numeric fractions, algebraic fractions can only be added when they are the same kind, that is when they have the same denominators

2 Algebraic fractions that do not have the same denominators can, as with numeric fractions, be changed to equivalent fractions with the same denominators so that they can then be added

Resources

Simplification

Use diagrams to reinforce what is happening when fractions are added and subtracted. Rectangles, subdivided into squares, are a convenient way of explaining the process for questions **1** and **4**.

Extension

Introduce mixed algebraic fraction questions. Begin with simple examples and ask if the fractions need to be converted into top heavy fractions or not. For example, $1\frac{x}{3} + x\frac{2}{3} = \frac{?}{3}$

Literacy

A reminder that denominator means kind of thing, as with denomination, may be useful.

A reminder that subtracting is just like addition with a negative value may also help.

Links

In chemistry, a fraction is a part of a mixture of liquids, generally with a different boiling point from that of other parts. The fractions in crude oil have individual names, (diesel, kerosene, petrol, *etc*.) and have different properties and uses. They are separated using a fractionating column. There is more information about oil fractions at http://www.bbc.co.uk/schools/gcsebitesize/science/edexcel/oneearth/fuelsrev3.shtml

Alternative approach

Only things that are of the same kind can be added (in zoo algebra, they must be the same kind of animal). If they are not, we will need to change them into the same kind of thing (students seem to have no problem with changing animals into the same kind) before we can add them.

Notice that the common denominators here are generally the product of the denominators we start with, so that the idea of LCM does not need to be emphasised. If students master these examples, then explore some other questions where the LCM would be needed to find the lowest common denominator.

Checkpoint

1 Simplify these algebraic fractions.

a $\frac{2x}{3} + \frac{x}{6}$ ($5x/6$)

b $\frac{3x^2}{4} - \frac{x}{2}$ ($x^2/2$)

c $\frac{4}{3ab} + \frac{1}{2a}$ ($(8 + 3b)/6ab$)

Starter

Draw a 4 × 4 table on the board to form 16 cells.

Label the columns with the terms, x, $3x$, $2y$, $-4x$, label the rows with the terms, $-2x$, $3y$, $5x$, $-y$.

Ask students to fill in the table by subtracting the left label term from the top label term. For example, the top row in the table would read $3x$, $5x$, $2y + 2x$, $-2x$.

Can be differentiated by the choice of terms.

Teaching notes

Recapitulate the methods of addition and subtraction of fractions covered in spread **1c**. The methods that apply to numbers can be extended to apply to algebra. Look at different ways of expressing a fraction of a term, for example, one and a half $x, 1\frac{1}{2}x, \frac{3}{2}x, \frac{3x}{2}$.

Which is the most common method of representation? What does $\frac{x}{5}$ actually mean? Discuss the fact that something that is cut into 5 is actually just one fifth.

Look at examples of adding and subtracting simple algebraic fractions with common denominators. Can any of the examples be simplified?

How can algebraic fractions be simplified if the denominators are different? Use the idea of equivalent fractions used for non-algebraic fractions. Is it possible to simplify the final answers?

Consider looking at examples that include **i** a mixed fractional part of a term, **ii** the combination of algebraic and non-algebraic fractions, **iii** three algebraic fractions with different denominators.

Plenary

Ask students to suggest a pair of equivalent fractions, similar to those in question **3**. Encourage students to be creative and think of complex possibilities. Does the rest of the class agree with the suggestions?

Exercise commentary

Questions 1 and **2** – These questions have common denominators. Students may need reminding that only fractions with common denominators can be added or subtracted.

Question 2 – Point out to students that parts **d** and **e** are a different way of writing a fraction, but can be treated as in part **c**.

Question 3 – Students can write out the algebraic fractions in full, splitting up x^2 $(x \times x)$ and 10 (2 × 5). This may make it easier to see how the fractions simplify.

Questions 4 and **5** – Suggest that students always look for the lowest common denominator. Ask them why this saves work.

Question 6 – Ask students how the denominators can be made the same. As a hint, show question **5** part **e** onwards with the denominators written as products of factors.

Question 7 – Ask students to re-phrase what Ashim and Aesha say. Encourage students to approach this algebraically, and not by any trial-an- improvement method, to give them practice in setting up and using equations.

Answers

1 **a** $\frac{4}{7}$ **b** $\frac{4}{9}$ **c** $\frac{4}{5}$ **d** $\frac{4}{11}$
e $\frac{1}{2}$ **f** 1 **g** $\frac{1}{4}$ **h** $1\frac{1}{2}$

2 **a** $\frac{2x}{3}$ **b** $\frac{x+y}{4}$
c $\frac{3a}{5}$ **d** $\frac{t}{7}$
e $\frac{1}{6}p+\frac{5}{6}q$ **f** $\frac{3}{x}$
g $\frac{5}{k}$ **h** $\frac{3}{x^2}$

3 $\frac{x}{5}$ pairs with $\frac{2x}{10}$
$\frac{x}{2}$ pairs with $\frac{xy}{2y}$
$\frac{x}{10}$ pairs with $\frac{x^2}{10x}$
$\frac{2}{x}$ pairs with $\frac{10}{5x}$

4 **a** $\frac{4}{9}$ **b** $\frac{5}{6}$ **c** $\frac{3}{10}$ **d** $\frac{3}{8}$
e $\frac{5}{6}$ **f** $\frac{2}{15}$ **g** $\frac{11}{20}$ **h** $1\frac{7}{12}$

5 **a** $\frac{3x}{4}$ **b** $\frac{p}{6}$ **c** $\frac{11a}{12}$ **d** $\frac{3b}{10}$
e $\frac{z}{5}$ **f** $\frac{5x^2}{8}$ **g** $\frac{5y^2}{27}$ **h** $\frac{3xy}{4}$

6 **a** $\frac{(6x-3)}{x^2}$ **b** $\frac{(2+3x)}{3x^2}$
c $\frac{(2z-3y)}{yz}$ **d** $\frac{(9+10y)}{15xy}$

7 **a** $\frac{c}{3}+\frac{2c}{7}=\frac{13c}{21}$ **b** 42 chocolates

3 Expressions and formulae – MySummary

Key outcomes	Quick check	
Use index notation and basic index laws.	Simplify each of the following. a) $x^3 \text{ x } x^4 \div x^5$ b) $1 \div (y^2 \text{ x } y^0)$ c) $(2a^5)^3$	 (x^2) (y^{-2}) $(8a^{15})$
Simplify algebraic expressions by collecting like terms.	Simplify these expressions a) $8p + 5 + 3q - 8 - 5p + 2q$ b) $5x^2 - 3x + 5x - 3x^2$ c) $8ab - 3ab^2 + 3ba + a^2b$	 $(3p + 5q - 3)$ $(2x^2 + 2x)$ $(11ab - 3ab^2 + a^2b)$
Expand single brackets.	Expand and simplify this expression. $5(x - 3) - 3(x - 2)$	$(2x - 9)$
Factorise an expression by taking out a common factor.	Factorise this expression fully. $6pq^3s - 9p^2q^2r$	$(3pq^2(2qs - 3pr)$
Derive and substitute into a formula.	$v^2 = u^2 + 2as$. Calculate v when $u = 3, a = 2$ and $s = 4$.	$(v = 5)$
Change the subject of a formula.	Make y the subject of the formula. $2x - 3y = x + 5y - 2$	$(y = (x + 2)/8\ )$
Add and subtract simple algebraic fractions.	What is 2 over x times 3 over x squared?	$(7/x^2)$

MyMaths extra support

Lesson/online homework			Description
Indices 1	1033	L7	Understanding indices; multiplying and dividing with indices; working out a power of a power

MyReview

3 MySummary

Check out

You should now be able to ...

		Test it ➡ Questions
✓ Use index notation and basic index laws.	7	1 - 3
✓ Simplify algebraic expressions by collecting like terms.		4
✓ Expand single brackets.		5, 6
✓ Factorise an expression by taking out a common factor.		7
✓ Derive and substitute into a formula.		8 - 10
✓ Change the subject of a formula.		11
✓ Add and subtract simple algebraic fractions.		12

Language	Meaning	Example
Index notation	A way to show repeated multiplication	$10^3 = 10 \times 10 \times 10 = 1000$ $x \times x \times x = x^3$
Reciprocal	The reciprocal of a number is $\frac{1}{\text{number}}$	The reciprocal of $\frac{5}{4}$ is $\frac{4}{5}$
Expanding brackets	Multiplying each term inside the bracket by the term outside the bracket	$3(5 + 2) = 3 \times 5 + 3 \times 2$
Simplify expressions	Rearrange or cancel common factors to arrive at an equation which is easier to solve!	$3b + 2b - 2 + b = 6b - 2$
Like terms	Terms that have the same variables and powers	$2x^2$ and $4x^2$ are like terms $2x^2$ and $2x$ are not like terms
Factorising expressions	This is the reverse of expanding brackets - divide each term in the expression by the HCF and write the answer inside the bracket	$4c^2 + 8c = 4c(c + 2)$
Algebraic fractions	Fractions whose numerator and/or denominator are algebraic expressions	$\frac{5x + 2y}{xy}$

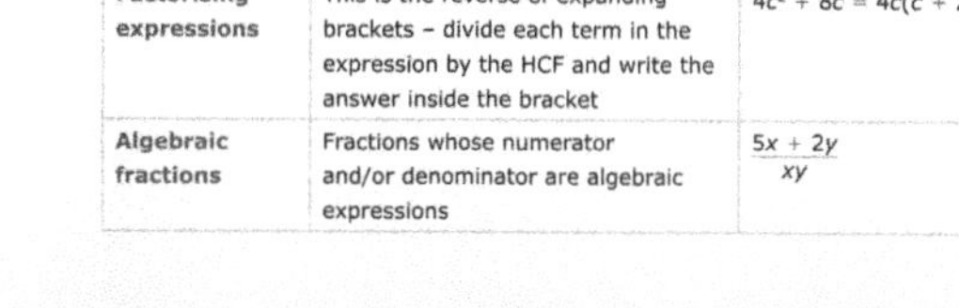

60 **Algebra** Expressions and formulae

3 MyReview

1 Evaluate these indices without a calculator.
a 5^0 **b** 3^{-2} **c** $(-5)^3$ **d** $(2^3)^2$

2 Given that $x = 2$ and $y = -3$, evaluate these expressions.
a x^4 **b** $2y^3$
c $(2xy)^{-1}$ **d** $(x^2 - y^2)^2$

3 Simplify each of these.
Use indices in your answers.
a $2 \times 2 \times 2$ **b** $1 \div (3^2 \times 3)$
c $x^6 \times x^4 \times x$ **d** $y^6 \div y^8$
e $\frac{x^3}{x^{-2}}$ **f** $(2a^4)^3$

4 Simplify these expressions.
a $16a - 12b + 9 - 15b - 18a$
b $3y + 4y^2 + 5y + y^2$
c $3cd + 5d + 8dc - 2c$
d $\frac{15pq^2}{30p^3q}$

5 Expand these brackets.
a $7(8 - 2a)$ **b** $-2(2b - 7)$
c $c(c + 1)$ **d** $-d(2d - 7)$

6 Expand these brackets and collect like terms.
a $3(r + 4) + 2(2r - 1)$
b $7(4s - 3) - 6(5s - 4)$

7 Factorise fully these expressions.
a $12x - 4$ **b** $7a + 14b$
c $15pq + 45p$ **d** $6st^2 - 9t$

8 $v = u + at$
Use this formula to find the value of v when $u = 5$, $a = 2$ and $t = 7$

9 A soft play area charges £50 to host a child's Birthday party, plus an additional cost of £3.50 per guest for food.
Derive a formula to find the cost, £C, of a party for n people.

10 Write a simplified expression for the shaded area.

$t + 2$, t, 1, 1, 1, 1

11 Make x the subject of the formulae
a $x - 2b = c$ **b** $7 + x = y - 12$
c $ax = b$ **d** $3x - y = 2y + 9$

12 Simplify
a $\frac{x}{5} + \frac{2x}{15}$ **b** $\frac{3a}{5} - \frac{a}{4}$
c $\frac{2}{x} + \frac{3}{xy}$ **d** $\frac{5}{p} - \frac{q}{p^2}$

What next?

Score		
0 - 5		Your knowledge of this topic is still developing. To improve look at Formative test: 2C-3; MyMaths: 1071, 1149, 1150, 1151, 1155, 1157, 1158, 1164, 1170, 1178, 1179, 1187, 1247, 2033 and 2034
6 - 10		You are gaining a secure knowledge of this topic. To improve look at InvisiPen: 145, 174, 184, 185, 212, 213, 214, 221, 222, 223, 251 and 256
11 - 12		You have mastered this topic. Well done, you are ready to progress!

MyMaths.co.uk 61

Question commentary

Question 1 – Emphasise that raising a positive number to a power will always give a positive answer, students often think 3^{-2} is -9 (or even -6).

Question 2 – Take care in part **c** when subtracting a negative, in **d** students may need reminding to raise 2 to the power 3.

Question 4 – In part **c**, there may need to be a discussion about cd being equal to dc.

Questions 5 and **6** – Students, when rushing, will sometimes neglect to multiply the second term inside the brackets by the term outside the brackets. Warn students to look out for double negatives.

Question 7 – Encourage students to think about the HCF of the terms

Question 10 – This question is tricky. Students should work out the area of both rectangles and subtract, taking great care with negatives or else they may find an answer of 0 which is clearly incorrect.

Question 11 – It is useful to recap dealing with non-algebraic fractions and emphasise the similarities with algebraic fractions.

Answers

1 **a** 1 **b** $\frac{1}{9}$ **c** -125 **d** 64

2 **a** 16 **b** -54 **c** $-\frac{1}{12}$ **d** 25

3 **a** 2^3 **b** 3^{-3} **c** x^{11} **d** y^{-2}
e x^5 **f** $8a^{12}$

4 **a** $9 - 2a - 27b$ **b** $8y + 5y^2$
c $11cd + 5d - 2c$ **d** $\frac{q}{2p^2}$

5 **a** $56 - 14a$ **b** $-4b + 14$
c $c^2 + c$ **d** $-2d^2 + 7d$

6 **a** $7r + 10$ **b** $3 - 2s$

7 **a** $4(3x - 1)$ **b** $7(a + 2b)$
c $15p(q + 3)$ **d** $3t(2st - 3)$

8 19

9 $C = 50 + 3.5n$

10 $4t$

11 **a** $x = c + 2b$ **b** $x = y - 19$
c $x = \frac{b}{a}$ **d** $x = y + 3$

12 **a** $\frac{x}{3}$ **b** $\frac{7a}{20}$ **c** $\frac{3+2y}{xy}$ **d** $\frac{5p-q}{p^2}$

3 MyPractice

3a

1 Evaluate these numbers without a calculator.

a 5^2 **b** 3^4 **c** 2^8 **d** 6^0 **e** 4^{-3} **f** 8^{-2} **g** $\left(\frac{1}{2}\right)^{-7}$ **h** $\left(\frac{3}{4}\right)^{-2}$

2 Given that $m = 3$ and $n = -2$, find the value of these algebraic expressions.

a $2m^3$ **b** $6n^2$ **c** $(2n)^2$ **d** $3m + n^4$ **e** mn^2 **f** $(m^2 - n^2)^2$

3b

3 Simplify these, giving your answer in index form.

a $2^3 \times 2^5$ **b** $4^8 \times 4^2$ **c** 7×7^4 **d** $5^7 \times 5^2$

e $a^4 \times a^6$ **f** $b^3 \times b^2 \times b$ **g** $2x^7 \times 5x^2$ **h** $3y^3 \times 4y^8$

4 Simplify these, giving your answer in index form.

a $6^7 \div 6^4$ **b** $10^6 \div 10$ **c** $\frac{8^4}{8^3}$ **d** $\frac{p^{10}}{p^3}$ **e** $16k^8 \div k^6$ **f** $12t^8 \div 6t^8$

5 Simplify these, giving your answer in index form.

a $(3^5)^2$ **b** $(12^3)^5$ **c** $(m^4)^9$ **d** $(n^2)^7$ **e** $(4d^5)^3$ **f** $(-2x^2)^5$

3c

6 Simplify these expressions, where possible, by collecting like terms.

a $3x + 8x - 2x$ **b** $4a^2 - 6a^2 + 10a^2$ **c** $10m + 7n - 3n - 5m$

d $4p^2 + 8 - 3p$ **e** $12ab - 6ba + ab$ **f** $3g^3 - 4g^3 + 2g^2$

7 Simplify these expressions as fully as possible.

a $\frac{20x}{5}$ **b** $\frac{12y}{4y}$ **c** $\frac{21pq}{7q}$ **d** $\frac{30k^2}{18k}$ **e** $\frac{24gh^2}{16h}$ **f** $\frac{3b + 12}{3}$

3d

8 Use brackets to write an expression for the area of this rectangle.
Then expand the brackets.

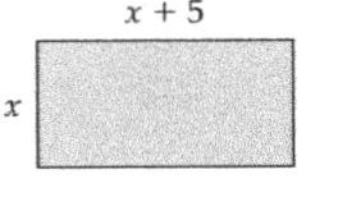
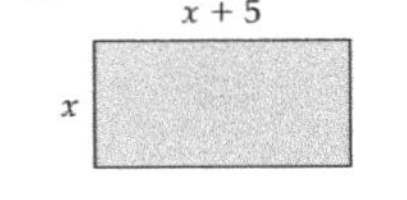

9 Expand and simplify these expressions.

a $5(a + 2) + 3(a + 4)$ **b** $3(4x + 1) + 6(2x - 1)$

c $3(4p + 3) + 7(1 - p)$ **d** $5(3b - 2) - 2(4b + 1)$

e $8(m + 2) - 3(2m - 3)$ **f** $6(4n - 3) - 4(5n - 4)$

3e

10 Factorise these expressions fully.

a $2x + 4$ **b** $5y + 20$ **c** $6g - 2$ **d** $8t - 12$

e $18 - 15k$ **f** $10p + 15q$ **g** $7a + ab$ **h** $15mn - 9n$

11 **a** Three consecutive numbers are summed. Using n to represent the first of these numbers, write and simplify an algebraic expression.

b Prove that the sum of three consecutive numbers is always equal to three times the middle number.

62 **Algebra** Expressions and formulae

3f

12 Entry to the Cheeky Monkeys play barn costs £3.50 per child, adults are free.

a Work out the cost of one child paying 4 visits to Cheeky Monkeys.

b Derive a formula for the cost, C, of one child paying n visits to Cheeky Monkeys.

A parent or carer can spend £10 for membership of Cheeky Monkeys for one year. Members pay only £2.50 entry fee per child.

c Derive a formula to work out the cost, C, of one child paying n visits to Cheeky Monkeys if their parent or carer is a member.

d Sam takes her only daughter, Aysha, to Cheeky Monkeys once a month. Work out whether or not it is worth Sam becoming a member of Cheeky Monkeys.

13 The diagrams show a pattern of red and white tiles.

a Write a formula to connect the numbers of white tiles, w, and red tiles, r.

b Explain why this formula works.

c Use your formula to find the number of red tiles surrounding 100 white tiles.

3g

14 Make x the subject of each of these formulae.

a $p = x + r$ **b** $a + b = x - c$ **c** $x + 3y = z$

d $3p + x = 5p$ **e** $a = x - a^2$ **f** $x - mn = p + mn$

15 Make y the subject of each of these formulae.

a $m = ny$ **b** $b^2y = a$ **c** $p - 3 = qy$

d $g = fy + h$ **e** $aby = x$ **f** $y(\pi + 2) = r$

3h

16 Write an algebraic expression for each missing length on this rectangle.

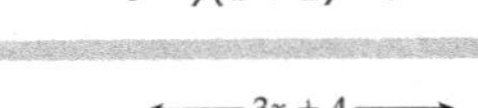
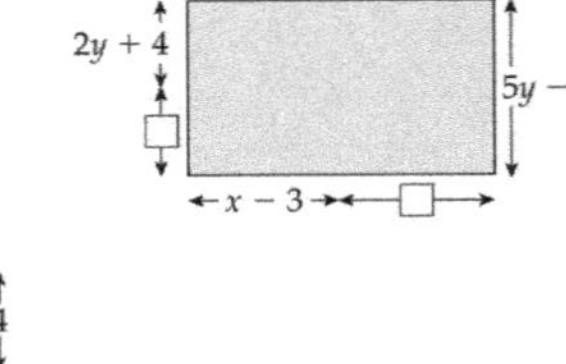

17 **i** Write an algebraic expression using brackets for the shaded areas in these rectangles.

ii Expand the brackets.

a

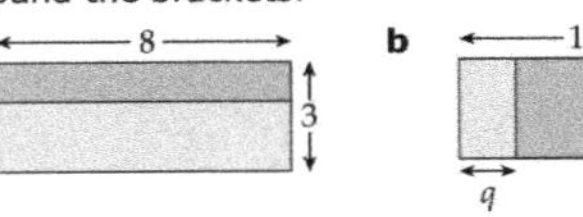

b

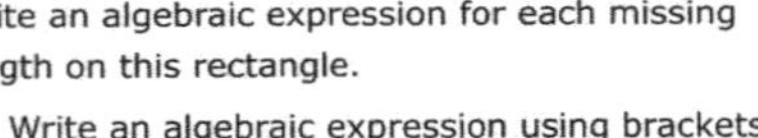

3i

18 Simplify these expressions.

a $\frac{x}{5} + \frac{2x}{5}$ **b** $\frac{p}{8} - \frac{q}{8}$ **c** $\frac{5}{9}a - \frac{1}{9}a$ **d** $\frac{10}{t} - \frac{3}{t}$

19 Simplify these using equivalent fractions.

a $\frac{k}{4} + \frac{k}{8}$ **b** $\frac{2y}{5} - \frac{y}{100}$ **c** $\frac{3}{8}m + \frac{1}{2}m$ **d** $\frac{3}{10}n - \frac{1}{8}n$

e $\frac{3}{a} + \frac{2}{b}$ **f** $\frac{6}{p} - \frac{1}{q}$ **g** $\frac{10}{t} - \frac{7}{t^2}$ **h** $\frac{5}{xy} - \frac{3}{x}$

MyMaths.co.uk 63

Question commentary

Questions 1–5 – It is important that students are able to recall and use the laws of indices.

Questions 6–10 – The importance of these algebraic skills, as they are so foundational for later algebra, cannot be overstated.

Question 11 – This may be the first proof question students have encountered. It is worth showing clearly what it means to prove something and why algebra has to be used, as it handles variables.

Questions 12 and **13** – Encourage students to write complete equations, and not just expressions.

Questions 14–19 – As above, the importance of students being very secure with these basic algebraic techniques cannot be overstated.

Answers

1 **a** 25 **b** 81 **c** 256 **d** 1
e $\frac{1}{64}$ **f** $\frac{1}{64}$ **g** 128 **h** $\frac{16}{9}$

2 **a** 54 **b** 24 **c** 16 **d** 25
e 12 **f** 25

3 **a** 2^8 **b** 4^{10} **c** 7^5 **d** 5^9
e a^{10} **f** b^6 **g** $10x^9$ **h** $12y^{11}$

4 **a** 6^3 **b** 10^5 **c** 8 **d** p^7
e $16k^2$ **f** 2

5 **a** 3^{10} **b** 12^{15} **c** m^{36} **d** n^{14}
e $64d^{15}$ **f** $-32x^{10}$

6 **a** $9x$ **b** $8a^2$
c $5m + 4n$ **d** $4p^2 - 3p + 8$
e $7ab$ **f** $2g^2 - g^3$

7 **a** $4x$ **b** 3
c $3p$ **d** $\frac{5}{3}k$
e $\frac{3gh}{2}$ **f** $b + 4$

8 $x(x+5) = x^2 + 5x$

9 **a** $8a + 22$ **b** $24x - 3$
c $5p + 16$ **d** $7b - 12$
e $2m + 25$ **f** $4n - 2$

10 **a** $2(x + 2)$ **b** $5(y + 4)$
c $2(3g - 1)$ **d** $4(2t - 3)$
e $3(6 - 5k)$ **f** $5(2p + 3q)$
g $a(7 + b)$ **h** $3n(5m - 3)$

11 **a** $n + (n + 1) + (n + 2) = 3n + 3$
b $3n + 3 = 3(n + 1)$

12 **a** £14
b $C = 3.5n$
c $C = 2.5n + 10$
d As a non-member cost is £42. As a member cost is £40. Just worth it!

13 **a** $r = 2w + 6$
b Twice the white tiles gives the tiles directly above and below and plus 6 gives the left and right ends.
c 206

14 **a** $x = p - r$ **b** $x = a + b + c$
c $x = z - 3y$ **d** $x = 2p$
e $x = a + a^2$ **f** $x = p + 2mn$

15 **a** $y = \frac{m}{n}$ **b** $y = \frac{a}{b^2}$
c $y = \frac{p-3}{q}$ **d** $y = \frac{g-h}{f}$
e $y = \frac{x}{ab}$ **f** $y = \frac{r}{\pi+2}$

16 $w = 2x + 7$ $l = 3y - 5$

17

	i	ii
a	$8(3 - p)$	$24 - 8p$
b	$4(10 - 3q)$	$40 - 12q$

18 **a** $\frac{3x}{5}$ **b** $\frac{p-q}{8}$
c $\frac{4a}{9}$ **d** $\frac{7}{t}$

19 **a** $\frac{3k}{8}$ **b** $\frac{39y}{100}$
c $\frac{7m}{8}$ **d** $\frac{7n}{40}$
e $\frac{3b+2a}{ab}$ **f** $\frac{6q-p}{pq}$
g $\frac{10t-7}{t^2}$ **h** $\frac{5-3y}{xy}$

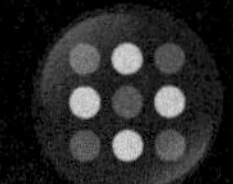

Case study 1: Energy in the home

Related lessons		Resources	
Percentage problems	4e	Percentages of amounts	(1030)
Mental multiplication and division	7d	Multiply triple digits	(1026)
Multiplication and division problems	11g	Newspapers	

Simplification	Extension
Most of the calculations required here are straightforward but some students might focus on two or three of the different items rather than considering the whole range. The numbers in tasks **2** and **3** could be simplified to aid the use of mental strategies.	All of the information given is about 'typical' costs and savings. Students could be asked to consider a *range* of savings and/or costs which will affect the time over which the savings/repayment costs are made. They could also investigate further the effects of the location of things like solar panels and wind generators in terms of their effectiveness at generating the required amounts of electricity.

Links

Most energy companies now offer government subsidised deals on things like new home insulation and solar panels. Private contractors also have access to these deals and students could look up the various offers on the Internet and in both local and national newspapers. Can they find a range of suppliers that could provide all of the various installations free of charge?

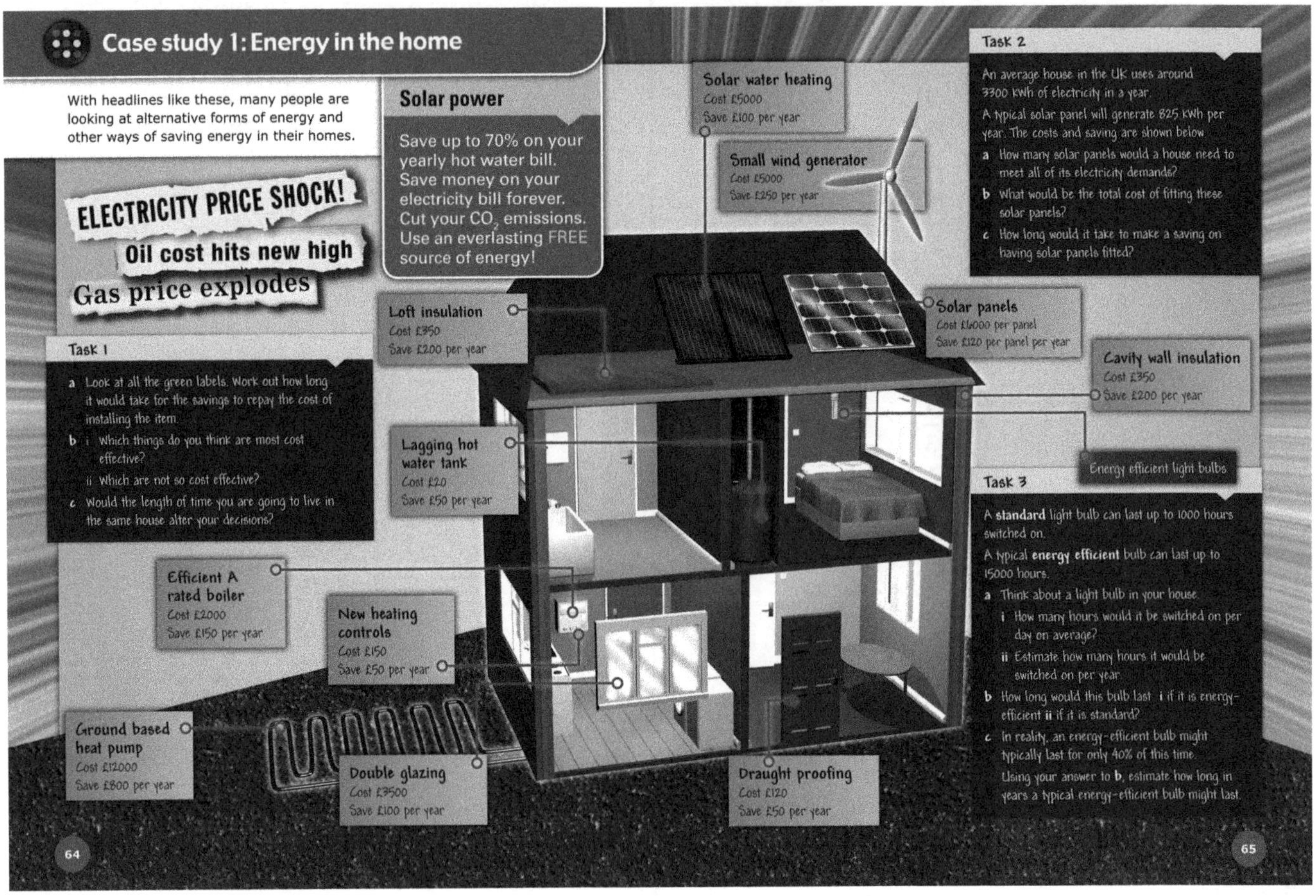

Case study 1: Energy in the home

With headlines like these, many people are looking at alternative forms of energy and other ways of saving energy in their homes.

ELECTRICITY PRICE SHOCK!

Oil cost hits new high

Gas price explodes

Solar power

Save up to 70% on your yearly hot water bill. Save money on your electricity bill forever. Cut your CO_2 emissions. Use an everlasting FREE source of energy!

Task 1

a Look at all the green labels. Work out how long it would take for the savings to repay the cost of installing the item.

b i Which things do you think are most cost effective?

ii Which are not so cost effective?

c Would the length of time you are going to live in the same house alter your decisions?

Solar water heating Cost £5000 Save £100 per year

Small wind generator Cost £5000 Save £250 per year

Loft insulation Cost £350 Save £200 per year

Lagging hot water tank Cost £20 Save £50 per year

Solar panels Cost £6000 per panel Save £120 per panel per year

Cavity wall insulation Cost £350 Save £200 per year

Energy efficient light bulbs

Efficient A rated boiler Cost £2000 Save £150 per year

New heating controls Cost £150 Save £50 per year

Ground based heat pump Cost £12000 Save £800 per year

Double glazing Cost £3500 Save £100 per year

Draught proofing Cost £120 Save £50 per year

Task 2

An average house in the UK uses around 3300 kWh of electricity in a year.

A typical solar panel will generate 825 kWh per year. The costs and saving are shown below.

a How many solar panels would a house need to meet all of its electricity demands?

b What would be the total cost of fitting these solar panels?

c How long would it take to make a saving on having solar panels fitted?

Task 3

A **standard** light bulb can last up to 1000 hours switched on.

A typical **energy efficient** bulb can last up to 15000 hours.

a Think about a light bulb in your house.

i How many hours would it be switched on per day on average?

ii Estimate how many hours it would be switched on per year.

b How long would this bulb last **i** if it is energy-efficient **ii** if it is standard?

c In reality, an energy-efficient bulb might typically last for only 40% of this time.

Using your answer to **b**, estimate how long in years a typical energy-efficient bulb might last.

64 65

Teaching notes

With energy prices rising and environmental concerns about the climate, there is much interest in reducing energy use around the house and obtaining energy in a cheaper or cleaner way.

This case study looks at a number of things that can be done to a house to make it more energy efficient. It looks at them in terms of how much they could reduce the cost of energy used over a year at current costs and considers their cost effectiveness by working out how long it would take for the savings to pay back the cost of purchase and installation of the items.

Look at the case study and explain that the house shows ways of either saving energy or of providing the energy in a different way. Ask the students some general questions such as: which items would save energy and which are alternative sources of energy? Do you have any of these things in your house? Why do you think that there is so much interest in saving energy these days? Establish that rising energy costs and concerns for the environment can both drive people to think about the way they use energy.

Task 1

Look at the information about loft insulation. What do you notice about the information that is given? Roughly how long would it take for the savings in costs to repay the cost of installing the insulation? Discuss how figures for items such as this are often given as ranges, as the actual figure will vary from house to house depending on its size, type and construction. Do you think that is a reasonable time in which to recoup the cost? What will happen for every year after that? Now look at the information for the A rated boiler and ask similar questions. The payback time is considerably longer. Discuss whether this is cost effective by asking questions such as if you have a perfectly good working boiler at the moment, do you think that it would be worth paying to have it changed for a new one? If you needed to change your current boiler, would it be worth having an A rated boiler as the replacement?

Task 2

Work through the section about the solar panels. When discussing answers, ensure that students comment on the fact that the payback time might shorten due to the electricity costs of supplied electricity increasing over time thereby increasing the annual savings.

Task 3

Look at the information about the energy efficient light bulbs. The students are guided through the working for both types of bulb using a series of estimates. Is there another way to save money when considering lighting the home? (Turn off the lights!)

Answers

1 **a** Loft insulation: 1.75 years; Lagging hot water tank: 0.4 years; Boiler: 13.3 years; Controls: 3 years; Heat pump: 15 years; Double glazing: 35 years: Draught proofing: 2.4 years; Cavity wall insulation: 1.75 years; Solar panels: 50 years; Wind generator: 20 years; Solar heating: 50 years.

b **i** Lagging hot water tank, loft insulation, cavity wall insulation.

ii Double glazing, efficient boiler, heat pump.

c More likely to buy expensive items like solar panels if you intend to stay longer. May not see the benefit, could increase the value of house.

2 **a** 4 panels

b £24 000

c 50 years

3 **a** **i** 4–5 hours/day **ii** 1500 hours/year

b **i** 10 years **ii** 8 months

c 4 years

Students' estimates may vary.

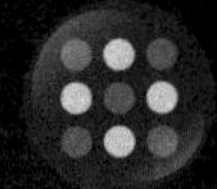

4 Fractions, decimals and percentages

Learning outcomes

N2 Order positive and negative integers, decimals and fractions; use the number line as a model for ordering of the real numbers; use the symbols =, ≠, <, >, ≤, ≥ (L6)

N4 Use the 4 operations, including formal written methods, applied to integers, decimals, proper and improper fractions, and mixed numbers, all both positive and negative (L6)

N9 Work interchangeably with terminating decimals and their corresponding fractions (such as 3.5 and 7/2 or 0.375 and 3/8 (L6)

N10 Define percentage as 'number of parts per hundred', interpret percentages and percentage changes as a fraction or a decimal, interpret these multiplicatively, express 1 quantity as a percentage of another, compare 2 quantities using percentages, and work with percentages greater than 100% (L7)

N11 Interpret fractions and percentages as operators (L7)

Introduction

The chapter starts by looking at ordering fractions and converting between decimals and fractions. Adding and subtracting fractions, including mixed numbers, is covered before work on multiplying and dividing fractions. It covers percentage change and then percentage problems before the final section on converting between fractions, decimals and percentages.

The introduction discusses places where fractions are used in everyday life. For example, one penny is one-hundredth of a pound and in telling the time one might say a quarter (of an hour) to four O'clock or half (an hour) past one O'clock. Up until 1984 halfpenny coins were legal tender and in pre-decimal currency a farthing – quarter penny – was used until 1960. Earlier coins included a half-farthing and a quarter-farthing.

It may be interesting to review the fractions that arise due to our units of time and money. A day is a seventh of a week, and hour a twenty-fourth of a day, a minute a sixtieth of an hour and a second a sixtieth of a minute. A shilling is a twentieth of a pound and a penny a fifth of a shilling. In pre-decimal currency a pound contained twenty shillings and a shilling contained 12 pence, so 240 pence in a pound.

NCTEM have produced a booklet on fractions which you might find useful.

https://www.ncetm.org.uk/public/files/257666/fractions_booklet.pdf

Prior knowledge

Students should already know how to…

- Interpret place notation for decimals
- Convert between decimals and fractions
- Add and subtract basic fractions
- Work out fractions of amounts
- Carry basic arithmetic including division

Starter problem

The starter problem introduces students to the idea of reverse percentage change. Adding 10% to the cost of a pair of trainers is straightforward: find 10% and then add it on. The new price will be £88.

Since we have to reduce the price of the trainers back to £80, we need to work out what percentage of 88 is 8. We can write this as a fraction in the form 8/88 and cancel it down to 1/11. Now what percentage is equivalent to 1/11?

We can convert it to a decimal by dividing 1 by 11 using a long division method:

$1 \div 11 = 0.09090909\ldots$

Since this decimal is recurring, we can get either an approximate, rounded, percentage equivalent (9.1%) or we can say it is 9.09 recurring percent.

Many students will simply assume the percentage reduction required following the increase is 10% so this worked example will help them to understand that this is not the case.

Resources

MyMaths

Frac dec perc 2	1015	Fractions to decimals	1016	Adding subtracting fractions	1017
Dividing fractions	1040	Multiply divide fractions intro	1046	Multiplying fractions	1047
Percentage change 1	1060	Mixed numbers	1074	Comparing fractions	1075
Change as a percentage	1302	Reverse percentages	1934		

Online assessment

Chapter test	2C-4
Formative test	2C-4
Summative test	2C-4

InvisiPen solutions

Multiplying by fractions	143	Dividing by fractions	144
Adding and subtracting fractions			145
Percentage increase and decrease			152
Calculating a percentage change			153
Reverse percentages	154	Fractions and decimals	161
Percentages, fractions and decimals			162

Topic scheme

Teaching time = 6 lessons/2 weeks

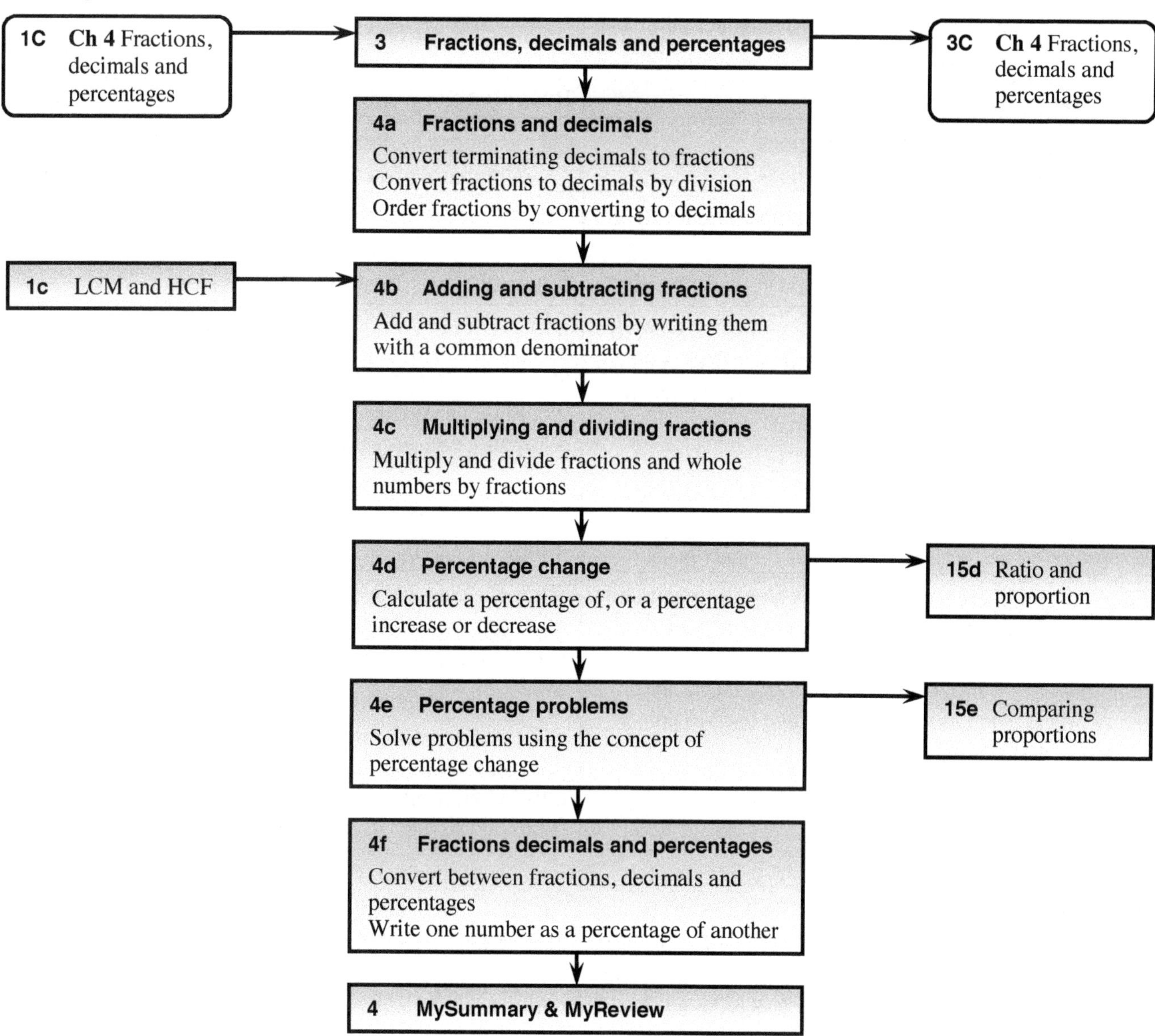

Differentiation

Student book 2A 66 – 85

Fractions
Fractions and decimals
Adding and subtracting fractions
Fraction of a quantity
Finding 10 percent
Percentages
Fractions, decimals and percentages

Student book 2B 60 – 77

Ordering decimals
Fractions and decimals
Adding and subtracting fractions
Fraction of a quantity
Percentages of amounts
Fractions, decimals and percentages

Student book 2C 66 – 83

Fractions and decimals
Adding and subtracting fractions
Multiplying and dividing fractions
Percentage change
Percentage problems
Fractions, decimals and percentages

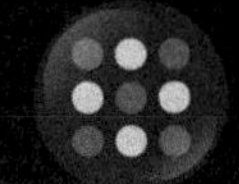

4a Fractions and decimals

Objectives	
• Convert terminating decimals to fractions	(L5)
• Use division to convert a fraction to a decimal	(L5)
• Order fractions by converting them to decimals	(L5)

Key ideas	Resources
1 Decimals can be written as fractions **2** Fractions can be written as decimals **3** Fractions can be conveniently compared once written as decimals	Fractions to decimals (1016) Comparing fractions (1075)

Simplification	Extension
Allow a calculator for all parts. Encourage students to use it not only to convert fractions to decimals, but also to check their answers. Remind students of the place value names tenths, hundredths, etc.	If $\frac{1}{3}$ is 0.33333... what is the decimal equivalent of $\frac{2}{3}$ and $\frac{3}{3}$? Are 0.999999... and 1 the same value? What would this mean about the fractional equivalent of 0.29999...? Same as $0.3 = \frac{3}{10}$. Make up other recurring decimals that recur with a 9 and challenge students to convert them to fractions.

Literacy	Links
Fractions, numbers smaller than 1, come in three main kinds: vulgar fractions, called fractions; decimal fractions, called decimals; and fractions with a denominator of 100, called percentages. There are many others, such as octals (US oktas) used to gauge the amount of cloud cover.	Show the class an imperial foot-long ruler. Foot-long rulers are marked in inches and fractions of inches. What does each division on the ruler represent? ($\frac{1}{8}''$, $\frac{1}{16}''$ or $\frac{1}{32}''$, depending on the ruler) How are different-sized divisions distinguished? (different length lines) A printable ruler can be found at http://www.vendian.org/mncharity/dir3/paper_rulers/UnstableURL/ruler_foot_a4.pdf

Alternative approach

The idea of last digits being all zero will need to be clarified. Show that a terminating decimal can have lots of zeros added, and agree that they do not need to be shown. But perhaps avoid discussion of which or where are the last digits, and simply say that a terminating decimal stops (there is a clue in the name, which may be worth a little discussion) after a few places. It may be necessary to show how some decimal fractions, by contrast, do not stop, in which case they are quite likely to be recurring. It may be appropriate or necessary, for inquisitive students, to give an example of a decimal that neither stops nor recurs, and in this case they can write their own, perhaps one that has never been written ever before. To illustrate, consider 0.1111454454445444445444445 ....
In question **2** part **e**, why might it be better not to simplify?

In question **4**, encourage students to look, even if only briefly, for short methods. For example, in part **a**, is $\frac{4}{7}$ obviously more than $\frac{1}{2}$? And in part **g**, how much less than 1 is $\frac{7}{9}$? And $\frac{8}{10}$? So which is closer to 1? This question would be a good opportunity to check their instincts, by asking for instant guesses for each part. Some students, often those for whom standard formal approaches are mystifying, have excellent mathematical intuition (even if they don't believe it), and this could be a good point to encourage some self-belief, especially if there are one or two such students in the class.

Can any time then be saved in the work of question **5**, or is it better here to simply change all to decimals? Perhaps especially if students know about the S↔D key on the calculator!

In question **6**, multiplying by the denominator (with an inequation, as for an equation) will be very helpful.

Checkpoint	
1 What is 1.24 as a fraction in its simplest form?	($1\frac{6}{25}$)
2 Convert 19 fortieths into a decimal.	(0.475)

Starter

Write nine decimal numbers in a 3 × 3 grid. Ask students to find

the sum of the top row

the product of the top left number and bottom right number

the difference between the middle left and middle right numbers, etc.

Can be differentiated by the number of decimal places in the chosen numbers.

Teaching notes

Use place value to remind students of the meaning of decimals. The place value columns could be written out and headings given. For example, 0.3 has a '3' in the 'tenths' column, so it represents '3 tenths' or $\frac{3}{10}$.

Discuss how we write decimals that have digits in more than 1 column. Include examples that simplify.

How can the process be reversed, what should fractions be out of to make them easy to recognise as decimals? Use examples of fractions that have denominators easily converted to powers of ten.

What about awkward fractions? Discuss the method of short division and why many students end up calculating the reciprocal instead. How can a calculator be used? What if the decimal does not terminate? Discuss how to represent recurring decimals.

When ordering fractions and decimals, will it be easier to convert them all to fractions or decimals to allow for comparison?

Plenary

When you look at a fraction in its simplest form, there is a way to tell if it will produce a recurring or terminating decimal. Give examples of both. For example, $\frac{1}{5}, \frac{7}{8}, \frac{3}{20}$ (terminating); $\frac{2}{7}, \frac{4}{15}, \frac{5}{12}$ (recurring). Can students give further examples of either? Can students spot how to tell? Answer: look at the product of prime factors of the denominator. If it is made of only 2s and 5s then the fraction will be terminating, otherwise it's recurring.

Exercise commentary

Question 1 – Orally, or with whiteboards. Encourage working to show how simplifying has been done.

Question 2 – Orally, or with whiteboards, but with discussion. For parts **e, i** and **j** encourage students to first simplify if possible.

Question 3 – Can be done without a calculator to practice short division if desired.

Question 4 – Use of a calculator is sensible here. Ensure students compare each decimal place separately. Some reminder of the inequality signs maybe needed.

Question 5 – Why is converting all values to a decimal easier than converting to a fraction?

Question 6 – A calculator is useful to convert fractions to decimals. The term *variable* may need explaining as may a two-sided inequality. Challenge students to come up with three fractions for each question.

Question 7 – Encourage the use of earlier parts of this question to help inform the later parts. For example, double part **a** to find part **c**.

Question 8 – Trial-and-improvement is likely to be effective.

Question 9 – Students will need guiding through this question. This is a technique they will come across later, so should be viewed as an extension. It involves subtracting one equation from another, which they will not have seen before. It is worth pointing out that any recurring decimal can be converted to a fraction.

Question 10 – New scientific calculators will show recurring decimals, even when repeating pattern cannot be fitted on the screen. Ask students which other fractions have a repeating pattern that is one less than the denominator, when converted to decimals. They are primes (but interestingly not all primes).

Answers

1 **a** $\frac{2}{5}$ **b** $\frac{28}{25}$ **c** $\frac{9}{25}$
d $\frac{49}{50}$ **e** $\frac{83}{500}$ **f** $\frac{21}{8}$

2 **a** 0.3 **b** 1.15 **c** 0.76 **d** 1.26
e 2.2 **f** 1.6 **g** 0.15 **h** 0.825
i 0.35 **j** 1.0625 **k** 2.44 **l** 4.625

3 **a** 0.3125 **b** 0.09375 **c** 0.36364
d 0.42857 **e** 2.83333 **f** 3.14286

4 **a** < **b** < **c** > **d** >
e < **f** > **g** < **h** >

5 **a** $0.425 < \frac{3}{7} < 0.43 < \frac{7}{16}$
b $0.11 < \frac{1}{9} < 0.12 < \frac{1}{8}$
c $\frac{4}{7} < \frac{571}{999} < \frac{19}{33} < 0.6$
d $\frac{2}{7} < 0.333 < 0.3$ recurring $< \frac{22}{63}$
e 0.08 recurring $< 0.09 < \frac{1}{11} < \frac{3}{29}$

6 **a** 0.5, 0.6, 0.7 **b** 0.3, 0.4, 0.5, 0.6, 0.7
c 0.4, 0.5, 0.6, 0.7, 0.8

7 **a** 0.1818181818181 **b** 0.27272727272727
c 0.36363636363 **d** 0.45454545454
e 0.5454545454 **f** 0.9090909090
They are all recurring decimals with the recurring digits the same as the digits for the numerator multiplied by 9.

8 $\frac{13}{19}$

9 **a** **i** 4.4444... **ii** 4/9
b **i** 5/9 **ii** 5/33

10 **a** 0.142857142857 **b** Students' explanations
c **i** 0.05263157895 **ii** 18 repeating digits. No.

Objectives

- Use efficient methods to add and subtract fractions (L7)

Key ideas

1 Fractions can only be added when they have the same denominators

2 Fractions that do not have the same denominators can be changed to equivalent fractions, with the same denominators, so that they can then be added

Resources

Adding subtracting fractions (1017)

Simplification

Finding a common denominator can be challenging for large numbers. Where needed, a calculator could be used to speed up the process of writing out lists of multiples to find a common multiple.

Extension

The diagonal length of a square of side 1 unit was thought by the ancient Babylonians (over three thousand years ago) to be roughly worked out by the following calculation. Can you find the answer as a mixed fraction? Use a calculator to check the approximation.

$$1+\frac{24}{60}+\frac{51}{60^2}+\frac{10}{60^3}=1\frac{8947}{21600} = 1.41421296$$

($\sqrt{2}$ = 1.41421356, to 9 sf)

Literacy

Note that the LCM of denominators is often referred to as the Lowest (or perhaps Least) Common Denominator, the LCD.

Remember that subtraction is really addition with a negative, so what goes for addition goes for subtraction.

Links

The Ancient Egyptians represented all their fractions as the sum of a number of unit fractions, where all the unit fractions are different. All positive rational numbers can be represented by Egyptian fractions. More information about Egyptian fractions, including a calculator to convert a fraction to an Egyptian fraction can be found at http://www.mcs.surrey.ac.uk/Personal/R.Knott/Fractions/egyptian.html

Alternative approach

Consider what other common denominators could be used in these examples. Is it necessary to find and use the LCM (or LCD) here? With the fairly large numbers being used in question **3**, for example, does it perhaps save work and avoid even larger numbers, which would make for a greater chance of errors?

Students may question the relevance of calculating such small fractional parts, but the concepts and techniques are related to other work to come, and, of course, the stretching of the brain to cope with such work is good for the individual, good preparation for even harder material in the future, and great evidence of an ability to cope with difficult work.

If accuracy does matter, then an estimate and the use of a calculator would seem very sensible.

Checkpoint

1 A piece of wood measures $35\frac{1}{4}$ inches. It is shortened by $8\frac{5}{8}$ inches. What is the new length? ($26\frac{5}{8}$ inches)

Starter

Challenge students to find two numbers

with a sum of 1.1 and a product of 0.24 (0.3, 0.8)

with a sum of 0.12 and a product of 0.0035 (0.05, 0.07)

with a sum of 0.76 and a product of 0.042 (0.06, 0.7)

with a sum of 1.29 and a product of 0.108, etc. (0.09, 1.2)

Teaching notes

Reinforce the concept of adding and subtracting fractions using shaded parts of diagrams. Discuss common misconceptions. For example, $\frac{2}{3}+\frac{3}{7}=\frac{5}{14}$.

How can fractions with different denominators be added and subtracted? Use a range of examples that require either one or both denominators to be converted. When fractions are converted, will the overall answer change?

How can fractions greater than one whole be written? Look at examples of both 'top heavy/improper fractions' and 'mixed fractions'. Reinforce the concept with shaded diagrams.

How can fractions be added and subtracted when mixed fractions are used? Look at both the method in the student book and the method of treating the whole number parts separately. What are the advantages and disadvantages of each method?

Include examples where the integer parts are large and the fractional parts cause a negative fraction. For example, $23\frac{3}{5}-7\frac{5}{7}$. What is the best strategy?

Plenary

If I add $\frac{1}{2}$ then $\frac{1}{4}$ then $\frac{1}{8}$ and continue adding fractions in this pattern, what happens to my answer? Encourage students to look for a pattern in the consecutive results that eliminates the need to keep finding a common denominator (sum first n term = $2^{n-1}/2^n$).

Exercise commentary

Question 1 – Part **d** can be tackled by 'borrowing' from the first whole number. Ask students if they have an alternative method. For example, using a negative fraction to assist. Converting to improper fractions is the less efficient.

Question 2 – The lowest common denominator is the product of the denominators in all but part **h**. Students could use a calculator or choose only a few parts from this question to reduce the time needed.

Question 3 – Encourage students to look for the lowest common denominator, or at least a common denominator that does not involve an unnecessarily large value.

Question 4 – Parts **b**, **d** and **g**, are more difficult. Encourage more than one approach; see the examples. Although students need to be able to do this without a calculator, it is worth showing students how mixed numbers can be entered on a scientific calculator.

Question 5 – Encourage students to write a sum similar to questions at the start of the exercise.

Question 6 – Discuss what alternative methods can be used? In part **a**, ask if anyone added the two sides of the rectangle, then doubled? Or did they double the length, double the width, and then add? Which method is easier?

Question 7 – Encourage students to use 16 as a common denominator. In the investigation students will think they have exhausted all possibilities by adding different combinations of the weights. Challenge them by saying it is possible to measure a sixteenth, since weights can be put on both sides of the scales.

Answers

1 **a** 4/7 **b** 1/2
c $4\frac{1}{12}$ **d** $1\frac{2}{3}$

2 **a** 67/72 **b** $1\frac{9}{77}$
c 27/35 **d** 11/195
e 23/255 **f** 305/432
g 33/208 **h** 43/48

3 **a** 19/30 **b** $1\frac{23}{60}$
c 29/140 **d** $1\frac{17}{120}$
e 47/48 **f** 7/32
g $1\frac{11}{60}$ **h** 53/90

4 **a** $1\frac{7}{8}$ **b** $1\frac{7}{8}$
c $5\frac{1}{2}$ **d** 7/10
e $3\frac{55}{63}$ **f** $4\frac{4}{15}$
g 37/40 **h** $3\frac{19}{21}$

5 **a** **i** 37/56 **ii** 19/56
b $1\frac{9}{16}$ kg

6 **a** $16\frac{1}{6}$ inches **b** $2\frac{19}{40}$ km

7 **a** $2\frac{9}{16}$ kg **b** 3/4 kg and 3/16 kg
c Students' answers

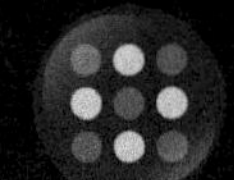

4c Multiplying and dividing fractions

Objectives

- Multiply and divide an integer by a fraction (L6)
- Use efficient methods to multiply and divide fractions, interpreting division as a multiplicative inverse (L7)
- Cancel common factors before multiplying or dividing (L7)

Key ideas

1 We can multiply fractions by multiplying numerators to give a new numerator, and denominators to give a new denominator

2 We can simplify the work by cancelling

3 Instead of dividing by a fraction, we can multiply by its reciprocal

Resources

Dividing fractions	(1040)
Multiply divide fractions intro	(1046)
Multiplying fractions	(1047)
Mixed numbers	(1074)

A dice

Simplification

Minimising the number of things to remember will simplify this exercise. Changing the integers to fractions over '1' will make multiplication easier. Not cancelling before multiplication will allow the correct answer to be achieved, but point out that cancelling needs to be looked at.

Extension

The √2 can be calculated as a 'continued fraction' which carries on forever! How far can students get calculating √2?

1/1, 3/2, 7/5, 17/12, 41/29, …

$$1+\cfrac{1}{2+\cfrac{1}{2+\cfrac{1}{2+\cfrac{1}{2+\cfrac{1}{\cdots}}}}}$$

Literacy

The 'of' key on the calculator has a cross on it so that it can easily be found. That 'of' is synonymous with times or multiply can be explained with a phrase such as 'two of', and so on.

Note that cancellation here can be taken as meaning cancelling, not that something is no longer happening. But why are the words so similar? (If the factors are written in full, then cancelling does indeed mean that something is no longer there.)

Links

Meteorologists use fractions to gauge and describe the amount of cloud cover. The sky is divided into eighths and an estimate made of how many eighths, or octals (US oktas), of the sky are covered in cloud. 0/8 octals means that the sky is clear, 8/8 means completely covered by cloud. There is more information about the symbols used to show cloud cover on weather charts at http://www.metoffice.gov.uk/education/secondary/students/charts.html

Alternative approach

Why do we multiply the numerators (because that's how many we now have) and the denominators (because this will show what the new fractions are – halves of thirds, or fifths of tenths, and so on) when we multiply fractions. So if we multiply by an integer, we change the number of fractions but not the kind of fraction: only the numerator changes. Writing an integer as a fraction with a denominator of 1 may clarify and reinforce this.

For division, consider such approaches as 'how many halves are there in 3', with oranges or whatever is needed, and establish that students will work these out by effectively carrying out a multiplication by the reciprocal. So that's what we do: division by a fraction is too hard, as a rule, but multiplication by the reciprocal is the same, and much easier, as long as we remember to reciprocate or invert the fraction we were dividing by.

Checkpoint

1 Calculate $\frac{16}{25} \div \frac{8}{15}$ ($\frac{6}{5}$ or $1\frac{1}{5}$)

Starter

Ask students to draw six boxes representing the numerators and denominators of three fractions side by side. Throw a dice six times. After each throw, ask students to place the score in one of their boxes. Students score points if the first fraction is bigger than the second fraction which in turn is bigger than the third fraction.

Teaching notes

When a fraction is multiplied what happens to the two numbers? For example, $\frac{2}{10}\times 3$ means what? $\left(\frac{6}{10}\right)$
Use shaded diagrams to establish the meaning. What possible error might some students make? Why is this incorrect?

What is the meaning of $\frac{3}{4}$ of 20? How can it be represented as a calculation? The word 'of' can be look at as meaning multiply, so $\frac{3}{4}\times 20$. Look at how this calculation can be simplified like the first example.

How can two fractions be multiplied? Use shaded diagrams to explain why this method works. Show how cancelling first can help.

How can two fractions be divided? What does $4 \div \frac{2}{5}$ mean? Express in words. Use diagrams to show that it is equivalent to multiplication by 5 and division by 2. Effectively the fraction has been 'turned upside down'. The following rhyme could useful to help divide with fractions: 'the one you are dividing by, turn upside down and multiply'.

Plenary

Check that question **10** outcome also holds true for negative fractions by trying a few examples. It works for any positive or negative fraction or integer (except -1, since division by zero is not possible). A very able student may be able to prove this.

Exercise commentary

Questions 1 and **2** – Watch for students multiplying both the numerator and denominator by the integer. Some students may prefer writing the integer as a fraction over '1'. This also makes it easier to look for cross simplifying.

Question 3 – Remind students that 'of' always means multiply in mathematics.

Question 4 – Encourage students to try to cancel before, rather than after, multiplying. Challenge students to try a question both ways and show that simplifying before multiplying is preferable.

Questions 5 and **6** – Again, some students may find it helpful to turn the integer into a fraction over '1'.

Question 7 – Some students may try to deal with the integer and fractional parts separately as can be done with addition and subtraction. Show them that they can use the grid method for multiplying, or convert the fractions to improper fractions first. Encourage experimentation and ask for students' conclusions.

Question 8 – Students may be tempted to add when they need to multiply the fractions. Again emphasise that whenever they see the word 'of' to think multiply.

Question 9 – Multiplying and dividing by mixed numbers will be covered in more detail in future years, so this question should be viewed as extension.

Question 10 – Seek many answers.

Question 11 – Encourage students to begin with simple fractions and to hypothesise about the result.

Answers

1 **a** $\frac{6}{7}$ **b** $\frac{4}{9}$ **c** $\frac{5}{8}$ **d** $\frac{9}{11}$
e $\frac{5}{7}$ **f** $1\frac{7}{8}$ **g** $2\frac{2}{5}$ **h** $4\frac{3}{8}$

2 **a** 4 **b** $4\frac{1}{2}$ **c** $7\frac{1}{2}$ **d** $13\frac{3}{4}$
e $5\frac{1}{4}$ **f** $7\frac{4}{5}$ **g** $22\frac{1}{2}$ **h** $2\frac{6}{7}$

3 **a** $3\frac{3}{4}$ feet **b** 24
c $5\frac{1}{3}$ inches **d** $93\frac{1}{2}$ minutes
e $35\frac{5}{8}$ GB **f** 297 m

4 **a** $\frac{6}{35}$ **b** $\frac{5}{16}$
c $\frac{5}{12}$ **d** $\frac{1}{4}$
e $\frac{1}{6}$ **f** $\frac{3}{8}$
g $\frac{4}{5}$ **h** $\frac{8}{35}$

5 **a** 6 **b** 10 **c** 15 **d** 21
e $11\frac{1}{4}$ **f** $17\frac{1}{2}$ **g** $16\frac{1}{2}$ **h** $16\frac{1}{4}$

6 **a** $1\frac{1}{20}$ **b** $\frac{3}{4}$ **c** $1\frac{1}{6}$ **d** $\frac{49}{50}$
e $\frac{1}{4}$ **f** 27

7 **a** $34\frac{7}{8}$ inches^2 **b** $1\frac{23}{40}$ kg

8 **a** 250 g **b** $\frac{1}{4}$

9 **a** 8 **b** $1\frac{31}{32}$

10 **a** Students' answers **b** Students' answers

11 **a, b, c** Students' investigations
d

$$\frac{a}{b} \to \frac{1-\frac{a}{b}}{1+\frac{a}{b}} = \frac{(b-a)/b}{(b+a)/b} = \frac{b-a}{b+a}$$

$$\frac{b-a}{b+a} \to \frac{1-(b-a)/(b+a)}{1+(b-a)/(b+a)} = \frac{b+a-(b-a)}{b+a+(b-a)} = \frac{2a}{2b} = \frac{a}{b}$$

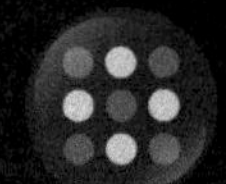

4d Percentage change

Objectives

- Calculate percentages and find the outcome of a given percentage increase or decrease (L6/7)
- Extend mental methods of calculation working with percentages (L5)
- Solve problems involving percentage changes (L6)

Key ideas

1. Finding percentages of amounts is done by multiplication
2. Percentage increase or decrease involves finding a percentage, so is also done by multiplication

Resources

Percentage change 1 (1060)

Simplification

For percentage decreases, ask 'What percentage is left? Therefore what percentage are you trying to find?' Encourage the use of decimal multiplication for percentage change, but allow the practice of adding or subtracting the required percentage.

Extension

How can these two answers be written?

a Increase £50 by x% $50 + \frac{x}{2}$ or $\frac{100+x}{2}$

b Increase £y by x% $y + \frac{xy}{100}$ or $\frac{100y+xy}{100}$.

An algebraic approach is likely to be very difficult, encourage an investigative approach with various values for x. Part **b** is even more demanding and most students will need support.

Literacy

Ensure no student is still ignorant of the difference between 'of' and 'off'; this may never have been explained. The original BODMAS included the 'of'; but 'off' means working out the new percentage that needs to be calculated … by multiplication.

Links

Forests are important to the world environment as they absorb carbon emissions but every year vast areas are lost to logging and agricultural clearance. A table showing the total percentage loss of primary forest, those undisturbed by human activity, for 17 countries from 1990 to 2005 can be found at http://rainforests.mongabay.com/primary_annual.html

Alternative approach

Take any amount offered, and any percentage increase offered (within limits), and ask students to increase the amount by this percentage, and again, and again. Or more times if they think they can cope or seem to be coping (depending on whether this is being discussed, or actually attempted). Then show how they can go directly to the answer with a suitable multiplier and the power key on the calculator, and a single press of the = or equivalent key. Question **6** does the same job quite well, and this could be a starting point, or the step after question **1**. Either way, the idea that all percentage calculations involve multiplication is vital and likely to be not only new to some students but resisted, if they have been well trained in different beliefs and processes that they have struggled to master.

It may not be necessary for students to do all of question **1**, but some may need the practice. Once the central concept (see checkpoint below) is firmly grasped, much of the rest of the exercise may seem fairly routine. So take time with the introduction to and fundamental point of question **2**.

Checkpoint

1 A company offers an 8% discount for concert tickets bought online. The tickets cost £56. How much are they if bought online? (£51.52)

Starter

Write the following fractions on the board.

$\frac{14}{49}, \frac{2}{12}, \frac{7}{42}, \frac{18}{30}, \frac{10}{35}, \frac{4}{24}, \frac{21}{35}, \frac{6}{21}, \frac{5}{30}, \frac{24}{40}, \frac{4}{14}, \frac{15}{25}$

Ask students to sort the fractions into three sets of equivalent fractions.

Can be extended by asking students to make up their own fraction sort puzzle.

Teaching notes

As a paired activity, write the figure £120 in the centre of an A3 sheet and circle it. Write 100% at the edge of the circle. Branch off from the circle and create another percentage of £120, for example, 50% = £60. Explain that different percentages can be found by drawing in multiple branches, branches off other branches or combining results. Challenge students to come up with as many as possible including unusual ones, for example, $3\frac{1}{4}\%$.

A percentage of an amount can be found using a calculator. When would a calculator be useful? Ensure students are confident expressing percentages as decimals. Look at the method of decimal multiplication as outlined in the first example. Encourage students to show the stages of their working. Consider a discussion of the method of performing a percentage change with just one multiplication. For example, × 1.23 for a 23% increase, or × 0.77 for a 23% decrease.

Plenary

Choose a simple starting amount. Increase it by a specific simple percentage. Now decrease the new amount by the same percentage. Why don't you get back to the original amount? What calculation do you have to do to increase then decrease by the same percentage? Encourage students to consider both the equivalent fraction and equivalent decimal method from the worked example. Make clear that multiplication and division are reverse processes.

Exercise commentary

Question 1 – Encourage students to try all three methods. Remind students that 'of' means multiply.

Question 2 – Encourage students to use the decimal multiplication method for all these questions, as they will need to know this method when they encounter reverse percentage change questions later.

Question 3 – An opportunity to explore payment schemes and credit. Ask why monthly payments are generally more expensive.

Question 4 – For these practical applications of percentage increase and decrease, get students to check to see if the answer is reasonable.

Question 5 – A function machine/arrow diagram may help students to realise how the reverse process works. Students who subtract 13% for part **b** should check their answer by adding on 13%.

Question 6 – This question introduces the idea of repeated percentage change, which students will encounter later. Encourage an organised approach in laying out the working, identifying the age and height. Discuss how growth rates change during your childhood and why this model is unlikely to continue for many years. Also discuss why finding 9% of 90 cm and just multiplying by the number of years that pass is inaccurate.

Answers

1 **a** £10.50 **b** 45 m
c 45.24 kg **d** 84 ml
e £61.38 **f** 29.75 GB
g \$26.10 **h** 98.01 m
i 3.6 mm **j** 43.75 MB
k 0.105 m **l** £1282.50
m 147 km **n** 698.25 g
o 0.66 tonnes **p** £50 000

2 **a** £44.80 **b** £284.40
c 50.4 km **d** 30.6 mm
e 147.5 kg **f** £2405
g £22.33 **h** 64.94 kJ

3 Paying in instalments costs more (£317.70)

4 **a** 48.6 kg **b** £9.10
c 46 marks **d** £184.80

5 **a** 319 225 **b** 250 000

6 **a** 98.1 cm **b** 127.0 cm
c 213.1 cm **d** Students' answers

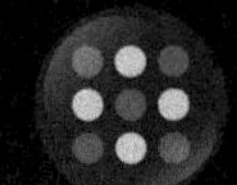

4e Percentage problems

Objectives	
• Calculate an original amount when given the transformed amount after a percentage change	(L8)
• Use calculators for reverse percentage change calculations by doing an appropriate division	(L8)

Key ideas	Resources
1 Percentage problems can be solved by multiplying or dividing by decimals.	Reverse percentages (1934)

Simplification	Extension
Provide students with an arrow diagram to help reinforce the reverse operation of percentage change. For example, original × 1.2 → new amount increased by 20% original amount before 20% increased ← new amount ÷ 1.2.	Solve question **4** using an algebraic method. Call the initial value x. A decimal multiplication method is useful here and students may need prompting to form an equation. For example, $0.8x = 0.7x + 15$.

Literacy	Links
The idea of an inverse function might need a little explanation. If students have been studying cost and sale prices in business studies, or similar, they may need a little clarification here of what is meant by original price – just the price before the sale. And if anyone happens to be well versed in such matters, they may be able to tell the class what does and does not count as an original price, in law.	The Consumer Price Index (CPI) is an official measure of the average price of goods and services including travel costs, food, heating and household goods. The index number is calculated each month by finding the price of a sample of goods that a typical household might buy, and comparing the price to a reference value. The percentage change in the CPI from the previous month is a measure of inflation. The latest figures for the CPI can be found at http://www.statistics.gov.uk/cci/nugget.asp?ID=19

Alternative approach

In the left hand side of the first example, show how ÷ 80 and × 100 can be written as $\times\frac{100}{80}$, or $\div\frac{80}{100}$, i.e. divide by 80% or ÷ 0.8 …which is the same figure that appears on the right hand side, where there will need to be some additional clarification. The sale price is obtained by multiplying the original price by 80%, so what do we do to the sale price to go back to the original price? The opposite or inverse?

The vital point here is that the multiplying (or dividing) factor, the ratio, does not change – it's just a question of whether we are multiplying or dividing by it. The figure to multiply or divide by is given by the change in the original amount, which always starts as 100%.

Emphasise that if the thinking can be done first, then the calculation becomes quite simple.

Checkpoint

1 Ali receives a pay rise of 3%. His salary is now £18 746.
What was it before the increase? (£18 200)

Starter

Ask students to find the fraction that is half-way between

$\frac{3}{5}$ and $\frac{7}{10}$, $\frac{3}{8}$ and $\frac{1}{2}$, $\frac{1}{3}$ and $\frac{5}{6}$, $\frac{1}{4}$ and $\frac{1}{3}$.

Can be extended by asking for other fractions in the given ranges.

Can be differentiated by the choice of fractions.

Answers: $\frac{13}{20}, \frac{7}{16}, \frac{7}{12}, \frac{7}{24}$.

Teaching notes

How can a percentage increase be performed on a calculator in one step? Since the new amount is over 100%, a decimal of over 1 can be used as the multiplier. If this is illustrated on an arrow diagram, then a discussion could follow as to the method of reversing the initial percentage increase. Explain this in terms of a 'reverse process'.

Consider examples of percentage decrease in the same way. If an amount is decreased by 15%, what percentage is being found? What multiplication is required? Once the change has been applied, how can it be reversed?

Why is a percentage increase by 10% not reversed by a percentage decrease of 10%?

Look at practical problems of finding the new amount using a single decimal multiplier. Look at practical problems of finding the original amount that require the use of the reverse process. Could these sorts of questions be solved without a calculator? Look at a possible example.

Plenary

An amount is increased by 44% over 2 years. If the increase was the same each year, what was the yearly percentage increase? (20%) Repeat for 21%. (10%) Is there a better way to find the answer than trial-and-improvement? This need not be followed to using $\sqrt{1.44}$ or $\sqrt{1.21}$. Investigation of how to achieve × 1.44 in 2 equal multiplications would demonstrate a clear understanding.

Exercise commentary

Question 1 – Showing an arrow between columns to demonstrate the method of increasing by 4% may help to inform students of the reverse process. × 1.04 Stress the inverse of multiplication is division.

Question 2 – Encourage the use of both multiplicative and ratio methods. For non-calculator questions the ratio method is often simpler.

Question 3 – Ask students how this question differs from 1 and 2? The amount of the change is given rather than the new or original amount. Ask how this changes the way the question is handled.

Question 4 – A trial-and-improvement approach is a good initial method. Some students will accept that 10% is £15, but is this correct? Algebra can be used to prove this is the case.

Question 5 – Encourage the efficient use of a calculator. It may be appropriate to introduce the power function. For further investigation look at http://en.wikipedia.org/wiki/World_Population

Also, students might like to see what the population would have been in the year AD 864 if a 2% increase had continued throughout history. Reduce by 2% (÷ 1.02) 1143 times. The population is just below 1!

Answers

1

Name	Old Wage	New Wage
James	£300	£312
Bernie	£275	£286
Vikki	£500	£520
Rufus	£350	£364

2 **a** £120 **b** £460 **c** 240 g

3 **a** £20 **b** 500 g

4 **a** £150 **b** £120 **c** £105

5 **a** 6 939.2 million **b** 5581.0 million

c Students' answers

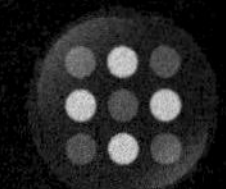

4f Fractions, decimals and percentages

Objectives

- Use the equivalence of fractions, decimals and percentages to compare proportions (L6)
- Interpret percentage as the 'so many hundredths of' and express one given number as a percentage of another (L6)

Key ideas

1 Fractions, decimals and percentages are interchangeable

Resources

Frac dec perc 2 (1015)
Change as a percentage (1302)

Newspapers and magazines

Simplification

Avoid simply giving students an algorithm to use. Focus on the meaning and understanding of fractions, decimals and percentages. For example, what does the line in a fraction mean when using a calculator? What does the first decimal place of a decimal tell us about the percentage it represents? Before you find the 'percentage increase', it makes sense to find the 'increase', etc.

Extension

A pub might buy a pint of lemonade for 20p and a pint of lager or beer of 80p and sell them each for £2. What percentage profit is this? (900% and 150%) Try this without a calculator. Why do pubs charge a similar price for soft drinks and alcoholic drinks if the percentage profit is so different? How much of the difference is due to tax? Or to overheads?

Literacy

The Links activity could lead to some analysis of the literary style of newspapers and magazines, and students could consider whether the style used helps to communicate the mathematical concepts clearly. Consider how some headlines appear to be deliberately misleading.

Links

Bring in some newspapers or magazines for the class to use. Ask students to find any article or advertisement where a decimal, percentage or fraction is used. Which format is used most frequently? Would the article or advertisement have the same affect if, for example, a decimal was used in place of a percentage, or a percentage in place of a fraction? Are there any examples where a conversion has been used?

Alternative approach

The second example can be worked as the reverse process of the last spread, and the subtraction of 357 from 420 avoided in the same way. All that ever needs to be asked in such questions as these is, What, out of what? It's either 357 out of 420, or the converse. One clue as to which is that it should always be out of the original. But if this is ever not clear, considering whether the ratio should be greater or less than 1 (ask here: if it is reduced in price, what sort of percentage should we have?) could help.

Once the question What, out of what? has been answered, we have a fraction, which is easy to turn into a decimal on a calculator (or perhaps without), and then easy to turn into a percentage.

In the example given, keying 357 ÷ 420 into the calculator (perhaps easiest with the fraction key or function) will give $\frac{17}{20}$, the S↔D key will give 0.85, which is 85%, which means a reduction of … with very little effort, and less opportunity for making an error.

So in order to find a percentage decrease, it makes sense to avoid the trouble of finding the decrease. Similarly with an increase, for example in question **3** part **b**: what is 2369 ÷ 2300? (No calculator needed?) This very easily gives the percentage increase. Similarly in question **4** part **a** – and again, no calculator really necessary.

Checkpoint

1 A school population increased from 1050 to 1134.
   a What was the percentage increase? (8%)
   b Express this as a fraction. (2/25)

Starter

Ask students to draw a 3 × 3 grid and enter nine amounts from the following list:

£2, £3, £4, £5, £6, £7, £8, £9, £10, £11, £12, £13, £14, £15, £16, £17

Give questions, for example, 12% of £75, 68% of £25, 44% of £25.

Winner is the first student to cross out all 9 amounts.

(Hint: 12% of 75 = 75% of 12.)

Teaching notes

If a fraction is out of 10 or 100, etc. show how place value tells us the decimal equivalent. Look to see if the denominators can be easily converted. What does a fraction need to be out of to see it as a percentage?

The other conversions between decimals, fractions and percentages are covered in the previous spreads in Chapter 4.

Look at examples of expressing one amount as the percentage of another amount. Include calculator and non-calculator examples. Encourage students to see the decimal solution as a percentage rather than relying on a further multiplication by 100. For example, express 4 as a percentage of 15: 4 ÷ 15 = 0.26666... which is 27%. Express 3 as a percentage of 20: $\frac{3}{20} = \frac{15}{100} = 15\%$

Look at examples of finding the percentage change. Emphasise that the change is **always** out of the **original**.

$$\text{Percentage change} = \frac{\text{change}}{\text{original}}.$$

But this gives a decimal. What is the last step? Convert the decimal to a percentage.

Plenary

Another use of percentages is in percentage errors. For example, attendance at a football game is 20 454 but a paper might quote 20 000. How might you calculate the percentage error? Ask students to estimate the size of the percentage error. Which value seems correct to divide by? True value or error value? Answer 2.22% (2 dp) but students will get 2.27% if they divide by the wrong amount.

Exercise commentary

Question 1 – To improve technique, encourage students to only use a calculator when necessary. An interesting investigation is to find out which denominators terminate and which recur.

Question 2 – Discuss what factors apart from the score in a test will give an indication of how well someone has done? Discuss class average, position in class, last year's results, difficulty of the test, etc. Is it possible to give a sensible answer to parts **b** or **c** without such information?

Question 3 – Encourage students to check their result by working out the new amount from the answer they achieve for the percentage change. Allow students to use a mental method of finding convenient percentages of the original amount and combining them to try to find the percentage change.

Question 4 –Challenge students to work without using a calculator. Encourage them to show how their fraction is being simplified.

Question 5 – Ask students whether people are better or worse off based on this table of figures. Discuss the relevance of salary and house increases in particular.

Answers

1

Fraction	7/40	7/100	27/20	7/12	19/400
Decimal	0.175	0.07	1.35	$0.58\dot{3}$	0.0475
Percentage	17.5%	7%	135%	$58.\dot{3}\%$	4.75%

2 **a**

Engineering	37.5%	(P)
Maths	35%	(P)
Media	80.4%	(P)
German	36.7%	(P)
Art	34.3%	
Geography	34.7%	
Sports Studies	34%	

b Sports studies

c Sports Studies, Art, Geography, Maths, German, Engineering, Media

3 **a** 15% **b** 3% **c** 5%

4 9%

5 **a**

Object	% increase/decrease
House	747.8% increase
Salary	228.6% increase
TV	50% decrease
Petrol	205.9% increase
Marz bars	181.3% increase
Milk	80% increase
Season ticket	582.8% increase
Music player	75% decrease

b, c Students' answers

Key outcomes	Quick check
Convert between decimals and fractions and order them.	Put these fractions in order of size from the biggest to the smallest. 3/7, 9/20, 1/3, 7/15, 5/12 (7/15, 9/20, 3/7, 5/12, 1/3)
Add and subtract fractions with different denominators.	Subtract $2\frac{4}{5}$ from $7\frac{2}{3}$ ($4\frac{13}{15}$)
Multiply and divide fractions.	Calculate $\frac{5}{12} \div \frac{15}{16}$ ($\frac{4}{9}$)
Calculate percentages of an amount and percentage changes.	In May the cost of petrol was £1.28 per litre. By September the price had increased by 6¼%. How much did it cost in September? (£1.36 per litre)
Calculate an original amount from the result of a percentage change.	In a 15% off everything sale a shirt costs £32.81. What was the original cost of the shirt? (£38.60)
Convert between percentages, fractions and decimals.	What is 5/16 as a percentage? (31.25%) Convert 92.5% to a fraction. (37/40)

MyMaths extra support

Lesson/online homework			Description
Frac dec perc 1	1029	L4	Converting well known fractions, decimals and percentages
Frac dec perc 2	1015	L6	Converting fractions, decimals and percentages
Fractions of amounts	1018	L5	Finding fractions of whole numbers
Percentages of amounts 2	1031	L5	Finding harder percentages such as 72% of 150
Ordering decimals	1072	L4	Putting decimals into size order

MyReview

4 MySummary

Check out

You should now be able to ...

	Test it ➡ Questions
✓ Convert between decimals and fractions and order them.	1 - 3
✓ Add and subtract fractions with different denominators.	4, 5
✓ Multiply and divide fractions.	6 - 8
✓ Calculate percentages of an amount and percentage changes.	9, 10
✓ Calculate an original amount from the result of a percentage change.	11, 12
✓ Convert between percentages, fractions and decimals.	13, 14

Language	Meaning	Example
Terminating decimal	A decimal whose last digits are all zero	0.125
Recurring decimal	A decimal whose last digits have a repeating (non-zero) pattern	$0.\dot{3} = 0.3333...$
Percentage	A fraction where the denominator is 100	50% of 10 is 5
Numerator	The number on the top of a fraction	In $\frac{2}{3}$ 2 is the numerator 3 is the denominator
Denominator	The number on the bottom of a fraction	
Common denominator	If two fractions have the same denominator they are said to both have a common denominator	$\frac{3}{4}$ and $\frac{1}{4}$ have a common denominator of 4.
Mixed number	A mixed number is written in terms of both integers and fractions	$2\frac{1}{2}$ is an example of a mixed number
Improper fraction	A fraction in which the numerator is larger than the denominator	$\frac{7}{5}$ is an improper since $7 > 5$
Equivalent fractions	Fractions that have the same value	$\frac{3}{5}$ and $\frac{15}{25}$

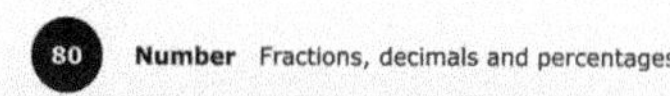

4 MyReview

1 Write these fractions as decimals
Do not use a calculator.
a $\frac{19}{25}$ **b** $\frac{36}{60}$ **c** $\frac{2}{9}$ **d** $\frac{13}{11}$

2 Write these decimals as fractions.
Do not use a calculator.
a 0.625 **b** 0.16 **c** $0.\dot{6}$ **d** 3.2

3 Put these numbers in order from lowest to highest.
a $\frac{1}{9}$ $\frac{1}{9}$ 0.1 $\frac{2}{15}$
b $\frac{3}{7}$ 3.4 $\frac{5}{12}$ 0.4

4 Calculate these and give your answer as a fraction in its simplest form
a $\frac{2}{7} + \frac{4}{21}$ **b** $\frac{9}{10} - \frac{2}{15}$
c $\frac{4}{5} + \frac{5}{6}$ **d** $\frac{11}{18} - \frac{2}{27}$

5 Calculate these; write your answers as improper fractions.
a $1\frac{2}{3} + 3\frac{1}{7}$ **b** $4\frac{1}{10} - 2\frac{5}{6}$

6 Use a mental method to calculate these.
a $\frac{2}{7}$ of £56 **b** $1\frac{2}{3}$ of 2 m

7 Calculate these using a mental or written method; simplify your answers.
a $14 \times \frac{5}{21}$ **b** $\frac{2}{11} \times \frac{33}{40}$

8 Calculate and simplify your answers.
a $12 \div \frac{3}{4}$ **b** $\frac{3}{10} \div \frac{4}{15}$

9 Calculate these percentages using a suitable method.
a 35% of 880 **b** 98% of 1230
c 110% of 752 **d** 5.7% of 24

10 Calculate these percentage changes.
a Increase 70 by 5%
b Decrease 17 by 32%

11 A car is reduced in price by 30%.
The new price is £5250.
What was the original price?

12 This year a school has 240 students in year 7, an increase of approximately 12% from the year before. How many students were there the year before?

13 An oil painting increases in value from £1200 to £1560.
What is the percentage increase?

14 A colour printer is reduced in price from £250 to £180.
What is the percentage reduction?

What next?

Score		
	0 - 5	Your knowledge of this topic is still developing. To improve look at Formative test: 2C-4; MyMaths: 1016, 1017, 1030, 1060 and 1073 - 1075
	6 - 16	You are gaining a secure knowledge of this topic. To improve look at InvisiPen: 143, 144, 145, 152, 153, 154, 161 and 162
	12 - 14	You have mastered this topic. Well done, you are ready to progress!

MyMaths.co.uk 81

Question commentary

Question 1 – Students will need to use short division for parts **c** and **d**, in part **b** suggest they simplify the fraction first.

Question 3 – Students should convert all the fractions to decimals first.

Question 4 – Ensure students are using the LCM. For part **a**. Some students will think 42 is the lowest common denominator.

Question 5 – Either method, of converting to improper fraction or handling fraction part and integer part separately, is acceptable. Students will have their own preference.

Questions 6 and **9** – Remind students that 'of' always means multiply.

Questions 6–8 – Encourage students to always check for cross simplification first.

Question 10 – Suggests students always use a decimal multiplier when calculating percentage change.

Questions 11–12 – Some students will calculate a new percentage change rather than reverse the given one. Make sure students recognise the difference. Dividing by the decimal multipliers is the best method.

Questions 12 and **13** – Show students that new ÷ old gives the decimal multiplier.

Answers

1 **a** 0.76 **b** 0.6 **c** $0.\dot{2}$ **d** $1.\dot{1}\dot{8}$

2 **a** $\frac{5}{8}$ **b** $\frac{4}{25}$ **c** $\frac{2}{3}$ **d** $3\frac{1}{5}$

3 **a** $0.1, \frac{1}{9}, \frac{2}{15}, \frac{1}{7}$
b $0.4, \frac{5}{12}, \frac{3}{7}, 0.\dot{4}$

4 **a** $\frac{10}{21}$ **b** $\frac{23}{30}$ **c** $\frac{49}{30}$ or $1\frac{19}{30}$ **d** $\frac{29}{54}$

5 **a** $\frac{101}{21}$ **b** $\frac{19}{15}$

6 **a** £16 **b** $3.\dot{3}$ m or $3\frac{1}{3}$ m

7 **a** $\frac{10}{3}$ or $3\frac{1}{3}$ **b** $\frac{3}{20}$

8 **a** 16 **b** $\frac{9}{8}$ or $1\frac{1}{8}$

9 **a** 308 **b** 1205.4 **c** 827.2 **d** 1.368

10 **a** 73.5 **b** 11.56

11 £7500

12 214

13 30%

14 28%

4 MyPractice

4a

1 Change these fractions into decimals using division. Use an appropriate method.

Give your answers to 5 dp where appropriate.

a $\frac{9}{16}$ **b** $\frac{5}{17}$ **c** $\frac{3}{13}$ **d** $\frac{6}{7}$ **e** $\frac{11}{19}$

2 Place < or > between these pairs of numbers to show which number is the largest.

a $0.4 \square \frac{3}{7}$ **b** $\frac{6}{13} \square \frac{7}{15}$ **c** $\frac{5}{8} \square 0.6$ **d** $0.39 \square \frac{7}{19}$

3 Put these fractions and decimals in order from lowest to highest.

a $\frac{8}{13}$ 0.623 $\frac{5}{8}$ 0.63 **b** $\frac{3}{13}$ $\frac{4}{17}$ 0.229 0.23

4b

4 Work out

a $\frac{12}{15} - \frac{7}{18}$ **b** $\frac{13}{15} + \frac{11}{25}$ **c** $\frac{14}{27} + \frac{13}{18}$ **d** $\frac{7}{14} + \frac{7}{21}$

e $\frac{13}{16} + \frac{7}{20}$ **f** $\frac{24}{35} - \frac{5}{28}$ **g** $\frac{23}{36} + \frac{7}{54}$ **h** $\frac{13}{60} + \frac{8}{15}$

5 Hector has $2\frac{1}{2}$ litres of water. Jenny has $\frac{3}{5}$ of a litre of blackcurrant cordial. They mix the two drinks together. What is the total amount of liquid?

6 Work out

a $2\frac{1}{5} + \frac{1}{3}$ **b** $1\frac{1}{4} - \frac{5}{8}$ **c** $3\frac{2}{5} + 1\frac{2}{3}$ **d** $2\frac{5}{8} - 1\frac{11}{12}$

4c

7 Calculate

a $\frac{3}{4}$ of 5 yards **b** $\frac{5}{12}$ of 60 kg **c** $\frac{3}{8}$ of 20 mm **d** $\frac{4}{13}$ of 39 km

e $1\frac{5}{16}$ of 40 miles **f** $3\frac{7}{8}$ of 200 m² **g** $1\frac{5}{12}$ of 340 mℓ **h** $3\frac{8}{25}$ of 1 century

8 Calculate

a $\frac{4}{7} \times \frac{5}{3}$ **b** $\frac{2}{5} \times \frac{3}{8}$ **c** $\frac{5}{6} \times \frac{4}{5}$ **d** $\frac{7}{8} \times \frac{3}{4}$

e $\frac{14}{15} \times \frac{12}{35}$ **f** $\frac{12}{35} \times \frac{15}{21}$ **g** $\frac{22}{16} \times \frac{32}{18}$ **h** $\frac{5}{8} \times \frac{24}{15}$

9 Calculate

a $4 \div \frac{4}{7}$ **b** $12 \div \frac{4}{3}$ **c** $16 \div \frac{8}{9}$ **d** $10 \div \frac{5}{7}$

e $3 \div \frac{5}{11}$ **f** $14 \div \frac{7}{4}$ **g** $15 \div \frac{10}{11}$ **h** $18 \div \frac{9}{13}$

4c

10 Calculate

a $\frac{4}{7} \div \frac{5}{8}$ **b** $\frac{6}{9} \div \frac{6}{7}$ **c** $\frac{8}{11} \div \frac{3}{4}$ **d** $\frac{8}{13} \div \frac{4}{7}$

e $\frac{5}{6} \div \frac{4}{9}$ **f** $\frac{9}{10} \div \frac{3}{5}$ **g** $\frac{3}{14} \div \frac{12}{35}$ **h** $\frac{8}{9} \div \frac{32}{45}$

4d

11 Calculate these percentage changes.

a Increase £50 by 28% **b** Decrease £640 by 45%

c Increase 180 km by 6% **d** Decrease 270 mm by 3.5%

e Increase 85 kg by 8% **f** Decrease £9 000 000 by 1.2%

12 a Monica earns £35 each weekend, working in her mum's shop. Next weekend her pay will be increased by 4%. How much will Monica earn next weekend?

b In a sale all prices are reduced by 15%. A DVD costs £12.49 before the sale. What is the sale price of the DVD?

4e

13 a A laptop is on sale for £330 which is 60% of the original price. What was the original price of the laptop?

b A Porsche 911 increased in price from 1982 to 2007 by 263%. The price for a Porsche 911 in 2007 was £60 621. What was the price of the Porsche in 1982?

14 a Kerry bought a mobile phone in a sale and saved £12. The label said that it was a 15% reduction. What was the original price of the mobile phone?

b In a special offer, a packet of biscuits says that it contains 20% extra. The weight of the packet is 64 g heavier than it was before the special offer. How much did the packet of biscuits used to weigh?

4f

15 Copy and complete this table. Show clearly your working out.

Fraction	Decimal	Percentage
$\frac{7}{15}$		
	0.995	
		12.5%
$\frac{4}{13}$		
	1.0377	

Give your answers as
- decimals to 4 decimal places
- percentages to 2 decimal places
- fractions in their simplest form.

16 a An DVD costs £13. In a sale the price is reduced to £11.44. What is the percentage reduction?

b A laptop is reduced in price from £880 to £836. What is the percentage reduction?

Question commentary

Question 1 – Students may need help dividing by 17 and 19 in particular. It may be appropriate to write out the times table on the board or encourage them to jot it down.

Questions 2 and **3** – Remind students they need to convert to decimals first and that 3 dp will suffice.

Question 4 – Ensure students are using the LCM for their common denominator.

Questions 5 and **6 –** Either method, of converting to improper fraction or handling fraction part and integer part separately, is acceptable. Students will have their own preference.

Questions 7–10 – Remind students that 'of' means multiply and to always look to cross simplify first.

Questions 11 and **12** – Students should use decimal multipliers to calculate percentage change.

Questions 13 and **14** – Dividing by the decimal multiplier enables students to have a strong method that is always applicable, but these questions can be answered using a ration/unitary method.

Question 16 – New ÷ old gives the decimal multiplier.

Answers

1 **a** 0.5625 **b** 0.29412
c 0.23077 **d** 0.85714
e 0.57895

2 **a** < **b** < **c** > **d** >

3 **a** 8/13 < 0.623 < 5/8 < 0.63
b 0.229 < 0.23 < 3/13 < 4/17

4 **a** 37/90 **b** $1\frac{23}{75}$ **c** $1\frac{13}{54}$ **d** 5/6
e $1\frac{13}{80}$ **f** 71/140 **g** 83/108 **h** 3/4

5 $3\frac{1}{10}$ litres

6 **a** $2\frac{8}{15}$ **b** 5/8 **c** $5\frac{1}{15}$ **d** 17/24

7 **a** $3\frac{3}{4}$ yards **b** 25 kg
c 7.5 mm **d** 12 km
e $52\frac{1}{2}$ miles **f** 775 m^2
g $481\frac{2}{3}$ ml **h** 332 years

8 **a** 20/21 **b** 3/20 **c** 2/3 **d** 21/32
e 8/25 **f** 12/49 **g** $2\frac{4}{9}$ **h** 1

9 **a** 7 **b** 9 **c** 18 **d** 14
e $6\frac{3}{5}$ **f** 8 **g** $16\frac{1}{2}$ **h** 26

10 **a** 32/35 **b** 7/9 **c** 32/33 **d** $1\frac{1}{13}$
e $1\frac{7}{8}$ **f** $1\frac{1}{2}$ **g** 5/8 **h** $1\frac{1}{4}$

11 **a** £64 **b** £352
c 190.8 km **d** 260.55 mm
e 91.8 kg **f** £8 892 000

12 **a** £36.40 **b** £10.62

13 **a** £550 **b** £16 700

14 **a** £80 **b** 320 g

15

Fraction	Decimal	Percentage
7/15	0.4667	46.67%
199/200	0.995	99.5%
1/8	0.125	12.5%
4/13	0.3077	30.77%
10 377 / 10 000	1.0377	103.77%

16 **a** 12% **b** 5%

MyAssessment 1

These questions will test your knowledge of the topics in Chapters 1 to 4.
They give you practice in the questions that you may see in your GCSE exams.
There are 70 marks in total.

1 Here is a set of statements. Say whether each statement is true (T) or false (F).

- **a** One of the prime factors of 375 is 3. (1 mark)
- **b** The HCF of 20 and 30 is 2. (1 mark)
- **c** 121 is divisible by 3. (1 mark)
- **d** 51 is a prime number. (1 mark)
- **e** The LCM of 20 and 30 is 60. (1 mark)

2 Find the value of these roots where possible.

- **a** $\sqrt{25}$ (1 mark) **b** $\sqrt[3]{27}$ (1 mark)
- **c** $\sqrt[3]{-125}$ (1 mark) **d** $\sqrt{-49}$ (1 mark)

3 Simplify each of these. Leave your answer as a single power of the number.

- **a** $3^4 \times 3^2$ (1 mark) **b** $5^4 \div 5^3$ (1 mark)
- **c** $5^4 \div 4^5$ (1 mark) **d** $2^6 \times 2^3$ (1 mark)

4 Round these numbers to the accuracy stated.

- **a** 3698 to the nearest 100 (1 mark)
- **b** 14.978 to 2 dp (1 mark)
- **c** 32.95 km to the nearest 100 metres (1 mark)

5 Use a trial-and-improvement method to find the roots of these numbers to 2 dp.

- **a** 40 (2 marks) **b** $\sqrt[3]{60}$ (2 marks)

6 Arrange these quantities in order of size from smallest to largest.

2 cℓ 2 pints 2 mℓ 2 litres 2 gallons (3 marks)

7 The area of this triangle is 35 cm².
Calculate the vertical height of the triangle. (2 marks)

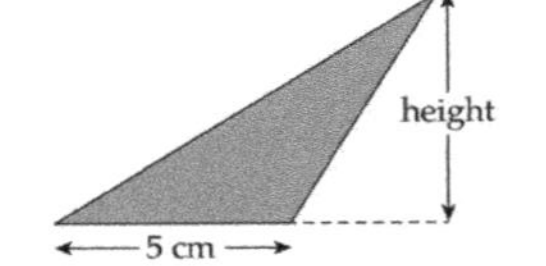

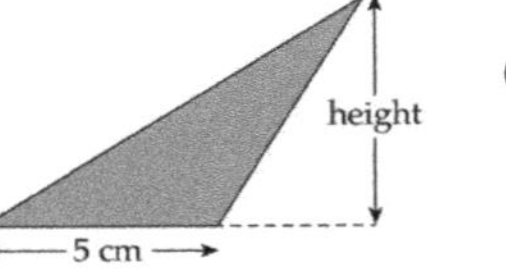

8 Each of these two shapes has the same area of 120 cm² and the same vertical height of 6 cm. Calculate

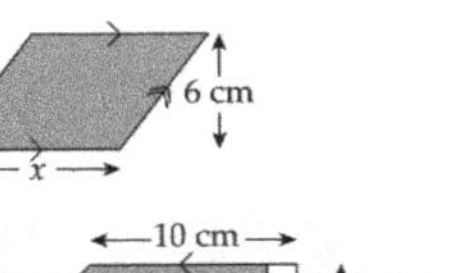

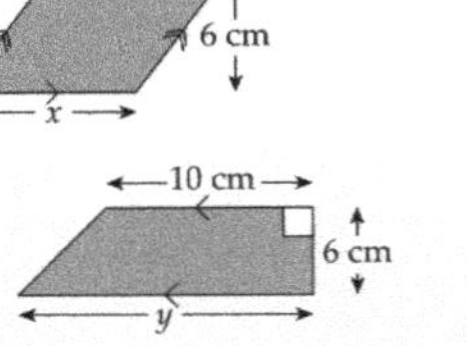

- **a** the base length, x of the parallelogram (2 marks)
- **b** the base length, y of the trapezium. (3 marks)

9 A circular hole, 5.4 cm in diameter, is being cut into a piece of wood 8 cm by 8 cm.

- **a** What is the circumference of the hole? (2 marks)
- **b** What is the area of wood that remains after the hole is drilled? Use $\pi = 3.14$. (3 marks)

10 Given that $x = 2$, find the value of these algebraic expressions.

- **a** $3x^2$ (1 mark) **b** $(3x)^2$ (1 mark)
- **c** $3x^{-2}$ (1 mark) **b** $(3x)^{-2}$ (1 mark)

11 Simplify these expressions, leaving your answer in index form.

- **a** $p^2 \times p^7$ (1 mark) **b** $3g^8 \div g^5$ (1 mark)
- **c** $(k^7)^2$ (1 mark) **d** $(5m^4)^3$ (1 mark)

12 Simplify these expressions by collecting like terms.

- **a** $3x^2 + 4x - x^2 + 9x - 3$ (1 mark) **b** $11p^3 - 4p + 3p^3 - p^2 + 9p$ (1 mark)
- **c** $-8t + 4t^2 - 5t + 8t^2 - t$ (1 mark) **d** $3n^2 - 4n - 7n^2 - 6n + 4n^2$ (1 mark)

13 A cuboid has side lengths x, $x + 3$ and $x - 1$.
Calculate the total surface area of the cuboid and give the answer in the simplest form. (4 marks)

14 Factorise these expressions.

- **a** $3x^2 + 4x$ (1 mark) **b** $10p^2 - 5pq$ (1 mark)

15 Rearrange these formulae to make the letter in bold the subject.

- **a** $v = u + \mathbf{a}t$ (1 mark) **b** $V = \pi r^2\mathbf{h}$ (1 mark)

16 A photographic image $8\frac{1}{2}$ inches long by $5\frac{1}{4}$ inches wide is being cropped by $\frac{1}{3}$ inch along its length and width.

- **a** What is area of the original image? (2 marks)
- **b** What is the new length and width of the new image? (2 marks)
- **c** What is the difference in area between the original and new images? (3 marks)

17 A new car was bought at a cost of £12 000. Each year the value depreciates by 15%.

- **a** What is the car worth after one year? (2 marks)
- **b** What is the car worth after three years? (3 marks)

18 A vase was bought at a car boot sale for £4.75 and was sold a year later at an auction for £67. What was the percentage profit? (3 marks)

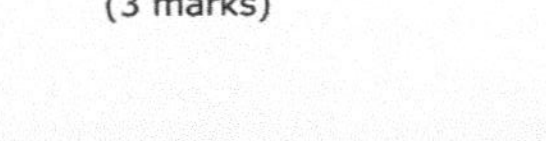

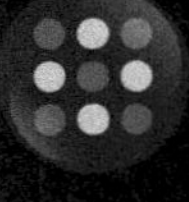

Mark scheme

Questions 1 – 5 marks

a 1 T
b 1 F
c 1 F
d 1 F
e 1 T

Questions 2 – 4 marks

a 1 5
b 1 3
c 1 -5
d 1 not possible

Questions 3 – 4 marks

a 1 3^6
b 1 5
c 1 not possible; 0.61 if done numerically
d 1 2^9

Questions 4 – 3 marks

a 1 3700
b 1 14.98
c 1 33.0 km

Questions 5 – 4 marks

a 2 6.32; must show evidence of trial and improvement method
b 2 3.91; must show evidence of trial and improvement method

Questions 6 – 3 marks

3 2 ml, 2 cl, 2 pints, 2 litres, 2 gallons

Questions 7 – 2 marks

2 14 cm; must see use of formula for both marks

Questions 8 – 5 marks

a 2 $x = 20$ cm; use of formula required
b 3 $y = 30$ cm; use of formula required

Questions 9 – 5 marks

a 2 16.96 cm; accept 17.0 cm but not 17 cm
b 3 41.1 cm^2; 2 marks for seeing 22.9 cm^2

Questions 10 – 4 marks

a 1 12
b 1 36
c 1 $\frac{3}{4}$ or 0.75
d 1 $\frac{1}{36}$ or 0.028

Questions 11 – 4 marks

a 1 p^9
b 1 $3g^3$
c 1 k^{14}
d 1 $125m^{12}$

Questions 12 – 4 marks

a 1 $2x^2 + 13x - 3$
b 1 $14p^3 - p^2 + 5p$
c 1 $8t^3 + 4t^2 - 14t$
d 1 $-10n$

Questions 13 – 4 marks

4 $2(3x^2 + 4x - 3)$ or $6x^2 + 8x - 6$
marks allocated to degree of simplification

Questions 14 – 2 marks

a 1 $x(3x + 4)$
b 1 $5p(2p - q)$

Questions 15 – 2 marks

a 1 $t = \dfrac{v - u}{a}$ **b** 1 $h = \dfrac{V}{\pi r^2}$

Questions 16 – 7 marks

a 2 $44\frac{5}{8}$ square inches
b 2 length $8\frac{1}{6}$ inches, width $4\frac{11}{12}$ inches
c 3 $4\frac{17}{36}$ square inches

Questions 17 – 5 marks

a 2 £10 200.00
b 3 £7369.50; must see successive application

Questions 18 –3 marks

a 3 1310.5%; 1 mark for profit of £62.25

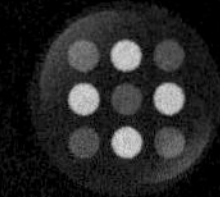

5 Angles and 2D shapes

Learning outcomes	
G5 Describe, sketch and draw using conventional terms and notations: points, lines, parallel lines, perpendicular lines, right angles, regular polygons, and other polygons that are reflectively and rotationally symmetric	(L6)
G7 Derive and illustrate properties of triangles, quadrilaterals, circles, and other plane figures (for example, equal lengths and angles) using appropriate language and technologies	(L6)
G10 Apply the properties of angles at a point, angles at a point on a straight line, vertically opposite angles	(L6)
G11 Understand and use the relationship between parallel lines and alternate and corresponding angles	(L6)
G12 Derive and use the sum of angles in a triangle and use it to deduce the angle sum in any polygon, and to derive properties of regular polygons	(L6)

Introduction

The chapter starts by looking at angles in parallel lines. Properties of triangles, quadrilaterals and other polygons are then covered before an introduction to the concept of congruence.

The introduction discusses the use of basic geometrical shapes, principally triangles, in the creation of 3D images for computer games. This process, which significantly simplifies the creation of 3D graphics, is used in many other areas as well such as architecture and 3D product design (e.g. in the design of cars).

Vector graphics, as opposed to 'bitmap' graphics, defines the points, lines and planes using simple mathematical equations rather than single point definitions and it significantly reduces the amount of computer power and storage requirements and can therefore be a lot more efficient, saving time and computational complexity for the designers.

This website gives a brief description of some of the differences between vector and bitmap graphics: http://www.animationpost.co.uk/tech-notes/bitmaps-vs-vectors.htm

Prior knowledge

Students should already know how to...

- Solve simple equations
- Measure and name angles
- Name and describe the basic properties of triangles and quadrilaterals

Starter problem

The starter problem is an investigation into tessellations using regular polygons. Students should be familiar with a standard 'tile' tessellation using squares and are invited to investigate which other regular polygons tessellate. By working out the internal angles of the regular polygons, they will be able to see that just two further polygons tessellate on their own: the equilateral triangle and regular hexagon. When it comes to tessellations involving more than one regular polygon (so-called semi-regular tessellations) it might be appropriate to provide the students with shapes to play about with. They will find some quite quickly but might need to be guided into working out possible combinations before trying them.

The following website gives all of the examples and also more detailed information on tessellation:

http://www.mathsisfun.com/geometry/tessellation.html

Resources

MyMaths

Angle sums	1082	Interior exterior angles	1100	Lines and quadrilaterals	1102
Angles in parallel lines	1109	Angle proofs	1141		

Online assessment

Chapter test	2C-5
Formative test	2C-5
Summative test	2C-5

InvisiPen solutions

Congruent shapes	317	Angles on a straight line	342
Types of triangles and angles			343
Properties of quadrilaterals and angles			344
Opposite angles	345	Polygon angles	346
Bearings	374		

Topic scheme

Teaching time = 4 lessons/2 weeks

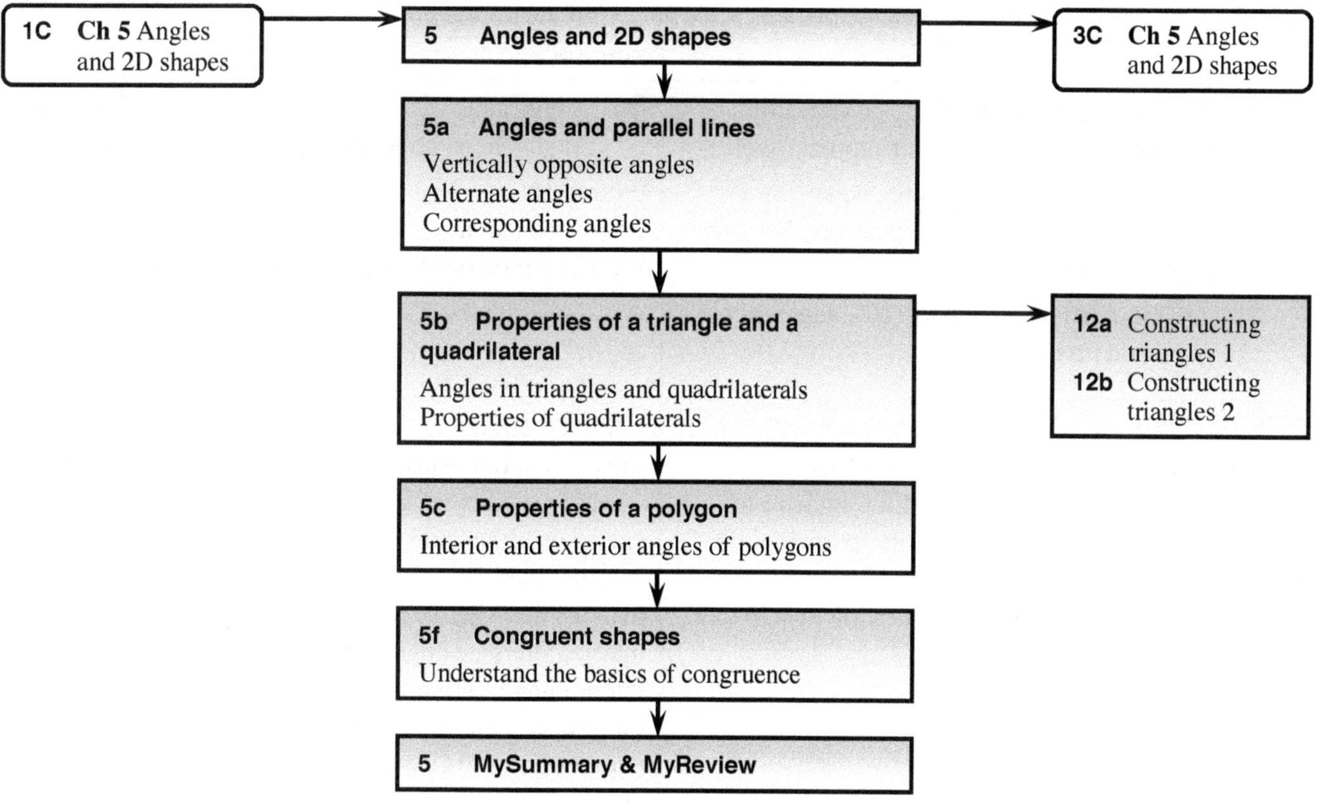

Differentiation

Student book 2A **88 – 105**

Angles
Opposite angles
Properties of triangles
Angles in a triangle
Parallel lines
Properties of quadrilaterals

Student book 2B **80 – 97**

Angles
Properties of a triangle
Angles in parallel lines
Properties of a quadrilateral
Properties of a polygon
Congruent shapes

Student book 2C **86 – 99**

Angles and parallel lines
Properties of a triangle and a quadrilateral
Properties of a polygon
Congruent shapes

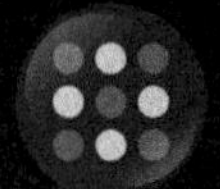

5a Angles and parallel lines

Objectives

- Solve problems using properties of angles, of parallel and intersecting lines, and of triangles and other polygons, justifying inferences and explaining reasoning with diagrams and text. (L6)

Key ideas

1. The naming and recognising of vertically opposite, corresponding and alternate angles
2. Vertically opposite angles are equal; corresponding angles are equal and alternate angles are equal
3. Angles on a line add up to 180°; angles about a point add up to 360°

Resources

Angle sums (1082)
Angles in parallel lines (1109)

Protractors
Board protractor
World map (showing latitude and longitude)

Simplification

Provide students with a copy of the exercise and encourage the use of annotation. Allow students to arrive at the results by not necessarily following the most efficient route. For example, students may calculate any of the angles in the question to help work towards the result.

Extension

There are a few unusual angle rules/names. Investigate what is meant by a) Exterior alternate angles (equal angles on either side of the transversal of a pair of parallel lines, lying outside the parallel lines rather than inside. Alternate angles are properly called interior alternate angles) b) Allied or consecutive interior angles (sum to 180°, on the same side of the transversal of a pair of parallel lines, lying inside the parallel lines) c) Complementary and supplementary angles (angles that sum to 90° or 180° respectively).

Literacy

The slightly technical nature of the 'vertically' in vertically opposite angles will need explaining. The word 'corresponding' may require discussion. Corresponding angles occupy the same position on identical sections of an image. The understanding of 'alternate' might also benefit from a little chat, to enhance recall and to assist in the coding of diagrams when trying to work out what is involved. For example, the taxonomical term, alternatifoliar, describes plants with leaves on alternating sides of the stem.

Links

Parallel lines are used in road markings. Yellow lines laid parallel to the kerb indicate no parking at certain times. Double yellow lines mean no waiting is permitted at any time. Red lines forbid all stopping, parking and loading. Double white lines down the centre of the road are used to discourage overtaking. There is more information about road markings at http://www.direct.gov.uk/en/TravelAndTransport/Highwaycode/Signsandmarkings/index.htm?IdcService=GET_FILE&dID=95931&Rendition=Web

Alternative approach

To reinforce the idea of an angle involving turning (and because a dynamic version is preferable for some students) it may be better to refer to there being 360° in a full turn, and 180° in a half turn or in a straight angle. This avoids the common misconception that the size of an angle is related to the length of the angle arms.

The term 'straight angle' can be handy since it is supplementary angles that add to 180°; and since complementary angles add to 90°, these are also in numerical/alphabetical order.

Share the advice that it is often best to attempt the missing angles in a diagram in their alphabetical order – the writer, or later examiner, is generally trying to be helpful. However, other orders will usually be possible.

Checkpoint

1 Calculate the value of $x°$ and $y°$.

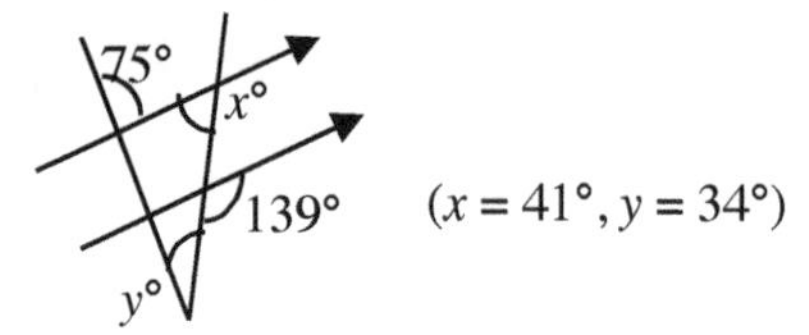

($x = 41°$, $y = 34°$)

Starter

Draw a mixture of acute, obtuse and reflex angles on the board.

Ask students to estimate the size of each angle in degrees then measure the angles.

Students score 6 points for an exact answer, 4 points for within 10° and 2 points for within 15°.

Teaching notes

Look at examples of angles at a point and on a straight line. What are the rules for the angle sum? Look at examples of vertically opposite angles. Are the rules for these three types of angles linked? Show their relationship to each other using an example of intersecting lines.

Draw a pair of parallel lines. Draw a *transversal*, a line that crosses the pair. What angles have been made? Ask students to measure the angles. Are some of the angles equal? Which ones? Are some of the angles equal and in the same position in relation to the parallel line and intersecting line? These angles 'match up' or *correspond* known as *corresponding angles*.

Are there angles that are equal but are on *alternate sides* of the intersecting line? Look particularly at angles inside the parallel lines. These are known as *alternate angles*.

How many pairs of corresponding and alternate angles are there for one pair of parallel lines and transversal? (4 pairs and 2 pairs)

Plenary

Discuss how longitude and latitude are used to fix your position on Earth. What do students know? Which one measures horizontally and which one vertically? Are these appropriate terms, or can we do better? What range of angles does each measure have? How are they written?

Exercise commentary

Question 1 – Ask students to give a simple statement of which rule they used: 'angles at a point = 360°', 'angles on a straight line = 180°' 'vertically opposite angles are equal'.

Question 2 – Ask students to use sentences and explain which rule they have used, for example, 'angle a and 64 are corresponding angles and are therefore equal'.

Question 3 – Finding angle c requires the sum of angles in a triangle. Part **b** may be made easier if the parallel lines are extended.

Question 4 – Ask students what is proved if the two values are replaced by variables. Sum of angles in (any) triangle is 180°. Look at other proofs, for example,

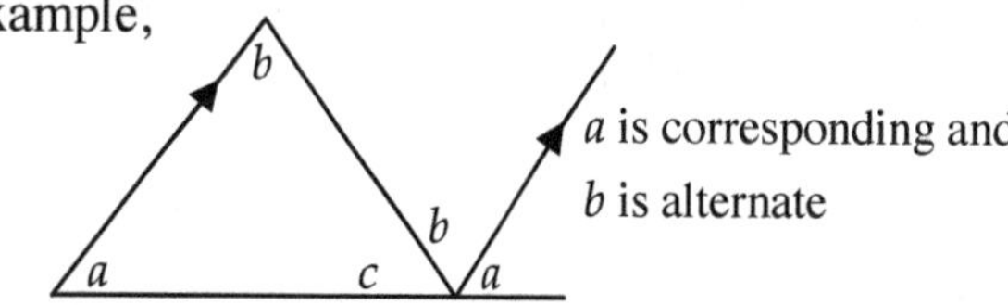

Answers

1 **a** $a = 146°$ **b** $b = 28°$
c $c = 57°, d = 123°, e = 57°$

2 **a** $a = 64°, b = 64°$
b $b = 110°, c = 110°, d = 110°$
c $c = 35°, d = 35°, e = 145°$
d $d = 108°, e = 108°, f = 108°$
e $e = 100°, f = 105°, g = 80°, h = 75°$
f $f = 80°, g = 75°, h = 105°, i = 100°$

3 **a** $a = 50°, b = 60°, c = 70°$
b $a = 56°, b = 72°, c = 52°$

4 **a** $a = 40°, b = 60°$ **b** $c = 80°$
c 180° **d** 180°
e Angles in a triangle add to 180°.

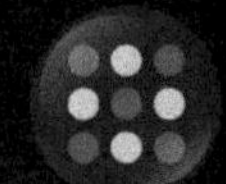

5b Properties of a triangle and a quadrilateral

Objectives

- Understand a proof that:
  – the angle sum of a triangle is 180° and of a quadrilateral is 360°
  – the exterior angle of a triangle is equal to the sum of the two interior opposite angles (L6)
- Classify quadrilaterals by their geometric properties (L6)

Key ideas	Resources
1 The name of a triangle can refer to the number of equal sides or the nature of the largest angle **2** Angle sum of triangle theorem **3** Exterior angle of triangle theorem **4** The description and classification of quadrilaterals	Interior exterior angles (1100) Lines and quadrilaterals (1102) Angle proofs (1141) Two sets of congruent quadrilaterals Dictionaries Enlarged copies of the image in question **2** of the student book

Simplification	Extension
Ensure checking strategies are used for the angle sum of triangles and quadrilaterals.	Using two congruent quadrilaterals, what types of quadrilateral can you construct? For example, two rhombuses can form a parallelogram. Students could use a set of shapes in this extension.

Literacy	Links
The word ‘symmetric’ will be relevant here; the word ‘equiangular’ is worth having here, too, and the word ‘regular’, for a shape that is both equilateral and equiangular. There needs to be an awareness of each new word used – even if not totally new – and a check made of comprehension.	Provide dictionaries for the class. The word *isosceles* derives from the Greek *isos* meaning ‘equal’, and *skelos* meaning ‘leg’. Ask the class to find other words beginning with *iso* that are related to the word equal. For example, *isobar* – a line on a map linking points of equal atmospheric pressure, *isometric* – having equal dimensions.

Alternative approach

Consideration of the ‘rect’ in ‘rectangle’ should show that a square is a special rectangle; we use rectangle when we do not know whether or not we have a square. We have the word ‘oblong’ for a rectangle that is known not to be a square, and similarly the word ‘diamond’ for a rhombus that is known not to be a square. Useful words.

It is necessary to persuade students of the truth of the exterior angle theorem (for example by labelling, but refusing to calculate, the angle of the triangle that is supplementary to the exterior angle, and seeing what can be said about the other angles), if they are to comprehend and accept it; but do then encourage students to now ignore the linking angle and see the theorem as a direct connection between the exterior angle and the opposite interior angles.

Question 7 and its sketch are good to deconstruct with the class. The rectangle extends to touch the circle and to *fit along* the radii means only to lie on, not be the same length as the radii. After giving the students time to work through the problem, all that is needed, with a magical dash of the board pen, is to draw the other diagonal, and there is the answer.

Checkpoint

1 A quadrilateral has two right angles. Which two shapes could it be? (Right-angled trapezium or kite)

Starter

Ask students to draw a 3 × 3 grid and enter nine angles from this list:

30°, 35°, 40°, 45°, 50°, 55°, 60°, 65°, 70°, 75°, 80°, 85°, 90°, 95°, 100°, 105°, 110°, 115°, 120°, 125°.

Give two angles of a triangle, for example, 83° and 42°. If students have the third angle in their grid, 55°, they cross it out.

The winner is the first student to cross out all nine angles.

Teaching notes

If not already covered in question **4** from spread **5a**, look at a proof of the interior angle sum of a triangle. Does this mean that you always need two angles to find a third? Counter this assertion by looking at examples of missing angles in isosceles triangles. So what is needed is two pieces of information, which could be of various sorts.

What is the interior angle sum for quadrilaterals? Show how this can be proved by splitting a quadrilateral into two triangles. Find the interior angle sum of another polygon using this method. Could you generalise? Interior angle sum of an n-sided polygon is $180(n - 2)$.

What types of quadrilaterals can students recall? Instead of saying the name of the quadrilateral, ask students to identify some of its properties. Can the other students correctly identify it, either by describing it or naming it?

A list of the most common quadrilaterals is given in the student book.

Plenary

Triangles can be further classified into acute-angled and obtuse-angled. What do these terms mean? How many different types of triangle can now be identified? (7) List them in a systematic way.

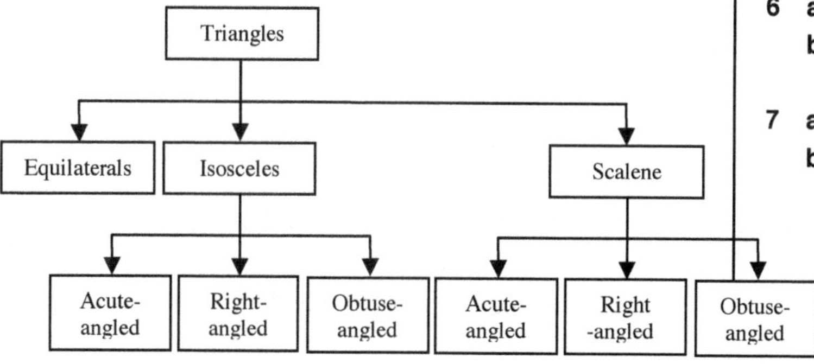

Exercise commentary

Questions 1 and **3** – Ask students to sketch their possible answers.

Question 2 – Ask students if all the eight quadrilaterals can be found. Their own enlarged copy would be useful. Encourage students to prove or disprove, identifying equal sides may help. (All shapes can be made except for parallelogram that isn't a rhombus.)

Question 4 – Sketching the diagrams offers a good opportunity to explain how the missing angles are found. Students should also be encouraged to show their numerical working.

Question 5 and **6** – Ask students to check their ideas by drawing a reasonable sketch. Encourage the use of the standard labelling techniques for equal angles, lengths, etc.

Question 7 – This challenge may need careful explanation. The language is quite technical. Encourage students to identify all possible measurements.

Answers

1 **a** 60°, equilateral **b** 33°, isosceles
c 90°, right-angled **d** 80°, scalene

2 isosceles trapezium, rectangle, kite, rhombus, trapezium, arrowhead

3 **a** 135°, isosceles trapezium, rhombus, parallelogram
b 125°, kite
c 255°, arrowhead
d 50°, arrowhead

4 **a** $b = 36°$ **b** $a = 122°$ **c** $c = 65°$ **d** $d = 100°$

5 **a** square, rectangle, rhombus, parallelogram, isosceles trapezium
b square, rhombus, kite
c square, rectangle, isosceles trapezium
d square
e rectangle, isosceles trapezium

6 **a** rhombus
b 4 equal sides, opposite angles are equal (60° and 120°), opposite sides are parallel.

7 **a** 6 cm (draw the other diagonal)
b Students' answers; yes, if the rectangles have the same length diagonal as the radius of the circle; no, if a rectangle with different dimensions but the same diagonal are required.

Objectives	
• Explain how to find, calculate and use: – the sums of the interior and exterior angles of quadrilaterals, pentagons and hexagons (L6) – the interior and exterior angles of regular polygons (L6)	
Key ideas	**Resources**
1 The naming of polygons **2** Exterior and interior angles of polygons	Interior exterior angles (1100) Protractors, pairs of compasses Scissors, tracing paper, square grid paper List of polygon names, chalk
Simplification	**Extension**
Provide tracing paper to help tessellation. Encourage students to first try to tessellate without reflection. Provide students with diagrams of regular polygons (pentagon to decagon) with edges extended to illustrate exterior angles.	There is a special relationship between the interior and exterior angles of a triangle. Try to find it. The exterior angle of a triangle at any vertex is equal to the sum of the interior angles at the other two vertices. Once students have discovered this they could try to prove this rule. The following diagram could be given as a hint.
Literacy	**Links**
The words supplementary, equilateral and equiangular may be used freely, but there needs to be an awareness of each new word used – even if not totally new – and a check made of comprehension when necessary.	The Giant's Causeway is a formation of thousands of columns of basalt which jut into the sea and resulted from a volcanic eruption 60 million years ago. The top surface of each column is polygonal, most columns having six sides but some having four, five, seven or eight sides. According to local legend, the Causeway was a bridge for two giants who wanted to cross the sea to do battle. There is more information at http://www.giantscausewayofficialguide.com/home.htm

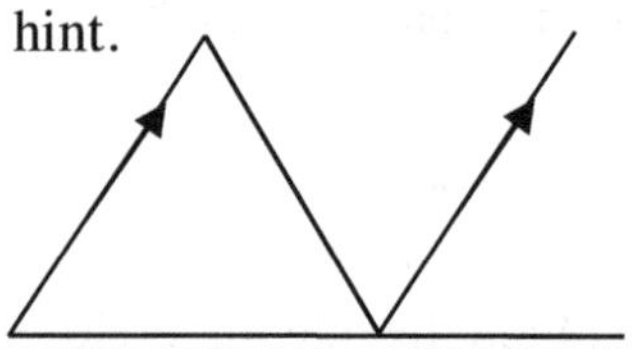

Alternative approach

Ask which of the shapes shown are equilateral (just the last two or three?) and which are equiangular (the hexagon, also?), and discuss this as needed.

The sum of the exterior angles can be shown by walking around any shape; or by simply placing a board pen flat on the board, pointing along the edge of a shape, and moving it around the shape, turning at each corner. A couple of demonstrations may be needed, but it will become apparent that the pen has turned through a full turn. How many degrees? Always, for any shape?

Similarly at the corners, draw some exterior angles and agree the interior angles are supplementary at each corner. Always?

The steps to equiangular and to regular shapes should be made very explicit, and are likely to be helped by the preliminary work above. Is being equilateral important here, or being equiangular? So being regular is not important, in this context. Sketch some equiangular, not equilateral, polygons, if not already done. Perhaps begin with an oblong.

Checkpoint

1 How many sides has a regular polygon with interior angles of 156°? (15)

Starter

Ask students questions based on the 180 times table. For example,

How many 180s in 1080? (6)
What is the angle sum of 8 triangles? (1440°)
How many triangles will give an angle sum of 900°? (5)
How many 180s are there in 4500? (25)

Teaching notes

Ask students if they have ever played the game 'Tetris'? It is likely that many of them will have played; generally it is played on a computer or mobile phone. Ask a student to describe how the game works. The goal is to fit whichever of the seven tetrominos next appear into the spaces available. Which of these will tessellate? How can you prove that a particular shape will tessellate? What sort of shapes will tessellate? Ask students to make suggestions and put them into three categories: certainly does (square), unsure (scalene triangle), certainly does not (circle).

Explain what is meant by an exterior angle. It could be described as the angle you turn through to get onto the next edge. As a way to demonstrate the sum of interior angles, students could be taken outside and walk round the edge of a chalk drawn polygon. If the exterior angles are marked, students will be able to see that having turned each angle they end up back at the start facing the initial direction. Hence the exterior angles sum to 360° for any number of sides.

Plenary

Explore the list of names of polygons. What patterns can students spot in the language? Can students pronounce any of the more complex names? Who can memorise the first 20? Who can pronounce a polygon name that is not in the list by using the clues in the given list?

Exercise commentary

Question 1 – Make sure students draw enough to show convincingly that the shape tessellates. As an extension activity, ask whether all quadrilaterals tessellate.

Question 2 – Encourage students to look for a pattern in the results to speed up the process of finishing the table of results. Can they establish a rule for the total angles in a polygon with n sides? Note that regularity does not matter here. ($180n - 360$)

Question 3 – Encourage them to look for a link between the exterior angle and the number of sides of the polygon. Again, can they establish a rule for the size of the exterior angle of a regular polygon with n sides? ($360 \div n$)

Question 4 – A sketch may prove useful here. Encourage students to label the information they find. Explain how the interior angle of a regular pentagon shows that it will not tessellate. Extend this idea to show that a regular hexagon must be the last regular polygon that can tessellate.

Question 5 – Ask what makes the regular hexagon special? (That it can be formed from six congruent triangles; this would explain why it is easier here, and possibly more accurate, to mark the points around the circle with a pair of compasses rather than a protractor.) Does this work with other regular polygons?

Answers

1 **a, b, c, d** Students' tessellations

2 **a** Students' drawings

b

Name	No. triangles	Sum int. angles
pentagon	3	3 × 180° = 540°
hexagon	4	4 × 180° = 720°
heptagon	5	5 × 180° = 900°
octagon	6	6 × 180° = 1080°
nonagon	7	7 × 180° = 1260°
decagon	8	8 × 180° = 1440°

3 **a** 120°, 60° **b** 60°, 120°
c 40°, 140° **d** 36°, 144°
e 20°, 160° **f** 15°, 165°

4 **a** 72° **b** 108°
c 36°, 36°,144°, 144°

5 **a** Students' drawings
b 120° **c** 120°

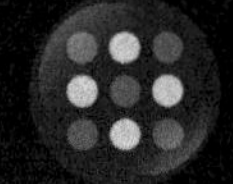

5d Congruent shapes

Objectives	
• Know that if two shapes are congruent, corresponding sides and angles are equal (L6)	
Key ideas	**Resources**
1 Identical shapes that are the same size are termed congruent 2 Matching, equal angles and sides in congruent shapes are termed corresponding	Tracing paper Square grid paper
Simplification	**Extension**
Supply tracing paper to make the comparison of shapes easier. Use an enlarged copy of the exercise to allow for easier measurement.	Consider four similarities between two shapes. **i** same number of sides **ii** same angles **iii** same perimeter **iv** same area. Is it possible to construct a pair of non-congruent shapes that still have all or some of these similarities? If so, which ones? Some possibilities: **i/ii/iii** only, **i/ii/iv** only, **i/iii/iv** only are all possible. **ii/iii/iv** only is impossible.
Literacy	**Links**
Return to the term corresponding angles. Remind students that we have previously used this term to describe angles that occupy the same position on identical sections of an image. Here, it is used to describe angles which occupy the same position on two congruent images. Emphasise that angles will continue to be corresponding if one drawing is rotated.	Patchwork is a form of needlework in which pieces of different fabric are cut into shapes and then joined together to form a larger design. Congruent shapes are often used and tessellated to form decorative quilts. There are examples of quilt patterns using congruent shapes at http://quilting.about.com/od/picturesofquilts/ig/Scrap-Quilts-Photo-Gallery/

Alternative approach

Note the distinction between directly congruent and oppositely congruent (an example of which is to hold up one's hands). Not vital per se, so much as for assisting in seeing congruence that happens to be opposite. Labelling three congruent shapes, such as right-angled trapeziums, one of which is oppositely congruent to the other two, could be helpful. Ask students to say which is labelled clockwise, which anticlockwise; another assistance when analysing diagrams.

Ask which in the first example are directly, and which oppositely congruent. The students might have to think a moment or two before answering; encourage students to think before they answer.

In the second example (which begins with oppositely congruent triangles), ask whether, if this was really badly drawn diagram, AC could be 5 cm, and BC 12 cm. Is there any reason, apart from appearance, for the measurements to be the other way around? And we cannot trust the appearance of diagrams, as is frequently made explicit in exam questions. On the other hand, could AB be anything but 13 cm? And why is this? The extra information here is that it is opposite the right angle … could any other angle also be 90°? So could any other side be 13 cm? (This issue of assumptions on the basis of appearance, versus known information, arises again in questions **3** and **4**; and be pleased if any student is alert enough to return to the directly and oppositely congruent shapes noted earlier, and require some measurements to establish which way round they are! Note that in both these questions the shapes are intended to be oppositely congruent.)

Regarding the extension, note that a square with a small triangle on one side, making a heptagon, would share all four similarities with another shape which had the triangle moved along a bit … without being congruent.

Checkpoint

1 Two triangles have at least two angles the same and at least one side the same length. Are they definitely congruent? Explain your answer.

(No, only if the equal sides are corresponding. Triangles must be similar.)

Starter

I am a regular polygon that will not tessellate. (For example, pentagon)

Each of my internal angles is exactly 120°. (Regular hexagon)
I have one pair of parallel lines and my angle sum is half of 720°. (Trapezium)
I have one internal angle of 90. All my other internal angles are less than this. (Right-angled triangle)
My angle sum is 900°. (Heptagon)

Starter can be extended by using students' own clues.

Teaching notes

Define the meaning of the word congruent. Are there some letters of the alphabet that might be congruent if they are drawn a certain way? For example, 'p' and 'd', 'W' and 'M'. How many examples can students find?

What can you say about the measurements on two congruent shapes? Look for responses that relate to the lengths of the sides and size of angles.

Combinations of certain congruent shapes can produce other familiar shapes. For example, two congruent isosceles right-angled triangles can produce either a square, a parallelogram or a larger isosceles right-angled triangle depending on how they are joined. What other examples can students find?

A certain special shape can be formed from six congruent equilateral triangles. What shape is it? Encourage students to experiment with sketches. (Regular hexagon) How can you be sure you have a *regular* hexagon?

Plenary

The term *directly congruent* applies to shapes that have been translated and/or rotated to produce the second shape. The term *indirectly congruent* applies to shapes that have been reflected and may also have been translated and/or rotated. Look at the exercise again. Which shapes are directly and indirectly congruent?

Exercise commentary

Question 1 – Discuss also when shapes have the same angles, but are a different size. Ask what the mathematical term for this is. (Similar)

Question 2 – Suggest that shapes with the same number of sides and same area must be congruent. Encourage students to prove you wrong.

Question 3 – Re-emphasise that congruent shapes must have identical angles.

Question 5 – Make it clear that each grid shows two shapes that are congruent to each other. Some students may think that they are to compare the grids with other grids. Encourage the use of curves – but note that straight line solutions will never be exhausted, if corners need not be at grid intersections. Note these shapes can also be tessellated.

Answers

1 **a** non-E shape **b** rhombus
c + shape **d** large circle

2 **a** B, C, D, G, I **b** A, E, H
c F

3 A = 36°, B = 144°, C = 36°, D = 144°

4 **a** AB = 15 cm **b** AC = 17 cm
c BC = 8 cm

5 **a** Students' drawings
b Students' observations; the shapes are rotations of each other

Key outcomes	Quick check
Reason geometrically using the properties of the angles at a point and on a line and intersecting and parallel lines.	Calculate the size of angles a, b, and c. 67° b° c° a 45° ($a = 113°$, $b = 67°$, $c = 45°$)
Recognise the different types of triangles and quadrilaterals and use their properties.	The diagonals of a quadrilateral cross at right angles. List all the shapes it could be. (square, rhombus, kite, isosceles trapezium)
Recognise the different types of polygons and calculate interior and exterior angles for regular polygons.	The interior angle of a regular polygon is 160°. How many sides does this polygon have? (18)
Identify and use congruence.	From the following list of transformations, which will result in a congruent shape? Reflection, rotation, enlargement. (Reflection and rotation)

MyMaths extra support

Lesson/online homework			Description
Angle reasoning	1080	L5	Looking for angle properties in well-known shapes
Interior exterior angles	1109	L6	Alternate angles, supplementary angles and corresponding angles on parallel lines

MyReview

5 MySummary

Check out

You should now be able to ...

	Test it ➡ Questions
✓ Reason geometrically using the properties of the angles at a point and on a line and intersecting and parallel lines.	1
✓ Recognise the different types of triangles and quadrilateral and use their properties.	2, 3
✓ Recognise the different types of polygons and calculate interior and exterior angles for regular polygons.	4, 5
✓ Identify and use congruence.	6

Language	Meaning	Example
Parallel lines	Lines that are always the same distance apart from each other	Railway tracks
Perpendicular lines	Two lines that are at right angles to each other	A crossroads
Quadrilateral	A shape with four straight sides	A parallelogram
Polygon	A two-dimensional shape with three or more straight sides	Triangles, rectangles and hexagons are all polygons
Regular shape	A shape that has equal sides and equal angles	A square
Interior angle	The angle between adjacent sides in a polygon	int ext
Exterior angle	The angle between one side and the next side extended in a polygon	
Congruent	Two shapes are congruent if they have both the same size and the same shape	Two triangles that are identical, but one is rotated or reflected relative to the other.

5 MyReview

1 Calculate the values of the labelled angles. State which geometric fact you used in each case.

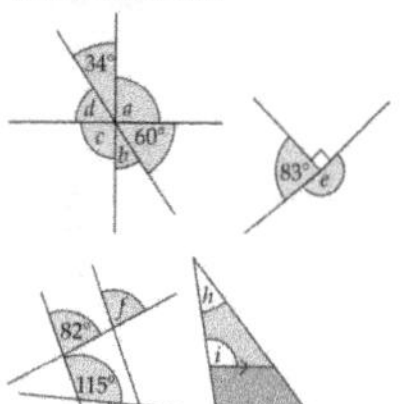

2 Calculate the value of the letters.

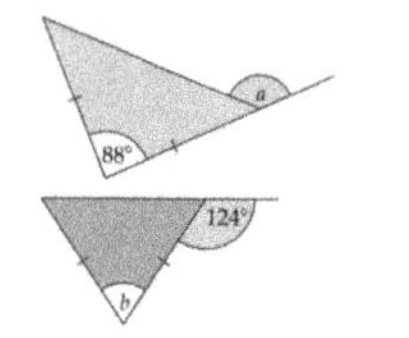

3 Which quadrilateral has
a 2 sets of equal sides, 2 pairs of equal angles and 2 sets of parallel sides?
b 1 set of equal sides, 2 pairs of equal angles and 1 set of parallel sides?

4 Calculate the size of
a the exterior angles of a regular nonagon
b the interior angles of a regular pentagon.

5 Accurately draw a regular hexagon.

6 The two parallelograms are congruent, state
a the length of AB
b the size of angle B
c the size of angle C

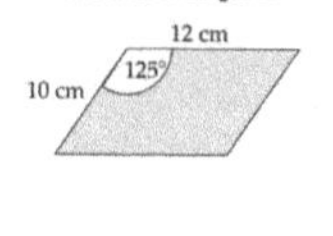

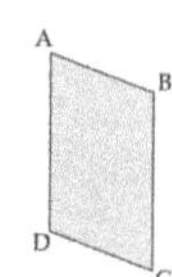

What next?

Score		
0 – 2	Your knowledge of this topic is still developing. To improve look at Formative test: 2C-5; MyMaths: 1081, 1082, 1086, 1100, 1141, 1148 and 1320
3 – 5	You are gaining a secure knowledge of this topic. To improve look at InvisiPen: 317, 342, 343, 344, 345, 346 and 374
6	You have mastered this topic. Well done, you are ready to progress!

 **Geometry** Angles

MyMaths.co.uk 

Question commentary

Students should be aware that diagrams will not, in general, be accurately drawn. They should be calculating angles, not measuring them.

Question 1 – It is important for students to give a reason for each answer, particularly for the questions involving parallel lines. For some of the angles there is more than one reason that can be given.

Question 2 – Students need to be able to identify which two angles are the same in isosceles triangles.

Question 3 – External exams can now penalise for incorrect spelling. It is important students learn how to spell the names of the quadrilaterals correctly.

Questions 4 and **5** – Students should learn the names for polygons with up to 10 sides. Septagon (a mixture of Latin and ancient Greek) is an acceptable name for a heptagon (pure Greek).

Question 5 – Tell students to only use a pair of compasses and a ruler.

Question 6 – Students may find it helpful to label the original diagram A, B, C, D.

Answers

1 $a = 86°$ Angles on a straight line add up to 180°.
$b = 34°$ Vertically opposite angles are equal.
$c = 86°$ Vertically opposite/straight line.
$d = 60°$ Vertically opposite/straight line/ angles around a point add up to 360°.
$e = 187°$ Angles around a point add up to 360°.
$f = 82°$ Corresponding angles are equal.
$g = 115°$ Alternate angles are equal.
$h = 29°$ Angles in a triangle add up to 180°.
$i = 99°$ Corresponding angles are equal.

2 $a = 134°$ $b = 68°$

3 **a** Parallelogram **b** Isosceles Trapezium

4 **a** 40° **b** 108°

5 Check interior angles are all 120°, allow ±2°.

6 **a** 10 cm **b** 125° **c** 55°

5 MyPractice

5a

1 Calculate the angles marked with a letter, giving a reason in each case.

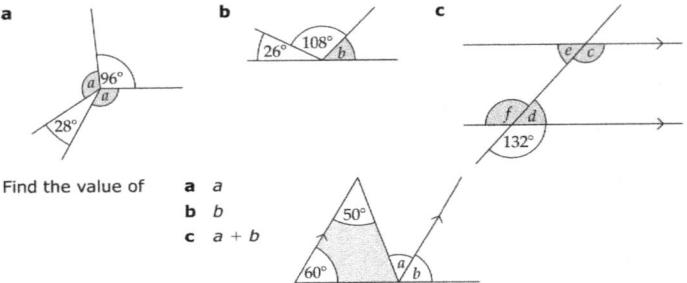

a **b** **c**

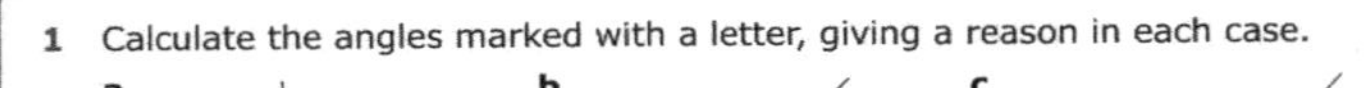

2 Find the value of

a a
b b
c $a + b$

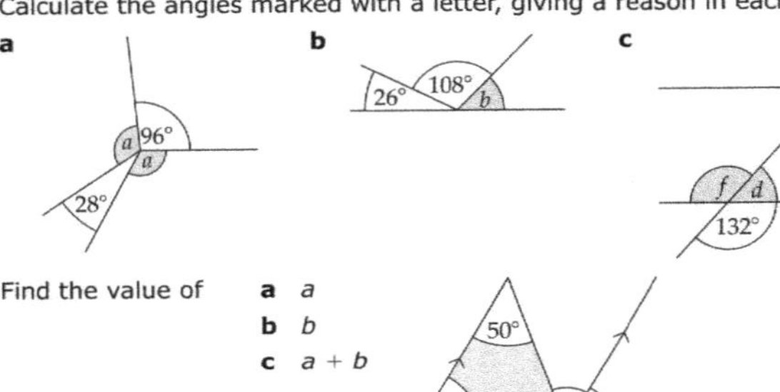

5b

3 Calculate the value of the unknown angles.
Give a reason in each case.

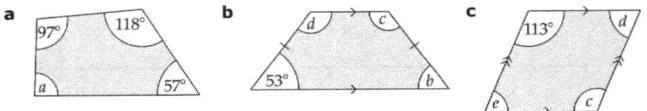

a **b** **c**

4 Two identical right-angled isosceles triangles are placed edge to edge.
Draw diagrams to show

a a square
b a right-angled isosceles triangle
c a parallelogram.

Use the properties of the right-angled triangles to show that each shape is the required quadrilateral.

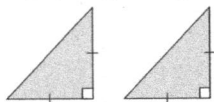

5 Calculate the value of the unknown angles.

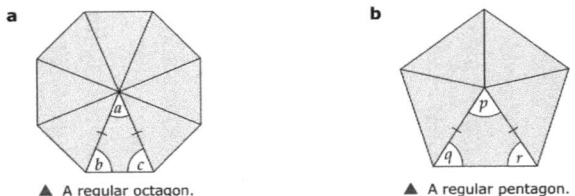

a

▲ A regular octagon.

b

▲ A regular pentagon.

5c

6 **a** Copy these shapes and draw all the diagonals from each vertex.

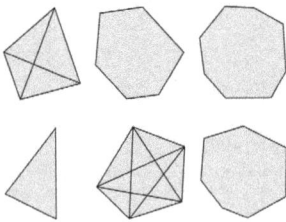

b Copy and complete the table.

Polygon	Number of sides	Number of diagonals
triangle	3	0
quadrilateral	4	2
pentagon	5	

5d

7 **a** Tessellate four congruent 'L' shapes on a 4 by 4 square grid.

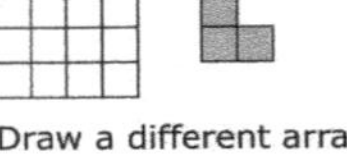

b Draw a different arrangement using the same shapes on the grid.

8 List the shapes which are congruent to one another.

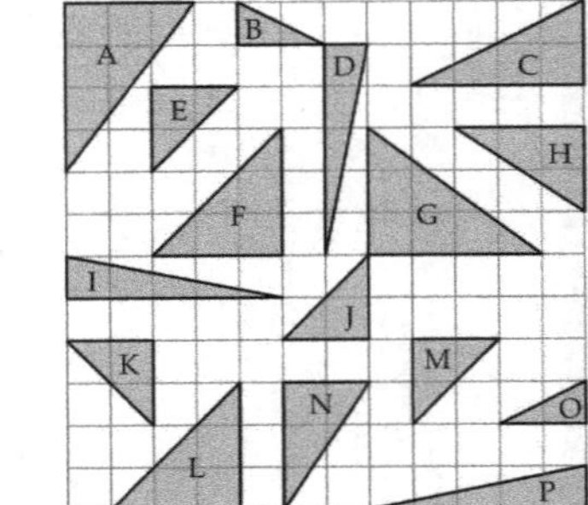

9 These two quadrilaterals are congruent.

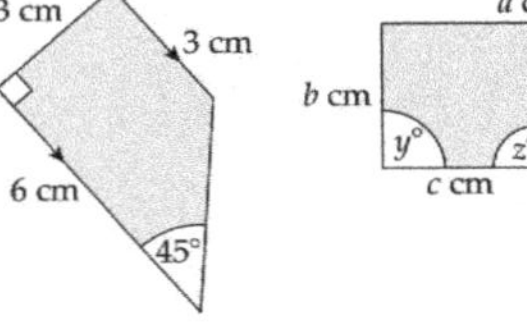

a State the size of angles x, y and z

b State the lengths of sides a, b and c

Question commentary

Questions 1 and **2** – Emphasise that a reason must be stated for each answer. Do not accept 'F' angle or 'Z' angle for corresponding and alternate angles.

Question 3 – Students must be familiar with angle properties of quadrilaterals.

Question 4 – Both triangles must be used for each part of the question, including the right-angled isosceles triangle required for part **b**. Ensure students can reason why this is a right-angled isosceles triangle.

Question 6 – Encourage students to notice a pattern. The number of diagonals is one less than triangular numbers.

Question 7 – There are only two possible arrangements. Only accept completely different arrangements and don't accept two that are congruent.

Answers

1 **a** $a = 118°$ Angles at a point add to 360°.
b $b = 46°$ Angles on a straight line add to 180°.
c $c = 132°$ Corresponding angles are equal.
$d = 48°$ Angles on a straight line add to 180°.
$e = 48°$ Angles on a straight line add to 180°/ Alternate angles are equal.
$f = 132°$ Vertically opposite angles are equal.

2 **a** $a = 50°$ **b** $b = 60°$
c $a + b = 110°$

3 **a** $a = 88°$ Angle sum of a quadrilateral is 360°.
b $b = 53°$ Isosceles trapezium.
$c = 127°, d = 127°$ Angle sum of a quadrilateral and isosceles trapezium angle properties.
c $c = 113°$ Opposite angles of a parallelogram are equal
$d = 67°, e = 67°$ Angle sum of a quadrilateral and parallelogram angle properties.

4 **a** Students' drawings of a square
4 equal sides and 2 right angles
45° + 45° = 90°
Must be a square
b Students' drawings of a right-angled isosceles triangle
2 equal sides and 45° + 45° = 90°
Must be a right-angled isosceles triangle
c Students' drawings of a parallelogram
45° + 90° = 135° for both opposite angles
Two sets of equal sides
Must be a parallelogram

5 **a** $a = 45°, b = 67.5°, c = 67.5°$
b $p = 72°, q = 54°, r = 54°$

6 **a** Students' drawings
b

Polygon	No. sides	No. diagonals
triangle	3	0
quadrilateral	4	2
pentagon	5	5
hexagon	6	9
heptagon	7	14
octagon	8	20
	n	$\frac{n(n-3)}{2}$

7 **a** Students' tessellations **b** Students' tessellations

8 A and G; B and O; D, I and P; E, J, K and M; F and L; H and N. C is not congruent to any other shape.

9 **a** $x = 45°, y = 90°, z = 135°$
b $a = 6$ cm, $b = 3$ cm, $c = 3$ cm

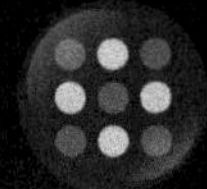

6 Graphs

Learning outcomes

A6 Model situations or procedures by translating them into algebraic expressions or formulae and by using graphs (L6)

A9 Recognise, sketch and produce graphs of linear and quadratic functions of one variable with appropriate scaling, using equations in x and y and the Cartesian plane (L6/7)

A11 Reduce a given linear equation in two variables to the standard form $y = mx + c$; calculate and interpret gradients and intercepts of graphs of such linear equations numerically, graphically and algebraically (L6)

A12 Use linear and quadratic graphs to estimate values of y for given values of x and vice versa and to find approximate solutions of simultaneous linear equations (L6)

Introduction

The chapter starts by looking at graphs of linear functions before exploring the equation of a straight-line graph in a more general sense. Curved graphs are introduced before a section on the midpoint of a line segment. Graphs of implicit functions, real-life graphs and time series graphs are covered in the final three sections.

The introduction discusses how meteorologists use mathematical formulae and graphs to predict future weather patterns. By plotting historical data onto time series graphs, the meteorologists can look for patterns in the data and use this to predict long-term trends. They can then model this going forwards in time in order to predict the future patterns that we might experience. Meteorology is far more than the weather man on the evening news and is an extremely complex scientific pursuit. The work of the United Kingdom 'Met Office', along with examples of meteorological data, can be seen at: http://www.metoffice.gov.uk/

A specific example of a time series graph plotting weather patterns can be seen at: http://www.metoffice.gov.uk/climate/uk/summaries/actualmonthly

Prior knowledge

Students should already know how to...

- Substitute numbers into simple formulae
- Plot coordinates on a standard Cartesian grid

Starter problem

The starter problem is a classic problem where the students are invited to find the maximum area given by a fixed perimeter. In this problem, the fourth side of the rectangle is not required so the students will have to divide the 40 m of fencing into three amounts, two of which are equal. An example might be 5, 5 and 30. This gives an area equal to 150 m^2. Increasing the short sides by one metre reduces the long side by two each time. 6, 6 and 28 gives an improved area of 168 m^2, as does 7, 7 and 26 (182 m^2).

Further experimentation with dividing the fencing up should lead them to the conclusion that the maximum area able to be enclosed is when the rectangle is 10 m by 20 m since going to 11 m by 18m reduces the area for the first time. 10 m by 20 m gives an area equal to 200 m^2.

Resources

MyMaths

y = mx + c	1153	Plotting graphs 3 – quadratics	1168
Real life graphs	1184	Midpoint and line length 1	1394
Plotting graphs 1 – lines	1395	Plotting graphs 2 – lines	1396
Time series	1939		

Online assessment

Chapter test	2C–6
Formative test	2C–6
Summative test	2C–6

InvisiPen solutions

Changing the subject of a formula			256
Equation of a straight line	265	Midpoints	266
Quadratic graphs	273	Real life graphs	275
Graphs of implicit functions	278		

Topic scheme

Teaching time = 7 lessons/3 weeks

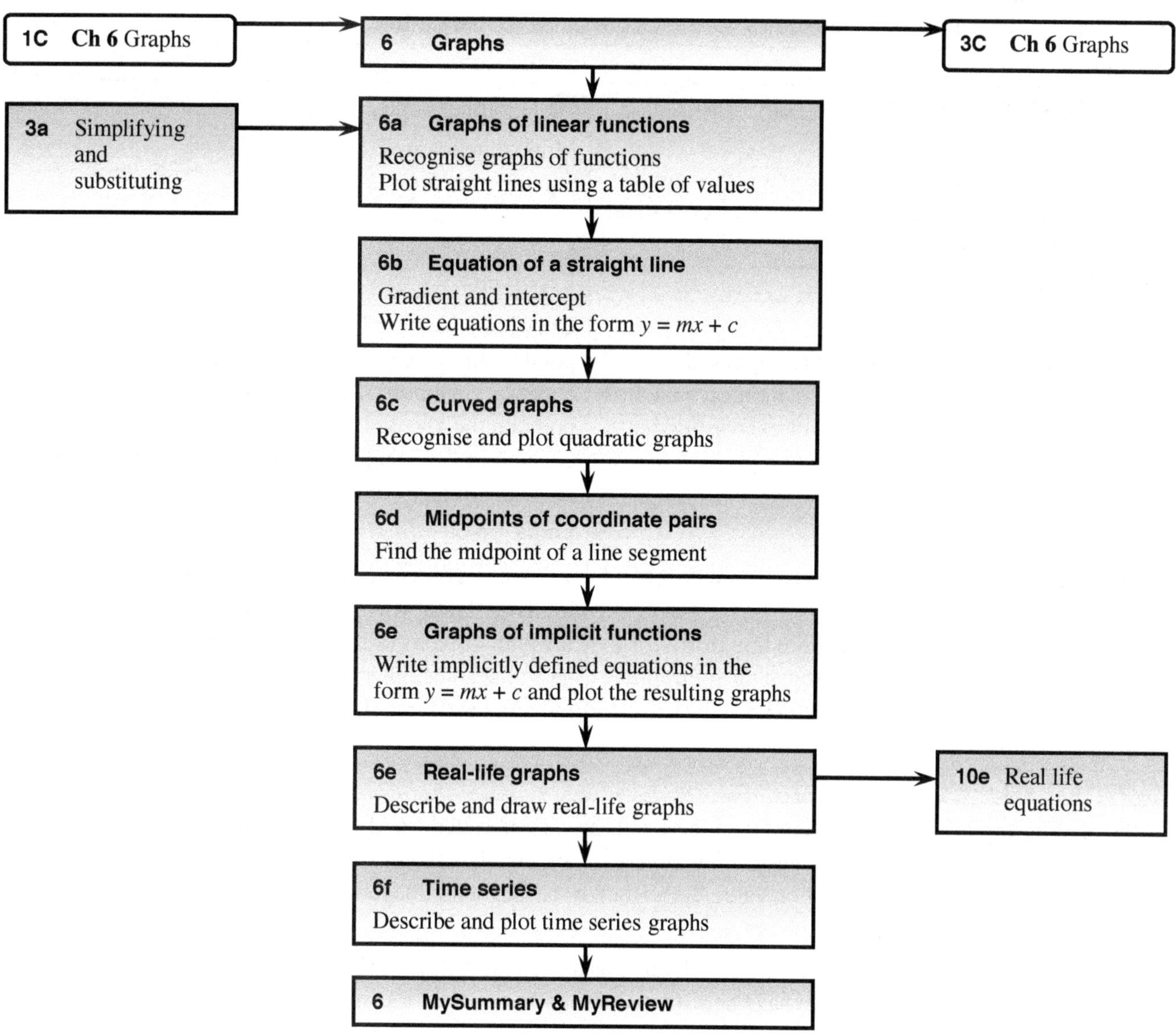

Differentiation

Student book 2A 106 – 125

Coordinates in four quadrants
Coordinates and straight lines
Drawing graphs
Horizontal and vertical graphs
Real-life graphs
Conversion graphs
Graphs and formulae

Student book 2B 98 – 113

Drawing straight-line graphs
Equation of a straight line
Real-life graphs 1
Real-life graphs 2
Time series graphs

Student book 2C 100 – 119

Graphs of linear functions
Equation of a straight line
Curved graphs
Midpoints of coordinate pairs
Graphs of implicit functions
Real-life graphs
Time series

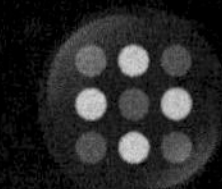

6a Graphs of linear functions

Objectives

- Plot the graphs of linear functions, where y is given explicitly in terms of x, on paper (L6)
- Recognise that equations of the form $y = mx + c$ correspond to straight-line graphs (L6)

Key ideas	Resources
1 Linear relationships can be represented graphically **2** Equations of the form $y = c$ or $x = c$ where c is a number produce horizontal graphs or vertical graphs respectively	Plotting graphs 1 – lines (1395) Mini whiteboards Square grid paper

Simplification	Extension
Provide students with examples of equation/table/graph for three different types of equation, $x = c$, $y = c$ and $y = mx + c$. Reinforce the link between the three alternative ways of expressing the function algebraic/mapping diagram/graph.	Question **6** has four lines that all intersect at the same point on the y-axis. Challenge students to create four equations that produce lines that intersect at the same point on the x-axis. For a harder challenge, can they create four lines that intersect at a point not on either axis? Encourage students to discuss their approaches.

Literacy	Links
A discussion about function machines would be a good introduction to the term 'function'. Discuss the colloquial use of the word line (for example 'wiggly line') and the mathematical meaning; the shortest distance between two points. Why are linear functions called linear?	The word *axes* is a heteronym as it can be pronounced in two different ways, each with a different meaning: the plural of axis or the plural of axe. Ask the class to try to list some other heteronyms. Some examples are minute, lead, wind, buffet, refuse, tear, wound and sow.

Alternative approach

If the relationship is between variables, then these will usually be called x and y, and the axes of the graph can be labelled accordingly. If we are talking of a function of a variable, then there is only one variable, usually x, and the vertical axis would be the function value, $f(x)$. But we are lazy with this terminology, and we muddle these two different things. Not often a problem.

In a similar way, there is perhaps really no such thing as an equation of a straight line: an equation can be solved, to find a missing value, whereas we have here a relationship that is true for many values, and cannot be solved to find any particular solution until we have more information. This is why function terminology is to be preferred. But for convenience, and in the absence of an easy alternative, we'll continue to talk of the equation of a straight line. Again, not often a problem.

Why does the book say three values? How many points do we need to fix the position of a straight line? So why the third point? Students will probably agree that it is good practice.

In the example, ask students to look carefully at the green line. Can they see the 2 and the -1 anywhere along the line, in any way at all? Maybe if they look up and down? Maybe if they look beyond the diagram?

If this goes well, the same can be tried in the exercise – maybe in question **2**, **4** and **5**. If it does not produce any result, it can be left hanging for the next spread.

Checkpoint

1 On the same graph draw the lines $y = \frac{1}{2}x + 3$ and $y = 2x$.
State the coordinates where these two lines cross. ((2,4))

Starter

A CD player and batteries together cost £23.The CD player cost £20 more than the batteries. How much do the batteries cost? (£1.50)

Ask students to explain their methods. Encourage the use of algebra.

Teaching notes

How can a function be represented as a diagram? Write a function as an equation and represent the input (x) and the possible outputs (y) on a set of Cartesian axes.

Show how the table of values helps us to organise the possible points. What pattern do they seem to make? Ensure students extend their lines all the way through the axes and label the function.

How many points are needed if we believe the function will produce a straight line?

What do the functions y = a number and x = a number look like? Establish that they in fact go in the perpendicular direction to the y-axis and x-axis. Therefore, ask students what are the equations of the x- and y- axes?

Is it possible to tell if an equation will produce a straight line or not? Use the previous spread as a guide, where, with the exception of question **1d**, they all produce straight lines.

Plenary

Is this equation, $y = \sqrt{25 - x^2}$ going to produce a straight line? What shape might it produce? Try to complete this table of values and join the points.

x	-5	-4	-3	0	3	4	5
y							

Note that the square root sign strictly means the positive square root. The points produce a semi-circle when joined.

Exercise commentary

Question 1 – Use mini whiteboards. Have the students write each of the four options top and bottom on each side and hold up the correct response for each question.

Question 2 – Some students may be confused by the $-2x$ term. Substitution and the BIDMAS rule could be used to help in the evaluation. For example, $3 - 2x$ becomes $3 - 2 \times 2$. Ask where the line cuts the y-axis.

Question 3 – Some students will find it counter-intuitive that $x = a$ is a vertical line and $y = b$ is a horizontal line. Stress this teaching point.

Question 4 – Highlight that lines are just a series of coordinates joined together. Make the link between (x, y) coordinates and equations for lines.

Question 5 – When drawing straight lines only two points are needed. Encourage students to plot a third to ensure no mistake has been made. This question is designed for students to make the link themselves that all these lines are parallel and have $2x$ in the equation.

Question 6 – Students are expected to notice that all these lines cross at the y-axis and notice the aspect each equation has in common.

Answers

1 **a** Vertical line **b** Sloping line
c Sloping line **d** Horizontal line
e Not a straight line **f** Sloping line
g Vertical line **h** Sloping line

2 **a**

x	0	1	2
y	3	1	-1

b Students' graphs

c $(1\frac{1}{2}, 0)$

3 **a** Students' graphs of $x = 1$ and $y = 3$. Lines intersect at $(1, 3)$.

b **i** $(2, 4)$ **ii** $(3, -1)$ **iii** $(\frac{1}{2}, 1)$

4

Line	$y = x + 3$	$x + y = 7$	$y = 3x$	$y = 2x - 1$	$y = \frac{3}{2}x + 2$
Yes/No	Yes	Yes	No	No	Yes

5 **a** **i**

x	0	1	2
y	-1	1	3

ii.

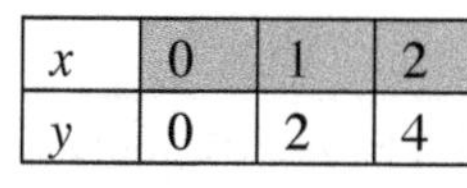

x	0	1	2
y	0	2	4

iii

x	0	1	2
y	1	3	5

iv.

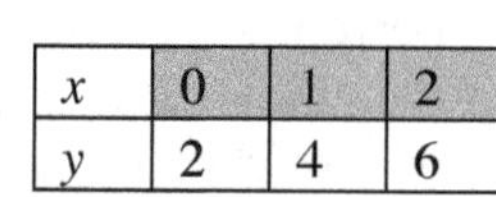

x	0	1	2
y	2	4	6

b **i–iv** Students' graphs of tables in **a** plotted on the same set of axes.

c The graphs are all parallel. All graphs have the same slope and the y-intercept for each graph is given by the '$+ c$' part of the equation.

6 **a** **i**

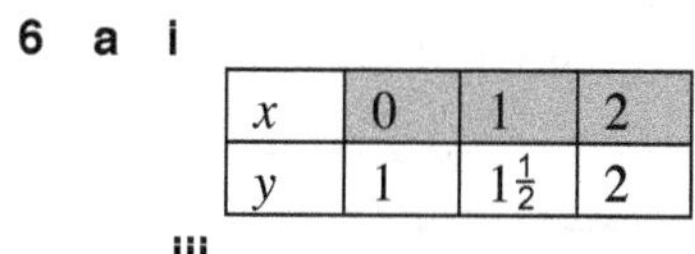

x	0	1	2
y	1	$1\frac{1}{2}$	2

ii.

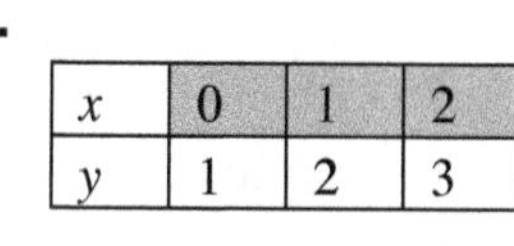

x	0	1	2
y	1	2	3

iii

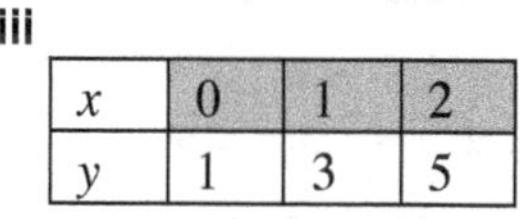

x	0	1	2
y	1	3	5

iv.

x	0	1	2
y	1	4	7

b **i–iv** Students' graphs plotted on the same set of axes

c The graphs all have different slopes. The y-intercept for each graph is given by the '$+ c$' part of the equation. For each graph it is '+1' and all the graphs intersect at $(0, 1)$.

7 $y = x$ pairs with $y = x + 2$
$y = 2x + 1$ pairs with $y = 2(x + 1)$

The odd equation out is $y = \dfrac{x+1}{2}$

An equation that pairs with this is of the form: $y = \frac{1}{2}x + c$ where c is a number.

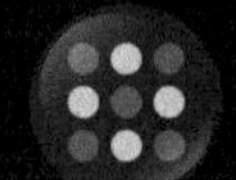

6b Equation of a straight line

Objectives

- Find the gradient of lines given by equations of the form $y = mx + c$, given values for m and c (L7)
- Understand that equations in the form $y = mx + c$ represent a straight line and that m is the gradient and c is the value of the y-intercept (L6)
- Construct functions arising from real-life problems and plot their corresponding graphs (L6)

Key ideas

1 When the equation of a straight line is written as $y = mx + c$, m is the gradient and c the y-intercept of the line.

Resources

$y = mx + c$ (1153)

Square grid paper

Simplification

When using the equation of a line, consistently use the form

$y = mx + c$ or $y = \frac{a}{b}x + c$. Show how equations can be re-written in this form if needed. This will help to reduce problems with distinguishing 'm' from 'c' and also help to find fractional gradients.

Extension

Give students examples of implicit straight-line equations with negative y terms. Ask them to say what they think 'm' and 'c' are before drawing the lines. What method could be used? What about the method of completing a table of values used in lesson **6a**? How can the initial thoughts on the values of 'm' and 'c' be checked? If students made an error, can they say what made the equation difficult to read? Is there a way to find 'm' and 'c' without drawing the line? For example how could $4x - 2y = 10$ be rearranged?

Literacy

The coefficients of polynomials, sums of multiples of powers of a variable (such as x) are generally not italicised (for example, see Exercise **6c** question **4**); why might they be here? Perhaps to emphasise that they can vary?

In the real world, would gradient be measured as vertical divided by horizontal or as vertical divided by length along the surface, of the road or whatever? Does this matter? (Even for the steepest roads, the angle is small enough for the tangent and sine ratios to be close for the accuracy involved, so no, it doesn't matter.)

Links

On maps, contour lines can be used to calculate the gradient of hills. Every point on a contour line is at the same height. The closer the contours are together, the steeper the slope. On roads a double arrow shows a gradient of 1 in 5 or steeper, that is, the road rises 1 m for every 5 m along, and a single arrow shows a gradient of between 1 in 7 and 1 in 5. A map showing these features can be found using grid reference SS871466 at http://getamap.ordnancesurvey.co.uk/getamap/frames.htm

Alternative approach

Take time to show the 1 along, 2 up (and other examples) repetitively and frequently, and then try 2 along, 4 up (etc) to show that it is a ratio we are considering here.

In part **c** of the example, and perhaps for some other examples, show that once the equation is found (this will still seem a bit like prestidigitation to some students) it will generate points on the line, including the y-intercept; and, when a few points have been labelled, that each time the x value is increased by 1, so the y value has changed, by the amount of the gradient. A few pennies might drop.

Students can easily learn to identify the m and c in such equations as those in question **1**, but good students will not be happy to do this without some grasp of what is going on. If they are happy to do this now, light may dawn later but this topic is often opaque even for bright students and more mature students, so anticipate slow going.

It may be necessary to explicitly discuss the way we go from left to right here; this is somewhat arbitrary, but essential to agree if we are to talk of positive and negative gradients.

Checkpoint

1 On a graph join the points (1, 1) and (5, 9) with a straight line. What is the equation of this line?

($y = 2x - 1$)

Starter

If $A = 3, B = 4, C = 7, D = 9$ ask students to form as many equations as they can in four minutes.

Score 1 point for each different operation or brackets and 2 points for each different letter used. For example, $2(B^2 - A) = AC + 5$ scores 11.

Teaching notes

Draw the lines with equations $y = 2x - 3$ and $y = -3x + 1$. What is meant by their gradients? *Gradient* is a measurement of the steepness of the slope. How can it be measured? Describe the method and give the formula gradient $= \frac{\text{height}}{\text{base}}$. It can be remembered by the fact that the 'height' goes 'high up' in the formula and the 'base' goes at the 'base'.

Find the gradients of the two lines. What major difference is there between the lines? One slopes uphill, the other downhill. How might this be represented in the value of the gradient? Discuss negative gradients.

An alternative way of looking at gradient is to see how far the line moves for every unit along. Test this on the two examples. The gradient is represented by the letter 'm'. The place where the line *intercepts* the y-axis is represented by the letter 'c'.

Is there a link between the values of m and c for these two lines and their corresponding equations? Establish the general rule $y = mx + c$.

Plenary

Why do students think that 'm' and 'c' are used to represent the gradient and y-intercept? Why not use 'g' and 'i'? Unfortunately, 'g' and 'i' are already taken to represent other values. In fact no-one knows why 'm' is used.

Exercise commentary

Question 1 – Emphasise that the gradient is the number that x is being multiplied by and that the y-intercept is the number that is being added or subtracted. Make sure that brackets are expanded so equations are in the form $y = mx + c$.

Question 2 – Highlight to students that if the gradient is negative, the y-intercept can be written first.

Question 3 – Not all straight lines are most easily written in the form $y = mx + c$. Students should look for any relationship they can for x and y – part **c** in particular.

Question 4 – Ask which line does not have an equation that looks like $y = mx + c$? What is the gradient of that line?

Question 5 – Ask what the values of the gradient and y-intercept mean when applied to 'Fab Cabs'? Ask students to interpret what type of journey a high c and low m might be better for.

Question 6 – Emphasise again that for the gradient and y-intercept to be interpreted from an equation, the equation of the straight line must be in the form $y = mx + c$.

Answers

1

	Equation	Gradient	Coordinate of y-intercept
a	$y = 3x + 2$	3	(0, 2)
b	$y = 4x - 1$	4	(0, -1)
c	$y = 2x$	2	(0, 0)
d	$y = \frac{1}{2}x + 3$	$\frac{1}{2}$	(0, 3)
e	$y = \frac{1}{2}x - 5$	$\frac{1}{2}$	(0, -5)
f	$y = 3(x + 2)$	3	(0, 6)
g	$y = 4 - \frac{3}{2}x$	$-\frac{3}{2}$	(0, 4)
h	$y = 10 - x$	-1	(0, 10)

2 **a** $y = 2x + 1$ **b** $y = x - 4$
c $y = \frac{1}{2} - 3x$

3 **a** $y = 5$ **b** $y = 2x$
c $x + y = 5$ **d** $y = 3x + 2$

4 **a** $y = 4$ **b** $y = x + 2$
c $y = 3x - 1$ **d** $y = -2x + 3$

5 **a, c** Students' graphs of fare equations for 'Fab Cabs' and 'Fair Fares'
b $y = 2x + 2$ so company charges £2 per mile and puts £2 on the meter at the start of the journey.
c If the mileage is less than 3, use Fab Cabs.
If the mileage is more than 3, use Fair Fares.
If the mileage is equal to 3, choose either taxi company.

6

Equation	Gradient	Coordinate of y-intercept
$y = 10 - x$	-1	(0, 10)
$y = \frac{1}{2}x + 2$	$\frac{1}{2}$	(0, 2)
$y = \frac{4}{3}x - 1$	$\frac{4}{3}$	(0, -1)
$y = 3 - \frac{1}{2}x$	$-\frac{1}{2}$	(0, 3)
$y = \frac{3}{4} - \frac{1}{2}x$	$-\frac{1}{2}$	$(0, \frac{3}{4})$

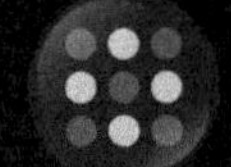

6c Curved graphs

Objectives	
• Plot graphs of simple quadratic functions	(L7)

Key ideas	Resources
1 Functions of the form $y = ax^2 + bx + c$, where a is non-zero, are termed quadratic 2 Graphs representing quadratic relationships are parabolic curves	Plotting graphs 3 – quadratics (1168) Graphing software Squared paper Mini whiteboards

Simplification	Extension
The main assistance is needed in using the table of values. Encourage students to primarily use the positive x values. Once the graph is partly drawn, the negative x values can be checked to see if they fit the general shape of the curve.	Draw the graph of $y^2 = x$. How can you change the table of values to make this easier? How can you transform the graph of $y = x^2$ into $y^2 = x$? If Chapter **9** has been covered, encourage the use of the language associated with reflection.

Literacy	Links
The word quadratic is linked to the Latin *quadrare* meaning to make square. Students may identify 'quad' with the number four, which is linked to the Latin *quattuor* meaning four and in turn *quadrum* meaning square. The link with the number four is helpful in other areas of this topic, for instance when two linear brackets are multiplied to give a quadratic expression we initially obtain four terms. For example $(x + 2)(x - 4) = x^2 - 4x + 2x - 8$.	A television satellite dish is a type of parabolic antenna. The inside surface of the dish is parabolic in shape. The incoming radiation reflects off the inside of the dish and is focussed on to a central antenna called a feedhorn. The signal is then transmitted electrically from the feedhorn to the television. There is an applet demonstrating how parabolic reflectors work at http://www.analyzemath.com/parabola/parabola.html

Alternative approach

What is the most obvious difference between the two graphs in the examples? And what in the equations corresponds to this? If x is very large, positive or negative, what is x^2? So what happens to the graph, as we move out to the left or right? And what is $-x^2$? So what would the graph look like if the x^2 term was negative?

Conclude that a positive coefficient of x^2 will give a happy parabola (a smile), and a negative coefficient, an unhappy parabola (a frown).

When using tables to generate coordinates, some students will find it helpful to write not just y, but $y = x^2 + 2$, or whatever the function or formula is, on the bottom row.

When drawing the curves, encourage students to not put pen or pencil to paper until they have assured themselves (maybe with pen or pencil upside down) that they will be able to move smoothly through the points they have marked. It is usually easiest to have the hand inside the curve (the joints of fingers, wrist, etc., lend themselves best to this), and turning the page upside down for happy parabolas can give happier curves.

Checkpoint

1 On the same axes draw the graph $y = x^2 + x - 2$ and $y = 3x + 1$.
Write down the coordinates of the two places where they cross. ((-1,-2) and (3,10))

Starter

Ask students to give three sets of coordinates that lie on the following lines:

$2y = 5x + 9$ for example (-1, 2) (1, 7) (3, 12)

$3x + y = -1$ for example (-1, 2) (-2, 5) (1, -4)

$y - x = 3$ for example (-1, 2) (1, 4) (-5, -2)

Encourage students to think of negative values.

Ask students what they notice when $x = -1$. (The lines intersect at (-1, 2).)

Teaching notes

Look at a table of values for a straight line (linear) graph. If the x values rise at a constant rate, what do you notice about the y values? What would happen if the y values did not rise evenly? The graph would not be a straight line.

One particular group of non-linear functions are known as the *quadratics*, they produce a type of graph known as a parabola. Give the students some examples of functions where all except one are quadratic. Can students tell which is the odd one out?

Establish what makes a function 'quadratic' and look at how a table of values can be used to organise possible points on the graph. Why do you need so many points?

Look at the shape of the parabola, does it ever flatten out? Use the example of $y = x^2 - x$ and x values from -1 to 3. It appears that the curve is flat between $x = 0$ and $x = 1$. Is this the case? Taking x as 0.5 and using a calculator will help demonstrate that the curve continues to 'dip'. If you are using graphing software, judicious use of the zoom feature may help to make this point. Is the curve symmetric?

Plenary

Use a graphing package with the whole class. Ask students to suggest a quadratic equation that will pass between two given fixed points. Initial guesses can be further refined by editing the equation. This could be done in the context of a 'football' landing in a 'goal'. A further challenge could be set to obtain a quadratic curve that passes through two 'goals'.

Exercise commentary

Question 1 – Remind students they need to expand any brackets. Mini whiteboards could be used here.

Question 2 – Some students may be confused both by squaring a negative and by the third row requiring '2' to be repeated across the row. A simpler example could be used to demonstrate how the table works, for example,

$y = 2x + 1$

x	2	3
$2x$	4	6
1	1	1
$y = 2x + 1$	5	7

Question 3 – The subtraction of $2x$ may cause problems for students, especially with negative x values. Allow students to make errors in their table, but to always question points which seem out of place when plotting the graph.

Question 4 – Encourage students to discuss their graphs with their partners and to try and make conclusions about the effect of changing a, b or c.

Answers

1 **a** Linear **b** Linear **c** Linear **d** Quadratic
e Quadratic **f** Linear **g** Linear **h** Quadratic

2 **a**

x	-3	-2	-1	0	1	2	3
x^2	9	4	1	0	1	4	9
+ 2	2	2	2	2	2	2	2
y	11	6	3	2	3	6	11

b Students' graphs of points in **a**

c (0, 2) **d** (0, 2)

3 **a**

x	-2	-1	0	1	2	3	4
x^2	4	1	0	1	4	9	16
$-2x$	4	2	0	−2	−4	−6	−8
y	8	3	0	-1	0	3	8

b Students' graphs of points in **a** joined with smooth curve

c (0, 0) and (2, 0) **d** $x = 1$

4 **a** Students' investigations using graph plotting tool

b $(0, c)$ is where the curve intersects the y-axis so increasing/decreasing c moves this point up/down the y-axis.
The curve intercepts the x-axis in two places if $b^2 > 4ac$. If $b = 0$ and a is positive then this happens when c is less than 0.

c If a is positive, increasing b from 0 moves the minimum of the curve down and to the left.
Decreasing b from 0 moves the minimum of the curve down and to the right.

d $x = -\dfrac{b}{2a}$
As b increases the line moves to the left.
As b decreases, the line moves to the right.

6d Midpoints of coordinate pairs

Objectives	
• Find the midpoint of the line segment *AB*, given the coordinates of *A* and *B*	(L6)

Key ideas	**Resources**
1 The coordinates of the midpoint of a line segment are given by the mid-values for the *x* and *y* coordinates of the ends of the line segment.	Midpoint and line length 1 (1394) Graph paper Graph paper on stiff card

Simplification	**Extension**
Drawing the points on graph paper will help with the questions. Check students are confident plotting points in all four quadrants and with the rules for adding and subtracting negative numbers.	A triangle *ABC* has coordinates *A*(2, 0), *B*(0, 4) and *C*(10, 8). Find the midpoints of the three sides, M_{AB}, M_{BC} and M_{CA}. Now find the point P which is one third of the way from M_{AB}, and the opposite vertex *C*. Likewise, *Q* a third of the way from M_{BC} and *A* and *R* a third of the way from M_{CA} and *B*. The common point (4, 4) is the centre of gravity. If the diagram is drawn on stiff card and cut out it should balance on a (pencil) point placed at *P*. Further, if the shape is allowed to pivot freely about any point then *P* will hang directly below the pivot point.

Literacy	**Links**
Distinguish a line from a line segment, and perhaps also from a half-line. Be clear that the midpoint is merely halfway along, both in the *x* and *y* directions.	René Descartes (1596–1650) was a polymath who made major contributions to several subjects. He developed a philosophy of knowledge starting from 'Je pense, donc je suis' (I think, therefore I am). In the sciences he showed that the angle between the centre and edge of a rainbow is 42°. In mathematics he is famous for *analytical geometry* which combines geometry with algebra and is why we use the name *Cartesian* coordinates. For more information see the MacTutor site http://www-groups.dcs.st-and.ac.uk/~history/Mathematicians/Descartes.html

Alternative approach

This topic could be approached through the concept of similar triangles. Draw a slanted line segment on a grid, marking the endpoints *A* and *B*, such that the horizontal distance and the vertical distance between *A* and *B* are both multiples of 6. Add a line through *A* parallel to the *x*-axis and a line through *B* parallel to the *y*-axis to form a right-angled triangle *ABC* with hypotenuse *AB*. Mark a fourth point *N* at an arbitrary position on *AB* and draw a vertical line to join *N* to *AC*. The right-angled triangle with hypotenuse *AB* is an enlargement of the right-angled triangle with hypotenuse *AN*, can the students prove this? Angle rules for parallel lines could be reinforced here to good effect. Encourage students to consider where *N* would need to be placed for the scale factor of enlargement from the triangle with hypotenuse *AN* **to** triangle *ABC* to be 3, 2, ½ (for this last one the line segment will need to be extended beyond *B*).

Students should then focus on the position of *N* when the scale factor of enlargement is 2; introduce this as the midpoint of *AB* and emphasise that the *x* coordinate and *y* coordinate of *N* are the midpoints of *AC* and *BC* respectively.

Checkpoint	
1 What is the midpoint of (-7, 3) and (4, -2)?	((-1.5,0.5))

Starter

Ask students to draw a quadrilateral from the list given in lesson **5b** and then join the midpoints of neighbouring sides, what shape do they get?

Kite → rectangle, rectangle → rhombus,
rhombus → rectangle, square → square,
parallelogram → parallelogram,
isosceles trapezium → kite.

The procedure can be iterated to give a nested sequence of quadrilaterals. Repeating this for a parallelogram results in a similar parallelogram of half the original size.

Teaching notes

Draw a slanted line segment *AB* with given end coordinates (in the first quadrant) on a grid and ask students how they would find its midpoint. Can they do better than using a ruler to measure the distance along the line?

Suggest they look at the line from above, where would the end points of its shadow be: $(x_A, 0)$ and $(x_B, 0)$. Agree that to find the point half way between x_A and x_B you calculate $\frac{(x_A + x_B)}{2}$. Ask the students to do the same for the *y*-coordinate. Check understanding with a further numerical example.

Pose the problem: given a point *A* and a midpoint *M*, how would you find *B*? Two approaches are possible. Formally based on setting up and solving two linear equations ($x_B = 2x_M - x_A$ and $y_B = 2y_M - y_A$). Informally based on working out how far in *x* you have to go to get from x_A to x_M and then adding this onto x_M, likewise for *y*. Check understanding with a numerical example.

Plenary

Pair students and ask them to set a question that gives *A* and *M* and asks you to find *B*. Swap with another pair and then check answers. As a class discuss cases where the pairs disagree or found a question hard.

Exercise commentary

Questions 1 and **2** – For the questions involving decimal coordinates point the students towards using the formula. Explain the formula as the midpoint being the average value for both *x* and *y*.

Question 3 – Remind students that a line joining opposite vertices of a quadrilateral is called a diagonal. As an extension, ask students which quadrilaterals have diagonals which cross at their midpoints.

Question 6 – Help students to notice than the equation for finding the midpoint can be easily modified to find any fraction of the way along the line.

Question 7 – Having card available will help students investigate the centres of mass. This method will work for all triangles, but not for all quadrilaterals. An isosceles trapezium is a good counter example.

Answers

1 **a** (3, 5) **b** (4, -3)
c (0, 0) **d** (-4, -5)
e $(-1\frac{1}{2}, 4\frac{1}{2})$ **f** (4.2, 1.05)

2 **a** (4, 6) **b** (7, 5) **c** (-4, 4) **d** (-3, -3)
e (-9.1, -3.7)

3 **a** **i** Parallelogram **ii** $M_{AC} = (2\frac{1}{2}, 2) = M_{BD}$
iii Diagonals bisect one another.
b **i** Rhombus **ii** $M_{AC} = (-3, -1) = M_{BD}$,
iii Diagonals bisect one another.
c **i** Isosceles trapezium
ii $M_{AB} = (3\frac{1}{2}, -\frac{1}{2})$, $M_{CD} = (3\frac{1}{2}, -3\frac{1}{2})$
iii The lines do not bisect one another.

4 **a** M (1, 0) **b** $M(1\frac{1}{2}, 4)$
c M (3, 0) **d** $M(\frac{1}{2}, 3\frac{3}{4})$

5 (3, 9)

6 **a** (1, 0) **b** (0, 4) **c** (3, 4) **d** (-3, -1)
e $(2, -3\frac{1}{3})$ **f** (1, 1.6)

7 Students' answers

Objectives

- Generate points and plot graphs of linear functions, where y is given implicitly as a function of x (e.g. $ay + bx = 0$, $y + bx + c = 0$) on paper and using ICT (L7)
- Interpret the meaning of various points and sections of straight-line graphs, including intercepts and intersections, e.g. solving simultaneous linear equations (L7)

Key ideas

1. Linear implicit functions can be rearranged to give explicit functions
2. Linear graphs can be drawn by finding their intercepts on the axes

Resources

Plotting graphs 2 – lines (1396)

Graphical software or graphical calculators

Simplification

When rearranging implicit functions, it may be helpful to use arrow diagrams that show the function beginning with y. Then by reversing the operations y can be made the subject.

Extension

Plot linear functions that are expressed implicitly, but do not have a convenient set of integer solutions. For example, $3x + 4y = 7$. If an accurate drawing is required, how can the points and scale be chosen to avoid the need for decimals? For this example use seven intervals per unit on each axis.

Literacy

The term implicit will need some explanation: the point being that y will be some function of x here, and x will be some function of y, but we may not be able to see what that function is, until we rearrange the function given. In the meantime, the function can be regarded as implied by what we see; i.e., implicit.

Links

An oscilloscope is a test instrument often used to troubleshoot electrical equipment that is malfunctioning. The instrument has a screen which can display a graph of voltage against time for the part of the circuit that is being tested. There is more information about oscilloscopes at http://en.wikipedia.org/wiki/Oscilloscope

Alternative approach

Present students with the following list of equations: $3x + 2y = 8$, $y = 4 - 1.5x$, $8 - 2y = 3x$, $x = 8/3 - \frac{2}{3}y$, $2y = 8 - 3x$. Are any of these functions linear? How can you tell? Emphasise that there are no powers on the variables. Instruct students to sketch each function on a set of -10 to 10 axes, what do they notice? Can they prove algebraically that these functions all describe the same relationship between x and y?

Discuss the relative advantages and disadvantages of explicit and implicit forms. When working with linear functions, one advantage of the explicit form $y = mx + c$ is that we can easily see what the gradient and y-intercept of the line are. On the other hand, a function such as $7y + x = 15$ may be much easier to plot if we leave it in this form; we can easily spot two pairs of coordinates that the line passes through ((1, 2) and (15, 0)) but the y-intercept would be tricky to plot accurately.

Checkpoint

1. Draw $3x + 4y = 24$ and $y = \frac{1}{2}x + 1$ on the same axes.
   Where do the lines cross? ((4,3))

Starter

Gareth observes a group of pigeons and rabbits. He counts the number of heads and feet. There are 26 heads and 74 feet.

How many pigeons and how many rabbits are there? (15 pigeons, 11 rabbits)

This can be extended by asking students to make up their own bird and animal puzzles.

Teaching notes

Recapitulate work covered previously on rearranging formulae in lesson **3g**. Continue to insist on working being shown on both sides. Keep comparing with the method of solving linear equations. Look briefly at examples that include all four operations.

Recapitulate work on drawing graphs of linear functions covered previously in lesson **6a**. Previously the equation was given 'explicitly', that is, it began with $y =$. Look at examples of 'implicit' linear functions. How can a table of values be completed for these? Encourage different approaches. First, by choosing different x or y values, can the matching y or x value be found to make the equation 'correct'? What difficulties does this create? Some values may be hard to find or give decimal/fractional answers that will be difficult to plot. Second, if explicit functions are easier to work with, what other method might be useful? Rearrange the function to make y the subject first.

Plenary

Is it possible to tell if a function will be linear before you draw it? Ask the students to suggest some functions they believe are linear. Encourage different looking functions. Can students suggest some that are not linear?

Exercise commentary

Question 1 – Encourage the balance method, manipulating equations by doing the same to each side of the equation. In part **h**, show students that adding $4y$ to both sides will eliminate the negative y.

Question 2 – Some students may want to make y the subject. Ask them if this is necessary?

Question 3 – Show students that by substituting $x = 0$ and then $y = 0$ the two points where the line crosses each axis can be easily found and joined to draw the line.

Question 5 – Note it is possible to have $x - y = 3$ or $y - x = 3$. Both clearly lead to the same solution as which is the larger number is not specified. Allow students to explore this for themselves.

Question 6 – Show students that this can also be solved logically. (Don't use simultaneous equation language, just argue logically). If $2a + 2c = 50$, then $a + c$ must equal 25. Compare this with $a + 3c = 45$. In both of these one adult ticket is being bought. So the extra £20 can only be for the 2 extra child's tickets. There a child's ticket must cost £10 etc.

Answers

1 **a** $y = 8 - x$ **b** $y = 1 - 2x$
c $y = 4x + 3$ **d** $y = 2 - 3x$
e $y = \frac{1}{2}x + 3$ **f** $y = 1 - \frac{2}{3}x$
g $y = 3x$ **h** $y = \frac{1}{4}x + 3$

2

	i	ii	iii
a	$\frac{3}{4}$	$-\frac{3}{2}$	$2\frac{1}{4}$
b	4	$11\frac{1}{2}$	-1
c	2	3	$\frac{4}{3}$
d	15	9	19

3 **a** Students' graphs of function given by table of values

x	0	2	4
y	4	2	0

b Students' graphs of function given by table of values

x	0	2	4
y	8	4	0

c Students' graphs of function given by table of values

x	0	3	6
y	2	1	0

4 **a** **i** (2, 4) **ii** (3, 3) **iii** (0, 1)
b **i** $2 + 4 = 6$ and $2 \times 4 - 3 \times 2 = 2$
ii $3 + 3 = 6$ and $3 \times 3 - 2 \times 3 = 3$
iii $2 \times 1 - 3 \times 0 = 2$ and $3 \times 1 - 2 \times 0 = 3$

5 **a** $x + y = 7$ and $x - y = 3$
b Students' graphs of functions given by these tables of values:

$x + y = 7$

x	0	3	7
y	7	4	0

$x - y = 3$

x	0	3	7
y	-3	0	4

c (5, 2)
(or (2, 5) if $y - x = 3$ used)
$5 + 2 = 7$ and $5 - 2 = 3$

6 **a** $2a + 2c = 50$ and $a + 3c = 45$
b Students' plots of equations in **a**
c Adult's ticket = £15 and child's ticket = £10

Objectives	
• Construct functions arising from real-life problems and plot their corresponding graphs; interpret graphs arising from real situations	(L6)
• Interpret graphs arising from real situations, e.g. time series graphs	(L6)
• Use compound measures to compare in real-life contexts (e.g. travel graphs)	(L7)

Key ideas	Resources
1 Graphs representing real-life situations can be sketches, or more precise models of reality	Real life graphs (1184) Graph paper

Simplification	Extension
Ask students to explain verbally what is happening at the various parts of the graphs. Encourage use of phrases like, 'increasing more and more'.	Draw a speed time graph for the journey in question **2**. Find the area underneath the graph. Look at the graph in question **2** again. Can you see what the value of the area represents in this journey?

Literacy	Links
In this topic students will encounter sections of text describing sequences of events. Encourage students to break down the text into bullet points and highlight the time or duration associated with each event to help them visualise what is happening.	Racing drivers use real-life graphs to analyse their own driving skills and the performance of the car during a race. The graphs can show features such as the engine speed and degree of steering as the car progresses around the bends in the track. There are examples of graphs used in motor sports at http://autospeed.com/cms/A_108255/article.html and at http://www.advantagemotorsports.com/WS.htm

Alternative approach

In 2012 Felix Baumgartner set a world record for completing the highest skydive, jumping from a balloon more than 39 km above the surface of the earth.

http://www.redbull.com/uk/en/adventure/stories/1331615604283/fly-with-felix-red-bull-stratos-pov-video

Students could use this video to sketch a graph of altitude against time for his descent. Where is the graph steepest? What does the graph look like at the moment when the parachute is opened? Students could sketch a more comprehensive graph including Baumgartner's ascent into the stratosphere.

In the first example, encourage students to look for possible variations to this graph. How would the graph change if the sink had a slow leak? What if the sink had an overflow drain placed at a certain position on the side? In the second example discuss speed as rate of change of position and encourage students to use the units on both axes to obtain the units for speed. This strategy serves as a quick check that they are calculating the speed correctly as the units and calculation should both be in the form distance ÷ time. How precise is this graph? Does it take account of real-life variations of speed, time taken to accelerate and brake, and so on? In this example we only need a simplified version, but in general could we make much use of a more complicated model? What do students think of the word 'model' here?

Be clear in use of terms such as 'constant rate', trying to always indicate what (volume, depth, etc.) it is that is changing at a constant rate.

Checkpoint

1 Water is poured at a constant rate into a nearly spherical goldfish bowl. Sketch the graph of the level of water against time.

(The graph is a smooth 'S' shape with gradients steepest at beginning and end and least in the centre.)

Starter

Ask students to imagine two unmarked containers. One holds exactly 3 litres; the other holds exactly 5 litres. Jamie says he can use these containers to get exactly 4 litres. Ask students to work out how this can be done. How about 1 litre?

What if the capacities are 5 litres and 7 litres?

Teaching notes

Look at a distance–time graph for a swimmer doing laps in a pool. Use the vertical axis for the distance from the start point. Show variations in speed and points were the swimmer stops. Ask students to suggest explanations for the shape of the graph.

Draw the graph of another swimmer on top of the previous graph. Use an example that shows the second swimmer initially swimming faster, but ultimately swimming the same distance in a slower time. Ask, who is the faster swimmer? Discuss the parts of the graph that provide us with the evidence.

Look at an example of the depth/time graph for filling a container at a constant rate. Use an example container such as

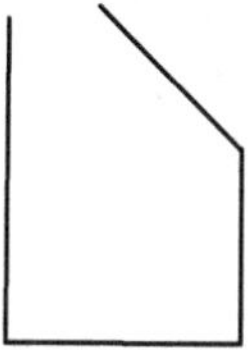

How can the change in the speed of the increase of depth be shown in the graph?

Plenary

What would a speed–time graph look like for the journey in question **2**? What scales are needed on the axes? Between the distance–time and speed–time graphs, which gives a clearer representation of the journey?

Exercise commentary

Question 1 – To begin with, students could match the statements and points of the graph that show an increase/decrease/constant depth and then investigate further to put the statements in order. Allow students to simplify part **b** by approximating to straight lines. Some may realise intuitively that the rate of loss of temperature is greater the hotter the tea is.

Question 2 – Students may need support with speed, distance, time calculations, especially with part **c** and giving an answer in km/hr.

Question 3 – Ask students to describe what happens when they fill a water bottle from the tap at home. Elicit why the bottle fills up much quicker at the end.

Question 4 – Ensure the containers are not too complicated, combinations of the ones used in question **3** will work well.

Answers

1 **a** A to vi B to ii C to iii D to iv E to v F to i

b Students' graphs showing temperature of cup of tea plotted against time, including changes when splash of cold water added and cup topped up with more tea.

2 **a** Students' distance–time graphs

b 12:05 **c** 24 km/h

3 A and 4, B and 2, C and 1, D and 3

4 Students' answers; compare to question **3**.

6g Time series

Objectives	
• Select, construct and modify, on paper and using ICT, suitable graphical representations to progress an enquiry and identify key features present in the data. Include line graphs for time series (L6)	

Key ideas	Resources
1 Construct time series graphs **2** Read from and interpret time series graphs	Time series (1939) Graph paper Life expectancy data (source: Office for National Statistics): http://www.ons.gov.uk/ons/dcp171776_253938.pdf

Simplification	Extension
Some students may find it difficult to write down their observations. Encourage them to verbalise their conclusions to the teacher. Allow students to make very short sentences if they need to, that is, just statements.	How do you think the number of smokers in the UK has changed over the last 20 years? Sketch a time series graph and use the Internet to check your prediction. Can you explain the changes and trends you observe? How do you think the number of smokers will change over the next 20 years? What factors will have an impact?

Literacy	Links
This section is a good place to introduce the terms *periodic*, *seasonal variation* and *trend*. The tide graph illustrates *periodic* and the quarterly electricity bill shows *seasonal variation*. Discuss with the class other things they know that are periodic or show seasonal variation.	For every 100 girls born in the UK, there are around 105 boys. What ratio is this of male to female? What percentage of all babies born in the UK are boys? In 2011 the population of the UK was 31 million males and 32.2 million females. What percentage of the population is male? Why is this different to the percentage at birth? (Life expectancy for females is longer than for males.)

Alternative approach

Reverse the order of the two key ideas. By focusing on the drawing elements of the time series graphs (question **3**) it links back to previous sections on drawing graphs. Once the time-series have been drawn, then students can work through interpreting the time series by completing questions **1** and **2**.

Checkpoint

1 Sketch a graph that shows seasonal variation for the cost of flights to Alicante in Spain.

(Graph should show more expensive tickets in the summer, with peaks at school holiday times)

Starter

Write a list of times and temperatures on the board:

6 a.m. -2°; 9 a.m. 9°; 12 noon 17.5°; 3 p.m. 14°; 6 p.m. 10.5°; 9 p.m. 8°.

Give students quick-fire questions, for example,

What is the biggest temperature difference?
By how much did the temperature change between 9 a.m.and 12 noon?

This can be differentiated by the choice of temperatures.

Teaching notes

Ask students how they think life expectancies have changed since 1911; will they be different for men and women? Ask them to sketch a graph to illustrate their ideas and then see how this compares to that given.

Look at the example of weight plotted against age in the student book. Do students expect this trend to continue? If it did, how much would you expect a 40-year-old to weigh? Discuss how rate of growth varies throughout a human's life. Sketch a more precise graph on the board showing the variation in an individual's weight over the course of a week; should we include this level of detail in the long term graph? Time series graphs are often used to indicate longer term trends and the level of detail required will depend in part on the timespan being covered.

Look at the example of tide height plotted against time; why is it important to have information about the tide? Discuss the impact of this data on safety, and on transport. Do students recognise this pattern? Use graphical software to demonstrate the sine curve and show that by altering the equation as needed we can fit a trigonometric function to a set of data of this nature. Emphasise that this is just one example of mathematical modelling being used in industry to make predictions and to solve practical problems.

Plenary

Carry out a confidential survey into the percentage of students in the class who have dropped litter during yesterday. Ask students to note yes/no and male/female and hand in their folded answers. Ask the class to suggest hypotheses. For example, over 50% of the class have dropped litter yesterday, or more boys than girls dropped litter yesterday. What do the actual results reveal? Can the results be trusted, will people have been honest?

Exercise commentary

Question 1 – Encourage use of language from the 'literacy' section above. Discuss what reasons cause the behaviour seen in the graph.

Question 2 – Encourage rich use of language in describing part **a** in particular.

Question 3 – Again encourage associated language described in 'literacy' section.

Answers

1 **a** The graph shows an overall downward trend in coal production, with peaks in production for 1910, 1930 and the mid-1950s.

b The quarterly gas bill shows highest consumption in the winter quarters and lowest consumption in the summer quarters.

2 **a** Sasha's phone use peaks every Saturday. Towards the end of the month her usage starts to fall. Even the peak for Saturday is much lower.

b After Sasha checked her phone usage she reduces the amount she uses it probably to try to keep within her 300 free minutes allowance for the month. By the end of the month her usage has dropped to almost zero minutes.

3 **a** **i** Students' time series graphs of monthly ice cream sales

ii Ice cream sales rose from their lowest in March to their highest in August. Sales then fell again in September with another peak in December, possibly corresponding the Christmas period.

b **i** Students' time series graphs of Thomas's quarterly earnings for three consecutive years

ii For each of the three years Thomas earned the most in the summer and the least in the winter. His earnings in the autumn, while less than in the summer, were always more than in the spring. Overall his earnings have risen steadily since 2010, with 2012 being his best year.

Key outcomes	Quick check
Plot the graph of a linear function and use the equation of a straight line.	Draw $y = \frac{1}{4}x + 2$ and $y = 2x + 9$ on the same graph. Where do the lines cross? ((-4, 1))
Plot the graph of a non-linear function.	Draw $y = x^2 - 6x - 8$ and $y = x^2 + 2x$ on the same graph. At what point do these quadratics cross? ((-1, -1))
Find the midpoint of a pair of coordinates.	What is the midpoint of (-3.2, 4.6) and (2.4, -3.2)? ((-0.4, 0.7))
Plot the graph of an implicit function.	Draw the lines $x + 4y = 6$ and $y = 3x - 5$ on the same graph. Where do these lines meet? ((2, 1))
Plot and interpret graphs of real-life situations.	Sketch a graph showing the speed of a cyclist going from school into the centre of town. (Check for correct features in the graph)
Plot and interpret time series graphs.	Sketch a graph showing how the number of music downloads have changed over the last five years, including any seasonal variation each year. (Upward trend, possibly getting steeper, showing peaks at Christmas time)

MyMaths extra support

Lesson/online homework			Description
Conversion graphs	1059	L6	Using conversion graphs
Coordinates 2	1093	L5	Coordinates in the four quadrants, midpoint of a line

Question commentary

Question 1 – Allow students to choose the most suitable scale for themselves. Check they number each axis evenly.
Question 2 – Remind them to check by substituting $x = 5$ into the equation and calculating the y value.
Question 3 – Use the word *gradient* when describing the steepness of the slope.
Question 4 – Remind students that gradient means how many squares the line moves up or down for every square it moves across.
Question 5 – Encourage good sketching techniques, even from this stage. Later, in external exams, marks will be lost for joining with straight lines and feathering. Encourage a smooth, single curve. It does take practice.
Question 8 – Students can rearrange equations using the balance method, when dividing or multiplying make sure they do it to *every* term, e.g. **d** is not $y = 26 + 7x$ or $y = 13 + 14x$ (watch out for students dividing by 2 instead here also).
Question 9 – Students should not need to rearrange or draw a table of values, just work out where the graph crosses the coordinate axes.

Question 10 – It would be best to make the y-axis 'distance from home' but 'distance from school' would also work (graph would be 'upside-down').

MyReview

6 MySummary

Check out
You should now be able to ...

	Test it ➡ Questions
✓ Plot the graph of a linear function and use the equation of a straight line.	1 - 4
✓ Plot the graph of a non-linear function.	5
✓ Find the midpoint of a pair of coordinates.	6, 7
✓ Plot the graph of an implicit function.	8, 9
✓ Plot and interpret graphs of real life situations.	10
✓ Plot and interpret time series graphs.	11

Language	Meaning	Example
Linear function	A function whose graph is always a straight line	$y = mx + c$
Gradient	The slope of a line	If $y = mx + c$, m is the gradient
Intercept	Where a line touches the x-axis or y-axis	If $y = mx + c$, c is the intercept with the y-axis
Midpoint	The point that lies halfway between its two endpoints	The midpoint of the line joining (1, 4) and (7, 8) is (4, 6)
Parabola	The shape you get if you plot a quadratic function	$y = x^2$
Explicit equation	An equation where y is the subject	$y = 2x + 1$, $y = mx + c$, $y = 3x^2$
Implicit equation	An equation where y is not the subject	$2y + 3x = 5$, $y - c = mx$, $y = x + y^3$
Distance-time graph	A graph where time is plotted on the x-axis and distance is plotted on the y-axis	See p. 112

6 MyReview

1 For the equation $y = 4x - 5$

a copy and complete the table

x	0	1	2	3
y				

b plot the graph of the equation.

2 Does the line $y = 5x - 2$ pass through the point (3, 12)?

3 For each equation write down its slope and where it crosses the y-axis.

a $y = 7x + 3$ **b** $y = x - 4$

c $y = 8 - 2x$ **d** $y = \frac{1}{2}x$

e $y = 5$ **f** $y = 5x + 4$

4 Find the equations of each of these straight lines.

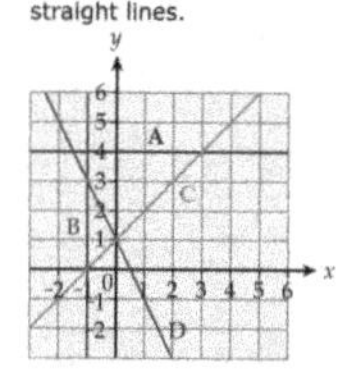

5 **a** Copy and complete the table of values for the equation $y = x^2 - 1$

x	-3	-2	-1	0	1	2	3
x^2							
-1							
y							

b Use the table to draw the graph of the equation

6 Find the midpoints of these pairs of points.

a (5, 8) and (13, 11)

b (3, -6) and (-8, -2)

7 M (8, 3) is the centre of the square ABCD. The coordinates of A are (5, 7).

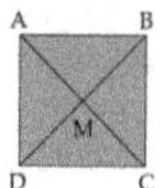

What are the coordinates of C?

8 Rearrange these to make y the subject.

a $x + y = 11$ **b** $2x + 3y = 18$

c $15 - 5y = 10x$ **d** $\frac{y}{2} - 7x = 13$

9 Plot the graph of $3x + y = 9$

10 Kat leaves her school which is 3 km from her home at 15:15. She takes 25 minutes to walk 2 km towards her home with a friend. She then stops at the friend's house for 15 minutes. Kat walks the rest of the way home at a speed of 6 km per hour.

Draw this journey on a distance-time graph.

What next?

Score		
0 - 4		Your knowledge of this topic is still developing. To improve look at Formative test: 2C-6; MyMaths: 1153, 1168, 1184, 1311, 1312, 1314, 1316 and 1322
5 - 8		You are gaining a secure knowledge of this topic. To improve look at InvisiPen: 256, 265, 266, 273, 275 and 278
9 - 10		You have mastered this topic. Well done, you are ready to progress!

Answers

1 a

x	0	1	2	3
y	-5	-1	3	7

b

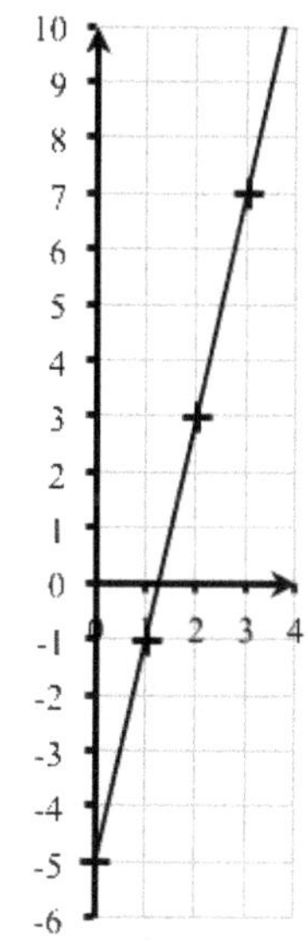

2 No

3 a Slope 7, y-axis 3

b Slope 1, y-axis -4

c Slope -2, y-axis 8

d Slope $\frac{1}{2}$, y-axis 0

e Slope 0, y-axis 5

f Slope 5, y-axis 4

4 Line A $y = 4$

Line B $x = -1$

Line C $y = x + 1$

Line D $y = 1 - 2x$

5 a

x	-3	-2	-1	0	1	2	3
x^2	9	4	1	0	1	4	9
−1	−1	−1	−1	−1	−1	−1	−1
y	8	3	0	-1	0	3	8

b

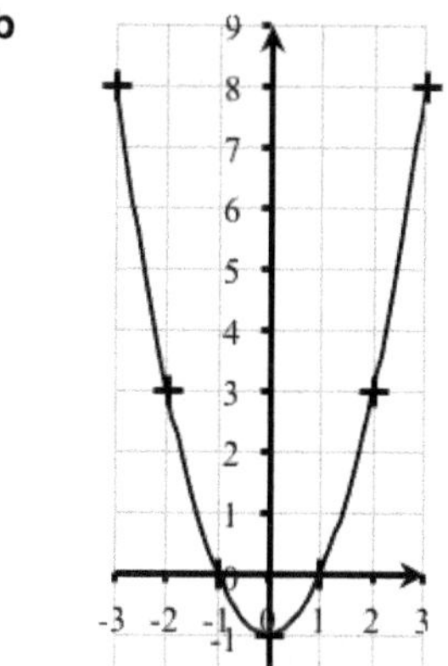

6 a (9, 9.5) **b** (-2.5, -4)

7 (11, -1)

8 a $y = 11 - x$ **b** $y = 6 - \frac{2}{3}x$

c $y = 3 - 2x$ **d** $y = 26 + 14x$

9

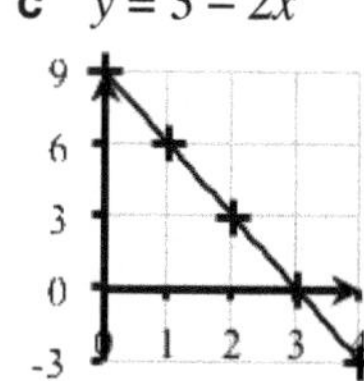

10 Students' distance–time graphs of Kat's journey

6 MyPractice

6a

1 **a** Copy and complete the table of values for the equation $y = 2x + 1$.

x	0	1	2
$2x$			
$+1$			
y	1		

b Plot these points on a set of coordinate axes with x and y values from 0 to 8. Join your points with a straight line.

c On the same set of axes, plot the graph of $y = 7 - x$.

d Write the coordinates of the point of intersection of these graphs.

2 True or false?
The graphs of the functions $x = 2$ and $y = -3$ intersect at the point (-3, 2).

6b

3 Write the gradient and y-intercept of these straight lines.

a $y = 2x + 1$ **b** $y = 3x - 2$

c $y = \frac{1}{2}x + 5$ **d** $y = 8x$

e $y = x - 2$ **f** $y = 4 - 3x$

g $y = 1 - \frac{1}{3}x$ **h** $y = 3(2 - x)$

4 Find the equation of each of these straight lines.

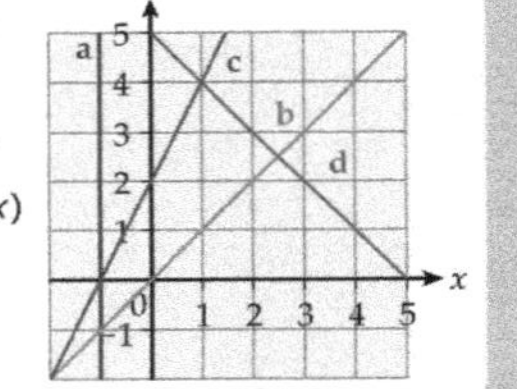

6c

5 True or false?
The graph of the function $y = x^2 + 5x + 6$ passes through the point (1, 12).
Explain your answer.

6 **a** Copy and complete the table of values for the equation $y = x^2 - x$.

x	-2	-1	0	1	2	3
x^2	4					
$-x$	2					
y	6					

b Plot these points on a set of coordinate axes with x-values from -3 to 4 and y-values from -1 to 8.
Join the points with a smooth curve.

c Write the coordinates of the points where the line $y = x^2 - x$ cuts the x-axis.

d Write the equation of the vertical line about which $y = x^2 - x$ is symmetrical.

6d

7 M is the midpoint of the line segment AB.
Find M or B given the following information.

a $A(4, 2)$ $B\,(6, 4)$ **b** $A(-1, 7)$ $B\,(3, 3)$

c $A(5, 6)$ $B\,(1, -2)$ **d** $A(-2, -3)$ $B\,(-4, 2)$

e $A(-2, -1)$ $M\,(0, 1)$ **f** $A(6, 4)$ $M\,(2, 2)$

6e

8 **a** Copy and complete the tables and plot the graphs of these implicit functions on the same set of axes.

$x + y = 5$

x	0	1	2
y			

$5x - y = 1$

x	0	1	2
y			

b Write the coordinates of the point of intersection of these graphs.

c Show that the coordinates of the point of intersection satisfy each equation.

6f

9 Patrick leaves his home at 08:00. He jogs 3 km in 20 mins and then stops for 30 mins to have breakfast at a local café. Patrick sprints home in 10 mins. Patrick's wife, Giselle, leaves home at 08:15. She runs to the same café as Patrick in 15 mins and joins her husband for breakfast. Giselle leaves at the same time as Patrick and quickly walks back home, arriving at 09:15.

a Draw each of these journeys on the same distance-time graph.

b How long did Patrick and Giselle spend together over breakfast?

c Calculate the average speed at which

i Patrick ran home **ii** Giselle walked home.

6g

10 Karim runs a newsagent which sells CDs. The time series graph shows the number sold recently in each quarter. Describe two features of the graph.

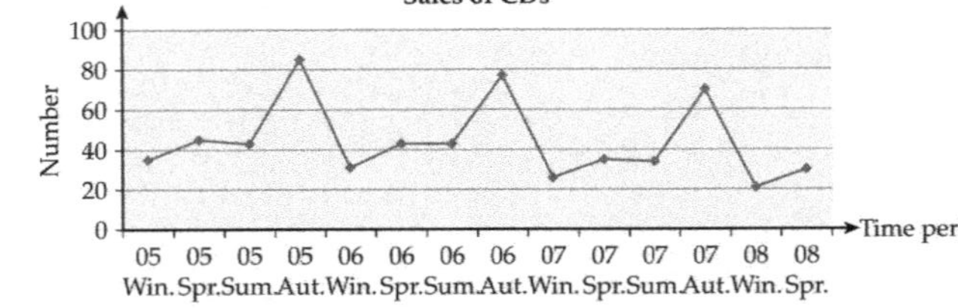

Question commentary

Question 2 – Ask students to justify their answer.

Question 4 – Remind students that gradient means how many squares up or down for every square across from left to right.

Question 5 – Remind students to substitute $x = 5$ into the equation and check the value of y.

Question 6 – Drawing graphs is a skill that students will need practice on. Encourage students to draw single curves without feathering.

Question 10 – Encourage associated language.

Answers

1 **a**

x	0	1	2
$2x$	0	2	4
$+1$	1	1	1
y	1	3	5

b Students' graphs of function given by table of values

c Graph of $y = 7 - x$ plotted on the same axes

d (2, 5)

2 False. The lines intersect where $x = 2$ and $y = -3$, (2, -3)

3 **a** 2, 1 **b** 3, -2 **c** $\frac{1}{2}$, 5 **d** 8, 0

e 1, -2 **f** -3, 4 **g** $-\frac{1}{3}$, 1 **h** -3, 6

4 **a** $x = -1$ **b** $y = x$

c $y = 2x + 2$ **d** $y = 5 - x$

5 True. When $x = 1$, $y = 1^2 + (5 \times 1) + 6 = 12$.

6 **a**

x	-2	-1	0	1	2	3
x^2	4	1	0	1	4	9
$-x$	2	1	0	−1	−2	−3
y	6	2	0	0	2	6

b Students' graphs of function given by table of values joined in a smooth curve

c (0, 0), (1, 0)

d $x = \frac{1}{2}$

7 **a** M (5, 3) **b** M (1, 5)

c M (3, 2) **d** M $(-3, -\frac{1}{2})$

e B (2, 3) **f** B (-2, 0)

8 **a**

x	0	1	2
y	5	4	3
x	0	1	2
y	-1	4	9

b (1, 4) **c** $1 + 4 = 5, 5 - 4 = 1$

9 **a** Students' distance–time graphs of Patrick's and Giselle's journeys

b 20 minutes

c **i** Patrick 18 km/h **ii** Giselle 7.2 km/h

10 Sales peaked each autumn. There has been a downward trend in sales from 2005 to 2007.

Related lessons		Resources	
Properties of a triangle and a quadrilateral	5b	Interior exterior angles	(1100)
Properties of a polygon	5c	Sum of angles in a polygon	(1320)
Congruent shapes	5d	Symmetry	(1230)
Symmetry	9c	Congruent triangles	(1148)
		Examples of patchwork	
		Isometric paper	

Simplification	Extension
Task **2** parts **b** and **c** could be scaffolded or omitted. Students could work on squared or isometric paper for task **3** to aid their designing. Patterns based on shapes other than the square could be omitted.	Ask students to find the internal angles in regular polygons, from equilateral triangle to dodecagon. ($60°, 90°, 108°, 120°, 128\frac{4}{7}°, 135°, 140°, 144°, 147\frac{3}{11}°, 150°$) Using knowledge of these angles ask students to see how many polygons of one type they can fit exactly around a point. (6 equilateral triangles; 4 squares; 3 hexagons). If you can use two polygons how many possibilities are there now? (2 squares and 3 equilateral triangles (two ways); 1 or 2 hexagons and 4 or 2 equilateral triangles; 2 octagons and 1 square; 2 dodecagons and 1 equilateral triangle) Can you use this knowledge to create six semi-regular tessellations? Can you find the other two semi-regular tessellations? (Based on 1 equilateral triangle, 2 squares and 1 hexagon or 1 square, 1 hexagon and 1 dodecagon)

Links

Students could research the work of the Dutch artist M C Esher and identify any of his work that they think is based on tessellation. Alternatively, they can look at tessellations they meet in everyday life or the Islamic art of the Alhambra Palace in Spain. http://www.alhambra-patronato.es/

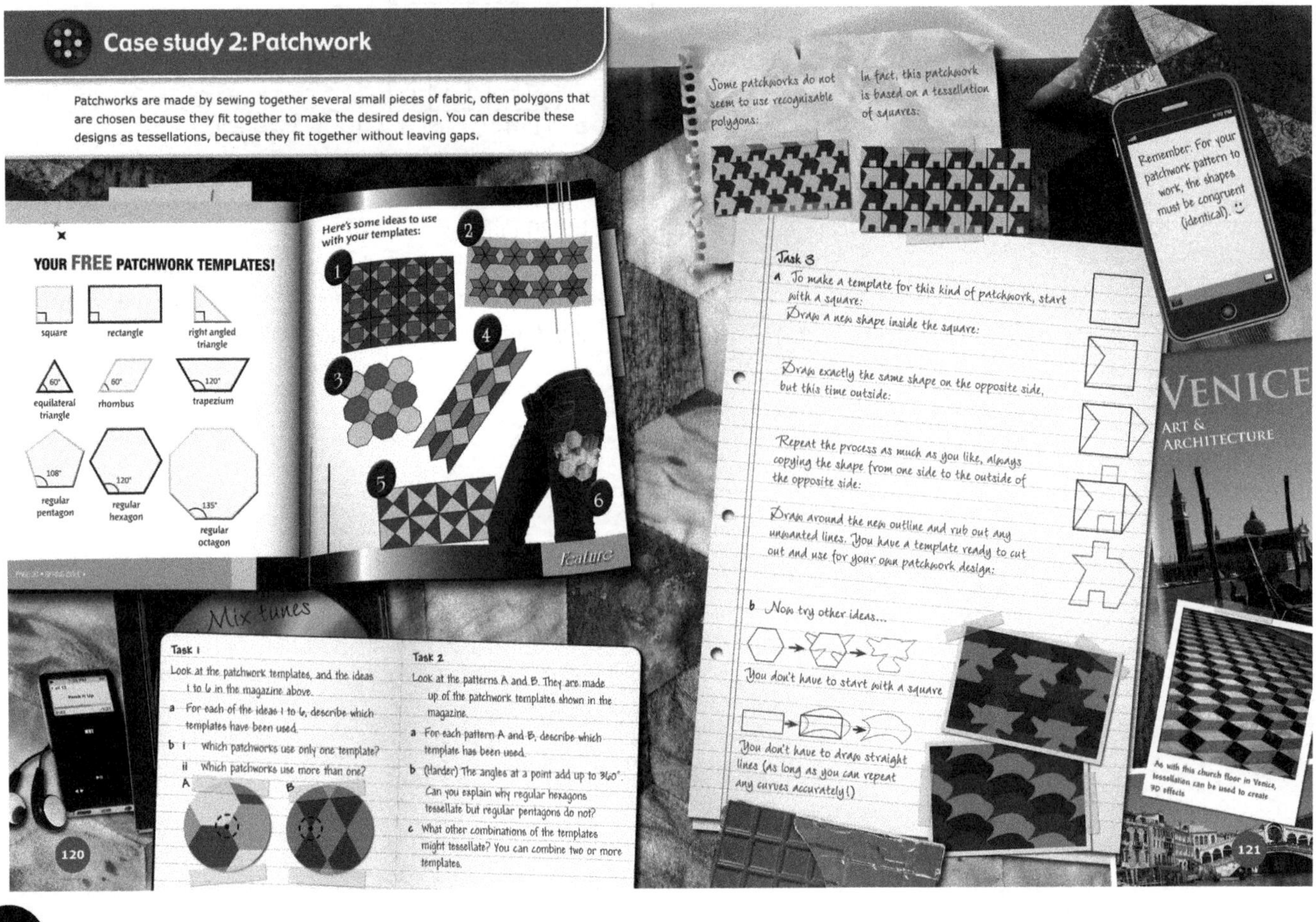

Case study 2: Patchwork

Patchworks are made by sewing together several small pieces of fabric, often polygons that are chosen because they fit together to make the desired design. You can describe these designs as tessellations, because they fit together without leaving gaps.

YOUR FREE PATCHWORK TEMPLATES!

square, rectangle, right angled triangle, equilateral triangle, rhombus, trapezium, regular pentagon, regular hexagon, regular octagon

Here's some ideas to use with your templates:

Some patchworks do not seem to use recognizable polygons:

In fact, this patchwork is based on a tessellation of squares:

Remember: For your patchwork pattern to work, the shapes must be congruent (identical).

Task 3

a To make a template for this kind of patchwork, start with a square: Draw a new shape inside the square:

Draw exactly the same shape on the opposite side, but this time outside:

Repeat the process as much as you like, always copying the shape from one side to the outside of the opposite side:

Draw around the new outline and rub out any unwanted lines. You have a template ready to cut out and use for your own patchwork design:

b Now try other ideas...

You don't have to start with a square

You don't have to draw straight lines (as long as you can repeat any curves accurately!)

VENICE ART & ARCHITECTURE

As with this church floor in Venice, tessellation can be used to create 3D effects

Task 1

Look at the patchwork templates, and the ideas 1 to 6 in the magazine above.

a For each of the ideas 1 to 6, describe which templates have been used.

b i Which patchworks use only one template?

ii Which patchworks use more than one?

Task 2

Look at the patterns A and B. They are made up of the patchwork templates shown in the magazine.

a For each pattern A and B, describe which template has been used.

b (Harder) The angles at a point add up to 360°. Can you explain why regular hexagons tessellate but regular pentagons do not?

c What other combinations of the templates might tessellate? You can combine two or more templates.

Teaching notes

Patchworks are mainly done as hobbies these days. In times of hardship, patchworks have been used as a way of recycling old clothes to make blankets and such like. Patchworks are often quite geometric in design. A person making the patchwork needs to consider how shapes fit together and often uses a template to make pieces of consistent size and shape. Similar considerations apply to designs using paving stones. This case study uses this geometric nature of patchworks to look at a shapes' internal angles and consider how these determine if a given shape will tessellate.

Introduce the idea of patchworks and remind students about tessellation. Look at the shapes that are used in typical patchworks and discuss what makes the shapes suitable for this purpose.

Look at the case study, focusing initially on the magazine and its free templates. What do you notice about the sizes of the templates? Agree that their dimensions are such that any shape will fit exactly with another.

How long do you think the rectangle is compared with its width? Establish that it is twice as long as it is wide so that it can be used alongside two squares or other shapes. How do you think the lengths of the sides of the trapezium relate to each other? The longer side is twice as long as the shorter sides, which are all the same length as each other. Why do you think the rhombus and the trapezium have both been made with an angle of 60°? Establish that the equilateral triangle has to have an angle of 60° and that if the rhombus and trapezium are going to fit with the triangle, they too have to have an angle of 60°.

Task 1

Now look at the example patchworks and ask students to think about which templates have been used in each patchwork. Give the students a few minutes to note their answers to this before discussing answers. Some students might have considered the lighter spaces in patchworks 2 and 3 as gaps while others might have included them as shapes and named their templates.

Task 2

Use the questions to initiate thinking about the angles in shapes and how these determine whether the shape will tessellate. Ask questions such as why will some shapes tessellate and others not? Is it just to do with the length of their sides or is it also to do with their angles? What is it about the angles of shapes that allow them to be used on their own?

Task 3

To make a template based on a square follow the instructions. Make sure that students understand how the method requires a new shape to be drawn **inside** the shape on one side and **outside** the shape on the other, and that the two shapes are aligned with each other. Look at the two tessellation examples at the end of the instructions to see how the original shape doesn't have to be a square. What shapes could you start with? Establish that the initial shape needs to be one that tessellates.

Answers

1 a 1 Square, right-angled triangle
2 Isosceles trapezium and rhombus
3 Regular octagon and square
4 Square and isosceles trapezium
5 Right-angled triangle
6 Regular hexagon

b i 5, 6 **ii** 1, 2, 3, 4

2 a **A** Hexagon **B** Rhombus

b To tessellate, a shape's interior angle must divide evenly into 360, since there are 360° at a point.

Hexagon: $\frac{360}{120} = 3$, therefore hexagons tessellate;

Pentagon: $\frac{360}{108} = 3.333\ldots$, therefore pentagons do not tessellate.

c Lots of possible answers

3 Students' own answers

7 Mental calculations

Learning outcomes

N2 Order positive and negative integers, decimals and fractions; use the number line as a model for ordering of the real numbers; use the symbols $=, \neq, <, >, \leq, \geq$ (L5)

N4 Use the 4 operations, including formal written methods, applied to integers, decimals, proper and improper fractions, and mixed numbers, all both positive and negative (L6)

N5 Use conventional notation for the priority of operations, including brackets, powers, roots and reciprocals (L6)

N14 Use approximation through rounding to estimate answers and calculate possible resulting errors expressed using inequality notation $a < x \leq b$ (L6)

Introduction

The chapter starts by looking at negative number arithmetic. Multiplying and dividing by powers of 10 are then covered before moving on to mental methods for addition and subtraction of decimals. Multiplication and division of decimals using mental methods is covered in the final section.

The introduction discusses the historical background of calculation and gives a brief history of mechanical calculation devices, including the first mechanical calculator invented by Blaise Pascal in 1642. The development of machines to help perform complex calculations has been a major part of the history of calculation over the last 300 years and eventually led to the development of the high-powered calculators and computers that we use today. Mathematicians such as Ada Lovelace (1815-1852), Charles Babbage (1791-1871) and Alan Turing (1912-1954) are all credited with significant contributions to the development of mechanical calculators and the eventual development of computers as we know them today. Biographies of these eminent mathematicians can be found at:

http://www-history.mcs.st-and.ac.uk/Biographies/Lovelace.html

http://www-history.mcs.st-andrews.ac.uk/Biographies/Babbage.html

http://www-history.mcs.st-andrews.ac.uk/Biographies/Turing.html

Prior knowledge

Students should already know how to...

- Add, subtract, multiply and divide whole numbers and decimals
- Use written methods for multiplication and division, including decimals

Starter problem

The starter problem is a classic example of a 'Route inspection' problem, often called 'The Chinese Postman' problem (so-called not because of a Chinese postman, but because it was originally studied by a Chinese mathematician, Kwan Mei-Ko, in 1962).

The development of efficient algorithms to solve this kind of problem forms part of a branch of mathematics called 'discrete mathematics'.

Beginning and ending at A, the postman must cover all of the streets at least once. It can be shown that he will not be able to cover each street once only, but that he must walk along some streets more than once. If he repeats streets DE and HF, he can complete the route in the shortest distance. This is equal to the total length of all the streets, plus 0.9 km (DE again) and 1.5 km (HF again). The total distance is therefore16.7 km.

A possible route would be: AHFHGFEGABCDEDA but there are many others.

More able students could be asked to work out a route which visits each vertex once (the 'Travelling salesman' problem) or be given more complex examples of these kinds of problems.

Resources

MyMaths

Estimating introduction	1002	Multiplying decimals by 10 and 100.	1013
Multiply triple digits	1026	Negative numbers 2	1068
Adding decimals mental	1380		

Online assessment

Chapter test	2C–7
Formative test	2C–7
Summative test	2C–7

InvisiPen solutions

Negative numbers	113
Mental methods of addition and subtraction	121
Mental multiplication	122
Powers of 10	182

Topic scheme

Teaching time = 4 lessons/2 weeks

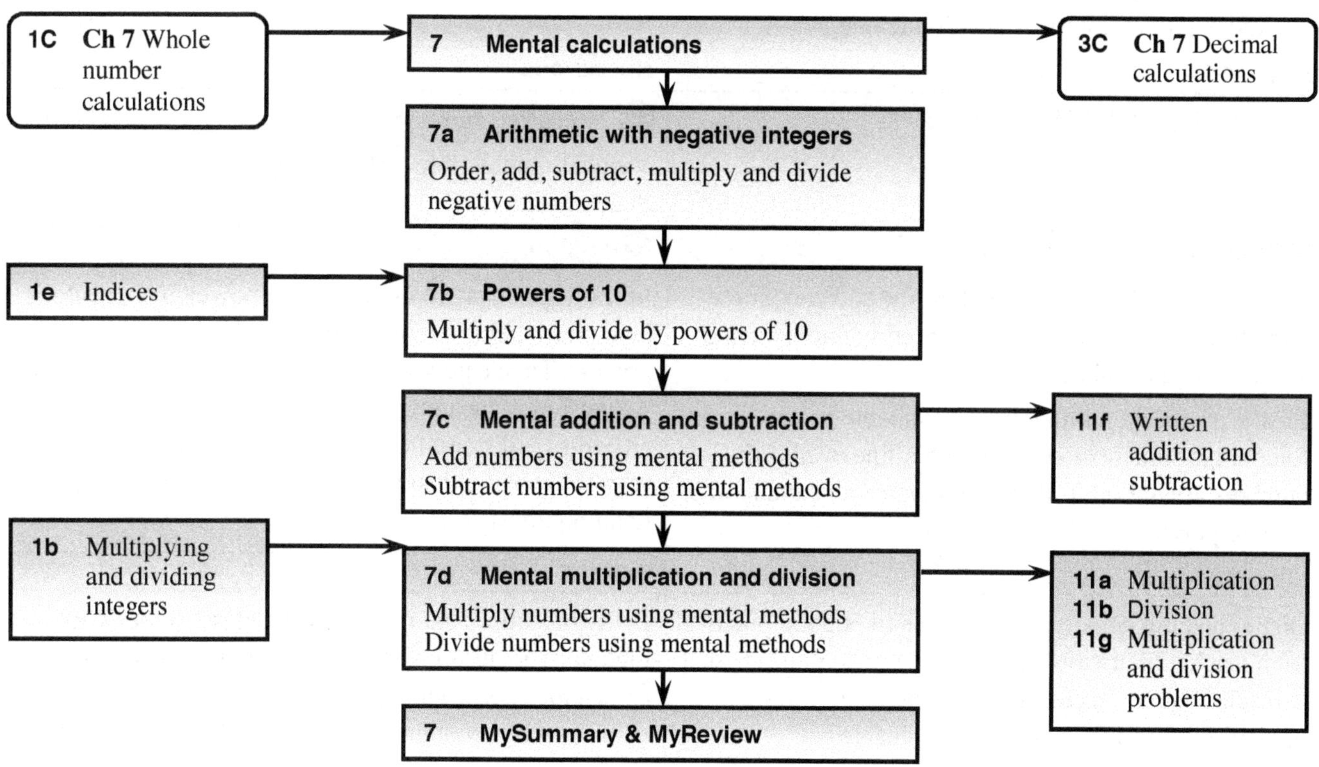

Differentiation

Student book 2A 128 – 143

Order of operations
Mental addition and subtraction
Mental multiplication and division
Addition and subtraction problems
Multiplication and division problems

Student book 2B 116 – 133

Rounding
Mental addition and subtraction
Multiply and divide by powers of 10
Mental multiplication and division
Mental addition and subtraction problems
Mental multiplication and division problems

Student book 2C 122 – 135

Arithmetic with negative integers
Powers of 10
Mental addition and subtraction
Mental multiplication and division

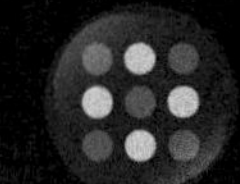

7a Arithmetic with negative integers

Objectives	
• Order decimals	(L5)
• Add, subtract, multiply and divide integers	(L5)

Key ideas	Resources
1 Four operations with negative integers	Negative numbers 2 (1068) Vertical number line (-10 to +10) Sheet music

Simplification	Extension
Give students a copy of a number line and encourage them to write on it to help with ordering numbers and also adding and subtracting. Ensure a vertical number line is available somewhere. Encourage students to use a number line even if the numbers are not on it: they can imagine an extension of it, as required.	Investigate negative numbers to a power. This could lead on to the difference between odd and even powers. Take care with the notation -2^2 which can have two different meanings, and can give two different answers on different calculators. Can students tell why? How should such calculations be entered, unambiguously?

Literacy	Links
Distinguishing negative from minus (it is good practice for a teacher to always use 'negative' when this is what is meant, but not necessary to ask pupils to do so), perhaps as adjective and verb, is valuable.	Bring in some sheet music for the class to use. The inequality signs are similar to the musical symbols *crescendo* (becoming louder) and *decrescendo* or *diminuendo* (becoming softer). Ask the class to find examples on the music.

Alternative approach

Check that students are looking at the sign associated with the number, on its left. Ask students why there is no sign in front of zero or positive numbers – in example **2**, for example. Show that when there are two adjacent –ve signs, one can be turned to be vertical and placed on the other, to make a +ve sign.

Seeing whether calculators can do this work correctly can be helpful – because it then becomes necessary to distinguish negative from minus (as well as necessary to key into the calculator in a way that will work), which helps with use of the number line.

Focus on the procedure of starting point, then up for adding, and down for minus or subtracting (the movement matching the idea of a verb), establishing this firmly; and then, perhaps as with negatives of photos (if enough of them know what these are), or as in the concept of negative (check what they understand by this idea, separately from numbers), simply say that adding or subtracting negative numbers goes the opposite way, in each and every case.

The difference between the smallest to biggest continuum and the least to greatest continuum is important for questions **1** and **2**. It is good practice for a teacher to use 'least' and 'greatest' rather than 'smallest' and 'biggest', when that is what is meant.

Checkpoint	
1 Calculate $(-8 \times -3) - (56 \div -4) + (9 \times -4)$.	(2)

Starter

Choose a number with one digit after the decimal place between -15 and +15.

Invite students to guess the number.

After each guess say whether the next guess should be higher or lower.

This can be extended by increasing the number of decimal places.

Teaching notes

A time counter begins to count down from 10 seconds to minus 10 seconds in thousandths of a second. Three people separately have a go at stopping the timer exactly on zero. Suggest three times and decide who is closest by comparing place value. Does the largest error correspond to the largest number, whether positive or negative? But which is the greatest value?

When adding and subtracting with negatives, many students confuse the rules. '*Two minuses make a plus*' is a common misconception, but -3 + -6 makes a negative result. Rules will always have such drawbacks. However, explain that '*adding a negative*' means '*take away*', but '*subtracting a negative*' means add. The first number is where you **start**, the second number is **how far** you move. Using the number line as an aid, students should write down question/working/answer. For example, -3 + -6 → -3 – 6 → -9.

When multiplying and dividing ensure students realise the rules are different from adding and subtracting. The rules '*signs different, so negative*', '*signs same, so positive*' can be used. Multiplying by -1 can be seen as a reflection in the number line about zero. This can help explain why minus × minus gives a positive result.

Plenary

Add the numbers 1, -2, 3, -4, etc., up to a certain limit. Is there a quick way to find the result? Is the rule different if the last number is odd or even? Encourage students to examine the positive and negative numbers as two different sets. If the sequence summed to 100 could you tell what the last number was? (199)

Exercise commentary

Question 1 – Students may need help remembering which way the < and > signs go. Tell them to remember the greedy crocodile always tries to eat the biggest number.

Question 2 – If any student is struggling with the concept of negative numbers and wants to put the modulus in order, rather than the actual number, make use of number lines. Vertical number lines can help clarify even further.

Question 3 – When helping students, avoid the phrase 'two minuses make a plus'. This often leads to confusion. The idea of directed number is much more helpful. The first number gives the starting place on the number line. Start going up and then every negative sign means change direction.

Question 4 – Again avoid the phrase 'two minuses make a plus' although it does lead to less confusion with multiplying and dividing. Amplify the phrase by saying 'If one number is positive and one negative then the answer is negative. If they are both the same then it is positive.' Expressing this symbolically is helpful: + × + = +, + × - = -, etc.

Question 5 – Answers can be checked by asking a partner to work out the answer, for example **5a**, ask 'what is 8 + -8?'

Question 6 – Tell students they must use at least one negative number in each sum, to ensure they are practising using directed number.

Question 7 – Ask the students to place their numbers along the top of the grid in ascending order and down the side in descending order. Also, if they include two positive numbers and two negative each time, the products will produce a clear pattern, with the negative products in the top left and bottom right. This visually helps re-enforce the rules for multiplying and dividing negative numbers.

Question 8 – Although this question does not need a calculator, it is good to show students how to enter negative numbers on a scientific calculator. Using the subtraction operation button to enter a negative number can lead to error. Have students always enter negative numbers using the (-) function button.

Answers

1 **a** < **b** > **c** > **d** <
e > **f** <

2 **a** -3 -2 -1.8 1.5 5
b -3.8 -3.4 -3.2 -3 -2.7
c -5.3 -5.28 -5.25 -5.2 5.4

3 **a** -4 **b** -21 **c** 7 **d** 9
e -34 **f** 6 **g** -5 **h** -7
i -7

4 **a** -36 **b** -180 **c** 84 **d** 105
e 50 **f** -51 **g** 23 **h** -32

5 **a** 8 **b** -2 **c** 15 **d** -91
e -16 **f** -14 **g** -30 **h** -6
i 24

6 Students' answers

7 **a**

×	-8	2	-7	3
-6	48	-12	42	-18
-5	40	-10	**35**	-15
-4	32	-8	28	-12
9	-72	18	-63	27

×	8	2	-7	-3
-6	-48	-12	42	18
-5	-40	-10	**35**	15
4	32	8	-28	-12
-9	-72	-18	63	27

b Students' multiplication grids and suggestions for what is the least information required for a unique solution.

8 **a** -30 **b** 256 **c** -1 **d** -1
e -22 **f** 54

7b Powers of 10

Objectives	
• Extend knowledge of integer powers of 10	(L6)
• Recognise the equivalence of 0.1, 1/10 and 10^{-1}	(L6)
• Multiply and divide by any integer power of 10	(L6)

Key ideas	Resources
1 Multiplying and dividing by powers of 10	Multiply decimals by 10 and 100 (1013)

Simplification	Extension
It is very important that students 'understand' what is being asked and are not just getting answers correct by replicating a method. Focus on the simpler questions and ask students to show that they understand by explaining what is being asked for. Encourage the breaking up of a question into stages.	Write the conversions for the standard metric measurements of length, mass and capacity using standard form. For example, 1×10^2 cm = 1 m, 1×10^5 cm = 1 km, etc.

Literacy	Links
A reminder of what is meant by powers, and by index notation, could be appropriate.	Number 10 Downing Street in London is the official residence of the First Lord of the Treasury, who is usually also the prime minister of Great Britain. See, http://www.number10.gov.uk/history-and-tour

Alternative approach

Before considering the rules offered, ask students what happens when multiplying by a number greater than 1, and by a (positive) number less than 1, first in general terms of size – will the number multiplied become larger, or smaller? – and then in terms of the ratio. Then, what about dividing by a number greater than 1, and by a number smaller than 1, in the same way.

Checkpoint

1 Use the fact that $123 \times 456 = 56\,088$ to write down the following.

a	12.3×45.6	(560.88)
b	1230×4.56	(5608.8)
c	$56.088 \div 4.56$	(12.3)
d	$1.23 \times 10^{-2} \times 4.56 \times 10^4$	(560.88)

Starter

Ask students to add up numbers you read out that are **not** multiples of 7. For example,

16, 21, 23, 7, 28, 34, 15, -3, 35, 11, 5, 14, -11, 49, 17 (total excluding multiples of 7 = 107)

This can be differentiated by the choice of multiple and numbers.

Teaching notes

Look at the sequence created by descending power of 10, beginning with 10 cubed

$$10^3 \xrightarrow{\div 10} 10^2 \xrightarrow{\div 10} 10^1 \xrightarrow{\div 10} 10^0 \xrightarrow{\div 10} 10^{-1} \xrightarrow{\div 10} 10^{-2} \xrightarrow{\div 10} 10^{-3}$$

1000   100   10   1   0.1   0.01   0.001

What happens when you multiply by a positive power of 10? Look at integer and decimal examples. What happens to a number when you multiply it by a number between 0 and 1?

What happens when you divide by a positive power of 10? Look at integer and decimal examples. What happens to a number when you divide it by a number between 0 and 1? For example, 4 ÷ 0.01. What does 0.01 represent? What does the question mean? How many hundredths in 4 units? Since the answer is 400, what effect does ÷ 0.01 have? Multiplication by 100. This question can also be written as $4 \div 10^{-2}$.

Question students' understanding of what is happening when multiplying or dividing by a number between 0 and 1. Discourage students from just slavishly following the rules.

Plenary

This method can be used for writing very large numbers in a simpler way. For example, the world's population, to the nearest million, was estimated to be 7 189 000 000 (October 2013). In what ways could this be written using a power of ten? Should you include the six zeros? Which is called the '**standard**' way and is used around the world? Ask students for their views.

Exercise commentary

Question 1 – Ask students to try and explain the meaning of the questions. For example, 26 × 0.1 is 26 lots of 0.1 making 2.6. What has happened to the starting number 26? For example, 388 ÷ 0.1 is how many 0.1s or tenths in 388?

Questions 2–4 – Show students that the power of ten indicates how many places the digits must be moved. When multiplying, a positive index moves the digits from right to left and a negative index moves them from left to right. When dividing, the reverse is true.

Question 5 – Again encourage students to recognise that the power of 10 indicates how many places and in what direction the digits have been moved. Supplement with more quick fire questions if needed.

Question 6 – This is a popular way for examiners to test understanding, so it is worth spending extra time on this.

Question 7 – Use this question to reinforce the properties of powers of 10.

Question 8 – This question lays the foundation for writing numbers in standard form. You may wish to make mention of this, explaining that this is how scientists write very big or very small numbers. For example the number of atoms in the universe is approximately 10^{89}. Chose a student to write this number out in full on the board!

Answers

1 **a** 2.6 **b** 3380 **c** 0.47 **d** 53
 e 2850 **f** 82 **g** 2.54 **h** 0.038

2 **a** 2800 **b** 3000 **c** 2.75 **d** 4.17
 e 8300 **f** 420 **g** 3.77 **h** 2.51
 i 320 **j** 1070 **k** 0.041 **l** 3.8

3 **a** 2.9 **b** 0.38 **c** 0.51 **d** 0.032
 e 360 **f** 92 **g** 6500 **h** 51
 i 31.7 **j** 29.9 **k** 0.0815 **l** 0.00602

4 **a** 3300 **b** 24 000
 c 47 000 **d** 630 000
 e 27 000 000 **f** 0.0047
 g 0.000029 **h** 1 010 000 000

5 **a** 10^2 **b** 10^{-2} **c** 10^2 **d** 10^{-2}
 e 10^{-3} **f** 10^{-1}

6 **a** 2322.6 **b** 2.3226 **c** 232.26
 d Students' answers **e** Students' answers

7 **a** Students' answers
 b Students' answers; move the digits to the right.

8 **a** 4 800 000 **b** 2000
 c 200 **d** 0.9

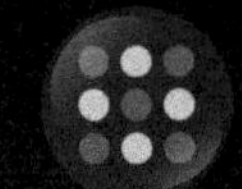

7c Mental addition and subtraction

Objectives	
• Extend mental methods of calculation, working with decimals	(L5)
• Solve problems mentally	(L6)
• Make and justify estimates and approximations of calculations	(L6)

Key ideas	Resources
1 Mental addition and subtraction of integers and decimals	Adding decimals mental (1380)

Simplification	Extension
Encourage students to see that there are many different methods available, for example by asking them to mentally add 17 and 25.Students should not say the answer, but say how they did it. Did anyone try two 20s + 5 – 3? Or 17 + 23 + 2? And so on. Help students to identify the order in which the information needs to be taken in question **4**.	Calculate this series as far as you can. 12.8 – 6.4 + 3.2 – 1.6 + 0.8 – 0.4 + 0.2 – 0.1 +… What do you think you get if you go on forever? (6.4, 9.6, 8, 8.8, 8.4, 8.6, 8.5, 8.55, 8.525, 8.5375, 8.53125, 8.534375, 8.532813, 8.533594, 8.533203, 8.533398, 8.533301, 8.533350, 3.533325, 8.533337, … $8\frac{8}{15}$ = 8.53333…)

Literacy	Links
Partitioning here could be represented as 'one bit at a time', and compensation as 'a bigger bit, then back a bit'. In practice, more imaginative variations may be appropriate. The terms are probably of little consequence; the important thing is to always look for neat methods.	The world record for adding 100 single digit numbers randomly generated by a computer is 19.23 seconds and is held by Alberto Coto from Spain. Details of other mental calculation World records can be found at http://www.recordholders.org/en/list/memory.html#adding10digits

Alternative approach

Try the first example, part **a**, by compensation (+ 9, – 0.2). Is this as good a method? How about part **b**, by partitioning? Encourage students to always try to spot which is the easiest method for them.

In the second example, is there any point in taking any notice of the £8, when we are approximating a figure in the thousands? Would £1000 do as an estimate?

Checkpoint

1 Jack lives 3.8 km from school. Amir lives 2.6 km further away.

a How far from school does Amir live? (6.4 km)

Maisie lives 8.2 km from school.

b How much closer does Amir live than Maisie? (1.8 km)

Starter

Ask students

to estimate the number of seconds in July

to calculate the number of seconds in July

(2 678 400)

How close were their estimates? What was the average error? Are older students more likely to be accurate than younger students? Are girls more accurate than boys?

Teaching notes

Ask students what number bonds they use to help with addition, such as, $4 + 6 = 10$, $8 + 7 = 15$. When summing decimals, ask students to describe any mental methods they use, for example,
$6.9 + 12.3 = (7 + 12.3) - 0.1$,
$3.42 + 5.5 = (3 + 5) + (0.42 + 0.5)$. When subtracting decimals, ask students for their strategies, for example, $4.24 - 1.98 = (4.24 - 2) + 0.02$.

When adding or subtracting with different units, what strategies do students use?
For example, 1.23 m + 43 cm + 0.54 m

When summing a long line of figures, what strategies can be used? For example, 2, **5**, 7, 2, 9, 12, 3, 6, 4, 9, 7, 1, 4, 10, 3, 12, **5**, 4, 6 looking through the list in order, focusing on the units you can see:
$(5 + 5) + (7 + 3) + (9 + 1) + (3 + 7) + (6 + 4) + (4 + 6) + (2 + 2 + 2 + 4) + 9 + 2 + 3 \times 10 = 111$.

Alternatively, you could add the numbers in pairs making,
$7 + 9 + 21 + 9 + 13 + 8 + 14 + 15 + 9 + 6$ then repeat
$16 + 30 + 21 + 29 + 15$
and finally sum the units and tens separately.

Plenary

Estimate the total mass of one each of the British coins in circulation; include the commemorative £5 coin. (A 10p weighs 6.5 g). Using mental, written or a combination of methods, calculate the total weight (83.21 g).

How much would £1 million in 1p pieces weigh? (356 tonnes, roughly 20 double decker buses or six tanks.)

£5	£2	£1	50p	20p	10p	5p	2p	1p
28.28	12	9.5	8	5	6.5	3.25	7.12	3.56

Exercise commentary

Questions 1 and **2** – Ask students which method is easier, partitioning or compensation. Are there times when one method is better than the other?

Question 3 – Encourage students to look for shortcuts. Point out that if they record the distance from Pi to Gamma, they can use it when going via Beta or Phi, without having to re-calculate.

Question 4 – Students may need reminding how to write 7 cm in metres. This could be solved using people maths where students take on the roles of the characters and position themselves in the correct order.

Question 5 – Ensure students realise that each offer is better in certain situations. Ask them to explain when special offer 1 is better and when special offer 2 is better.

Answers

1 **a** 21.3 **b** 13.68 **c** 16.75 **d** 11.28
e 11.81 **f** 3.83

2 **a** 1.27 **b** 13.15 **c** 5.97 **d** 47.01
e 22.35 **f** 6.24

3 **a** pi, delta, gamma, alpha, beta, epsilon
b 236.5 km

4 **a** Liam 1.93 m
b 0.36 m
c Giuseppe 1.42 m < Hanif 1.50 m < Ian 1.63 m < Jason 1.75 m < Kiefer 1.86 m < Liam 1.93 m

5 Special offer 1 looks like the better offer provided you want three of one item. You save 33.3% of the total cost of the three items.
With Special offer 2, the greatest saving is only achieved when you buy four of the same item, and then the saving is only 25%.

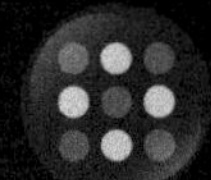

7d Mental multiplication and division

Objectives

- Extend mental methods of calculation, working with decimals (L5)
- Break down substantial tasks to make them more manageable (L6)
- Make and justify estimates and approximations of calculations (L6)

Key ideas

1 Mental multiplication and division with integers and money

Resources

Estimating introduction (1002)
Multiply triple digits (1026)

Simplification

Encourage students to make suggestions as to ways in which they might use shortcut/mental methods. Discuss possible miscomprehensions, for example, $13 \times 24 = (10 \times 20) + (3 \times 4)$. If necessary allow students to work with suitable approximations to make calculations more manageable.

Extension

Set students divisions that can be solved more simply by using product of prime factors. Students may find it useful to set out the division as a fraction first. For example, $315 \div 126$

$$\frac{315}{126} = \frac{3 \times 3 \times 7 \times 5}{2 \times 3 \times 3 \times 7} = \frac{5}{2} = 2.5$$

Literacy

Students may think the term 'page' is ambiguous (could be a single sheet, a double sheet, or each side of a sheet, and so on), but it does not matter here, since we have the cost. And sometimes we can do the mathematics for a question without any idea of what the question is about – we need not always panic when we do not understand a question! But to avoid any confusion you may wish to explain that in printing terminology a page is a single side and a leaf is two sides, or two pages. Therefore the guidebook is 112 pages long = 56 leaves.

Links

The cost of football tickets for all Premiership clubs can be found at http://www.footballticketprices.co.uk/index.php/premier-league. Find the cost of three adult tickets at the most/least expensive clubs and compare with the cost in the example. Is £115 enough to buy three adult tickets?

Alternative approach

In the second example, once the figure of £226 is reached we have finished the work and can answer the question. The exact calculation is unnecessary, as it would be in practice in real life. (Incidentally, to answer this question, do we need to know what a football match is? Or even a ticket? Or even an adult or a child? Could we guess what to do, if English was not our first language? Which part of the question would we actually need to understand?)

Checkpoint

1 A fruit farmer buys 28 fruit trees for £238.56. Without using a calculator, work out how much he paid for each tree. (£8.52)

Starter

Ask students for

three numbers where the sum is the same as the product ($1 + 2 + 3 = 1 \times 2 \times 3$)
four numbers where the sum is the same as the product ($1 + 1 + 2 + 4 = 1 \times 1 \times 2 \times 4$)
five numbers where the sum is the same as the product ($1 + 1 + 2 + 2 + 2 = 1 \times 1 \times 2 \times 2 \times 2$)

Is there more than one solution? Hint: the same number may be used more than once.

Teaching notes

When solving problems involving multiplication, what mental and shortcut strategies do students use? Suggest examples and examine various possibilities. For example,

$12 \times 34 = 10 \times 34 + 68$

$92 \times 66 = 100 \times 66 - 10 \times 66 + 2 \times 66$

Encourage students to consider estimates before they perform a calculation. What would the estimates be for the examples considered so far?

When a number of figures need to be multiplied together, is there a useful strategy than can be adopted? For example, $7 \times 5 \times 12 \times 2 \times 4 \times 7$
Pick the numbers that are easiest to work with
$(5 \times 4) \times (12 \times 2) \times (7 \times 7) = 20 \times 24 \times 49 = 480 \times 49$.
Now look at a strategy for multiplying by 49.

$480 \times 100 = 48000$

$480 \times 50 = 24000$

$480 \times 49 = 24000 - 480 = 23520$

Look at examples of division that can be cancelled to make them significantly easier by writing the division as an equivalent fraction.

Plenary

Discuss mental methods for calculating multiples of common prices charged in shops. For example, 7 × £8.99 or 8 × £4.98 or 3 × £899. What are common prices for cars and houses? For example, £11 995 or £195 000. How can you mentally calculate multiples of these amounts?

Exercise commentary

Questions 1–6 – It is important that students have one preferred method for multiplication and division. These may include the grid method for multiplication and repeated subtraction (chunking) for division, as well as traditional column methods.

Question 1 – Encourage the use of a mental/shortcut method where possible. For example, for 83×15 use $83 \times 10 = 830$ so 83×5 is half that answer 415, add results together. Encourage students to write down their methods.

Question 2 – Encourage students to simplify divisions by cancelling down. E.g. $25\,200 \div 700 = 252 \div 7$

Question 3 – Tell students to use the method they are most secure with.

Question 4 – Suggest to students that they work in pence and cancel the division sum to $975 \div 15$.

Question 5 – Remind students to state any approximations they make.

Question 6 – Again remind students to state any approximations they make. Ask if their approximate answer is too big or too small.

Answers

1	**a** 180	**b** 112	**c** 56 100	**d** 13 815
	e 703	**f** 2108	**g** 1.84	**h** 0.0511
2	**a** 56	**b** 237	**c** 562	**d** 36
	e 21	**f** 32	**g** 17	**h** 0.055

3 Cycling 1245 beats
Running 1183 beats
Swimming **1275 beats**

4 16 pages

5 **a** Alesha's order costs £73.51; so she has enough money.
b Jameela's order costs £295.77; so she has enough money.
c Bert's order costs £380.58; so he does NOT have enough money.

6 **a** 7 portions with 100 ml left over
b **i** 4.2 litres
ii 4 cartons
c £340 (£341.84)

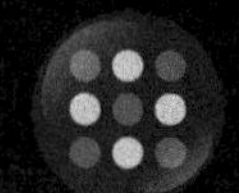

7 Mental calculations – MySummary

Key outcomes	Quick check
Use the rules of arithmetic with negative numbers.	Calculate (-4 × 3) + (-5 × -7) – (240 ÷ -8). (53)
Calculate with positive and negative powers of 10.	Write the following answers as decimals: a) $0.000\,056 \times 10^5$ (5.6) b) $2.56789 \div 10^{-4}$ (25 678.9)
Perform mental addition, subtraction, multiplication and division.	Calculate each of the following: a) 5.76 + 8.5 (14.26) b) 124.35 – 9.57 (114.78) c) 23.7 × 3.8 (90.06) d) 5 966 ÷ 38 (157)

MyMaths extra support

Lesson/online homework			Description
Rounding decimals	1004	L5	Rounding numbers to the nearest whole number and to 1 decimal place
Multiple decimals by whole numbers	1010	L5	Multiplying decimals by a whole number
Mixed sums all numbers	1345	L4	Adding and subtracting with numbers of different sizes
Word problems	1393	L3	Solving word problems with one or two steps

MyReview

7 MySummary

Check out

You should now be able to ...		Test it ➡ Questions
✓ Use the rules of arithmetic with negative numbers.	5	1, 2
✓ Calculate with positive and negative powers of 10.	6	3
✓ Perform mental addition, subtraction, multiplication and division.	6	4 - 7

Language	Meaning	Example
Negative integer	Whole numbers less than 0	-2
Index notation	A way of writing numbers as 'powers'	360 can be written as either $2 \times 2 \times 2 \times 3 \times 3 \times 5$ or as $2^3 \times 3^2 \times 5$
Compensation	Using number bonds to find the sum or difference	$8.49 - 1.97$ $= 8.49 - 2 + 0.03$ $= 6.49 + 0.03$ $= 6.52$
Partition	A way of working out maths problems that involve large numbers by splitting them into smaller units so they're easier to work with.	$9.6 + 8.8 = 9.6 + 8 + 0.8$ $= 17.6 + 0.8$ $= 18.4$
Approximation	The use of rounding to simplify a calculation. An approximate answer can be used to check an exact calculation.	2.19×32.6 $\approx 2 \times 33 \approx 66$ Exact = 71.394 ≈ 66 ✓

132 **Number** Mental calculations

7 MyReview

1 Place < or > between these pairs of numbers to show which number is the larger.
 a -8.9 and -8.7
 b -0.031 and -0.1

2 Copy and complete these calculations.
 a $12 + \square = 5$
 b $\square \times 8 = -32$
 c $-9 - \square = -14$
 d $-23 - \square = 5$
 e $-45 \div \square = 9$

3 Calculate
 a 6.51×10^3 b $0.34 \div 10^2$
 c 240×10^{-3} d 0.62×10^{-1}
 e $35.7 \div 10^{-2}$ f $10.4 \div 10^{-3}$

4 Use a mental method to do these calculations.
 a $5.76 + 3.4$ b $11.9 + 13.7$
 c $17.6 - 6.45$ d $6.78 - 0.79$

5 Four babies are weighed at a clinic.
Jack weighs 8.6 kg.
Emily weighs 1.2 kg more than Jack but 500 g less than Sophie.
Alex weighs 1.5 kg less than Sophie.
 a Who is the heaviest baby and what is their weight?
 b How much heavier is Emily than Alex?
 c Put the babies in order of weight from lightest to heaviest.

6 Use a mental method to do these calculations.
 a 5×24.1 b 6.99×8
 c $96.3 \div 1.5$ d $£169 \div 7$

7 Harry is taking his three children ten-pin bowling.
The cost per game is £7.99 per adult and £4.99 per child. If you pay two games the second is half price.
Harry has £35, is this enough to pay for two games?
Explain how you know.

8 Use a written method to do these calculations.
 a $0.435 + 11.03$
 b $12.6 + 7.89 + 172$
 c $23.67 - 5.478$
 d $56.89 - 7.98 + 32.7$

9 A box and its contents weighs 4.562 kg in total.
Inside the box are four books that weigh an average of 670 g, a torch that weighs 1.3 kg and some socks that weigh 105.2 g.
What is the weight of the empty box?

What next?

Score		
0 - 3	Your knowledge of this topic is still developing. To improve look at Formative test: 2C-7; MyMaths: 1013, 1026, 1068, 1338, 1341, 1374 and 1380
4 - 7	You are gaining a secure knowledge of this topic. To improve look at InvisiPen: 113, 121, 122 and 182
8 - 9	You have mastered this topic. Well done, you are ready to progress!

MyMaths.co.uk 133

Question commentary

Question 1 – If students are unsure, refer them to a number line.

Question 2 – Encourage students to always view addition and subtraction as moving up or down the number line. A negative sign means change direction.

Question 3 – Beware that manipulating the numbers can lead to confusion. Encourage a single method; knowing that the powers of 10 indicate how many places and in what direction the digits are moved.

Question 5 – Students should be doing all the calculations in their head, but can write down the weights as they work them out.

Question 6 – Part **d** is not a whole number. Ask students to give the answer as a fraction, and not attempt to give it as a decimal without a calculator.

Questions 8 and **9** – Students should be using standard column method. They may need reminding how many grams are in a kilogram.

Answers

1 **a** < **b** >

2 **a** -7 **b** -4 **c** 5 **d** -28
 e -5

3 **a** 6510 **b** 0.0034 **c** 0.24 **d** 0.062
 e 3570 **f** 10 400

4 **a** 9.16 **b** 25.6 **c** 11.15 **d** 5.99

5 **a** Sophie, 10.3 kg **b** 1 kg
 c Jack, Alex, Emily, Sophie

6 **a** 120.5 **b** 55.92 **c** 64.2 **d** £24.14

7 Yes. Approximating the prices: $1 \times £8 + 3 \times £5 = £23$
Including the second game at half price gives:
$1.5 \times £23 = £34.5$ (which is less than £35)
As the prices were rounded up to start with we can be sure Harry has enough money.

8 **a** 11.465 **b** 192.49 **c** 18.192 **d** 81.61

9 476.8 g

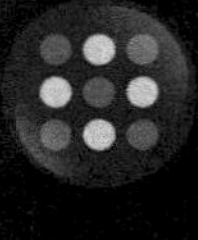

7 MyPractice

7a

1 Put these numbers in order from smallest to largest.

a	-0.5	-3	2	0.5	-2
b	-2.5	-3.5	-4.5	-1.5	-0.5
c	-4.5	-4.6	-5	-5.2	3

2 Calculate

a 5 + -10 **b** -11 + -13 **c** -6 − -18 **d** -5 − -12
e -17 + -13 **f** 13 + -19 **g** -24 + -23 **h** -35 − -38
i 48 − -52 **j** -37 + -35.5 **k** -7 − 8 − 9 **l** -7 − -8 − -9

3 Calculate

a 7 × -9 **b** -8 × 9 **c** -11 × -7 **d** -13 × -9
e -12 × 15 **f** 17 × -15 **g** -18 × 13 **h** -19 × -9
i -15 × -23 **j** -21 × 19 **k** -150 ÷ -6 **l** -231 ÷ 7
m -216 ÷ -8 **n** -306 ÷ -9 **o** 372 ÷ -12 **p** -345 ÷ -15

7b

4 Calculate

a 39×10^3 **b** 7×10^2 **c** $416 \div 10^1$ **d** $3703 \div 10^2$
e 5.3×10^{-1} **f** 7.7×10^1 **g** $562 \div 10^3$ **h** $327 \div 10^3$
i 0.49×10^{-2} **j** 2.7×10^{-1} **k** $6.4 \div 10^{-2}$ **l** 0.057×10^{-2}

5 Write each number as a decimal

a 4.7×10^3 **b** 3.9×10^{-2} **c** 8.2×10^4 **d** 2.9×10^5
e 7.3×10^6 **f** 8.07×10^{-4} **g** 6.3×10^5 **h** 2.05×10^7

7c

6 Here are the distances in kilometres between six towns.
Helen walks from Aley to Bright to Deeton to Fite.
Jenny walks from Aley to Ceough to Esville to Fite.
Who walks the furthest distance and by how much?

Aley					
3.17km	Bright				
5.86km	6.45km	Ceough			
3.7km	4.08km	1.74km	Deeton		
6.32km	5.04km	2.64km	1.84km	Esville	
6.10km	6.03km	4.93km	4.56km	3.75km	Fite

7c

7 Calculate these mentally.

a 11.8 + 7.4 **b** 2.68 + 8.9 **c** 4.8 + 5.92 **d** 3.07 + 2.98
e 13.7 − 8.88 **f** 6.99 − 3.49 **g** 8.71 − 4.8 **h** 9.67 − 3.85
i 0.867 − 0.577 **j** 1.006 − 0.756 **k** 8.349 − 2.022 **l** 19.73 − 7.605

8 Calculate these mentally.

a 109.9 + 12.2 **b** 99.9 − 45.5 **c** 28.3 − 7.49 **d** 15.78 + 7.9
e 899.5 − 98.6 **f** 41.8 − 38.9 **g** 1.37 + 5.69 **h** 12.85 + 19.55

9 Sayed has a 4m length of cable. If he uses 197cm how much does he have left?

10 Alexis sells used cars. She has four cars ready to sell at £3999; £5449; £7950 and £1750.

a What is the difference between the highest and lowest priced cars?
b What is the total price of all four cars?

7d

11 Calculate these mentally.

a 7.3 × 11 **b** 6.4 × 9 **c** 14 × 5.2 **d** 13 × 31
e 4.7 × 21 **f** 406 ÷ 7 **g** 3.4 × 13 **h** 300 ÷ 9
i 235 ÷ 4 **j** 16 × 1.9 **k** 576 ÷ 8 **l** 3.7 × 15

12 Calculate these mentally

a 5.02 × 6 **b** 9.9 × 12 **c** 3.4 × 5 **d** 1.49 × 4
e 98 × 7 **f** 2.6 × 3 **g** 0.22 × 5 **h** 0.06 × 0.5
i 376 ÷ 8 **j** 585 ÷ 15 **k** 7.2 ÷ 0.12 **l** 13.8 ÷ 0.6
m 2272 ÷ 4 **n** 0.0063 ÷ 0.9 **o** 0.64 ÷ 128 **p** 1365 ÷ 21

13 Calculate the cost of a day out for the Adams family:
two adults and three children

Adult £29.50
Child £4.90

Question commentary

Question 1 – Encourage students to always visualise a number line.

Question 2 – Ensure students are viewing addition and subtraction as moving up and down the number line, when a negative sign means change direction. Avoid the often misquoted 'two minuses make a plus'.

Questions 4 and **5** – Expect students to be able to give answer by only considering the power of 10 as indicating the number of places and direction the decimal point is moved.

Question 6 – Using a traditional column method is the best method. Ensure students are lining up the decimal points.

Questions 11–13 – At this stage students should use the method for which they feel most secure. For many this will be the grid method for multiplication and repeated subtraction method (chunking) for division.

Answers

1 **a** -3 -2 -0.5 0.5 2
b -4.5 -3.5 -2.5 -1.5 -0.5
c -5.2 -5 -4.6 -4.5 3

2 **a** -5 **b** -24 **c** 12 **d** 7
e -30 **f** -6 **g** -47 **h** 3
i 100 **j** -72.5 **k** -24 **l** 10

3 **a** -63 **b** -72 **c** 77 **d** 117
e -180 **f** -255 **g** -234 **h** 171
i 345 **j** -399 **k** 25 **l** -33
m 27 **n** 34 **o** -31 **p** 23

4 **a** 39 000 **b** 700 **c** 41.6 **d** 37.03
e 0.53 **f** 77 **g** 0.562 **h** 0.327
i 0.0049 **j** 0.27 **k** 640 **l** 0.00057

5 **a** 4700 **b** 0.039
c 82 000 **d** 290 000
e 7 300 000 **f** 0.000807
g 630 000 **h** 20 500 000

6 Helen walks 11.81 km, Jenny walks 12.25 km. Jenny walks 0.44 km further.

7 **a** 19.2 **b** 11.58 **c** 10.72 **d** 6.05
e 4.82 **f** 3.50 **g** 3.91 **h** 5.82
i 0.29 **j** 0.25 **k** 6.327 **l** 12.125

8 **a** 122.1 **b** 54.4 **c** 20.81 **d** 23.68
e 800.9 **f** 2.9 **g** 7.06 **h** 32.4

9 203 cm

10 **a** £6200 **b** £19 148

11 **a** 80.3 **b** 57.6 **c** 72.8 **d** 403
e 98.7 **f** 58 **g** 44.2 **h** $33.\dot{3}$
i 58.75 **j** 30.4 **k** 72 **l** 55.5

12 **a** 30.12 **b** 118.8 **c** 17 **d** 5.96
e 686 **f** 7.8 **g** 1.1 **h** 0.03
i 47 **j** 39 **k** 60 **l** 23
m 568 **n** 0.007 **o** 0.005 **p** 65

13 £73.70

Learning outcomes

S1 Describe, interpret and compare observed distributions of a single variable through: appropriate graphical representation involving discrete, continuous and grouped data; and appropriate measures of central tendency (mean, mode, median) and spread (range, consideration of outliers) (L6)

S2 Construct and interpret appropriate tables, charts, and diagrams, including frequency tables, bar charts, pie charts, and pictograms for categorical data, and vertical line (or bar) charts for ungrouped and grouped numerical data (L6)

S3 Describe simple mathematical relationships between 2 variables (bivariate data) in observational and experimental contexts and illustrate using scatter graphs (L6)

Introduction

The chapter starts by looking at planning a statistical investigation before moving on the methods of collecting data. Grouped frequency tables are covered before work on constructing stem-and-leaf diagrams. Basic averages are covered along with finding averages from grouped data. **8g** is a section on interpreting statistical diagrams. Scatter diagrams and correlation are covered before the final spread on comparing distributions.

The introduction discusses the principle of a census. This is where everyone living and working in the country is asked a number of questions about their lifestyles, etc. in order to build up a complete picture of the population of the country. This is as opposed to a sample where only a selection of people is asked. Censuses are useful for governments since they have to make important decisions that affect all of our lives. Understanding attitudes, behaviours and the needs of the population help them to make the correct decisions.

Censuses in the UK take place every ten years and the last UK census took place in 2011. Details can be found at: http://www.ons.gov.uk/ons/guide-method/census/2011/index.html

Prior knowledge

Students should already know how to...

- Criticise survey questions
- Find the mean, median, mode and range from simple discrete data sets

Starter problem

The starter problem poses four statistical questions for students to consider. In all cases, these questions could be answers (partially at least) from surveying the students in the class. This also provides a good opportunity to discuss how representative such a survey is. How might it be improved? How could we collect a more representative sample from the school year, or the whole school, or the local area?

The idea of a hypothesis, rather than a question, could also be discussed. This is where a statement is made about what you expect to find. For example, the first question could be converted into a hypothesis by saying that you believe 'most students travel to school by bus.' The third question could likewise be converted into a hypothesis such as 'boys take less time to get to school than girls.'

The methods of analysis available once the data is collected could also be discussed. Completion of the data cycle could be by using this analysis to reach a conclusion.

Resources

MyMaths

All averages	1192	Grouping data	1196
Mean of grouped data 1	1201	Median and mode from a frequency table	1202
Reading pie charts	1206	Scatter graphs	1213
Stem and leaf diagrams	1215	Questionnaires	1249

Online assessment

Chapter test	2C-8
Formative test	2C-8
Summative test	2C-8

InvisiPen solutions

Grouping data	412	Collecting data	413
Planning an enquiry	414	Scatter graphs	427
Stem and leaf diagrams			431
Interpreting graphs and charts			444
Comparing data sets	445	Averages from freq tables	446
Averages of a list	454	Averages of a list	455

Topic scheme

Teaching time = 9 lessons/3 weeks

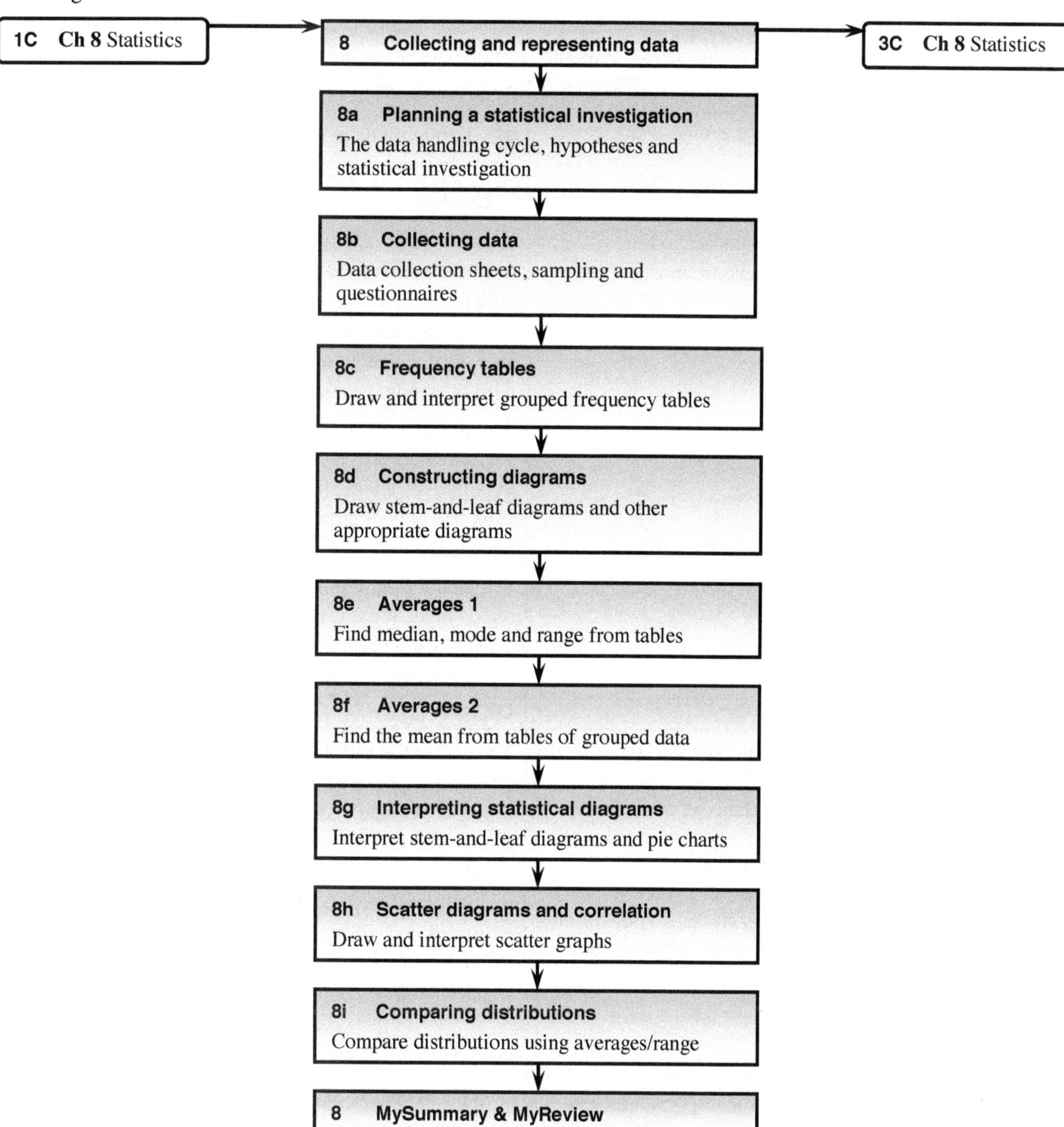

1C Ch 8 Statistics
8 Collecting and representing data
3C Ch 8 Statistics
8a Planning a statistical investigation
The data handling cycle, hypotheses and statistical investigation
8b Collecting data
Data collection sheets, sampling and questionnaires
8c Frequency tables
Draw and interpret grouped frequency tables
8d Constructing diagrams
Draw stem-and-leaf diagrams and other appropriate diagrams
8e Averages 1
Find median, mode and range from tables
8f Averages 2
Find the mean from tables of grouped data
8g Interpreting statistical diagrams
Interpret stem-and-leaf diagrams and pie charts
8h Scatter diagrams and correlation
Draw and interpret scatter graphs
8i Comparing distributions
Compare distributions using averages/range
8 MySummary & MyReview

Differentiation

Student book 2A 144 – 169

Planning a survey
Collecting data
Frequency tables
Bar charts
Pie charts
Mode, median and range
The mean
Averages from frequency tables
Comparing data sets
Statistical reports

Student book 2B 134 – 155

Planning a data collection
Collecting data
Pie charts
Bar charts and frequency diagrams
Averages
Averages from frequency tables
Scatter graphs and correlation
Stem-and-leaf diagrams

Student book 2C 136 – 159

Planning a statistical investigation
Collecting data
Frequency tables
Constructing diagrams
Averages 1
Averages 2
Interpreting statistical diagrams
Scatter diagrams and correlation
Comparing distributions

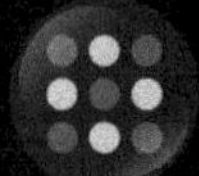

8a Planning a statistical investigation

Objectives	
• Discuss a problem that can be addressed by statistical methods and identify related questions to explore	(L6)
• Suggest a problem to explore using statistical methods, frame questions and raise conjectures	(L7)

Key ideas	Resources
1 Investigations that will involve statistics can be seen as cyclical	Grouping data (1196) Questionnaires (1249)

Simplification	Extension
Suggest a number of possible responses to the questions. Which do students think are most appropriate?	If you want to discover if GCSE results have improved over the last five years at your school, how would you look at the data? Could you just see how many students passed? If possible, obtain the results and analyse them. Why are you unlikely to be provided with the students names? (confidential data) A manufacturer claims that there are 40 matches on average in a box. What is the alternative to this hypothesis? There are less than 40 matches on average. Why does the alternative not include more than 40 matches? A manufacturer claims that their nails are 3.2 cm long on average. What is the alternative to this hypothesis? The nails are not 3.2 cm long on average. Why does the alternative include both longer and shorter nails?

Literacy	Links
Is the *evidence* we gather to test a hypothesis *statistical*? (Do we gather statistics? What do we gather? Evidence/*data*. What counts as evidence?) In the second example the term *critical factor* should be discussed. Where have students seen the word 'critical' before? Are traffic lights set to behave differently at different times? Do students know of any badly designed junctions? How could they be better?	The traffic light was invented before the motor car. In 1868 a gas-powered lantern was used to control the horse-drawn and pedestrian traffic at a junction outside the Houses of Parliament in London. The lantern had rotating red and green lamps which were turned manually to face the oncoming traffic. The lantern exploded on January 2, 1869 and injured its operator. There is more information about traffic lights at http://www.bbc.co.uk/dna/h2g2/A9559407

Alternative approach
Students should be clear that in statistical work, at nearly all levels, it is easier to regard the measurable as important than to try and make the important measurable or in any way assessable and analysed, and that is what nearly always happens. It is important to make sure the data we choose to gather is relevant and provides a fair way to investigate the question at hand, and to be aware of other factors that may affect the data. It may be that data which can be measured objectively is all that we have that we can agree on when it comes to discussions and decisions. So the statistics matter a great deal.

Checkpoint
1 Use the data handling cycle, including stating a hypothesis, to plan a statistical investigation to find whether girls in you class receive more money as an allowance than boys. (Look for key features: a clear hypothesis that is a statement and not a question; a simple data collection question; a suggestion how they will process that data and how they will use this to make a conclusion.)

Starter

Ask questions based on 'Today's number', for example,

What is one third of 72 and add 3? (27)
What is the nearest prime number to 72? (73)
How many factors of 72 are square numbers? (4)
What is 17.5% of 72? (12.6)
The square root of 72 lies between which two whole numbers? (8, 9)

Teaching notes

Discuss an issue that is relevant at the students' school/college. If students' views were to be sought in a survey, what factors would be of importance/relevance?

What sort of information would you need to collect? For example, age, ethnicity, gender. Are these factors relevant to the issue being discussed? Consider a wide range of factors.

Pick a completely different issue that is unrelated to the school, but relevant to young people. What factors are relevant in this case?

Will it be possible to collect information from people relating to these factors? Can students see any potential problems? For example, is some of the information of a personal nature? Can students suggest a way round this? A confidential questionnaire or response sections that include a range of responses, for example, income £20–30 per week.

When collecting this information, will it be easy to analyse it? Can it be averaged or easily to put categories?

Plenary

With the whole class, look at the Office for National Statistics (ONS) website. What sort of information can be found? Encourage students to suggest a common line of enquiry and see if the ONS website can offer any data to help investigate further.

Exercise commentary

Question 1 – Discuss the students' tests from the point of view of the answers they may give. In part **b**, students should restrict themselves to factors that can be measured and have a likely bearing on memory. Do not allow factors like 'favourite movie', 'hair length'.

Question 2 – Emphasise that the best statistical investigations approach the task with no pre-conceptions. Even though they may suspect young males in sports cars as being the worst offenders, their survey must include all types of drivers.

Question 3 – Students should try to keep the factors to those that can be measured. Focus on physical factors of the subject involved.

Question 4 – Encourage students to write the hypothesis that they believe is true. Ask them to suggest reason why they believe their hypothesis to be true. Ensure all hypotheses are statements and complete sentences.

Question 5 – Include in this discussion things that can be done at the collection stage to make processing the data easier. Also discuss whether quantitative data is better that qualitative.

Answers

The answers in this exercise should be taken as indicative of the type of factors to consider rather than an exhaustive list of all the possibilities.

1 **a** Apply the same memory test to a group of males and a group of females.
b General memory: age, intelligence, type of job, general health, specific brain diseases
Temporary effects: tiredness, alcohol or drug consumption

2 Driving groups: young people – especially young males, business people late for a meeting, high mileage drivers.
Types of car: sports performance models, convertibles, high-powered executive cars.

3 Body weight, age, whether the usual level of alcohol consumption, time since alcohol consumed, tiredness, time since last meal

4 **a** Males have better memories than females.
b Older people have worse memories than young people.
c People under 22 drive faster than older people.
d Drivers of performance cars drive faster than drivers of family cars.
e The same amount of alcohol has a bigger effect on people who do not normally drink alcohol.
f The time of day affects how long it will take to make a delivery to a client.

5 Students' answers
Question **1**
Straightforward: gender, age, type of job.
Difficult: intelligence, health (exam/medical records or tests)
Controlled experiments: tiredness, alcohol consumption, drugs (legal?)
Question **2**
Use police records but would miss aware drivers who avoid speed traps. Observation on a road (without cameras or radar) would provide data on car types but not drivers.
Question **3**
In an experiment, it is easy to measure body weight, gender and age and to control for time of eating and drinking and tiredness. Accurate self-reporting of how much people regularly drink may not be reliable (though the context is not judgemental).

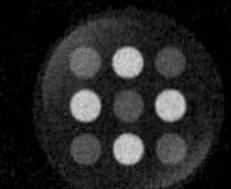

8b Collecting data

Objectives

- Design a survey or experiment to capture necessary data from one or more sources (L6)
  Design, trial and if necessary refine data collection sheets (L6)
- Determine the sample size and most appropriate degree of accuracy (L6)
- Decide which data to collect to answer a question and the degree of accuracy needed (L6)
- Identify possible primary or secondary sources (L6)

Key ideas

1 Before any statistics can be worked out, data is required

2 An effort should be made to only collect relevant data

Resources

Questionnaires (1249)

Office for National Statistics website

http://www.ons.gov.uk/ons/index.html

Simplification

Allow students to work in pairs and make use of each other's answers for question **2**. Encourage students to discuss why they are choosing a particular factor to be sampled.

Provide students with an outline of a questionnaire and a data record sheet for question **3** to help emphasise the difference. Allow the students to select the appropriate detail.

Extension

What are the advantages/disadvantages of the following methods of data collection: postal questionnaire, telephone canvassing, email questionnaires, asking people in the street, asking your friends? How do companies improve the response rate for each of these methods?

Investigate different methods of sampling: for example, systematic, convenience, quota, cluster, random. A GCSE Statistic textbook is a good reference to use if available.

Literacy

Is the word 'variable' being used in much the same way as before, or does it have different meaning?

Will the word 'population' always refer to people, or must we allow it to be used for whatever it is we are considering? So the population here could refer to plants.

Links

The UK Census has been held every ten years since 1801, except in 1941. It covers the entire population of the UK on one particular day. Information from a past census is useful to people trying to research their family history as it lists all the people living in a particular household on the day the census was taken. Information from censuses taken up until 1901 can be seen at http://www.nationalarchives.gov.uk/census/

Alternative approach

In the example, finding out about gender is described as 'straightforward'. Is this why this data is collected or is it important to see if gender is a relevant factor here? Gender, and other factors that are easy to measure, are often considered in investigations. Researching statistics presented in the media can help students to critically examine whether the data collected is suitable for the hypothesis under investigation. Can they think of any improvements? A look at reports in the media could reveal the shallowness of much of what is reported. But, is this a true reflection of what researchers do?

Checkpoint

1 Lucia is designing a survey about her school canteen. What is wrong with her questionnaire?

1. How much money do you spend on school lunches?

☐ £1.00 - £2.00 ☐ £2.00 - £3.00 ☐ £3.00 - £4.00

2. Are you overweight?

3. Do you have chips more often, or fruit?

4. Everyone knows our canteen is not very good. Rate it from 1 to 5.

(Q1 Overlapping, no box for < £1.00 or > £4.00; Q2 too personal; Q3 too vague; Q4 biased)

Starter

Draw a Venn diagram on the board with three different attributes, for example, brown eyes, cereal for breakfast, did homework last night.

Enter possible numbers or enter students' own data and ask questions. For example, how many students have brown eyes, did not have cereal for breakfast and did their homework last night?

Teaching notes

Collecting data is a multi-million pound international business. Why is collecting data so important to so many companies? Discuss what companies do with their data. For example, design new products, improve their advertising methods, open new branches.

Some types of data are difficult to collect. Ask students for examples of types of data would be difficult for the following reasons, take too long, cost too much, too much effort, too personal/confidential, access would be denied, can't be measured effectively.

In each case suggest a way in which an attempt could be made to collect the data. For example, using a convenience sample to cut down on cost or applying to the police for data to help in your investigation.

What are students' experiences of taking part in surveys? How were they approached? What tactics do street surveyors use to try to stop people and encourage them to take part in a survey? (EP)

Plenary

Ask the class for their ideas on the relative importance of the factors in question **1**. Is there much agreement between the pupils? Is there a good statistical way to measure the amount of agreement between the students?

Exercise commentary

Question 1 – Discuss ranking the variables from hardest to collect data for to the easiest. Also rank in terms of reliability of the data collected.

Question 2 – The term 'botanist' may need explaining. Encourage students to be imaginative even if they lack the botanical knowledge necessary. For example, moisture in the soil, hours of sunlight, distance from nearest plant, noise level.

Question 3 – Explain that the questionnaire should be clear so that anyone can complete without further explanation. Each question needs to make sense and a clear space needs to be made for the possible responses. The data record sheet needs to have space to collect data from many individuals. Well-designed tally charts are often best.

Question 4 – The main criticism relates to using 'convenient' data. Why is this a problem? This may need careful discussion. Use more obvious examples of convenience data being biased. For example, a professional footballer wants to investigate people's average salary.

Answers

1 **i** Ask them / birth records
ii Observation
iii Measure
iv Measure
v Ask them – if confidential, probably reasonably reliable
vi Ask them – very subjective descriptions

2 Carry out a controlled greenhouse experiment not field observations.
Soil: acidity, amount of fertiliser, mineral content, type (clay/sandy/ ...)
Amount of ground water – control
Humidity – control
Temperature – control
Depth of planting – control

3 **a** Gender: male / female
Age: ____________ years
Do you have any brothers or sisters? yes / no
How long did you sleep last night? _________ hours

b

Name	Gender (M/F)	Age (years)	Siblings (Y/N)	Sleep (hours)
Auther M.	M	12	N	7.5

4 **a** Friends are a 'special group' who may act alike and not be typical. Also they may give answers they think he wants to hear.

b There are very few 14- or 15-year-olds and the difference between 12- and 13-year-olds is not likely to be big enough to show up, so looking at gender differences and whether having siblings makes a difference are probably the best.

c Students' answers, e.g. Christiano needs to choose a random sample of children from each year group so he has equal numbers in each age group.

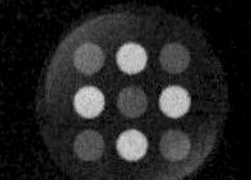

8c Frequency tables

Objectives

- Construct tables for gathering large discrete and continuous sets of raw data, choosing suitable class intervals (L6)

Key ideas

1 Data can be gathered in frequency tables

2 Large amounts of data may need grouped frequency tables

Resources

Grouping data (1196)

Copies of the data in question **1**

Simplification

Provide students with a copy of the data to allow them to cross off the data as they go. Ask students to check with partners to see if they agree on the number of data results in each interval. Can they work together efficiently?

Extension

Challenge students with a data set that does not lend itself easily to be converted into a grouped frequency table. For example, a skewed data set. What solutions can they come up with? For example, variation in group width.

Literacy

The word 'frequency' may benefit from discussion. What do we mean when we use this in everyday conversation? The idea of discrete values will need to be checked, and most of the first example will probably need to be read together carefully.

Links

Ask the class if they know the location of any speed cameras in the local area. There is a map showing the location of all speed cameras in the UK at http://www.speedcameramap.co.uk/

Are any shown locally on the map that the class didn't know were there?

Alternative approach

Ask students to consider the results in the first example critically. Is the median a fair value to take to represent each group? Is the difference between 36 and 33 big enough to count as evidence of a genuine difference between the groups? (Accept any answer, if with justification.) Is this difference in scores, in any case, enough to conclude there is a difference in, say, health, or would this need more consideration? In effect, do we trust the health score to be an accurate measure of health? What might be included in this health score?

Note that since the national speed limit on single carriageways is 60 mph, the sign shown in the 'Did you know?' box and in the picture will not be seen on the road. What sign will be seen? Where might students see the 60 sign? (Many students will have seen one version of it on the M25; some others may have been seen.)

Checkpoint

1 The table shows the results of a maths exam for a whole school year. In which group is the median?

Mark	≤ 49	50 - 59	60 - 64	65 - 69	70 - 74	75 - 79	80 - 89	≥ 90
Frequency	7	17	19	25	30	38	22	14

(70 - 74)

Starter

Ask students to imagine a bag containing 10 cubes numbered 1, 2 or 5. Cubes are drawn out of the bag and replaced each time. Write numbers on the board, for example,

5, 1, 5, 5, 2, 2, 2, 5, 2, 5, 2, 2, 2, 2, 5, 2, 2, 2, 5, 2

Ask students to estimate how many of each number there are in the bag (for example, $1 \times 1, 2 \times 6, 5 \times 3$).

Are there several possibilities? Which possibilities can we rule out? Which numbers are possible, but unlikely?

What is the mean of the numbers pulled out? (3)

Teaching notes

Look at a set of ordered, raw, skewed data. How can the data be represented in a grouped frequency table? How many groups would be sensible? As a guide suggest between 4 and 8. Ask students to suggest group widths. How can the group widths/class intervals be written in so that overlapping does not occur? Make use of inequality signs if necessary.

Would an ungrouped frequency table have been of more use in the case of this data? Which of these two types of table would be more useful for representing the number of goals scored by a single player over an entire season? Hint that they are only likely to have ever scored between 0 and 4 goals in a match.

How can the group/interval containing the median result be found for the first set of data? If the data is skewed it will probably not lie in the middle interval. Discuss the method of counting through the data to the 'middle' value.

Plenary

Discuss the various strategies used by members of the class to handle large amounts of data. What did students find successful and unsuccessful? Is there a broad agreement in as to the most efficient method?

Exercise commentary

Question 1 – The inequality signs may need explaining. Encourage students to include a row for a tally. Students who try and count all the values in each frequency group will be prone to errors. Some students may suggest that the middle grouping is the median. Ensure they realise why this is not case.

Question 2 – Comparing the median is not the only way to compare this data. Elicit from the students that a frequency polygon will also make comparisons clear.

Question 3 – The table shows that the maximum speed was less than 85. Grouping as suggested would not give this detail. Students may need reminding that percentage is a good way of expressing proportion.

Question 4 – Expect students to say that reducing speeding is a clear safety issue, whilst it is hard to argue that parking has that many safety implications.

Answers

1 a

Speed (mph)	≤ 54	55–59	60–64	65–69	70–74	75–84	≥ 85
No. cars	7	21	19	3	3	5	2

b 60–64

2 a 55–59

b Before, less than half the cars travelled at less than 60 mph and 10/60 = 16.7% travelled at over 70 mph. After, almost 2/3 of cars respected the speed limit and only 2/100 = 2% travelled over 70 mph. Speeds have been reduced.

3 a The actual speed makes a big difference to the level of danger; combining a 73 mph and a 111 mph driver loses important information.

b Before 13/60 = 26.7%, after 10/100 = 10%.

4 There is a major safety component in cameras for speeding (although there are arguments whether this is the main consideration in where cameras are placed), but not for parking. These are more social issues relating to keeping traffic moving. Fines are intended to act as a deterrent and cover the cost of running the detections services needed to make them work.

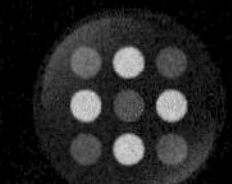

8d Constructing diagrams

Objectives	
• Select, construct and modify, on paper and using ICT, suitable graphical representations to progress an enquiry and identify key features present in the data	(L6)
• Include	
– pie charts for categorical data	(L6)
– bar charts and frequency diagrams for discrete and continuous data	(L6)
– stem-and-leaf diagrams	(L6)

Key ideas	**Resources**
1 Data can be displayed in various ways, each having their advantages and disadvantages	Stem and leaf (1215) Spreadsheet for help with discussion at end of exercise.

Simplification	**Extension**
Provide students with a copy of the data to allow them to cross off the data as they go. Encourage students to check with partners to see if they agree on the ordering of the data. Can they work together efficiently?	Challenge students with more difficult data sets, for example, including decimals to various orders of accuracy. Ask them to construct a stem-and-leaf diagram. They may need to consider rounding data.

Literacy	**Links**
Some explanation may be needed of the example, in particular of the 'order' in the middle. Encourage the students to keep their 'leaves' in columns to facilitate finding the median and so on. Discuss the need to use a key; it may be helpful to present a simple example involving decimals to emphasize that without a key there are multiple interpretations.	The first known use of a pie chart was in 1801 by William Playfair. He was a Scottish engineer who also invented the bar chart and line graph. There is a copy of one of his pie charts at http://en.wikipedia.org/wiki/Image:Playfair-piechart.jpg Stem-and-leaf diagrams are a much later innovation, being invented in 1969 by American statistician John Wilder Tukey.

Alternative approach

Note that there is no need to turn a stem-and-leaf diagram on its side for it to be used as a line graph or bar chart; there is no requirement that these be vertical.

Because the stem-and-leaf diagram arrangement organises the data, it is a handy way of first grouping and then rewriting in order; this process also has a built-in check, since the data is looked at twice, giving an extra chance of spotting errors such as missing values.

Checkpoint

1 Forty students were entered for music and dance exams. The table shows the results. Draw a comparative bar chart to show this data.

Mark	Fail	Pass	Merit	Distinction
Music	2	24	8	6
Dance	5	15	12	8

(Check that axes are correctly labelled and accuracy of graph)

Starter

Write a list of anagrams on the board and ask students to unscramble them. Possible anagrams are

VURSEY, DOME, TAAD, ATORSIINENQUE, UNNSUITCOO, NAME, MAPLES, CERTSIDE (survey, mode, data, questionnaire, continuous, mean, sample, discrete)

This can be extended by asking students to make a data handling word search.

Teaching notes

Look at a set of data. Is it clear how many results are in the 20s, 30s, etc. Is the way that the data is spread obvious? Look at the way in which a stem-and-leaf diagram is constructed. The example illustrates this. Encourage an unordered stem-and-leaf diagram as a first draft, putting in the data as it appears in the raw list. Next, convert to an ordered diagram. Why is this a good approach? Show how the key is used to explain the value of the data entries. What can you tell about the spread of the data from the diagram?

Discuss the difference between a bar chart and a comparative bar chart. For example, percentage of people who smoke in different age categories (bar chart) and percentage of males and females who smoke in different age categories (comparative bar chart)

Remind students of the method of finding the angle for the sectors of a pie chart.

Plenary

Look at some examples of frequency graphs on the internet (search on 'frequency diagrams'). Discuss which graphs give clear information and which do not. Which types were not covered in the exercise? Can students make guesses into how they work? For example, cumulative frequency graphs.

Exercise commentary

Question 1 – Note that stem-and-leaf diagrams are no longer part of the National Curriculum. When organising the data, encourage students to make two passes. On the first pass just sort into 10s, then on the second pass put each term in order.

Question 2 – A back-to-back stem-and-leaf diagram could be used. Ask students to make use of both the median and the range when making comparisons.

Question 3 – Students could be told they may use each type of graph only once. The term 'proportions' may need explaining for part **b**. Proportion should indicate a pie chart. Highlight this advantage of pie charts, actual values do not need to be shown to see proportion.

Question 4 – Use a spreadsheet application to view a comparative bar chart for different numbers of schools. Ask the class to give their opinion on the most appropriate number of bars.

Answers

1
5 | 3 8 8 9
6 | 1 1 1 3 3 4 7 8 8 8   Key
7 | 1 2 3 3 4 4 7 7 8 9   7 | 1 means 71 mph
8 | 1 2 3 4 9
9 | 1

2 **a** Males
2 | 9
3 | 1 2 4 5 5 6 7 9   Key
4 | 1 1 3 4 5 6 6 9   5 | 1 means 51 years old
5 | 1 7
6 | 0 1

b Females
2 |
3 | 4 7 8 9   Key
4 | 1 2 7 7 9 9   5 | 2 means 52 years old
5 | 2 5 7
6 | 1 3

c Males 41, females 47

d There are more males than females and the males tend to be younger.

3 **a** Comparative bar chart for comparing numbers in groups. Students can group the data in two different ways: either showing all the data for each school side by side or the data for each level for both schools side by side.

b Pie chart for school B

c Bar chart for school C

4 To compare a large number of schools the second of the charts (showing all the schools results together) will make it easier to see what is going on. 6 or 7 schools is OK, 10 is quite a lot to work with and more than that gets difficult unless there are big differences.

Objectives

- Calculate statistics for small sets of discrete and continuous data, including with a calculator (L6)

Key ideas

1. Popular statistics include measures of location, or central tendency or representative value (such as mode and median) and of spread (such as range)
2. Versions of these statistics can be found for grouped frequency tables

Resources

All averages (1192)
Median and mode from a frequency table (1202)

Copy of exercise

Simplification

Provide students with a list of the raw data for question **2** (or, maybe, have them produce a possible list themselves) and the outline of the grouped frequency table for question **3**. Encourage students to explain how the raw data and grouped data each help to find the mode and median in different ways.

Extension

Look again at question **2**. Find a good estimate for the median from the table. How many results are there? (35) Which result is the median? (18th result) Where might you find the 18th result? What assumption would you have to make? That the 18 results in the second interval were evenly spread.
(9 4/9 min = 9.4 min to 1 dp)

Literacy

Some revision of the terminology 'mode', 'median' and 'range' will be appropriate here. Encourage students to work out the meaning of 'modal class' and 'median class'.

Students could be asked whether they have any suggestions for why the statistics are described as 'summary statistics'. Any answers acceptable, up to a point.

Links

The word *average* comes from the French word *averie* which means 'damage sustained at sea'. Costs of losses at sea were shared between the ship owners and the cargo owners and the calculations used to assess the individual contributions gave rise to the modern sense of the word *average*.

Alternative approach

There is nothing rough about the idea the range gives of the spread of data: it is quite precise. But it is unreliable, because of the effect on it of unusually high or low values: ask students (but not too early in this work), if there happens to be a strangely high or low value, what happens to the range? What if we had two very similar sets of data, which differed only in this one value? So, what can we say about the range as a statistic?

Checkpoint

1. The table shows the heights of 40 Year 8 students. Find the modal class, the class containing the median and the largest possible range.

Height (cm)	$140 \le h < 145$	$145 \le h < 150$	$150 \le h < 155$	$155 \le h < 160$	$160 \le h < 165$	$165 \le h < 170$
Frequency	2	15	10	7	4	2

($145 \le h < 150$; $150 \le h < 155$; 30 cm)

Starter

Ask students to find six non-zero single digits that have the same value for the mean, median, mode and range. (Possible answer: 3, 5, 6, 6, 7, 9 average = 6)

What other mean values can they make?

Teaching notes

Recapitulate the work on medians and ranges looked at previously. Recall work in year seven on the mode (modal average). Why can't the mode or median actually be found from a grouped frequency table? Ask, what is the modal class interval? Which interval contains the median?

How can the median be roughly located in a grouped table? Show a list of raw data and clearly identify the median. Then put the data into a grouped frequency table. Ensure the median does not lie in the middle interval. Show how you can count through the data to find the 'middle' data value. What should you know before you start counting through the table? The number of data values.

Discuss where exactly the middle data value lies for an odd or even number of data values. The method of adding 1 and dividing by 2 to find the position of the median value could be used, but there is a variety of formulae available.

Plenary

If the interval widths were not all of the same size, would it still make sense to find the modal class interval and the interval containing the median? No and yes. What other type of average have students come across? Mean. Why is it not possible to find the (exact) mean average from a grouped frequency table?

Exercise commentary

Question 1 – Warn students to be careful about units.

Question 2 – Ensure students give the class name as their answers, and not the frequency. Discuss why the range can only be an estimate.

Question 3 – Recommend that students add a middle row to their table for a tally.

Question 4 – When finding the range, tell students that the world record is just under 13 min.

Question 5 – Some students may argue that the median does not change, because the person who got the median mark doesn't change. Use this to illustrate that medians are always numerical.

Answers

1 Mode = 45 cm, median = 67.5 cm, range = 130.5 cm

2 **a** $5 \le t < 10$ **b** $5 \le t < 10$

c $20 - 0 = 20$ min

3 **a**

Amount raised (£)	30–39	40–49	50–59	60–69	70–79	80–89
No. of friends	2	12	5	4	2	1

b 40–49 **c** 40–49 **d** £49

4 **a** $20 \le t < 25$ **b** $20 \le t < 25$

c $35 - 10 = 25$ min

5 **a** False. Rank order is the same, so the median person is the same but the median mark is increased by 10. Highest and lowest marks both increased by 10 so range stays the same.

b True.

c False. Highest mark = 80 + 10 = 90

Objectives

- Calculate statistics and select those most appropriate to the problem or which address the question posed (L6)

Key ideas

1 The arithmetic mean as a measure of location, or central tendency

2 The mean can be found using a frequency table

Resources

Mean of grouped data 1 (1201)

Copies of the table in the exercise

Simplification

Provide students with a separate copy of the grouped tables with space to include a further column for frequency × value. Also make a further box for the total frequency to reduce the risk of division by the number of intervals rather than the total frequency.

Extension

Construct a grouped frequency table with more than ten results that has the modal class interval, class interval containing the median and the mean all occurring in different class intervals. Note, students should try to keep the class intervals the same width if possible.

Literacy

Some students may need to be told what a radio is; it could be fun to first tell them it is the same as a wireless, and then watch and listen while they explain to each other.

Links

The average at rest pulse for an adult human is about 70 beats per minute but animals have widely differing pulse rates depending on their size. Smaller animals usually have faster pulse rates. An elephant has a pulse rate of about 25 beats per minute, a dog's pulse is 90–100 beats per minute, while a shrew's pulse rate is over 600 beats per minute. However, an elephant has a much longer life span than a shrew, so the total number of heart beats in both animals' life span is roughly the same. What does this suggest about size and heart rate?

Alternative approach

The mean is mean, because we have to work it out (although calculators will do this for us).

On the other hand, it is fair, because it treats all data equally. How is this different from the range (which will reflect extreme values) or the median (which ignores extreme values) or the mode (which may be just two values that happen to be the same, or have no value)? Which of these statistics is the odd one out, in any case? (The range measures something quite different from the others.) So is the mean the best measure of location or central tendency (or whatever phrasing works best for the class)? And would we perhaps like to have a measure of spread that included all values, fairly?

However, this may seem like a lot of work when there is a lot of data. The use of a frequency table, gathering identical values, can be seen as a way of coping, since it is the mean that we really want to use. And if this still seems a bit tiresome, then we have the statistical functions on calculators, there for the same reason, to make the calculation of the statistics we want (rather than of those, such as mode, that we sometimes do not want) practicable. If these have not yet been introduced, this might be a good time – for example for question **4**.

Checkpoint

1 Harry conducted a survey of 40 people from his year group. One question was the number of siblings each person had. The table shows his results. What is the mean number to 1 dp of siblings for this group?

No of siblings	0	1	2	3	4	5
Frequency	2	15	13	6	3	1

(1.9)

Starter

Ask students to calculate the mean, median and range of the playing times of the following DVDs:

Harry Potter and the Chamber of Secrets	2 hours 34 minutes
Lord of the Rings	3 hours 21 minutes
Toy Story 2	1 hour 29 minutes
Spiderman	2 hours 1 minute
Billy Elliot	1 hour 46 minutes
Batman Begins	2 hours 20 minutes

(Mean = 2 hr 15 min 10 sec, median = 2 hr 10 min 30 sec, range = 1 hr 52 min)

Teaching notes

Work through an example like question **1** involving a change of units. Emphasise that you add up the values and divide by the number of values. Then give a long (~30 items) list of discrete values with multiple copies of certain numbers and ask students to find the mean. Can they think of ways of organising the calculation? Suggest putting the data in order (always useful for finding the mode and median). Can anyone spot how multiplication might help? Show how the calculation can be set out in a table. Again, emphasise that you divide the total of the values by the number of values and **not** the number of 'intervals'.

Consider splitting the class in two for question **3a**. One half to first tally the values, the second half to 'scan' the data and go straight to finding the frequency. Which group was more successful getting the right answer? Can any errors be traced to getting the frequencies wrong?

Plenary

Look back at the data in exercise **8e**. What is the best average to use to represent the data? Is there more than one good option? Can students think of examples where each of the averages would be appropriate/inappropriate? For example, a professional footballer scores the following number of goals in five matches, 0, 1, 0, 2, 3. His modal score is zero; is he a good player by this measure of average?

Exercise commentary

Question 1 – Warn students to be careful about units. Remind students that scientific calculators follow BIDMAS. Tell students that after adding all the numbers press '=' and see the total on their screen, before dividing by 6.

Question 2 – For part **a**, students need to show the calculations they are performing; since the easiest way of doing this work is to add another column to their table, this is no problem. In an exam, this type of question may be worth 3 marks. One small error and no working will lose all the marks. Look for the common mistake of dividing by 5 rather than 30. Encourage students to always check their mean is a sensible value. In part **b**, ask what might be the effect of rounding measurements to the nearest 5 cm.

Question 3 – In part **a**, again encourage an approach as in the second example, with a tally column and a frequency column. Check that students divide by 30, not 7. In part **b** students should definitely compare means but could also plot bar charts and look at distributions.

Question 4 – Again, check their method. Ensure they are adding another column for time × frequency and are not dividing total by 5.

Question 5 – Encourage students to test their theory on a small set of data, although some students will see this intuitively.

Question 6 – This question is worth supplementing with further practise. This could form part of the starter.

Answers

1 800 + (43 ÷ 6) = 807.2 g (1 dp)

2 a 225 ÷ 30 = 7.5 cm (1 dp)

b The calculated mean is an estimate as we do not know the exact lengths of the pieces of fabric.

3 a

n	f	$n \times f$
0	2	0
1	5	5
2	6	12
3	9	27
4	6	24
5	1	5
6	1	6
Total	30	79

Mean = 2.63 (2 dp)

b On average each household has more televisions than radios. The number of television has a wider distribution than that for radios.

4 96 200 ÷ 3899 = 24.7 min (1 dp)

5 The mean mark will increase by 10.

6 12

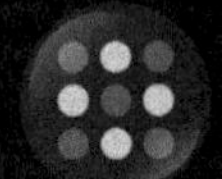

8g Interpreting statistical diagrams

Objectives

- Select, construct and modify, on paper and using ICT, suitable graphical representations to progress an enquiry and identify key features present in the data (L6)
- Include
  - pie charts for categorical data
  - stem-and-leaf diagrams (L6)
- Interpret graphs and diagrams and make inferences to support or cast doubt on initial conjectures (L6)

Key ideas

1 Two sets of data can be compared with back-to-back stem-and-leaf diagrams or with pie charts

Resources

Reading pie charts (1206)
Stem and leaf diagrams (1215)

Protractors

Simplification

Provide students with a copy of the data from the exercise to allow them to cross off values as they go. If necessary, begin the formation of the pie chart and stem-and-leaf diagram. Create extra rows for the data in question **3** to allow for the calculations of the angles for the pie charts. Give these rows headings.

Extension

Draw pie charts to show comparisons between the times for the men and women in question **1**. How should the data be grouped to be able to show a clear comparison? Use exactly the same intervals, ensuring that each data set has at least one result in the intervals chosen. How many intervals should be used? Rough estimate maybe over 2 and under 7.

Literacy

Pulse rate will need to be explained to some students. They may be interested in finding their pulses.

What is the force of the 'able to conclude' in the second example? Some clarification may be needed.

Links

The history of the World record for running the 100 m can be found at http://en.wikipedia.org/wiki/World_record_progression_100_metres_men and http://en.wikipedia.org/wiki/World_record_progression_100_metres_women

This data could be used to produce time series graphs. Can students explain why there are 'steps'? Can they make predictions for what the records will be in 2050?

Alternative approach

Reading the back-to-back stem-and-leaf diagrams needs to be taken carefully; in the first example, such questions as 'What was the third highest (or lowest) pulse rate before exercise' will catch out some students at first. Do students agree with the conclusions in the first example that the spreads are similar, but the medians different?

There have been some developments in recent years in the use of pie charts and other circular symbols in the media to represent data – examples in reports from such papers as the Guardian have been impressive, and perhaps some can be found for display and discussion. Students will quite probably have seen maps, where towns and cities of different sizes are indicated by circles of different sizes, and a lot of what has appeared can be seen as a development of this idea; which will also provide an idea of how to answer question **4**.

Checkpoint

1 The table shows the number of medals won by Great Britain and Germany at the London 2012 Olympics. Draw pie charts and comment on whether 'home advantage' makes a difference.

Medal	Gold	Silver	Bronze
Germany	11	19	14
Great Britain	29	17	19

(Data shows a higher proportion of gold medals for Great Britain, but data selection too limited.)

Starter

Ask students to find

Four numbers with a mean of 15 and a range of 11 (11, 12, 15, 22)

Four numbers with a mean of 16 and a range of 14 (9, 13, 19, 23)

Five numbers with a mean of 14, a median of 12 and a range of 9 (10, 12, 12, 17, 19)

Possible solutions given, there are others.

Teaching notes

Recapitulate the method of finding the angles of the sectors for a pie chart previously covered in lesson **8d**. Advise students to write their angles to 1 decimal place and then decide how to round them in case rounding leads to the sum not equalling 360°. For example, 1800 people are asked which party they will vote for, the votes for parties A, B and C are 267, 632 and 901. Once the angles are calculated you obtain 53.4°, 126.4° and 180.2°. What problem has this created? How can it be solved?

If the pie chart is shown without any numbers, does it demonstrate a large support for party C? Discuss the fact that the pie chart does not say the number of people it represents, it might only be a very small survey, and therefore unreliable.

Plenary

Statistical graphs can be used to mislead people. In what ways can this be done? For example, change class widths on grouped frequency tables, omit the scale on a bar chart, record results over selected time periods, etc.

Exercise commentary

Question 1 – Stem-and-leaf diagrams are no longer assessed at GCSE, but can be useful in identifying the basic shape of a distribution.

Question 2 – Ask for comparisons for each age group. Also suggest students make comparisons for under 18 and over 18. Highlight that pie charts do not show the total numbers represented, and that this information is sometimes needed.

Question 3 – The total for the school is a convenient number (120), but the total for the county is not (1049). Encourage students to draw the pie chart for the school first. Try to employ the same method for the county, although the numbers are more awkward. You may wish to show them similar data for your school's results compared with the county.

Question 4 – The best way is to make the area for each sector proportional to the number they represent, but this in practice is difficult to do.

Answers

1 a

	Men	Stem	Women		Key
(2)	9 7	11		(0)	1 |12| 5 means
(6)	8 7 7 4 2 1	12	8	(1)	12.1 s for men
(6)	7 6 6 3 0 0	13	2 5 6 7 7 9	(6)	12.5 s for women
(2)	2 1	14	0 2 3 5 6 8	(6)	
(0)		15	5 6	(2)	
(0)		16	0	(1)	

b 12.9 s men,14.1 s women

c The women are typically a second slower than the men; the two distributions have similar shapes, with slightly more variation in the women's times (a longer tail for longer times).

2 a There is a higher proportion of young children at Camp B and of older children at Camp A.

b Only the proportion of young children is higher at Camp B. There may be many more children at Camp A.

3 a Students' pie charts of school's results and county's results

b The school has got higher proportions of high levels in Maths than were found across the County.

4 Students' answers

Make the areas (radius squared) of the two pie charts proportional to the total number of entries in each pie chart. Sizes of the sectors would then reflect the absolute sizes of the category.

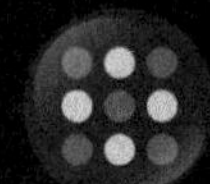

8h Scatter diagrams and correlation

Objectives

- Select, construct and modify, on paper and using ICT, suitable graphical representations to progress an enquiry and identify key features present in the data (L6)
- Include scatter graphs to develop further understanding of correlation (L6)
- Have a basic understanding of correlation (L6)

Key ideas

1 Linear correlation is apparent in scatter graphs

Resources

Scatter graphs (1213)

Spreadsheet

Graph paper

Simplification

Help students by outlining the axes needed for the scatter diagram in question **3**.

Extension

The official points system for the decathlon uses the following formulae.

100 m: points = $25.4347(18 - \text{time (s)})^{1.81}$

long jump: points = $0.14354(\text{distance (cm)} - 220)^{1.4}$

shot put: points = $51.39(\text{distance (m)} - 1.5)^{1.05}$

The points are rounded down to the nearest integer. Calculate athletes' scores from question **3** and then rank them in descending order (A, B, D, C, E, H, F, G, I, J). This could be done using a spreadsheet.

Literacy

Correlation is not, of course, a property of scatter graphs but a description of the relationship between two variables, which may perhaps be evident in a scatter graph.

Look out for the word decathlon in the exercise; a little reminder of recent Olympics and of individuals should be enough to bring an explanation to students' minds, but still they might recall only, say, heptathlons, and not decathlons.

Links

Bring in some advertisements for the class to use from local car dealers showing prices for second hand cars. Alternatively prices can be found at http://www.autotrader.co.uk/ or http://www.exchangeandmart.co.uk/iad

Choose a particular brand of car and find prices for models of different ages. Is there any correlation between the age of the car and the price? What other factors affect the price of the car? (Mileage, model, condition)

Alternative approach

Note that it is *linear* correlation that is being considered here. Correlation does not have to be linear, although this is the only sort that we attempt to analyse numerically, at least up to A level. For the last diagram, there is clearly a strong correlation … but not linear. This may be best not mentioned, unless it arises. However, with graphs such as this, it should be an unavoidable issue for any reasonably bright and engaged class.

Question **3** could be completed using a graphical calculator or similar to display the various scatter graphs without needing to input or plot any more data. The focus can then be on understanding and interpreting what is seen.

Checkpoint

1 Some students took two maths papers. One pupil scored 74% on paper 1, but was absent for paper 2. By drawing a scatter diagram and line of best fit, give an estimate for her paper 2 mark.

Paper 1	70	76	60	45	68	90	92	76	88	85	68	77	74	62	48
Paper 2	62	66	54	41	56	82	80	71	82	75	61	66	58	62	40

(Between 64% and 68% acceptable)

Starter

Ask students to draw a 3 × 3 grid and enter nine numbers between 15 and 40 inclusive.

Give two numbers and ask students to give the mean or range of the numbers, for example, range of 17, 41; mean of 11, 25.

The winner is the first student to cross out all their numbers.

Teaching notes

If there is a pattern in the results then we say that there is a correlation, if no pattern is obvious then there is no correlation. If the rough pattern lies in a straight line then there is a linear correlation.

The type of linear correlation depends on the direction of the line. Ask students what they think would be a good name for the increasing and decreasing lines. You could hint that this is related to the equations of straight lines. Establish that, like gradients, you have positive and negative correlation.

Emphasise that the strength of a correlation relates to how closely the data clusters about a line, not how steep the line is.

Plenary

Draw a scatter diagram showing a strong correlation between two obviously unconnected variables. For example, a person's height (between ten years ago and this year) and the price of a pint of milk. Ask the students, what can you say about the correlation? (Positive) Does this mean that the increase in one of the variables is causing an increase in the other? Although there is correlation, this does not automatically mean that the two variables are connected; we need to use common sense as well.

Exercise commentary

Question 1 – This question will provide opportunity to discuss 'outliers'. Encourage students to describe the relationship in words before stating the type of correlation.

Question 2 – Encourage the use of descriptive terms: strong, weak, curved as well as positive/negative correlation.

Question 3 – It might be necessary to explain what the decathlon is. Before students complete the question ask what type of correlation they expect.

Question 4 – Encourage students to justify the reasons for choosing which athlete is the best based on these three events.

Answers

1 **a** Students' scatter graphs of data using different colours for men's and women's point.
  b Blood pressure tends to be higher in older men.
  c (70, 32). Blood pressure and age may have been swapped.
  d Women's blood pressure tends to increase less as they get older and becomes slightly less than men of the same age above 45.

2 **a** No correlation
  b Negative correlation
  c Negative correlation

3 **a, b** Students' scatter graphs
  c A fast time for the 100 m correlates with longer distance in long jump and shorter distance in shot-put.

4 **a** Students' answers, e.g.
  A – he came first in both events; I and J occupied the last two places in the two events. J performed worse in the 100 m compared to the general performance.
  b Hard given negative correlation and absence of consistent standout performances in all three events. This is why the decathlon has a 'points' system of scoring for the 10 events. Contenders for best are A, B and E (best in shot, reasonable in other two) and for worst are F, I and J (F is poor in shot, only reasonable in others).

Objectives

- Compare two or more distributions and make inferences, using the shape of the distributions and appropriate statistics (L7)

Key ideas

1 Sets of data can be compared by use of statistics

Resources

Visit the Met Office website:

http://www.metoffice.gov.uk/learning/learn-about-the-weather/how-weather-works/tides

Simplification

Provide students with ordered data for question **2**. Keep emphasising the type of response needed when comparing the sets of data. Give examples of poor statements such as 'women perform better (or worse)'. Remind students that we do not know what is normal for women, or for men, or whether the difference noted is significant. We could find out in a more thorough comparison; and note that without knowing what LDL stands for, we do not even know what is desirable here Recommend statements that attempt to describe what has actually been seen, but no more, such as 'women have a higher average'.

Extension

In question **2**, instead of comparing the ranges (max. – min), compare the difference between the results that are a quarter and three quarters of the way through the data. Does this change the conclusions?
Range = 0.6 females, 0.9 males; conclude that there is more variation of cholesterol levels in males.
IQR = 0.3 females 0.25 males; conclude that there is no real difference in the variation of cholesterol levels between men and women. Why is this second measurement possibly a more reliable one? It is not affected by extreme results. Why is the IQR less informative? It ignores the values we are probably most interested in, and includes only the central values.

Literacy

Some discussion of tides will be necessary if students are to fully engage with the example. Possibly some mention of neap and spring tides (see Met Office website), but at least an explicit clarification that not all high tides are the same height. This will be news to a fair number of students, and (although good classes should by now be proactive in asking about anything that is not clear to them) without it there is a good chance that it will seem to them like so much gobbledegook, which will then prevent them from accessing the points about statistical analysis.

Links

The highest tides in the UK are in the Bristol Channel where in extreme cases the water can rise up to 15 m between low and high tide. Before Bristol's floating harbour was built at the beginning of the 19th century, boats unloading at Bristol were stranded in the mud for a considerable length of time at low tide, and would keel over. Goods had to be well stowed to avoid movement and damage, giving rise to the second part of the phrase 'shipshape and Bristol fashion'. A graph showing current tide information for Bristol can be found at http://www.bbc.co.uk/weather/coast/tides/west.shtml

Alternative approach

It is important to convey clearly the distinction between general comparison of statistics and comparison of distributions. Students could be presented with two sets of data with the same mean, median, mode and range (but different standard deviations and inter-quartile ranges) and asked to describe the differences. Encourage students to use their common sense to develop strategies, such as leaving extreme values out of certain calculations and determining the impact this will have.

The second speech bubble provides an interesting point for discussion. Note that once the information available has been reduced to simply the summary statistics we can no longer tell whether this extra information is true.

Checkpoint

1 The table shows the heights of a group of Year 7 boys and girls. Compare the heights of the two groups.

Height (cm)	$135 \le h < 140$	$140 \le h < 145$	$145 \le h < 150$	$150 \le h < 155$	$155 \le h < 160$	$160 \le h < 165$
Girls	0	6	10	18	8	0
Boys	6	12	15	11	3	1

(Use of averages and range to make sensible conclusions)

Starter

Write a list of anagrams on the board and ask students to unscramble them and then make their own anagrams or word search. Possible anagrams are

AGRAVEE, CQUEENFRY, GAREN, TRAINCOROLE, CASTISITT, EDAMIN, MISTIREESE (2 words), ACIPERTH (2 words) (average, frequency, range, correlation, statistic, median, time series, pie chart)

Teaching notes

Look at the example for the high tide depths. When trying to compare the average high tide, why is the median a more reliable measure than the mean? Discuss the fact that the mean is calculated from all the results, so one unusual result will have an effect on the mean, but not on the median.

What type of measure is the range? Establish that it gives an idea of the degree of variation in the data. Is the range a reliable measure of the overall degree of variation in the results? Establish that the range is also affected by one extreme result that might not reflect the rest of the data. In more advanced statistics, there are better measures of the variation that are not affected so extremely by one result.

Recall the method of finding the interval that contains the median result from a grouped frequency table, previously covered in lessons **8c, 8d** and **8e**.

Plenary

Look at a frequency polygon for the data in question **3**. Would it have been possible to make the same conclusions from these graphs as from the data in the table?

Exercise commentary

Question 1 – Students need to comment on the changes in the mean and the range, and interpret what this tells us about the training, rather than their numeric values. In part **b**, ask students to take into account sample size and the participants' familiarity with the test.

Question 2 – When drawing a comparison, encourage students to make use of both the median and the range. Ensure comments relate to the differences rather than just the numerical results.

Question 3 – When finding the interval containing the median, some students may pick the middle interval (30 – 35). Clarify why this strategy is wrong.

Question 4 – The term constituency may need explaining. Use this question to discuss the concept of data being 'representative.'

Answers

1 **a** The difference in means (12.7) is substantial compared to the range of scores on the two tests, so this group have done much better on the test after the training.

b The improvement could be down to practice rather than training. The sample is small.
The time scale is important – if they were tested again in a year would they show the same improvement (if not, would you say the training was effective?).

2 **a** Male 3.1, female 3.55

b There are many more males with low cholesterol levels than females. Only 2 females below 3.4; only 3 males above 3.4.

3 **a** A has median in $25 \leq v < 30$
B has median in $30 \leq v < 35$

b Range = 20 mph for A and B

c The speeds approaching B tend to be higher on average and more variable than A (although range is the same for both).

4 Students' answers
The patients in a doctor's surgery are not representative of the general population – since cholesterol is an important health indicator this is a biased sample.

Key outcomes	Quick check
Plan a statistical investigation using the data handling cycle.	Ask students to plan and carry out a statistical investigation of their chosing for their class. Allow suffecient time and expect them to include all the elements listed here in their investigation. This is a useful exercise at this stage to enable students to view statistics as a whole, rather than individual skills that can lose meaning when separated from a larger context. Gender is usually the best way to generate two sets of data to compare. Guide the students to use numerical data and make suggestions as to what data needs to be collected to be able to draw a scatter diagram, etc. Encourage students to use statistical language throughout. Note that stem-and-leaf diagrams are no longer included in the National Curriculum.
Collect suitable data using questionnaires, data sheets and samples.	
Create and interpret a grouped frequency table.	
Create and interpret a stem-and-leaf diagram.	
Calculate averages, including from a frequency table.	
Create and interpret scatter diagrams and time series commenting on correlations and trends.	
Compare distributions.	

MyMaths extra support

Lesson/online homework			Description
Mean and mode	1200	L5	Working out the mean and mode of a small set of data
Median and range	1203	L5	Working out the median and range of a small set of data
Reading pie charts	1206	L5	Solving problems by reading information from a pie chart
Mean from frequency tables	1254	L7	Finding the mean from a frequency table

Question commentary

Question 1 – Students often confuse data collection sheets with questionnaires.
Question 2 – Discuss with students why the groupings are handled differently for discrete data and continuous data.
Question 3 – Students will be more accurate if they use the frequency table to calculate the mean, rather than the raw data.
Question 4 – Remind students when calculating the mean to divide by the number of packets and not the number of rows in the table.
Question 6 – Although this type of diagram is still useful, if time is short this question can be omitted as stem-and-leaf diagrams are no longer included on the National Curriculum.

8 MySummary

Check out

You should now be able to ...

	Test it ➡ Questions
✓ Collect suitable data using questionnaires, data sheets and samples.	1
✓ Create and interpret a grouped frequency table.	2
✓ Create and interpret a stem-and-leaf diagram.	3
✓ Calculate averages, including from a frequency table.	4
✓ Create and interpret scatter diagrams and time series commenting on correlations and trends.	5
✓ Compare distributions.	6

Language	Meaning	Example
The data handling cycle	A way to organise a statistical investigation	Specify the problem; collect the data; process the data; interpret the data
Hypothesis	A testable statement that is either true or false	In Year 8 boys are taller than girls
Population	The complete set of 'objects' being studied	Population: the students in your school
Sample	A sub-set of a population	Sample: the students in Year 8
Scatter diagram	A graph showing paired data plotted as (x, y) points	See p. 152
Correlation	A measure of how close points are to lying on a straight line	Can be positive or negative, strong or weak, or no correlation
Time series	A scatter diagram with time as x-coordinate	The weekly rainfall over a year

156 **Statistics and probability** Statistics

8 MyReview

1 Pippa plans to stand at the entrance to a supermarket and record how customers travelled to the shop, their gender and if they have come alone or not.
Design a record sheet for her to use.

2 The list gives the ages of people at a gym.

21 32 24 55 18 33 42 49
59 50 63 28 26 30 38 44
47 53 68 27 30 32 41 45

Construct a grouped frequency table for this data. Use the groups: ≤15, 16–19, 20–29, 30–39, 40–49, 50–59, ≥60.

3 Use the data from question **2**.

a Draw an ordered stem and leaf diagram to represent the ages of people in a gym.

b Find the mean age.

4 Jason records how many cakes are in lots of different packets.

Cakes, c	Frequency
1	5
2	8
3	0
4	25
5	1
6	43

Find the

a mean **b** median **c** mode.

5 The table shows the number of scarves sold at a shop and the outside temperature.

Temperature (°C)	-2	9	3	0	5	8
Scarves	15	2	11	14	5	3

a Draw a scatter diagram for this data.

b Describe the correlation.

6 The back-to-back stem-and-leaf diagram gives reaction times for girls and boys.

Boys		Girls
9	3	
1 8	4	9
2 4 6 8 8 9	5	2 4 4 7 8
3 4 4 7 8	6	0 4 5 5 8 9
0 3 5	7	1 3 3 7 8 8
2	8	0 1 4
8	9	0 1

Key 2 | 9 | 8 means 0.92 for a boy and 0.98 for a girl

a Find the median for girls and for boys.

b Find the range for girls and for boys.

c Compare the reaction times of girls and boys.

What next?

Score	
0 – 2	Your knowledge of this topic is still developing. To improve look at Formative test: 2C-8; MyMaths: 1192, 1193, 1196, 1201, 1202, 1207, 1213, 1215 and 1249
3 – 5	You are gaining a secure knowledge of this topic. To improve look at InvisiPen: 412, 413, 414, 427, 431, 444, 445, 446, 454 and 455
6	You have mastered this topic. Well done, you are ready to progress!

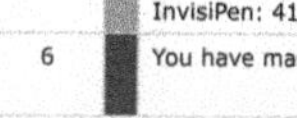

Answers

1

Transport	Gender (M/F)	Alone (Y/N)

2

Age	Frequency
≤ 15	0
16–19	1
20–29	5
30–39	6
40–49	6
50–59	4
≥ 60	2

3 **a**

1	8
2	1 4 6 7 8
3	0 0 2 2 3 8
4	1 2 4 5 7 9
5	0 3 5 9
6	3 8

b 39.79

4 **a** 4.68 **b** 6 **c** 6

5 **a**

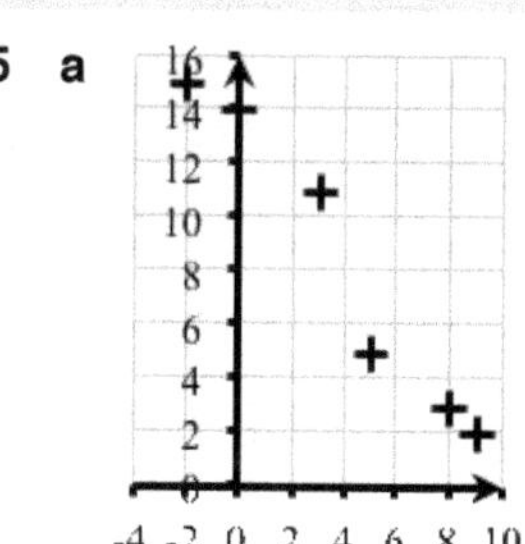

b Negative correlation

6 **a** Girls 0.69 Boys 0.63

b Girls 0.42 Boys 0.59

c Median lower for boys so boys' reactions were slightly quicker on average. Range is higher for boys so girls' times were more consistent.

8 MyPractice

8a

1 A drug company wants to test the effectiveness of different doses of a new drug and whether the drug will affect some groups of people differently.

> A patient's general health is important when taking medication.
> You may wish to consider factors affecting general health.

a Suggest six ways to group people you think might react differently to the drug, for example, by gender if you think males and females might react differently.

b For each of your groups, write down a hypothesis which could be investigated.

8b

2 **a** Make a list of the variables the company will need to collect data on in order to investigate the hypotheses you wrote for question **1**.

b If the initial trials are to be done with groups of volunteers, say how easy you think it will be to get the information for each variable.

c Are there any of the variables you think will be harder to get information on when the people involved are not volunteers?

d The drugs company says you can only investigate three variables, which three variables do you think will be most important and why?

8c

3 The ages of a group of patients in a nursing home who were given the new drug are given below.

67, 63, 52, 49, 71, 82, 71, 59, 61, 57 64, 72, 56, 48, 59,64, 70, 53, 49, 67,
81, 80, 56, 53, 59, 63, 67, 64, 47, 51 60, 76, 70, 61, 53, 52, 59, 72, 86, 49,
73, 71, 59, 62, 57, 46, 62, 70, 49, 57 62, 70, 49, 80, 66, 47, 55, 90, 53, 61

a Summarise this information in a grouped frequency table using the intervals ≤ 54, 55–59, 60–64, 65–69, 70–74, 75–84, ≥ 85.

b In which interval does the median lie?

8d

4 A sample consisting of the first half of the population used in question **3** is taken.

a Draw a stem and leaf diagram to show the ages of these patients.

b Hence find the median of this sample.

8e

5 The table shows the times taken, in minutes, for a group of Year 8 students to complete a cross-country run.

Time, t	$10 \le t < 12$	$12 \le t < 14$	$14 \le t < 16$	$16 \le t < 18$	$18 \le t < 20$
Frequency	7	24	15	6	2

a Find the modal class for the time taken for the run.

b Find the class containing the median time taken for the run.

c Estimate the range of the times taken for the run.

8f

6 Sally sells some raffle tickets. Using the table calculate the mean number bought per person.

Number of tickets	1	2	3	4	5
Frequency	8	5	2	1	9

8g

7 100 people in London and in Belfast were asked to choose which food they preferred. The results are shown in the pie charts.

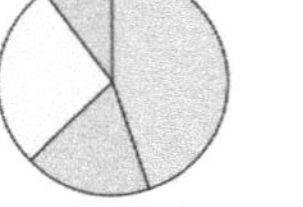

a Compare the food preferences of people in London and Belfast.

b In which city do you think most Chinese food was eaten? Explain your answer.

8h

8 Choose three pairs of variables and sketch the corresponding three scatter graphs to show each type of correlation (positive, negative and no correlation).

8i

9 A careers teacher has collected data from some sixth form pupils who left school to start a job on whether they did A-level maths and their starting salary (in £'000s).

> Y15.7, N13.7, Y13.5, Y14.2, N14.0, Y14.8, Y13.9, N13.7, Y13.9, N14.2, Y14.6, Y13.9, N13.8, N14.3, Y14.8, Y13.9, Y15.1, N13.6, Y14.3, Y14.1

a Find the range and median starting salaries for the two groups.

b Is it reasonable to say that on average people with an A-level in maths earn more than those without one?

> Y15.7 means yes did A-level maths, starting salary £15.7k

Question commentary

Questions 1 and **2** – Some students may struggle to come up with six. Allow gender to be one. Others may include age, height, weight, smoking, alcohol consumption, blood pressure, etc. Ensure the hypotheses are always complete sentences and statements.

Question 3 – Encourage students to add a tally row to their table.

Question 4 – Although stem-and-leaf diagrams are no longer included in the National Curriculum, they can prove useful in certain situations.

Question 6 – Remind students to divide by the number of people and not by 5.

Question 9 – Encourage students to be systematic when processing this data.

Answers

1 a Age, gender, body weight, how severe their illness is, any medication they already take, other health issues, e.g. do they smoke/drink (how much), lifestyle, e.g. how much exercise they take.

b Students' answers
Hypotheses should be a clear statement about the effectiveness of the drug on different groups being equal (or giving a direction of expected difference – but this is much more difficult to do in this context without expert medical knowledge).

2 a Students' answers based on their choice of variables

b Drug trials are usually conducted through clinics or through GP surgeries so some medical background information is likely to be available; volunteers are likely to co-operate.
Age: ask/records – easy
Gender: observation/records – easy
Body weight: measure – relatively easy
Severity of illness: expert opinion – will depend on what the disease is.
Medication: medical records (reliable) or ask (reasonably reliable)
Other health issues: do they smoke/drink (how much), lifestyle – how much exercise they take.

c Even if they have not volunteered they probably have to agree to take part in the trial so there should not be too much difficulty here.

d Students' answers

3 a

Age	≤ 54	55–59	60–64	65–69	70–74	75–84	≥ 85
No. patients	16	11	12	4	10	5	2

b 60–64

4 a
4 | 6 7 9 9
5 | 1 2 3 6 7 7 7 9 9 9
6 | 1 2 2 3 3 4 7 7
7 | 0 1 1 1 3
8 | 0 1 2

Key
7 | 1 means 71 years old

b Median is 61.5 years

5 a $12 \le t < 14$ b $12 \le t < 14$

c 10 min

6 2.92

7 a There are many ways to talk about this:
Italian is more popular in London and Chinese is more popular in Belfast (others are similar). In London, Italian is by far the most popular then Indian, Chinese, Thai. In Belfast, Italian is slightly more popular than Chinese and Indian and Thai is the least popular.

b London, as population considerably larger.

8 Students' answers

9 a Median is £13 800 and range is £700 without A-level Maths; median is £14 200 and range is £2200 with it.

b This is just a small sample and it is only the starting salary, so while it is true for this group the statement is too strong for the evidence of this sample.

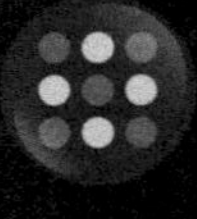

MyAssessment 2

These questions test your knowledge of the topics in chapters 5 to 8.
They give you practice in the questions that you may see in your GCSE exams.
There are 55 marks in total.

1 Calculate the value of the four angles marked with a letter. (4 marks)

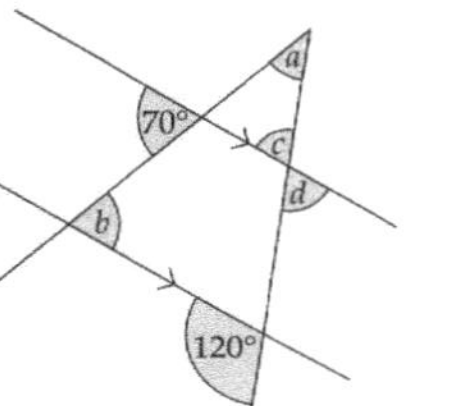

2 Name the quadrilateral that has these three properties. (2 marks)

- Only one pair of parallel sides.
- Only one line of symmetry.
- No rotational symmetry.

3 Look at this shape which shows four regular pentagons joined together.

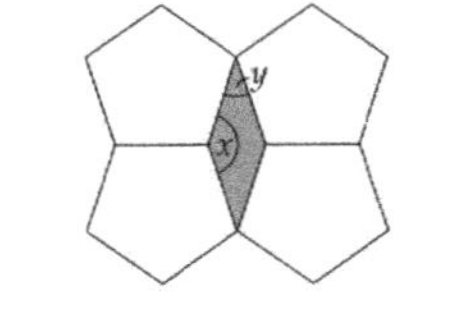

a What is the name of the shape that forms the gap in the centre? (1 mark)

b Calculate the two angles marked with a letter. (3 marks)

4 **a** State the gradient and y-intercept of the following straight lines. (4 marks)

i $y = 2x + 5$ **ii** $y = -1 - 2x$ **iii** $2y + 3x = 3$ **iv** $12 = 3x + 4y$

b On a graph with x-axis from -3 to 3 and y-axis from -4 to 12 draw the lines given by the equations in parts **a i** and **iii**. (5 marks)

c What are the coordinates of the point where the two lines intersect? (1 mark)

5 **a** Copy and complete the table of values for the equation $y = x^2 + 3x$ (2 marks)

x	-4	-3	-2	-1	0	1
y						

b Plot these points on a set of coordinate axes with x-values from -5 to 2 and y-values form -3 to 5. Join the points with a smooth curve. (4 marks)

c What name do we give to this shaped curve? (1 mark)

d What is the equation for the line of symmetry for this curve? (1 mark)

e Write the coordinates of the points where the curve cuts the x-axis? (2 marks)

6 Calculate

a $264 \div 0.01$ (1 mark) **b** 0.61×10^2 (1 mark)

c 8.7×10^{-1} (1 mark) **d** $1.71 \div 10^{-2}$ (1 mark)

7 On my birthday I received £65 in cash and decided to spend it on a book for £7.99, a memory pen for £6.99 and a DVD for £9.99.

a How much did I spend altogether? (2 marks)

b How much change did I have left? (2 marks)

c With the remaining money I bought some artists materials including six pencils costing 65p each and 8 sheets of drawing paper at £1.20 each. How much did I spend on art materials? (2 marks)

8 A survey was carried out to record the time taken to travel to school (to the nearest minute).

7	35	21	44	31	46	25	20	21	11
15	19	27	8	40	57	23	14	15	31
38	41	16	29	33	9	35	43	17	11

a Draw a stem-and-leaf diagram to show this information. (3 marks)

b Summarise this information in a grouped frequency table using the intervals 1 – 9, 10 – 19, 20 – 29, 3 – 39, 40 – 49 and 50 – 59 (3 marks)

c Answer these questions using the information in the frequency table.

i In which interval does the median lie? (1 mark)

ii In which interval does the mode lie? (1 mark)

iii What is the range of the data? (1 mark)

9 The table shows the number of competitors taking part in the Winter Olympic Games between 1952 and 2002.

1952	1956	1960	1964	1968	1972	1976
694	820	665	1091	1158	1006	1123
1980	1984	1988	1992	1994	1998	2002
1072	1274	1423	1801	1737	2302	2400

a Plot a scatter graph to show this data. (3 marks)

b Describe any trend you see in your graph. (1 mark)

c Draw the best straight line through the points. (1 mark)

d What type of correlation does this scatter represent? (1 mark)

Mark scheme

Questions 1 – 4 marks

a 1 $a = 50°$

b 1 $b = 70°$

c 1 $c = 60°$

d 1 $d = 60°$

Questions 2 – 2 marks

2 isosceles trapezium; 1 mark for trapezium

Questions 3 – 5 marks

a 1 Rhombus (accept kite)

b 2 $x = 144°$

2 $y = 36°$

Questions 4 – 10 marks

a 4 **i** 2, 5 **ii** -2, -1 **iii** $-\frac{3}{2}, \frac{3}{2}$ **iv** $-\frac{3}{4}, 3$

b 5 Students' graphs of $y = 2x + 5$ and $2y = 3x + 3$

c 1 (-1, 3)

Questions 5 – 10 marks

a 2 y values : 4, 0, -2, -2, 0, 4

b 4 Students' graphs of correctly plotted points joined with a smooth curve

c 1 Quadratic or parabolic

d 1 $x = -1.5$

e 2 (-3, 0) and (0, 0)

Questions 6 – 4 marks

a 1 26 400

b 1 61

c 1 0.87

d 1 171

Questions 7 – 6 marks

a 2 £24.97; has to be a mental calculation

b 2 £30.03; has to be a mental calculation

c 2 £13.50; has to be a mental calculation

Questions 8 – 9 marks

a 3

0| 7 8 9
1| 1 1 4 5 5 6 7 9
2| 0 1 1 3 5 7 9
3| 1 1 3 5 5 8
4| 0 1 3 4 6
5| 7

Key
1 | 1 = 11 min

b 3 Frequencies tabulated : 3, 8, 7, 6, 5, 1
Results should be tabulated correctly

c i 1 20–29

ii 1 10–19

iii 1 50

Questions 9 – 6 marks

a 3 Students' scatter graphs

b 1 The number of competitors is increasing

c 1 Best straight line drawn through the points using a ruler

d 1 Strong positive correlation

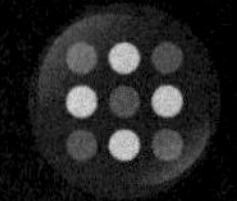

9 Transformations

Learning outcomes	
G5 Describe, sketch and draw using conventional terms and notations: points, lines, parallel lines, perpendicular lines, right angles, regular polygons, and other polygons that are reflectively and rotationally symmetric	(L6)
G8 Identify properties of, and describe the results of, translations, rotations and reflections applied to given figures	(L6)
G9 Identify and construct congruent triangles, and construct similar shapes by enlargement, with and without coordinate grids	(L6)

Introduction

The chapter starts by looking at rotations, reflections and translations before moving on to look at combining these transformations. Rotational and reflective symmetry is then covered before the concept of an enlargement is introduced. Enlargements from a given centre are covered as well as enlargements with fractional scale factors.

The introduction discusses the idea of symmetry in art. Buddhist sand mandalas are the main focus but it also mentions Islamic and Hindu art as well as contemporary artists such as M C Escher. Symmetry in the natural world is also considered. There are many great examples of traditional and contemporary art that uses extensive symmetry to create what is referred to as 'formal' art, designed to affect the viewer through the appreciation of the patterns, rather than the emotions that the art stirs.

The following websites provide a wealth of examples that could be used to illustrate these art forms:

http://patterninislamicart.com/

http://www.mysticalartsoftibet.org/mandala.htm

http://en.wikipedia.org/wiki/Rangoli

http://www.mcescher.com/

Prior knowledge

Students should already know how to...

- Convert metric units
- Perform simple transformations
- Recognise the symmetry properties of simple shapes

Starter problem

The starter problem gives the students a simple rectangle reflection in the line $y = x$ and asks them to consider how the coordinates are transformed under the reflection. They are told that the x- coordinate and the y-coordinate are interchanged.

Students could be directed to test this hypothesis by carrying out their own reflection in the line $y = x$ for another shape.

The second part of the starter activity asks students to consider the effect of other transformations such as a reflection in the line $y = -x$. Here, not only are the coordinates interchanged, but the signs of the coordinates are also changed. Positive y-coordinates become negative x-coordinates, for example. Again, students could be directed to try out their hypothesis on other shapes reflected in the line $y = -x$.

Reflecting in the x-axis has the effect of changing the sign of the y-coordinate and reflecting in the y-axis has the effect of changing the sign of the x-coordinate.

As an extension, students could be asked to investigate the effects of rotating a shape through 90° or 180°.

Resources

MyMaths

Enlarging shapes	1099	Reflecting shapes	1113	Lines of symmetry	1114
Rotating shapes	1115	Rotational symmetry	1116	Transformations	1125
Translating shapes	1127	Symmetry	1230		

Online assessment

Chapter test	2C–9
Formative test	2C–9
Summative test	2C–9

InvisiPen solutions

Reflection and rotation symmetry			361
Reflection	362	Translation	363
Rotation	364	Enlargements	366
Combined transformation not enlargement			368

Topic scheme

Teaching time = 5 lessons/2 weeks

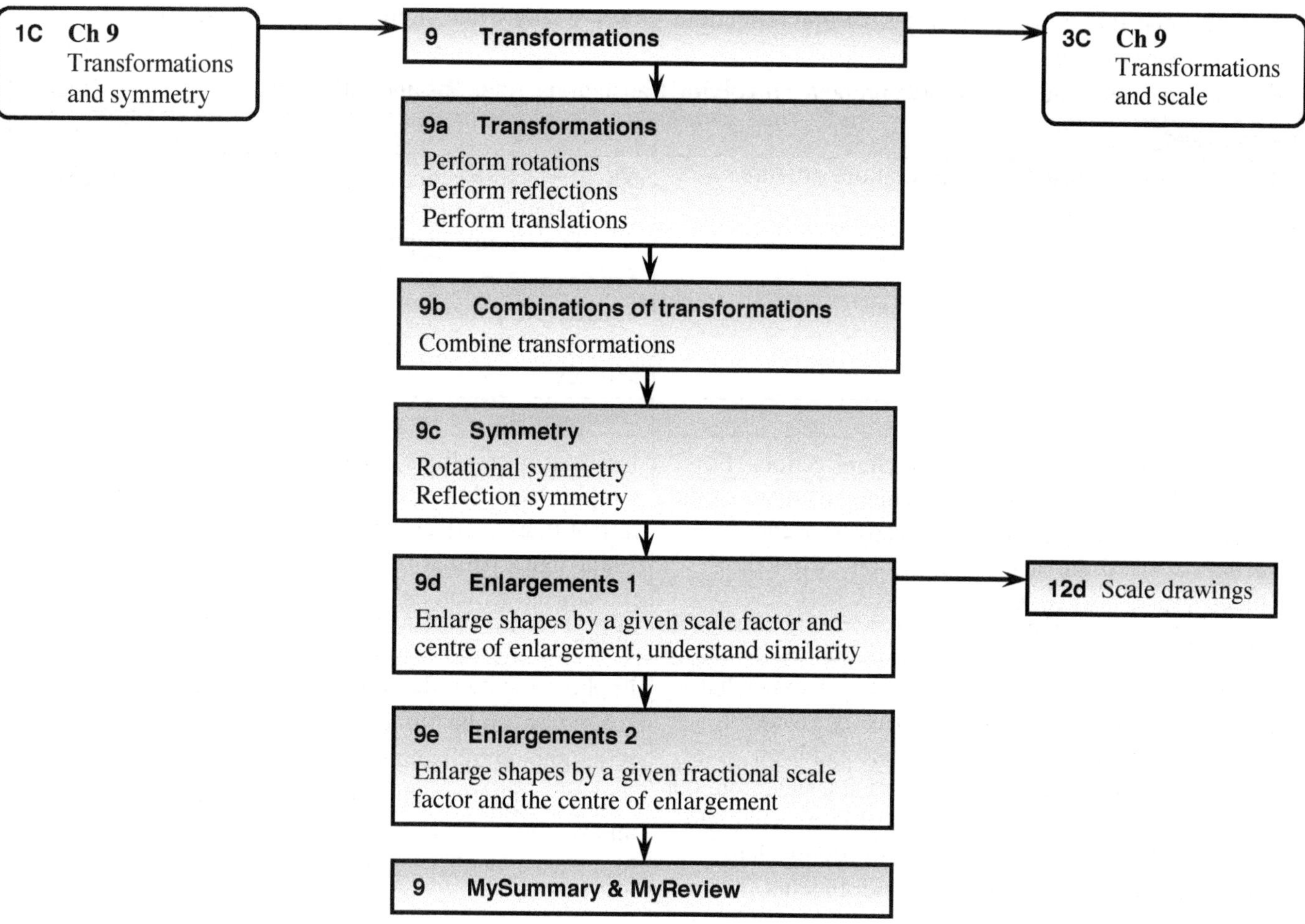

Differentiation

Student book 2A 172 – 189

Reflection
Reflection symmetry
Rotation
Rotational symmetry
Translation
Tessellation

Student book 2B 158 – 173

Transformations
Combinations of transformations
Symmetry
Enlargements 1
Enlargements 2

Student book 2C 162 – 177

Transformations
Combinations of transformations
Symmetry
Enlargements 1
Enlargements 2

Objectives	
• Transform 2D shapes by rotation, reflection and translation	(L5)
• Recognise that translations, rotations and reflections preserve length and angle, and map objects in to congruent shapes	(L6)
• Use the coordinate grid to solve problems involving translations, rotations and reflections	(L6)

Key ideas	Resources
1 Reflections, translations and rotations are three kinds of transformations	Reflecting shapes (1113) Rotating shapes (1115) Translating shapes (1127) Tracing paper Square grid paper Image of 2 faces/a vase Mirrors
Simplification	**Extension**
Allow the use of mirrors to help with reflections. For those with poor motor skills, use enlarged copies of the exercise and tracing paper that already have the vertices of the original shape drawn on. Allow the students to add the edges.	Use four mirror lines, $y = 0, x = 0, y = x, y = -x$. Draw a simple shape that actually crosses over one of the mirror lines. Reflect the shape in each of the lines. Challenge a partner to the same problem and see if there is agreement as to the solution.
Literacy	**Links**
The word transformation is used here in a somewhat technical sense; to transform is normally to alter intrinsically (if we were told someone had been transformed, we would be a bit puzzled if we found out that they had just walked into the next room), but here we are dealing with extrinsic changes. Being clear about this may be necessary for some students. Recall that congruency may be direct or opposite; ask students which, with which transformations.	In photography reflections are used to add interest. Examples can be found at http://photography.nationalgeographic.com/photography/photos/patterns-nature-reflections.html and at http://www.danheller.com/mirrors.html

Alternative approach

It can be helpful to classify these three transformations in the order reflections (one piece of information required), translations (two pieces of information, whether Cartesian or polar) and rotations (three pieces of information; unless it's a half turn).Students may be advised to copy, or be given copies, rather than trace over the textbook or jab pens into it in an attempt to find centres of rotation. This does matter because otherwise the marks give the game away to the next cohort, significantly reducing the educational activity for them.

Note that some different transformations can look the same – for example, in question **1**, A could be reached by reflection or rotation, if we have no labels on the corners.

For tracings, accurate lines are not necessary, provided the vertices are marked well enough (blobs will do quite well), since students will nearly always be dealing with corners that are on intersections of grid lines.

On the other hand, connecting shapes to the centre of rotation (whether known, or current guess) with a line or with an L-shaped connector makes the rotating a lot easier.

Checkpoint

1 A triangle has coordinates $A(2, 4)$, $B(4, 3)$ and $C(1, 0)$. Draw this on a grid and carry out the following transformations. Write down the new coordinates in each case.

a Reflection in the x-axis. ($A'(2, -4)$, B' $(4, -3)$, C' $(1, 0)$)

b Rotation 90° anti-clockwise about (1, 1). (A' $(-2, 2)$, B' $(-1, 4)$, C' $(2, 1)$)

c Translation of 8 squares to the right. (A' $(10, 4)$, B' $(12, 3)$, C' $(9, 0)$)

Starter

First November 2010 is palindromic if written using two digits for the day, month and year: 01.11.10

Ask students to find other palindromic dates occurring within the next 50 years. (11.11.11, 21.11.12, 02.11.20, 12.11.21, etc.)

Teaching notes

What are the four main ways in which a shape can be transformed? Translation, Rotation, Reflection, Enlargement. What do students think is meant by a translation? Give an example of a shape and its translated image. Ask students to describe the transformation. Note that some students mistakenly count the gap between the two shapes rather than count the distance that a common point has moved.

How should a rotation be described? For example, is rotate 90 degrees a clear instruction that will give a unique answer? Establish that an angle, direction and centre of rotation are all needed to define the rotation properly.

Allow students to use tracing paper to help perform and describe rotations including finding the centre of rotation through trial and improvement.

How can reflections in lines of the form $y = \pm x + c$, where c is a real number, be performed? Use an example and demonstrate the method of counting perpendicular to and across the mirror line. What alternative method of counting is useful? Look at counting vertically and horizontally either side of the mirror line.

Plenary

Look at question **4** again. What other shapes can be made from rotating other types of triangle? If time allows, consider all classifications of triangle, there are seven: scalene (acute-angled, right-angled, obtuse-angled), isosceles (acute-angled, right-angled, obtuse-angled) and equilateral. The class could be divided to spread the work load.

Exercise commentary

Question 1 – When describing transformations, encourage students to write as complete answers as possible, for example, reflect in a vertical line, or rotate 90° clockwise, or move a given number of squares in specific directions.

Question 2 – Many students find diagonal reflection tricky. Ask students if they have different ways of counting the squares. Elicit that reflection always keeps the perpendicular distance from the line equal.

Question 3 – Allow students to use tracing paper. Emphasise the importance of a sharp pencil.

Question 4 – Students may find it helpful to label the angles *a, b, c*. Encourage the use of the standard method of labelling equal sides, that is, single/double dashes on corresponding sides.

Question 5 – Before commencing this activity, the class could be shown the completed picture for a few seconds and asked to write down the very first thing they see. Some will have seen it before.

Question 6 – If lines are parallel leads to a translation. Otherwise leads to a rotation of twice the angle between the lines.

Answers

1 **a** Reflection or rotation **b** Translation
c Translation **d** Rotation
e Rotation or reflection

2 **a, b** Students' drawings of double reflection in the mirror lines given

3 **a** (0, 0), 90° anticlockwise
b (-1, 2), 90° clockwise
c **i** Translation of 3 to the right and 1 down
ii Translation of 3 to the left and 1 up

4 **a, b** Students' diagrams of rotated scalene triangle forming a parallelogram, with equal angles and equal sides marked
c Opposite angles equal
2 sets of equal sides
Must be a parallelogram

5 Students' drawings showing reflection of line to form vase/face

6 **a** Students' drawings
b Rotation 90° clockwise, about the intersection of the mirror lines.
c The single transformation that is equivalent to two reflections is a rotation through twice the angle between the mirror lines, about the intersection of the mirror lines.

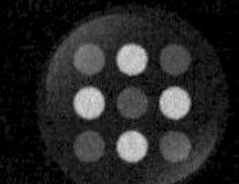

9b Combinations of transformations

Objectives	
• Explore and compare mathematical representations of combinations of translations, rotations and reflections of 2D shapes (L6)	
Key ideas	**Resources**
1 Transformations can be combined, one following another	All transformations (1125) Isometric paper Tracing paper Square grid paper Coloured pencils Mirrors
Simplification	**Extension**
Allow the use of mirrors to help with reflections. For those with poor motor skills, use enlarged copies of the exercise and tracing paper that already has the vertices of the original shape drawn on. Allow the students to add the edges.	Is it ever possible to perform a reflection, then a rotation, then a translation to return at the end to the starting shape? (Yes, if the order of the corners is ignored.) Is it always possible, or does it depend on the type of shape you begin with? (It depends.) Will the original order of the transformations make any difference?
Literacy	**Links**
Tessellations were investigated in lesson **5c** but it may be necessary to recapitulate the definition. Students could investigate other meanings of the word 'translate'; when we translate a word from one language to another the meaning does not change but it is moved from one language to another. Similarly, when we translate a shape its orientation does not change, but its position does.	Islamic art does not use images of living things, but instead uses geometric patterns and tessellations. The Alhambra palace in Granada, Spain, is richly decorated with Islamic art. For more information about the Palace see http://en.wikipedia.org/wiki/Alhambra There are examples of the patterns found at Alhambra at http://www2.spsu.edu/math/tile/grammar/moor.htm

Alternative approach

Tracing paper can be useful for nearly all this work, most efficiently if no attempt is made to trace the entire shape but only to mark the corners. This acts as a quick guide or a quick check, the counting of grid lines and gaps being more precise for the actual drawing. Even for question **2**, just marking the corners will be best but students should mark them very carefully on the tracing paper, as crosses or dots in circles or similar, to press through to mark on the paper, so that the dimples can then be joined neatly. For question **3**, two fold lines can be used to see what is happening, before any accurate drawing is done, and also to see the final result.

Checkpoint

1 A trapezium $A(-4, 0)$, $B(-3, 2)$, $C(-1, 2)$, $D(0, 0)$ is rotated 90° clockwise about (0, 0) and then the new image is reflected in the x-axis. Draw this transformation on a grid and describe the single transformation that matches the first shape onto the last. (A reflection in the line $x = y$)

Starter

Ask students to plot (or imagine) a triangle with vertices at (1, 1) (2, 1) (1, 5). Then ask students to imagine the x-coordinates are multiplied by -1, that is, (-1, 1) (-2, 1) (-1, 5).

What transformation has taken place?
(Reflection in y-axis)
What if the x and y coordinates are reversed?
(Reflection in $x = y$)
What transformation has taken place if the coordinates are changed to (-1, 3) (0, 3) (-1, 7)?

Teaching notes

Students may already be familiar with the term tessellation. If not then follow the second example as a way to introduce tessellation.

Look at examples of repeated transformations like the first example. Will two reflections always be able to be represented by a single transformation? Investigate. (A rotation centred on where the mirror lines cross, through twice the angle between the lines. Or if the mirror lines are parallel a translation perpendicular to and through twice the separation between the mirror lines.) Encourage students to consider vertical/horizontal/slanting lines of refection. What difference, if any, would it make if the mirror line passes through the shape being reflected? What sort of shape should be used for the investigation?

Encourage students to share their findings with others and try to convince their neighbours of their conclusions.

Plenary

What words in the English language read the same when they are rotated 180°? Use only capital letters. Begin by examining what letters make sense when rotated 180°. Examples are SIS, MOW, SWIMS, NOON. These are known as a type of ambigram. These could be further researched.

Exercise commentary

Question 1 – Students may need to be helped in understanding that the isometric paper allows for the rotation of 60° at a time.

Question 2 – Some students may prefer to label the equal angles, a, b, c, d. Ask students to investigate whether all quadrilaterals tessellate using this method of rotation.

Question 3 – Insist that students use the word translation to describe the transformation. Do not accept slide or shifted or moved, etc.

Question 4 – Encourage students to name the mirror line in part **c** either y-axis or $x = 0$.

Question 5 – The removed triangle is actually rotated through 90° anti-clockwise. The tessellation is not easy to see. The final pattern is alternating rows of upright upside down 'horses'. Allow students to experiment, without the expectation that they should know how it tessellates quickly.

Answers

1 Equilateral triangle

2 **a, b** Students' drawings of tessellated quadrilaterals with equal angles coloured

c Alternate angles are equal for parallel lines.
Sum of the angles in a quadrilateral is the same as the sum of the angles at a point.

3 **a, b** Students' drawings of multiple reflections of the flag in parallel mirror lines

c Translation of 8 to the right.

4 **a, b** Students' drawings of the rotation and then reflection of the green triangle

c Reflection in the y-axis

5 Students' drawings showing tessellations of the given shape

9c Symmetry

Objectives

- Identify all the symmetries of 2D shapes (L5)

Key ideas	**Resources**
1 Shapes with one or more lines of symmetry are said to have reflection symmetry **2** Shapes which fit onto themselves two or more times in a full turn are said to have rotational symmetry	Lines of symmetry (1114) Rotational symmetry (1116) Symmetry (1230) Protractors Tracing paper Square grid paper Mirrors Cut-out copy of a parallelogram Set of name cards for common polygons

Simplification	**Extension**
Provide tracing paper to help identify rotational symmetry. Provide mirrors to help identify line symmetry.	If possible construct hexagons that have 0, 1, 2, 3, 4, 5 lines of symmetry. Hint that 0, 1, 2 are certainly possible.

Literacy	**Links**
Lots of familiar terminology is used here including names of common polygons and the mathematical adjective 'regular'. A game of 'What am I?' is a fun way to recapitulate the terminology; students take turns to select a card holding the name of a shape, the student with the card describes features of the shape, for example 'two pairs of parallel sides', to the class and the class attempt to work out the name of the shape.	The kaleidoscope was invented in 1816 by David Brewster in Scotland. Kaleidoscopes are usually thought of as toys but are also used by designers and artists. There are instructions for making a simple kaleidoscope at http://www.zefrank.com/dtoy_vs_byokal/index.html and an interactive kaleidoscope at http://www.kaleidoscopesusa.com/makeAscope.htm

Alternative approach

Recollection can be assisted by such questions as 'What would the rhombus be if it had rotational symmetry of order 4, instead of 2' and 'what else could you then say about it?' It is worth spending a little time on the parallelogram to assure students it has no lines of symmetry. Asking students what shape is made when a parallelogram is reflected in a line that bisects the shape is usually worthwhile.

Use the terms mirror line and fold line as well as line of symmetry. The physicality of folding will assist some students, and is in any case a valuable technique in some real-life applications (such as finding the centre of a circle).

Checkpoint

1 On squared paper use three squares to draw a hexagon. Firstly, arrange two of these shapes to give a new shape that has one line of symmetry and no rotational symmetry. Then arrange two more of these hexagons so that the new shape has two lines of symmetry and order of rotation of two.

(Check shapes match given conditions)

Starter

Ask students to draw hexominoes that will fold up to form a cube.

How many can they find? (11 possible nets)
How many nets show line symmetry?
How many nets show rotation symmetry?

Teaching notes

When a parallelogram is rotated about its centre, will its edges and angles appear in exactly the same place more than once when it has completed a full turn? If so how many times? (Twice) Introduce the term 'order of rotational symmetry'. A parallelogram is said to have order of rotational symmetry 2.

Look at some other common 2D shapes and comment on their orders of rotational symmetry. What order do shapes that have no rotational symmetry have? (Order 1)

How many lines of symmetry do rhombuses and parallelograms have? Demonstrate that a parallelogram has no lines of symmetry by attempting to fold a cut out copy. Consider rectangles and squares; is there a connection between the number of lines of symmetry and the order of rotational symmetry? They are the same value here. However, consider rhombuses and parallelograms, where this rule does not apply.

Plenary

A cuboid can be sliced in half to produce two 3D shapes that are reflections of each other. The 'slice' acts like a mirror. How many different ways can this be done? Encourage a new sketch to show each possibility. Three if no faces are square, or five if two opposite faces are square, or nine if it is in fact a cube. You could use the term 'planes of symmetry'.

Exercise commentary

Question 1 – Encourage the use of dashed lines of symmetry to avoid confusion with the diagram itself.

Question 2 – Students could make accurate drawings of the regular shapes using a protractor and given the interior angles. Alternatively a reasonable sketch could be used. Elicit the connection between regular polygons and their symmetry.

Question 4 – Help students recall any angle facts they need. Compare the original shape with the symmetry of both the trapeziums and the rhombus.

Question 5 – Encourage students to generalise. These numbers must be made up of the digits 0, 1 or 8.

Question 6 – You may wish the students to research longest English palindromic sentences, such as 'Norma is as selfless as I am, Ron'.

Answers

1 Students' drawings of
- **a** cross hatch symbol showing 4 lines of symmetry; rotation symmetry = order 4
- **b** rectangle showing 2 lines of symmetry; rotation symmetry = order 2
- **c** three intersecting lines showing 6 lines of symmetry; rotation symmetry = order 6
- **d** phone symbol showing 1 line of symmetry; rotation symmetry = order 1
- **e** arrow symbol showing 1 line of symmetry; rotation symmetry = order 1
- **f** open book symbol showing 1 line of symmetry; rotation symmetry = order 1

2 Students' drawings of
- **a** **i** equilateral triangle with 3 lines of symmetry
  ii rotation symmetry = order 3
- **b** **i** square with 4 lines of symmetry
  ii rotation symmetry = order 4
- **c** **i** regular pentagon with 5 lines of symmetry
  ii rotation symmetry = order 5
- **d** **i** regular hexagon with 6 lines of symmetry
  ii rotation symmetry = order 6
- **e** **i** regular octagon with 8 lines of symmetry
  ii rotation symmetry = order 8

3
- **a** Students' drawings of three coloured squares on the grid showing 2 lines of symmetry; rotation symmetry = order 2
- **b** Students' drawings of four coloured squares on the grid showing 1 line of symmetry; rotation symmetry = order 1
- **c** Students' drawings of five coloured squares on the grid showing no lines of symmetry; rotation symmetry = order 2

4 $a = 130°$, $b = 100°$, $c = 100°$, $d = 80°$, $e = 50°$

5 1881

6 Both diagonals are lines of symmetry.

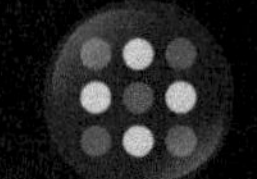

9d Enlargements 1

Objectives	
• Enlarge 2D shapes, given a centre of enlargement and a positive integer scale factor	(L6)
• Identify the scale factor of an enlargement as the ratio of the lengths of any two corresponding line segments	(L6)
• Use the coordinate grid to solve problems involving enlargements	(L6)

Key ideas	**Resources**
1 Shapes can be transformed by enlargement; we sometimes use a specified centre of enlargement	Enlarging shapes (1099) Transformations (1125) Isometric paper with lines drawn Graph paper

Simplification	**Extension**
Provide students with enlarged copies of the shapes from the exercise.	Explore enlargements of shapes that include arcs. Once students have decided on a shape, challenge them to enlarge it from different centres of enlargement. Advise students to keep their shape simple to begin with.

Literacy	**Links**
Enlargement is used here for any scale factor – we will not always know whether the scale factor is greater than 1, or less than 1, so we just stick to the one word, even though the image may be smaller than the object. So, a slightly technical use of the work enlargement. The word similar should be used at some point here.	Magnifying glasses and microscopes are used to make objects appear larger. The magnification value is the scale factor. There are microscope images at different magnification values at http://micro.magnet.fsu.edu/primer/java/scienceopticsu/virtual/magnifying/index.html

Alternative approach

Is the size of the shape always altered? Since any scale factor is possible, 1 is possible. (Can students think of any other scale factor that would leave size unchanged? If they suggest -1, fine; perhaps leave the question with them, if no suggestions are made.) What happens if the scale factor is 0? Do angles still stay the same? Or does this question simply have no meaning here? (The idea of meaninglessness is important for later understanding.)

A shape can simply be enlarged, made larger (or maybe smaller), without any specified centre of enlargement, in which case it can be drawn wherever is convenient. Or, there may be a specified centre of enlargement, in which case the enlargement has to be in the correct place relative both to the centre of enlargement and to the object. (Conversely, if the position of the image relevant to the object is specified, then there is a centre of enlargement somewhere, fixed, that can be located.)

The ratio of distance from the centre of enlargement to the image, to that from the centre to the object, is the scale factor, and this needs to be made very clear. It can be considered for any point on image and object. (The requirement that the points be corresponding will be mentioned in passing, but may not need any elaboration, since it will be taken for granted by most or all students.) And then, of course, this same scale factor is also the ratio of image size to object size, again for any corresponding lengths. So, we could regard the entire shape-with-rays drawing as one entity, where all corresponding lengths of image and object are in the same ratio.

Note that in question **2** parts **a** and **c** each have the same alternative negative scale factor, and that the centre of enlargement involved with these may be more obvious to students that the intended one; the idea of negative enlargements may be unavoidable, but still does not need to be discussed in detail.

Checkpoint

1 On squared paper draw the triangle $A(4, 2)$, $B(3, 5)$ and $C(7, 3)$. Enlarge this triangle with a scale factor of 3 and the centre of enlargement at $(2, 1)$. Give the new coordinates of A, B and C.

($A'(8, 4)$; B' $(5, 13)$ and C' $(17, 7)$)

Starter

Ask students to draw

- shapes that have rotational symmetry of order six but no reflection symmetry
- shapes that have rotational symmetry of order six and do have reflection symmetry.

Ask students how many lines of symmetry these shapes have.

This can be extended using different orders of symmetry.

Teaching notes

How can an enlargement be described? Discuss the term 'scale factor'. What scale factors are likely to be used in questions? (2, 3, 1.5, 2.5, 0.5) Do negative scale factors exist? (Yes, but they are normally covered in Year 10.)

Why is a scale factor not enough to tell you all you need to know about the image? (Because the position has not been stated.)

Describe how a slide projector works. Describe how the light from the bulb strikes the slide and continues in 'rays' to the screen. The centre of enlargement is like a light source with the rays of light coming out to strike at the vertices of the shape. Use an example on coordinate axes and show how a scale factor of 2 is produced. Emphasise that the distance from the centre of enlargement to the corners of the original shape has doubled. Note that many students double the distance from the vertex of the original shape rather than from the centre of enlargement.

Plenary

If a shape is enlarged using the origin as the centre of enlargement, what pattern can you establish when comparing the original and new coordinates of the vertices of the shape? Answer, each x and y coordinate has been multiplied by the scale factor. What do you expect if the centre of enlargement had been somewhere else, for example, (1, 0)?

Exercise commentary

Question 1 – Reinforce the concept that in an enlargement the length of every line is multiplied by the scale factor. Students may choose any line to be able to calculate the scale factor.

Question 2 – Remind students that the centre of enlargement can be on the edge, inside or outside a shape. Ask students to check that all dimensions have been enlarged by the same scale factor. Students should get used to counting squares when using construction lines, rather than use a ruler.

Question 3 – Many students will prefer finding the location of one vertex and then drawing the enlargement relative to that point, rather than referring every vertex back to the centre of enlargement. For more complicated shapes it is worth suggesting to students that they add guidelines and make sure they all pass through the centre of enlargement.

Question 4 – Some students might see this as a scale factor of 3 since the point has moved 3 squares on. Remind students that they are comparing the distance from the centre of enlargement to a point on the original shape, with the distance from the centre of enlargement to a point on the enlarged shape.

Question 5 – Ask students to start with a scale factor of 3 and then a scale factor of 4 and see if they can generalise. Repeat with an example of the area of a rectangle. Ensure students conclude that scale factors are squared to find out how much area has been increased by.

Answers

1 **a** s.f. 2 **b** s.f. 3 **c** s.f. 2.5

2 **a** s.f. 2, centre (5, 5) **b** s.f. 3, centre (1, 3)
c s.f. 2, centre (2, 5) **d** s.f. 2, centre (0, 0)

3 **a** Students' drawings of s.f. 2 enlargement of L shape
b Students' drawings of s.f. 3 enlargement of triangle
c Students' drawings of s.f. 4 enlargement of L shape from one corner
d Students' drawings of s.f. 2 enlargement of shape given

4 **a** s.f. 4
b (4, 5) (4, 1) (12, 1) (12, 5)

5 **a** 100 small triangles
b Students' drawings of s.f. 10 enlargement of equilateral triangle on isometric paper

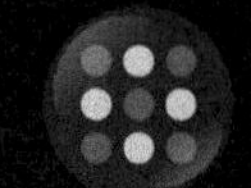

9e Enlargements 2

Objectives

- Enlarge 2D shapes using positive, fractional scale factors (L7)
- Recognise that enlargements preserve angle but not length, and understand the implications of enlargement for perimeter (L7)

Key ideas	Resources
1 Enlargement scale factors can be less than 1	Enlarging shapes (1099) Transformations (1125) Multi-link cubes Square grid paper

Simplification	Extension
Provide students with enlarged copies of the shapes from the exercise. Remind students to keep measuring/counting from the centre of enlargement every time.	Set questions involving fractional scale factors greater than 1. If students tried the previous extension, can they apply fractional scale factors to shapes with arcs?

Literacy	Links
As mentioned for the previous lesson, enlargement is used here for any scale factor – we will not always know whether the scale factor is greater than 1, or less than 1, so we just stick to the one word, even though the image may be smaller than the object. So, a slightly technical use of the word enlargement.	Pictures can be copied and enlarged or reduced using a device called a pantograph. A pantograph consists of several hinged rods joined together in a parallelogram shape with extended sides. One end is traced over the image and a pencil attached to the other end reproduces the image to the desired scale. Pantographs are often sold as toys. There is more information about pantographs at http://en.wikipedia.org/wiki/Pantograph and an interactive pantograph at http://www.ies.co.jp/math/java/geo/panta/panta.html

Alternative approach

As for the previous spread, ask if the size of the shape is always altered? Since any scale factor is possible, 1 is possible. (Can students think of any other scale factor that would leave size unchanged? If they suggest -1, fine; perhaps leave the question with them, if no suggestions are made.)

A shape can simply be enlarged, made larger (or maybe smaller), without any specified centre of enlargement, in which case it can be drawn wherever is convenient. Or, there may be a specified centre of enlargement, in which case the enlargement has to be in the correct place relative both to the centre of enlargement and to the object. (Conversely, if the position of the image relevant to the object is specified, then there is a centre of enlargement somewhere, fixed, that can be located.)

The ratio of the distance from the centre of enlargement to the image, to the distance from the centre of enlargement to the object, is the scale factor, and this needs to be made very clear. It can be considered for any point on image and object. (The requirement that the points be corresponding will be mentioned in passing, but may not need any elaboration, since it will be taken for granted by most or all students.) And then, of course, this same scale factor is also the ratio of image size to object size, again for any corresponding lengths. So, we could regard the entire shape-with-rays drawing as one entity, where all corresponding lengths of image and object are in the same ratio.

Checkpoint

1 On squared paper draw this quadrilateral, $A(5, 5)$, $B(5, 8)$, $C(8, 8)$ and $D(11, 2)$. What is the special name given to this quadrilateral? Enlarge this shape by a scale factor of ⅓ with a centre of enlargement at (2, 2). Give the new coordinates of the quadrilateral. (kite; $A'(3, 3)$, $B'(3, 4)$, $C'(4, 4)$, $D'(5, 2)$)

Starter

Write a list of anagrams on the board and ask students to unscramble them and then make their own anagrams or word search. Possible anagrams are

ATTORNIO, SNATTINAROL, AGEMI, GRONNTUCE, INFLECETOR, JOTBEC, TRYSMYME, DERRO, GLAMENNTREE, RECENT (rotation, translation, image, congruent, reflection, object, symmetry, order, enlargement, centre)

Teaching notes

What do enlargements by scale factors 1 and 2 mean? Establish that scale factor 1 will keep a shape the same size in the same position. What must a scale factor or 1.5 or $\frac{1}{2}$ represent? What mistake is common when performing an enlargement by scale factor $\frac{1}{2}$? Enlarging by scale factor 1.5 rather than reducing the lengths to half the size.

Look at an example of an enlargement between 0 and 1 on coordinate axes. Consider putting the centre of enlargement inside the original shape. How can the enlargement be reversed to return to the original shape? Is there a connection between the 2 scale factors that would be used? They are reciprocals.

How could you enlarge a circle or ellipse? What ideas do students have? Which point is the most important one to locate for the image? (Centre point)

Plenary

If a 3D shape is enlarged, what happens to its volume? Experiment with cuboids initially. What conclusion do students reach? This could be made more interesting by using multilink cubes. Students could build small shapes and then an enlarged shape using a specified scale factor. How has the volume changed?

Exercise commentary

Question 1 – The term 'enlargement' may cause confusion when the shapes are in fact being reduced in size. Discuss this problem with the language if necessary. Ask students to investigate how angles change during enlargement, and conclude they remain unchanged.

Question 2 – Encourage students to count vertically and horizontally in squares. Many will prefer to start with the easiest vertex and then draw the enlargement relative to that point. For questions where the new vertex is not on the lines on the grid, show students that adding guidelines through the centre will enable them to mark these vertices accurately.

Question 3 – Show students how they can check whether lines are parallel on squared paper and confirm with them this shape is a trapezium.

Question 4 – Ask students to try with a simple shape. Many students will recognise this intuitively.

Question 5 – Use this to reinforce the concept that any distance, even a compound distance like the perimeter, is changed by the same factor.

Question 6 – Remind students of the term similar and that any enlargement will produce a similar shape. Ask them to try another shape and check whether this method always produces the same result. Classroom projectors provide a good illustration of enlargement.

Answers

1 **a** Students' drawings of s.f. $\frac{1}{3}$ enlargement of triangle
b Students' drawings of s.f. $\frac{1}{4}$ enlargement of square
c Students' drawings of s.f. $\frac{1}{2}$ enlargement of arrow

2 **a** Students' drawings of s.f. $\frac{1}{2}$ enlargement of L shape
b Students' drawings of s.f. $\frac{1}{3}$ enlargement of square
c Students' drawings of s.f. $\frac{1}{2}$ enlargement of rectangle

3 **a** Students' drawings of trapezium using coordinates given
b Trapezium
c Students' plots of the trapezium and its s.f. $\frac{1}{2}$ enlargement about (2, 4)
d (2, 3) (5, 2) (7, 6) (3, 5)

4 s.f. $\frac{1}{4}$

5 **a** s.f. $\frac{1}{3}$ **b** $x = 5$ cm **c** 12 cm, 36 cm

6 Yes, s.f. $\frac{1}{2}$

Key outcomes	Quick check
Carry out and specify reflections, rotations and translations.	The trapezium $A(3,2)$, $B(4,4)$, $C(6,4)$, $D(7,2)$ is transformed onto $A'(2,-3)$, $B'(4,-4)$, $C'(4,-6)$, $D'(2,-7)$. Describe fully this transformation. (Rotated 90° clockwise about $(0,0)$)
Carry out combinations of transformations.	A shape is reflected in the y-axis and then rotated 180° about (0,0). What is this as a single transformation? (Reflection in the x-axis)
Recognise rotation and reflection symmetry.	Put two identical isosceles trapeziums together to create a shape that has rotational order of symmetry of 2 and no lines of symmetry. Put two identical isosceles trapeziums together to create a shape that has rotational order of symmetry of 2 and 2 lines of symmetry. (Side by side to form a parallelogram; one above the other to make a hexagon or an hourglass)
Carry out and specify an enlargement.	A flag $A(2,0)$, $B(2,4)$, $C(4,4)$ $D(2,3)$ is enlarged by a scale factor of 3, with centre of enlargement at $(1,3)$. What are the new coordinates for the flag? ($A'(4,-3)$; $B'(4,9)$; $C'(10,6)$; $D'(4,3)$)

MyReview

9 MySummary

Check out
You should now be able to ...

Check out		Test it ➡ Questions
✓ Carry out and specify reflections, rotations and translations.	5	1, 2
✓ Carry out combinations of transformations.	6	3
✓ Recognise rotation and reflection symmetry.	5	4, 5
✓ Carry out and specify an enlargement.	7	6, 7

Language	Meaning	Example
Object	The starting shape	p. 164
Image	The resulting shape after the transformations have been applied	
Reflection	The object is flipped over a given mirror line	Looking at this book in a mirror is a reflection.
Rotation	Rotates an object around a central point (like a car wheel turning)	Turning this book through 90° clockwise about its bottom right corner is a rotation.
Translation	A transformation which slides an object	Sliding this book across your desk is a translation.
Enlargement	A transformation that changes the size of the object.	If you enlarged this book by scale factor 2 about its centre, it would grow to twice its size
Scale factor	In an enlargement, the number that you multiply lengths on the object by to get corresponding lengths on the image	

9 MyReview

1 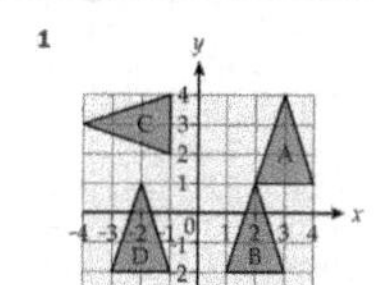

Describe the transformation that moves
a A to B **b** A to C **c** B to D

2 Copy this shape on squared paper. Reflect the shape in the mirror line.

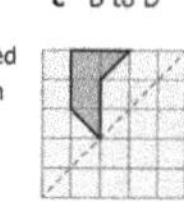

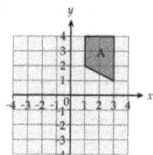

3 Copy the diagram.
a Rotate the trapezium 180° about (0, 0) and label the image B.
b Reflect B in the line $x = 0$ and label the image C.
c Describe fully the single transformation that moves A to C.

4 How many lines of symmetry do the following have?
a Regular decagon **b** Rectangle

5 State the order of rotation symmetry of
a an isosceles triangle
b a regular nonagon.

6 B is enlarged to give B′, calculate the scale factor and find the coordinates of the centre of enlargement.

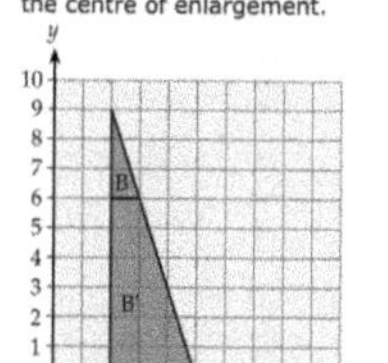

7 Copy the shape onto squared grid paper and enlarge it by scale factor $\frac{1}{2}$ using the dot as the centre of enlargement

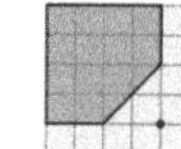

What next?

Score		
0 – 3		Your knowledge of this topic is still developing. To improve look at Formative test: 2C-9; MyMaths: 1099, 1113 – 1116, 1125, 1127, 1148 and 1230
4 – 6		You are gaining a secure knowledge of this topic. To improve look at InvisiPen: 361, 362, 363, 364, 366 and 368
7		You have mastered this topic. Well done, you are ready to progress!

Question commentary

Question 1 – Ensure students describe the transformation fully. Allow them to use tracing paper for rotation.

Question 2 – Emphasize that perpendicular distance must stay the same. Some students find counting diagonal squares helpful.

Question 3 – Remind students that the $x = 0$ line is NOT the same as the x-axis. Again have students use tracing paper for the rotation and insist they describe the transformations fully.

Question 4 – Students sometimes draw diagonals on rectangle thinking they are lines of symmetry. Have a piece of rectangular paper and show them what happens when it is folded along its diagonal.

Question 5 – Remind students to say that a shape has rotational symmetry of order 1, rather than saying no rotational symmetry.

Question 7 – Some students will prefer to find the new location of one vertex and then find the other points relative to that one, rather than referring back to the centre. If they use this method suggest they add guidelines at the end to check.

Answers

1 a Translation of 1 unit left and 3 units down
b Rotation of 90° anti-clockwise about (0, 0)
c Reflection in the y-axis, line $x = 0$

2

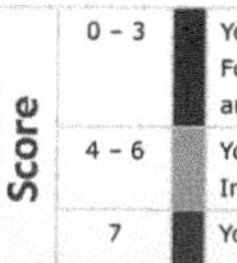

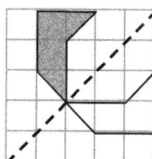

3 a, b Trapezium labelled A with vertices at (1, 2), (1, 4), (3, 1), (3, 4)
Trapezium labelled B with vertices at (-1, -2), (-1, -4), (-3, -1), (-3, -4)
Trapezium labelled C with vertices at (1, -2), (1, -4), (3, -1), (3, -4)
c Reflection in the x-axis, line $y = 0$

4 a 10 **b** 2

5 a 1 **b** 9

6 Scale factor 3, centre of enlargement (2, 9)

7

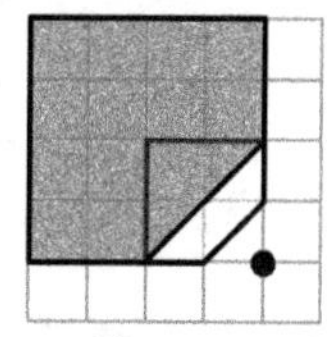

8 a 50 m **b** 6 cm

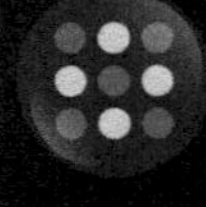

9 MyPractice

9a

1 Copy the diagram on square grid paper.
Describe fully the transformation that moves the pink shape to

- **a** shape A
- **b** shape B
- **c** shape C.

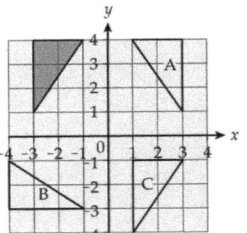

2 Copy the diagram on square grid paper.

- **a** Reflect the green hexagon in the line $y = x$.
  Colour the image orange.
- **b** Describe a different transformation that moves the green hexagon to the orange hexagon.

9b

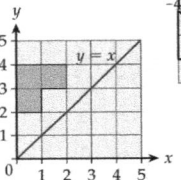

3 **a** Tessellate a regular hexagon using repeated translations.
b Which other repeated transformations can you use to tessellate a regular hexagon?

4 The pink triangle is rotated clockwise through 90° about (0, 0).

- **a** Draw the image and label it I_1.
- **b** The triangle I_1 is reflected in the y-axis.
  Draw the new image and call it I_2.
- **c** The triangle I_2 is reflected in the x-axis.
  Draw the new image and call it I_3.
- **d** Describe the single transformation that moves the pink triangle to I_3.

9c

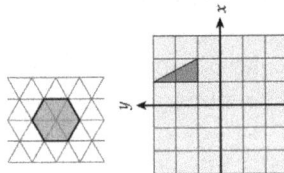

5 Draw these currency symbols.
Draw any lines of reflection symmetry and state the order of rotation symmetry for each symbol.

a € **b** $ **c** S **d** ¥ **e** ₦

6 This triangle has one vertical line of symmetry.

- **a** State the values of a and b.
- **b** Explain your reasoning.

9d

7 Copy the shapes on square grid paper.
Draw the enlargement of each shape using the dot as the centre of enlargement and the given scale factor.

a scale factor 3 **b** scale fator 2 **c** scale factor 4

8 Copy each diagram. The blue shape has been enlarged to give the green shape.
Calculate the scale factors and give the coordinates of the centre of enlargement.

a **b** **c**

9e

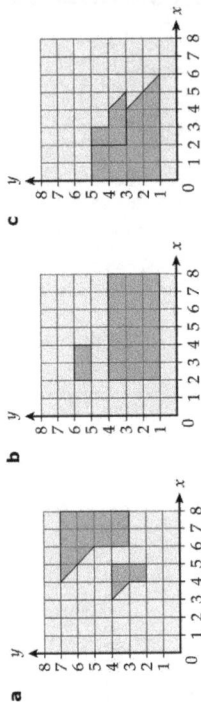

9 **a** Plot the points A (4,0), B (7,0) and C (4,6) on the coordinate axes.
b What is the mathematical name of the shape ABC?
c Using (1,3) as the centre of enlargement, enlarge the shape ABC by scale factor $\frac{1}{3}$.
d Write down the coordinates of the image A′B′C′.

10 **a** The smaller triangle is an enlargement of the larger triangle, what is the scale factor?

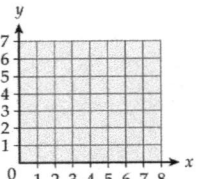

w cm, 4 cm, 6 cm, perimeter = x cm

y cm, 10 cm, z cm, perimeter = $32\frac{1}{2}$ cm

b Find the values of w, x, y and z.

Question commentary

Questions 1 and **2** – Again emphasise that perpendicular distance must stay the same. Tracing paper can be used to support students who find this difficult. To use tracing paper, turn paper upside down and match up line of reflection, to show position of image.

Questions 3 and **4** – Encourage students to describe each transformation fully.

Question 5 – Remind students that all shapes have rotational symmetry of an order of at least 1.

Question 7 – Encourage students to have the habit of checking enlargements by drawing guidelines.

Question 10 – Use the word 'similar' in your explanations. Remind students that in similar shapes every length is increased by the same factor, the factor of enlargement.

Answers

1 **a** Reflection in the y-axis
b Anticlockwise rotation of 90° about (0, 0)
c Translation of 4 to the right and 5 down

2 **a** Students' drawings of reflection of L shape in $y = x$
b Rotation of 180° about (2, 2)

3 **a** Students' drawings of tessellation of regular hexagon
b Reflections or rotations

4 **a, b, c** Students' drawings of triangle I_1 and its transformations to I_2 and I_3
d Anticlockwise rotation of 90° about (0, 0)

5 Students' drawings of
a euro symbol showing 1 line of symmetry; rotation symmetry = order 1
b dollar symbol with no lines of symmetry; rotation symmetry = order 2
c capital letter S with no lines of symmetry; rotation symmetry = order 2
d yen symbol showing 1 line of symmetry; rotation symmetry = order 1
e naira symbol with no lines of symmetry; rotation symmetry = order 2

6 **a** $a = 65°$, $b = 90°$
b The two triangles are congruent and so $a = 65°$. Angles on a straight line add to 180° and so $2b = 180°$ and so $b = 90°$.

7 **a** Students' drawings of s.f. 3 enlargement of flag
b Students' drawings of s.f. 2 enlargement of square
c Students' drawings of s.f. 4 enlargement of rectangle

8 **a** s.f. 2, centre (2, 1) **b** s.f. 3, centre (2, 7)
c s.f. 2, centre (4, 5)

9 **a, c** Students' drawings of right-angled triangle and its s.f. $\frac{1}{3}$ enlargement
b right-angled triangle **d** (2, 2) (3, 2) (2, 4)

10 **a** s.f. $\frac{2}{5}$
b $z = 15$ cm, $y = 7\frac{1}{2}$ cm, $w = 3$ cm, $x = 13$ cm

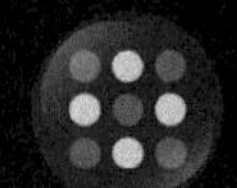

Case study 3: Food crops

Related lessons		Resources	
Real-life graphs	6f	Add and subtract decimals	(1007)
Constructing diagrams	8d	Real life graphs	(1184)
Written addition and subtraction	11f	Examples of graphs from newspapers	

Simplification	Extension
Students may need structured guidance working through the table in task **1**.	Students could be asked to look at the percentage changes of wheat production, consumption and stocks and the percentage change of the price of wheat and the production of biodiesel. Further research could also be carried out into misleading graphs that appear in the press or online.

Links

Students should be encouraged to look in more detail at the range of crops that are being used for various purposes and research the effects this is having worldwide on food prices and levels of availability. There is much useful data on the internet, for example www.hgca.com or www.ukagriculture.com/crops/crops.cfm.

Students could be organised to research different aspects to bring together as a class.

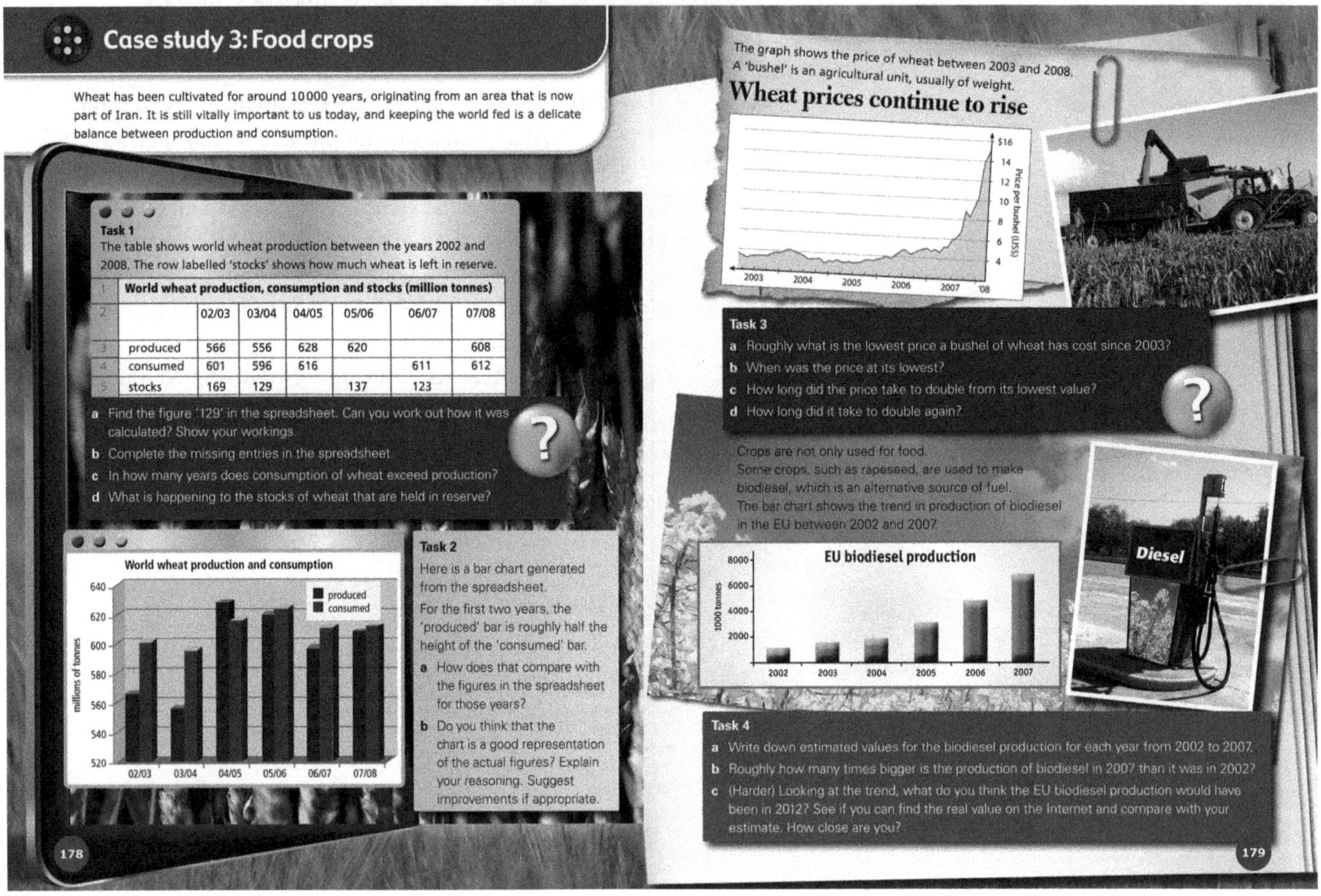

Case study 3: Food crops

Wheat has been cultivated for around 10000 years, originating from an area that is now part of Iran. It is still vitally important to us today, and keeping the world fed is a delicate balance between production and consumption.

Task 1

The table shows world wheat production between the years 2002 and 2008. The row labelled 'stocks' shows how much wheat is left in reserve.

1	World wheat production, consumption and stocks (million tonnes)					
2		02/03	03/04	04/05	05/06	06/07	07/08
3	produced	566	556	628	620		608
4	consumed	601	596	616		611	612
5	stocks	169	129		137	123	

a Find the figure '129' in the spreadsheet. Can you work out how it was calculated? Show your workings.

b Complete the missing entries in the spreadsheet.

c In how many years does consumption of wheat exceed production?

d What is happening to the stocks of wheat that are held in reserve?

World wheat production and consumption

(millions of tonnes; 520–640; 02/03, 03/04, 04/05, 05/06, 06/07, 07/08; produced, consumed)

Task 2

Here is a bar chart generated from the spreadsheet.

For the first two years, the 'produced' bar is roughly half the height of the 'consumed' bar.

a How does that compare with the figures in the spreadsheet for those years?

b Do you think that the chart is a good representation of the actual figures? Explain your reasoning. Suggest improvements if appropriate.

178

The graph shows the price of wheat between 2003 and 2008. A 'bushel' is an agricultural unit, usually of weight.

Wheat prices continue to rise

(Price per bushel (US$); 4–$16; 2003, 2004, 2005, 2006, 2007, '08)

Task 3

a Roughly what is the lowest price a bushel of wheat has cost since 2003?

b When was the price at its lowest?

c How long did the price take to double from its lowest value?

d How long did it take to double again?

Crops are not only used for food.
Some crops, such as rapeseed, are used to make biodiesel, which is an alternative source of fuel.
The bar chart shows the trend in production of biodiesel in the EU between 2002 and 2007.

EU biodiesel production

(1000 tonnes; 2000–8000; 2002, 2003, 2004, 2005, 2006, 2007)

Diesel

Task 4

a Write down estimated values for the biodiesel production for each year from 2002 to 2007.

b Roughly how many times bigger is the production of biodiesel in 2007 than it was in 2002?

c (Harder) Looking at the trend, what do you think the EU biodiesel production would have been in 2012? See if you can find the real value on the Internet and compare with your estimate. How close are you?

179

Teaching notes

Many students will be aware of the rising use of biofuels through hearing about cars that run on chip fat and other oils. Some may have experienced it or know adults who use biofuels. Running cars in this way is often portrayed as being 'alternative' and 'green'. Students might also be aware that prices for wheat and other crops have recently been rising quite rapidly, and know that there is a shortage of food crops in some parts of the world.

This case study focuses on production figures for wheat and biodiesel to raise the possibility that there could be a partial link between the increasing use of biodiesel and the increasing price and shortage of wheat.

Task 1

Introduce the case study and look at the spreadsheet shown at the top left. Discuss what is meant by 'produced', 'consumed' and 'stocks' and look at the first two columns to see how the figures relate to each other. Discuss how you have to find the surplus or deficit of production compared with consumption and then adjust the stocks level accordingly. Give the students a few minutes to work out the missing values on the spreadsheet and answer the related questions.

Task 2

When the students have considered the questions relating to this bar chart, discuss their opinions about the reasonableness or otherwise of the vertical scale. For example, the differences would be very hard to determine if the vertical axis started at zero. However, starting the axis at 520 million tonnes means that the shortfall between wheat production and consumption appears exaggerated. In the first two columns the production appears to provide only about half the amount of wheat that is needed.

Task 3

Look at the graph showing wheat prices for the past few years. What do you notice about the graph? The most obvious thing is that the prices rise very rapidly in the last two years shown on the graph. Students should then work through the questions about the graph.

Task 4

Look at the final graph on the spread that shows figures for biodiesel production in Europe. Do you notice anything familiar about this graph? Elicit that the shape is very similar to the shape of the wheat price graph, increasing only slowly for a while and then increasing much more rapidly. Conclude by considering whether the production of biofuels could be having an influence on the cost of wheat and other crops.

Answers

1 **a** 169 – (596 – 556)

b

	02/03	03/04	04/05	05/06	06/07	07/08
Produced	566	556	628	620	597	608
Consumed	601	596	616	624	611	612
Stocks	169	129	141	137	123	119

c 5 years

d Decreasing trend

2 **a** Appears to be half the height but should be 95% of the height.

b Students' answers. The suppressed zero makes the size of the difference misleading, but allows it to be seen.

3 **a** Just over $3

b May, 2004

c $2\frac{1}{2}$ years

d $\frac{1}{2}$year

4 **a** 1300, 1800, 2000, 3200, 4800, 6600

b 5

c Students' own answers

Learning outcomes	
A3 Understand and use the concepts and vocabulary of expressions, equations, inequalities, terms and factors	(L6)
A4 Simplify and manipulate algebraic expressions to maintain equivalence by: collecting like terms, multiplying a single term over a bracket, taking out common factors, expanding products of 2 or more binomials	(L6)
A6 Model situations or procedures by translating them into algebraic expressions or formulae and by using graphs	(L6)
A7 Use algebraic methods to solve linear equations in 1 variable (including all forms that require rearrangement)	(L6/7)

Introduction

The chapter starts by looking at equations which require two steps, those with brackets and those with the unknown on both sides and then moves on to solving equations with a negative algebraic term. Equations with fractions are then introduced before a section on trial and improvement. The final section looks at equations which might appear in real life.

The introduction discusses how biologists use equations to model things like population growth among species of animal. This concept uses a form of equation known as an exponential equation where the growth (or decline) in a population is related to the population present at the time (among other factors). There are many other things that behave according to these kinds of rule. Bacteria growth can be modelled using exponential equations, for example. Radioactive substances which 'decay' over time can also be modelled using the concept of exponential decay. Each radioactive substance has what is called a 'half-life': the length of time it takes for the radioactivity to halve. Carbon-15 has a half-life of 2.449 seconds so its rate of decay is very fast, whereas titanium-44 has a half-life of close to 63 years. The longest half-life known is that of the isotope tellurium-128 which has a half-life of 2.2×10^{24} years – over 100,000,000,000,000 times longer than the universe has been in existence!

Prior knowledge

Students should already know how to…

- Perform simple arithmetic operations on positive and negative whole numbers
- Solve simple two-step equations
- Collect like terms and expand single brackets

Starter problem

The starter problem is a spider diagram showing s simple equation which has been modified in six different ways. Students are invited to describe the six changes and continue each one a further step.

In order, clockwise from top left:

- 1 has been subtracted from both sides
- both sides have been doubled
- 1 has been added to both sides
- x has been added to both sides
- both sides have been halved
- x has been subtracted from both sides

Students are then directed to invent some changes of their own. These could be further examples of changes to the original equation given, or they could be invited to make up their own equation and complete a similar exercise to this one.

Resources

MyMaths

Trial and improvement	1057	Equations 2 - multi-step	1154	Rules and formulae	1158
Equations 3 - both sides	1182	Equations 4 - brackets	1928	Equations 5 - fractions	1929

Online assessment

Chapter test	2C–10
Formative test	2C–10
Summative test	2C–10

InvisiPen solutions

One-step equations	234	Two-step equations	235
Equations with brackets	236	Unknowns on both sides	237
Equations with negative terms			241
Solving equations with fractions			242
Solving algebraic fractions cross mult			243

Topic scheme

Teaching time = 5 lessons/2 weeks

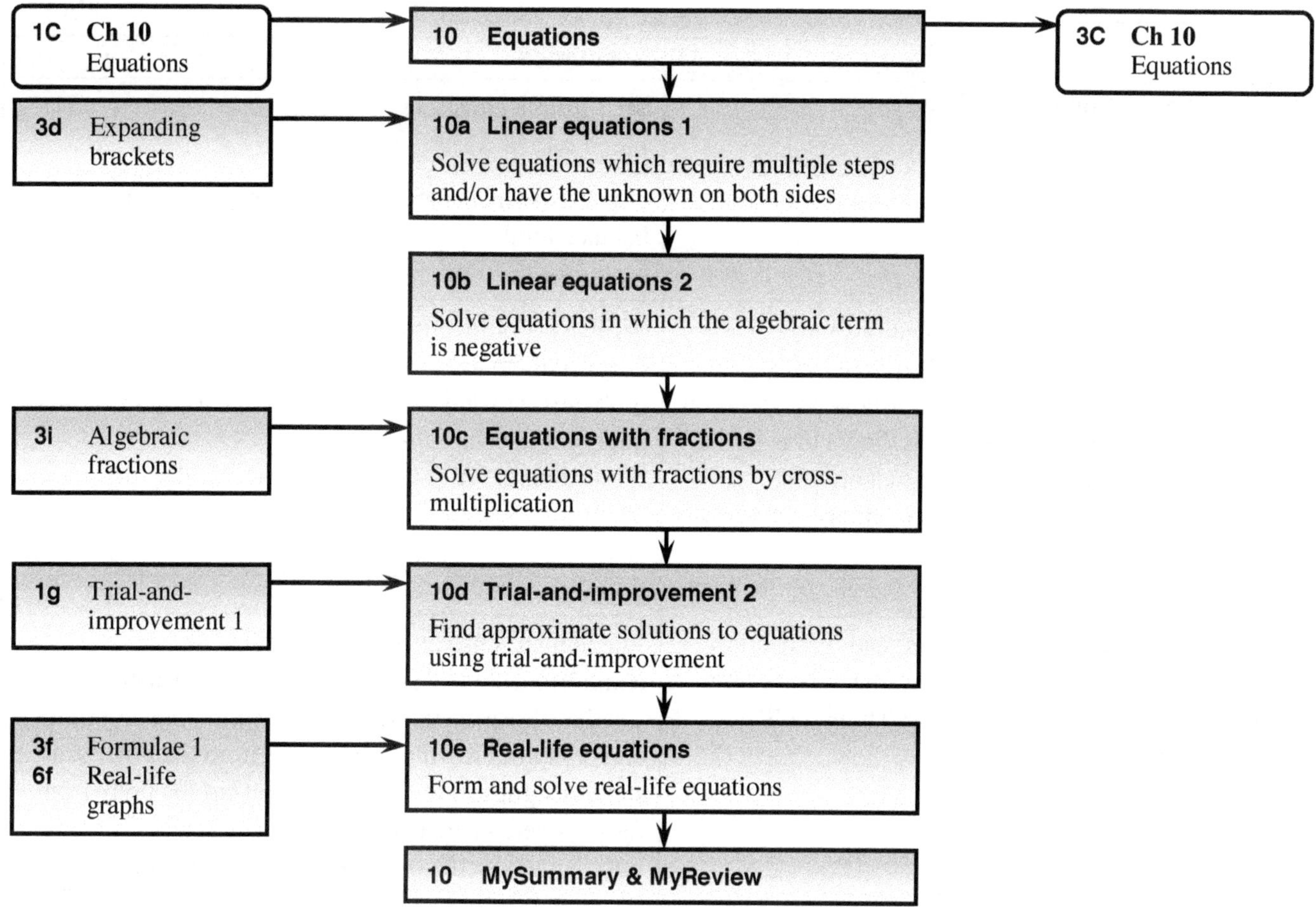

Differentiation

Student book 2A 192 – 205

One-step equations
Equation puzzles
Two-step equations
Making equations

Student book 2B 176 – 189

Solving one-step equations
Solving multi-step equations
Equations with brackets
Real-life equations

Student book 2C 180 – 195

Linear equations 1
Linear equations 2
Equations with fractions
Trial-and-improvement 2
Real-life equations

Objectives	
• Construct and solve linear equations with integer coefficients (with and without brackets, positive or negative solution) (L6)	
Key ideas	**Resources**
1 The solving of linear equations	Simple equations (1154) Interactive scales http://www.mathsisfun.com/algebra/add-subtract-balance.html
Simplification	**Extension**
Pictorial representations of the equations through 'balances', where possible, may help to reinforce understanding. The method of performing an operation on both sides of an equation can be shown in both the algebraic and pictorial approach. Students will however become aware of the disadvantages of the latter approach.	Write a set of identities for students to solve, but disguise them as equations. Ask students what problems they have encountered? What makes these questions special? For example, $3(2x - 4) = 4 + 2(x + 1) + 4x - 18$.
Literacy	**Links**
The difference between 'both sides' and 'each side', and the clarification that the former, in the book here, means the latter, could be another small point that assists understanding.	The human sense of balance is called equilibrioception. The brain collects information from a series of organs in the inner ear called the labyrinth and combines it with information from the other senses such as sight and touch to help prevent the body from falling over. There is more information at http://en.wikipedia.org/wiki/Equilibrioception

Alternative approach

Encourage students to always spend a moment seeing whether the solution is obvious, and perhaps a bit longer guessing and checking. This will be fine for the first equation and for much of question **1**.

When the answer can be seen quickly, this gives a feeling of confidence; and as students find that this does not work quickly they will both be more responsive to suggestions of more formal algebraic techniques and also be likely to deduce these for themselves, albeit not explicitly, because the steps of analysis they will naturally develop (with a little help) will be the same steps. These will begin with inverse functions, and it will then be important to emphasise the need to always do the same thing to each side, so that they stay equal, and also to write each line of working afresh, so that students do not find themselves writing things (such as $7h = 20 + 1 = 21 = 3$) that are not true.

And then, return to the examples in the book, which should make sense and be more appealing, and students should be in a better position to see the most efficient way of solving each equation, or at least choosing a method that suits them.

In question **3**, encourage students to spot that some cancelling can take place (in parts **a**, **d** and **f**) before the brackets are expanded. This should allow some discussion and elucidation of when cancelling can occur and when not.

For question **5**, do not insist on formal methods; if the words do not provide much of an obstacle, the algebra is simple.

For question **7**, show that terming the middle number x, rather than the first number, makes life easier.

Checkpoint

1 The sum of four consecutive odd numbers is 96. By making x the first number, form and solve an equation to find the value of x and the other numbers. ($x = 21$)

Starter

Each consonant scores 2 and each vowel scores 1. Multiply the total consonant score by the square of the total vowel score to get the word score.

Ask students to write down mathematical words and find their scores. Bonus points for scores that equal 72.

This can be differentiated by the score allocated to a consonant or vowel.

Teaching notes

Using the idea of balancing scales, show how an equation can be solved by performing operations to both sides of the scales (equal sign). Use the example in the student book.

Show how equations can be solved algebraically without drawing balances, but strongly emphasise the need to show working on both sides.

Introduce the four basic methods of showing working, describe them as 'reverse' or 'inverse' operations. For example

$x + 4 = 7$	$-2 = x - 3$
$-4 \qquad -4$	$+3 \qquad +3$
$x = 3$	$1 = x$
$3x = 1$	$\frac{x}{4} = 2.5$
$\frac{3x}{3} = \frac{1}{3}$	$4 \times \frac{x}{4} = 2.5 \times 4$
$x = \frac{1}{3}$	$x = 10$

Include examples where you need to perform two stages of operations. Progress onto examples that involve expanding brackets and having letters on both sides. Suggest that with letters on both sides, it is better to deal with the letters first. Note that students may well introduce an extra unnecessary step if they deal with the numbers first when solving an equation with letters on both sides.

Some students may need reminding of the rules for multiplying with negatives in order to be able to expand the brackets correctly.

Plenary

Is there more than one solution for the isosceles triangle in question **6**? Yes, $x = 3, 4.5, 6$ are all correct Point out that the diagram can't be assumed to be anything other than what it is said to be – and nothing is said about which two sides are equal. Write a similar question, but for an equilateral triangle.

Exercise commentary

The balance method illustrated is conceptually the best method for solving equations. Use language consistent with the balance method, e.g. 'Always do the same to both sides.' Avoid language like 'just move x to the other side' as conceptually this will cause confusion.

Question 1 – Some solutions are negative.

Question 2 – Some students will prefer to expand brackets first. Show them that it is more efficient if they don't, but allow them to use the method with which they are most comfortable.

Question 3 – Unlike the previous question, brackets must be expanded first in order to solve. Make sure students are looking out for occasions where they need to subtract a negative.

Question 4 – With unknowns on both sides students must expand brackets and then use the balance method. Tell them to remove the variable from whichever side has the least, so that there is a positive co-efficient, as negative co-efficients are harder to deal with.

Question 5 and **6** – Encourage students to translate the words into a maths sentence, making sure each stage is included. Note in **6b** there are 3 possible solutions.

Question 6 – In part **a**, are brackets needed? In part **b**, most students will assume that the base is the unique side of the isosceles triangle.

Question 7 – The term 'consecutive even' may need explaining. You may wish to use this question to ask them to prove why the sum of three consecutive numbers must be in the three times table.

Answers

1 **a** $x = 3$ **b** $z = 4$ **c** $n = 5$ **d** $p = 3$
e $t = 0$ **f** $h = 3$ **g** $k = \frac{1}{2}$ **h** $y = -1$

2 $3(x + 5) = 21$ pairs with $\frac{5x+4}{7} = 2$

$\frac{x}{2} + 9 = 8$ pairs with $\frac{2x+7}{3} = 1$

$12 = 4(x - 3)$ pairs with $\frac{x}{3} + 5 = 7$

The odd one out is $2(10 + x) = 8$

3 **a** $x = 2$ **b** $a = 4$ **c** $p = 6$ **d** $k = 1$
e $y = 5$ **f** $n = 7$

4 **a** $x = 5$ **b** $q = 5$ **c** $a = 2$ **d** $b = 4$
e $m = \frac{1}{2}$ **f** $n = -4$

5 **a** The number is 5 **b** $x = 3$
c $x = 35$. The angles are 35°, 65° and 80°.

6 **a** $5n + 4 = 3n + 14, n = 5$.
b $3x + 4 = 5x - 8$ so $x = 6$

7 $x + (x + 2) + (x + 4) = 3x + 6 = 48$ hence $x = 14$

10b Linear equations 2

Objectives

- Construct and solve linear equations with integer coefficients (with and without brackets, negative signs anywhere in the equation, positive or negative solution) (L6)
- Solve linear equations that require prior simplification of brackets, including those with negative signs anywhere in the equation (L7)

Key ideas	Resources
1 Linear equations with negative algebraic terms can be solved by adding the negative term to both sides	Equations 3 - both sides (1182) Equations 4 - brackets (1928)

Simplification	Extension
Some students may find that using inverse operations is useful although this can be hard to use for negative terms. Continually emphasise the importance of removing the negative term to make the equation simpler.	A rectangle is said to have sides $4 - x$ and $2 + 2x$, and perimeter 22 cm. Find x. (5). Is there anything wrong with your answer? Try finding the area. What can you say about the possible value of x? And of the perimeter? Look at the lengths of the sides. If the perimeter can't be 22, what values can it take? ($-1 < x < 4$, $10 <$ perimeter < 20)

Literacy	Links
There were negative terms in the previous exercise, in question **3**, for example. Can students see, and say, what is different about these questions?	The equals sign was first used by the Welsh mathematician and physician Robert Recorde in 1557 in his book The Whetstone of Witte. He used two parallel lines in the symbol because 'noe 2 thynges, can be moare equalle' However, other symbols for 'is equal to' were still used until the 1700s including the Latin abbreviation *ae* or *oe* (for *aequalis* or equal). There is more information about Robert Recorde at http://en.wikipedia.org/wiki/Robert_Recorde

Alternative approach

Note that, again, the first examples and many of the first questions in the exercise can be solved by inspection.

Note also that all these questions can be solved in the same way as the previous lesson, if students are happy to divide by a negative coefficient. This is not liked by most students, but there are quite likely to be some for whom this presents no problem, and who might therefore prefer to do things this way. It should at least be shown – perhaps for both examples in the first box – so that students know of this option.

The speech bubble suggests that $-2x$ is smaller than $3x$. Ask students how much smaller. Even if they are happy with this terminology, it may be worth mentioning the terminology of less than, as something they can expect to need to understand one day. In either case, can they explain why it is the most negative term that, it is suggested here, should be removed by addition of a positive equivalent? And again, they can be asked whether this seems like a good idea to them. It probably does, for most.

Checkpoint

1 A square measures $3x + 4$ by $19 - 2x$. What is the area of this square? (169 cm^2)

Starter

Draw a 4×4 table on the board.

Label the columns with the terms: $4a, b, a^2, 7$. Label the rows with the terms: $a, 2ab, b^2, 3c$.

Ask students to fill in the table with the products, for example, the top row in the table would read $4a^2, ab, a^3, 7a$.

This can be differentiated by the choice of terms.

Teaching notes

Look at examples of equations that have a negative term. How can this be dealt with? Compare the way in which we solve examples like $2x - 3 = 5$ by +3 to each side. Establish that adding the negative term to each side will 'improve' the equation.

$$25 - 2x = 7$$
$$+ 2x \quad + 2x$$
$$25 = 7 + 2x$$

Encourage students to always deal with the negative x's as soon as possible.

Look at examples that have terms on both sides and include one or both as negative.

If both terms are negative, how much should you add onto each side? Try students' suggestions on an example and establish a good rule. Include examples that have brackets and/or fractions. For example,

$$\frac{14 + 2x}{3} = 2 \qquad 3(1 - 2x) = 4x$$

Why is it not possible to $+2x$ to each side and deal with the negative x term immediately? What must the first step be in each case?

Plenary

I think of a number, double it, add 6, then half the answer I have so far, finally I subtract the number I started with. What result do I get? (3). Why do you always get 3? Encourage students to try to explain in words. Is there an algebraic way to prove that the result is always 3? Encourage students to form the expression and simplify.

Exercise commentary

Question 1 – Remind students of the rules of arithmetic for negative numbers.

Question 2 – Some students will solve the easiest and then check the others by substitution. Encourage them to make sure they can solve the other equations.

Question 3 – With unknowns on both sides encourage students to eliminate the negative coefficient by adding to both sides. With the latter questions, brackets will need to be expanded first.

Question 4 – Encourage students to check that they are translating each piece of information into their equation.

Question 7 – Students will need to know the formula for the circumference of a circle for this question. If students have not yet covered circle, then it is better to omit this question.

Question 8 – The concept of two solutions will be new. Encourage students to associate quadratic equations with two solutions. Part **f** is harder than the others. Tell students to again deal with the negative coefficient by adding $3x^2$ to both sides and then solving.

Answers

1 **a** $x = 7$ **b** $a = -2$ **c** $n = 1$ **d** $m = 4$
e $t = 5$ **f** $p = 2$ **g** $k = 0.5$ **h** $y = -1$
i $b = -2$ **j** $d = 2.5$

2 The solution is $x = 3$ for all.

3 **a** $x = 2$ **b** $t = 1$ **c** $p = 2$ **d** $k = 3$
e $n = 0$ **f** $a = 6$ **g** $b = 5$ **h** $m = 2$
i $y = 4$ **j** $d = 3$ **k** $q = \frac{1}{8}$ **l** $x = -1$

4 **a** $2n + 4 = 19 - n, n = 5$ **b** $10 - 2n = 4n - 8, n = 3$

5 The length is 32 ($x = 6$)

6 The length is 6 ($x = 2$)

7 Radius = 2.39 (2 dp)

8 $x = \pm 4$
a $x = \pm 2$ **b** $x = \pm 5$ **c** $x = \pm 10$ **d** $x = \pm 3$
e $x = \pm 8$ **f** $x = \pm 3$
Equations that have x^2 as their highest order term are called quadratic equations.

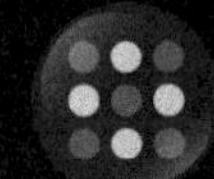

10c Equations with fractions

Objectives	
• Solve linear equations within one unknown with integer and fractional coefficients (L7)	
Key ideas	**Resources**
1 Cross multiplication can be used to solve linear equations containing fractions	Equations 5 - fractions (1929)
Simplification	**Extension**
This is a challenging exercise: direct students to those parts that only involve a simple denominator, for example, questions **1**, **2a–g**. Writing out all workings should be encouraged. Cross multiplication is often very poorly recalled and confused with addition/subtraction and multiplication of ordinary fractions. In question **3,** part **a,** start students off by writing $4x = 2(x + 6)$.	Challenge students with examples that include three fractions. How can the denominators be removed? Can cross multiplication still be used? If so, how? Are the methods used in spread **3i** helpful? For example, $\frac{x}{5}+\frac{2x}{3}=\frac{1}{2}$.
Literacy	**Links**
In view of some of the questions in the previous spread, some caution is now due when declaring that 'multiplication and division are inverse operations': what is the inverse of 'subtract from 10', as met in the previous exercise? And what is the inverse of 'divide into 24'? This does not have to be addressed here, but be on the lookout for misconceptions about inverses popping up.	There is no proof yet for the existence of extra-terrestrial life, but in 1960 scientist Frank Drake produced an equation to estimate the number (N) of civilisations in our galaxy who might be capable of communicating with us. The equation is $N = R \times f_p \times n_e \times f_l \times f_i \times f_c \times L$ where R is the rate of formation of stars, f_p is the fraction of stars with planets, n_e is the number of planets per star capable of sustaining life, f_l is the fraction of those planets where life develops, f_i is the fraction of f_l where intelligent life develops, f_c is the fraction of f_i where technology develops and L is the length of time that civilizations release radio waves into space. Find out more at http://www.pbs.org/wgbh/nova/origins/drak-flash.html

Alternative approach

Cross-multiplication, if taught as a rule, may not be clearly understood in the absence of rationale. There is no need to mention the term 'cross-multiplication', instead emphasise the need to multiply by both (or all) denominators (or LCDs), until either a student comments on this feature or the process is grasped well enough for the giving of this name to not detract from the understanding gained. It may be helpful to complete some preliminary work in this area before students attempt the exercise in the textbook. The first pair of examples is well suited to this purpose.

One way of approaching the solving of equations is to first ask what is least desirable about what is there, and then to deal with that. In the first example box, part **b**, this may mean multiplying by 3 as a first step; which works fine provided students understand the need to multiply every term, and is a perfectly acceptable alternative to the reverse process approach shown.

In the second example box emphasise that when multiplying by 5, on the left hand side we can simply remove the denominator, and similarly on the right hand side when multiplying by 3. And then see how multiplying by the denominators on each side of the equation is much the same as following the 'change the side, change the sign' rule; i.e., cross-multiplication.

Checkpoint

1 I'm thinking of a number. When I add 6 to double that number and divide by 5 I get the same answer as when I times the number by 4, add 3 and divide by 7. What is my number? (4.5)

Starter

Siobhan and Rachel are twins. Siobhan multiplied her age by 3 and subtracted 6. Rachel got the same answer when she multiplied her age by 2 and added 6.

Ask students to work out the age of the twins by forming an equation and solving it. (12 years)

Challenge students to make up their own puzzles.

Teaching notes

Recapitulate work covered for solving equations in exercises **10a** and **10b**. Focus on equations that have fractions. Include examples of different types and discuss the best steps to find solutions. Remind students to eliminate negative terms of the unknown value as soon as possible. For example,

$$\frac{x}{3}+5=12,\ \frac{5(3-2x)}{4}=3,\ \frac{7}{x}=8,$$

$$5-\frac{3x}{2}=7,\ \frac{2}{x}+7=18,\ \frac{10}{x+1}=4$$

How can the fractions be eliminated? Should you multiply both sides by the denominator as the first step in every case? Encourage students to look for ways to simplify the equation by adding or subtracting from both sides if possible.

Look at an equation of the type in question **3**. What will happen if you multiply both sides by one of the denominators? When a fraction is multiplied, which part of the fraction changes? Top, bottom, both? Look at the example of $\frac{1}{4}\times 3=\frac{3}{4}$. Only the top is multiplied. Perform two multiplications to eliminate both denominators. Ask, could this have been achieved in one step? Discus the method of cross-multiplying.

Plenary

Challenge students to construct a question similar to question **5**. Area or perimeter could be used. Can the rest of the class answer some of the proposed questions? Is it possible to construct this sort of question and end up with an impossible answer? For example, a negative area or length of a side.

Exercise commentary

Questions 1–3 – Explain to students that fractions in algebra are always problematic, but they can be easily 'got rid of' by multiplying by the denominator. To enable students to have a consistent method, tell them to always 'get rid of' denominators as the first step. The need to make sure that every term is multiplied by the denominator. Highlight that fractions sometimes have invisible (implicit) brackets.

Question 4 – Make sure students read the information carefully and set up the correct equation.

Question 5 – Students may struggle to set up this equation. Encourage them to think how they can best use the rule for working out the area of a triangle to help them set up this equation.

Question 6 – If students have already covered external angle of polygons in their syllabus then this question should be straight forward and provide opportunity for revision. Otherwise the term external angle will need explanation. The first equation does have two unknowns. Model this to students.

Answers

1 **a** $x=63$ **b** $a=40$ **c** $y=1\frac{1}{3}$ **d** $k=1\frac{4}{5}$
e $n=10$ **f** $p=8$ **g** $t=21$ **h** $b=9$
i $m=11$ **j** $q=14$ **k** $d=11$ **l** $g=6$

2 **a** $a=2$ **b** $y=5$ **c** $k=\frac{2}{3}$ **d** $t=1\frac{3}{4}$
e $b=2$ **f** $x=5$ **g** $p=1\frac{1}{2}$ **h** $m=1\frac{1}{3}$
i $n=1$ **j** $d=2$ **k** $g=1$ **l** $q=\frac{1}{3}$

3 **a** $x=6$ **b** $y=5$ **c** $t=3$ **d** $p=10$
e $a=3$ **f** $k=5$ **g** $m=4$ **h** $b=2$

4 $m=38$

5 $x=3$, area = 12 square units

6 **a** $a=\frac{360}{n}$ where a is the external angle and n is the number of sides
b **i** 5 **ii** 10 **iii** 8
c Impossible. The equation does not give integer value for n.

Objectives	
• Use systematic trial-and-improvement methods and ICT tools to find approximate solutions to equations such as $x^2 + x = 20$ (L6)	
Key ideas	**Resources**
1 Improved values of roots can be found by a trial-and-improvement process **2** Equations involving reciprocals and exponents can be solved using trial-and-improvement	Trial and improvement (1057)
Simplification	**Extension**
Prepare the table of values for some of the questions and include an initial close estimation. Allow students to work to the nearest integer rather than 1 dp for questions **4–6**, but point out that they must still check half of the final interval.	Solve these problems using trial-and-improvement and the power button on the calculator. $9^x = 3, 100^x = 10, 36^x = 6, 8^x = 2, 1000^x = 10, 125^x = 5$ What does a power of $\frac{1}{2}$ or $\frac{1}{3}$ do to a number? (square and cube root)
Literacy	**Links**
Does any student remember why we say trial-and-improvement, rather than trial-and-error, even though this is easier to say? The meaning of root, as a solution to an equation, should perhaps be mentioned here.	Trial by ordeal is an ancient form of trial practised by the Anglo-Saxons up until the Middle Ages. The defendant was forced to walk over red-hot coals/plunge their hand into boiling water/be thrown into a river or pond to see if they sank/ take part in a fight (trial by fire/hot water/cold water/combat). In each case, it was believed that God would intervene to protect the innocent.

Alternative approach

For trial-and-improvement, first rearrange the equation to equate to zero. It is then far simpler to see whether a result is positive or negative, or when a positive and a negative bracket the solution, or which of two values (one positive, one negative) is closer to zero, in order to allow an intelligent choice (linear interpolation, formally, but a general idea of which is closer is fine) for the next step. The teaching notes for spread 1g give some illustration of why equating to zero may be easier for some students than the approach described. This approach also ties in with the idea of roots of equations, which will be important later when solving such equations as these by algebraic rather than numerical methods.

It is essential that students are discouraged from going too far in one step; insist that they improve the accuracy of their bounds one significant figure at a time, or they can become very confused, even if equating to zero (much more, if not); and also that all steps are shown – this is a matter of process, rather than a matter of result.

Encourage students to spot answers if they can, but then to use the trial-and-improvement approach if they cannot. Questions **1** and **2** are all amenable to inspection for bright students, especially if the entire class is applied to the task, but it is just as valuable for students to realise once they have spent a long time on a question that the solution was in fact obvious, so there is no need to alert them to this fact beforehand.

The answers to these questions can be found with a graphical calculator emulator or some other software, and this may be useful in showing the relationship between answers. Always input functions once equated to zero, of course. Graphing will also show that there are two answers to question **4** part **d**, and also to the second example in the book. Students may like to have a rough sketch of a function, once equated to zero, before trying to solve by the trial-and-improvement process.

Checkpoint

1 One side of a rectangle is 2 cm longer than the other. Find the sides of the rectangle to 2 dp using trial-and-improvement, if the area of the rectangle is 20 cm^2. (3.58 cm by 5.58 cm)

Starter

Ask students to write equations for 'Think of a number' problems and find the starting numbers, For example,

I multiply by 3 and subtract 7. I get the same answer if I double and add 2. (9)

I double my number, add 14 and divide by 2. I get the same answer if I double and subtract 5. (12)

Teaching notes

Recap work on trial-and-improvement covered previously in lesson **1g**. Remind students that the x in the examples that gives the closest estimate is not necessarily the correct answer. The midpoint of the x values **must** be checked and then the correct x value decided upon.

Look at alternative approaches to constructing a table to record the trials. The example uses two additional columns of working for x^2 and $\frac{1}{x}$. Are these necessary? Encourage students to give advantages and disadvantages to showing this extra working. Which students in the class feel more comfortable showing all the working?

Solving equations like $x^4 = 60$ can be made much easier by using the power function on a calculator. Ensure all students are aware of how it is displayed on their own calculator, appearing as any of [y^x] [^] [x^n] [x^y].

Plenary

The equation $x^3 - 4x = 0$ has three solutions (-2, 0, 2). Find all of them using trial-and-improvement. What value of x should you begin with? What are the limitations of the method of trial-and-improvement? In this case trial-and-improvement gives the exact solution – does this indicate that there may be another way to approach this question?

Exercise commentary

Questions 1–6 – All newer scientific calculators have a table mode. Using this is a very effective way of solving these types of equation, and the results can be manipulated into a table to make it seem a more traditional trial-and-improvement method has been used!

Question 1 – Insist students show all their working in tabular form, including the first estimates, even if they are a long way from the solution.

Question 2 – Encourage a tabular layout as in question **1**. Part **d** is an exponential equation and may need some explaining. Remind students how to use the power function on scientific calculators.

Questions 3 and **4** – Ask students what level of accuracy they feel is appropriate.

Question 4 – Again be aware that parts **a** and **c** are exponential.

Questions 5 and **6** – Encourage students to write an equation before using trial-and-improvement.

Question 7 – Students will need reminding how to enter equations in a spreadsheet. Show them that by dragging cells all the cell references are adjusted accordingly. Challenge them to see if they can make this spreadsheet more sophisticated. (By making the initial value and increment separate variables).

Answers

1 $x = 15$

2 **a** $x = 10$ **b** $x = 9$ **c** $x = 8$ **d** $x = 10$
e $x = 49$ **f** $x = 5$

3 $x = 4.8$ (1 dp)

4 **a** $x = 2.8$ (1 dp) **b** $x = 6.7$ (1 dp)
c $x = 3.6$ (1 dp) **d** $x = 7.7$ or 1.3 (1 dp)

5 $w = 9.5$ (1 dp)

6 **a** $V = k^3 + k^2$ **b** $k = 4.2$ (1 dp)

7 $x = 3.6$ (1 dp)

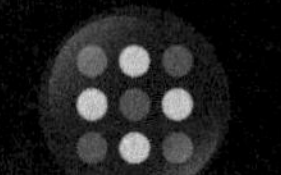

10e Real-life equations

Objectives	
• Construct and solve linear equations with integer coefficients (L6) • Use formulae from mathematics and other subjects (L6)	
Key ideas	**Resources**
1 Using equations applied to real-life contexts **2** To link abstract algebraic skills to applied contexts	Equations 2 - multi-step (1154) Rules and formulae (1158) Mini whiteboards
Simplification	**Extension**
Reading values from graphs is an easier skill than using equations. Start with a simple currency conversion graph, and show how that can be shown by a simple equation. Then introduce a cost that includes a standing charge in a graph. A mobile phone tariff could provide a good example. Again show how it is more efficient to use algebra, and link this with question.	Ask students to look for non-linear relationships. Familiarising them with some of the acceleration / distance equations (SUVAT equations) and linking them with police accident investigation work would provide a real-life context for harder equations.
Literacy	**Links**
Some of these questions can be wordy, and a challenge to decipher. Encourage students to highlight key terms and make sure every piece of information is used. Ask them to translate these words into complete mathematical sentences.	Some real-life quadratic equations can be found here: http://www.mathsisfun.com/algebra/quadratic-equation-real-world.html Students can use trial-and-improvement methods from previous section to solve these (rather than quadratic formula this website suggests).

Alternative approach

Introduce the idea of students responding to questions of the format 'Give me an example of…', 'now a peculiar example of', 'now a general example of…'. Ask for examples of an even number; odd number; multiple of 5; a fraction. Share and discuss the results fully using mini whiteboards, addressing any misconceptions that are exposed. Using algebraic pyramid puzzles or number walls is a good way to rehearse construction strategies. Suggestions for variations of these can be found in the Y8 booklet on Constructing Linear Equations (DCSF). Finding expressions for the perimeters of shapes is useful to assist students creating their own equations. Investigations such as matchstick shapes can also generate valuable practice in generalisation. Compile a list of some common formulae, including conversion ones such as $p = 22k/10$ (kilograms to pounds). Which are familiar to the students? What others have they found in other subjects? Use some for rehearsing substitution skills in order to find a particular value.

Checkpoint

1 Two local electricians have different charges. The first has a call out charge of £20 and then charges £30 per hour. The second has a call out charge of £30 and then charges £25 per hour. For what length of job is there total fee the same? (2 hours)

Starter – Upside-down pyramid

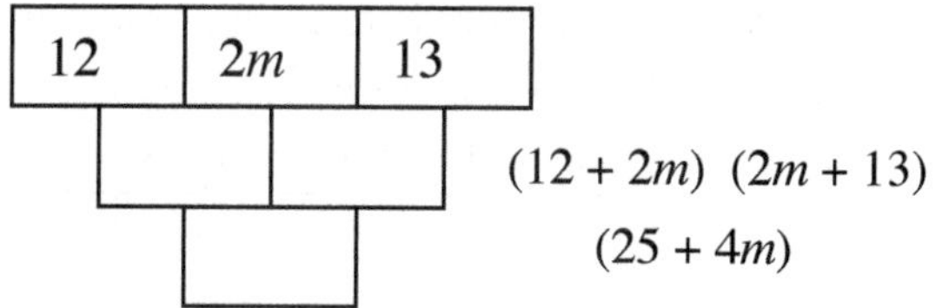

Ask students to complete the number pyramid on mini whiteboards. Check grid entries with a neighbour. Now tell students that the final box is actually 52, so what particular value is m? ($m = 6.75$)

Teaching notes

There is lots of scope for mini whiteboard work at the start of the lesson with problems such as 'I think of a number...' and substitutions into simple formulae. Dice can be used to generate 'random' numbers.

The topic naturally splits into two key areas: using given equations to find missing values and writing down equations from a context.

The first part of this can be done again using quick-fire question and answer before allowing students to complete further examples of their own from the textbook. Encourage them to substitute first and then solve when working backwards.

The second aspect of the lesson can be modelled using examples similar to those in the textbook. Provide a scenario for the students and show how this translates into an equation which can then be solved.

Plenary

Further quick-fire examples can be provided for the students to complete 'against the clock' or in a race with a partner. Points can be awarded for correct answers to ensure that the students focus on getting the question right rather than racing through the questions making careless mistakes.

Exercise commentary

Question 1 – Students will need to be able to change the subject of equations, in order to answer parts **c** and **d**. Use this to link abstract algebraic skill with an applied context.

Questions 2 and **3** – Have students show all these graphically on the same graph. Link this graph with $y = mx + c$ and asks students which company they think offers the best tariff.

Question 4 – Use www.xe.com to investigate other currency conversion rates.

Question 5 – Again representing these equations in a graph will help students understand the information shown in the equation. A graph is only useful if needing to use the same equation repeatedly.

Answers

1 **a** 212 °F **b** -40 °F
c 60 °C **d** -17.8 °C (1 dp)

2 **a** $T = 3 + 0.25m$ **b** $T = 2.5 + 0.35m$
c $T = 2 + 0.4m$ **d** $T = 0.48m$

3

	i	ii
a	£6.00	12 miles
b	£6.70	10 miles
c	£6.80	10 miles
d	£5.76	12.5 miles

4 **a** \$153.20 **b** \$383.00
c \$1256.24 **d** £489.56
e £1000.00 **f** £6853.79

5 **a** **i** $y = 5 + 0.15x$
ii $y = 10 + 0.1x$
b **i** CheapTalk (£8)
ii CheapTalk (£12.50)
iii BargainPhone (£25)
c **i** $5 + 0.15x = 10 + 0.1x$, so $0.05x = 5$ (or $x = 100$)
ii 100 minutes
d If you use less than 100 minutes a month, choose CheapTalk; if you use more than 100 minutes a month choose BargainPhone.

Key outcomes	Quick check
Solve linear equations that involve brackets.	My sister is four years older than me. My mum is four times older than me and three times older than my sister. Write this imformation as an equation and solve it to find out how old I am. $(3(x+4)=4x;\ x=12)$
Solve linear equations that involve the unknown appearing more than once.	Solve $5(x+2)=4(16-x)$. $(x=6)$
Solve linear equations that involve negative numbers.	The coldest ever temperature, recorded in Antartica in August 2010, was -138.5° F. Using the conversion equation F = 1.8C + 32 convert this temperature to degrees Celsius. (-94.7 °C)
Solve linear equations that involve fractions.	I'm thinking of a number. If I multiply it by 8 and then add two and then divide by 5, I get the same answer as if I double it and subtract 3. What is my number? $(x=8.5)$
Solve nonlinear equations using a trial-and-improvement method	Use trial-and-improvement to solve $x^3 - \sqrt{x} = 40$ to 2 decimal places. $(x=3.47)$

MyMaths extra support

Lesson/online homework			Description
Single brackets	1247	L5	Expanding single brackets such as $3(3x-2)$

MyReview

10 MySummary

Check out

You should now be able to ...

Check out		Test it ➡ Questions
Solve linear equations that involve ✓ Brackets		1
✓ The unknown appearing more than once		2, 3
✓ Negative numbers		2
✓ Fractions		3, 4
✓ Solve nonlinear equations using a trial and improvement method		5 - 7

Language	Meaning	Example
Expression	A mathematical statement	$3y + 6x$
Equation	A mathematical statement that two expressions are equal	$3y = 6$
Linear equation	An equation where the highest power is 1	$2x = 4$
Expand	To multiply out all brackets and then collect like terms	Expanding $2(3x + 5) - 7 + 4x$ gives $10x + 3$
Trial and improvement	A method for solving complex equations by making a guess, then improving on that guess until you are very close to the correct answer.	The equation $x^3 + x = 245$ can be solved by trial and improvement

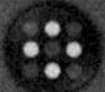

10 MyReview

1 Solve these equations.
- **a** $6 + 5a = 6$
- **b** $4(2b - 5) = 12$
- **c** $3(2c - 7) + 4(3c - 2) = 61$
- **d** $8(2d + 5) - 3(8d - 9) = -21$
- **e** $4e - 9 = 3e - 2$
- **f** $6(2f - 13) = 5(10f - 8)$

2 Solve these equations.
- **a** $28 - 9g = 4$
- **b** $3h + 7 = 23 - h$
- **c** $21 - 6i = 69 + 2i$
- **d** $4(6j - 15) = 6(38 - 2j)$
- **e** $12 - 5k = -66 - 11k$
- **f** $3(12 - 4m) = 21 - 13m$

3 Solve these equations.
- **a** $\frac{n + 2}{5} = 11$
- **b** $\frac{3p - 2}{4} = 7$
- **c** $3 + \frac{q}{4} = 0$
- **d** $11 = \frac{3}{4}r - 19$
- **e** $\frac{15}{s} = 3$
- **f** $20 - \frac{8}{t} = 18$
- **g** $\frac{45}{1 - 2u} = 5$
- **h** $\frac{40 + v}{3(5 + v)} = 2$

4 Solve these equations.
- **a** $\frac{w}{3} = \frac{w + 2}{4}$
- **b** $\frac{x}{5} = \frac{x - 3}{4}$
- **c** $\frac{y + 3}{3} = \frac{5y - 1}{7}$
- **d** $\frac{5(z - 4)}{11} = \frac{3z + 1}{4}$

5 Copy and complete this table to find a solution of $x^3 - 2x = 329$.

x	x^3	$x^3 - 2x$	result
10	1000	980	high

6 Use a trial and improvement method to find a positive solution of the following equations. Give your answers correct to 1 decimal place.
- **a** $x^5 = 19$
- **b** $4^x = 37$
- **c** $2x - \frac{5}{x} = 13$
- **d** $x^3 + x^2 = 3$

7 A cuboid has side lengths p, p and $p-1$. The volume of the cuboid is $40\,\text{cm}^3$. Find p correct to 1 decimal place.

What next?

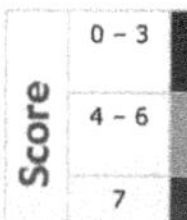

Score	
0 - 3	Your knowledge of this topic is still developing. To improve look at Formative test: 2C-10; MyMaths: 1057, 1158, 1154, 1182 and 1183
4 - 6	You are gaining a secure knowledge of this topic. To improve look at InvisiPen: 234, 235, 236, 237, 241, 242, 243, 362, 363 and 364
7	You have mastered this topic. Well done, you are ready to progress!

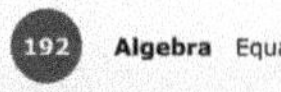

192 **Algebra** Equations

MyMaths.co.uk

193

Question commentary

Question 1 – Remind students they need to expand brackets first, being careful to notice times they need to subtract a negative.

Question 2 – Students should add the negative algebraic term to ensure positive coefficients.

Question 3 – When multiplying by a denominator students should take care to multiply every term in the equation.

Question 4 – Students should start by 'cross-multiplying', although it is important they understand precisely what they are doing and why it works.

Questions 5–7 – Students should show their working in tabular form. Using the table mode on scientific calculators can be very useful in solving these types of equation.

Question 7 – Students should first form an equation and expand the brackets: $p^3 - p^2 = 40$ then solve using trial-and-improvement as in **6**.

Answers

1 **a** $a = 0$ **b** $b = 4$ **c** $c = 5$ **d** $d = 11$ **e** $e = 7$ **f** $f = -1$

2 **a** $g = -2$ **b** $h = 4$ **c** $i = -6$ **d** $j = 8$ **e** $k = -13$ **f** $m = -15$

3 **a** $n = 53$ **b** $p = 10$ **c** $q = -12$ **d** $r = 40$ **e** $s = 5$ **f** $t = 4$ **g** $u = -4$ **h** $v = 2$

4 **a** $w = 6$ **b** $x = 15$ **c** $y = 3$ **d** $z = -7$

5 $x = 7$

6 **a** $x = 1.8$ **b** $x = 2.6$ **c** $x = 6.9$ **d** $x = 1.2$

7 $p = 3.8$

10 MyPractice

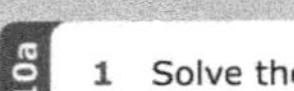

10a

1 Solve these equations.

a $7x + 3 = 6x + 8$
b $6y + 9 = 4y + 17$
c $2a + 5 = 5a - 7$
d $5b - 3 = 9b - 7$
e $p + 24 = 7p$
f $4(q - 1) = 6q - 5$
g $3(k - 4) = 2(4k - 1)$
h $\frac{2}{3}t - 2 = \frac{1}{3}t + 2$

2 For each of these questions, form an equation and solve it to find the answer to the problem.

a Find the length of this rectangle.

b The areas of these shapes are equal.

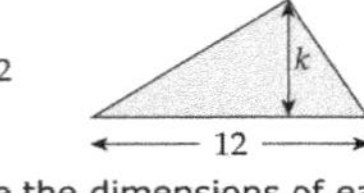

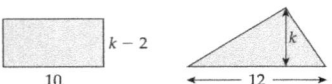

Find k and hence the dimensions of each shape.

3 a Think of a number, multiply it by 5 and then subtract 3. If you double the same number and add 15, you get the same answer. Find the number.

b This mobile is made from different shapes. It can hang from the ceiling. If the square shape has a mass of 60 grams, find the masses of all the other shapes.

10b

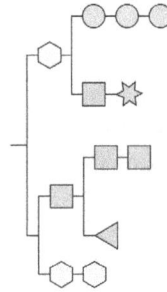

4 Solve these equations.

a $10 - x = 7$
b $15 - 2y = 5$
c $11 = 21 - 5m$
d $0 = 18 - 6n$
e $9 - 3d = 8$
f $4 - 7f = 11$
g $8 - 2k = 5$
h $12 - 3t = 7$

5 Solve these equations.

a $4x + 3 = 8 - x$
b $2k + 5 = 17 - 4k$
c $3p - 5 = 5 - 2p$
d $10 - 3t = t - 2$
e $7 - a = 15 - 2a$
f $11 - 5b = 5 - 2b$
g $8(3 - y) = 2 + 3y$
h $2(7 - 2g) = 3(4 - g)$

10c

6 Solve these equations.

a $\frac{a}{3} = \frac{a + 4}{5}$
b $\frac{b - 1}{3} = \frac{2b}{7}$
c $\frac{x + 5}{3} = \frac{x + 11}{5}$
d $\frac{y + 6}{9} = \frac{y - 2}{5}$
e $\frac{2p - 1}{9} = \frac{p - 3}{2}$
f $\frac{5q - 1}{4} = \frac{7q - 5}{5}$
g $\frac{3m + 1}{7} = \frac{5m - 6}{4}$
h $\frac{3n - 2}{5} = \frac{5n - 8}{6}$

7 Tim and Tom are identical twins.

Tim says "My age is three years less than one quarter my mum's age".

Tom says "If you take 6 from my mum's age then my age is two-fifths of the result".

a Write two equations for Tim's and Tom's ages in terms of their mother's age.
b Hence find the ages of Tim and Tom and their mother.

10d

8 Copy and complete this table to find a positive solution of $x^3 - x = 50$, correct to 1 dp.

x	x^3	$x^3 - x$	Result
4	64	60	high
3	27	24	low

9 A number plus ten times its square root is equal to one thousand.

a Write down an equation whose solution gives this number.
b Solve your equation using trial and improvement.
Give your answer to 2 decimal places.

Question commentary

Question 1 – Remind students to subtract the smaller variable in order to avoid negative coefficients.

Question 3 – Each row of the mobile must be balanced in order for the whole mobile to balance. This is a good question for illustrating the balance method.

Questions 4 and **5** – Ensure students are in the habit of eliminating negative coefficients by adding to both sides.

Questions 6 and **7** – Ensure students are using a consistent method. Cross-multiplying and then expanding brackets is the best method.

Question 6 – Remind students that the table mode on scientific calculators can be used in these questions.

Answers

1 **a** $x = 5$ **b** $y = 4$ **c** $a = 4$ **d** $b = 1$
e $p = 4$ **f** $q = \frac{1}{2}$ **g** $k = -2$ **h** $t = 12$

2 **a** $3x + 2 = 8(x - 1)$, $x = 2$ so the length of the rectangle is 8
b $10(k - 2) = 6k$, $k = 5$ so the rectangle has length = 10 and width = 3 and the triangle has base = 12 and height = 5

3 **a** 6
b Triangle = 120 g
Hexagon = 150 g
Circle = 75 g
Star = 165 g

4 **a** $x = 3$ **b** $y = 5$ **c** $m = 2$ **d** $n = 3$
e $d = \frac{1}{3}$ **f** $f = -1$ **g** $k = 1\frac{1}{2}$ **h** $t = 1\frac{2}{3}$

5 **a** $x = 1$ **b** $k = 2$ **c** $p = 2$ **d** $t = 3$
e $a = 8$ **f** $b = 2$ **g** $y = 2$ **h** $g = 2$

6 **a** $a = 6$ **b** $b = 7$ **c** $x = 4$ **d** $y = 12$
e $p = 5$ **f** $q = 5$ **g** $m = 2$ **h** $n = 4$

7 **a** Tim = $\frac{m}{4} - 3$ Tom = $\frac{(m-6)}{5}$
b Tom and Tim are 6. Mum is 36.

8 $x = 3.8$

9 **a** $x + 10\sqrt{x} = 1000$ **b** $x = 729.85$

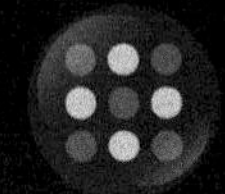

11 Written and calculator methods

Learning outcomes		
N4	Use the 4 operations, including formal written methods, applied to integers, decimals, proper and improper fractions, and mixed numbers, all both positive and negative	(L6)
N5	Use conventional notation for the priority of operations, including brackets, powers, roots and reciprocals	(L6)
N15	Use a calculator and other technologies to calculate results accurately and then interpret them appropriately	(L6)

Introduction

The chapter starts by looking at methods multiplication and division (including decimal numbers) before two sections focusing on using a calculator. The order of operations is covered before formal written methods for addition and subtraction of decimals. The final section contains problems which require methods of multiplication and/or division to solve.

The introduction discusses the different types of way in which cultures write. The right to left conventions of the Arabic and Hebrew cultures and the top to bottom conventions of the Chinese and Japanese mean that they have very different ways of setting out text. Obviously since mathematics is a 'universal' language, we have to agree to a convention in which everyone follows the same method. The use of left to right conventions in setting out mathematical calculations, the use of BIDMAS and some of the standard methods are the same throughout the world.

However, different cultures still have different methods for carrying out calculations, many of which are as efficient as the ones we are used to using in a typical mathematical classroom. Chinese multiplication, for example, is a nice alternative to our standard method and can be used to show the students a different way.

http://www.youtube.com/watch?v=n97nmGGlBf4

Prior knowledge

Students should already know how to…

- Add, subtract, multiply and divide numbers using mental methods
- Add, subtract, multiply and divide whole numbers

Starter problem

The starter problem invites students to make up an 'amazing' story using a series of two sets of number facts, one about the masses of animals and one about the eating habits of people. Obviously, there is no right answer to this, but the information given can be used to stimulate discussion about scale or the relationships between numbers of different magnitudes, or in the case of the eating example, the value of calculating with complex information.

The first set of information tells us that the mass of a blue whale is $120 \div 7.5 = 16$ times that of an elephant whereas the elephant is $7500 \div 0.022 = 340\,909$ times that of a mouse. This makes the blue whale over 5 million times heavier than a mouse!

The second set of information tells us that the average meal weighs $9 \times 62 = 558$ grams and that it takes on average $19.3 \times 62 = 1197$ seconds (nearly 20 minutes) to eat, assuming that we just keep shovelling the food in without a break!

If we were to contemplate eating the whale or the elephant, imagine how long it would take!

Resources

MyMaths

Adding and subtracting decimals	1007	Dividing decimals by whole numbers	1008
Multiply decimals by whole numbers	1010	Multiply two decimals	1011
Multiply triple digits	1026	Long division	1041
Order of operations	1167	Short division	1905
Short and long multiplication	1914	Long multiplication	1916
Introducing long division	1917	Calculator methods 1	1932

Online assessment

Chapter test	2C–11
Formative test	2C–11
Summative test	2C–11

InvisiPen solutions

Mental multiplication	122	Mental division	123
Order of operations	124	Written multiplication	126
Written division	127	Calculator methods	128
Adding and subtracting decimals	131		
Written methods multiplying decimals	133		
Written methods dividing decimals	134		

Topic scheme

Teaching time = 7 lessons/3 weeks

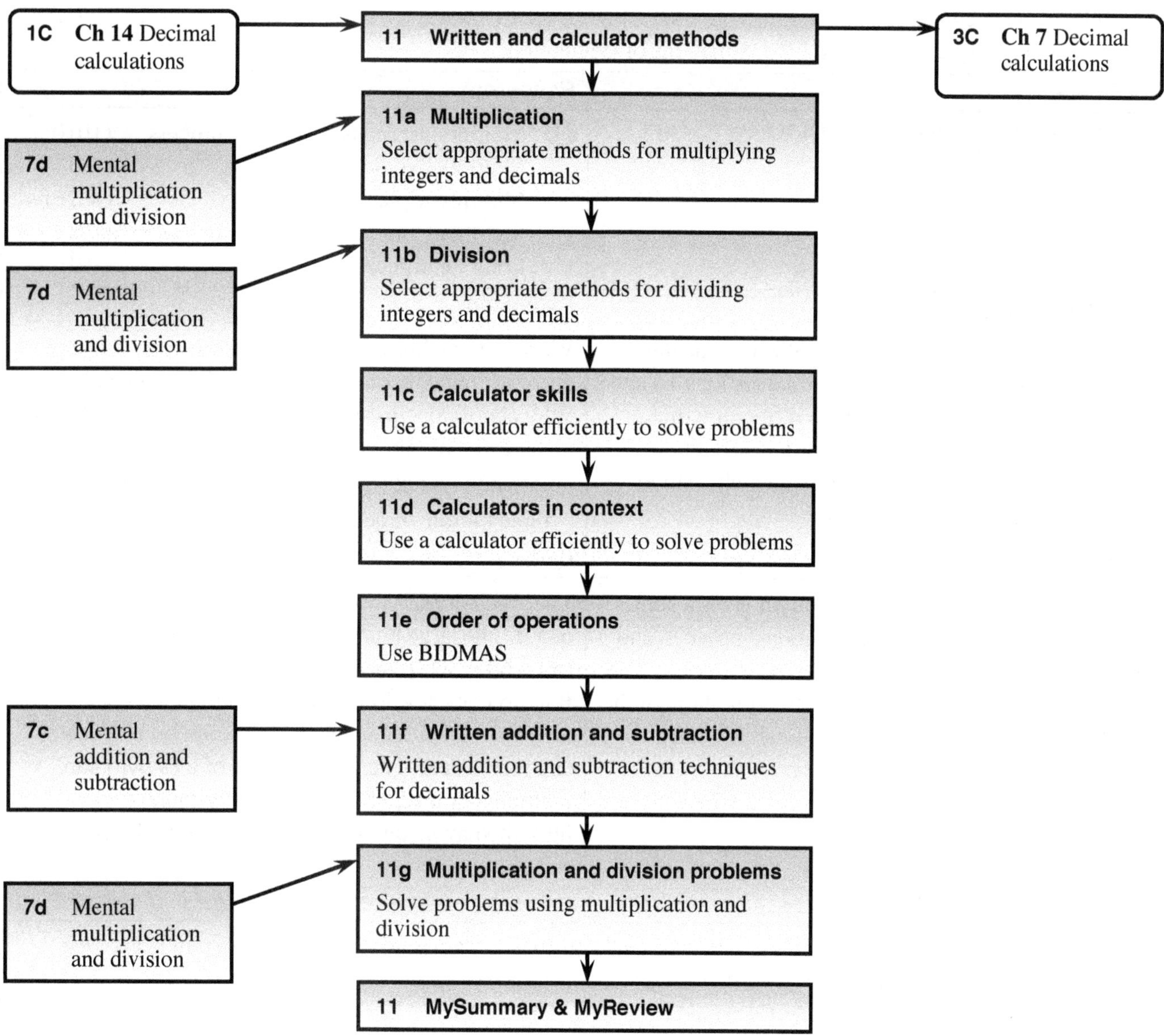

Differentiation

Student book 2A 206 – 223

Written addition and subtraction
Written multiplication
Written division
Written arithmetic problems
Calculator skills
Interpreting the display

Student book 2B 190 – 209

Written addition and subtraction
Written methods of multiplication
Written methods of division
Order of operations
Addition and subtraction problems
Multiplication and division problems
Calculation methods

Student book 2C 196 – 215

Multiplication
Division
Calculator skills
Calculators in context
Order of operations
Written addition and subtraction
Multiplication and division problems

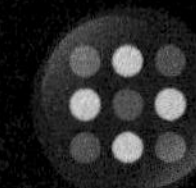

11a Multiplication

Objectives	
• Extend mental methods of calculation, working with decimals	(L5)
• Multiply by decimals	(L5)
• Make and justify estimates and approximations of calculations	(L6)

Key ideas	Resources
1 Multiplications can be done in a variety of ways	Multiply decimals by whole numbers (1010) Multiply two decimals (1011) Multiply triple digits (1026) Short and long multiplication (1914) Long multiplication (1916)

Simplification	Extension
Focus on a select few examples to illustrate mental short cut approaches. For example in questions **1d** and **2a** ask students to experiment with different written methods for multiplication. Perhaps try different methods for the same question to see which method makes them feel most comfortable.	Work out one billion, one million, one thousand and one multiplied by one million, one thousand and one. Why choose one particular method over another? What methods would prove too cumbersome? (1 002 003 003 002 001 – one quadrillion, two trillion, three billion, three million, two thousand and one).

Literacy	Links
A reminder may be timely that addition gives a sum, subtraction a difference, multiplication a product, and division a quotient. Give students the opportunity to both think through the question on their own and discuss possible strategies with others.	The Ancient Babylonians used a number system based on 60. The large number of multiplication facts ($60 \times 60 = 3600$) made multiplication difficult so the Babylonians developed multiplication tables. The tables were written in cuneiform script on clay tablets and then baked. There is a picture of a Babylonian multiplication tablet for the 35 times table at http://it.stlawu.edu/~dmelvill/mesomath/tablets/36Times.html

Alternative approach

Always encourage students to find their own ways and consider any alternatives that come to mind. The first example could be solved in the many different ways:

You could use doubling and halving. For example, $26 \times 0.05 = 13 \times 0.1 = 1.3$

Or rewrite the decimal as a fraction. For example, $26 \times 0.05 = 26 \times 5 \div 100$

A method used a few centuries ago – the **Gelosia** method – which requires only knowledge of times tables and ability to add single digits, is often liked by one or two students who have never been happy with other methods they have been shown. With the Gelosia method – known also as 'lattice multiplication', the calculation is set out in a grid. For example, Decimal example,

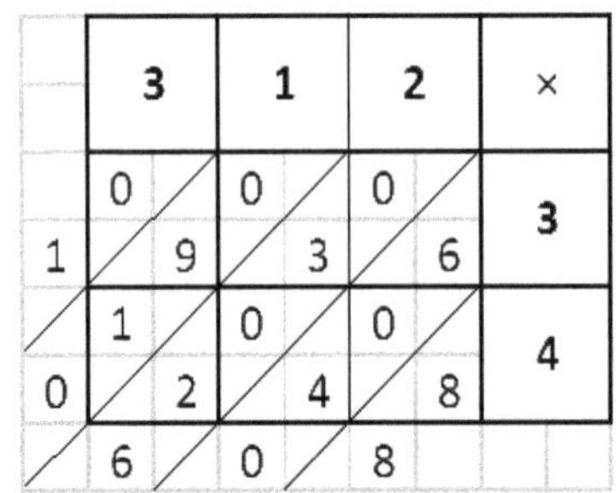

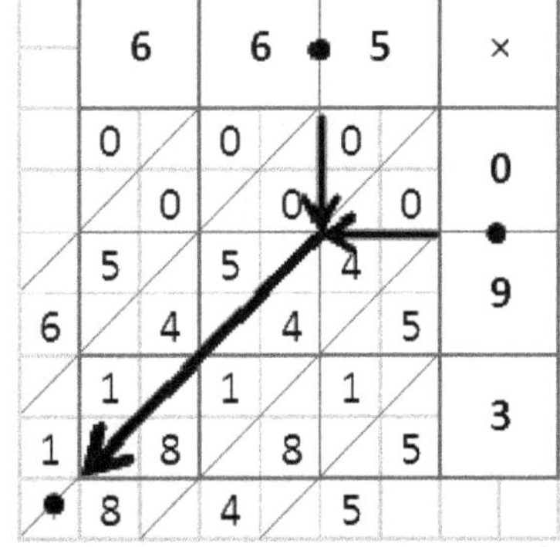

Decimal points can be inserted by counting places, or by following the points down from the top, left from the right, and then down the diagonal.

Checkpoint

1 Without a calculator work out 42.57×6.7. (285.219)

Starter

Ask students to make 105 by

- **i** the product of two odd numbers (3 × 35)
- **ii** the product of three odd numbers (3 × 5 × 7)
- **iii** the product of four odd numbers (1 × 3 × 5 × 7)
- **iv** the sum of a square number and a prime number (64 + 41)
- **v** the difference between two square numbers (169 – 64)

Can any be done in more than one way?

Teaching notes

Look at examples of multiplication that can be simply solved by using the method of factors. You can look at the method used in the student book as a guide. Introduce an example where factors are more difficult to use. Look at the method of partitioning and examples where it is useful.

Look at the three most common methods of written multiplication

- **i** long multiplication in rows
- **ii** lattice method
- **iii** grid method.

How can you use a written method to tackle decimal multiplication?
Advise students to remove the decimal points from the calculation and insert it back in at the end.

How can you tell where to put the decimal point?
Count the number of decimal places after the point in the numbers you are multiplying and use this to identify how many places to move the decimal point in the final answer.

Would an estimate help?
Conclude that it will help if an estimate is possible. For example, 4.3 × 8.34 is approximately $4 \times 8 \approx 32$, but 1.3 × 0.032 is harder to estimate.

Plenary

Pull together the various methods that students have used in the exercise. Is there a common feeling for methods that are more or less effective, or do different students have different preferences? Does the choice of method depend on the question itself? Ask students to explain where they find the greatest difficulty.

Exercise commentary

Question 1 – Encourage students to practise their preferred method. Some students will expect parts **g** and **h** to have the same answer. Make sure they realise the answers are different.

Questions 2–4 – Although some grid methods can accommodate the decimal point, suggest students work out answer without decimal point, and then add it later.

Question 5 – Suggest students work in pence first and the convert final answer to pounds and pence.

Question 6 – The terms 'product' and 'sum' may need explaining. Students may well restrict themselves to integers. Discuss this. When investigating for part **b**, allow the use of a calculator. Encourage a generalisation expressed in words for the maximum product. Ask students to test their ideas.

Answers

1 **a** 1204 **b** 4836 **c** 29 666 **d** 23 886
e 12 780 **f** 13 604 **g** 71 104 **h** 78 144

2 **a** 121.8 **b** 0.48 **c** 10.23 **d** 347.9
e 142.6 **f** 66.7 **g** 3.75 **h** 0.91

3 **a** 46.62 **b** 27.44 **c** 124.2 **d** 158.4
e 7.28 **f** 25.2 **g** 2269.8 **h** 265.74
i 109.15 **j** 440.91 **k** 129.08 **l** 113.24
m 16.932 **n** 5.705 **o** 15.675 **p** 36.27

4 **a** 69 104 **b** 622 521
c 1694.35 **d** 15.1165
e 1.80514 **f** 2.3055

5 **a** £57 **b** £36.96
c **i** £45.14 **ii** 743.28 km
d **i** £9.60 **ii** £499.41
e **i** $6487.12 **ii** $8554.89

6 **a** $(19 \div 2)^2 = 90.25$
b $(19 \div 3)^3 = 254.04$ (2 dp)
c Students' answers; largest value for equal divisions.

Objectives	
• Extend mental methods of calculation, working with decimals	(L5)
• Divide by decimals by transforming to division by an integer	(L5)
• Make and justify estimates and approximations of calculations	(L6)

Key ideas	Resources
1 Divisions can be done in a variety of ways	Dividing decimals by whole numbers (1008) Long division (1041) Short division (1905) Introducing long division (1917)

Simplification	Extension
Focus on a select few examples to illustrate mental shortcut approaches. For example, questions **1a**, and **2h**. Ask students to experiment with the different written methods for division, trying different methods for the same question to see which method makes them feel most comfortable.	1 inch is exactly 25.4 mm. Without a calculator, convert 1 mm into inches. (0.039 370 078 740 157 5 inches to 16 dp) Can students express this as a fraction of an inch? Did any student divide by a number other than 254?

Literacy	Links
Make sure that students take seriously the instruction to always try to work out divisions in their heads.	Question **5** refers to Fair Trade coffee. Fair Trade is a trading partnership that ensures that farmers and producers in developing countries are paid a fair price for their goods. There is more information about Fair Trade at http://www.fairtrade.org.uk/

Alternative approach

In the first example in the student book there are many possible ways to solve these two questions.

For example in **a**, $435 \div 15 = (450 - 15) \div 15 = 450 \div 15 - 1 = 30 - 1 = 29$

Or, $435 \div 15 = 870 \div 30$ (double *both* numbers) $= 87 \div 3 = (90 - 3) \div 3 = 29$

In **b**, you could use trial-and-improvement,

$30 \times 13 = 390$ (remainder 60)

Then, $3 \times 13 = 39$ (remainder 21 = 1 r 8)

$390 \div 13 = (30 + 3 + 1)$ r 8 = 34 r 8

As an extension ask the class to do the division in second example together in their heads using trial-and-improvement.

$532 \div 3.9 \approx 532 \div 4 \approx 262 \div 2 \approx 133$

$133 \times 3.9 = 133 \times (4 - 0.1) = 532 - 13.3 = 518.7$ (remainder 13.3)

$3 \times 3.9 = 3 \times (4 - 0.1) = 12 - 0.3 = 11.7$ (remainder 1.6)

Which gives, $532 \div 3.9 = (133 + 3)$ r 1.6

$1.6 \div 3.9 \approx 1.6 \div 4 \approx 0.4$

Finally, $532 \div 3.9 = 136.4$ 1dp

Similarly for **1a** $84 \div 6 = (90 - 6) \div 6 = 90 \div 6 - 1 = 15 - 1 = 14$

For question **3e**, try 4×18, as closer than 3×18, and lo!, we have 72, which is 1.8 more than 70.2, and therefore the answer is 0.1 less than 4.

There are many approaches and the class should spend time sharing any methods, for particular questions, that they like. The standard premise should always be, that there are several methods available, that one of those methods will be easier than the others, that we should always make some effort, even if only brief, to find an easy method, and that practice at this will lead to us becoming better and better at it.

Checkpoint

1 Without a calculator, work out $299.86 \div 4.7$. (63.8)

Starter

Ask students to draw a 3 × 3 grid and enter four factors of 48, three factors of 36 and two factors of 52.

Give possible answers, for example, 6. The winner is the first student to cross out all their factors.

This activity can easily be differentiated by the choice of numbers.

Teaching notes

Look at examples of division that can be simply solved by using the method of factors. Include examples with remainders if appropriate. Look at the method used in the student book as a guide. Introduce an example where factors are more difficult to use. Look at the method of partitioning and examples where it is useful.

Look at the method of short division.
For example, 2399 ÷ 17. Why is it helpful to write down part of the times table? Show how this example can be extended to allow the solution to 1 decimal place.

$$17\overline{)2\,3^{6}9^{1}9}\quad 0141 \text{ r } 2$$

1 × 17 = 17

2 × 17 = 34

4 × 17 = 68

8 × 17 = 136

Look at an example of division by a decimal. How can expressing the question as a fraction help to simplify the problem?
Show how an equivalent fraction without a decimal denominator will be easier to solve. Will the numerator and denominator always have to be multiplied by a power of ten? Consider 56 ÷ 2.5. (22.4)

Plenary

What numbers were easier to divide by in the exercise? Why? Before the invention of electronic calculators, division could take a very long time, many clever inventions were made to help improve efficiency.
For example, Napier's Bones.

Exercise commentary

Questions 1 and **2** – Encourage a use of a variety of mental approaches. Students should share their method with a partner and discuss which methods work best. Allow students to jot numbers down to support their mental method.

Question 3 – Most students will prefer to use the 'bus stop' method for short division and the repeated subtraction method (chunking) for harder divisions. Although, traditional long division is a difficult method and can sometimes confuse understanding of place value encourage students to practice this now.

Question 4 – Encourage students to remove the decimal point from the divisor by multiplying both numbers by powers of 10.

Question 5 – Note that repeated subtraction enables remainders to be expressed as fractions, but not decimals. In part **a** encourage students to see how they can simplify the question, since dividing by 98 is difficult. Suggest they halve the number and then divide by 7 twice.

Question 6 – Encourage students to view division as a fraction. Viewing the numbers as numerator and denominator will help them see the effect of multiplying and dividing any number in the question by powers of 10.

Answers

1 **a** 14 **b** 15 **c** 13 **d** 21
e 22 **f** 45 **g** 52 **h** 33
i 56 **j** 89 **k** 32 **l** 93

2 **a** 17 r 2 **b** 19 r 7 **c** 11 **d** 23
e 18 r 9 **f** 23 r 3 **g** 29 r 1 **h** 56 r 8
i 10 r 22 **j** 30 r 14 **k** 51 r 2 **l** 221 r 20

3 **a** 7.6 **b** 7.6 **c** 9.8 **d** 4.6
e 3.9 **f** 5.1 **g** 1.6 **h** 13.1
i 19.2 **j** 18.9 **k** 2.6 **l** 2.8

4 **a** 131.9 **b** 163.6 **c** 376.8 **d** 163.7
e 145.4 **f** 250 **g** 140 **h** 355.5

5 **a** 10.20 m/s
b 233 packs, remainder 0.5 kg
c £40.72

6 **a** **i** 0.57, inverse of the multiplication
ii 5.7, value in calculation is 10 times greater
iii 570, value in calculation is 1000 times greater

b Students' spider diagrams showing related division calculations

11c Calculator skills

Objectives	
• Use a calculator efficiently and appropriately to perform complex calculations	(L6)
• Use the sign change key	(L5)
• Use the function keys for powers roots and fractions	(L5)
• Make and justify estimates and approximations of calculations	(L6)

Key ideas	Resources
1 Calculators are useful if you know how to use them	Calculator methods 1 (1932) Calculators

Simplification	Extension
For estimations, encourage the use of rounding to one significant figure before calculation. Suggest a range of values that students can use to investigate the statements in question **3**.	Using the fraction button on your calculator evaluate $\dfrac{1}{2+\dfrac{3}{4+\dfrac{5}{6+\dfrac{7}{8+9}}}}=\dfrac{1}{2+\dfrac{3}{4+\dfrac{5}{6\frac{7}{17}}}}=\dfrac{1}{2+\dfrac{3}{4\frac{85}{109}}}=\dfrac{1}{2\frac{327}{521}}$ $=\dfrac{521}{1369}$ Can the same be done using the negative integers from -1 to -9 instead of 1 to 9? Will the answer just be the same but negative? (No, the answer is $\frac{59}{61}$.)

Literacy	Links
Students will need to check the picture and notes in the spread and then perhaps make a short list of features that are different on their calculators.	The first widely available hand-held battery-operated calculator was the Sharp LC-8 (also known as EL-8) which was introduced in January 1971. The calculator measured 100 mm × 163 mm × 67 mm and was advertised as the world's smallest electronic calculator. Ask the class to compare the size of their own calculator.

Alternative approach

The calculator is likely to be a student's best friend in an examination, when it is permitted, but only if they have come to know it well. Calculators that are well looked after and used will be better friends, because they will be better understood.

Some students are likely to have calculators that are at least one generation newer than that shown. This will mean that some buttons are more advanced or will look different from the buttons on older calculators.
For example, the a b/c fraction button to input fractions looks like the equation editor symbol for a fraction and S ⇔ D is used to change between the fraction and decimal answer. They will be able to key in and see recurring decimals and see a fraction written out in full.

Checkpoint

1 Use a calculator to work out the answer to $\dfrac{3^2+(5\times7-2)}{(7-5)\times\sqrt{2^2+5}}$ (7)

Starter

A clock chimes every 6 minutes. A second clock chimes every 7 minutes. The clocks chime together. How many minutes before the clocks chime together again? (42 min)

What if a third clock chimes every 26 min? (5 hr 6 min)

This can be extended by asking how many times the clocks will chime together in 24 hours. (2 clocks 34 times, 3 clocks twice)

Teaching notes

Many of the calculator functions will have been used by students if they have tackled the previous chapters in the student book. Use examples to illustrate the use of the following functions/operations:

- the negative button (–)
- fractions, both mixed and vulgar
- square, cube and higher powers
- square root, cube root and power root
- brackets for protecting fractions and negatives

What use is the square root function?
The area of a square can be found by squaring the side length. To find the length of a side reverse the process and square root the area of the square.

Plenary

Investigate how to change hours, minutes and seconds into hours or vice versa. Make use of the D°M′S″ and DEG functions.
For example, 2.82 hr = 2 hr 49 min 12 sec.

Exercise commentary

Question 1 – Students will tend to trust an answer on the calculator blindly. Explain how this question is an important part of using a calculator. Students should always have an approximate answer in mind, as it is easy to mistype.

Question 2 – Note that newer scientific calculators have a more intuitive fraction button. There are still scientific calculators sold with the old style a b/c button. Highlight the implicit brackets when using the √ button on newer calculators.

Question 3 – Discourage the use of trial-and-improvement. Ask students to look for an alternative method as described in the teaching notes. Use simpler areas of other squares to re-enforce the link between area, side length, squaring and square-rooting.

Question 4 – Ensure students give consideration to numbers between 0 and 1; -1 and 0; negatives and the numbers 0 and 1. Does the student's conclusion cover all possible numbers?

Question 5 – There are 5! = 120 different rearrangements of the numbers, but only one solution. When using calculators with the new fraction button this question can be entered once and then edited to try other combinations of numbers.

Answers

1 **a** 88 209 **b** 250

2 **a** $1.\dot{2}\dot{1}$ **b** 0.6068 **c** 96.0467 **d** 2075.94
e -68.2656 **f** 20.48 **g** 1.2454 **h** 2.8037

3 **a** 8.66 cm
b Width of changing room = 6.2 m
Area of changing room = 96.1 m^2
Areas of sports hall = 496.9 m^2
Length of sports hall = 22.29 m

4 **a** Students' answers: numbers between 0 and 1
b Students' answers: numbers between 0 and 1
c Students' explanations
d **i** Students' graphs
ii Students' comments on graphs

5 $\frac{\sqrt{17^2+35}}{9} = 2$

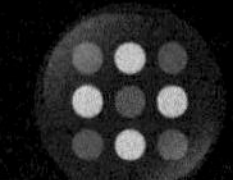

11d Calculators in context

Objectives

- Enter numbers and interpret the display in different contexts (extend to time) (L6)
- Use a calculator efficiently and appropriately to perform complex calculations with numbers of any size, knowing not to round during intermediate steps of a calculation (L6)

Key ideas

1 Calculators are useful if you know how to use them and can interpret the context

Resources

Calculator methods 1 (1932)

Calculators

Flow chart (see simplification)

Table of imperial and metric conversions

Simplification

For question **2**, a single flow diagram could be designed to help conversion from seconds to minutes to hours to days to weeks to years that could be applied to all the parts. For example,

4365 sec into hr, min, sec (1 hr 12 min 45 sec)

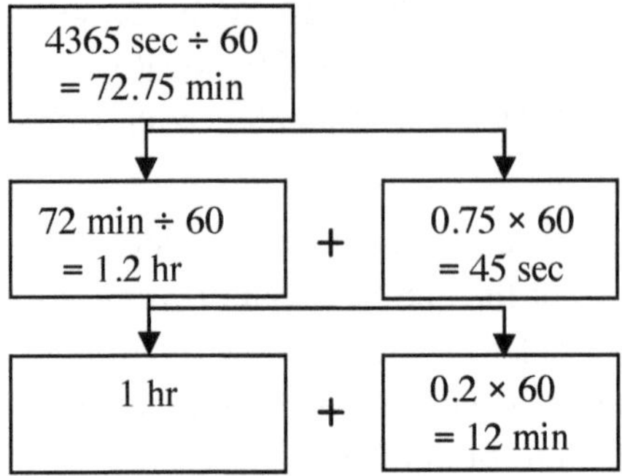

Extension

A light year, $9.46073047258\ 3\ 10^{15}$ metres, is the distance that light travels in one year. Using appropriate units, what is the speed of light? A light year is based on a Julian year. (365.25 days)

(299 792 458 m/s or 1 079 252 849 km/hr or 670 616 629 mph).

These are the standard International Astronomical Union values but other variants exist.

Literacy

Does the £166.67 have any useful meaning here in the first example?

Although the individual cost price of each game might not have a useful meaning on its own, it could be used to compare against the sale price the shop owner sets.

Links

An abacus is a mechanical calculator that consists of a frame containing rows of beads threaded onto wires. Usually, two of the beads in each row are separated from the remaining five by a crossbar. Versions of the abacus are still widely used in the Far East and Africa. There is more information about the abacus and an online abacus at http://www.educalc.net/144267.page

Alternative approach

In the second example, make it clear that the 0.6666… should never be keyed in, but should be obtained by subtracting the integral (whole number) part of the 166.6666…; however, when time is involved, there is no need for this approach. The sexagesimal key (° ′ ″), intended for angle calculations, can be used for time calculations as shown in the 'Did you know?' box. Keying in as 0 (° ′ ″) 0 (° ′ ″) 10000 (° ′ ″) and pressing the equals button will give the answer in hours, minutes and seconds as required.

The fraction key can sometimes be used in a similar way, but less specifically. For example, in checkpoint question **1** the 111 hours can be entered as a fraction, $\frac{111}{24} = 4\frac{5}{8} = 4\frac{15}{24} = 4$ days 15 hours.

For question **1e**, note that the one exact metric to imperial conversion is 1 inch = 2.54 cm.

Checkpoint

1 Convert 11 hours to days and hours. (4 days, 15 hours)

2 Around the world there are on average 44 strikes of lightning every second. How many times does lightning strike each year? (1 387 584 000 or nearly 1.4 billion times)

Starter

Anwar received £10 pocket money each week.
Bryony's pocket money started at £5 and increased by 50p each week: £5 in week 1, £5.50 in week 2, etc.
Charlie said he would be happy if his pocket money started with 1p and it doubled each week:
1p, 2p, 4p, etc.

Ask students who would get the most money after 10 weeks. (Anwar)
How about 20 weeks? (Charlie)
In which week will Charlie get more than £10? (Week 11)

Teaching notes

Show a table of metric-metric, imperial-imperial and metric-imperial conversions with blanks. Ask students which they already know. Fill in as many of the blanks as possible. Are there some patterns in the answers that will make them easier to remember?
For example, grams—kg—tonnes all go in thousands.
Are there any rhymes or helpful tips that students know for remembering any other ones?
For example, two and a quarter pounds of jam is roughly a kilogram.

Use a square metre to show that this 100 cm squared is not the same as 100 square centimetres. Express the side length in cm to establish that 1 m^2 = 10 000 cm^2.

Use a calculator to show how units of time can be subdivided for examples like those in the student book.

Plenary

Is there a quick way to convert from metres per sec to km per hour or mph? Investigate.

Exercise commentary

Question 1 – Students may need reminders of metric and imperial measures and their conversions. Beware of students not making the distinction between length and area conversions.

Question 2 – Encourage students to show all their working in breaking down the time measurements. The standard number of days in a year is 365; leap years are usually ignored in this type of calculation.
Show students they can use the ° ′ ″ button to convert decimals into hours, minutes and seconds.

Question 3 – Expressing part **c** as a percentage is useful, but discuss with students why this does not answer the question, and what other information is needed. For example, is this result good for Ben in the context of his past performance?

Question 4 – Converting m/s to km/hr may need explaining. Ask if more distance is covered in a second than an hour, to show students the need to multiply to convert the time part of this compound unit. Use other compound units like miles per gallon, or measures of density to illustrate.

Answers

1 **a** 38 m and 65 cm
b 3 km, 730 m and 68 cm
c 7 litres and 427 ml
d 15 tonnes, 863 kg and 320 g
e 490 inches = 40 feet and 10 inches
f 5.8 m^2
g 55 pounds
h 4 cm^2

2 **a** 16 min and 40 s
b 1 hour, 30 min and 20 s
c 4 days, 15 hours, 6 min and 40 s
d 274 years, 37 weeks and 5 days
e 0 years, 16 weeks, 3 days, 17 hours, 46 min and 39 s

3 **a** £11 929.40 or more realistically 'under £12 000'
b 5.88 so they need to order 6 coaches
c 38/60, which is about 63%

4 **a** 10.1 m/s **b** 36.3 km/h
c Students' answers:
400 mph = 640 km/h
110 km/h = 30.6 m/s
105 m/s = 378 km/h = 236 mph
17 000 mph = 27 200 km/h = 7556 m/s

Objectives	
• Understand the order of precedence of operations, including powers	(L5)
• Use a calculator efficiently and appropriately to perform complex calculations	(L6)
• Use the function key for powers and roots	(L5)
• Use brackets	(L5)

Key ideas	Resources
1 BIDMAS rules OK?	Order of operations (1167) Calculators Dictionaries

Simplification	Extension
For question **1**, encourage students to use a calculator to find the correct answer. Remind them that a calculator obeys the BIDMAS rule. Then attempt to find how the incorrect answer is made by adjusting/removing some of the operations. Why do they think that mistakes may have been made? Would they have made the same mistake without a calculator?	Use the digits 1, 2, 3, 4, 5 each only once. Use the operation 1, 2, 3, 4, cube and one set of brackets to make the answer -23. You could hint that the answer is in the style of question **2b.** $\left(\frac{4\times5+3}{(1-2)^3}\right)$ Other solutions are also possible.

Literacy	Links
Note that $-3^2 = -9$, $(-3)^2 = 9$ is perhaps ambiguous. Emphasise that brackets ensure clarity.	Bring in some dictionaries for the class to use. The word order can have several meanings and can be used as a noun or a verb. In which curriculum subject would each sense of the word most likely be used?

Alternative approach

All the calculations given as examples, including the last, can probably be entered as they are on the calculators the students have, without any need for extra brackets. Put some similar questions on the board, but with numbers that can be worked without a calculator. For example, using exact squares to square root, this will mean that they can be worked faster without a calculator and might encourage students to consider the order of operations.

If we look at the example $\frac{3^2+(5\times7-2)}{(7-5)\times\sqrt{2^2+5}}$ from a couple of lessons ago, it is clear that the BIDMAS rule now needs a little updating, in one way or another. It seems we must accept that the calculator knows what to do without the need for brackets around the numerator and around the denominator; or perhaps we could suppose there were invisible brackets there, or that the dividing line takes priority here.
See what suggestions students have: IBIDMAS, or DLBIDMAS, perhaps? Or TBIDMASB, for top and bottom?

The most tempting method used to be to work out separate parts of the question. The more unattractive but much preferred method, to find the answer in just one calculation, is now fairly straightforward with a calculator. Since this does not require any comprehension or application of the BIDMAS rule, it is important that students practise both with and without a calculator. Do emphasise the parity of additions and subtraction, and of multiplication and division; and, more importantly, the priority of indices over these, as in πr^2.

Checkpoint

1 Calculate each of the following without a calculator. $\frac{7+(6\div2)^2}{(5-3)^3\div2}$, $\frac{8-(8\div4)^3}{\sqrt{7^2-3(4.3+6.7)}}$, $\frac{4+\sqrt{5^2-4^2-3^2}}{2-\sqrt{5^2-4^2-3^2}}$

(4; 0; 2)

Starter

Ask students to think of a four-digit number (four different digits), for example, 4512.

Ask them to reverse the digits, 2154.
Subtract the smaller number from the larger number, $4512 - 2154 = 2358$.
Add the answer digits together until a single digit obtained $2 + 3 + 5 + 8 = 18$, $1 + 8 = 9$.
Repeat with another four digit number.

Ask students what they notice. (Always 9)

Teaching notes

Ensure students are familiar with all the main functions of their calculator. Previous exercises in this chapter and previous chapters will have already practiced the use of all the main functions.

Does a calculator follow the BIDMAS rule? Establish that it does by using a few examples, $3 + 4 \times 5^2 = 103$.

How can you evaluate expressions like $\frac{3+5^2}{1.6\times2.5}$?

What will happen if you type this into the calculator in one go and how will the calculator decide on the order of priority? ($3 + 5^2 \div 1.6 \times 2.5 = 42.0625$)
Check this answer by calculating the numerator and denominator of the original question and then dividing them. (7)
Why has this gone wrong? Discuss what the calculator thinks is the correct calculation. How can you ensure that the correct calculation is performed? Discuss how brackets can be used to 'protect' the numerator and denominator.
What are the advantages/disadvantages of using brackets around the numerator and denominator compared to working the top and bottom out separately?

Plenary

Put brackets into the expression $2 + 3 \times 4 - 5$. What different answers can you make? Allow the use of one or more sets of brackets. (-5, -1, 9, 15)

Exercise commentary

Question 1 – Ask students to work these out without a calculator initially. If they use a calculator they will not be recalling BIDMAS.

Question 3 – It is important that students explain each error made, and how BIDMAS was not followed.

Question 4 –Encourage students to hypothesise how part **b** can be simplified. Ask if they can generalise and if they can find any other (irrational) square roots that when multiplied produce an integer.

Answers

1 **a** -24 **b** -1 **c** -10 **d** 2.78
e 2.88 **f** 10

2 **a** 71.40 **b** -27.24 **c** 35.28 **d** 0.394517
e 4.43 **f** 16.88

3

	Correct answer	Incorrect working
a	38	$(3 + 4)^2 \times 2$
b	-7	$(5 - 3)^2 - 3$
c	-19	$6 + 5^2$
d	31	$-(5)^2 + 6$
e	25	$60 \div (4 + 8 - 7) + (5 - 2)^3$
f	5	$(3 \times 5)^2 \div (3 \times 5)$
g	96	$[(3 \times 8) \div (3 \times 2)]^2$

4 **a** Students' answers: $\frac{a}{b}\times\frac{a}{b}=\frac{a^2}{b^2}$

b **i, ii** $3^2 \times 5^2 = (3 \times 5)^2$
iii $\sqrt{12} \times \sqrt{3} = \sqrt{(12 \times 3)} = \sqrt{(2 \times 3)^2} = 2 \times 3 = 6$
iv $\sqrt{12} \div \sqrt{3} = \sqrt{(12 \div 3)} = \sqrt{2^2} = 2$

Objectives

- Use efficient written methods to add and subtract integers and decimals of any size (L5)
- Break down substantial tasks to make them more manageable (L6)

Key ideas	Resources
1 Questions might need a mixture of addition and subtraction, perhaps in more than one step	Squared paper Pre-drawn columns for decimal calculation

Simplification	Extension
Provide students with pre-drawn columns for writing in decimal numbers. This may help students to keep their decimal points lined up and assist with subtraction and addition.	An unusual plant keeps increasing in size. At the end of the first day after germinating it is 0.1 cm high; at the end of the next four days it is 0.2, 0.4, 0.7, 1.1 cm high. The pattern of growth forms a mathematical sequence. $\left(0.1(1+\frac{1}{2}n(n-1))\right)$ Compare this to triangular numbers. $\left(\frac{1}{2}n(n+1)\right)$ How long before the plant grows to over 100 cm? (46 days, 103.6cm)

Literacy	Links
Talk about the decimal point and what it represents. Why is it important to make sure that your decimal points line up when doing a column addition or subtraction?	By 2008 over 120 US space shuttle flights had been made since the space shuttle Columbia made its first test flight into space in 1981. There is more information about the US space shuttle at http://www.nasa.gov/mission_pages/shuttle/main/index.html

Alternative approach

Before looking at part **b** of the first example with students, present a simpler question to them first. For example, 123.4 – 2.7 – 3.7 – 25.4. (91.6)
Ask the class what different methods they used, some may have tried to perform the calculation in one go with 4 rows of numbers. Discuss a better method. For example summing the answers that are to be subtracted and then performing a single subtraction as shown in part **b**. Discuss the advantages of this method.

In question **6** give students a chance to do this question in their heads but allow them to jot down numbers on paper. Lead them through together, from the third picture, to the second to the first.

Checkpoint

1 Without using a calculator, work out 0.65 + 13.867 + 3.4 – 6.78. (11.137)

Starter

Seven students estimated the number of sweets in a jar. Their estimates were:
135, 139, 141, 145, 149, 158 and 162.

The errors in their estimates (not necessarily in the same order) were: 2, 6, 7, 11, 15, 17 and 21.

Ask students how many sweets were in the jar. (156)

You can extend this by asking students to explain their strategies and make their own puzzles.

Teaching notes

Recall work previously covered in lesson **7c**. What errors might students make when adding a column of decimals? Discuss the problem of getting the decimal point in the correct place and forgetting about carry marks. Do you need to insert extra trailing zeros to make all the numbers have the same number of decimal places? Discuss.

What errors might students make when subtracting with decimals? Discuss the problems of blank spaces created by mismatched numbers of decimal places. Show that a calculation is incorrect by using the inverse operation of adding. For example,

$$\begin{array}{r} 79.8 \\ -\ \underline{6.54} \\ 73.34 \end{array} \qquad \begin{array}{r} 73.34 \\ +\ \underline{6.54} \\ 79.88 \end{array}$$

Therefore an error has occurred. How can the calculation be performed correctly? Try the calculation again with a trailing zero after the '8'.

What strategy can be employed to calculate questions like 12.43 – 2.12 – 4.32 – 3.075? Will this work in one long column? Is there a simple alternative? (2.915)

Plenary

Discuss the strategies used in questions **4** and **6**. In question **4**, what can be calculated first from knowing the entire perimeter? In question **6**, how does one diagram help add meaning to the next one?

Exercise commentary

Question 1 – Ensure students are very careful when lining up the digits in their correct place value. Make sure students show carry marks clearly.

Question 2 – In some cases students will need to add zeros into empty place value columns to enable subtraction.

Question 4 – Ask students to sketch the building diagram. Encourage students to fill in every length from the diagram on their sketch.

Question 5 – Students will need to remember simple metric conversions.

Question 6 – The logic required to work out Kirsty's weight is not immediately obvious. Avoid telling students and allow them to enjoy puzzling it out for themselves.

Answers

1 **a** 568.6 **b** 622.42 **c** 776.15 **d** 691.6
e 286.53 **f** 221.06

2 **a** 538.02 **b** 220.17 **c** 542.748 **d** 1371.45
e 110.1 **f** 152.83

3 Risotto Twist 239.065 g
Spiced Rice Cakes 235.65 g

4 **a** $y = 52.805$ m **b** $x = 8.055$ m

5 **a** 8.935 kg **b** 3.35 km
c 0.072 litres **d** 3.372625 tonnes
e 3.100346 km

6 58.3 kg

11g Multiplication and division problems

Objectives	
• Multiply decimals	(L5)
• Divide by decimals by transforming to division by an integer	(L5)
• Check results using appropriate methods	(L6)

Key ideas	Resources
1 Problems involving multiplication and division may need careful reading, some careful thought and maybe even tackling in parts	Dividing decimals by whole numbers (1008) Multiply two decimals (1011) Long division (1041) Long multiplication (1916)

Simplification	Extension
To help students with multiplications or divisions involving decimals, use a simple approximation to judge the order of magnitude. Discourage multiplication and division methods that include calculations with decimals. Encourage students to remove decimals before calculating.	Look at question **3a** again. What is the percentage increase in the journey time? (25%) What happens to the speed? (-25%) Can students see any connection between these two percentages? Try other examples. The time is increased by $\frac{1}{3}$ that is, multiply by $\frac{4}{3}$. The speed decreased to $\frac{3}{4}$ of the original, the fraction is inverted. This is difficult so encourage a range of responses.

Literacy	Links
Spend a little time reading the table in the first example carefully. Students do not have lots of practice with these and can easily misread tables. Try to catch some of them misreading and make the point that reading such things is not quite as easy as it seems.	The division symbol ÷ is called an obelus, as are other symbols such as – and †. These symbols were originally used in manuscripts to mark passages containing errors, and this one first appeared as a division symbol (having been used previously to represent subtraction) in a book called *Teutsche Algebra* by Johann Rahn in 1659. There is more information about mathematical symbols at http://www.encyclopediaofmath.org/index.php/Mathematical_symbols

Alternative approach

Ask students what other methods they could use for the first example. For example, students could first estimate the answer to find its order of magnitude (in this case, a couple of hundred pounds). Then use this information to replace the decimal point in the correct place at the end of the calculation.

In question **2**, students could write the answer as an expression before doing any calculations. You might need to help students to write $\frac{342 \times 1.18}{9.8}$, but it should not be too challenging. Ask the students to remove the decimal points from this calculation and ask them to cancel before solving. A factor of 49 might be spotted by some students who remember their cubes! Finally, don't forget to remind students to put the decimal point back at the end of the calculation.

For question **4**, hopefully someone will point out that $10 \times 28 = 280$, so that 9×28 is 28 less, and then follows that through to a conclusion. If not, point this out to the class.

Checkpoint

1 A small business signs up to a communication package that charges 3.8p per text. Their first bill shows £120.27 for texts. Without a calculator work out how many texts they sent. (3165 texts)

Starter

Write the following list of times on the board:

3 days, 192 hours, 1 fortnight, 47 hours, 24 600 seconds, 8 days, 1 leap year, 17 hours, 12 300 minutes, 1020 minutes, 169 200 seconds, 8784 hours, 336 hours, 4320 minutes, 410 minutes, 205 hours.

Challenge students to match up eight pairs in the shortest possible time.

Teaching notes

Recall work previously covered in lesson **11a**. What written methods are students most confident using? Use this as a starting point. Students can then compare their favourite method with long multiplication and build their confidence this way.

How can decimal multiplication be dealt with? Should the decimal point be removed? If so, how can you tell where it is to be placed at the end of the calculation? Discuss the use of estimates to help place the decimal point. Is this the only way to tell?

How can you divide by a decimal? Can the decimal point be removed and inserted later? Will an estimate help to place the decimal point correctly? Is there a good alternative? Discuss eliminating the decimal from the denominator by a suitable multiplication to give an equivalent fraction.

Plenary

Discuss the methods that students used for multiplying with decimals. Did any students attempt to multiply with the decimals still in place? Did this lead to any incorrect answers? Ask the same question with respect to division with decimals.

Exercise commentary

Question 1 – This question allows for practice of multiplying decimals. Do not insist on a particular method but make sure that students have some practice with long multiplication.

Question 2 – Dividing by 98 is challenging. Encourage students to look for easier methods. Some will see that halving and dividing by 7 twice is easier, but may want to experiment as to whether it is quicker. Many students will find repeated subtraction (chunking) a more secure method but encourage them to practice long division.

Question 3 – Some students may need help with linking speed, distance and time. The D/S/T triangle might be useful here.

Question 4 – This question focuses on how to handle remainders in division in different contexts. Ensure students understand why these remainders are treated differently in different situations.

Answers

1 **a** 1.75p
  b **i** 72p **ii** £37.44
  c **i** ≈36 texts, Four
   ii ≈77 texts, Skyte
   iii ≈145 texts, Skyte

2 **a** £41.30
  b About £2000 (She might not spend any on her holidays etc.)

3 **a** 48 mph **b** t (hours) = $\frac{360}{v}$ (mph)

4 **a** No, 11 × 58 = 638 people
  b Yes, 250 ÷ 9 = 27.8, but this would mean 7 classes of 28 and 2 classes of 27.

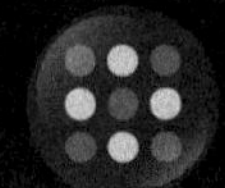

11 Written and calculator methods – MySummary

Key outcomes	Quick check
Use mental methods for division and multiplication.	How many times bigger is 4.5 ÷ 0.04 than 4.5 × 0.04? (625)
Use standard written methods for addition, subtraction, multiplication and division.	A school shelf is 70 cm long. MyMaths 2C student books are 17 mm thick. How many student books can fit along the shelf? (41 books)
Use a calculator to calculate with powers, roots, brackets and fractions.	Lisa's Dad is offering her an incentive for her GCSEs. She is going to be rewarded for each grade 8 or 9 and can choose one of the three following schemes. Lisa thinks she will achieve 9 GCSEs at grade 8 or 9. Which option should she choose? Option A) 1p for the first and then quadrupled for each one after that. Option B) 10p for the first and then tripled for each one. Option C) £1.50 for the first and the doubled. (Option B worth £984.10)
Interpret the results of a calculation in context.	How old (in years) is someone when they celebrate their billionth birth second? (31 years old)
Use the BIDMAS rules to do a calculation in the correct order.	What is the square root of -12 squared plus -5 cubed take away 3? (4)

MyMaths extra support

Lesson/online homework			Description
Multiply decimals by whole numbers	1010	L5	Multiplying decimals by a whole number
Word problems	1393	L3	Solving word problems with one or two steps

MyReview

11 MySummary

Check out

You should now be able to ...

		Test it ➡ Questions
✓ Use mental methods for division and multiplication.	5	1
✓ Use standard written methods for addition, subtraction, multiplication and division.	6	2 - 6
✓ Use a calculator to calculate with powers, roots, brackets and fractions.	6	7
✓ Interpret the results of a calculation in context.	7	8, 9
✓ Use the BIDMAS rules to do a calculation in the correct order.	6	10

Language	Meaning	Example
Equivalent calculation	A way to write a decimal calculation as a whole number calculation	$0.13 \times 2.3 = (13 \times 23) \div 10$
Order of magnitude	Two numbers are the same order of magnitude if the difference between them is much smaller than either number	106 and 95 because 106 − 95 = 11 and 11 is much less than 106 or 95
Inverse operation	The operation, + − × ÷, that undoes the effect of another operation	The inverse of − 7 is + 7 ÷ 3 is × 3
BIDMAS	The correct order for working out operations – Brackets, Indices, Divide, Multiply, Add, Subtract	$(3 + 2^2) + 2 \times 4 = 9 + 8 = 17$
Long division	A way of setting out workings when dividing by a multi-digit number	12)1324 = 110 r 4 12 12 12 04
Long multiplication	A way of setting out workings when multiplying	317 × 51 15850 + 317 16167

11 MyReview

1 Calculate these using a mental method.
- **a** 28×0.04 **b** 19×2.2
- **c** $555 \div 15$ **d** $50.4 \div 0.24$

2 Calculate these using a written method.
- **a** 12×4.31 **b** 8.3×90.4
- **c** 54.8×0.78 **d** 0.57×0.894

3 Calculate these, give your answer to 1 dp.
- **a** $35.2 \div 6$ **b** $823 \div 12$
- **c** $19 \div 8$ **d** $718 \div 1.8$
- **e** $839 \div 0.62$ **f** $10.5 \div 4.5$

4 Rob is going to bake 178 cakes. Each cake requires 65 g of butter. The butter costs £1.45 for a 250 g pack.
How much does the butter for all the cakes cost in total?

5 Joe runs the 110 m hurdles in 16.2 s, what is his speed in metres per second? Give your answer to 2 dp.

6 Vijay's energy bill shows that he used 1224.89 kWh (kilowatt hours) of gas and 1133 kWh of electricity in one quarter of the year.
The price of gas was 4.217p per kWh and the price of electricity was 12.139p per kWh
In addition, he must pay a standing charge of 23.276p per day for gas and 15.219p per day for electricity.
There were 91 days in the quarter.
VAT at 5% of the total must also be added on.
Calculate the total cost of his energy bill (including VAT).

7 Use your calculator to work out
- **a** $\sqrt{132.5 - 4.2^3}$
- **b** $\dfrac{-5 - \sqrt{5^2 - 4x - 2 \times 3}}{2x - 2}$
- **c** $\dfrac{\sqrt{25 - 3^2}}{4^2 - 8}$
- **d** $\dfrac{10.9 - 2.3 \times 1.4}{0.3(7.3 - 2.4)^2}$

8 Convert
- **a** 7520 minutes to days, hours and minutes.
- **b** 1 000 000 seconds to weeks, days, hours, minutes and seconds.

9 Convert these imperial measurements to the metric measurements indicated.
- **a** 14 pounds to kg
- **b** 5 feet, 9 inches to m

10 The following calculations are incorrect. Give the correct answer and explain the mistake.
- **a** $(2 \times 3 + 5)^2 - 7 = 249$
- **b** $(-4)^2 \div 18 = 2$
- **c** $72 \div (3 \times 2^2) - 5 + (7 - 8)^3 = 12$
- **d** $(5 \times 8)^2 \div (5 \times 2) = 16$

What next?

Score		
0 – 4		Your knowledge of this topic is still developing. To improve look at Formative test: 2C-11; MyMaths: 1007, 1008, 1011, 1026, 1041 and 1167
5 – 8		You are gaining a secure knowledge of this topic. To improve look at InvisiPen: 122, 123, 124, 126, 127, 128, 131, 133 and 134
9 – 10		You have mastered this topic. Well done, you are ready to progress!

Question commentary

Encourage students to estimate the answers to questions they calculate using written methods to ensure the order of magnitude correct.

Questions 1 and **2** – Allow students to use whichever written method they prefer.

Question 3 – Encourage students to look for how divisions can be simplified first.

Question 4 – Some students will round down to the nearest number of packs, but this will not be enough butter. Check that they have rounded up.

Question 5 – Encourage students to notice that halving and the dividing by 9 twice is easier than dividing by 162.

Question 6 – Help students to organize all the information provided in the question.

Question 7 – The fraction button on newer calculators should make this question straightforward.

Question 9 – Students may need reminding that there are approximately 2.2 pounds in a kg, 12 inches in a foot and approximately 2.5 cm in an inch.

Question 10 – Students should do this without a calculator.

Answers

1 **a** 1.12 **b** 41.8 **c** 37 **d** 210

2 **a** 51.72 **b** 750.32 **c** 42.744 **d** 0.50958

3 **a** 5.9 **b** 68.6 **c** 2.4 **d** 398.9
e 1353.2 **f** 2.3

4 £68.15

5 6.79 m/s

6 Gas = $1224.89 \times 4.217 = 5165.36113$
Electricity = $1133 \times 12.139 = 13\,753.487$
Standing charge gas = $23.276 \times 91 = 2118.116$
Standing charge electricity = $15.219 \times 91 = 1384.929$
Total charge = 22 421.89313p
Add VAT at 5% gives 23 542.98779p
So £235.43

7 **a** 7.64 **b** 3 **c** 0.5 **d** 1.07

8 **a** 5 days, 5 hours and 20 minutes
b 1 week, 4 days, 13 hours, 46 minutes and 40 seconds

9 **a** 6.36 kg **b** 1.725 m

10 **a** 114 $2 \times 3 + 5 = 6 + 5$ not 2×8
b 34 $(-4)^2 = -4 \times -4 = 16$ not -4×4
c 0 $6 - 5 - 1$ not $6 + 5 + 1$
d 160 $(5 \times 8)^2 \div (5 \times 2) = 5 \times 8 \times 4$ not 4^2

11a

1 Calculate these using a written method.
Remember to do a mental approximation first.

a 82×0.65	**b** 64×0.57	**c** 82×91.3	**d** 93×26.5
e 36×1.86	**f** 72×9.51	**g** 16×2.19	**h** 8.3×86.7
i 63.7×0.91	**j** 38.4×0.69	**k** 57.2×0.61	**l** 93.9×0.93

11b

2 Calculate these using an appropriate method.
Give your answer as a decimal to 1 dp where appropriate.

a $48.6 \div 6$	**b** $67.4 \div 8$	**c** $82.8 \div 7$	**d** $38.5 \div 14$
e $62.5 \div 15$	**f** $31.2 \div 16$	**g** $327 \div 4.6$	**h** $912 \div 5.6$
i $304 \div 2.4$	**j** $441 \div 2.1$	**k** $327 \div 8.2$	**l** $955 \div 3.7$

11c

3 Use your calculator to work out the answers to these sets of instructions.

a Input the number 12. Square your answer. Add 23.
Find the square root. Add -8. Cube your answer.

b Input the fraction $\frac{7}{8}$. Square your answer. Divide by 2.
Add 14. Square root your answer.

c Write the sets of instructions in parts **a** and **b** as calculations using the correct order of operations.

11d

4 Solve these problems.
Give each of your answers in a form appropriate to the question.

a Jasmine's syndicate wins £3 454 123.23 on the Euro millions. There are 17 people in the syndicate. How much does each person receive?

b The population of Smalltown is 48. Each year the population is predicted to increase by 6%. What will the population be in one year's time?

11e

5 Calculate these, giving your answer to 2 dp where appropriate.

a $\frac{(7-2)^3}{(8-3)^2}$ **b** $\frac{(4^2-1.2)(7-2.5)^2}{(9-4.1)^3}$ **c** $\frac{(3^2-2)^2\sqrt{(31-2^3)}}{(17-5)^2}$

6 Use a calculator to work out these calculations.
Give your answers to 2 dp where appropriate.

a $[1.8^3 + (17 - 2.3^2)]^2$ **b** $8.2 + [3.7^2 - (12.7 \div 2.6)]$

c $9.2 \times (1.05 - 2.1)^3$ **d** $\frac{5.03 \times 1.9^3}{4.23 \times (8.7 - 3.3)^2}$

11f

7 Calculate these using an appropriate method.

a $7.6 + 4.3 + 11$	**b** $79 + 115.6 + 41$	**c** $9.27 + 0.9 + 9 + 0.95$
d $999.9 + 99.99 + 0.099$	**e** $33.3 + 333.3 - 3.33$	**f** $2473.5 + 40.79 - 4.6$

8 An airline baggage handler has 1.35 tonnes of capacity left on a plane. Can she load all of the following packages?

car parts, 560 kg	cut flowers, 34.6 kg	a sack of letters 76 kg
two sacks of parcels 98 kg each	a crate of mangoes 425 kg	

9 Darren is having trouble with his arithmetic. For each problem

i work out the correct answer **ii** explain Darren's probable mistake.

a $346.95 + 564.32$	Darren's answer, 811.27
b $1.0046 - 0.045$	Darren's answer, 1.0001
c $627.43 - 451.62$	Darren's answer, 275.81
d $126.6 + 59.3 + 384.13$	Darren's answer, 4027.2

11g

10 Calculate these using the standard method.

a 19×3.68	**b** 27×4.18	**c** 46×5.53	**d** 62×7.26
e 49×5.69	**f** 74×8.57	**g** 79×8.37	**h** 99×9.99

11 Calculate these using an appropriate method. Give your answer as a decimal rounded to 1 decimal place where appropriate.

a $36.7 \div 8$	**b** $43.6 \div 7$	**c** $25.6 \div 6$	**d** $35.7 \div 9$
e $50.4 \div 24$	**f** $52.7 \div 39$	**g** $91.6 \div 24$	**h** $41.8 \div 17$

12 Depak is driving the 249 miles home from holiday.

a His average speed is 45 miles per hour. How long will it take him?

b His fuel consumption is 33 miles per gallon. How much fuel will he need?

c When full his petrol tank holds 14 gallons but at the start of this journey it is only five-eighths full. Can he make it home without having to fill up?

d Depak doesn't know it but his car has a leak, and it is losing 0.15 gallons of petrol every hour. Will he still make it home?

13 **a** Elliot is cooking an 8.5 kg turkey for his family. The instructions say cook at a high heat for 5 min per kg, then turn the heat down and cook for 25 min per kg and finally cook for 30 min at the high heat again.
How long will it take to cook the turkey?

b After cooking the turkey must rest for 45 min. It will take Elliot a further 20 min to carve and serve. If Elliot wants to serve dinner at 4 o'clock in the afternoon, when should he put the turkey in the oven?

MyMaths.co.uk

Question commentary

Question 1 – Students should use their preferred written method for multiplication.

Question 2 – Encourage students to look for how the division can be simplified.

Questions 3 and **4** – Allow calculators for both these questions.

Questions 5 and **6** – By using the fraction button on newer scientific calculators, these questions should be straight forward.

Questions 7–13 – Calculators should not be used for any of these questions. Students must feel secure in any written methods they choose to use.

Answers

1 **a** 53.3 **b** 36.48 **c** 7486.6 **d** 2464.5
e 66.96 **f** 684.72 **g** 35.04 **h** 719.61
i 57.967 **j** 26.496 **k** 34.892 **l** 87.327

2 **a** 8.1 **b** 8.4 **c** 11.8 **d** 2.8
e 4.2 **f** 2.0 **g** 71.1 **h** 162.9
i 126.7 **j** 210 **k** 39.9 **l** 258.1

3 **a** 119.3 **b** 3.79
c $[\sqrt{(12^2+23)}-8]^3$ $\sqrt{[(7\div 8)^2]\div 2+14}$

4 **a** £203 183.72 **b** 51

5 **a** 5 **b** 2.55 **c** 1.63

6 **a** 307.72 **b** 17.01 **c** -10.65 **d** 0.28

7 **a** 22.9 **b** 235.6 **c** 20.12 **d** 1099.989
e 363.27 **f** 2509.69

8 Total mass of parts = 1.2916 tonnes so she can load the plane

9 **a** 911.27 Answer 100 too low so didn't carry hundreds correctly
b 0.9596 Got place value wrong and took away 0.0045 instead of 0.045
c 175.81 Answer 100 too high so didn't exchange hundreds correctly
d 570.03 Added the numbers without regard for place value and then put decimal point in at the end.

10 **a** 69.92 **b** 112.86 **c** 254.38 **d** 450.12
e 278.81 **f** 634.18 **g** 661.23 **h** 989.01

11 **a** 4.6 **b** 6.2 **c** 4.3 **d** 4.0
e 2.1 **f** 1.4 **g** 3.8 **h** 2.5

12 **a** 5 h 32 min **b** 7.55 gallons
c Yes. He has 8.75 gallons
d Yes. He will lose 0.83 gallons and use 7.55 gallons which is less than the 8.75 he has in the tank.

13 **a** 285 min = 4 h 45 min **b** 10:10

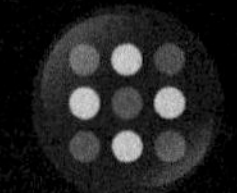

12 Constructions

Learning outcomes

G3 Draw and measure line segments and angles in geometric figures, including interpreting scale drawings (L6)

G4 Derive and use the standard ruler and compass constructions (perpendicular bisector of a line segment, constructing a perpendicular to a given line from/at a given point, bisecting a given angle); recognise and use the perpendicular distance from a point to a line as the shortest distance to the line (L6/7)

Introduction

The chapter starts by using a ruler and protractor to construct triangles before developing a method that uses a pair of compasses. The construction of bisectors and perpendiculars are then covered along with scale drawings before the constructions are contextualised through an introduction to loci. The final section covers bearings.

The introduction discusses how supermarket companies make use of geometrical construction methods to find ideal sites to locate things like warehouses. For example, if there are three supermarkets located in a particular area, it would make sense for the distribution warehouse to be an equal distance from each one. This can be done by using a map (drawn to scale) and constructing the perpendicular bisectors of each pair of supermarkets. The rules of triangulation tell us that these three lines should cross at a single point and this should be our warehouse location.

The idea of triangulation as a method of location goes beyond this practical use. Map makers, navigators and the people who make mobile phone location apps and GPS all use triangulation methods to help them. In GPS, for example, the phone (or satnav) transmits a signal to three masts (or towers) or satellites, and the distance the signal travels to each one can be used to calculate (accurate to a few metres) the location of the device.

Prior knowledge

Students should already know how to…

- Measure lengths and angles using a ruler and protractor
- Use a pair of compasses to draw circles and arcs

Starter problem

The starter problem demonstrates to the students that in an equilateral triangle the perpendicular bisectors of each side meet at the centre of the triangle and go through the vertices. By finding the point where all if these bisectors meet, a circle can be drawn which fits exactly through the vertices of the triangle (the circumcircle, drawn using the circumcentre as the fixed point). Students are invited to try the technique on a range of different triangles. In general, the bisectors of the sides will all meet at a common point (the circumcentre) and a circle can be drawn through the vertices (the circumcircle) but the bisectors will *not* go through the vertices themselves.

The idea of triangle 'centres' has fascinated mathematicians right back to the days of classical geometry in Ancient Greece. There are several different centres, all of which can be constructed using simple techniques.

The incentre is the meeting point of the angle bisectors of the triangle and a circle drawn using this centre as its fixed point will fit exactly inside the triangle (the incircle).

If each vertex of the triangle is joined to the midpoint of the opposite side you get what is called the centroid of the triangle, or the barycentre. This is the centre of mass of the triangle and if it was to be suspended from any point on its edge, the direct line to the ground would pass through this point.

Resources

MyMaths

Bearings	1086	Constructing shapes	1089	Constructing triangles	1090
Map scales	1103	Scale drawing	1117	Drawing loci	1147

Online assessment

Chapter test	2C–12
Formative test	2C–12
Summative test	2C–12

InvisiPen solutions

Constructing a triangle	371	Constructing bisectors	373
Bearings	374	Loci	375

Topic scheme

Teaching time = 6 lessons/2 weeks

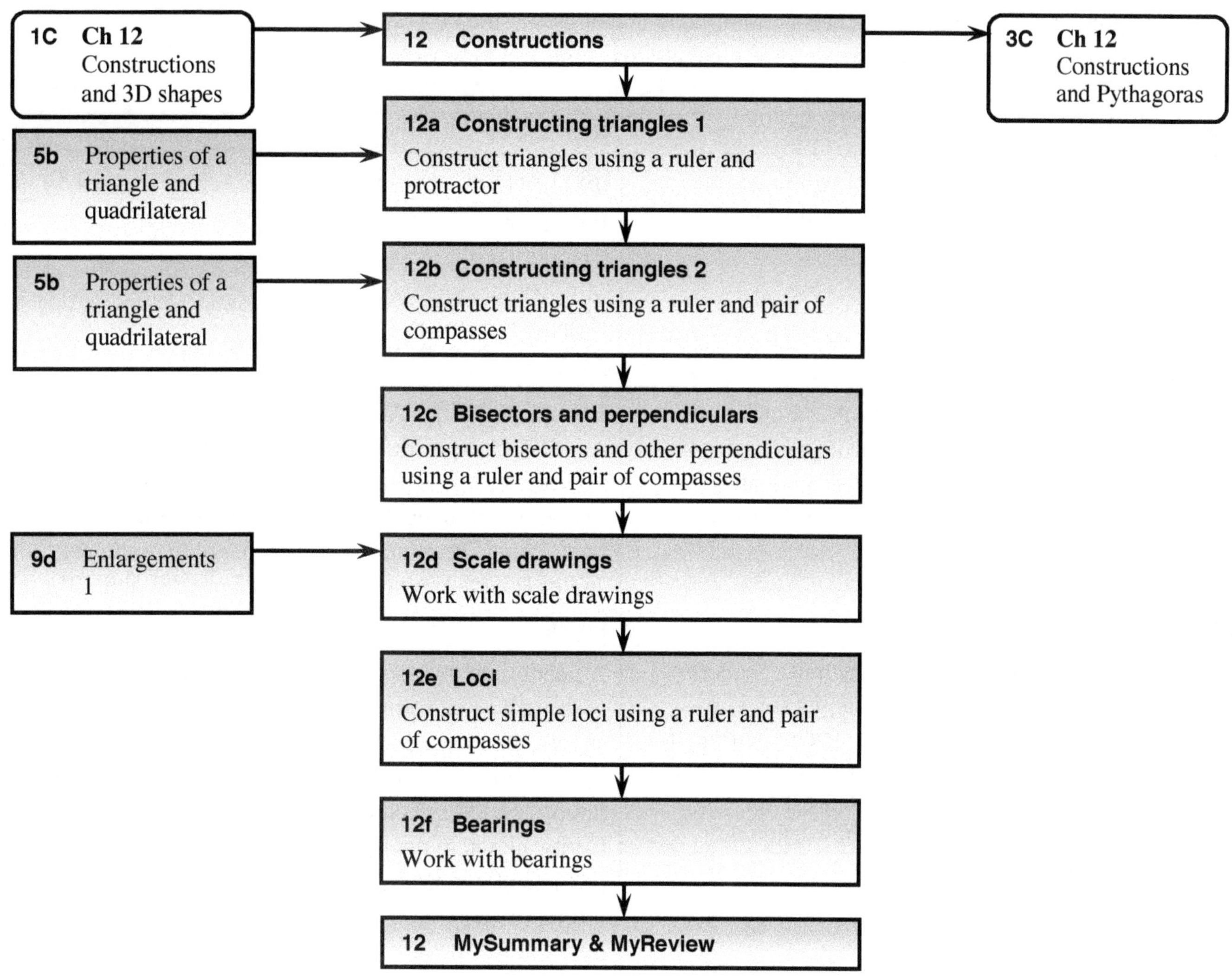

1C Ch 12
Constructions and 3D shapes
5b Properties of a triangle and quadrilateral
5b Properties of a triangle and quadrilateral
9d Enlargements 1
12 Constructions
12a Constructing triangles 1
Construct triangles using a ruler and protractor
12b Constructing triangles 2
Construct triangles using a ruler and pair of compasses
12c Bisectors and perpendiculars
Construct bisectors and other perpendiculars using a ruler and pair of compasses
12d Scale drawings
Work with scale drawings
12e Loci
Construct simple loci using a ruler and pair of compasses
12f Bearings
Work with bearings
12 MySummary & MyReview
3C Ch 12
Constructions and Pythagoras

Differentiation

Student book 2A 224 – 237

Lines and angles
Constructing a triangle 1
Constructing a triangle 2
Scale drawing

Student book 2B 210 – 229

Constructing triangles 1
Constructing triangles 2
Bisectors
Constructing perpendiculars
Loci
Scale drawings
Bearings

Student book 2C 216 – 233

Constructing triangles 1
Constructing triangles 2
Bisectors and perpendiculars
Scale drawings
Loci
Bearings

Objectives	
• Use a ruler and protractor to – measure and draw lines to the nearest millimetre and angles to the nearest degree (L5) – construct a triangle given two sides and the included angle (SAS) or two angles and the included side (ASA) (L6)	
Key ideas	**Resources**
1 Construct to an accurate level of within ±1 mm **2** Construct to an accurate level of within ±1 °.	Constructing triangles (1090) Protractor Ruler Mini whiteboards Dynamic geometry software
Simplification	**Extension**
Provide students with the base of the triangle drawn accurately on a worksheet. Leave adequate space for them to layout all their solutions. Ask students to initially label the vertices of the base of the triangle.	Triangle ABC has AC = 8 cm, BC = 6 cm and angle A = 30°. One person says angle B is 42° and another says angle C is 12°. How could they both be correct? Encourage students to sketch the triangle then draw it accurately. There are in fact two possible triangles, angles B and C could 42° and 108° or 138° and 12°.
Literacy	**Links**
The key term in this section is 'construct'. Students must be aware of the particular meaning for mathematicians. Construct simply means to make an accurate drawing. They will also need to use side/angle terminology and recognise for example that ASA means angle-side-angle; that the known side is between the two known angles.	A geodesic dome is a structure comprised of a network of triangles that form a surface shaped like a piece of a sphere. Geodesic domes are very strong but are lightweight and can be built very quickly. There are famous geodesic domes at the Eden Project in Cornwall and at the Epcot Centre in Florida There are pictures of geodesic domes at http://www.geo-dome.co.uk/ and at http://en.wikipedia.org/wiki/Geodesic_dome

Alternative approach

Present the construction task of each example as a challenge to pairs of student, using only the information and without a diagram. First ask students to sketch the possible triangle on mini whiteboards. Students should then compare their sketches. Raise the question does it matter if your sketch is 'left' or 'right handed? Are these shapes congruent? Why? Some students may have established the size of the third angle in the first example, which can provide further discussion, and alternate ways to construct. Now ask students to plan how they would construct their triangles, step by step. Discuss, share and compare where there are differences. Follow with all students carrying out the construction, and then checking by comparing the resulting sizes of the unknown aspects. Quick demonstrations of student suggested steps may help using your IWB tools, and/or dynamic geometry software.

It may be a helpful addition to tackle using a compass when marking a length on a line. Later in the lesson, ask students to consider whether it matters where the measure detail — side length or angle — exists in order to establish the nature of SAS and ASA. Students can sketch triangles with the three pieces of information in different positions, then compare and discuss which might be congruent or not, which can be constructed with ease, and so on.

Checkpoint

1 Two triangles have two sides and an angle that are the same. Explain why these two triangles are not necessarily congruent. (They may be ASS and not SAS)

Starter – How many angles?

Two lines meet exactly at a point. Excluding reflex angles, one angle is made. Ask students how many non-reflex angles will be made if three lines meet at a point. (3)

What if four lines meet at a point? (6)

five lines? (10)

n lines? $\left(\frac{1}{2}n(n-1)\right)$

Teaching notes

Recover the sum of the interior angles of a triangle and quadrilateral seen previously in spread **5b**.

Look at the proper use of protractor. What mistakes do many students make when measuring and drawing angles? Invite comments from students. These may include: placing the centre of the base of the 180° protractor at the vertex of the angle, rather than the marked cross — using a 360° protractor will remove this error. It could also include, not lining up zero degrees with one of the arms of the angle, but squaring the protractor to the page instead and reading the protractor in the wrong direction and so finding the supplementary angle instead. Or finally, taking insufficient care over accuracy and misreading by more than 1°.

Ask students to construct this triangle as carefully and accurately as possible.

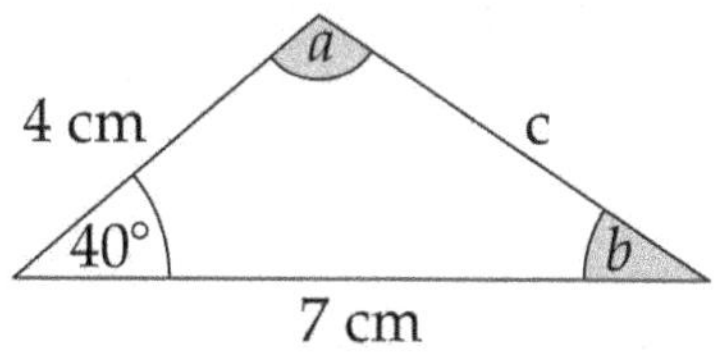

Measure the missing values.

Good accuracy has been achieved if:

a is in between (72, 74)°, b is in between (66, 68)° and c is in between (4.6, 4.8) cm.

Plenary

How much information is needed in order to draw a unique triangle? Try to find all the combinations of sides and angles.

For example are three angles and one side needed, or can just two angles and one side be given?

This could lead to a discussion of ambiguous triangles, for example, the ASS triangle 30° – 8 cm – 5 cm.

Missing side/angles: 9.9 cm – 53° – 97° or 3.9 cm – 127° – 23°.

Exercise commentary

Remind students to use a sharp pencil and to be accurate to the nearest mm and degree. Examiners will generally allow tolerances of 1 mm and 1° either way.

Question 1 – The diagrams in the exercise are roughly to scale. Check that the students' drawings are similar. The most common error is likely to be reading 95° as 85°.

Question 2 – Challenge students if they can recognise the type of triangle before they construct it.

Question 3 – Ask the students why is it necessary to find the unknown angles first? They might need help recalling the meaning of the marks on the side of the triangle in part **c**.

Question 4 – Elicit from the students that the bottom triangle is equilateral, so therefore all three sides are 6 cm.

Question 5 – Since both are right-angled triangles it is clear the resulting kite must have the same area as the rectangle. Ask students to investigate making a kite from any two congruent triangles.

Question 6 – If constructed accurately OD should be a whole number. At this stage students may not have encountered Pythagoras so will not be able to understand why.

Answers

1 Students' constructions
- **a** 141 mm **b** 14.5 cm
- **c** 17.1 cm

2 Students' constructions
- **a** isosceles **b** right-angled
- **c** scalene **b** right-angled isosceles

3 Students' constructions
- **a** 50° **b** 130° **c** 75°, 75° **d** 120°, 30°

4 **a** Students' constructions
- **b** 60°, 85°, 90°, 125° **c** 20.5 cm

5 **a** Student activity
- **b** Kite constructed from the two triangles
- **c** 20 cm^2

6 **a** Students' constructions
- **b** The sides OA, OB, OC have side lengths in the ratio $\sqrt{1}, \sqrt{2}, \sqrt{3}$ etc.

12b Constructing triangles 2

Objectives

- Use straight edge and compasses to construct a triangle, given three sides (SSS) (L6)
- Use straight edge and compasses to construct triangles, given right angle, hypotenuse and side (RHS) (L6)

Key ideas	Resources
1 Introducing the use of compasses for length markers.	Constructing shapes (1089) Rulers Compasses Protractors Dynamic geometry software

Simplification	Extension
Provide students with the base of the triangle drawn accurately on a worksheet. Leave adequate space for them to lay out all their solutions. Ask students to initially label the vertices of the base of the triangle. In question **2** draw the lines BC, PR, EF and label the vertices to assist with the initial stages of the triangle construction.	Construct an isosceles trapezium and an arrowhead accurately. Measure all the sides and angles to see how good your drawing is. What equipment is necessary? If possible group students into threes, allow each a ruler and then give one just a pair of compasses, one a protractor and the other both a protractor and a pair of compasses. Who has the most accurate drawing? What conclusions can you draw?

Literacy	Links
As well as the terms 'construct' and congruent, which students have already met, they will need to know the word 'hypotenuse'. This is an important term which they will need for trigonometry in the future.	A hexaflexagon is a flat hexagon-shaped paper toy that can be folded or flexed along its folds to reveal and conceal its faces alternately. It was invented in 1939 in the USA by Arthur Stone and its construction is based on equilateral triangles. There are instructions to make a hexaflexagon at http://hexaflexagon.sourceforge.net/ and at http://www.flexagon.net/flexagons/hexahexaflexagon-c.pdf

Alternative approach

An approach similar to that of the previous section may be used, starting with a discussion – with sketches – of drawing triangles either with all three sides given or with all three angles given. Use the results to reinforce previous points about congruent shapes and similar shapes, thus establishing that 3 angles are insufficient information for accurate construction. Another point that might arise is which length to choose as the start or base of the construction. There is common sense in choosing the longest given side for placement purposes, but discussing whether it really matters, and also if the 'left' or 'right' aspects of length matters. It is worthwhile to use dynamic software for a quick comparison of congruence.

Checkpoint

1 Construct a triangle with side lengths of 2.5 cm, 6 cm and 6.5 cm. What do you notice about this triangle?
(It is a right-angled triangle)

Starter – Take three

Ask students to make triangles from six rods that are exactly 1 cm, 2 cm, 3 cm, 4 cm, 5 cm and 6 cm long (only 1 of each rod).

How many different triangles can they find? (7)

Which rod does not get used at all? (1 cm)

Why?

What if there was a seventh rod 7 cm long?

Teaching notes

Look at the proper use of a pair of compasses.

What mistakes do many students make when drawing arcs and circles?

Invite comments from students. These may include:

- Holding the compass poorly so that the point moves around.
- Using a loose compass so the arms move and the arc is not accurate.
- Measuring the radius of the arc for the compass on a ruler by starting at the end of the ruler rather than a few mm in where the zero marker lies.

Look at the method described in the student book. Since you can't be sure where the 5 cm and 4 cm sides go, draw a picture of possible locations for each side.

Ask students to construct this triangle as carefully and accurately as possible using a compass and ruler. Which side should be constructed first?

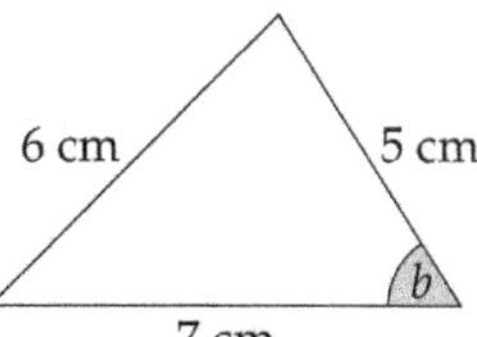

Measure the angle b, if it is between 56° and 58° then good accuracy has been achieved.

Plenary

Discuss real-life examples of when a scale drawing is necessary. For example, when designing a new product that you intend to sell, when landscaping your garden, when demonstrating team tactics for a ball game to your team or drawing pictures to help with the construction of something you have purchased like a chest of drawers.

Exercise commentary

Remind students to use a sharp pencil and be accurate to the nearest mm and degree. They will also need to ensure their compasses are properly tightened to improve accuracy. Do not assume students can use a pair of compasses accurately. This is a skill that needs practice.

Questions 1–3 – Tell students that the arcs are part of the construction and that they must never rub them out. They communicate to the observer that this is an accurate construction.

Question 3 – Suggest that the shared side should be the first one they draw.

Question 4 – Discuss the advantages of changing the scale.

Question 5 – Ask students to explain why this method does not work for other regular polygons. Tell them that after the next section they will be able to construct regular octagons.

Answers

1 Students' constructions
 a 39°, 70.5°, 70.5° **b** 39°, 55°, 86°
 c 37°, 53°, 90°

2 Students' constructions

3 Students' constructions
 a 5.8 cm and 6 cm **b** 4.5 cm and 9.2 cm

4 **a** Students' constructions
 b 3.46 cm representing 1.73 m
 c 60°

5 Students' constructions
The hexagon is made from 6 equilateral triangles of length 4 cm.
The construction of each triangle is SSS.

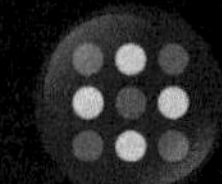

12c Bisectors and perpendiculars

Objectives	
• Use straight edge and compasses to construct – the midpoint and perpendicular bisector of a line segment (L6) – the bisector of an angle (L6) – the perpendicular from a point to a line (L6) – the perpendicular from a point on a line (L6)	
Key ideas	**Resources**
1 Understanding and constructing an angle bisector **2** Understanding and constructing a perpendicular bisector	Constructing shapes (1089) Rulers Protractors Compasses Prep-prepared worksheet (Simplification)
Simplification	**Extension**
Use a prepared worksheet with the first line and, if appropriate, the first intersection of arcs to help with the construction. With this initial assistance for the first few questions, it might help students to feel more confident to try the later questions on their own.	The perpendicular bisectors of the sides of an equilateral triangle all pass through the same point. Is this true of all triangles?
Literacy	**Links**
Keywords in this section are 'perpendicular' and 'bisector'. Students should have come across the word perpendicular before. To introduce the word 'bisect' talk about medical dramas on television and ask if they know what doctors mean by 'a section'. Highlight that 'sect' in Latin means cut, so bisect must mean cut in two.	Perpendicular recording is a new technology that increases the storage capacity of hard drives. It is predicted that perpendicular recording will allow information densities of up to around 1000 Gbit/in2 compared with 100–200 Gbit/in2 using conventional technology.

Alternative approach

Ask students, in pairs, to try to work out how to construct a rhombus. You may add detail of a particular rhombus if and when the students are more comfortable with greater structure. Establish possible steps, so students can construct the rhombus. Request that they now explore the diagonals, and what effect the diagonal has on the interior angles. Now request that they use their findings to come up with steps for constructing angle bisectors. Check and share the results, probing understanding through questions such as would the diagonals of a parallelogram bisect? Perpendicular bisector construction may also be posed as a challenge.

Checkpoint

1 Only using a straight edge, sharp pencil and a pair of compasses, construct a regular octagon.

(First construct a perpendicular bisector and then bisect each right angle)

Starter – Quad bingo

Ask students to draw a 3 × 3 grid and enter nine angles from the following list:

30°, 35°, 40°, 45°, 50°, 55°, 60°, 65°, 70°, 75°, 80°, 85°, 90°, 95°, 100°, 105°, 110°, 115°, 120°, 125°.

Give questions, for example, one of the angles in a rhombus is 135°, what is the smallest angle?

The winner is the first student to cross out all nine angles.

Teaching notes

If available, use the compass tool on an interactive whiteboard to demonstrate the method of constructing

- the perpendicular bisector of a line
- the perpendicular of a line through a point on a line
- the perpendicular of a line through a point off the line
- the angle bisector

Use a pre-prepared worksheet to give students an opportunity to try each of the four constructions in turn once they have seen a demonstration. Remind students to make sure their compasses are extended to over half the length of the line in the case of the perpendicular bisector. Highlight the similarities between the first three constructions, the second and third construction in fact being perpendicular bisectors of a 'shortened line'. In the case of the angle bisector, warn students against using the ends of the arms of the angle to create their 'middle point'. Point out that the ends of the arms are not necessarily equidistant from the vertex of the angle. Two equidistant points should be found using the compass.

Plenary

Do the perpendicular bisectors of the sides of an isosceles triangle cross at the same point? If instead you join the midpoint of each side to the opposite vertex do the lines cross at the same point? Is it the same point? Are either of these points the centre of gravity of the triangle? Can this be tested with an actual triangle?

Exercise commentary

Use plain rather than square paper so that the grid cannot be used to draw perpendiculars.

Question 1 – Remind students that to construct a perpendicular bisector they need to open the compasses to beyond halfway.

Question 2 – Look out for students who may wish to bisect the angle by using the protractor only.

Question 3 – Students may need help in how to modify the perpendicular bisector technique to accommodate this question.

Question 5 – The term diamond might be used, but encourage the use of the term rhombus. Link this back to work on symmetry and area of quadrilaterals.

Question 6 – Ensure students draw a sufficiently large diagram. Allow students to add colour. Ask if they can see how this can be used to construct a regular octagon.

Answers

1 Students' constructions
2 Students' constructions
3 Students' constructions
4 **a** Students' constructions
b Perpendicular distance on students' diagrams
5 **a** Students' constructions
b Rhombus
c Students' constructions
d PR is the perpendicular bisector of SQ
6 Students' constructions

Objectives	
• Use and interpret maps and scale drawings in the context of mathematics and other subjects (L6)	
Key ideas	**Resources**
1 Scale drawings can be thought of as enlargements	Map scales (1103) Scale drawing (1117) Rulers
Simplification	**Extension**
Treat the ratio similarly to the way an equation is treated. Show working on each side to create an equivalent ratio. Ask, what does the ratio tell you initially? What length are you trying to represent? How can the ratio be changed to get the number you want? For example 1 : 50 000 tells you 1 cm represents 50 000 cm. If you want to find 5 cm, you multiply each side by 5. 1 : 50 000 × 5 × 5 5 : 250 000	The most popular map scales are 1 : 25 000 and 1 : 50 000 for walking. What length on each map represents a mile? Give your answer both in cm and inches. (6.437376 cm or 2.5344 inches and 3.218688 cm or 1.2672 inches respectively).
Literacy	**Links**
Scale drawings are enlargements with small — or very small — scale factors.	Model railways are available in different gauges. OO gauge means that the model is built to a scale of 1 : 76, or 1 cm on the model represents a distance of 76 cm in real life. 1 cm on an N-gauge model represents a distance of 146 cm. If an N-gauge model locomotive is 5 cm long, how long is the real-life locomotive? (730 cm)

Alternative approach

Is this all we need to know about scale drawings? What other features should we know about? The projective nature of the drawings, perhaps, where things are necessarily flat, whether the drawings are of land or of helicopters. This gives a representation that is a bit like a cartoon.

Different phrases can be confusing for some students so consider the language you use carefully. For some, the phrase '4 times bigger than 3' would suggest 15; '4 times as large as 3' is unambiguously 12; and '4 times larger than 3' is somewhere between, with only a small chance of being thought of as 15. It might be worth checking the understanding of students, especially if there are some whose first language is not English.

Checkpoint

1 How many kilometres are represented by 38 mm on a 1 : 50000 map? (1.9 km)

Starter

Ask students to draw a 3 × 3 grid and enter nine quadrilaterals or polygons.

Give properties. For example,

This is a regular shape with six lines of symmetry. (Hexagon)

This shape has two pairs of equal sides with perpendicular diagonals. (Kite)

The winner is the first student to cross out all nine shapes.

Teaching notes

Show how a scale can be represented in words, for example, 2 cm represents 1 m. How can this be represented by a ratio? Show how the units would be removed on the ratio written in its simplest form.

A map scale might be written as 1 : 100 000. What does this actually mean? Is this a useful way to think of the scale if you are trying to measure distances on a map? Write this ratio in words.

A model maker of sailing ships knows the area of canvas needed for the sails of the full size ship. He is building a model using the ratio 1 : 100. How can he work out the area of the canvas he needs to use in the model?

Are the areas and lengths of a scale drawing in the same ratio? Use two rectangles in the scale 1 : 3. What are their corresponding areas when their lengths are in the ratio 1 : 3? $(1 : 3^2 = 1 : 9)$

How can this help the model maker?

Plenary

Investigate the different scales used on ordnance survey maps. You can visit the site https://www.ordnancesurvey.co.uk/shop/ to see the different scales and types of maps available.

Exercise commentary

Question 1 – Encourage students to consider what units to give their final answers in.

Question 2 – Point out that when calculating distances on the scale drawing the inverse operation is needed.

Question 3 – Most students will use 4 cm by 3 cm, but suggest a larger drawing to enable a more accurate measurement. Ensure they state the scale of their drawing.

Question 4 – Discuss what shape initially could be used to represent the boat. Discuss how wide canal boats are. Presumably they can pass. Students may wish to cut out a 'boat' to see if it can pass these two bends.

Answers

1 **a** 70 cm **b** 175 cm **c** 87.5 cm

2 **a** 12 cm **b** 8 cm **c** 5 cm

3 Students' scale drawings that must include the scale used

4 **a** Students' scale drawings

b Maximum length at zero width = 14 m.
Length reduces as the width of the boat increases.

12e Loci

Objectives	
• Find the locus of a point that moves according to a simple rule, by reasoning (L7)	
Key ideas	**Resources**
1 Understanding that loci are about exploring the paths traced by a moving point **2** Beginning to visualise possible resulting paths from simple conditions given	Drawing loci (1147) Area of a triangle (1129) Rulers Compasses Protractors Tracing paper Mini whiteboards Counters Graphing software Pre-prepared worksheet with questions drawn out
Simplification	**Extension**
Use a prepared worksheet with the question already drawn in place and, if appropriate, the first intersection of arcs to help with the construction. With this initial assistance for the first few questions, it might help students to feel more confident to try the later questions on their own.	Construct perimeters around shapes that are equidistant at all points from the shape. Include challenging shapes like concave polygons and compound shapes made from arcs and straight lines.
Literacy	**Links**
As this section includes new terminology, literacy must be viewed as central to the topic. The key term is 'locus' and its plural 'loci'. Link it with the word location. A locus is any location an object can take when following a rule. Although a locus can be a path, as described in the student book, be aware it can also be an area.	Spirograph is a toy invented by the British engineer Denys Fisher in 1965. The pattern drawn is the locus of a pen attached to one circle rolling around the inside circumference of another and is called a hypotrochoid. There is an interactive Spirograph at http://perl.guru.org/lynn/apps/index.html

Alternative approach

This concept is quite a challenging one for many students, so it is helpful to take a practical approach and let students work in twos or threes to support each other. Begin by describing some very simple situations, such as those given in question **1**, and encourage the students to trace what they think will be the paths in the air with their finger. Follow this up with sketching on mini whiteboards. You could also get students to stand at key points to mark out a diagram and then get other students to walk what they think the locus would be. Alternatively students could use counters to mark the positions of a moving point.
Different scenarios or problems could be given in card form for a group of students to work on. A variety of strategies including physically walking the locus, counter marking/tracing and sketching can then be applied. Finally, using a moving demonstration, for example, with GeoGebra, following discussion about each scenario will help to establish the concept for the whole class.

Checkpoint

1 A garden shed measures 2 m by 3 m. A dog is tied to the outside of the shed at a corner, with a 2 m long lead. On a scale diagram draw the locus of the dog if the lead remains tight.

(Appropriate scale diagram showing a locus of ¾ a circle)

Starter – Clock angles

Ask students to give the angle between the hour and minute hands at the following times: 7.00, 4.00, 9.30, 1.30, 3.15 and 4.45. Hint: The hour hand moves as well as the minute hand!

(150° or 210°, 120°, 105°, 135°, 7.5° and 127.5°)

Teaching notes

Look back at the initial work from the previous spread. In the case of the perpendicular bisector, where would you have to stand in order to be an equal distance (equidistant) from the two end points of the line?
(On the perpendicular bisector)

In the case of the angle bisector, where would you have to stand in order to be equidistant from the two lines? (On the angle bisector)

The word locus (singular) or loci (plural) comes from the Latin word for 'position' or 'place'. So 'find the locus' means 'find the place'.

What does the locus of the points an equal distance around the outside of a rectangle look like?
Invite students' comments and then look carefully at the solution. Why are the corners 'rounded off'?
What would the locus around an equilateral triangle look like?

Plenary

Examine the locus of points that can be reached by a dog on a lead when tied to different positions along two walls at right angles. Look at solutions that involve being tied at one point and other solutions that allow the dogs lead to move along a rail on the wall. Include problems that let the dog go round to the next wall, thereby 'shortening' the lead and resulting in an arc of smaller radius.

Exercise commentary

Question 1 – Allow students to extend the line and not concern themselves with it being 'too long'. Make sure students leave their construction lines as part of their answer.

Question 2 – Students may need coaching on how to use a pair of compasses. Make sure compasses are tight and pencils are sharp. Remind students they don't have to press hard and only to touch the very top of the compass when drawing the circle.

Question 3 – Make sure that students learn that equidistant from two points always results in a perpendicular bisector.

Question 4 – Likening this to a running track may help students visualize the locus of a fixed distance from a line.

Question 6 – There is a useful graphic of this on mymaths.co.uk in the area of a triangle lesson. (1129) Re-interpret this graphic using the language of locus.

Question 7 – The activity could be aided by the use of tracing paper. Ask students to anticipate what they think will be the shape of the path. Did they expect the shape of the locus?

Answers

1 Students' constructions of the bisector of angle ROQ

2 Students' constructions of a circle of radius 35 mm

3 **a** Students' scale drawings
  b Students' constructions of the perpendicular bisector of AB

4 **a** Students' constructions of three parallel lines, length 3 cm, 1 cm apart, with a semicircle (radius 1 cm), centred on each end of the middle line so that they join the ends of the outer two lines

5 **a** Students' scale drawings of two parallel lines, 4 cm apart
  b Students' drawings of a straight line parallel to the existing lines, 2 cm from each

6 Students' constructions of a straight line parallel to AB, 4 cm from AB

7 Student activity

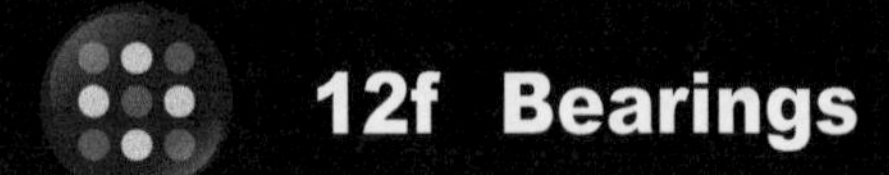

12f Bearings

Objectives

- Use bearings to specify direction (L6)

Key ideas

1 Bearings are measured clockwise from North, and should be expressed with three digits or figures

Resources

Bearings (1086)

Enlarged copies of questions **1** and **2**

Protractors

Simplification

Consider giving students two copies of question **1** to allow them to add an arc for the bearings without over complicating the diagram.

Provide students with accurate drawings of question **2** as well as a copy of the exercise. Ask students to try to use the printed exercise to find the other angles in the question, but check their answers using the scaled copy.

Extension

In question **2** the bearing from A to B was 120°, the bearing from B to A (a reverse bearing) was 300°. By examining the bearings and reverse bearings of each point in question **2**, write a formula that connects a bearing and reverse bearing. If the bearing is:

$< 180°$, then the reverse bearing = bearing + 180°,

$\geq 180°$ then the reverse bearing = bearing – 180°.

Note, a bearing of 360° is not used; instead, 000° is used for North.

Literacy

Why do we call them three-figure, and not three-digit, bearings? Get students to come up with their own suggestions.

Beware of occasional variations from 'the bearing of B from A', the usual phrasing, with 'the bearing from A to B', or similar … which, here, is the same thing.

Links

Magnetic compasses measure bearings in relation to the Magnetic North Pole rather than the geographical North Pole. The Earth's magnetic field changes and the position of the Magnetic North Pole moves approximately 40 km each year. There is more information about the Magnetic North Pole at http://en.wikipedia.org/wiki/Magnetic_north_pole

Alternative approach

Are the angles in the photograph proper three-figure bearings? Might this matter, as the board becomes worn and less clearly legible over time? Does it help to have three digits? Why else might we need to use three digits, always? For example, over the radio, or on the telephone?

Is it acceptable to have angles in the diagrams, in the usual way, as long as we use three digits whenever we are actually saying or writing bearings?

Note that the example shows how to find reverse bearings, which can be very important for working out where one is, from the bearings of visible landmarks; the reverse bearings can be transferred to a map, to pinpoint the viewpoint the bearings are taken from. In the example, what is the first step in finding the reverse bearing?

(Either drawing the new North line … or, just adding 180°!)

Checkpoint

1 Jack walks 3 km on a bearing of 060°. He then turns and walks 5 km on a bearing of 280°.
On a scale diagram, measure how far and on what bearing he must walk to get back to where he started.

(4.7 km on a bearing of 124°)

Starter

Ask students to find a triangle where all the angles are square numbers. (100°, 64°, 16°)
Can they find any quadrilaterals where all the angles are square numbers?
(144°, 100°, 100°, 16° and others)
Any pentagons? (196°, 144°, 100°, 64°, 36°)

Teaching notes

What does a bearing measure? An angle.
Where do the arms that make the angle of the bearing go? One always points to the North, the other points in the direction of the point you are finding the bearing of.
Where do you always begin counting from?
The North line.
Which direction do you count in? Always clockwise.
How many digits are there in a bearing? Three.
How can bearings be measured if they are over 180°?

Remind students of the common mistakes made using protractors, such as:

- placing the centre of the base of the 180° protractor at the vertex of the angle, rather than the marked cross (a 360° protractor will prevent this error)
- not lining up zero degrees with one of the arms of the angle, but squaring the protractor to the page instead
- reading the protractor in the wrong direction and finding the supplementary angle
- taking insufficient care over accuracy and misreading by more than 1°.

Plenary

Suppose a ship is in a storm and is attempting to transmit its bearing from a lighthouse over the radio. If the radio communication fails part of the way through the message, what possible bearing could the ship be on?
Use examples and invite students to give possible solutions. 'we are on bearing 2…!' Some students may give the solution 20 or 25, is this possible?
Is it clearer now why three figures are used by everyone around the world? For clarity and safety the first figure is always the hundreds.

Exercise commentary

Question 1 – Constantly remind students that bearings are always measured clockwise and are given as 3 figures.

Question 2 – The diagrams are not drawn to scale. The shading will help them to measure bearing in a clockwise direction. Challenge students to be able to work out reverse bearing quickly.

Question 3 – Suggest students only consider bearings less than 180°. Some students will find 021° to 029° relatively quickly but challenge them that there are other sets.

Question 4 – This question will challenge their accuracy as a small error in measuring the bearing can have a significant effect on the distance.

Answers

1 **a** 095° **b** 260° **c** 345° **d** 135°
e 315° **f** 290° **g** 030°

2 **a** 120° **b** 230° **c** 040° **d** 225°
e 325° **f** 300° **g** 050° **h** 220°
i 045° **j** 145°

3 Examples include bearings from 020°/200° to 029°/209° and from 130°/310° to 139°/319°

4 5.7 km, bearing of C from A is 015°

Key outcomes	Quick check
Construct ASA, SAS, SSS and RHS triangles.	Construct a triangle with sides 5 cm, 7 cm and 7 cm. Use a protractor and measure each angle to the nearest degree. (69°, 69°, and 42°)
Construct an angle bisector, the perpendicular bisector of a line, the perpendicular from a point on a line and the perpendicular from a point to a line.	Construct an equilateral triangle of sides 10 cm and then construct a perpendicular bisector along the base. By bisecting angles draw an isosceles triangle with base 10 cm and 2 angles of 30°. Measure the height of this triangle. (2.9 cm)
Interpret scale drawings and maps using ratios.	How far is 3.5 km when represented on a 1 : 25000 map? (14 cm)
Construct simple loci	A square animal enclosure at a zoo measures 3 by 3 m. A Safety rail must be put all the way around and must always be 1 m from the enclosure. Draw a scale diagram to show this. (Square with rounded corners around enclosure)
Use three figure bearings	Olivia walks 6 km on a bearing of 200° and then turns and walks 9 km on a bearing of 070°. From a scale diagram measure how far and on what bearing she needs to walk to return to where she started. (6.7 km on a bearing of 292°)

MyMaths extra support

Lesson/online homework			Description
Constructing triangles	1090	L5	Constructing triangles using a ruler and protractor
Scale drawing	1117	L5	Draw scale plans and read measurements from scale plans

MyReview

12 MySummary

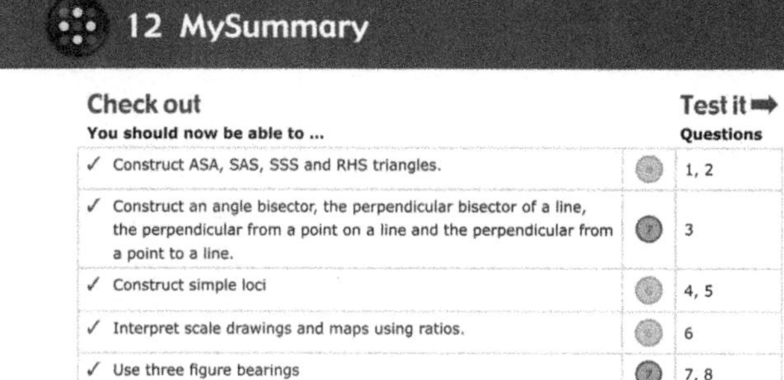

Check out
You should now be able to ...

You should now be able to ...	Test it ➡ Questions
✓ Construct ASA, SAS, SSS and RHS triangles.	1, 2
✓ Construct an angle bisector, the perpendicular bisector of a line, the perpendicular from a point on a line and the perpendicular from a point to a line.	3
✓ Construct simple loci	4, 5
✓ Interpret scale drawings and maps using ratios.	6
✓ Use three figure bearings	7, 8

Language	Meaning	Example
Perpendicular bisector	A line that cuts a second line at 90°	P, A, B, C
Locus	The path made by the point of an object as it moves	A, B, 1 cm, 1 cm
Congruent	Shapes that are identical: corresponding lengths and angles are the same	ASA, SAS, SSS and RHS triangles are congruent
Construct	To draw accurately using a ruler, protractor and compasses	Bisecting an angle is a construction
Three figure bearing	A direction given as an angle, measured clockwise from north, using three digits	East is 090°

230 **Geometry** Constructions

12 MyReview

1 Construct these triangles.

a

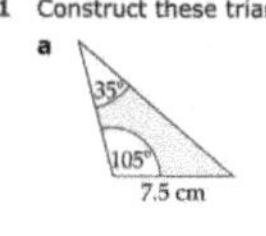

b

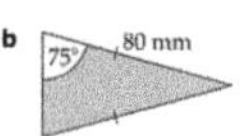

2 Construct these triangles.

a 8 cm, 15 cm, 11 cm

b

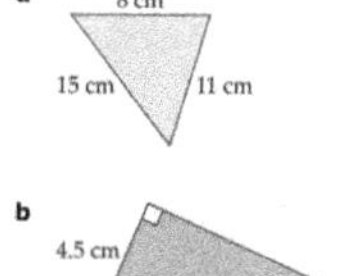

3 Use a ruler and compasses to add the following lines to your earlier constructions.

a On **1b**, the bisector of the angle between the equal sides.

b On **2b**, the perpendicular to the hypotenuse passing through the opposite vertex.

4 Copy this rectangle and construct accurately the locus of a point that is 1 cm from the edge of the rectangle.

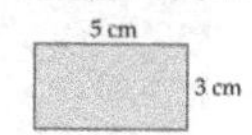

5 Two fences meet at 90° as shown. Copy the diagram and construct the locus of the point which is equidistant from both fences.

6 A circular pond has a radius of 1 m.

a Draw a scale drawing using a scale of 1 : 40

b Draw the locus of the point that is 0.5 m from the edge of the pond.

7 Find the bearings of

a B from A c C from D

b A from B d D from C

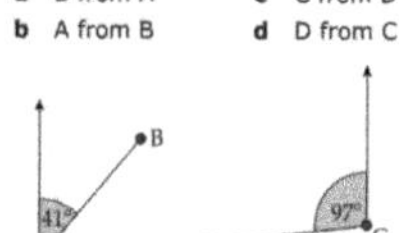

8 Draw the following bearings of B from A and state the bearing of A from B in each case.

a 076° b 195° c 308°

What next?

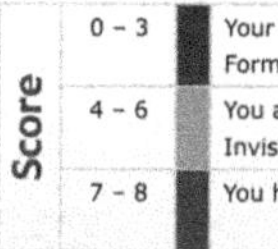

Score		
0 – 3		Your knowledge of this topic is still developing. To improve look at Formative test: 2C-12; MyMaths: 1086, 1089, 1096 and 1147
4 – 6		You are gaining a secure knowledge of this topic. To improve look at InvisiPen: 371, 373, 374 and 375
7 – 8		You have mastered this topic. Well done, you are ready to progress!

MyMaths.co.uk 231

Question commentary

Ensure students have a protractor, rule, a pair of compasses and a sharp pencil. Allow ±1° and ±1 mm on all constructions.

Question 1 – Students will need to find the missing angles before they can construct the triangles. They should know that they require SAS or ASA.

Question 2 – Remind students to show their construction lines clearly.

Question 3 – Remind students to show their construction lines clearly.

Question 4 – Corners must be rounded using a pair of compasses.

Question 6 – Ensure students draw both circles, with the same centre, one of radius 2.5 cm and the second with a diameter of 7.5 cm.

Question 7 – Remind students that bearings must always be measured in a clockwise direction and have three figures.

Question 8 – Students should be able to calculate reverse bearings without measuring.

Answers

1 Students' constructions of triangles

a ASA: 105°, 7.5 cm, 40°

b SAS: 80 mm, 30°, 80 mm or ASA: 75°, 80 mm, 30°

2 Students' constructions of triangles:

a SSS: 8 cm, 15 cm, 11 cm

b RHS: 90°, 7.5 cm, 4.5 cm

3 **a** Students' constructions. The half angle is 15° and the line is the perpendicular bisector of the base.

b Students' constructions. The line should cross the hypotenuse at 2.7/4.8 cm.

4 Students' constructions of rectangle with either a second rectangle drawn inside it, 1 cm from each edge, or four lines drawn parallel to and 1 cm from each edge outside the rectangle, with quarter circles linking these lines.

5 Students' constructions. The locus is the angle bisector at 45°.

6 **a** Students' scale drawings of pond, a circle radius 2.5 cm

b Students' scale drawings of a concentric circle on **a**, radius either 3.75 cm (outside pond) or 1.25 cm (inside the pond)

7 **a** 041° **b** 221° **c** 083° **d** 263°

8 Students' constructions of bearings given. Bearings of A from B are:

a 256° **b** 015° **c** 128°

12a

1 Construct these triangles.

a

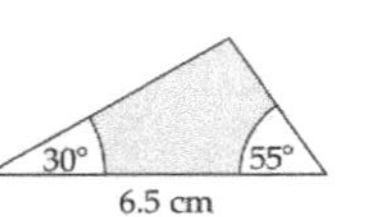

b

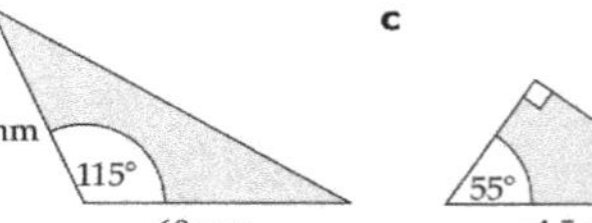

c 55°, 4.5 cm

12b

2 Construct these triangles.

a 7 cm, 4 cm, 9 cm

b 4 cm, 8.5 cm

3 Construct these nets, using ruler and compasses.
Each triangle is equilateral.
State the name of the 3-D shape formed by the net.

a

b

12c

4 Make an accurate copy of this diagram of an isosceles triangle.
Construct the perpendicular bisector of the base AB.
Comment on your result.

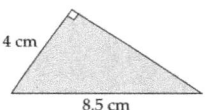

A, B, 8 cm, 6 cm

5 Draw a horizontal line and a point P above the line.

a Using compasses, construct the perpendicular to the line passing through P.

b Label your diagram A, B, P and C as shown.

c What is the mathematical name of the quadrilateral APBC?

d Explain why this construction gives a perpendicular line.

P, A, B, C

12d

6 The Naze Tower in Essex is 26 metres high and 6 metres wide.

a Draw a scale drawing of the tower using a scale of 1 : 500.
Show your calculations for the height and the width of the tower in a scale drawing.

b Estimate the height of the person in the photograph.

c Calculate the height of the person in the scale drawing and draw the person on your scale drawing.

7 Jules is using a map with a scale of 1 : 50 000.
What is the actual distance in kilometres, if the length on the map is

a 1 cm **b** 5 cm **c** 1.5 cm **d** 3.5 cm **e** 4.8 cm?

12e

8 A goat is tethered to a post with a 3 metre length of rope.

a Using a scale of 1 : 100, draw a scale drawing showing all the grass the goat can reach to eat.

b The goat is now tethered with the same rope to a wall. Draw another scale drawing with the same scale, showing all the grass the goat can now eat.

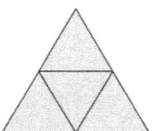

3 m

12f

9 The map shows three villages in Derbyshire.
Measure the bearing of

a Baslow from Bakewell

b Ashford from Bakewell
Centre your protractor at Bakewell.

c Baslow from Ashford
Centre your protractor at Ashford.

d Bakewell from Baslow

e Ashford from Baslow.
Centre your protractor at Baslow.

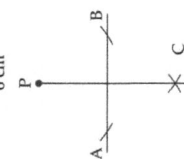

N, N, N, Baslow, Ashford, Bakewell

10 Point B is 6 km East of point A.
Point P is on a bearing of 050° from A and 330° from B.
Using a scale drawing, with 2 cm representing 1 km, find the distance of P from A and from B.

232 **Geometry** Constructions

MyMaths.co.uk

233

Question commentary

Questions 1–5 – Encourage students to focus on accuracy. This means using a sharp pencil. Also remind them to leave all their construction marks.

Question 6–7 – Tell students to make sure they leave their answers in appropriate units.

Question 8 – This is the first question students have come across where locus is an area, rather than a line.

Question 9 – Remind students of the three things they must remember about bearings; measure from north; measure clockwise; and always give bearings as three figures.

Answers

1 Students' constructions of triangles

2 Students' constructions of triangles

3 Students' constructions of nets

a Tetrahedron **b** Octahedron

4 Students' constructions of equilateral triangle with perpendicular bisector of AB. This passes through the apex of the triangle.

5 **a** Students' constructions

b Correct labelling of diagram

c Rhombus

d The diagonals of a rhombus are perpendicular.

6 **a** Students' scale drawings, height = 5.2 cm, width = 1.2 cm

b 2.5 m

c 2.1 m, person added to scales drawing

7 **a** 0.5 km **b** 2.5 km **c** 0.75 km **d** 1.75 km

e 2.4 km

8 **a** Students' constructions indicating the interior of a circle of radius 3 cm

b Students' constructions indicating the interior of a semicircle of radius 3 cm

9 **a** 045° **b** 300° **c** 070° **d** 225°

e 250°

10 Students' scale drawings, AP = 5.3 cm, BP = 3.9 cm

Related lessons		Resources	
Properties of a triangle and a quadrilateral	5b	Lines and quadrilaterals	(1102)
Properties of a polygon	5c	Properties of triangles	(1130)
		Examples of folded figures Prepared squares of paper Other examples of origami from books, etc.	

Simplification	Extension
Prepared origami squares can be used to help students get started with the activities. Pre-folded templates can also be given to students.	Students could be challenged to make further origami shapes from instructions in books or found on the internet. Some students may already be able to make origami patterns and these students could be used as 'experts' to teach others.

Links
Links could be made to design technology, considering the practical uses of folding. For example, there has been much research on effective ways of folding a map so that adjacent sections can be made visible without unfolding the whole map and one such fold has been used with large solar panel arrays on satellites where the panel opens up once the satellite is in orbit. See: http://math.serenevy.net/?page=Origami-ApplicationLinks

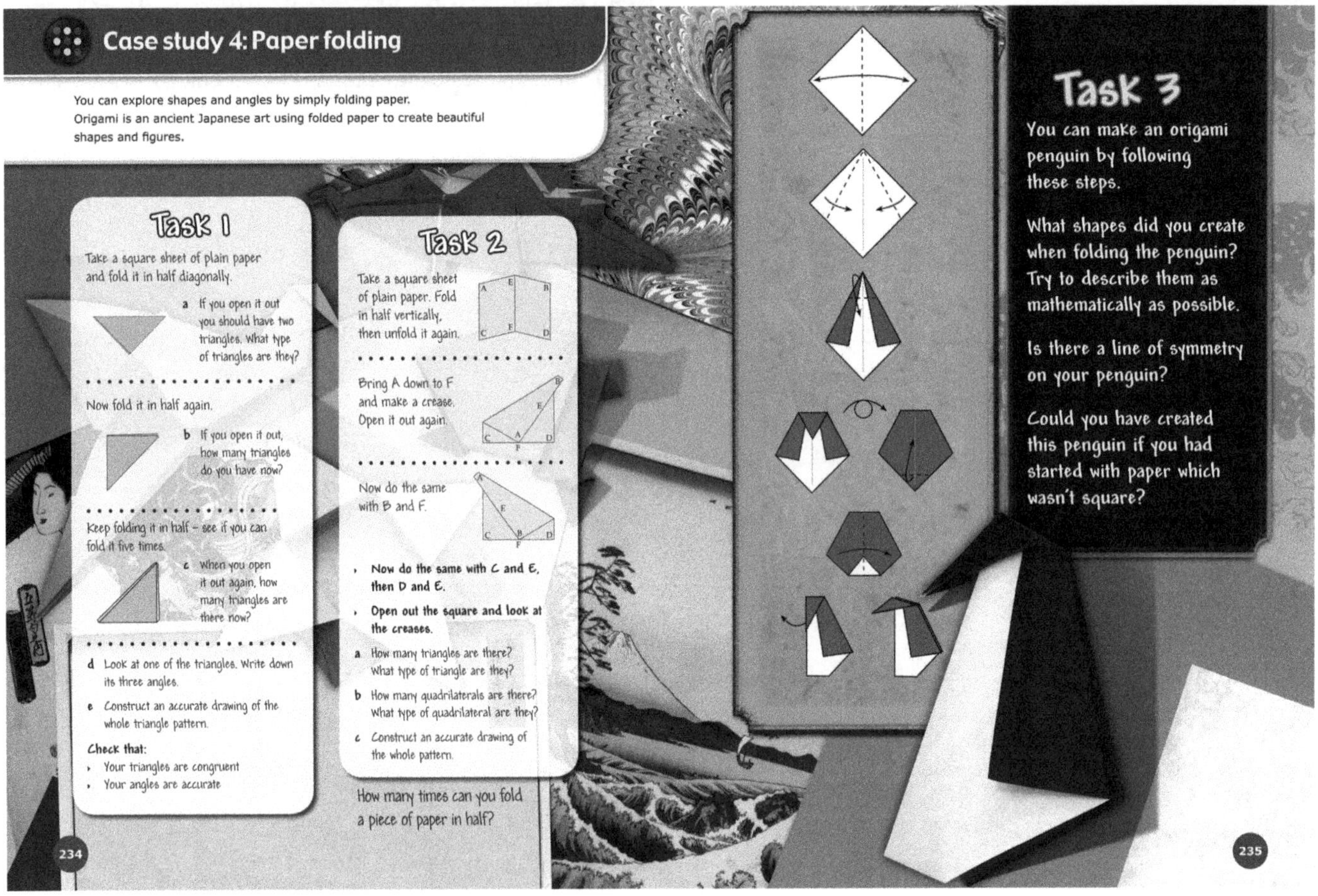

Case study 4: Paper folding

You can explore shapes and angles by simply folding paper.
Origami is an ancient Japanese art using folded paper to create beautiful shapes and figures.

Task 1

Take a square sheet of plain paper and fold it in half diagonally.

a If you open it out you should have two triangles. What type of triangles are they?

Now fold it in half again.

b If you open it out, how many triangles do you have now?

Keep folding it in half – see if you can fold it five times.

c When you open it out again, how many triangles are there now?

d Look at one of the triangles. Write down its three angles.

e Construct an accurate drawing of the whole triangle pattern.

Check that:
- Your triangles are congruent
- Your angles are accurate

Task 2

Take a square sheet of plain paper. Fold in half vertically, then unfold it again.

Bring A down to F and make a crease. Open it out again.

Now do the same with B and F.

- **Now do the same with C and E, then D and E.**
- **Open out the square and look at the creases.**

a How many triangles are there? What type of triangle are they?

b How many quadrilaterals are there? What type of quadrilateral are they?

c Construct an accurate drawing of the whole pattern.

How many times can you fold a piece of paper in half?

234

Task 3

You can make an origami penguin by following these steps.

What shapes did you create when folding the penguin? Try to describe them as mathematically as possible.

Is there a line of symmetry on your penguin?

Could you have created this penguin if you had started with paper which wasn't square?

235

Teaching notes

Origami is the art of paper folding and has been practised in Japan since the 17th century. It uses a combination of folds and creases to produce designs from paper, without cutting or sticking. This case study looks at several such designs and gives students the opportunity to consider the shapes within them.

Task 1

Encourage students to fold their paper using sharp creases. This will mean that the triangles formed are easy to see. Can the students see other sizes of triangle as well as the small ones created from the repeated folding?

Task 2

Again, stress the importance of sharp folds. Students should be encouraged to compare their patterns with others to check the constructions and also to enable discussion of the end results.

Task 3

Look at the pictures showing how to make a penguin. Check that the students understand how they show the stages for folding the paper. Ask them to use the instructions to make a penguin, stressing the importance of making sharp folds. When they have made their penguins, ask them to answer the questions in the panel. To answer the last question, they might want to try folding a penguin from a rectangular piece of paper. When they have had sufficient time, discuss their answers.

Answers

1 **a** Isosceles

b 4

c 32

d 45°, 45°, 90°

e Students' own drawings

2 **a** 4; Isosceles

b 8; Trapeziums

c Students' own drawings

3 Discuss task with students

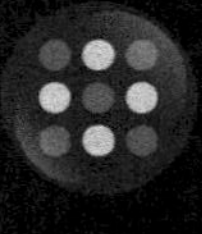

MyAssessment 3

MyAssessment 3

These questions will test you on your knowledge of the topics in chapters 9 to 12.
They give you practice in the questions that you may see in your GCSE exams.
There are 70 marks in total.

1 Make an accurate copy of this diagram.

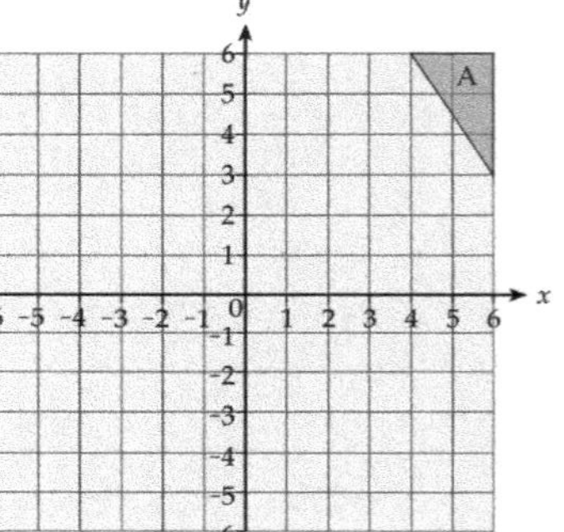

- **a** Reflect the triangle A in the x-axis and label it B. (1 mark)
- **b** Reflect triangle B in the y-axis and label it C. (1 mark)
- **c** Rotate triangle C through 180° about the centre (0, 0). What do you notice about this new position? (2 marks)

2
- **a** On a coordinate grid with x and y values from 0 to 10, plot the points A (1, 1), B (5, 1), C (5, 3), D (3, 3), E (3, 5) and F (1, 5) and join successive points AB, BC ... FA to make a shape. (4 marks)
- **b** Enlarge the shape by a scale factor of $\frac{1}{2}$ using point (8, 8) as the centre of enlargement. (2 marks)
- **c** Write down the coordinates of the new points A′, B′, C′, D′, E′ and F′. (4 marks)

3
- **a** Using only five squares draw a shape that has
  - **i** Only four lines of reflection symmetry.
  - **ii** Only two lines of reflection symmetry.
  - **iii** No lines of reflection symmetry. (3 marks)
- **b** In each case state the shape's order of rotational symmetry. (3 marks)

4 The length of sides of a triangle are $x + 3$, $2x - 1$ and $3x - 4$.
- **a** Write down the simplified expression for the perimeter of the triangle. (2 marks)
- **b** The perimeter of the triangle is 22 cm.
  - **i** Write down an equation for the perimeter. (1 mark)
  - **ii** Solve this equation and hence state the lengths of each side. (3 marks)
  - **iii** What is the mathematical name of this triangle? (1 mark)

5 Solve these equations.
- **a** $3(2p - 1) = 33$ (2 marks)
- **b** $15 - 3y = 3(y - 1)$ (2 marks)
- **c** $\frac{m}{4} + 3 = 7$ (2 marks)
- **d** $\frac{(3x - 2)}{11} = 2$ (2 marks)

6 A rectangle has a length $3n$ and a width $(2n - 3)$.
The area of the rectangle is 80 cm^2.
Use trial and improvement to find n to two decimal places (5 marks)

7 For these calculations
- **i** Give an estimate of the answer (6 marks)
- **ii** Use your calculator to find the accurate answer to 2d.p. (4 marks)

- **a** $\frac{2 \times 3.142 \times \sqrt{2.6^2 + 7.1^2}}{\sqrt{9.8}}$
- **b** $\frac{\sqrt{5^2 + 2.1} \times (8 - 3.5)}{4 \times 3^2}$

8 A 4 × 4 driver calls in at a petrol station and buys £25 worth of diesel at 139.6 pence per litre.
- **a** How many litres of diesel is bought at this station? (2 marks)
- **b** The next time they buy diesel it costs 140.2 pence per litre. If they fill the 4 × 4 with the same amount of fuel, how much more does it cost? (3 marks)

9 The plan of a local sailing course forms a triangle as shown.
Using a ruler and compasses make an accurate scale drawing of the course.
Use a scale of 1 cm = 100 m.
Leave on all your construction arcs. (4 marks)

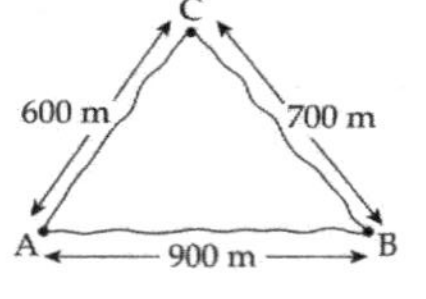

10 A map has a scale 1 : 25 000.
- **a** Two points on the map are 88 mm apart, how far apart are they in real life? (2 marks)
- **b** A road is 5 km long. How long is the road on the map? (2 marks)

11 A cable is to be laid that is equidistant from two fences AB and AC, as shown.
Copy the diagram and then construct the locus of the cable.
Leave on all your construction arcs. (3 marks)

12 The diagram shows a short sailing course.
The race starts at S, goes around the buoy at A and around a second buoy at B before heading back to the start.
- **a** Find the bearing of A from S. (1 mark)
- **b** Find the bearing of S from A. (1 mark)
- **c** Find the bearing of A from B. (2 marks)

Mark scheme

Questions 1 – 3 marks

a 1 Students' reflections of A, labelled B

b 1 Students' reflections of B, labelled C

c 2 Students' rotations of C about (0, 0). It is the same position as original triangle A.

Questions 2 – 11 marks

a 4 Students' plots of points A to F joined by straight lines

b 2 Students' s.f. $\frac{1}{2}$ enlargements about (8, 8) showing construction lines

c 4 A′($4\frac{1}{2}$ $4\frac{1}{2}$), B′($6\frac{1}{2}$, $4\frac{1}{2}$), C′($6\frac{1}{2}$, $5\frac{1}{2}$), D′($5\frac{1}{2}$, $5\frac{1}{2}$), E′($5\frac{1}{2}$, $6\frac{1}{2}$), F′($4\frac{1}{2}$, $6\frac{1}{2}$)

Questions 3 – 6 marks

a i 1 Students' drawings showing four lines of symmetry

ii 1 Students' drawings showing only two lines of symmetry

iii 1 Students' drawings showing no symmetry

b i 1 Order 4

ii 1 Order 2

iii 1 No order of rotational symmetry

Questions 4 – 7 marks

a 2 $6x - 2$; 1 mark for an attempt at simplification

b i 1 $6x - 2 = 22$

ii 3 $x = 4$ cm; hence sides are 7 cm, 7 cm, 8 cm

iii 1 Isosceles

Questions 5 – 8 marks

a 2 $p = 6$

b 2 $y = 3$

c 2 $m = 16$

d 2 $x = 8$

Questions 6 – 5 marks

5 4.48 cm; 1 mark for $6n^2 - 9n$; 1 mark for $6n^2 - 9n - 80 = 0$; remainder for trial-and-improvement method

Questions 7 – 8 marks

a i 2 16; or whole numbers around this value

ii 2 15.18; or values close to this

b i 2 0.5 or values close to this

ii 2 0.5

Questions 8 – 5 marks

a 2 17.91 litres

b 3 £0.11 or 11p

Questions 9 – 4 marks

4 Students' scale drawings of triangle ABC showing accurate measurement of AB; compasses used to find position C; ruler used to connect AC and BC.

Questions 10 – 4 marks

2 **a** 2.2 km

2 **b** 20 cm

Questions 11 – 3 marks

Students' diagrams showing compasses used to bisect the angle; line formed is stated as the locus of points

Questions 12 – 4 marks

a 1 074°

b 1 254°

c 2 124°

Learning outcomes	
A14 Generate terms of a sequence from either a term-to-term or a position-to-term rule	(L5)
A15 Recognise arithmetic sequences and find the *n*th term	(L6)
A16 Recognise geometric sequences and appreciate other sequences that arise	(L7)

Introduction

The chapter starts by looking at the term-to-term and position-to-term rules for arithmetic and other sequences before looking at sequences in context. Recognising and working with geometric sequences and recursive sequences are also covered.

The introduction discusses the presence of sequences inside the human body, specifically related to the sequence of bases in DNA which determine the physical characteristics of each cell in the body. The use of DNA sequencing can help us to treat specific diseases and also in the solving of crimes by using DNA profiling of both the physical evidence and the suspects in the crime. This kind of profiling is known as DNA fingerprinting since each person has a unique genetic sequence in their DNA.

The study of the human genome has been a huge part of modern scientific research and scientists have spent many years developing their techniques to allow them to determine the sequence of chemical base pairs which make up human DNA. There are 3 billion bases of genetic information found in human cells and it has therefore been a massive undertaking. Information on the human genome project, its uses and future developments can be found at:

http://www.wellcome.ac.uk/Our-vision/Research-challenges/Genetics-and-genomics/index.htm?gclid=CMyQu9Xagr0CFerpwgod62cAOw

Prior knowledge

Students should already know how to…

- Recognise patterns in sequences of numbers
- Continue simple sequences

Starter problem

The starter problem considers how a specific sequence in context grows. The girl is asking for just 50 pence in the first week but then 20 pence more each week thereafter. At first it seems like she is taking a significant cut in pocket money but if you watch the sequence grow, you can see how long it takes her to get more than the original £3:

50p, 70p, 90p, £1.10, £1.30, £1.50, £1.70, £1.90, £2.10, £2.30, £2.50, £2.70, £2.90, £3.10

After 14 weeks, she gets more than the original, but remember that this will keep growing by 20 pence per week thereafter.

The father is clearly getting a good deal at the start, but it will not take him long after this period of time to be 'out of pocket'. Questions could be posed to the students such as:

How much does the girl lose out on in the first 13 weeks?

How long will it take her after her pocket money exceeds £3 to get this back?

How much pocket money would she get in one year?

How much *more* pocket money would she get in one year?

Resources

MyMaths

Arithmetic sequences	1165	Sequences	1173	Geometric sequences 1	1920
Generating sequences	1945				

Online assessment

Chapter test	2C–13
Formative test	2C–13
Summative test	2C–13

InvisiPen solutions

Next terms in a sequence	281	Term-to-term rules	282
Position-to-term rules	283	nth term	286

Topic scheme

Teaching time = 4 lessons/2 weeks

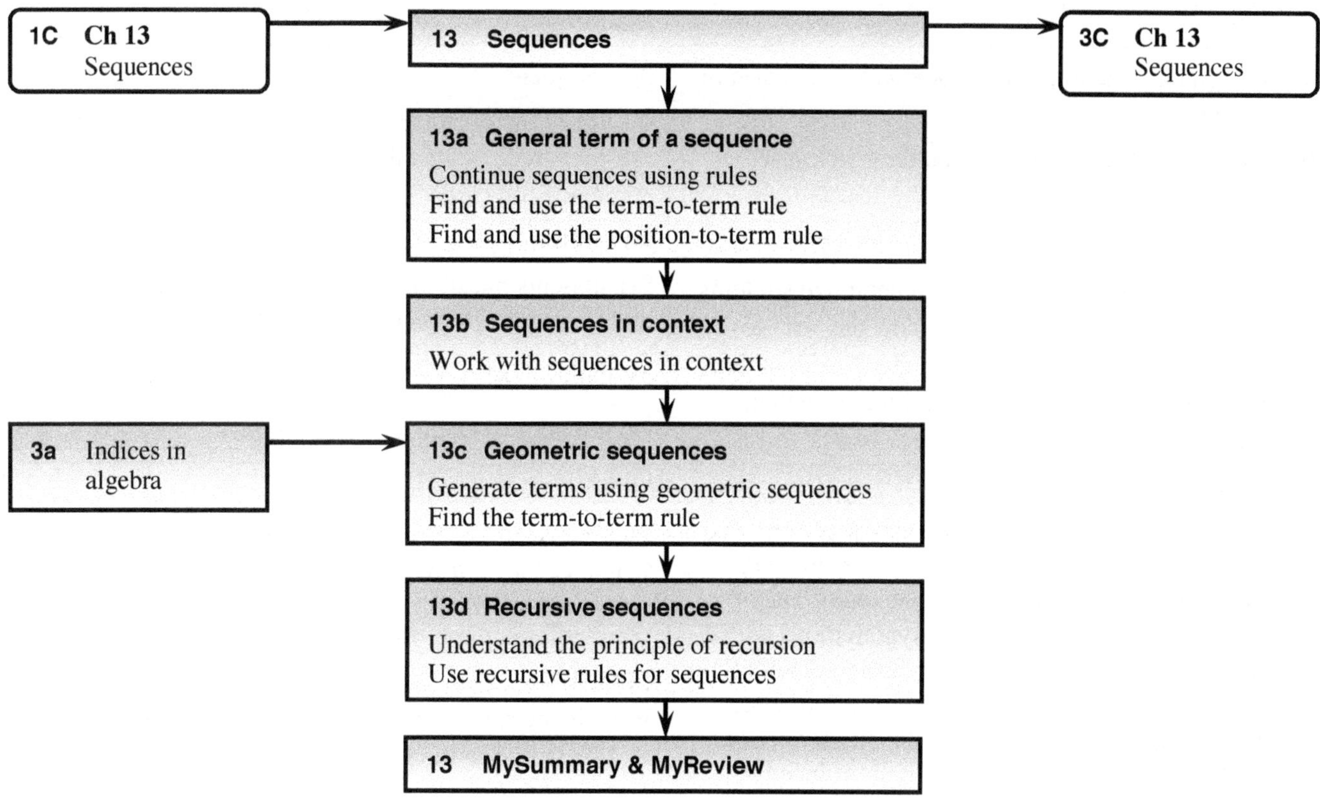

Differentiation

Student book 2A 242 – 255

Term-to-term rules
Position-to-term rules
Real-life sequences
Triangular numbers

Student book 2B 234 – 247

Term-to-term rules
Position-to-term rules
Sequences in context
Geometric sequences

Student book 2C 238 – 251

General term of a sequence
Sequences in context
Geometric sequences
Recursive sequences

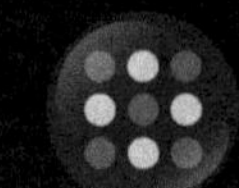

13a General term of a sequence

Objectives	
• Generate terms of a sequence using term-to-term and position-to-term rules (L6)	
Key ideas	**Resources**
1 Recognising the importance of a term's position in a sequence **2** Recognise, describe and use patterns in linear sequences	Sequences (1173) Copies of the exercise Pre-prepared results tables Sequences on cards
Simplification	**Extension**
Provide a copy of the exercise and encourage students to annotate the sequences to help show the term-to-term rule. Alternatively, provide students with tables so they can insert the sequences and organise their results more clearly.	Set students questions similar to those in question **6** but that require the terms to be left in fractional form, for example, $T(n)=\frac{n}{n+1}$. Do not allow a calculator to be used.
Literacy	**Links**
Sequences have a lot of associated language. The two phrases term-to-term and position-to-term are very useful to help students understand the topic. They should also link '*n*th term rule' as synonymous with position-to-term rule. Students will be happy with the term linear, but it is useful at this stage to introduce that linear sequences are called arithmetic sequences, especially as later in chapter they are introduced to geometric sequences.	The 'Look and Say' sequence is a famous non-linear sequence that sometimes appears in puzzle books. The first seven terms are: 1, 11, 21, 1211, 111221, 312211, 13112221, 1113213211. What is the rule for moving from one term to the next? (Describe the previous term in words and then write it in numbers, so one one; two ones; one two, two ones etc.). Try starting the sequence with 2 or 3 instead of 1. See, http://en.wikipedia.org/wiki/Look_and_say_sequence

Alternative approach

Begin by giving students three terms of a number sequence: 1, 2, 4, … and ask them to find at least two different sequences with these three first terms. (Most obvious sequences are 1, 2, 4, 7, 11, 16…; or 1, 2, 4, 8, 16, …). Can student partners spot the pattern when they are given the fourth term? An alternative approach is to explore patterns and position to term rules together, with growing levels of sophistication. Prepare a variety of sequences presented on separate cards, for students to group together, thus all the ones that involve for example 'adding 3', 'subtracting 2', 'doubling', 'multiplying by 10', where the initial terms are all different. Students can then be encouraged to identify the nature of 'linear' sequences, by being informed which are linear. Students can then be encouraged to examine a term's position to help establish rules for each linear sequence.

Checkpoint

1 A position-to-term rule is given as T(n) = 100 – 3n. Which term is the first negative term? (33rd)

Starter – Connections

Ask students to give three sets of coordinates that lie on the following curves:

$y = x^2 + 3$	for example (0, 3) (-1, 4) (2, 7)
$y = x^2 + 3x + 3$	for example (0, 3) (1, 7) (-2, 1)
$y = 3 - x - x^2$	for example (0, 3) (2, -3) (-2, 1)

Ask students what they notice when $x = 0$.

(The point (0, 3) lies on all three curves.)

Teaching notes

Give the first few terms of a sequence. Can students spot the next two terms in the sequence by first describing the term-to-term rule? Do students know the name of the type of sequence? Give examples of

- Linear sequences, ascending and descending
- Square number sequence
- Triangular number sequence
- Fibonacci sequence
- Prime number sequence

A sequence can be defined by giving the first term and the term-to-term rule or by giving a position-to-term rule. We normally let the letter 'n' stand for the position of the term in the sequence. Examine the sequences generated by various position-to-term rules. The position-to-term rule is known as the nth term and can be written as $T(n)$. What is meant by $T(6)$? What is the advantage of the nth over the term-to-term rule?

Plenary

How is question **6** related to drawing graphs? Make the analogy with graphs of the form $y = mx + c$ and $y = x^2$. Experiment by drawing some of the graphs. What does the x-axis represent? (Position)

What does the gradient and y-intercept represent?

(m represents the term-to-term rule, c represents the independent number in the $T(n)$ rule)

Exercise commentary

Question 1 – In each case ask the students to give the term-to-term rule and identify which ones are arithmetic.

Question 2 – Point out that term-to-term rules need a first term. Position-to-term rules do not.

Question 3 – Extend this question by giving students a 5 term sequence that is arithmetic, but only give them the first and last term.

Question 4 – Challenge students to generalise about the first term in each case.

Question 5 – Encourage students to use a table, listing the position numbers first. Draw an analogy with a table of values for the coordinates of a straight line graph.

Question 6 – Ask what does the 'n' represent in $T(n)$?

Question 7 – Encourage students to show their workings in an organised way. Each solution is possible without using a calculator. Will the position they stand in ever change after $T(100)$? Students may find drawing a graph useful.

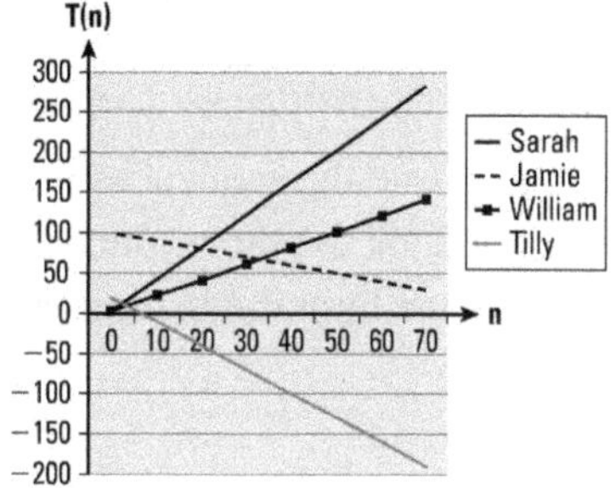

Answers

1 **a** 26, 31 **b** 64, 128 **c** 2.5, 2 **d** 0, -3
e 1, $\frac{1}{3}$ **f** -32, 64

2 **a** 1, 5, 9, 13, 17, … **b** 20, 17, 14, 11, 8, …
c 5, 10, 20, 40, 80, …
d 10 000, 1000, 100, 10, 1, …
e 2, $2\frac{1}{4}$, $2\frac{1}{2}$, $2\frac{3}{4}$, 3, …
f 100, 50, 25, 12.5, 6.25, …

3

	i	ii
a	Add 4 to the previous term	12
b	Add 3 to the previous term	5
c	Add 7 to the previous term	10, 17
d	Subtract 3 from the previous term	25, 22
	i	**ii**
e	Add 6 to the previous term	16, 28
f	Subtract 5 from the previous term	3, -7

4 **a** Any even integer **b** Any multiple of 4
c Any odd integer **d** Any fraction

5 **a** 11, 12, 13, 14, 15 **b** 5, 10, 15, 20, 25
c 7, 9, 11, 13, 15 **d** 4, 7, 10, 13, 16

6 **a** 4, 5, 6, 7, 8 **b** 0, 1, 2, 3, 4
c 8, 16, 24, 32, 40 **d** 11, 21, 31, 41, 51
e 5, 7, 9, 11, 13 **f** 49, 48, 47, 46, 45
g $\frac{1}{2}$, 1, $1\frac{1}{2}$, 2, $2\frac{1}{2}$ **h** 1, 4, 9, 16, 25
i 0, $\frac{1}{2}$, $\frac{2}{3}$, $\frac{3}{4}$, $\frac{4}{5}$ **j** 2, 4, 8, 16, 32

7 **a** Jamie (99), Tilly (17), Sarah (7), William (4)
b Jamie (90), Sarah (43), William (22), Tilly (-10)
c Sarah (403), William (202), Jamie (0), Tilly (-280)

13b Sequences in context

Objectives	
• Generate sequences from practical contexts and write and justify an expression to describe the *n*th term of an arithmetic sequence (L6)	
Key ideas	**Resources**
1 Investigating a simple situation systematically recording, analysing observations, generalising and testing conclusions.	Arithmetic sequences (1165) Generating sequences (1945) Copies of the tables of sequences
Simplification	**Extension**
Provide a copy of the sequences in tables and encourage students to annotate the sequences in the way shown in the student book example. Encourage the use of arrows to show the thinking behind the patterns.	How many squares in each of these patterns? Pattern 1 Pattern 2 Pattern 3 Note, there are not four in the second pattern! Give students a few minutes to search for the number of squares in the *n*th pattern. Ask them to see if $\frac{1}{6}n(n+1)(2n+1)$ works. $(1, 5, 14, \ldots)$
Literacy	**Links**
The keywords the same as the previous section. Students should realise that *n*th term rule and position-to-term rule are synonymous, as are linear sequence and arithmetic sequence.	Chronophotography is the art of taking a sequence of photographs of a moving object at regular time intervals. It was very popular with the Victorians.

Alternative approach

Students may work in pairs on an investigation which has the capability of resulting in linear relationships, and perhaps others. Matchstick growth patterns are a good source, and these could be used as a starting activity to a for full investigation such as 'Rotten Apples', where the placement of one initial rotten apple can be varied for more complex rules. A simple starting point here is for the one rotten apple to be placed in a corner. On successive days surrounding apples become rotten as shown in the diagram::

Day 1 one apple; Day 2 three apples, Day 3 six apples...

Checkpoint

1 Write the *n*th term rule for the following two sequences:

a 3, 7, 11, 15, 19 $(T(n) = 4n - 1)$

b 43, 36, 29, 22, 15 $(T(n) = 50 - 7n)$

Starter – Connections

If $x = -2$, $y = -5$ and $z = 7$, ask students to write down ten equations connecting x, y and z.
For example, $x - 2y = z + 1$

Encourage students to use all three letters in their rules.

Teaching notes

Write a linear sequence and ask students for the term-to-term rule. Show the term-to-term rule as the differences between successive terms and write the positions of the terms under the term values. For example,

	+3	+3	+3	+3	
	5,	8,	11,	14,	17
positions	1	2	3	4	5

Is there a link between the positions and the value of the terms? Hint that the rule has something to do with the term-to-term rule. Establish that you need to multiply the positions by 3 to get close, but an extra +2 is needed in each case.

This rule is known as the 'position-to-term rule' or 'nth term'. What letter is normally used for the positions? How is this rule written in algebra? ($3n + 2$) Will this approach work for all sequences? Will it depend on the type of sequence? Try a linear and non-linear sequence to establish the answer.

Look at an example of a linear sequence constructed from a series of diagrams. For example, triangles made from matchsticks. How can the number of 'matchsticks' be found for the 80th diagram? What sort of rule for the sequence will be most helpful in finding the answer?

Plenary

When dealing with the nth term in a linear sequence, how can you quickly tell what n needs to be multiplied by? Look at the term-to-term rule. Is there a quick way, which does not involve a table of values, to tell what number to add? Using any linear sequence from the exercise, extend it backwards from the first term. Can anyone spot a connection? Why can you use the 'zeroth' term?

Exercise commentary

Question 1 – Some teachers prefer to talk about a 0th term when finding the nth term. This book presents the more natural link of arithmetic sequence to times tables. The times tables students learned from a very early age are sequences, and so form a better basis for nth term rules.

Question 2 – Remind students of the link between term-to-term rules and position-to-term.

Question 3 – Encourage the approach in question **1**. Some students may jump straight to the answer. Ensure this is checked against at least two of the terms.

Question 4 – Encourage students to adopt the same method as used in questions **1** and **3**. Tell them it is acceptable to refer to the half times table or the minus 2 times table.

Question 5 – Some students may expect the rule to be $5n$. Highlight that part **b** shows the big advantage of position-to-term rules. If term-to-term then the previous 49 terms would need to be worked out first.

Question 6 – Students may need help with their algebraic notation. Insist on a complete equation.

Question 7 – Encourage students to think about area, as measured in small circles.

Question 8 – Ask which arrangement they have seen more often and ask why. The top option requires far fewer tables.

Answers

1 **a** 2

b

Position number	1	2	3	4	5
2 times table	2	4	6	8	10
Term	5	7	9	11	13

c **i** Multiply position number by 2 and add 1,
ii $T(n) = 2n + 1$

2 **a** $10n$ **b** n^2 **c** $n - 1$ **d** $4n$
e n^3 **f** $2n + 1$

3 **a** $T(n) = 3n$ **b** $T(n) = 10 + n$
c $T(n) = 2n + 5$ **d** $T(n) = 5n - 1$

4 **a** $T(n) = 3n - 8$ **b** $T(n) = 1 + \frac{n}{2}$
c $T(n) = 10 - n$ **d** $T(n) = 5 - 2n$

5 **a** $m = 4n + 1$ **b** 201
c Each new pentagon adds 4 straws to the previous one plus one straw to complete the first pentagon.

6 $w = r + 4$ Each pattern has one more red and one more red tile between the two white tiles at each end.

7 Each pattern is made up of an array of $2 \times n$ dots, plus two more. $2 \times n + 2$ can be simplified to $2(n + 1)$.

8 Option 1: each table adds four more chairs, with a chair at each end, $c = 4t + 2$. For 54 people, she would need 13 tables: $4 \times 13 + 2 = 54$
Option 2: each table adds two more chairs with two chairs at each end, $c = 2t + 4$. For 54 people, she would need 25 tables: $2 \times 25 + 4 = 54$

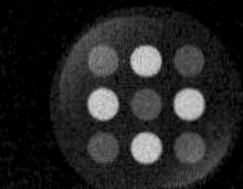

13c Geometric sequences

Objectives	
• Recognise geometric sequences and appreciate other sequences that arise (L6)	
Key ideas	**Resources**
1 Describe the term-to-term rule for geometric sequences **2** Generate terms in a geometric sequence	Geometric sequences 1 (1920) Graphing tool
Simplification	**Extension**
Introduce as an extension to the work competed on term-to-term rules. If arithmetic sequences are where you add the same number each time, then geometric sequences are ones where you multiply by the same number each time. Avoid referring to indices at an early stage.	Challenge students how geometric sequences can be notated. Allow them to make the link with indices themselves. Introduce the idea of a common ratio and encourage them to use recognized notation of Ar^n. Draw the link between geometric sequences and repeated percentage change.
Literacy	**Links**
The key term in this section is 'geometric'. Students are expected to recognise geometric sequences, even when the common ratio is not an integer.	One interesting link is population growth and 'doubling time'. A culture being grown in a lab will have a doubling time based on which organism it is. Also the half-life of radioactive isotopes is clearly defined as a geometric sequence. This could lead to an interesting investigation into radiometric dating, especially with Uranium_{238}, which has a half-life of 4.5 billion years. http://science.howstuffworks.com/dictionary/geology-terms/radioactive-dating-info.htm

Alternative approach

A real-life context could be used to stimulate discussion of geometric sequences. Consider, for example, a petri dish full of bacteria. The number of bacteria doubles each minute. How long ago was the dish half full? (1 minute: since the dish is now full, it was half full one minute ago so that when it doubled it is now full). This is a classic 'brainteaser' which shows the power of the geometric sequence.

Another alternative could be to just give students some 'random' term-to-term rules and ask them to work out the sequence following a function machine approach similar to question **2**. These can be mixed arithmetic and geometric sequences and then the sequences can be split into two groups using observation of patterns and reference back to the original rules.

Checkpoint

1 The population of rats, if unchecked, doubles every 20 days approximately. Taking a year to be 360 days, what would an initial population of 10 be in a year's time? ($10 \times 2^{18} = 2\ 621\ 440$)

Starter – Rice on a chessboard

A classic mathematical puzzle is where a single grain of rice is placed of the first square of a chessboard and then two, four, eight, etc. grains on the next squares. Challenge students to work out how many grains are on the 6th square, the 10th square, the 20th square, etc., or to find the total number of grains of rice on, say, the first five squares.

Teaching notes

The concept of a geometric sequence can be developed from the idea in the starter. The phrase 'common ratio' is not used but could be introduced if students become familiar with the principle of multiplicative sequences. Model the sequences in the introduction or develop the starter to show the pattern of simple sequences.

It is important that students appreciate that geometric sequences can be formed by dividing — multiplying by a fractional ratio — and also by multiplying by negative numbers (so that the signs alternate +/-).

The contextual example about birds of prey is useful to discuss since it combines both a geometrical element and an arithmetical element.

Plenary

Consider: If the first term of a geometric sequence is 2 and the third term 8, how can you find out the term-to-term rule? (Square root the ratio of the given terms)

What about if you have a first term of 3 and a fourth term of 24? (Cube root the ratio of the given terms)

Can this pattern be used to develop a method for working out the answers to question **4** without writing all the terms out?

Exercise commentary

Question 1 – Ask students how they can work out the multiplier in a geometric sequence. You may wish to use the term common ratio.

Question 2 – Highlight the negative common ratio resulting in a sequence that oscillates between positive and negative values.

Question 3 – Although not required, challenge students to see if they can come up with a position –to-term rule. Give them the clue that it will involve indices.

Question 4 – Challenge students to see if they can use indices and the power button on their calculator to work out the tenth term without knowing the previous nine terms. For part **e** show students what this sequence looks like graphically. Ask them to predict what is going to happen as the sequence continues.

Question 5 – Ask students to represent each option on the same graph and estimate after how long does option A overtake option B. Explain to them that this kind of growth is called exponential.

Question 6 – Students may wish to show this graphically. It might be useful to use a graphing tool to show the whole class what the solution would look like graphically when discussing the solution.

Question 7 – Make sure students know and can justify why these sequences are NOT geometric.

Answers

1 **a** 96, 192 **b** 972, 2916
c 7776, 46 656 **d** 100 000, 1 000 000
e 31.25, 15.625 **f** -1, -0.5

2 **a** 3, 6, 12, 24, 48 **b** 4, 20, 100, 500, 2500
c 2, 16, 128, 1024, 8192 **d** -5, -15, -45, -135, -405
e 8, -16, 32, -64, 128 **f** 32, 80, 200, 500, 1250

3 **a** Start at 2 multiply by 5
b Start at 3 multiply by 6
c Start at 0.5 multiply by 3
d Start at -4 multiply by 4
e Start at 2 multiply by $1\frac{1}{2}$
f Start at -2 multiply by -5

4 **a** 2560 **b** 7 812 500
c -524 288 **d** -8
e -3072 **f** $\frac{5}{128}$

5 Option A: money doubles each week so total earnings = 5 + 10 + 20 + 40 + 80 + 160 = £315
Option B: 6 weeks at £50 = £300
Cassie should choose Option A. This way she will earn more money after 6 weeks even though the weekly amount is much lower to start with.

6 A: T(6) = 7776 T(7) = 46 656
B: T(6) = 12 150 T(7) = 36 450
So A overtakes B after term 6.

7 **a** 1, 4, 9, 16, 25 square numbers
b 1, 8, 27, 64, 125 cube numbers
c **i** $1^7, 2^7, 3^7, 4^7, 5^7$ **ii** 2 097 152

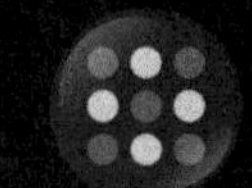

13d Recursive sequences

Objectives	
• Recognise geometric sequences and appreciate other sequences that arise (L6)	
Key ideas	**Resources**
1 Link to term-to-term rules **2** Find terms in sequences using a recursive formula **3** Generate recursive formulae	Mini whiteboards Card sort activity
Simplification	**Extension**
It is important that students recognise that recursive sequences are simply an attempt to be more mathematical in describing term-to-term sequences. Simplify things by being consistent in setting out recursive definitions, always linking them to the term-to-term rules.	Challenge students if they can convert a recursive definition for an arithmetic rule into an *n*th term rule and the vice versa. Also give them harder sequences, such as those generated by question **2**, and challenge them to work out the recursive formula.
Literacy	**Links**
The key new word is recursive. Ask for words that sound like recursive. Elicit recurring and recur. Ask what 'to recur' means. Show that the concept of going back to go forward is what a recursive formula is doing.	The classic recursive definition is the Fibonacci sequence. Of particular interest is how Fibonacci tends to a geometric sequence for larger numbers where the common ratio is the golden ratio. http://www.mathsisfun.com/numbers/fibonacci-sequence.html

Alternative approach

Students could be provided with two sets of cards (or two jumbled lists), one set with the recursive formulae on and one set with the terms of sequences. They can then try and work out, in pairs or threes, how the two sets link together and match them up. This will encourage discussion about the structure of the algebraic formulae and how they link to the generation of recursive sequences.

Checkpoint

1 A recursive definition is given as $T(n + 1) = 5 - 2T(n)$ with $T(1) = 1$. Write down the first 7 terms.

(1, 3, -1, 7, -9, 23, -41)

Starter – Number Jumble

These numbers belong to two different arithmetic sequences but have been jumbled up. Sort them into two sets and write down the two sequences:

1, 17, 4, 13, 7, 10, 8, 11, 5, 14, 16, 2

(1, 4, 7, 10, 13, 16 and 2, 5, 8, 11, 14, 17)

Teaching notes

Since the recursive formula is basically a formal algebraic way of writing the term-to-term rule, students could be asked to look back at **13a** where term-to-term sequences are introduced. Can they think of a way of writing the 'wordy' rule using symbols? Describe the structure of the algebraic statements and show, using a few simple examples, the way that a recursive formula works. Show the difference between a linear sequence and a geometric sequence. Students can then complete selected questions from the exercise and work through the practical problems in questions **5** to **7**. There is scope for students to 'invent' their own sequences and challenge a partner to find the recursive formula, or to generate terms with their own formula.

Plenary

Are the following sequences (a) linear, (b) geometric, or (c) neither?

$T(n+1) = T(n) + 4, T(1) = 7$ (arithmetic)

$T(n+1) = 3T(n) - 1, T(1) = 1$ (neither)

$T(n+1) = 4T(n), T(1) = 4$ (geometric)

$T(n+1) = -T(n), T(1) = 5$ (geometric)

$T(n+1) = T(n) - \frac{1}{2}, T(1) = 7$ (arithmetic)

Vary the sequences and order to suit student ability and time available.

Exercise commentary

Question 1 – Ask whether these sequences are arithmetic, geometric or neither. Then ask what is the key feature of a recursive formula that will lead to an arithmetic sequence.

Question 2 – Ask again whether these sequences are arithmetic, geometric or neither. Then ask what is the key feature of a recursive formula that will lead to a geometric sequence. It is important that students recognize that most of these sequences are neither arithmetic or geometric.

Question 3 – All of these sequences are arithmetic.

Question 4 – Re-enforce the difference between arithmetic and geometric sequences when writing them recursively.

Question 5 – Link this with compound and simple interest. They are both 1% interest per month, but one is simple and the other is compound. You may wish to use this to highlight the dangers of payday loan companies.

Questions 6 and **7** – Students may find it interesting to represent both these questions graphically.

Answers

1 **a** 2, 3, 4, 5, 6, ... **b** 0, 2, 4, 6, 8, ...
c 3, 7, 11, 15, 19, ... **d** -1, -3, -5, -7, -9, ...
e $1, \frac{1}{2}, 0, -\frac{1}{2}, -1, \ldots$
f 0.5, -0.25, -1, -1.75, -2.5, ...

2 **a** 2, 4, 8, 16, 32, ... **b** 0, 1, 3, 7, 15, ...
c 3, 5, 9, 17, 33, ... **d** 1, 2, 5, 14, 41, ...
e 1, 2, 0, 4, -4, ... **f** 1, 1, 1, 1, 1 ...

3 **a** $T(1) = 2, T(n+1) = T(n) + 2$
b $T(1) = 3, T(n+1) = T(n) + 4$
c $T(1) = -2, T(n+1) = T(n) + 6$
d $T(1) = 4, T(n+1) = T(n) - 3$
e $T(1) = -5, T(n+1) = T(n) - 4$
f $T(1) = \frac{1}{2}, T(n+1) = T(n) + \frac{3}{4}$

4 **a** $T(1) = 5, T(n+1) = T(n) + 6$
b $T(1) = 7, T(n+1) = T(n) + 8$
c $T(1) = 13, T(n+1) = T(n) + 17$
d $T(1) = 1, T(n+1) = 3T(n)$
e $T(1) = 1, T(n+1) = 4T(n)$
f $T(1) = 5, T(n+1) = 2T(n)$

5 **a** $T(1) = 300, T(n+1) = T(n) + 3$
b £303.00, £306.03, £309.09, £312.18, £315.30
c Zadie

6 **a** 54 **b** 30 714

7 Yes, by the end of the 8th month (remembering the number of frogs and lily pads were counted at the beginning of the first month).

Key outcomes	Quick check
Describe a linear sequence using a term-to-term rule.	What is the term to term rule for this sequence? 4, 12, 36, 108, 324 (multiply by 3)
Describe a linear sequence using a position-to-term rule.	Write the *n*th term for this sequence? 32, 27, 22, 27, 12 $(37 - 5n)$
Recognise and describe geometric sequences.	What is the position-to-term rule for this geometric sequence? 7, 49, 343, 2401, 16807 (7^n)
Describe a general sequence using a recursive formula.	Write the first 5 terms for this reursive formula, $T(n+1) = 3T(n) - 5$ where $T(1) = 5$. (5, 10, 25, 70, 205)

MyMaths extra support

Lesson/online homework			Description
Comparing fractions	1075	L5	Comparing fractions

MyReview

13 MySummary

Check out

You should now be able to ...		Test it ➡ Questions
✓ Describe a linear sequence using a term-to-term rule.	5	1
✓ Describe a linear sequence using a position-to-term rule.	6	2 - 4
✓ Recognise and describe geometric sequences.	7	5 - 6
✓ Describe a general sequence using a recursive formula.	7	7 - 8

Language	Meaning	Example
Sequence	An ordered set of terms	2, 4, 6, 8
Term	A number in a sequence	Any of the numbers in the sequence 2, 4, 6, 8
Term-to-term rule	A formula for the next term in a sequence as a function of the current term.	For 2, 4, 6, 8, ... $T(n+1) = T(n) + 2$
Position-to-term rule	A formula for the term at position n as a function of n	For 2, 4, 6, 8, ... $T(n) = 2n$
General term nth term	Other names for a position-to-term rule.	
Geometric sequence	A sequence in which the next term is a fixed multiple of the current term.	2, 4, 8, 16, ... $T(n+1) = 2T(n)$ $T(n) = 2^n$

13 MyReview

1 Find the term-to-term rule and the next two terms for each of these sequences.

a 5, 2.5, 0, -2.5, ...
b 64, 32, 16, 8, ...
c 3, -6, 12, -24, ...

2 Generate the first 5 terms of the sequences given by these position-to-term rules.

a $T(n) = 5n - 1$ **b** $T(n) = \frac{1}{2}n + 1$
c $T(n) = n^2 + 2$ **d** $T(n) = 100 - n^2$

3 Consider this arrangement of tables and chairs.

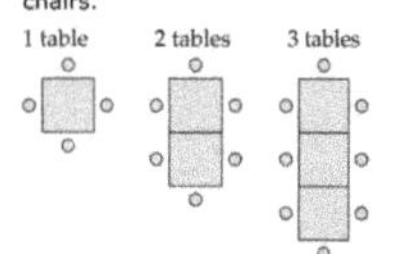

a Copy and complete this table.

Number of tables, t	1	2	3	4
...... times table				
Number of chairs, c	4			

b Find a rule that relates the number of tables, t, to the number of chairs, c.
c How many chairs will be needed if there are 10 tables?
d How many tables are there if there are 16 chairs?

4 Find the nth term rule for these sequences.

a 19 26, 33, 40, ...
b 10, 21, 32, 43, ...
c 7.5, 8. 8.5, 9, ...
d -5, -10, -15, -20, ...

5 Find the term-to-term rule and the next two terms for each geometric sequence.

a 5, 0.5, 0.05, 0.005, ...
b 0.25, -0.5, 1, -2, ...
c 4, 6, 9, $13\frac{1}{2}$, ...
d 2048, -1024, 512, -256, ...

6 Find the 10th term of the sequence described by each rule.

a Start at 512 and multiply by $\frac{3}{2}$
b Start at 1 000 000 and multiply by -0.1

7 Write out the first 5 terms for each of these sequences.

a $T(n+1) = 4 - 3T(n)$, $T(1) = 0$
b $T(n+1) = 2T(n) - 1$, $T(1) = 1$
c $T(n+1) = 2T(n) - 1$, $T(1) = 2$
d $T(n+1) = [T(n)]^2 - 1$, $T(1) = 2$

8 Describe each of these sequences using a recursive formula.

a 14, 17, *, 23, *, 29, ...
b *, 62, 47, *, *, 17, 2, ...
c *, -9, 27, -81, *, 729, ...
d 3, *, 6, 9, 13, ...

What next?

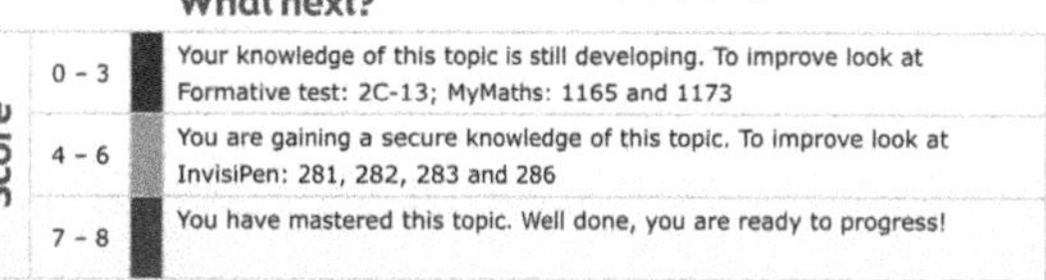

Score		
0 - 3		Your knowledge of this topic is still developing. To improve look at Formative test: 2C-13; MyMaths: 1165 and 1173
4 - 6		You are gaining a secure knowledge of this topic. To improve look at InvisiPen: 281, 282, 283 and 286
7 - 8		You have mastered this topic. Well done, you are ready to progress!

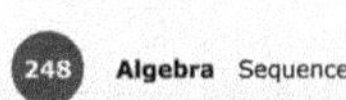

MyMaths.co.uk 249

Question commentary

Question 1 – Term-to-term rules to be described in words. For part **c**, if students are struggling get them to ignore the negative signs to start with.

Question 2 – Warn students to consider BIDMAS in part **d.**

Question 3 – Make sure students describe the sequence with a complete equation. In answering part **d**, encourage them to rearrange the equation rather than guess and check.

Question 4 – Encourage students to think which times table goes up or down by the same amount as the sequence, so then see which times table the sequence is connected to.

Questions 5 and **6** – Highlight what happens when the common ratio is negative.

Question 7 – Ensure students realise these sequences are neither arithmetic nor geometric.

Question 8 – If students are struggling tell them that **a** and **b** are arithmetic and **c** and **d** are geometric.

Answers

1 a Subtract 2.5 from previous term; -5, -7.5
b Halve previous term; 4, 2
c Multiply previous term by -2; 48, -96

2 a 4, 9, 14, 19, 24 **b** 1.5, 2, 2.5, 3, 3.5
c 3, 6, 11, 18, 27 **d** 99, 96, 91, 84, 75

3 a

Number of tables, t	1	2	3	4
2 times table	2	4	6	8
Number of chairs, c	4	6	8	10

b $c = 2t + 2$ **c** 22 **d** 7

4 a $7n + 12$ **b** $11n - 1$ **c** $\frac{1}{2}n + 7$ **d** $-5n$

5 a Divide previous term by 10; 0.0005, 0.00005
b Multiply previous term by -2: 4, -8
c Multiply by $\frac{3}{2}$: $20\frac{1}{4}$, $30\frac{3}{8}$
d Divide by -2: 128, -64

6 a 19 683 **b** -0.001

7 a 0, 4, -8, 28, -80 **b** 1, 1, 1, 1, 1
c 2, 3, 5, 9, 17 **d** 2, 3, 8, 63, 3968

8 a $T(n+1) = T(n) + 3$ $T(1) = 14$
b $T(n+1) = T(n) - 15$ $T(1) = 77$
c $T(n+1) = -3T(n)$ $T(1) = 3$
d $T(n+1) = T(n) + n$ $T(1) = 3$

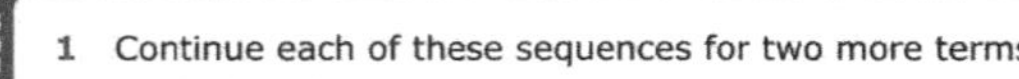

13 MyPractice

13a

1 Continue each of these sequences for two more terms.

- **a** 3, 6, 9, 12, 15, ...
- **b** 2, 5, 8, 11, 14, ...
- **c** 1, 10, 100, 1000, 10 000, ...
- **d** 50, 44, 38, 32, 26, ...
- **e** 1, $1\frac{1}{2}$, 2, $2\frac{1}{2}$, 3, ...
- **f** 1024, 512, 256, 128, 64, ...
- **g** 2, 1.8, 1.6, 1.4, 1.2, ...
- **h** 1, 8, 27, 64, 125, ...

2 **i** Write the term-to-term rule for each of these linear sequences.

ii Fill in the missing numbers.

- **a** 4, □, 14, 19, 24, ...
- **b** 2, □, □, 14, 18, ...
- **c** □, □, -1, -4, -7, ...
- **d** 5, □, 19, □, 33, ...

3 Generate the first five terms of each of these sequences given by their position-to-term rules.

- **a** $T(n) = n + 10$
- **b** $T(n) = 2n$
- **c** $T(n) = n - 5$
- **d** $T(n) = \frac{n}{3}$
- **e** $T(n) = 2n + 1$
- **f** $T(n) = 10 - n$
- **g** $T(n) = 5n - 2$
- **h** $T(n) = 23 - 3n$

13b

4 Find the nth term of each of these sequences.

- **a** 5, 10, 15, 20, 25, ...
- **b** 1, 4, 7, 10, 13, ...
- **c** -2, 0, 2, 4, 6, ...
- **d** 5, 4, 3, 2, 1, ...

5 **a** For this pattern of tiles, find a rule that relates the pattern number, n, to the number of tiles, t.

b Use your formula to find the number of tiles in pattern number 100.

c Explain why your rule works by referring to the diagrams.

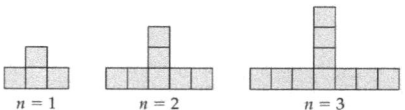

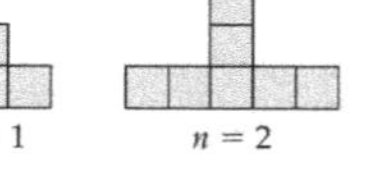

6 **a** For this pattern of tiles, find a rule that relates the number of red tiles, r, to the number of white tiles, w.

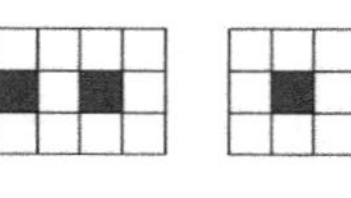

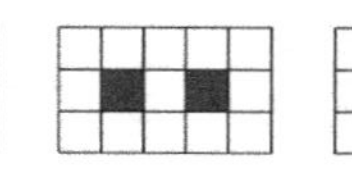

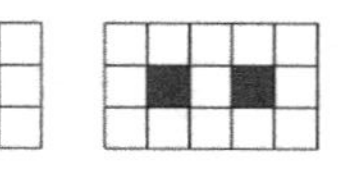

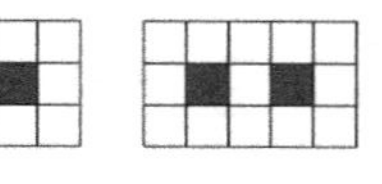

b Use your formula to find the number of tiles in pattern number 100.

c Explain why your rule works by referring to the diagrams.

13c

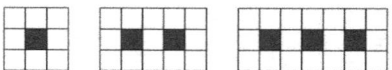

7 Generate the first five terms of each sequence.

- **a** Start at 3, multiply by 3
- **b** Start at 2, multiply by 4
- **c** Start at 4, multiply by 5
- **d** Start at 16, multiply by $\frac{1}{2}$

8 Find the term-to-term rule and the next two terms for each of these geometric sequences.

- **a** 99, 9.9, 0.99, 0.099, ...
- **b** 2, 6, 18, 54, ...
- **c** 3, -6, 12, -24, ...
- **d** $\frac{5}{16}, -\frac{5}{8}, \frac{5}{4}, -\frac{5}{2}, ...$

9 Find the eighth term in each of these sequences.

- **a** Start at 64 and multiply by $-\frac{3}{2}$.
- **b** Start at 1 and multiply by 0.2
- **c** $T(1) = 0.01$ $T(n + 1) = 5T(n)$
- **d** $T(1) = 200$, $T(n + 1) = \frac{T(n)}{2}$

13d

10 Write out the first five terms for each of these sequences.

- **a** $T(n + 1) = 17 - 4T(n)$, $T(1) = \frac{1}{4}$
- **b** $T(n + 1) = 3T(n) + 2$, $T(1) = 1$
- **c** $T(n + 1) = 3T(n) + 2$, $T(1) = 0$
- **d** $T(n + 1) = 1 - [T(n)]^2$, $T(1) = 2$

11 Describe each sequence using a recursive formula.

- **a** 4, 7, 10, 13, 16, ...
- **b** 3, -1, -5, -9, -13, ...
- **c** 2, 8, 32, 128, 512, ...
- **d** 3, -9, 27, -81, 243, ...

12 Describe each of these recursive sequences using a formula.

- **a** 15, 12, *, 6, *, 0, ...
- **b** *, 57, 46, *, 24, 13, ...
- **c** *, -16, *, -4, 2, -1, ...
- **d** 81, *, 78, 75, *, 66, ...

Question commentary

General comments that apply to all questions go at the start.

Question 2 – Term-to-term rules should be written fully in words.

Question 4 – Expect answers to be written in the same format as question **3**.

Questions 5 & 6 – Make sure students write complete equations when describing the sequences.

Question 9 – Encourage students to find the 8th term using indices rather than multiplying repeatedly.

Question 10 – Ensure students know that none of these sequences are either arithmetic or geometric.

Question 12 – Allow students to know whether the sequence is arithmetic or geometric if struggling.

Assessment

For algebra, successfully answering

questions 1 – 3 is evidence of level 6 work
questions 4 – 9 is evidence of level 7 work.

Answers

1 **a** 18, 21 **b** 17, 20
c 100 000, 1 000 000 **d** 20, 14
e $3\frac{1}{2}$, 4 **f** 32, 16
g 1.0, 0.8 **h** 216, 343

2

	i	ii
a	Add 5 to the previous term	9
b	Add 4 to the previous term	6, 10
c	Subtract 3 from the previous term	5, 2
d	Add 7 to the previous term	12, 26

3 **a** 11, 12, 13, 14, 15 **b** 2, 4, 6, 8, 10
c -4, -3, -2, -1, 0 **d** $\frac{1}{3}, \frac{2}{3}, 1, 1\frac{1}{3}, 1\frac{2}{3}$
e 3, 5, 7, 9, 11 **f** 9, 8, 7, 6, 5
g 3, 8, 13, 18, 23 **h** 20, 17, 14, 11, 8

4 **a** $T(n) = 5n$ **b** $T(n) = 3n - 2$
c $T(n) = 2n - 4$ **d** $T(n) = 6 - n$

5 **a** $t = 3n + 1$ **b** 301
c 3 tiles are added on each new diagram, one on each 'arm'. Then add on one for the central tile.

6 **a** $w = 5r + 3$ **b** 503
c 5 white tiles in a 'C' shape for each red tile plus 3 tiles in a vertical line at the right-hand end.

7 **a** 3, 9, 27, 81, 243
b 2, 8, 32, 128, 512
c 4, 20, 100, 500, 2500
d 16, 8, 4, 2, 1

8 **a** Divide previous term by 10; 0.0099, 0.00099
b Multiply previous term by 3; 162, 486
c Multiply previous term by -2; 48, -96
d Multiply previous term by -2; 5, -10

9 **a** -1093.5 **b** 0.0000128
c 781.25 **d** 1.5625

10 **a** $\frac{1}{4}$, 16, -47, 205, -803 **b** 1, 5, 17, 53, 161
c 0, 2, 8, 26, 80 **d** -3, -8, -63, -3968

11 **a** $T(1) = 4, T(n + 1) = T(n) + 3$
b $T(1) = 3, T(n + 1) = T(n) - 4$
c $T(1) = 2, T(n + 1) = 4T(n)$
d $T(1) = 3, T(n + 1) = -3T(n)$

12 **a** $T(1) = 15, T(n + 1) = T(n) - 3$
b $T(1) = 68, T(n + 1) = T(n) - 11$
c $T(1) = 32, T(n + 1) = T(n) \div -2$
d $T(1) = 81, T(n + 1) = T(n) - (n - 1)$

14 3D shapes

Learning outcomes	
G1 Derive and apply formulae to calculate and solve problems involving: perimeter and area of triangles, parallelograms, trapezia, volume of cuboids (including cubes) and other prisms (including cylinders)	(L6/7)
G15 Use the properties of faces, surfaces, edges and vertices of cubes, cuboids, prisms, cylinders, pyramids, cones and spheres to solve problems in 3D	(L6)

Introduction

The chapter starts by looking at 3D shapes in general: naming the shapes and looking at the number of faces, edges and vertices that each shape has. The second section covers plans and elevations of 3D shapes. Surface area and volume of a prism are then covered.

The introduction discusses how companies use an appreciation of surface area and volume to design environmentally-friendly packaging for their products. If you look around the supermarket, you can see packaging designed as cubes, cuboids, cylinders and other prisms, each of which is designed to suit the purpose of the packaging and also to add some aesthetic value while being only as big as necessary to safely package the goods. The use of efficient packaging can also help companies to reduce costs since customers do not buy the products for the packaging alone. The cost incurred from the packaging is a 'throw away' cost to the company since the packaging is rarely useful to the consumer and almost always gets thrown away or at best recycled.

Higher level mathematics can help companies solve what are referred to as 'optimisation' problems. Mathematicians use what is called differential calculus to find the minimum surface area for a given volume, or to solve similar problems. This type of mathematics will be covered in A level.

Prior knowledge

Students should already know how to...

- Carry out simple arithmetic
- Work out the areas and perimeters of plane figures, including compound shapes
- Find volumes of cuboids

Starter problem

The starter problem requires students to work with the volume of a cuboid formula in order to reduce the surface area of a given package, for the fixed volume stated. Trial-and-improvement is clearly going to be the method of choice for most students and they should easily be able to determine that a package measuring 10 cm by 6 cm by 6 cm will work. Here the surface area is $4 \times 10 \times 6 + 2 \times 6 \times 6 = 312\text{ cm}^2$ as opposed to the original of $2 \times 12 \times 6 + 2 \times 12 \times 5 + 2 \times 6 \times 5 = 324\text{ cm}^2$.

There is an interesting link to prime factorisation. There are many possible (whole number) combinations of side length for the cuboid and some will be better than the original and some worse. By finding the prime factorisation of 360 we can actually work out how many combinations there will be and also what these combinations are. We *could* therefore try them all.

$360 = 2^3 \times 3^2 \times 5$ so if we split this prime factorisation into three parts, lots of different ways, we can find all the combinations. The one given in the question is $2 \times 2 \times 3$, 2×3 and 5. The one stated above is 2×5, 2×3 and 2×3. An alternative could be $2 \times 2 \times 2$, 3×5 and 3 and more able students could be invited to come up with others and check their surface areas.

Resources

MyMaths

3D shapes	1078	Plans elevations	1098	Nets of 3D shapes	1106
Nets, surface area	1107	Volume of prisms	1139		

Online assessment

Chapter test	2C–14
Formative test	2C–14
Summative test	2C–14

InvisiPen solutions

Properties of 3D shapes	321	Isometric grids	324
Nets of simple 3D shapes			325
2D representations of 3D solids			326
Prisms	327	Surface area of a prism	328

Topic scheme

Teaching time = 4 lessons/2 weeks

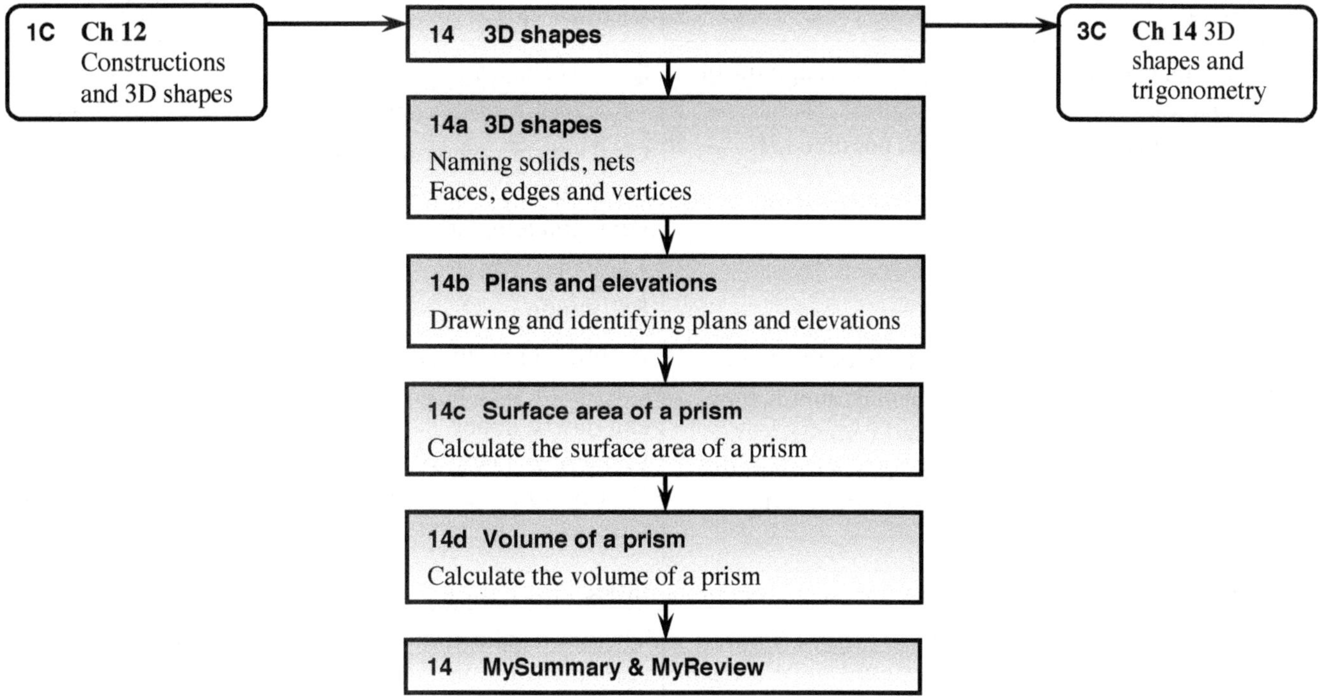

Differentiation

Student book 2A 256 – 271	Student book 2B 248 – 263	Student book 2C 252 – 265
3D shapes	3D shapes	3D shapes
Isometric drawings	Plans and elevations	Plans and elevations
Nets of 3D shapes	Surface area of a cuboid	Surface area of a prism
Surface area of a cuboid	Volume of a cuboid	Volume of a prism
Volume of a cuboid	Prisms	

Objectives

- Visualise and use 2D representations of 3D shapes (L6)

Key ideas	Resources
1 Read, understand and begin to use 2D diagrams of 3D shapes **2** Begin to link a 3D shape with its possible net	3D shapes (1078) Nets of 3D shapes (1106) Card nets of common 3D shapes Card, rulers, scissors, glue for making nets Pentagon templates Cardboard cartons

Simplification	Extension
Provide students with an enlarged copy of the exercise and encourage them to annotate the diagrams as they count the number of faces, edges and vertices. Provide pre-prepared nets for folding to help with the understanding of how the nets fold to produce the 3D shapes.	A cube can be sliced in half to produce two congruent 3D shapes. How many different ways can this be done? (9) Encourage a new sketch to show each possibility. You could use the term planes of symmetry to describe the slices.

Literacy	Links
There is a lot of language associated with 3D shapes. Make sure students are clear on the terms 'face', 'edge' and 'vertex' (plural 'vertices'). Highlight that the terms prism and pyramid describe a family of shapes.	There is a collection of nets for paper models of more complex solids at http://www.korthalsaltes.com/index.html

Alternative approach

If there is a set of 3D shapes in your department use these with groups of three students. Label them and circulate them for student groups to examine carefully, decide whether the shape is a prism, pyramid or other, name it if possible and record the number of faces, edges and vertices. This activity can be carried out with a collection of cardboard cartons of a variety of shapes. Share and discuss the students' results fully. Cardboard cartons can be used for a different task where students are required to 'undo' the carton in order to sketch its net.

Checkpoint

1 Name the 3D shape that has 5 faces, 8 edges and 5 vertices. (Square-based pyramid)

Starter – SHP!

Write words on the board missing out the vowels, (for example, SHP). Ask students for the original words – shape. Possible 'words':

NGL, PRLLL, RHMBS, LTRNT, RCTNGL, DGNL, SSCLS, CTGN, PRPNDCLR, QLTRL.

(angle, parallel, rhombus, alternate, rectangle, diagonal, isosceles, octagon, perpendicular, equilateral).

This can be extended by asking students to make up their own examples.

Teaching notes

Using the resources detailed earlier get students to draw one of the nets from question **1**. Use a pentagon template for the pyramid. Students will need to think creatively about where they will put the tabs for gluing together the edges. Encourage students to think about this before drawing out the net.

Challenge students to produce a net of another 3D shape of their choice. Can students tell how many faces, vertices and edges the shape has from looking at the net? Compare these answers with the 3D model once it has been constructed.

Is there more than one possible net for the shapes in question **1**? If so, challenge students to find alternative representations for the nets. How can you be certain they will work? Show how labelling the faces of the net can lead you to accept or reject it as a possible solution. Normally begin by labelling the middle one as the base.

Plenary

Visit http://maths.ac-noumea.nc/polyhedr/index_.htm, a French website with an English translation for exploring polyhedra of many types.

Exercise commentary

Question 1 – Point students towards the description of the shapes in the student book, there is a clue to an alternative name for shape A elsewhere in the exercise. Can students find it?

Question 2 – Make sure students count the unseen faces, edges and vertices.

Question 3 – Students will often find the 6 nets with a spine of 4 squares relatively quickly. Finding the other 5 is more challenging.

Question 5 – This shape is used as a dice in certain games. Ask how students think it is numbered and how the score is decided upon. One sophisticated option is shown here.

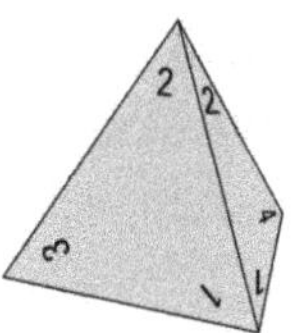

Question 7 – Ask if there is more than one way to number the octahedron. This could be used as a dice. How would the score be read on this dice?

Answers

1 **a** A tetrahedron, B triangular prism, C cube, D pentagonal pyramid, E cuboid

b

	A	B	C	D	E
i faces	4	5	6	6	6
ii vertices	4	6	8	6	8
iii edges	6	9	12	10	12

2 **a** 10 faces **b** 16 vertices
c 24 edges

3 11 nets of a cube

4 **a** Square-based pyramid or triangular prism
b 6 vertices, 9 edges

5 **a** 1 edge **b** 4 edges **c** 1 edge

6 **a** Rectangle **b** Yes. Cut one corner off.

7 **a** **i** 8 faces **ii** 6 vertices
iii 12 edges
b Various answers possible

Objectives

- Analyse 3D shapes through 2D projections, including plans and elevations (L6)

Key ideas

1 Being able to match a 2D diagram to the corresponding 3D shape
2 Understanding the aspects of elevations and plans

Resources

Plans elevations (1098)
Isometric paper
Set of solid models of 3D shapes
Multi-link cubes
Sketches of platonic solids

Simplification

Provide students with solid models of the 3D shapes used in the exercise. Advise students to look 'head on' at the models from a distance to give the idea of the elevated view.

Extension

Attempt to draw plans and elevations of the five platonic solids. How do you decide which is the plan view? Students could be sent to investigate what they look like, or they could be provided with the sketches.

tetrahedron cube octahedron
dodecahedron icosahedron

Literacy

Ask students what a dimension is. When might they have used that word outside maths? Why is it important to consider dimensions in maths?
Also consider elevation. This is a more technical word and students need to appreciate its specific mathematical meaning.
Look at the root of the word isometric: iso (same) metric (measure). Ask why this is a good name for this kind of paper?

Links

Engineers and architects use drawings showing plan and elevation views of parts, products and buildings. Traditionally drawings were produced by hand but computers have revolutionised the process and most drawings are now produced using CAD (computer-aided design). There is an example of an engineering drawing showing plan and elevation views at http://en.wikipedia.org/wiki/Image:Schneckengetriebe.png

Alternative approach

The Standards Unit resources, including the software, Build, provide a strong alternative and active approach to this section. A further approach could be to set up pairs of students to build and draw plans and elevations, and challenge another pair to recreate their shape from the plans. This can also be set up as a team 'collective memory' game, where one student from the group is allowed to view the shape for a short amount of time, and then reports back to the group. The group challenge is to produce a set of plans and elevations for the 'hidden' shape based on the team's observations and feedback.

Checkpoint

1 Draw to scale a plan view, front elevation and side elevation of a cone with diameter 4 cm and a height of 4 cm.
(Plan is a circle with radius 2 cm and centre marked, both elevations are isosceles triangles, base and height 4 cm)

Starter – Faceless

Ask students questions involving the numbers of faces, edges and vertices of 3D shapes. For example,

What is the sum of faces on a cuboid and vertices on a triangular prism? (12)
What is the product of edges on a cube and faces on a square based pyramid. (60)
Subtract the edges on a pentagonal pyramid from vertices on a cuboid. (-2)

Teaching notes

Draw three views of a cuboid. Label them as the 'front elevation', 'side elevation' and 'plan view'. Is it possible to draw the resulting cuboid? Show how it can be drawn both on plain paper and on isometric paper.

Given a 3D object, attempt to construct the three views of it. A pentagonal prism in the standard shape of a house is a good example. How is the sloping roof of the side elevation depicted? How is the top of the roof to be shown on the plan view? Why are elevations important to designers? Why can't you just draw a 3D picture of the shape you are describing?

Draw a plan view of a 3D shape, ask students to suggest what it might be? Now add the front elevation, does this make it completely clear? If not, add the side elevation.

Plenary

Ask students to sketch a plan view of the ground floor of their house. Remind students they can't show height in any way. What are common ways that architects use for showing details like, windows, doors, etc.?

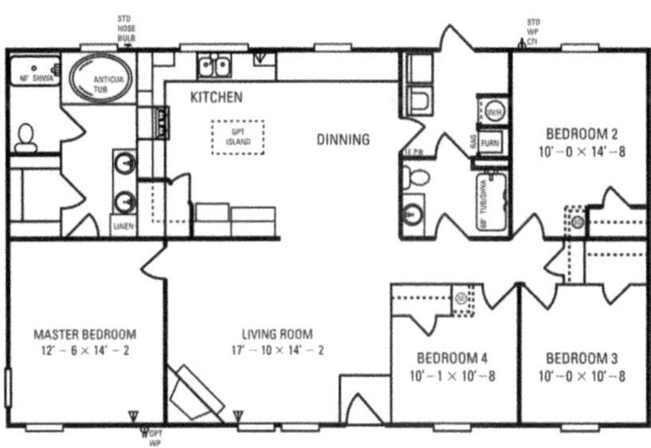

Exercise commentary

Question 1 – Discuss whether these three views are unique to the cuboids shown. It is possible to have the unseen corner removed.

Question 2 – Remind students that a depth is not shown in an elevation. A face that slopes away from you appears upright. Students may be tempted to curve the edges of the cylinders side view.

Question 3 and **4** – Some students struggle to use isometric paper. As a guide tell them that there are no right angles on isometric paper. Right angles in reality are not represented as such. Make sure they can draw a unit cube – an upside down 'Mercedes' hexagon.

Question 4 – Use of multi-link cubes would help. Extend and ask them if their partner can make their shape from 6 cubes from their drawings.

Question 5 – Emphasise that lengths (dimensions) must match up in different views.

Answers

1 Students' sketches of front elevation, side elevation and plan view of
- **a** 4 cm × 1 cm × 2 cm cuboid
- **b** 2 cm × 2 cm × 3 cm cuboid
- **c** 5 cm × 1 cm × 1 cm cuboid

2 Students' sketches of front elevation, side elevation and plan view of
- **a** hexagonal prism
- **b** triangular prism
- **c** cylinder

3
- **a** Students' drawings of 3D solid on isometric paper
- **b** Students' drawings of front elevation and side elevations

4
- **a** Students' drawings of 3D solid on isometric paper
- **b** 5 cubes

5 Students' sketches of 2 cm cube and 4 cm × 3 cm × 2 cm cuboid

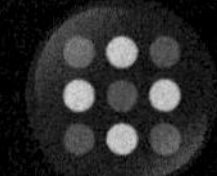

14c Surface area of a prism

Objectives	
• Visualise and use 2D representations of 3D objects	(L6)
• Calculate the surface area of right prisms	(L7)

Key ideas	Resources
1 Calculate the surface areas of a variety of prisms	Nets, surface area (1107) Multi-link cubes Calculators

Simplification	Extension
Set students to initially work out surface area of cuboids that have integer length sides. Show how the faces can be split into unit squares. This 'counting' method may help to re-enforce the more general method of finding the surface area.	A cuboid has integer lengths for its sides. The ratio of surface area to volume is 13 : 6. Suggest possible dimensions for the cuboid. One possible solution is 2 × 3 × 4. Other solutions might be possible. One possible strategy could be to write an equivalent ratio to 13 : 6 and look for possible values of the sides that have a product of the volume.

Literacy	Links
The key term is surface area. Encourage students to come up with their own definition. Challenge them to not include the word 'area' in their definition. Also the word 'integer' in question **7** is one that students often forget the meaning of.	Human skin has a total surface area of about 1.8 m^2. It accounts for between 15% and 20% of the total weight of the human body and helps to protect the body from the environment. It constantly renews itself. Over 90% of common house dust is made up of dead skin cells.

Alternative approach
Models of prisms can be used to generate initial discussion about what it is to be 'a prism'. Students could be invited to think up their own examples from experience (cereal or chocolate boxes, for example) and asked to come up with an informal definition of what a prism is. Develop this into the standard definition with reference to a constant cross-section and highlight special cases such as the cuboid and cylinder.

Checkpoint	
1 What is the surface area of a cuboid that measures 8 cm by 10 cm by 12 cm?	(592 cm^2)

Starter – Puzzle pairs

Write the following lists on the board.

Measurements in cm: 15 and 9; 7 and 6; 12 and 7; 12 and 9; 7 and 7; 14 and 2.5.
Areas in cm^2: 84, 54, 135, 21, 24.5, 35.

The measurements are either the lengths and widths of rectangles or the bases and heights of triangles. Ask students to match up the triangles and rectangles with their areas and then make their own puzzle.

Teaching notes

Use multi-link cubes to build a cuboid from 24 cubes. Count the area of each of the six faces/surfaces in square faces of the multi-link cubes. What is the total? This is known as the surface area.
Is it possible to construct the cuboid in such a way as to make the surface area equal to any of these values 52, 56, 68, 70, 76, 98?

Look at a sketch of a cuboid. How can the surface area be found? Encourage students to look for an efficient method of calculating. What units are likely to be used?

Draw a net for the example just looked at. Is it possible to tell the surface area from the net? Would drawing in the squares on the net be helpful?

Recap the formula for the area of a triangle. What can students recall about the definition of a prism? Use the term cross-section to describe the ends of the prism.

Plenary

Calculate the surface area of a prism with a circular cross section. Can a formula be constructed for the surface area of these types of prisms? Explore different ways of expressing the formulae.

Exercise commentary

A calculator would be useful for the exercise, but is not essential. For a more demanding exercise students could attempt some or all of the questions without a calculator.

Question 1 – Encourage students to view the six faces as three pairs. Opposite faces in a cuboid always have the same area.

Question 2 – Give students time to puzzle out a solution. Don't be too hasty in providing support.

Question 3 and **4** – Encourage students to always sketch the nets of the shapes, to make sure they include every face in calculating the surface area. This is especially the case with question **4**.

Question 5 – Link this question back to question **2**. In question **2** students were solving this equation.

Question 6 – Encourage students to first set up an equation and then solve to find the missing lengths.

Question 7 – Remind students what an integer is. This question is difficult. It may be useful to set up a spreadsheet to help with the repetitive calculations.

Answers

1 **a** 56 m^2 **b** 32 m^2 **c** 78.5 cm^2
2 **a** 15 cm **b** 4.5 cm **c** 1 m
3 **a** Students' sketches of net of triangular prism, 15 cm long with right-angled triangular side measuring 6 cm × 8 cm × 10 cm
b 408 cm^2
4 **a** Students' dimensioned sketches of net of L-shaped prism
b 950 cm^2
5 $6l^2$
6 $x = 5$ cm, $y = 7$ cm, $z = 9$ cm
7 1 cm × 2 cm × 10 cm
2 cm × 2 cm × 7 cm
2 cm × 4 cm × 4 cm

14d Volume of a prism

Objectives

- Calculate the volume of right prisms (L7)

Key ideas

1 Calculate the volume of common prisms

Resources

Volume of prisms (1139)

Calculators
Multi-link cubes
Mini whiteboards

Simplification

Set students to initially work out volumes of cuboids that have integer length sides. Show how the faces can be split into unit squares. This ‘counting’ method may help to re-enforce the more general method of finding the volume. Possibly use simple prisms in the same way, showing how the cubes are subdivided.

Extension

Find the volume of a regular hexagonal prism. Students may need reminding that six congruent equilateral triangles form a regular hexagon. Can students construct a formula for the volume? Without the use of Pythagoras students will have to consider the height of the triangles separately from the base.

Literacy

Ask students to write their own dictionary definition of volume. It is not an easy concept to define simply and can lead to an interesting discussion. Remind students that a prism has a regular cross-section. Each of these terms may need defining.

Links

The largest building in the world by volume is the Boeing aircraft factory at Everett, Washington in the USA. The volume of the building is 13.3 million m^3 and it has a floor area of 398 000 m^2 or 98 acres. There is more information about the factory at http://www.boeing.com/commercial/facilities/index.html

Alternative approach

If the formula for cuboid volume has been developed with students in terms of ‘base area’ multiplied by height then build on this concept in order to draw all prisms together with the one formula. Encourage students to identify the cross-section physically, using actual solid examples as well as visual images. Students may be encouraged to record how to find each cross-section area using mini whiteboards, providing instant feedback on area knowledge. This can then be extended to displaying solids and requesting how to find the volume using mini whiteboards, before consolidating and applying to problems.

Checkpoint

1 What is the volume (to 1 dp) of a cylinder with diameter 4 cm and a height of 4 cm? (201.1 cm^3)

Starter – Costly solids

A face cost 7p, an edge cost 8p and a vertex cost 9p.

Ask students to find the cost of different solids, for example, a cuboid, a square based pyramid and a pentagonal prism. (£2.10, £1.44 and £2.59)

Ask students to find a shape that costs £1.61?
(Triangular prism)

Teaching notes

Construct a cuboid from multi-link cubes. How can the number of cubes be found without having to count every single one? Establish that multiplication can find the area on the end 'slice' of the cuboid, and a final multiplication by the number of 'slices' can find the number of cubes.

Generalise this to produce a formula for the volume of a cuboid: volume = length × width × height or volume = area of the cross section × length.

Look at the volume of a right-angled triangular prism. Can its volume be found in a similar way to that of the cuboid? Try using the second formula. This gives half the answer that the cuboid formula would give.

Establish that the cross section can be of any shape, as long as it is continuous — same size and shape all the way along — to produce a prism.

Volume of a prism = area of the cross-section × length.

Plenary

Look at question **7** again. Is it possible to predict the volume from the net? Look at other nets of 3D shapes, beginning with cuboids, can students imagine the net being folded and calculate the volume?

Exercise commentary

Question 1 – Encourage students to view cuboids as a type of prism. Ask what is unique about prisms that are cuboids. When giving answer deliberately write cm^2 as the unit and ask students to spot the mistake.

Question 2 – Remind students how to calculate the area of compound shapes. Students will either view this problem as a rectangle and a square, or as a big square with a smaller square removed.

Question 3 – Encourage students to include right angled in their definition.

Question 4 – Ask if students can remember how to work out the area of a trapezium. If they cannot, have them treat it as a compound shape and then see if they can derive the formula.

Question 5 – Students will need to know the formula for calculating the area of a circle.

Question 7 – Remind students that all they need to identify to calculate the volume is the cross-section and the perpendicular distance to that cross-section.

Question 8 – Ask students to explain how they arrived at a solution. Encourage associated language, as in 35 has the fewest factors so I knew …

Answers

1 **a** 260 cm^3

2 **a** 1200 cm^2 **b** 120 000 cm^3

3 **a** Triangular prism **b** **i** 20 cm^2 **ii** 120 cm^3

4 **a** 450 cm^2 **b** 27 000 cm^3

5 **a** 78.5 cm^2 **b** 1177.5 cm^3

6 Volume of each container = 76.128 m^3
Total volume = 380 640 m^3

7 **a** 6 cubic units **b** 10 cubic units

8 280 cm^3

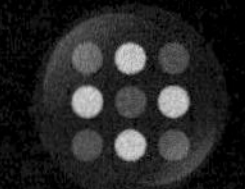

14 3D shapes – MySummary

Key outcomes	Quick check
Name 3D shapes and draw their nets.	Draw the two possible nets for a shape that has 4 faces, 5 edegs and 4 vertices. What is the mathematical name of that shape? (Two possible nets for a tetrahedron drawn)
Draw plans and elevations and isometric diagrams.	A shape made from 4 cubes has the same plan view as front and side elevation. Make an isometric drawing of that shape. Name another shape that has the same plan view as front and side elevation. (Shape is drawn on page 256 of student book; sphere)
Calculate the surface area of a prism.	A right-angled triangular prism is 12 cm long and the sides of the triangle measure 4 cm, 7.5 cm and 8.5 cm. What is the surface area of this prism? (843 cm^2)
Calculate the volume of a prism.	A right-angled triangular prism is 12 cm long and the sides of the triangle measure 4 cm, 7.5 cm and 8.5 cm. What is the volume of this prism? (180 cm^3)

MyMaths extra support

Lesson/online homework			Description
Volume of cuboids	1137	L6	Introduction to volume by counting cubes

MyReview

14 MySummary

Check out

You should now be able to ...

Check out	Test it ➡ Questions
✓ Name 3D shapes and draw their nets	1, 2
✓ Draw plans and elevations and isometric diagrams	3, 4
✓ Calculate the surface area of a prism	5
✓ Calculate the volume of a prism	6, 7

Language	Meaning	Example
Face	A flat surface of a solid shape	vertex, edge, face
Edge	The line where two faces meet	
Vertex	A point where three or more edges meet	
Net	A 2D shape that can be folded to form a 3D shape	
Front elevation	The view of the shape from the front	
Side elevation	The side view of the shape	
Plan view	The bird's eye view of the shape (the view from above).	
Prism	A 3D shape with the same cross-section throughout its length	Cylinder, cuboid

14 MyReview

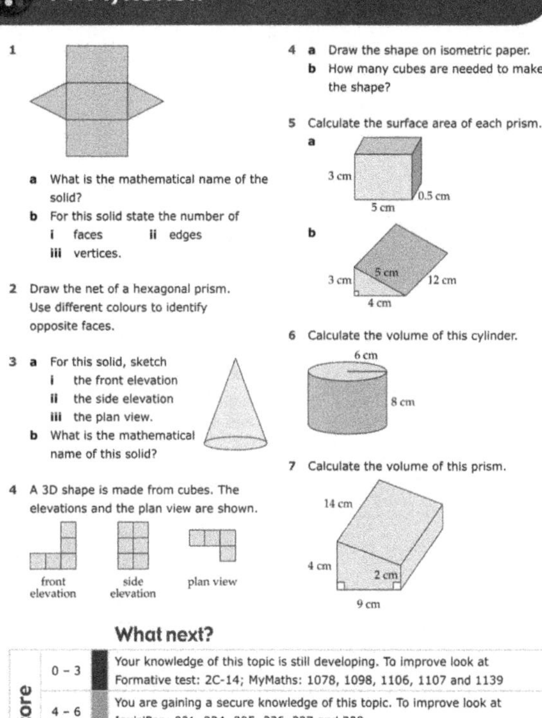

1 a What is the mathematical name of the solid?
b For this solid state the number of
i faces ii edges
iii vertices.

2 Draw the net of a hexagonal prism. Use different colours to identify opposite faces.

3 a For this solid, sketch
i the front elevation
ii the side elevation
iii the plan view.
b What is the mathematical name of this solid?

4 A 3D shape is made from cubes. The elevations and the plan view are shown.

front elevation, side elevation, plan view

4 a Draw the shape on isometric paper.
b How many cubes are needed to make the shape?

5 Calculate the surface area of each prism.
a 3 cm, 5 cm, 0.5 cm
b 3 cm, 5 cm, 12 cm, 4 cm

6 Calculate the volume of this cylinder. 6 cm, 8 cm

7 Calculate the volume of this prism. 14 cm, 4 cm, 2 cm, 9 cm

What next?

Score		
0 – 3		Your knowledge of this topic is still developing. To improve look at Formative test: 2C-14; MyMaths: 1078, 1098, 1106, 1107 and 1139
4 – 6		You are gaining a secure knowledge of this topic. To improve look at InvisiPen: 321, 324, 325, 326, 327 and 328
7		You have mastered this topic. Well done, you are ready to progress!

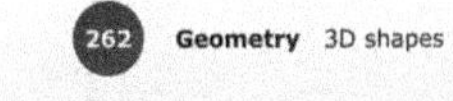
262 Geometry 3D shapes

MyMaths.co.uk 263

Question commentary

Question 2 – Some students may try to draw net as a fanfare. Show them that it is much easier to show rectangular faces as linked.

Question 3 – Remind students that elevations are 2D and they should not try to show perspective.

Question 4 – It will be useful to have multi-link cubes available to illustrate.

Question 5 – Remind students to know how many faces each shape has and to include all of them when calculating the surface area.

Question 6 – Students will need to know the formula for the area of a circle. Encourage students to use the π button on their calculators.

Question 6 – Encourage students to view the cross-section as a trapezium, rather than a rectangle and triangle.

Answers

1 **a** Triangular prism
b **i** 5 **ii** 9 **iii** 6

2 One possible net is

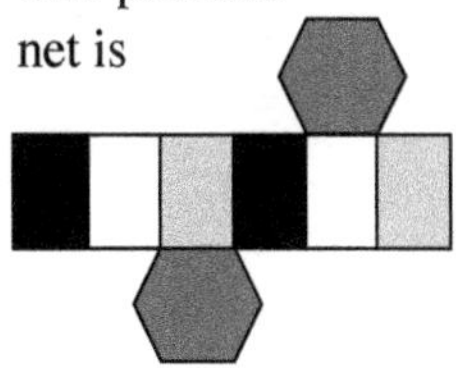

3 **a** **i** **ii** **iii**

b Circular pyramid or cone

4 **a** Shape like this drawn on isometric paper

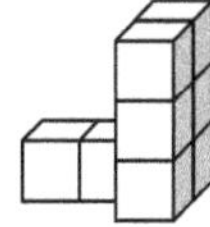

b 8

5 **a** 38 cm^2 **b** 156 cm^2

6 904.3 cm^3

7 378 cm^3

14 MyPractice

14a

1 On square grid paper, draw the net of a cuboid with dimensions 3 cm by 4 cm by 5 cm.

2 **a** Which shapes are the net of a square-based pyramid?

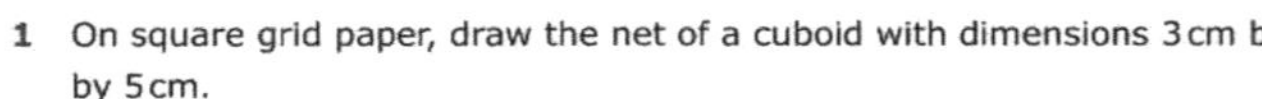
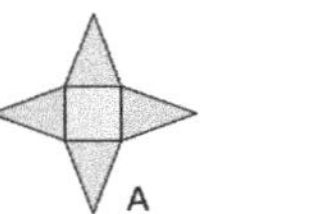
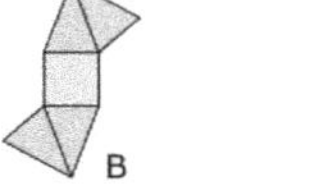

b For a square-based pyramid state the number of

i faces **ii** vertices **iii** edges.

3 On a standard dice the number of dots on opposite faces always adds up to seven. Draw a net for a dice showing the dots.

14b

4 On square grid paper, draw the front elevation (F), the side elevation (S) and the plan view (P) of each solid.

a

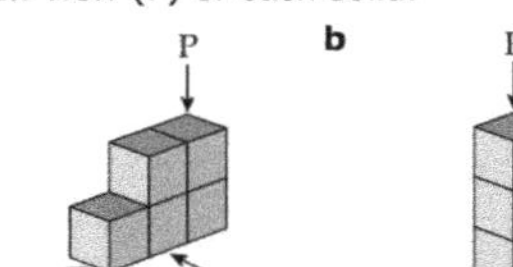

b

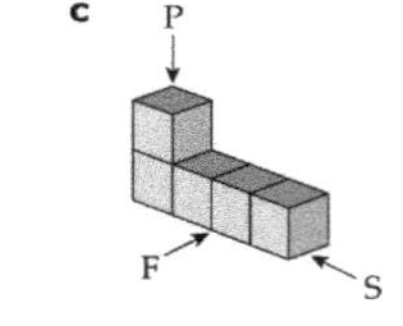

c

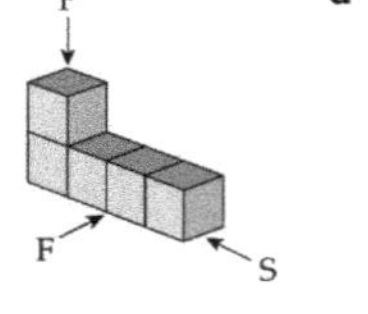

d

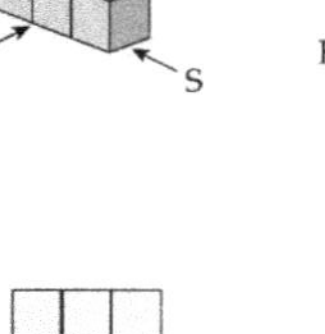

5 A 3D shape is constructed from cubes. The elevations and plan view are shown.

Front elevation Side elevation Plan view

a Draw the solid on isometric paper

b How many cubes are needed to make the shape?

14b

6 Calculate the surface areas of these prisms.

a

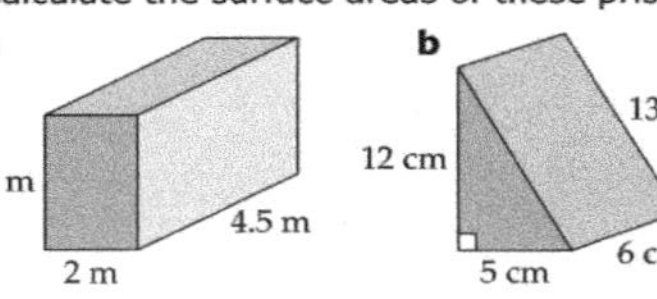

b

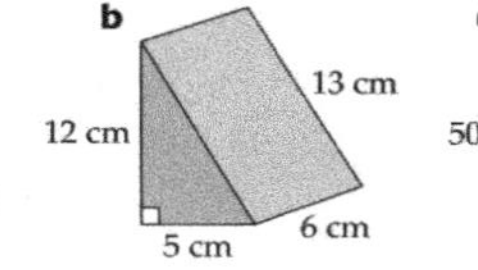

c

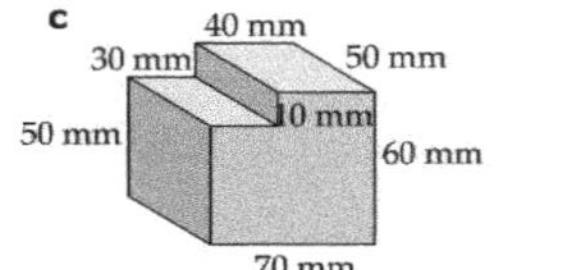

14c

7 **a** Find the nine possible cuboids that can be made using 48 one-centimetre cubes.

b Calculate the surface area of each cuboid.

c Which cuboid has the largest surface area?

d Which cuboid has the smallest surface area?

8 Find the volume of a cube with surface area 150 cm^3.

9 Find the volumes of these prisms.

a

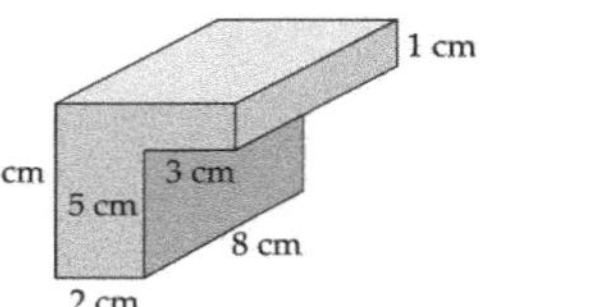

b

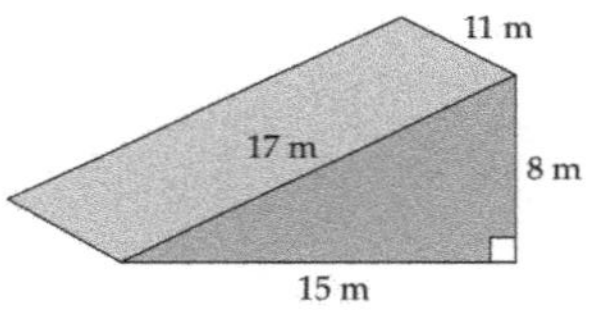

14d

10 A chocolate box has a cross-section of an equilateral triangle.

a State the mathematical name of the solid.

b Draw a sketch of the net, showing the dimensions.

c Calculate

i the surface area

ii the volume of the solid.

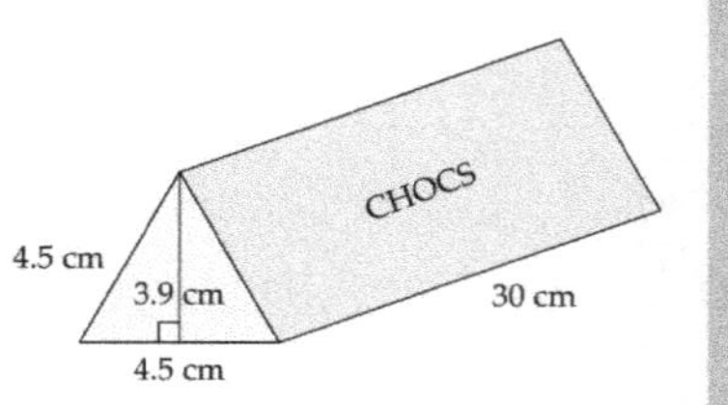

MyMaths.co.uk

Question commentary

Question 2 – Ensure students can see why drawing C is not a net.

Question 5 – Point out that the drawings do show different levels by using a darker line and that their elevations should also show this.

Question 6 – Encourage students to sketch nets to make sure they include every face in their calculation.

Question 7 – Have students first list all the factors of 48 to help them find the 9 combinations. You may wish to link volume surface area ratio to heat loss and its application in nature, e.g. why a giraffe could never survive in the Artic.

Question 9 – Some students may visualise part **b** as half a cuboid.

Answers

1 Students' constructions of 3 cm × 4 cm × 5 cm cuboid

2 **a** A and B

b **i** 5 faces **ii** 5 vertices **iii** 8 edges

3 **a** numbered net of dice

4 **a, b, c, d** Students' drawings of front elevation, side elevation and plan view of shapes given

5 **a** Students' drawings of 3D solid on isometric paper

b 7 cubes

6 **a** 57 m^2 **b** 240 cm^2 **c** 20 800 mm^2

7 All dimensions are in centimetres:

a, b $1 \times 1 \times 48$ (194 cm^2); $1 \times 2 \times 24$ (148 cm^2); $1 \times 3 \times 16$ (134 cm^2); $1 \times 4 \times 12$ (128 cm^2); $1 \times 6 \times 8$ (124 cm^2); $2 \times 2 \times 12$ (104 cm^2); $2 \times 3 \times 8$ (92 cm^2); $2 \times 4 \times 6$ (88 cm^2); $3 \times 4 \times 4$ (80 cm^2)

c $1 \times 1 \times 48$ **d** $3 \times 4 \times 4$

8 125 cm^3

9 **a** 120 cm^3 **b** 660 m^3

10 **a** Triangular prism

b Students' dimensioned sketches of net of triangular prism

c **i** 422.55 cm^2 **ii** 263.25 cm^3

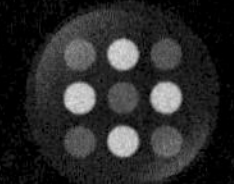

Case study 5: Perspective

Related lessons		Resources	
3D shapes	14a	3D shapes 2D and 3D shapes Cubes and cuboids Old newspapers or magazines	(1078) (1229)

Simplification	Extension
Prepared templates could be used for task **2**. Encourage students to complete one very good drawing rather than trying to complete too many of the tasks in the time available.	Students could look in old magazines or newspapers for examples of pictures that show single or two point perspective. They could draw guidelines on the pictures to find their vanishing points and eye-lines. Whilst searching for these, ask them to look out for pictures that seem to have more than two vanishing points. They might come across some such as looking upwards at an edge on a skyscraper that show tapering of the vertical edges as well as the horizontal ones. Students could also research the use of reverse perspective, where the exact opposite of perspective happens and the vanishing point would be behind or on the person viewing the picture rather than its more natural position in the distance away from the viewer.

Links
Design and technology uses perspective drawing when creating designs for objects to be manufactured. Links can be made to other types of technical drawing and the rationale behind them. Consider the need for such drawing techniques. http://en.wikipedia.org/wiki/Technical_drawing

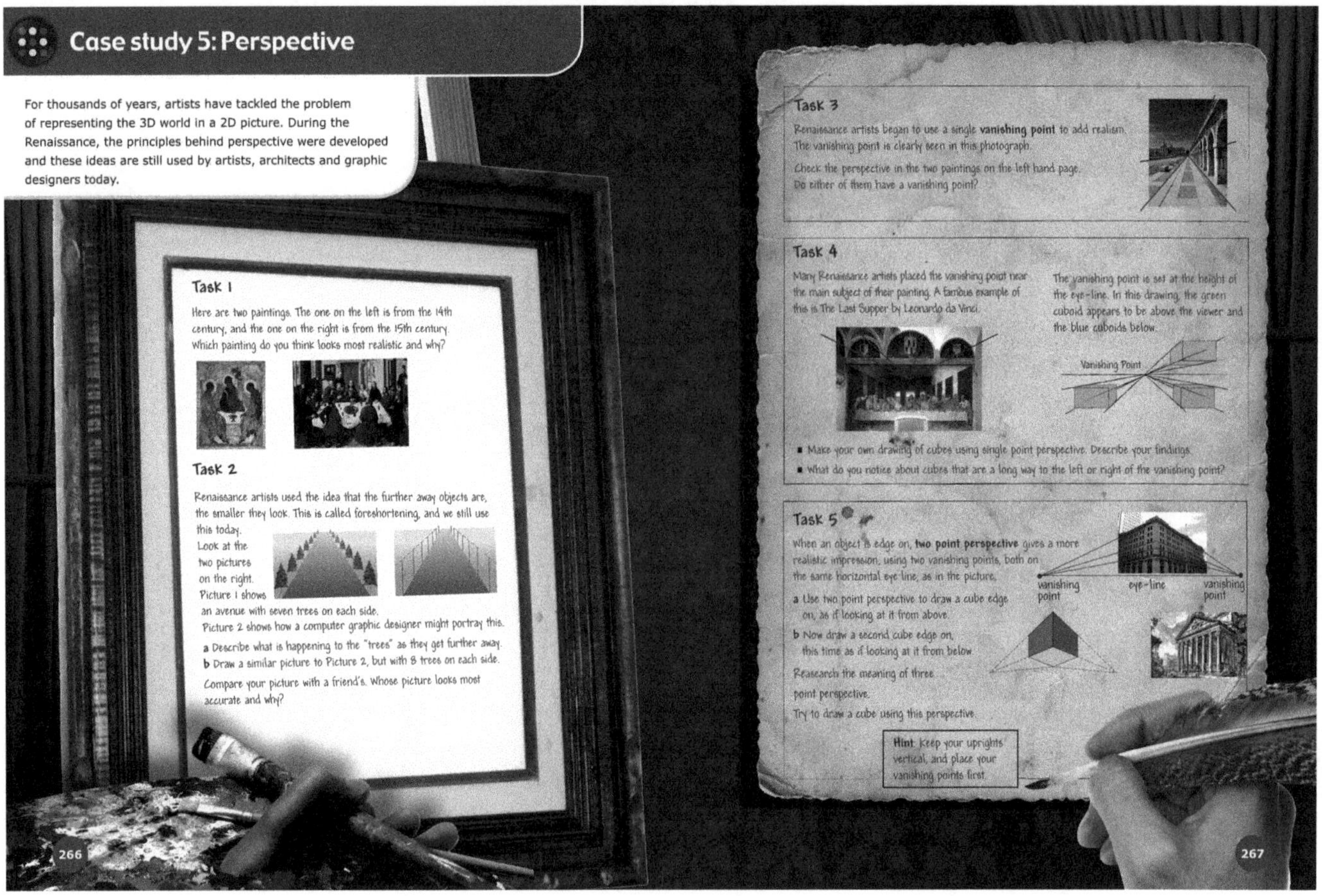

Case study 5: Perspective

For thousands of years, artists have tackled the problem of representing the 3D world in a 2D picture. During the Renaissance, the principles behind perspective were developed and these ideas are still used by artists, architects and graphic designers today.

Task 1

Here are two paintings. The one on the left is from the 14th century, and the one on the right is from the 15th century. Which painting do you think looks most realistic and why?

Task 2

Renaissance artists used the idea that the further away objects are, the smaller they look. This is called foreshortening, and we still use this today.

Look at the two pictures on the right. Picture 1 shows an avenue with seven trees on each side.

Picture 2 shows how a computer graphic designer might portray this.

a Describe what is happening to the "trees" as they get further away.

b Draw a similar picture to Picture 2, but with 8 trees on each side.

Compare your picture with a friend's. Whose picture looks most accurate and why?

266

Task 3

Renaissance artists began to use a single **vanishing point** to add realism. The vanishing point is clearly seen in this photograph.

Check the perspective in the two paintings on the left hand page. Do either of them have a vanishing point?

Task 4

Many Renaissance artists placed the vanishing point near the main subject of their painting. A famous example of this is The Last Supper by Leonardo da Vinci.

The vanishing point is set at the height of the eye-line. In this drawing, the green cuboid appears to be above the viewer and the blue cuboids below.

- Make your own drawing of cubes using single point perspective. Describe your findings.
- What do you notice about cubes that are a long way to the left or right of the vanishing point?

Task 5

When an object is edge on, **two point perspective** gives a more realistic impression, using two vanishing points, both on the same horizontal eye line, as in the picture.

a Use two point perspective to draw a cube edge on, as if looking at it from above.

b Now draw a second cube edge on, this time as if looking at it from below.

Reasearch the meaning of three point perspective.

Try to draw a cube using this perspective.

Hint: Keep your uprights vertical, and place your vanishing points first.

267

Teaching notes

During the Renaissance period (from the 14th century to the 17th century), artists strived to produce paintings that gave a more realistic representation of the world than had been the case in many paintings prior to the Renaissance period. In the Renaissance, artists became interested in using perspective to represent 3D objects in a 2D picture in a way that showed them as they were seen in the real world.

Talk about the Renaissance period and look together at the two paintings shown on the left hand page. Remind students that both pictures are painted on a flat 2D surface and are trying to show a 3D world. Ask them which one they think is more realistic and how this realism is created.

Task 1

Discuss angles in the pictures. In the right hand picture, lines that lie along the sight line and would be parallel in the real world are shown converging to a common point. In the left hand picture, the angle of the seat and the platforms under the feet are tapering in an unnatural looking manner, as are some parts of the building in the background. Discuss how sizes are used to create depth in the right hand picture. People in the foreground are shown slightly larger than those further away, windows that are closer are taller than those that are further away, etc. In comparison, the left hand picture looks almost flat, even though there are things in the background.

Task 2

Students will need to create the 'framework' onto which to put their trees. They should ensure that they consider the vanishing point along the sight lines.

Task 3

Talk about the vanishing point and look again at the original two paintings to see if either of those have a vanishing point (you should find that the right hand painting does). Discuss how the vanishing point is on the eye-line and how the angles converge from above for things that are above the eye-line and from below for things below the eye-line.

Task 4

Look at the diagram of cuboids and discuss with the students how to draw diagrams with single point perspective. Establish that, to draw a cube, you would set an eye-line and vanishing point and then draw the front face as a square. Then you would draw guidelines from the corners of this face to the vanishing point and use these to help construct the diagram. Give students time to draw their own diagram of cubes, positioning at least one above the eye-line and using different amounts of horizontal offset either side of the vanishing point.

Task 5

Discuss how, when the building is viewed edge on, the two walls either side of the edge appear to taper away in different directions to form two vanishing points that lie on the same eye-line. Discuss how you would use two point perspective to draw a cube edge on and give the students some time to make their own drawings as described.

Answers

1 The 15th century painting looks more realistic. The people in the foreground look larger than the people in the background.

2 a The trees get smaller

b Students' own answers

3 Yes, the right hand one

4 Students' own answers

5 Students' own answers

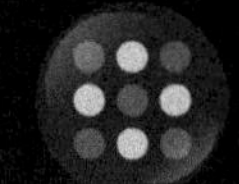

15 Ratio and proportion

Learning outcomes		
R2	Use scale factors, scale diagrams and maps	(L6)
R3	Express one quantity as a fraction of another, where the fraction is less than 1 and greater than 1	(L6)
R4	Use ratio notation, including reduction to simplest form	(L6)
R5	Divide a given quantity in two parts in a given part : part or part : whole ratio; express the division of a quantity into two parts as a ratio	(L7)
R7	Understand that a multiplicative relationship between two quantities can be expressed as a ratio or a fraction	(L7)
R8	Solve problems involving percentage change, including: percentage increase, decrease and original value problems and simple interest in financial mathematics	(L7)

Introduction

This chapter builds on ratio and proportion work done in Chapter 4. Students learn to: simplify ratios, solve ratio problems and divide a quantity in a given ratio; solve direct proportion problems using the unitary method; and solve problems that mix ratio and proportion. The chapter moves on to looking at comparing proportions as fractions or percentages before the final section which links algebraic and numerical relationships.

The idea of creating things which are in proportion is vital to art and architecture. However there is one number, called the 'Golden Proportion', which is supposed to be the most pleasing to the eye.

The Golden Proportion relates to a rectangle whose ratio of length to width is 1.6180339887 : 1. There is evidence that the ancient Greeks and Egyptians used this proportion in the design of many of their buildings, and Renaissance artists used it commonly in their paintings.

Prior knowledge

Students should already know how to…

- Simplify and use ratios
- Convert between fractions, decimals and percentages
- Calculate simple percentages of an amount

Starter problem

Students should be encouraged to collect their own data on height and head length as well as the sizes of other body parts (which could link to work in statistics). This data can then be used to quantify various ratios and proportions. Opportunities can be taken to emphasise the need to use common units and how to draw scale drawings. Posing the question 'In an accurate 10 cm tall model of an adult, how big should the head be?' allows a discussion of dividing in a given ratio. Similar modelling questions can be used to introduce direct proportion.

Students could investigate the age dependence of measurements. What are the percentage changes in the size of body parts as people grow? How should you compare relative proportions? At birth a baby is about four heads tall but only $7\frac{1}{2}$ heads tall as an adult.

The theory of art contains several examples of the ideal proportions for bodies and faces. How do you quantify these proportions and how realistic are they? One famous example is da Vinci's version of Vitruvian man. Manga comics illustrate the effect of modifying ratios.

Resources

MyMaths

Proportion unitary method	1036	Proportion	1037	Ratio dividing 1	1038
Ratio dividing 2	1039				

Online assessment

Chapter test	2C–15
Formative test	2C–15
Summative test	2C–15

InvisiPen solutions

Calculating a percentage change			153
Simplify and use ratio	191	Ratio and proportion	193
Direct proportion and unitary method			195

Topic scheme

Teaching time = 6 lessons/2 weeks

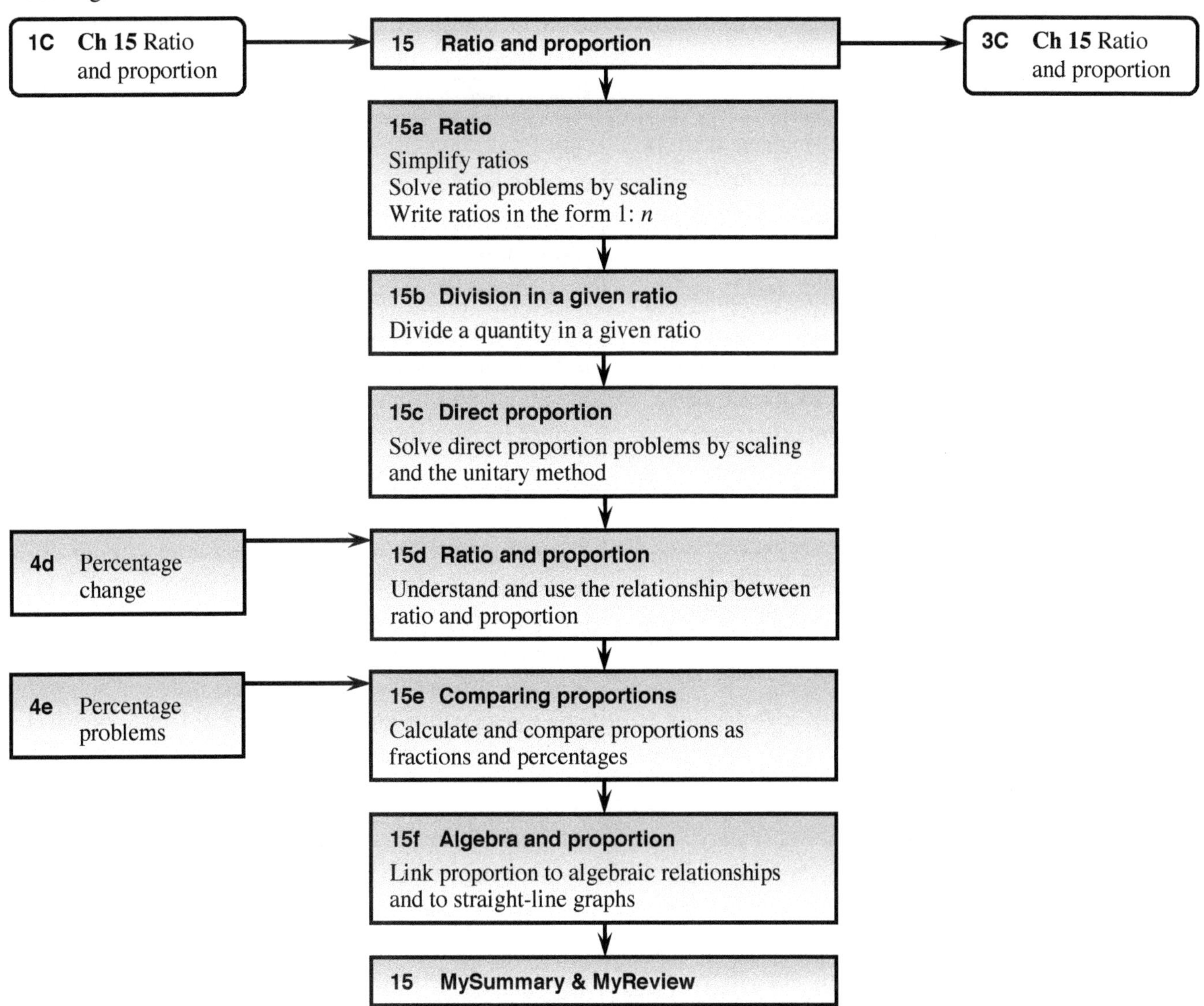

Differentiation

Student book 2A 274 – 293

Simplifying ratios
Dividing into ratios
Proportion
Proportion problems
Ratio and proportion problems
Comparing proportions
Calculations involving money

Student book 2B 266 – 283

Ratio
Division in a given ratio
Direct proportion
Ratio and proportion
Percentage increase and decrease
Comparing proportions

Student book 2C 268 – 285

Ratio
Division in a given ratio
Direct proportion
Ratio and proportion
Comparing proportions
Algebra and proportion

Objectives	
• Use ratio notation (L4) • Simplify ratios, including those expressed in different units, recognising the link with fraction notation (L5) • Compare two ratios (L6)	
Key ideas	**Resources**
1 Recognise and use proportional language flexibly 2 Understand what is expected of a ratio in its simplest form	Proportion (1037) Calculators
Simplification	**Extension**
Allow students to simplify their ratio without having to find the simplest form, for example, 8 : 20 to 4 : 10. If no calculator is used for the initial simplification, a calculator could then be used to go back over their answers and try to find the most simplified form.	Examine the ratio of the lengths of students little fingers to their middle fingers. Give answers to the nearest cm. Is the ratio the same for everyone? If the measurement was made to the nearest 2 cm, would that change the conclusions?
Literacy	**Links**
The most important aspect of this chapter is helping students to appreciate the difference between ratio and proportion. They are both comparison words. Ratio compares two quantities irrespective of the whole. Proportion is always comparing with the whole. Make sure this clear distinction in constantly maintained.	The aspect ratio of a screen or an image is the ratio of its width to its height. HD televisions and monitors have an aspect ratio of 16 : 9 (also known as 1.78 : 1) but older style screens use 4 : 3 (1.33 : 1). Common cinema film ratios are 1.85 : 1 and 2.35 : 1. When an image filmed in one aspect ratio is displayed on a screen with a different aspect ratio, the image has to be cropped or distorted.

Alternative approach

Students should be familiar with the vocabulary and notation, but will need to fully develop competence and confidence with using and applying these concepts. Begin by showing a diagram such as :

Ask students to describe what they see, using any proportional language. For example, 3/7 of the bar is grey; grey is 75% of white; the ratio of grey to white squares is 3 : 4; and so on. Gather, share and explore as many of these statements as is sensible. Equivalent proportion card sorting can also be used to widen students' appreciation of variety. Equivalent spider diagrams can also be developed by pairs of students, and may include equivalent ratios, simplest form as well as amounts with units.

Checkpoint

1 The ratio of silver to copper in ring A is 38 : 3. The ratio in ring B is 49 : 4. Which ring contains the highest proportion of silver? Explain your answer. (Ring A; 12.67 : 1 vs 12.25 : 1)

Starter – 9999

Ask students to make as many numbers as possible between 1 and 20 inclusive using four nines and any operation(s). For example, $1 = (9 + 9) \div (9 - 9)$.

Hint: $\sqrt{9} = 3$

Teaching notes

Ratio is always used to compare amounts to each other. Give examples of ratios that can be simplified to their simplest forms. Remind students that ratios do not give the 'value' of a particular measurement, but allow for comparisons only. Express a ratio in words. For example, £10 : £15 = 2 : 3, 'for every £2 of the first amount there are £3 for the second amount'.

Look at examples were the units are different and show how converting to a convenient common unit allows us to do away with the units. Include examples of triple ratios.

Sometimes it is helpful to express a ratio in an alternative form to the simplest one.

For example, £10 : £15 = 1 : 1.5. This tells us that every £1 compares to £1.50. This form in known as 1 : n. It can be an easier way to compare amounts and solve ratio problems.

Plenary

Write the answers to question **3** using mixed fractions instead of decimals. What advantage does this give? A calculator would not be needed.

Exercise commentary

Question 1 – Encourage students to show working on both sides of the ratio. Point out that they don't need the HCF but it is quicker if they do. Emphasise the only ratio in which decimals are allowed are those in the form of 1: n.

Question 2 – This is the only time that decimals can be written in ratios.

Question 3 – Ask what in this case does the 1: n mean. How would they express this in words?
(Shots per goal scored)

Question 5 – Ask students what other examples they can think of when conversion rates can be given as 1: n.

Answers

1 **a** 2 : 5 **b** 8 : 7 **c** 4 : 5 : 8 **d** 3 : 4 : 9
e 5 : 7 : 11 **f** 80 : 41 **g** 25 : 14 **h** 35 : 8
i 1 : 4 **j** 3 : 80 **k** 3 : 10 **l** 2 : 3
m 3 : 4 : 5 **n** 1 : 6 **o** 25 : 18 **p** 25 : 3

2 **a** 1 : 2 **b** 1 : 4 **c** 1 : 5 **d** 1 : 14
e 1 : 1.8 **f** 1 : 4.67 **g** 1 : 3.4 **h** 1 : 14.5
i 1 : 2.67 **j** 1 : 2.57 **k** 1 : 1.83 **l** 1 : 13.67
m 1 : 14 **n** 14 : 1 **o** 1 : 4 **p** 1.96 : 1

3 **a, b** Table ordered from most to least accurate. Most accurate person takes the fewest shots compared with the goals scored so has the lowest ratio.

Name	Goals : Shots	1 : n
Robin	16 : 35	1 : 2.19
Frank	21 : 50	1 : 2.38
Demba	17 : 43	1 : 2.53
Warren	13 : 34	1 : 2.62
Daniel	19 : 53	1 : 2.79

4 First T-shirt 1 : 2.66 or 0.375 : 1
Second T-shirt 1 : 2.8 0.357 : 1
The first T-shirt has the highest proportion of cotton.

5 **a**

miles	kilometres	miles: km	miles: km
10	16	5 : 8	1 : 1.6
24	38.4	5 : 8	1 : 1.6
31.25	50	5 : 8	1 : 1.6
50	80	5 : 8	1 : 1.6

b It is the conversion factor, i.e. miles × 1.6 = km

c, d Students' investigations and explanations

15b Division in a given ratio

Objectives	
• Divide a quantity into two or more parts in a given ratio (L6) • Interpret and use ratio in a range of contexts (L6)	
Key ideas	**Resources**
1 Dividing into given ratios with any appropriate method **2** Begin to consider more efficient ways of solving proportional problems	Proportion unitary method (1036) Ratio dividing 1 (1038) Ratio dividing 2 (1039) Spreadsheet to show results for investigation
Simplification	**Extension**
Keep the language of ratio in terms of 'parts' of the whole amount. Ask, 'How much is there to begin with?' 'How many groups is it being split into?' 'How many parts are their all together?' 'What is each part worth?'. When solving a question, help students to correctly label what they have found. For example, 1 part = 16 cakes for question **1a**.	In question **6,** how old would the girls have to be so that they all have received the same amount of money? A trial-and-improvement approach is likely to be the most effective; a linear equation could be formed but is very difficult to solve at this level. (999 997, 1 000 000 and 1 000 006)
Literacy	**Links**
Although the term 'unitary method' is used, it is not necessary that students understand or use the term. It is important that they understand what dividing by ratio is and know to calculate what one part is worth.	The Golden Ratio, 1 : 1.618 (to 3 dp), occurs in mathematics, art and in nature. It can be used to divide an object into two parts so that the ratio of the smaller part to the larger part is the same as the ratio of the larger part to the whole object. The ratio is used in architecture to produce buildings of aesthetically pleasing proportions. There are pictures of buildings built on the Golden Ratio at http://goldennumber.net/architecture.htm

Alternative approach

Group students into threes, and present them with a scenario that three people have jointly won £367 425 with a lottery ticket that they all contributed to. If they decided to share the money fairly, based on their contributions to the £1 ticket, find what they might receive for, say, three different situations. It is likely that students will begin with proportions which are likely to be solved with informal methods. Suggested further situations can be suggested and shared – with differentiation – and efficient use of a calculator explored.

Checkpoint

1 The ratio of male to female at a rowing club is 5 : 7. There are 96 members of the rowing club.
How many of the rowers are female? (56)

Starter – Countdown

Ask students for six numbers between 1 and 10, and one from 25, 50, 75 and 100.

Write the numbers on the board.

Throw a dice three times to generate a three-digit target number.

Challenge students to calculate this target number (or get as close as possible to it) using the five numbers and any operations.

Teaching notes

An amount can be split up/divided up in a certain ratio. First, identify how many parts the amount is being split up into. Two or three people may be sharing the amount, but that does not mean it is being split into two or three parts. Look at the total of all the parts of the ratio. Ask, what is one part worth? This is called the unitary method because it finds the value of one unit/part first. How many parts does each person receive? Use multiplication to find the amounts that are to go to each person. Look at examples that have integer solutions and include triple ratios.

An alternative way of looking at ratio is to ask what fraction/ proportion each person receives of the whole amount as shown in the second example. Look at the parts of the ratio in order to decide. Then that fraction/proportion of the total amount can be calculated.

Plenary

Investigate the ratio of elements in various alloys. For example, 'Nickel Silver' is 65 : 18 : 17 with respective parts being copper : nickel : zinc. Wikipedia's 'list of alloys' is a useful site as the ratios tend to be given as percentages. Can any of the ratios looked at be simplified?

Exercise commentary

Question 1 and **2** – Use language like 'how many parts are there in the ratio? So what is each part worth?'

Question 2 – Ask why the amounts might not add up to the original total.

Question 4 – Note that the question is different. It is no longer a straight forward divide by a given ratio question. Careful reading and deciphering is required.

Question 5 – For part **b** ask for the answer in the form of 1: n and then ask what the significance of this number is. Some will recognize it as the percentage multiplier used when calculating percentage increase.

Question 6 – A spreadsheet is a useful way of calculating the figures that the girls have each year. Ask why they are getting closer and why the youngest is getting more each year. Will her amount ever stop increasing? Will the amounts ever be the same?

Answers

1 **a** 32 cakes : 48 cakes **b** 65 km : 91 km
c £170.67 : £213.33 **d** 27p : 54p : 81p
e 16 sweets : 16 sweets : 64 sweets

2 **a** £4.88 : £8.13 **b** 87.5 m : 112.5 m
c 1.14 GB : 2.86 GB **d** £8.89 : £13.33 : £17.78

3 **a** 560 girls **b** 210 g

4 **a** 350 kg **b** 175 ml

5 **a** Not enough information to make a decision. Only know that:
Years 7 + 8 + 9 > Years 10 +11
b 1 : 1.1 or 10 : 11

6 **a, b**

Year	Zoe		Breeze		Jenny	
1	6	£200.00	9	£300.00	15	£500.00
2	7	£212.12	10	£303.03	16	£484.85
3	8	£222.22	11	£305.56	17	£472.22
4	9	£230.77	12	£307.69	18	£461.54
5	10	£238.10	13	£309.52	19	£452.38
6	11	£244.44	14	£311.11	20	£444.44
7	12	£250.00	15	£312.50	21	£437.50
8	13	£254.90	16	£313.73	22	£431.37
9	14	£259.26	17	£314.81	23	£425.93
10	15	£263.16	18	£315.79	24	£421.05

c Ratios $n + 6 : n + 9 : n + 15 \rightarrow 1 : 1 : 1$ as they get older

7 Large : small = 1 : 3

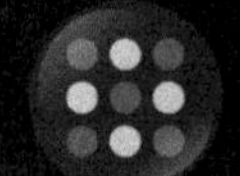

15c Direct proportion

Objectives

- Use the unitary method to solve problems involving ratio and direct proportion (L6)
- Use proportional reasoning to solve problems, choosing the correct number to take as 100%, or as a whole (L6)

Key ideas

1. Recognise when a problem involves direct proportion
2. Begin to spot the multiplicative relationship or scale factor in a direct proportion problem

Resources

Proportion unitary method (1036)

Card sort

Calculators

Simplification

Expressing the proportional questions as ratios may be an easier way to approach this exercise. How can the ratio be changed into the numbers asked for? Do you need two steps to achieve the result you want? This could lead the way to the unitary method with the use of a calculator.

Extension

If the exchange rate for £ : $ is 1 : 1.79 and £ : euros is 0.79 : 1, find the exchange rate for $: euros in the three forms

i	1 : n	(1 : 0.71 (2 dp))
ii	n: 1	(1.41 : 1 (2 dp))
iii	simplest	(14 141 : 10 000)

Are these exchange rates still accurate? The website www.xe.com is useful for current exchange rates.

Literacy

This section has a more natural meaning for the 'unitary method' than dividing by ratios. Discuss why it is called the unitary method. Elicit that unit means one or single. Representing direct proportion graphically will help their understanding. Stress that direct proportion results in a straight line graph through the origin.

Links

As part of the design process for a product, manufacturers draw up a 'parts list' of all the components used in the assembled product. The manufacturer decides how many of the product he is going to build and then orders the number of parts required. The number he needs is in direct proportion to the number on the parts list.

There are examples of parts lists at http://www.turbocharged.com/catalog/parts_list.html

Alternative approach

Use vertical bars to represent values in problems, for example in the given examples:

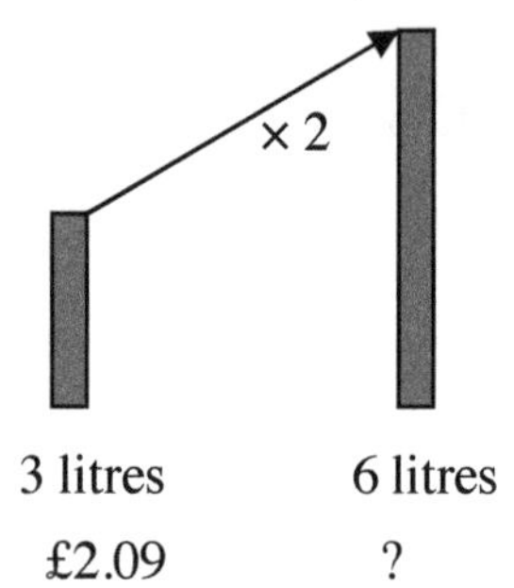

3 litres £2.09 6 litres ?

or

÷ 20 ×15

20 texts 48p 1 text ? 15 texts ?

This helps to secure the intuitive approaches that students may have when they recognize a simple 'scale factor', and develops a visual approach to using the unitary method. Students will have varying recognition of proportional facts that they may apply, which need to be encouraged. Further direct proportion problems including card sorts can be used.

Checkpoint

1. Use the following exchange rates to work out which is worth more, 100 Euros or 300 Turkish Lira.
   £1.00 = 1.26 Euros; £1.00 = 3.58 Turkish Lira

   (100 Euros = £79.37; 300 TL = £83.80; so 300 TL worth more)

Starter – Grandad Bob

Bob wanted to share £5555 between his four grandchildren. He decided give the money in the ratio of their ages. Simon was 16, Lucy and Jo were both 12 and Steven was 10.

Ask students how much money each grandchild received. (Simon £1777.60, Lucy £1333.20, Jo £1333.20, Steven £1111)

This can be extended by students making up their own ratio problems.

Teaching notes

Describe situations where two quantities are in direct proportion. What can be said about how the two amounts change? They rise and fall by the same factor. If one amount was zero, what would the other amount be?

Direct proportion and ratio are really the same thing. The unitary method (from the previous spread) can still be used, but another method maybe of more use. Look at examples that make easy use of the scaling method but would be more awkward when using the unitary method. For example, 6 pens cost 34p, the number of pens and cost are in direct proportion. What is the cost of 15 pens? Show how this problem can be scaled down and then up to the required solution. Illustrate this additionally using ratio notation. Ask students which of the methods of calculation and presentation would they be likely to use in this case.

Plenary

Without a calculator, why would the unitary method be a poor choice for solving the following question?
21 pencils can be purchased for £4.90.
How much would 45 pencils cost?
(Assume cost ∝ number of pencils). What non-calculator approach could be used? What is the advantage of using pence rather than pounds? Is it helpful to represent this question using ratio?

Exercise commentary

Question 1 – Even with the easier questions encourage students to use the unitary method and always ask themselves how much one part is worth.

Question 2 – When using the unitary method students may find it helpful to set out their work as ratio.
For example,
part **a**, 5 : £4.79 →1 : 95.8p → 18 : £17.24

Question 3 – Ask students to re-phrase what direct proportion means in this example, i.e. cost per text must be the same.

Question 4 – Many students will have come across this approximate conversion before and used it without considering direct proportion. Stress that all conversions are based on direct proportion. In discussing part **c** use the term 'reciprocal' and enable students to understand why for reverse conversions the reciprocal is used.

Answers

1 **a** 585p **b** 320 calories
c 500 ml

2 **a** £17.24 **b** 383.3 g
c **i** 270.8 km **ii** 9.6 litres
d **i** 2998.78 Croatian kuna
ii £108.38
e 2100 kg

3 Offer A Direct proportion (1 : 2.4)
Offer B No
Offer C Direct proportion (1 : 2.25)

4

Kilograms (kg)	Pounds (lb)	Pounds ÷ Kilograms	Ratio Pounds : Kilograms
1	2.2	2.2	5 : 11
2	4.4	2.2	5 : 11
5	11	2.2	5 : 11
10	22	2.2	5 : 11
23	50.6	2.2	5 : 11
50	110	2.2	5 : 11

a pounds ÷ kilograms = 2.2
pounds : kilograms = 5 : 11
b kilograms = pounds ÷ 2.2
c pounds = kilograms × 2.2
multiply by 11 and divide by 5

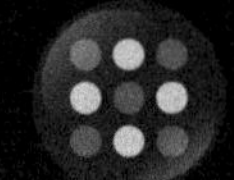

15d Ratio and proportion

Objectives	
• Apply understanding of the relationship between ratio and proportion (L6)	
Key ideas	**Resources**
1 Recognise that proportion is equality of ratios 2 Solving simple ration and proportion problems	Ratio dividing 1 (1038) Ratio dividing 2 (1039)
Simplification	**Extension**
Ask students to explain verbally what they understand by the information given. Allow students to draw sketches to visualise how the ratio is dividing the amounts. Allow the explanation and clear understanding of a question to stand as a substitute to answering it in some cases.	£140 is shared between Mr A, Mr B and Mr C in the ratio $x : x + 2 : x - 3$. The second largest share of the money is £49. How much does each person get? Many approaches are possible. Some students may want to try different values for x, ($x = 7$ in fact). Others may want to try using algebra, although this is difficult. (49 : 63 : 28)
Literacy	**Links**
The key is to emphasise the difference between ratio and proportion. They are both comparing words but ratio compares a quantity with another; proportion compares a quantity with the whole. Discuss which statistical chart fits best to help distinguish between the two: Ratio → Bar Chart; Proportion → Pie Chart.	Proportional representation is a system of election where the number of seats given to a particular party is proportional to the number of votes that it receives. In an election in the UK, only the winning candidate in each constituency becomes a Member of Parliament. Smaller parties might win a sizeable proportion of the vote without winning any seats.

Alternative approach

The key idea is not an easy one, so students need to explore and practise application fully. An alternative approach is to tackle this section after **15e** and directly followed by **15f** so that the ideas can be consolidated more firmly.

Checkpoint

1 The recipe for a health smoothie uses 70 ml almond milk and 50 ml of coconut milk. What is the ratio of coconut milk to almond milk and what is the proportion, given as a percentage, of coconut milk? (5:7; 41.7%)

Starter – Emergency!

Ask students to find as many ways as possible of arranging the digits 1 to 9 to make three 3-digit numbers that will add up to give 999.

(One possible way is 498 + 375 + 126 = 999)

Can a similar kind of puzzle be made using subtraction?

Teaching notes

Ratio can be used to compare the proportions of amounts to each other. For example, Mr A is 20 years old and Mr B is 35 years old. What proportion is Mr A's age of Mr B's age? How can their ages be compared to begin with? Ratio 20 : 35. Is this satisfactory? Simplifying the ratio gives 4 : 7. Therefore Mr A is $\frac{4}{7}$ of Mr B's age. Verify this from their actual ages. What fraction is Mr B's age of Mr A's age? What sort of answer is expected? Greater than one, actually $\frac{7}{4}$. Can this be expressed as a percentage?

Ratio can also be used to find the total amount. Look at examples where the ratio is given and the quantity of one side of the ratio is known. Consider examples like those in question **3**.

Plenary

The dimensions of a football pitch for international games must be 100 to 120 m long by 70 to 80 m wide. What ratios can be created from the possible pitch sizes? Simplify each answer

Exercise commentary

Question 1 – Emphasise that ratio is comparing one colour with another, while proportion is comparing one colour with the whole. In part **iii**, ask students which sum is ratio and which is proportion.

Question 2 – Point out that even though the original ratio compares three things, it is still a ratio when only two of them are compared.

Question 3 – Encourage students to consider the unitary method and convert the ratio to 1: *n* first.

Question 4 – Help the students see that fractions, decimals and percentages are all ways of expressing proportion and therefore belong together. Ratio is different, but can be calculated from proportion. This confusion often appears when dealing with probability, as bookies express odds as ratio, when mathematically probabilities should always be expressed as proportions.

Question 5 – Check that students recognise this as essentially a dividing by a ratio question.

Answers

1 **a** **i** 2 : 1 : 3

ii $\frac{1}{3}$ pink; $\frac{1}{6}$ yellow; $\frac{1}{2}$ blue

iii pink = 2 × yellow

pink = $\frac{2}{6}$ or $\frac{1}{3}$ × whole shape

b **i** 7 : 5 : 6

ii $\frac{7}{18}$ pink; $\frac{5}{18}$ yellow; $\frac{1}{3}$ blue

iii pink = $\frac{7}{5}$ × yellow

pink = $\frac{7}{18}$ × whole shape

2 **a** 15 : 6 : 19 **b** 2.5

c $\frac{19}{40}$ = 47.5%

3 **a** 18 kg **b** 68.75 m **c** 240 g **d** 2.4 g

4 **a** 4 : 5 **b** 3 : 5 **c** 5 : 6

d £4.20 child; £5.60 adult

5 72.7 cm

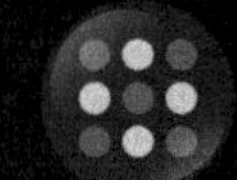

15e Comparing proportions

Objectives	
• Recognise when fractions or percentages are needed to compare proportions (L6) • Use proportional reasoning to solve problems, choosing the correct number to take as 100% or as a whole (L6)	

Key ideas	Resources
1 Recognising and using equivalence of fractions, decimals and percentage **2** Supporting the concept that proportion is an equality of ratio	Mini whiteboards Calculators

Simplification	Extension
Write one amount as a fraction of another amount before calculating the fraction. This may make it easier to perform the division in the correct direction. Ask students to say what they are calculating in words, for example, question **2a**, 5.5 out of 21 as a percentage. Encourage students to have an idea about the approximate value of the answer.	A pub landlord purchases 50 000 litres of lemonade for £1500. She sells the lemonade at £2.10 per pint. What is the percentage profit? How do you interpret an answer (much) greater than 100%? Will the same answer be achieved regardless of whether the numbers are converted to pints or litres? 1 litre $\approx 1\frac{3}{4}$ pints; a useful rhyme is 'a litre of water's a pint and three quarters!'. (buy at 3p/litre sell at 367.5p/litre or buy at £1500 and sell at £183 750, percentage profit is 12 150%)

Literacy	Links
This section again examines proportion. Use it to forge a strong link in students' minds between proportion and fractions, decimals and percentages and that these three ways of expressing number belong together.	Chocolate is made from the beans of the tropical cacao tree and was prized as a drink by the Aztecs. The first eating chocolate was produced by Joseph Fry in Bristol in 1848. On average, each person in the UK eats 10 kg of chocolate each year. The population of The United Kingdom is approximately 60 million. How many tonnes of chocolate are eaten in the UK each year? (600 000) If chocolate is ≈10% fat, how many tonnes of fat is this? (60 000)

Alternative approach
Useful ideas and activities for students can be found in the booklet 'What is a Fraction?', chapters 4 & 5, which cover these themes. http://www.nationalstemcentre.org.uk/elibrary/resource/4651/what-is-a-fraction. Also draw on examples from across the school's curriculum, as well as using sources of real (functional) contexts. Section 2 on Problem Solving from the referenced resource provides several appropriate problems. http://archive.excellencegateway.org.uk/pdf/T%20%26%20L%20Maths%20Apr%202009.pdf

Checkpoint
1 In a local primary school 124 children out of 180 ate school lunches. In the secondary school 744 students out of 1080 ate school lunches. Which school has the highest proportion of pupils eating school lunches? (Both schools the same, 68.9%)

Starter – Paper round

Sam earns £25 a week doing a paper round. As a bonus Sam was offered a choice of three options

- an extra lump sum of £10 for one week
- an extra £2 each week for five weeks
- a pay rise of 50% for one week followed by a pay cut of 50% the following week.

Ask students what choice Sam should make and why? What should the pay cut be? ($33\frac{1}{3}$%)

Teaching notes

A proportion of the whole amount can be expressed as a fraction or percentage. Look at examples that convert easily to denominators of 100 and other examples that require a calculator to change a fraction into a decimal. Recap equivalence between decimals and percentages. Encourage students to recognise a decimal as a percentage rather than rely on multiplying by 100.

Look at examples of finding the percentage change. Give the original and new amounts. Before finding the percentage change, what needs to be calculated first? (The change itself)

Is the change that has happened out of the new amount or out of the original? Establish that the change has come out of the original amount. Use the formula

$$\text{percentage change} = \frac{\text{change}}{\text{original}}$$

(Expressed as a decimal)

Include examples that can be solved mentally – denominators that can be easily converted to 100 – and those that require a calculator.

Plenary

Explore examples of expressing one number as a percentage of another where division in either direction is meaningful. Use non-calculator methods. For example, Mr A is 20 years old and Mr B is 25 years old. What is Mr A's age as a percentage of Mr B's age? (80% and vice versa 125%).
Use equivalent fractions to convert to a fraction out of 100. What do these results mean in words? Mr A is 80% of Mr B's age. Is there a connection between the two numbers? Explore other examples that can be done without a calculator.

Exercise commentary

Question 1 – Use this question to strengthen the link between proportion and fractions and percentages.

Question 2 – In part **b** it could be argued that the healthiest bar depends on total fat content, and not proportion. Open this up for discussion.

Question 3 – Discuss why in deciding which cereal is the healthiest is it right to look at proportion and it wasn't in question **2b**.

Question 4 – This question needs careful reading. Warn students to make sure they understand the information they are being given. Encourage them to translate into maths-speak
i.e. 175000 = 1.1% of 55% of the original rain forest.

Question 5 – Students will have been interested in value for money questions for a long time and generally find it the easiest application of proportion.

Answers

1 **a** **i** $\frac{1}{125}$ **ii** 0.8%

b **i** $\frac{23}{40}$ **ii** 57.5%

c **i** $\frac{2}{5}$ **ii** 40%

2 **a, c**

Chocolate	% fat	Fat / 150 g
Kit Kit	26.2%	39 g
Malties	23.0%	34 g
Venus	17.5%	16 g
Cream	15.9%	24 g
Twicks	24.0%	36 g

b Kit Kit is the least healthy because it contains the highest percentage of fat.

3 **a** Fruity fruit contains the least amount of fat as shown by the percentages in the following table.

Cereal	% fat	Fat / 40 g
Fruity fruit	2.2%	0.9 g
Nutty fruit	3.3%	1.3 g
Nuts to nuts	3.6%	1.4 g

b Fruity fruit is the healthiest as it contains the lowest proportion of fat.

c See table above

4 **a** Original area = 175 000 ÷ 0.011 ÷ (1 – 0.45)
= 28 925 619.83 = 29 000 000 km^2

b In 1997, area = 29 000 000 × 0.55
= 15 950 000 km^2
In 1997 + n, area = 15 950 000 × $(1 - 0.011)^n$
(in 2009, area = 13 970 000 km^2)

c About 91 years after 1997 at a constant rate of loss

5 A = 1.25 £/kg B = 1.22 £/kg C = 1.20 £/kg

Sack C is the best value for money because it costs least per kilogram.

Objectives

- Understand that a multiplicative relationship between two quantities can be expressed as a ratio or a fraction (L6)

Key ideas

1 Use algebra in proportion problems
2 Link to the equation of a straight line

Resources

Proportion unitary method (1036)

Mini whiteboards

Calculators

Simplification

Use mostly examples working only with direct proportion and use careful judgement as to whether to include question **5** and inverse proportion.
Always link A α B as being a straight line graph through the origin, so therefore being synonymous with $y = mx$ (as c is always 0).

Extension

In science many experiments involve discovering how one amount varies with another. Explain that there are other kinds of variation. Discuss for example A α B^2 then look at these results.

A	707	1500	2827	4000	5027	6000
B	15	21.9	30	35.7	40	43.7

Ask if students have any idea what A and B represent.
(A is the area of circle while B is the radius)

Literacy

Students by now should be comfortable with the term proportion as relating to the whole. The confusion now is that when we describe things as proportional, or being in the same proportion, we mean their ratio is constant. This section also introduces the concept of inverse proportion. It is worth at this stage highlighting that in direct proportion A over B is constant, whilst with inverse proportion A times B is constant.

Links

One of the most important things about learning to drive is knowing what the stopping distances are at different speeds. The chart provided by the Highway Code is interesting because the distance travelled during reaction time is proportional to speed, but braking distance is proportion to the square of speed. Use this link to explore, and also discuss what factors might affect stopping distance. For example, alcohol, wet conditions etc.

https://www.gov.uk/government/publications/the-highway-code-typical-stopping-distances

Alternative approach

Make links back to the work on the unitary method and show how the algebraic approach used here is equivalent to the unitary method. There is also a clear link to the work on real–life graphs, currency exchange and conversion graphs. These could all be used as the starting point with quick-fire question and answer before developing the generalised methods.

Checkpoint

1 In a physics experiment different weights are hung from 20 cm of copper wire, and the extension is measured. When a 2 kg mass was hung the extension was 1.2 cm. When a 5 kg mass was hung the extension was 3 cm.
Do these results show that mass α extension or not? Justify you answer. (Yes, since $1.2 \div 2 = 3 \div 5$)

Starter – Quick convert

The conversion from pounds (lb) to kilograms is to divide by 2.2. Give the students quick-fire (mini whiteboard) conversions to carry out. Calculators can be used to increase the speed. Questions could include:

11 pounds in kg

20 pounds in kg

3 kg in pounds

7 kg in pounds, etc.

Teaching notes

Emphasise what it means to 'be in proportion' and introduce the notation for proportionality. Engage the class in discussion about what it means to be proportional and get them to generate examples from everyday life.

Model an algebraic approach similar to the first example or using question **2** and show how the calculations can be done in one step.

Links to straight-line graphs can be developed using the second example and question **4** as models.

Plenary

Provide further examples such as that in question **3** and ask students to work out the heights of the similar triangles as quickly as possible. Mini whiteboards and calculators can be used for speed.

Exercise commentary

Question 1 – Discuss the properties of direct proportion. For example, when one value doubles so does the other value; when one value is zero, so is the other one, etc.

Question 2 – Encourage students to use a unitary method. Discuss how this method leads to what is called the constant of proportionality.

Question 3 – State explicitly that corresponding lengths in similar shapes are in direct proportion with each other.

Question 4 – Again make the link between A α B with $y = mx$ (+ c) highlighting that c is always zero if there is direct proportion. Discuss the meaning of 'm'. This is the constant of proportionality, and in this case is the exchange rate.

Question 5 – Include in your discussion the time taken to complete a job and the number of workers.

Answers

1 **a** Yes **b** No **c** No **d** Yes
e No or possibly!

2 **a** Yes. Ratio in both rows is 2 : 3 : 8.
b Yes. Ratio in both rows is 2 : 3 : 10.

3 14 cm

4 **a**

£	1	4	8	16
€	1.25	5	10	20

b Conversion graph of £ (x-axis) to €(y-axis)
c **i** €7.50 **ii** £14.40
d €= 0.8£
e €100 = £80 so this is better than £75

5 Any two quantities that are in inverse proportion, e.g.
Distance travelled and amount of fuel left in the tank
Temperature of hot water in a bowl and time from the start
The more workers there are to do a job, the shorter the time it takes
For the same motor, the lighter the car, the higher its top speed

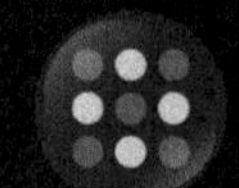

15 Ratio and proportion – MySummary

Key outcomes	Quick check
Simplify and compare ratios.	One company pays £33.60 for 5 hours work. A second company pays £35.84. Express their hourly rates as a ratio in its simplest form. (3:4)
Divide a quantity in a given ratio.	Divide £5.92 in the ration 3 : 5. (£2.22:£3.70)
Use the unitary method to solve direct proportion problems.	Which bottle of water is the best value for money, 500 ml for 55p, 1.75 litres for £1.90 or 5 litres for £5.45? (the 1.75 litre bottle)
Solve ratio and proportion problems.	A catering company charges £525 for 60 guests. How much do they charge for 75 guests? (£656.25)
Compare proportions.	In company A, 5 out of 40 employees earn more tan £50 000. In company B, 8 out of 60 employees do. Which company has the higher proportion of higher earners? (Company B)
Describe quantities in direct proportion using an equation or a graph.	It takes 24 seconds to download a 1.5 MB image over a phone network and 56 seconds to download a 3.5 MB image. Using this information is it possible to work out how long it will take to download a 3 MB image, and if so how long will it take? (Yes; 48 seconds)

MyMaths extra support

Lesson/online homework			Description
Comparing fractions	1075	L5	Comparing fractions to see which is biggest
Change as a percentage	1302	L7	Writing one number as a percentage of another, and working out the change as a percentage

MyReview

15 MySummary

Check out

You should now be able to ...		Test it ➡ Questions
✓ Simplify and compare ratios.	6	1 – 2
✓ Divide a quantity in a given ratio.	7	3 – 4
✓ Use the unitary method to solve direct proportion problems.	7	5 – 6
✓ Solve ratio and proportion problems.	7	7 – 8
✓ Compare proportions.	7	9 – 11
✓ Describe quantities in direct proportion using an equation or a graph.	8	12

Language	Meaning	Example
Ratio	A ratio is the relative size of one value to another	1:5
Simplest form	A ratio in which all units and decimals have been removed and the parts have been divided by their HCF	3 : 6 : 27 becomes 1 : 2 : 9
Proportion	A part given as a fraction of the whole	Success is 99% perspiration and 1% inspiration
Direct proportion	Two quantities are in direct proportion if when one quantity increases, the other increases by the same fractional amount	If 10 units of something costs £180, then 15 units will cost £270.
Unitary method	A technique for solving problems in which you first find the value of one unit	5 apples cost £1.20 So 1 apple costs 24p Hence 3 apples cost 72p

15 MyReview

1 Write each of these ratios in its simplest form.
a 63 : 18 : 54 **b** 3.6kg : 240g

2 Express each of these ratios in the form 1 : *n*.
a 12 : 102 **b** 7 : 1344

3 Divide 500m in the ratio 3 : 5.

4 Divide £80 in the ratio 2 : 5 : 4, give your answers to 1dp.

5 14 bananas cost £2.10, what is the cost of 40 bananas?

6 A driver fills up the tank of her car so it has 75 litres of diesel. On a full tank she can drive 900km.
a How far could her car travel on 65 litres of diesel?
b How much diesel would she need to travel 408km?

7 A small-animal area at a farm has rabbits and guinea pigs.
$\frac{5}{9}$ of the small animals are rabbits.
a What is the ratio of rabbits to guinea pigs?
There are 15 rabbits.
b How many guinea pigs are there?

8 A meringue is made using egg white and sugar in the ratio 6 : 11. The white from one egg weighs 30g. How much sugar do you need to make a meringue with 5 egg whites?

9 Davina is 1.6m, her husband is 15% taller than her.
What is the ratio of Davina's height to her husband's? Write the ratio in its simplest form using whole numbers.

10 Cereal A contains 9g of sugar per 30g serving and Cereal B contains 11g of sugar per 35g serving. Which cereal is higher in sugar?

11 There are 42 members of a maths society. 18 of these are women, what percentage of the society are men?

12 The distance that Joyce has driven is directly proportional to the journey time. Use ratios to complete the table.

Distance travelled, miles		40		100
Journey time, minutes	30	60	90	

What next?

Score	
0 – 5	Your knowledge of this topic is still developing. To improve look at Formative test: 2C-15; MyMaths: 1036 – 1039
6 – 10	You are gaining a secure knowledge of this topic. To improve look at InvisiPen: 153, 191, 193 and 195
11 –12	You have mastered this topic. Well done, you are ready to progress!

282 **Number** Ratio and proportion

MyMaths.co.uk 283

Question commentary

Question 1 – Remind students that units must be the same in a ratio and to make sure they simplify fully.
Question 3 – Remind students that they must divide by the total number of parts in the ratio.
Question 4 – Ask students why their answers do not add up to £80. Who should get the extra penny?
Question 5 – Use the term unit cost in explaining answer.
Question 6 – Encourage students to use the unitary method. In this case discuss fuel efficiency, given as km/litre.
Question 7 – Look out for students confusing ratio and proportion and giving a wrong answer of 5 : 9
Question 8 – Students will first need to calculate the total weight of the egg whites.
Question 9 – Suggest students consider Davina's height as 100% and her husband's as 115% and simplify that ratio.
Question 12 – Ask students to rephrase what direct proportionality means in this case – constant speed.

Answers

1 **a** 7 : 2 : 6 **b** 15 : 1
2 **a** 1 : 8.5 **b** 1 : 192
3 187.5 m, 312.5 m
4 £14.55, £36.36, £29.09
5 £6
6 **a** 780 km **b** 34 litres
7 **a** 5 : 4 **b** 12
8 275 g
9 20 : 23
10 Cereal B
11 57.1%
12

Distance travelled, miles	20	40	60	100
Journey time, minutes	30	60	90	150

15 MyPractice

15 MyPractice

15a

1 Write each of these ratios in its simplest form.

a 0.4 : 3 **b** 0.6 : 5 **c** 1.2 : 4
d 2.5 : 4 **e** 1.8 : 2.8 **f** 3.2 : 4 : 4.8
g 2 : 3 : 4.5 **h** 1.6 : 2.4 : 6.4 **i** 0.6 m : 360 cm
j 2.2 kg : 1100 g **k** £3.75 : 90p **l** 440 ml : 1.4 litres

2 Express each of these ratios in the form 1 : *n*.

a 3 : 15 **b** 8 : 12 **c** 10 : 25
d 9 : 12 **e** 15 : 21 **f** 5 : 19
g 6 : 21 **h** 15 : 100 **i** 7 : 12
j 26 : 9100 **k** 3.4 : 68 000 **l** 2.5 cm : 75 m

15b

3 Divide these quantities in the ratios given.

a Divide 140 km in the ratio 2 : 5 **b** Divide £640 in the ratio 3 : 5
c Divide $728 in the ratio 6 : 7 **d** Divide 30 cm in the ratio 4 : 3
e Divide 7 MB in the ratio 8 : 7 **f** Divide €3000 in the ratio 4 : 2 : 1

4 **a** In a school, the ratio of boys to girls is 7 : 9. There are 371 boys at the school. How many girls are there at the school?

b A metal alloy is made from zinc and iron in the ratio 7 : 2. How much iron is needed to make 792 kg of the alloy?

c Gina draws a pie chart to show how the pupils in her school travel home. The pupils travel home by walking, bus or car in the ratio 7 : 3 : 2. How big are the angles she needs to draw for each of the three sectors?

15c

5 **a** 7 litres of petrol cost £7.91. What is the cost of 35 litres of petrol?

b There are 15 cakes in a box. The cakes weigh 420 g. What is the weight of 25 cakes?

c Rene's mobile phone contract means she pays £3.60 for 150 text messages.

i How much would Rene pay for 500 text messages?

ii How many text messages could she have for £2?

6 A wholesaler advertises the following prices for fruit.

Apricots	
3 kg	£22
10 kg	£70
40 kg	£275

Blueberries	
5 kg	£62.50
12 kg	£150
32 kg	£400

Cherries	
4 punnets	£16.50
24 punnets	£99
60 punnets	£247.50

Which of the prices are in direct proportion? Explain your answer.

15d

7 **a** An alloy is made from lead and iron in the ratio 4 : 7. How much lead needs to be mixed with 8.4 kg of iron?

b The length and width of a netball court are in the ratio 9 : 5. The length of the court is 40.5 m. What is the width of the court?

c The ratio of pop music to rock music CDs in Jermal's collection is 4 : 11. If there are 28 pop music CDs, how many rock music CDs does Jermal have in his collection?

15d

8 **a** $\frac{2}{9}$ of the pupils at a school gym club are boys. What is the ratio of boys to girls at the gym club?

b Roldova scores $\frac{7}{11}$ of the time he shoots at the goal. What is Roldova's ratio of goals to missed shots?

c Hannah is 1.75 m tall. Ursula is 20% shorter than Hannah. What is the ratio of Hannah's height to Ursula's height?

d A bow and set of arrows costs £40.50. The bow is $1\frac{1}{4}$ times the price of the arrows. How much did the bow cost?

15e

9 **a** Copy and complete the table.

b Which is the least healthy food to eat? Explain and justify your answer.

c Which is the most healthy food to eat? Explain and justify your answer.

d How many grams of fat would there be in 250 g of each food? (Give your answers to the nearest gram.)

Type of food	Weight (grams)	Fat content (grams)	%fat
Lamb chops	28	5	
Chocolate bar	26	4.3	
Crisps	35	11.6	
Burger and bun	215	23	
Peas	60	0.4	

15f

10 To convert miles to kilometres, you use the direct proportion relationship

5 miles = 8 kilometres

a Copy and complete this table of values.

b Draw a graph to convert miles to kilometres.

Miles	5	7.5		20
Kilometres	8		16	

c Use your graph to estimate how many kilometres are equivalent to 7 miles.

d Write the equation of your line.

Question commentary

Question 1 – Remind students that ratios must have the same units and be simplified fully.

Question 2 – Warn pupils to take care with part **l**

Questions 3 and **4** – Remind students that they need to divide by the total number of parts in the ratio.

Questions 5 and **6 –** Refer to unit cost. If that is constant then there is direct proportionality.

Question 7 – Ensure students appreciate that these are not dividing by ratio questions.

Question 8 – Re-enforce link between fractions and proportion. Ratios are different.

Questions 9 – Ensure that discussion over which is healthiest includes comparison with amount eaten.

Question 10 – Highlight that when ratio is expressed as 1: *n* that *n* is the gradient of the line.

Answers

1 **a** 2 : 15 **b** 3 : 25 **c** 3 : 10 **d** 5 : 8
e 9 : 14 **f** 4 : 5 : 6 **g** 4 : 6 : 9 **h** 2 : 3 : 8
i 1 : 6 **j** 2 : 1 **k** 25 : 6 **l** 11 : 35

2 **a** 1 : 5 **b** 1 : 1.5 **c** 1 : 2.5 **d** $1 : 1.\dot{3}$
e 1 : 1.4 **f** 1 : 3.8 **g** 1 : 3.5 **h** $1 : 6.\dot{6}$
i 1 : 1.71 **j** 1 : 350
k 1 : 20 000 **l** 1 : 3000

3 **a** 40 km : 100 km **b** £240 : £400
c \$336 : \$392 **d** 17.1 cm : 12.9 cm
e 3.7 Mb : 3.3 Mb
f €1714.29; €857.14; €428.57

4 **a** 477 girls **b** 176 kg **c** 210°, 90°, 60°

5 **a** £39.55 **b** 700 g
c **i** £12 **ii** 83 text messages

6 Blueberries and cherries

7 **a** 4.8 kg **b** 22.5 m **c** 77 CDs

8 **a** 2 : 7 **b** 7 : 4 **c** 5 : 4 **d** £22.50

9 **a, d**

Food	% fat	Fat / 250 g
Chops	17.9%	45 g
Chocolate	16.5%	41 g
Crisps	33.1%	83 g
Burger	10.7%	27 g
Peas	0.7%	2 g

b Crisps are the least healthy because they have the highest proportion of fat.

c Peas are the most healthy because they have the lowest proportion of fat.

10 **a**

Miles	5	7.5	10	20
Kilometres	8	12	16	32

b Conversion graph for miles to kilometres

c 11 miles

d $k = 1.6m$ where k is number of kilometres and m is number of miles

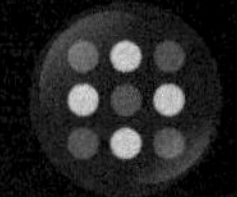

16 Probability

Learning outcomes

P1 Record, describe and analyse the frequency of outcomes of simple probability experiments involving randomness, fairness, equally and unequally likely outcomes, using appropriate language and the 0–1 probability scale (L6)

P2 Understand that the probabilities of all possible outcomes sum to 1 (L6)

P3 Enumerate sets and unions/intersections of sets systematically, using tables, grids and Venn diagrams (L7)

P4 Generate theoretical sample spaces for single and combined events with equally likely, mutually exclusive outcomes and use these to calculate theoretical probabilities (L6/7)

Introduction

The chapter starts by looking at how outcomes can be listed using sample space diagrams and tree diagrams. Mutually exclusive outcomes are then covered before experimental and theoretical probabilities. Simulating experimental probability is then covered before the final section which looks at Venn diagrams and probability.

The introduction discusses the use of probability in clinical trials for things like new drugs. The idea of giving a 'control group' a placebo in order to measure the effect of the real drug on the other patients relies heavily on the idea of probability. What is the probability, for example, of the drug failing to work on a patient who has the disease being looked at? What is the probability of the patient who takes the placebo actually recovering from the illness being tested on despite not getting the real drug?

Mathematicians can help the scientists and doctors solve these kinds of problems by working out the chances of 'false positives' and errors in the trial. This kind of statistical analysis goes way beyond Key Stage 3 mathematics, but the fundamentals are important to understand at this level by analysing the probabilities of single events and looking at the effect of combining probabilities into two or more sequential or related events.

Prior knowledge

Students should already know how to...

- Work with simple fractions and/or decimals
- Understand simple probability

Starter problem

The starter problem looks at the probability of picking numbered cards from a bag. The problem is a two-event situation where you pick one card, replace it and pick a second card. For the first card you pick, there is a 1/3 chance you will get each number. This probability is repeated for the second card and therefore we have three options which will give the desired result: 1 followed by 1, 2 followed by 2 and 3 followed by 3. The probability of 1 followed by 1 is $1/3 \times 1/3 = 1/9$ and this is the same for each of the other two successful results. So our overall probability is $1/9 + 1/9 + 1/9 = 3/9 = 1/3$.

This problem could be solved using a sample space diagram or a tree diagram and students could be invited to solve alternative problems using a similar approach. What if there were four cards in the bag, for example?

Resources

MyMaths

Listing outcomes	1199	Relative frequency	1211	The OR rule	1262
Experimental probability	1264	Venn diagrams 1	1921	Venn diagrams 2	1922
Frequency trees	1954				

Online assessment

Chapter test	2C–16
Formative test	2C–16
Summative test	2C–16

InvisiPen solutions

Averages			454
Experimental and theoretical probability			461
Tree diagrams	463	Simulations	466

Topic scheme

Teaching time = 7 lessons/3 weeks

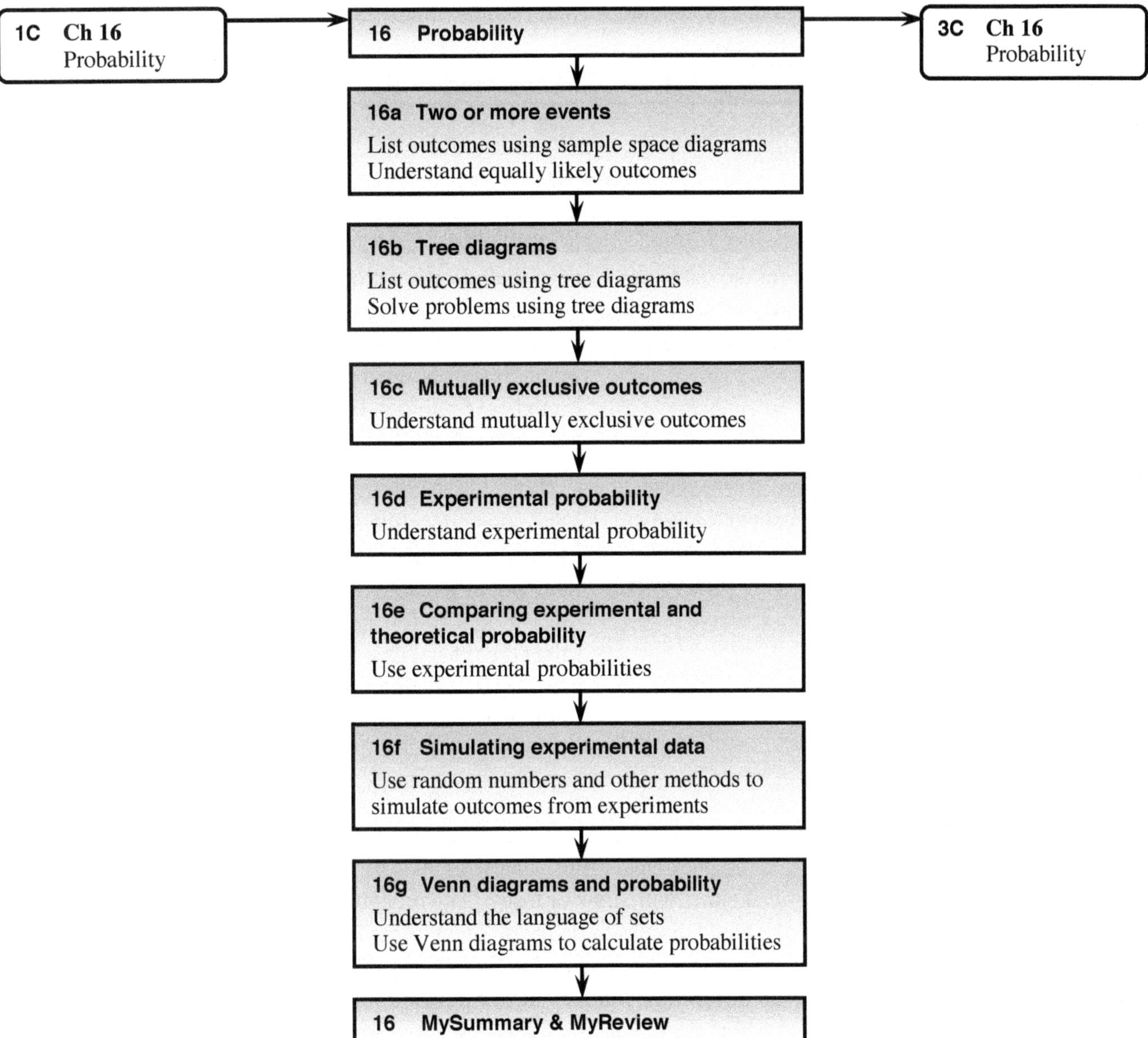

1C Ch 16
Probability
16 Probability
3C Ch 16
Probability
16a Two or more events
List outcomes using sample space diagrams
Understand equally likely outcomes
16b Tree diagrams
List outcomes using tree diagrams
Solve problems using tree diagrams
16c Mutually exclusive outcomes
Understand mutually exclusive outcomes
16d Experimental probability
Understand experimental probability
16e Comparing experimental and theoretical probability
Use experimental probabilities
16f Simulating experimental data
Use random numbers and other methods to simulate outcomes from experiments
16g Venn diagrams and probability
Understand the language of sets
Use Venn diagrams to calculate probabilities
16 MySummary & MyReview

Differentiation

Student book 2A 294 – 309

Likelihood and chance
The probability scale
Equally likely outcomes
Experimental probability
Venn diagrams

Student book 2B 284 – 299

Listing outcomes
Probability
Experimental probability
Theoretical and experimental probability
Sets

Student book 2C 286 – 305

Two or more events
Tree diagrams
Mutually exclusive outcomes
Experimental probability
Comparing experimental and theoretical probability
Simulating experimental data
Venn diagrams and probability

Objectives	
• Identify all the mutually exclusive outcomes of an experiment	(L5)
• Use diagrams and tables to record in a systematic way all possible mutually exclusive outcomes for single events and for two successive events	(L6)

Key ideas	Resources
1 Systematically recording all possible outcomes **2** Being able to interpret and use simple sample space diagrams	Listing outcomes (1199)

Simplification	Extension
Establish meaningful abbreviations for the outcomes and discuss a logical approach to listing. For example, with coins, no heads, then one head, then two heads, etc.	Set the following problem. There are 60 possible meals you can choose if you have one item from each course. There is a choice for each course. No course has more than 5 choices. Two of the courses have the same number of choices. How many courses are there? (4 courses: 2, 2, 3, and 5 choices for each course)

Literacy	Links
The term 'favourable outcomes' is coined to save space and may need some explaining. Favourable outcomes means the total number of ways the event can happen.	Dice that are deliberately biased are called crooked or loaded dice. Dice can be loaded by adding a small amount of metal to one side or by manufacturing the dice with a hollow gap inside so that one side is lighter than the others. One way of testing for a loaded die is to drop it several times into a glass of water. If it is hollow it will float with the hollow side uppermost; if it is weighted, it will sink with the same number always facing down.

Alternative approach

Begin by posing one or two Always/Sometimes/Never true statements such as 'the probability of a football club winning a match is 1/3 because they can either win, draw or lose'; 'The probability of having two boys in a family of two children is ¼'. Students should discuss these in pairs then some key points can be shared with the whole group. Display an example of a sample space diagram, perhaps using the members of the class as a starting point. The first outcome could be whether you are male or female and the second whether you are left or right handed. Use this for discussion before developing the ideas further by working through the lesson.

Checkpoint

1 Two 6-sided dice are rolled and the two numbers are multiplied together. Which two products are the most likely and what is the probability of getting them? (6 and 12, $\frac{1}{9}$)

Starter – Stamps

A package costs 60 pence to post. Ask students how many ways 60 pence can be made using 5p and 7p stamps. ($12 \times 5p, 5 \times 5p + 5 \times 7p$)

Challenge students to find the largest postage amount that cannot be made using 5p and 7p stamps. (23p)

What about 5p and 11p stamps? (39p)

Teaching notes

In a football match there are three possible results for a team, win, lose and draw. If a team plays two matches, how can we list all the possible outcomes?
Discuss suitable ways of abbreviating the outcomes. How can you set about listing all the outcomes in an organised way? Why is this necessary? How many possible outcomes are there for the two matches? ($3 \times 3 = 9$)

How many would it be for 3 matches? (27)

Give an example of the usefulness of a sample space diagram for two independent events in a two-way table. For example, a spinner (1–3) and a dice (1–4). Add the scores.

Ask questions like 'what is the probability of scoring over 5?'

What advantage does the sample space have over simply listing the outcomes? Is it possible to calculate answers to questions like these without a sample space? Would you recommend it?

Plenary

What is the most likely score when you roll two unbiased six-sided dice numbered 1 to 6 and add the scores of the two dice? Would listing all possible outcomes help? Establish that the most likely score is 7, but it is not likely (probability is $\frac{1}{6}$).

Does it make sense that 7 is the most likely outcome, but it is not likely to happen?

Exercise commentary

Stress that probabilities are fractions. Refer to the definition on page 288 to show this. As a result probabilities are best written as fractions, although they can be written as decimals or percentages (but never ratios). Decimals and percentages are useful if having to compare likelihood.

Questions 1 and **2** – Some students may need help deciding how to list outcomes. Part **1b ii** can be used to discuss the difference between HT and TH.

Question 3 – Encourage students to draw a sample space. Point out that a skirt and trousers cannot be worn at the same time!

Question 4 – Encourage abbreviations: C or T/V or S/F, Sp or N. Ask why a sample space as a two way table is not possible.

Question 5 – An example may be needed to help explain what is required: if a 4 and 6 are thrown, then record a 6 in the sample space for the higher score

Question 6 – Encourage students to calculate the number of outcomes without listing. Still allow listing if necessary, but challenge them to see if they can work out how the answer could have been achieved without listing. The word pâté on the set menu may need explaining.

Answers

1 a TT, TH, HT, HH

b i $\frac{1}{4}$ **ii** $\frac{1}{2}$ **iii** $\frac{1}{4}$

c Sum to 1.

2 a TTT, TTH, THT, THH, HTT, HTH, HHT, HHH

b i 3 **ii** 4

c $\frac{3}{8}$

3 $4 \times (1 + 3) = 16$

4 (C cone, T tub) × (V vanilla, S strawberry) × (F flake only, S sprinkles only, B both, N neither)
CVF, CVS, CVB, CVN,
CSF, CSS, CSB, CSN,
TVF, TVS, TVB, TVN,
TSF, TSS, TSB, TSN

5 a

High	1	2	3	4	5	6
1	1	2	3	4	5	6
2	2	2	3	4	5	6
3	3	3	3	4	5	6
4	4	4	4	4	5	6
5	5	5	5	5	5	6
6	6	6	6	6	6	6

b $\frac{7}{36}$

6 a $3 \times 4 \times 4 = 48$

b $3 \times 3 \times 3 = 27$ if the lasagne does not contain cheese
$3 \times 2 \times 3 = 18$ if the lasagne contains cheese

c $2 \times 1 \times 4 = 8$

16b Tree diagrams

Objectives	
• Use tree diagrams to represent outcomes for two or more events (L6)	
Key ideas	**Resources**
1 Systematically recording all possible outcomes **2** Being able to interpret and use simple tree diagrams	Frequency trees (1954) Empty tree diagrams
Simplification	**Extension**
Have available empty tree diagrams so that students can focus on deciding how to label them correctly. If drawing a diagram by hand it is often useful to start at the end of the tree to help ensure enough space is available.	Ask students to look at question **3** and see if they can relate the final probabilities to those along the set of branches followed (the product for independent events). This way of approaching the probabilities can be reinforced with further numerical examples.
Literacy	**Links**
Could tree diagrams be called something else that also is indicative of their appearance? How about tree and leaf diagrams or tree and branch diagrams? Or forks?	On the10th December 1868 the railway engineer J.P. Knight installed the world's first traffic lights outside the British houses of parliament. It employed semaphore arms and red and green gas lamps which were manually turned around by a policeman. The use of red, amber and green to code levels of satisfaction is widely used in the civil service's RAG rating and has been adopted by the Food Standards Agency to indicate the healthiness of foods.

Alternative approach

Emphasise the link with two-way tables and sample space diagrams by taking some of the examples from **16a** and developing them as tree diagrams instead. Question **4** is a particularly good example to work through using a tree diagram instead of a sample space diagram. Discuss also when it is more appropriate to use the different types of diagram.

Checkpoint

1 A family has four children. Assuming that there is an equal chance of having a boy or a girl draw a tree diagram and work out the probability that the family has two boys and two girls. ($\frac{3}{8}$)

Starter – Ice cream

Ask students how many different combinations of ice cream they could make choosing two different flavours from the following seven flavours: vanilla, strawberry, toffee, mint choc, pistachio, coconut and banana.
($\frac{7\times6}{2} = 21$)

What is the probability of choosing an ice cream with strawberry in it? ($\frac{6}{21} = \frac{2}{7}$)

Teaching notes

Explain that in a school register a student can be marked P for present, A for absent or L for late. Ask students to say how many possible combinations of marks there are for the entries for two lessons ($3 \times 3 = 9$) and how to list them all. Anticipate lists, such as PP, PA... or a two-way table. Did anyone come up with a tree diagram? Can they explain how to draw one? Show how one is drawn, focusing on the correct labelling of each tier of branches and the ends of each branch.

Challenge students to draw a tree diagram for two successive tosses of a coin. State that the coin is biased and P(heads) = ¼. What is P(tails)? (1 – ¼ = ¾)
Suppose the coin is tossed twice 64 times. How often do you expect heads to occur on the first toss?
(¼ × 64 = 16)

How often do you expect to get two heads?
(¼× 16 = 4)

Can students say how often the other outcomes are most likely to occur? Show how to find the probability of two heads. (4/64 = 1/16)
Challenge students to find the probabilities of the other three combinations.
(P(HT) = 12/64 = 3/16, P(TH)= 12/64 = 3/16 and P(TT) = 36/64 = 9/16)

Plenary

Explain the scenario in the 'Monty Hall problem' as introduced in the 'Did you know?'. Ask students to say if they would swap envelopes or not. Then discuss the reasons for their choices. After the discussion, ask students again ask if they would swap. The advantage to swapping can be seen by carefully listing all options. Essentially you have a 1/3 chance of initially guessing the car (don't swap) or 2/3 chance of guessingly wrongly but then the unopened envelope is guaranteed to contain the car (do swap).
See the discussion at
http://en.wikipedia.org/wiki/Monty_hall_problem

Exercise commentary

Question 1 – Check that students correctly label each set of branches 'first/second ball' and write the outcomes at the end of the branches 'red/blue/green' or 'R/B/G'.

Question 2 – This will involve a '3 × 2 tree diagram'. Introduce the language of with and without replacement and take the opportunity to discuss the idea of independent events.

Question 3 – Students may require further explanation with part **b**. Ask how students could check their answers to part **c**. Some students may rightly question whether these two events are independent, which could lead to an interesting discussion about traffic planning!

Question 4 – This is an opportunity to discuss expectation, which does not change, though considerations such as having a guaranteed £300 may change students' choices. This also leads into the 'Monty Hall' problem, which is an interesting one to share with students and led to very heated arguments between university level mathematicians!

Question 5 – This question is similar to question **3**. If question **3** has been modelled, encourage students to complete this without support.

Answers

1 **a** Tree diagram showing nine possible outcomes: RR, RB, RG, BR, BB, BG, GR, GB, GG
b **i** $\frac{5}{9}$ **ii** $\frac{4}{9}$

2 **a** Tree diagram showing six possible outcomes: RB, RG, BR, BG, GR, GB
b **i** $\frac{2}{3}$ **ii** $\frac{1}{3}$

3 **a, b** Tree diagram showing four possible outcomes and the number of times you would expect each to occur in 150 journeys:
GG (60), GR (40), RG (30), RR (20)
c **i** 60/150 = $\frac{2}{5}$
ii (40 + 30)/150 = $\frac{7}{15}$
iii 20/150 = $\frac{2}{15}$

4 Students' answers. In both cases the expectation is the same, (100 + 200 + 300) × 1/3 = £200
= 0 × 1/2 + (200 + 400 + 600) × 1/6

5 **a** **i** $\frac{2}{3}$ **ii** $\frac{1}{3}$
b, c Tree diagram showing eight possible outcomes and the number of times you would expect each to occur in 27 throws:
HHH (8), HHT (4), HTH (4), HTT (2), THH (4), THT (2), TTH (2), TTT (1)
d **i** $\frac{1}{27}$ **ii** $\frac{2}{9}$ **iii** $\frac{4}{9}$ **iv** $\frac{8}{27}$

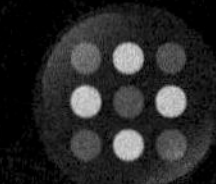

16c Mutually exclusive outcomes

Objectives	
• Identify all the mutually exclusive outcomes of an experiment (L6) • Know that the sum of probabilities of all mutually exclusive outcomes is 1 and use this when solving problems (L6)	
Key ideas	**Resources**
1 Understand mutually exclusive events **2** Understanding that the probability of all possible mutually exclusive events must add to one	The OR rule (1262) Dice
Simplification	**Extension**
Reinforce the idea that mutually exclusive means 'both events can't both happen at the same time'. Give the simple example that when you roll a dice the events (i) less than 3, (ii) over 4, are mutually exclusive because they can't both happen. BUT (i) rolling even, (ii) over 3, can both happen, so these events are not mutually exclusive.	If a coin is tossed n times, what is the probability of obtaining heads every time? $\left(\frac{1}{2^n}\right)$
Literacy	**Links**
'Mutually exclusive' is the key term and it is important students do not confuse this concept with independence. It is useful to ask students if they can come up with examples of events that are not mutually exclusive. Make sure these examples are true and are not simply two dependent events.	An impossible object is a type of optical illusion where the brain interprets a 2D image as a 3D object that cannot exist. Often the brain interprets different parts of the drawing in different ways which are incompatible with each other. There is a demonstration of an impossible object at http://www.michaelbach.de/ot/cog_imposs1/index.html and further examples at http://lookmind.com/illusions.php?cat=1

Alternative approach
Place emphasis on the links between equally likely, mutually exclusive, exhaustive and complementary probability. This holistic approach will encourage the students to focus on the language used and distinguish between all the different terms. Links to complementary probability and mutually exclusive events should be easy to see along with the concept of exhaustive events covering all possibilities.
Checkpoint
1 Matthew puts 12 red balls in a bag, Rosanna adds 4 green balls and David adds some blue balls. Alicia pulls a ball out at random. The probability she picks a blue ball is $\frac{1}{3}$. How many balls did David add to the bag? (8)

Starter – Dice bingo

Ask students to draw a 3 × 3 grid and enter nine numbers from 2 to 12 inclusive, duplicates allowed.

Throw two dice. Students add the scores and cross out the total if they have it in their grid (only one number at a time). The winner is the first student to cross out all their numbers.

Teaching notes

Give examples of events that are mutually exclusive. For example, rolling less than a 3 and rolling 5 or more on a dice. Show how it helps to list all the primitive outcomes that make up an event, {1, 2} and {5, 6}, and checking for common entries.

When two events take place it can be difficult to think about all the possible outcomes. The previous teaching notes used both a list and a tree diagram to look at all possible outcomes. Introduce a sample space that makes use of a two way table for rolling two dice. For example, two four sided dice where the scores are added together. Ask questions that relate to mutually exclusive events.
For example, P(score less than 2 OR over 3). Show how this can be obtained by counting.

This could lead to a discussion about why P(A or B) = P(A) + P(B) for mutually exclusive events. Why doesn't it work for non-mutually exclusive events? How could you fix the problem of counting the intersection twice?

Plenary

When it's sunny people are less depressed. Does this mean that peoples' depression is effected by sunlight? Does this mean that the sunlight is affected by peoples' depression? Are the two dependent? Can you use the term mutually exclusive here? If so, are the events mutually exclusive?

Exercise commentary

Question 1 – Encourage students to discuss each part fully. For example part **a** could be considered as mutually exclusive in our country but not necessarily throughout the world.

Question 2 – Allow students opportunity to disagree and discuss with each other, to establish a clear understanding.

Question 3 – Ask students to justify their conclusion for part **c** based on the properties of numbers, rather than rolling two dice.

Question 4 – Refer students to P(not A) = 1 – P(A), when A is mutually exclusive.

Question 5 – Ask students if they can repeat this question using the biased coin from question **5** on the previous page.

Answers

1 a These are extremely unlikely to happen in the same year but not impossible so not mutually exclusive.

b Yes. The only even prime is 2 and you cannot get this as the sum of three dice.

c No, if you take over a lifetime.
Yes, in a single season.

2 a A and B, B and D, C and D

b Students' answers: odd total and same score, odd and even, a 5 and less than 3, prime and multiple of 4

3 a

	Even	Odd
Even	E, E	E, O
Odd	O, E	O, O

b $\frac{3}{4}$

×	Even	Odd
Even	E	E
Odd	E	O

c $1 - \frac{3}{4} = \frac{1}{4}$

4 a Tree diagram showing eight possible outcomes: TTT, TTH, THT, THH, HTT, HTH, HHT, HHH

b i $\frac{3}{8}$ **ii** $\frac{4}{8} = \frac{1}{2}$

c i $\frac{4}{8} = \frac{1}{2}$ **ii** $1 - \frac{1}{2} = \frac{1}{2}$

d There is one outcome that is 3 heads (HHH) and one outcome that is no heads (TTT) so the probability of either event is the same.
There are three outcomes that give 2 heads and three outcomes that give 1 head. So the probability is the same.

5 a i 16 **ii** 4

b 32, 5

c Number of outcomes for n tosses = 2^n
Number of outcomes with exactly one head = n

Objectives	
• Compare estimated experimental probabilities with theoretical probabilities, recognising that – if an experiment is repeated the outcome may, and usually will, be different (L5) – increasing the number of times an experiment is repeated generally leads to better estimates of probability (L5)	

Key ideas	Resources
1 Understand that experimental results can provide an indication of probability **2** Begin to recognise the importance of the size of data and the validity of the conclusions	Relative frequency (1211) A pre-prepared frequency table Drawing pins Playing cards Numbered cards Piece of text

Simplification	Extension
A pre-prepared frequency table for question **1** would help students structure this question and provide a scaffold for drawing further frequency tables.	How could you estimate the probability of becoming Prime Minister? What sort of information might you wish to find? For example, number of Prime Ministers, number of males and females, age at the time of becoming PM. What would increase your probability of becoming Prime Minister? For example, joining a political party, watching the news, being on the school council, etc.

Literacy	Links
Relative frequency is another phrase which means an experimental probability. Ask students what kind of probability has been dealt with so far. Probability can either be approached theoretically of experimentally.	A substitution cipher conceals a message by consistently replacing one letter with another. This results in the frequency of the encrypted and original letters being the same. In English text, the most common letter is E, followed by T and A. Code breakers compare the relative frequencies in regular and the encrypted text to try to match original and substituted letters. An example is the cipher used in the Babington plot, which is featured in the 'Did you know?'. For more information on the Babington plot see http://www.simonsingh.net/The_Black_Chamber/maryqueenofscots.html and for information on letter frequencies see http://www.simonsingh.net/The_Black_Chamber/letterfrequencies.html

Alternative approach
Pose the question: what is the probability of being left-handed? Students may want to estimate answers to this and share thoughts on it, before a simple experiment about this takes place. Ask students if they are left-handed, and then use this information to suggest what the probability is from the class data. Now ask students to consider its validity. Ask how the result might be improved. Share discussion thoroughly with the group before informing them that it that it is generally 12% of males and 10% of females that are found to be left-handed. So overall there is a probability of 0.1 to 0.12 of being left-handed.

Checkpoint
1 300 hundred light bulbs were tested and 5 failed before burning for 100 hours. What is the probability that a light bulb will fail before burning for 100 hours? ($\frac{1}{60}$)

Starter – Higher or lower

Using either a set of playing cards or a set of numbered cards, show students the first card and ask whether they think the next card will be higher or lower.

Repeat several times. (As necessary, agree the values of face cards in advance).

This can be extended by being more specific. For example, asking what the chance of the next card being a square number.

Teaching notes

How likely is a drawing pin to land on its side or its head? How could the probability be discovered? Discuss the fact that only the experimental probability could be calculated. How many trials should be undertaken?

Conduct the drawing pin experiment to see what the experimental probability of 'side' and 'head' are? How should the experiment be conducted? Give students a few initial unrecorded trials to allow them to consider the problem. Ideas such as 'dropping from the same height' or 'dropping onto the same surface' might be considered. Once the rules are established, conduct the experiment and record the results.

Analyse the results. How many trials did students use? How many are needed for a reliable estimate? Discuss the fact that more trials mean a better estimate. Is it fair to pull all the results together for the whole class?

Plenary

The order of frequency for letter usage in the English language in descending order is ETAONIRSH. Choose a piece of English text and check this. The class could be subdivided and the whole class's results pooled. Why might the class result not agree?
The longer the text, the more reliable the findings.

Exercise commentary

Question 1 – Some students may think the actual times are significant. What would be the use of knowing these? (Finding average arrival time)

Question 2 – This will take time. Consider restricting this to a part of the page or have students pool results from different sections. EAOIU is the actual order of frequency for vowels in descending order for the English language.

Question 3 – Encourage students to use their experience from question **2** to improve their method for this question.

Question 4 – Encourage some reasoning to be shown. What if this book only had 199 pages? Does that produce a similar probability?

Question 5 – Highlight that historical data is a form of experimental probability.

Answers

1 $\frac{4}{22}$

2 **a** Accept answers in the region of the following

Vowel	a	e	i	o	u
Frequency	99	166	94	96	28

b 166/483= 0.344

3 **a** It is likely to be close, unlikely to be exactly the same because of sampling variability.

b Students' answers

c Students' answers, likely to vary.

d Make a larger sample by combining class results for non-duplicate pages.

4 **a** $\frac{11}{20}$

b No, pages containing 1 are not evenly distributed, they in groups 10–19, 100–199

5 **a** Divide the number of people in UK struck by lightning in past 70 years by 60 million.
Results may differ for other counties that are more or less prone to thunderstorms.

b Use historical weather records for the given day, or group of days centred on the birthday.

c Limited 'evidence' as only last 2–3 seasons relevant. Bookmakers' odds may reflect a pool of people's views (and the size of bets placed).

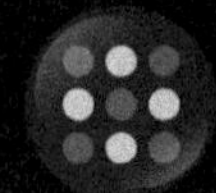

16e Comparing experimental and theoretical probability

Objectives

- Interpret results involving uncertainty and prediction (L6)
- Compare experimental and theoretical probabilities in a range of contexts (L7)

Key ideas

1. Understand the similarities and the differences between theory and experiment in probability
2. Understand that repeating experiments while perhaps resulting in similar outcomes may not be identical

Resources

Experimental probability (1264)
Introducing probability (1209)

Calculators
Dice
Blue tack
Counters in two different colours
Spreadsheet for results
Random generator

Simplification

Allow students to generate their own data for question **1** and ask them to calculate probabilities after 1, 4, 10, 20, 40, 100 trials. How does the reliability of their results change?

Extension

Would securing pieces of blue tack to the face of three sides of a dice cause it to be biased? Investigate. Consideration should be given to how the blue tack is secured and to which faces. Also to the number of trials. Also, is the dice biased to start with?

Literacy

Discuss whether experimental probability can ever become theoretical. The key issue is the number of trials. Experimental probability will tend to theoretical as the number of trials increase.

Links

Many superstitions are based on the belief that a particular action can bring good or bad luck and so increase the chance of an event happening. For example, breaking a mirror is supposed to bring seven years bad luck and catching a falling leaf on the first day of autumn prevents catching a cold during the winter. How many other superstitions do the class know? The origins of some common superstitions are explained at http://www.allsands.com/history/originscommons_ssd_gn.htm

Alternative approach

Use a simple experiment with the whole class, modelling and recording the data on a spreadsheet. For example, have a closed bag of 10 counters/cubes made up of 2 colours. Pose the question what is the probability of picking a red one? Draw out and replace a counter 10 times asking students to suggest probabilities, then enter the results on a spreadsheet showing a frequency bar chart of the two colours. A second spreadsheet can show the trials as a scale in 10s against an estimated probability. Now add a further 10 trials, perhaps done by two of the students, and carry on. The second chart will show clearly how there is a tendency to a consistent result the more trials take place. A random generated simulation can be set up on excel to replicate the experiment in order to speed the trials up.

Checkpoint

1. Arjun has a spinner made from 5 equal sections. He spins it 20 times. Here are his results.
   5 1 4 2 1 4 3 1 5 2 2 1 3 1 5 1 1 2 3 1
   Arjun calculates the experimental probability of getting a 1 and says this proves his spinner is biased.
   a What is the experimental probability of getting a 1? (P(1) = 0.4)
   b Is Arjun right? (No, not enough trials)
   c How could he make his case stronger? (Increase the number of trials)

Starter – Probability jumble

Write a list of anagrams on the board and ask students to unscramble them. Possible anagrams are

ANCHEC, COMETOU, TEENV, LIRAT, RODMAN, SLIPSOMBIE, KELLIY, TRAINCE

(chance, outcome, event, trial, random, impossible, likely, certain)

This can be extended by asking students to make a probability word search.

Teaching notes

Discuss the fact that a fair coin does not necessarily give 50 heads and 50 tails after being thrown 100 times. Why is this? Although 50 heads and 50 tails is the most likely outcome, it's not likely to happen. Encourage students to use the term random in their explanations.

What do students think is an estimate of the probability of 50 heads and 50 tails; choose from $\frac{22}{25}, \frac{8}{25}, \frac{2}{25}$. $\left(\frac{2}{25}\right)$

Look at the example in the student book relating to the ancient burial.

Discuss the sample sizes in parts **a** and **b**.

How should probability be expressed? Options are fractions, decimals, percentages, ratio. Discuss the advantages and disadvantages of each method. For example, decimals allow an easy comparison between different events. Note that ratio is generally not used in maths for probability, but is normally used on horse racing.

Plenary

Examine a graph of experimental probability for the throwing of one coin and recording the number of heads. Record results after every five trials. Use a decimal value for experimental probability. What do you notice about the graph?

Exercise commentary

Question 1 – It is important to discuss what constitutes proof. How many trials are necessary? There is a useful simulation on www.mymaths.co.uk of rolling a biased dice that illustrates this in 'Introducing probability' lesson (1209).

Question 2 – The term 'placebo' may need defining. Calculators could be used to find the percentage success. Could drug B (70%) be more effective than drug A (75%)? Why is the number of trials important?

Question 3 – Writing the probabilities as unsimplified fractions is likely to offer the most straightforward approach. This enables results to be easily compared. Note that the number 'zero' is shown in the illustration but not included in the record of results.

Question 4 – What does an increased number of trials mean for the experimental probability?

A more reliable answer, but not an exact answer. Eventually though it does produce the same answer rounded to an appropriate degree of accuracy.

Answers

1 **a** Students' answers. Outcomes HH, HT, TH, TT so P(1 head) = 2/4 = 1/2 ≠ 1/3

b Estimated probability = 21/40 = 0.525. Differs from 1/3 by 0.19167 whilst a single event contributes 1/40 = 0.025. Therefore data provides strong evidence but it is not a proof.

2 Estimated rates of cure are:
drug A 72/96 = 0.750 (1/96 = 0.010)
drug B 7/10 = 0.700 (1/10 = 0.100)
placebo 17/36 = 0.472 (1/36 = 0.0.278)
Both drugs appear beneficial but the results for drug B are less reliable. A better trial would randomly assign equal numbers of patients to the three groups.

3 **a** 12/37 for each group

b

	1–12	13–24	25–36	Total
1	38.3%	36.7%	25.0%	100%
2	28.3%	31.7%	36.7%	96.7%
3	26.7%	28.3%	45.0%	100%
4	33.3%	30.0%	36.7%	100%

c Wheel 3 gives a large number of high scores (27/60 – 12/37 = 0.126 compared to 1/60 = 0.17). Since cheaper to test than replace recommend more trials.

d Wheel 2, sum of probabilities = 58/60; two 0s must have occurred (the house won twice).

4 Students' answers. Not a proof but would provide much more compelling evidence. A list of outcomes/sample space or tree diagram could be used to give a proof.

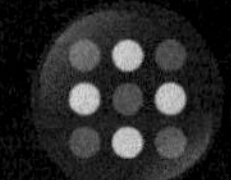

16f Simulating experimental data

Objectives	
• Appreciate the difference between mathematical explanation and experimental evidence (L7) • Justify the mathematical features drawn from a context and the choice of approach (L7)	
Key ideas	**Resources**
1 Understand simulation and carry out simulation **2** Understand that the more simulations that are carried out, the better the estimate	Experimental probability (1264) Calculators with a random function List of random numbers sheet Website http://www.random.org/ Dice
Simplification	**Extension**
Provide students with a list of random integers from 1 to 10. How can this help to decide a coin toss? When working through the exercise ensure students understand that they should work through in order without missing or repeating a position.	Four cars arrive at a crossroads. Each car has an equal probability of turning right, left or going straight on. Use a simulation to find an estimate of the probability that three of the cars turn down the same road. Note that a car can't do a 'U turn'. Theoretical probability is $\frac{8}{27}$. (0.30 to 2 dp). Simulation should give a close approximation if the number of trials is sufficient.
Literacy	**Links**
Asking if anyone has tried out any kind of simulator could lead to a stimulating discussion! For example, flight or golf simulators. Ask students to come up with their own definition of a simulation. Football players are sometimes accused of simulating. What does that mean?	Understanding how the Earth's future climate may change is now a pressing task given man's influence. Simulations are used but these make several assumptions and the effects of small changes to them need to be tested to be sure of any results. The distributed computing project climateprediction.net allows ordinary people to donate idle time on their personal computers to helping to solve this challenge. For details and how to get involved see http://www.climateprediction.net/index.php

Alternative approach

Focus on the links between theoretical probability, experimental probability and simulated experimental data. Take a coin, for example. The theoretical probability of a head is $\frac{1}{2}$. Get the students to then carry out an experiment to work out the experimental probability of getting a head. Repeat using a random number generator on a calculator or computer (or using a table of random numbers) to simulate the experiment. Compare and contrast the results of all three methods. Paired work and/or extensive class discussion can be used rather than working directly through the exercise.

Checkpoint

1 Chloe says 'I can simulate the roll of a fair six sided dice by using the random function on my calculator and multiplying by 6. Writing the number in the unit's column will simulate a dice roll.' Is she correct?

(No, because she will never get a 6 and will get a 0. She needs to add 1 for it to work.)

Starter – BIDMAS bingo

Ask students to draw a 3 × 3 grid and enter nine numbers from 20 to 40 inclusive, duplicates allowed.

Using a calculator (or dice), generate three random numbers from 1 to 6. Students cross out one of their numbers if they can make it using the numbers and the standard arithmetic operations; they should write their calculation in the square.

The winner is the first student to cross out all numbers.

Teaching notes

Simulation is used to help model traffic flow and reduce congestion on the roads, see the extension activity. Look at an example of traffic flow at a set of lights or road junction. Use probabilities that are multiples of $\frac{1}{6}$ at each junction. How can a calculator be used to help model the roll of a dice? Note that some calculators actually have a 'dice function'. Other calculators will have to use the [R#] or similar function.

Run the simulation. Where do the first 10 cars end up? What do you predict will happen for the first 40 cars? Run the simulation and encourage students to comment on the results.

If the simulation was run again, would the results be totally different?

How can the calculator be used to generate the outcome of heads or tails from a coin? What about an integer from 1 to 10?

Plenary

Investigate the types of random numbers you can generate using the website http://www.random.org/

Exercise commentary

Question 1 – Encourage students to explore the random function on their calculator. Part **b ii** may need discussion of an efficient rule. Also show that spreadsheets also have a random function and can be programmed to do the same.

Question 2 – Emphasise that the process is random, which means that a simulation won't necessarily give the same result twice. What advantage do you gain from a greater number of trials? Students could share data in order to increase the number of trials. Warn students that in order to be able to answer question **3**, they must record all their results and not just tally.

Question 3 – Discuss if their results did not show a run of 3 heads, does this mean that their estimate should be zero?

Question 4 – The graphs may need some explanation of what they show. The coin is tossed 300 times; does this give a reliable number of trials? If the experiment is thought to use a biased coin, is it biased towards heads or tails?

Question 5 – This question lends itself to using a spreadsheet. Show students the COUNTIF function, which will enable them to produce graphs for different probabilities at a touch of a button.

Answers

1 Students' answers

a Heads if tenths digit 0-4, else tails (expect ~5 heads)

b **i** Heads if first tenths 0–5, else tails (expect ~6 heads)

ii Heads if tenths digit 0–2, tails if 3–8, else repeat (expect ~3 heads)

2 Students' answers

a Estimated P(heads) = no. heads ÷ 10 (expect 0.60 ± 0.15)

b Very, very unlikely given the random nature of coin tosses.

c Estimated P(heads) = total no. heads ÷ 100 (expect 0.60 ± 0.05)

3 **a** Students' answers (fair coin P = $\frac{1}{4}-\left(\frac{1}{2}\right)^{10}$)

b Probability to increase with P(heads)

4 Students' answers

Distribution is skewed towards low numbers of heads; suggests coin is biased P(heads) < 0.5.

(Estimate P(heads) = 117/300 = 0.39, actual 0.4; compare 140/300 = 0.47 for fair coin)

5 Students' answers.

Reliable results will require repeat simulations for the same value of P(heads). Expect the centre of the distribution to be at 10 × P(heads), with an increasingly asymmetric distribution as P(heads) moves away from 0.5.

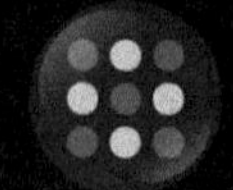

16g Venn diagrams and probability

Objectives
• Enumerate sets and unions/intersections of sets systematically, using tables, grids and Venn diagrams (L7)

Key ideas	Resources
1 List elements in sets, understand the language of sets and understand the notation associated with sets **2** Work with sets and Venn diagrams to calculate probabilities	The OR rule (1262) Venn diagrams 1 (1921) Venn diagrams 2 (1922) Pre-prepared Venn diagrams Calculators

Simplification	Extension
Use ready prepared Venn diagrams to illustrate. See http://www.cram.com/flashcards/venn-diagrams-notation-3411256 for examples.	Generate some data that has 3 sets and ask students to come up with the resulting Venn diagram. If the three sets are A, B and C ask them to use a Venn diagram to illustrate A ∩ B U C etc.

Literacy	Links
The key terms are universal set, union, intersection and complement. All of these will be new, as will their symbolic representations. Help students to remember these definitions by remembering that intersection means AND and union means OR.	Venn diagrams can be used to illustrate statistical data. http://www.mathsisfun.com/sets/venn-diagrams.html has some interesting examples. Students could then generate their own data from a group of their friends.

Alternative approach

A two-way table provides a good way to link previous work on sample spaces, with this work on Venn diagrams. For example consider a two-way table showing two types of chocolate split into 'like' and 'dislike':

	Like B	Dislike B
Like A	18	6
Dislike A	12	15

How can this information be translated into a Venn diagram? Students should be able to see that the four numbers in the table match the four regions in the Venn diagram and they can use this to complete the diagram. Follow-up questions can then be used such as 'What is the probability that…?'

Checkpoint

1 Represent the following information on a Venn diagram.
Ω={integers from 1 to 20}, M={Multiples of 4}, F={Factors of 24}
List the elements of
a F' ∩ M
b F' U M'

(F' ∩ M = {16,20}; F' U M' = {5,7,9,10,11,13,14,15,17,18,19})

Starter – How many people?

In a recent survey, 18 people said they liked rugby, 13 people said they liked hockey and 5 people said they liked both. 4 people said they liked neither. How many people were asked? (30)

Similar logic problems can be given like this and the level of challenge varied accordingly. For example, you might have no-one who liked both, or no-one who liked neither.

Teaching notes

Students need to be able to comprehend the general language of sets and the structure of the Venn diagram and explain, in words, what each region represents. Encourage them to do this first rather than diving straight into the questions. They should produce a glossary of terms since much of the language will be unfamiliar.

Walk the students through the examples to illustrate the key points before give them time to work through questions **1** and **2**.

In question **3**, encourage students to link all their work together and provide a full written explanation of what they are doing.

Plenary

Return to the starter problem. Can the students now draw a Venn diagram to illustrate the results of the survey? Questions can also be asked such as 'what is the probability that a person chosen at random likes hockey?' ($\frac{13}{30}$)

Exercise commentary

Question 1 – Instruct students to draw Venn diagrams for each part of the question. When they then list required elements, they will take them from the same part of the Venn diagram.

Question 2 – Highlight the subtle difference from Question **1**, the totals are listed in the Venn diagram, and not the individual elements. Encourage the students to shade Venn diagrams to show the different questions. Have them familiarize themselves with the idea that visually the patterns are the same.

Question 3 – Allow students to use calculator. Make sure they show their working clearly.

Question 4 – Discuss whether event A and event B are mutually exclusive or independent. Is it possible to tell from the Venn diagram?

Answers

1 **a** **i** $A = \{3, 6, 9, 12\}$
ii $A' = \{1, 2, 4, 5, 7, 8, 10, 11\}$
iii $B' = \{1, 2, 4, 5, 6, 8, 12\}$
iv $A \cap B = \{3, 9\}$
v $A \cup B = \{3, 6, 7, 9, 10, 11, 12\}$
vi $A \cap B' = \{6, 12\}$

b **i** $A = \{1, 2, 3, 5, 8, 13\}$
ii $A' = \{21, 34, 55\}$
iii $B' = \{5, 13, 21, 34, 55\}$
iv $A \cap B = \{1, 2, 3, 8\}$
v $A \cup B = \{1, 2, 3, 5, 8, 13\}$
vi $A \cap B' = \{5, 13\}$

c **i** $A = \{1, 3, 5, 7, 9, 11, 13, 15\}$
ii $A' = \{2, 4, 6, 8, 10, 12, 14, 16\}$
iii $B' = \{1, 4, 6, 8, 9, 10, 12, 14, 15, 16\}$
iv $A \cap B = \{3, 5, 7, 11, 13\}$
v $A \cup B = \{1, 2, 3, 5, 7, 9, 11, 13, 15\}$
vi $A \cap B' = \{1, 9, 15\}$

2 **a** $P(S \cap T) = \frac{10}{25} = \frac{2}{5}$

b Region $S \cap T'$ shaded (Circle S but not the overlap with T)

c $\frac{8}{25}$

d Region $S' \cap T'$ shaded

e $\frac{3}{25}$

3 8 students

4

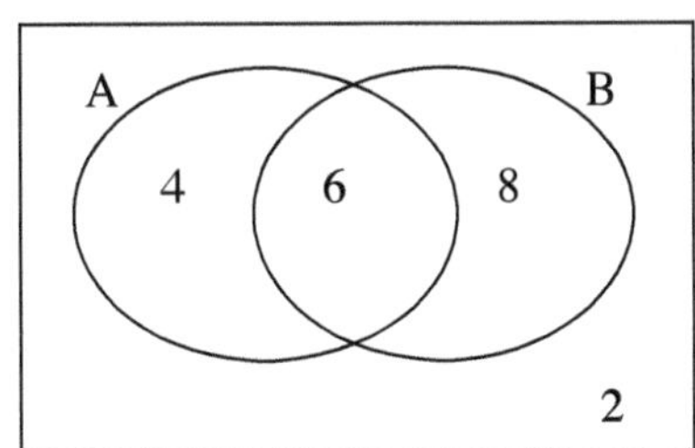

Key outcomes	Quick check
Systematically list the outcomes for combined events.	A catering company offers hot lunches. There are three choices of main; chicken, duck or vegetarian, which come with a choice of three types of potato; roast, new or wedges. Make a list of all the possible combinations. (CR, CN, CW, DR, DN, DW, VR, VN, VW)
Use tree diagrams to list outcomes and calculate probabilities.	The probability of it raining for any of the next three days is 30%. Draw a tree diagram and work out the probability that it will be dry for at least two of the next three days. (78.4%)
Identify mutually exclusive events and calculate their probabilities.	A bag contains red, blue and green counters. The probabilty of choosing a red counter at random is ¼ and a blue of ⅓ and there are 20 green counters. What is the probability of choosing a green counter and how many blue counters are there? (5/12, 16 blue counters)
Estimate probabilities using experiments and compare the results to theoretical models.	Rashid has twenty cards, from a pack of cards. He cuts the pack 20 times and never gets a diamond, so he assumes there can be no diamonds. Is he right? There are 8 clubs. What is the probability of drawing a club? (No, 0.4)
Use random numbers to simulate real world data.	Based on the last 10 results the probability that Aston Ham win their next game is 0.3. Explain how you can use your calculator to simulate whether they win at least 4 of their next 10 matches. (Use the random function where > 0.7 represents a win)
Use Venn diagrams to calculate probabilities.	Draw a Venn diagram based on the following information. A union B has 36 elements. $P(A \cap B) = 0.2$, $P(A) = 0.5$, $P(B) = 0.6$, $P(A' \cap B') = 0.1$. ($A \cap B'=12$, $A \cap B=8$, $A' \cap B=16$, $A' \cap B'=4$)

MyMaths extra support

Lesson/online homework			Description
Listing outcomes	1199	L6	Listing outcomes from two events using sample space diagrams
Relative frequency	1211	L7	Understanding relative frequency

Question commentary

Question 1 – Students should be methodical to avoid missing combination out, they should be aware of repeating combinations as, e.g. blue and black is the same as black and blue in this case.

Question 2 – Differences should be positive, the answer for **b** is $\frac{8}{36}$, but students should simplify.

Question 3 – Students will need to allow themselves plenty of space to draw the diagram, the non-simplified answer to **b** is $\frac{3}{9}$

Question 4 – Open up for a class discussion. Encourage students to debate before you state answer.

Question 5 – The total number of visitors is 177. Two dp is sufficient for part **a**, in part **b** the answer is 148.31 (2 dp) but need to round down to nearest whole person. It is worth discussing here if this is a suitable approach. There may be a reason why more women went to the library on the first day which doesn't apply on the second. How could they improve the estimate? For example, they could continue the survey over a week/month, etc.

Question 6 – Discuss how you could investigate further if the dice is fair, e.g. more trials.

Question 7 – Encourage students to suggest either using a scientific calculator or spreadsheet.

Question 8 – Ensure students have learned the new symbols associated with Venn diagrams

MyReview

16 MySummary

Check out

You should now be able to ...

Check out		Test it ➡ Questions
✓ Systematically list the outcomes for combined events.	6	1 – 2
✓ Use tree diagrams to list outcomes and calculate probabilities.	6	3
✓ Identify mutually exclusive events and calculate their probabilities.	6	4
✓ Estimate probabilities using experiments and compare the results to theoretical models.	7	5 – 6
✓ Use random numbers to simulate real world data.	7	7
✓ Use Venn diagrams to calculate probabilities.	7	8

Language	Meaning	Example
Sample space	A list of all the simplest outcomes of an event or combination of events	If you toss 2 coins the outcomes are HH, HT, TH, TT
Independent probability	Two events are said to be independent if and only if the occurrence of one event happening has absolutely no effect on the chances of the other event happening	What you have for tea and who wins the next World Cup
Mutually exclusive outcomes	Outcomes are mutually exclusive if they cannot happen at the same time	Rolling a dice once and getting a 6 and a 2
Relative frequency	The empirical probability of an event, based on the actual frequency relative to the total possible frequencies	If you have 10 hurdles to jump and succeed at jumping 8, your relative frequency is 80%
Experimental probability	P(event) = $\frac{\text{number of times the event occurs}}{\text{number of trials}}$	P(heads) = $\frac{28}{50}$ = 0.56 = 56%
Simulation and Model	Simulation is the imitation of the operation of a real-world process or system over time. The act of simulating something first requires that a model be developed; this model represents the key characteristics of the selected physical or abstract system or process. The model represents the system itself, whereas the simulation represents the operation of the system over time	Computer simulations are a key feature of most of the working world and the gaming industry

16 MyReview

1 Jack has a drawer of loose socks. There are lots of black, grey and brown socks. He selects two socks at random. List of all the possible combinations he could choose.

2 Two fair dice are thrown.

a Construct a sample space diagram which shows the difference between the two scores.

b Calculate the probability of getting a difference of 2.

3 The letters from the word CAT are written on individual cards. One card is selected at random then replaced and another card is selected.

a Draw a tree diagram to show all the possibilities outcomes for the two cards.

b What is the probability of drawing the same letter twice?

c What is the probability of drawing the letter C at least once?

4 Two dice are thrown. Are the following pairs of events mutually exclusive?

a *'One of the dice shows a 2.'* and *'The sum of both dice is 9.'*

b *'The product of the two dice is odd.'* and *'The sum of the two dice is even.'*

c *'The difference between the two dice is 1.'* and *'The sum of the two dice is greater than 4.'*

5 A librarian observes that 72 men and 105 women use his library on one particular day.

a Estimate the probability that a visitor to the library is a man.

b The next day there are 250 visitors to the library. Estimate how many will be women.

6 A dice is rolled 20 times and 8 sixes are scored.

a Calculate the experimental probability of scoring a six

b Assuming the dice is fair what is the theoretical probability of scoring a six?

c Does this prove the dice is not fair? Explain your answer.

7 A biased coin has P(heads) = 0.6

a Explain how you could simulate tossing the coin 10 times.

b Explain how you could estimate the probability of getting more than 5 heads in 10 tosses of the coin.

8 **a** Draw a Venn diagram to show the following sets.

Ω = {Whole numbers from 1 to 16}

A = {Factors of 48}

B = {Multiples of 3}

b List the elements in

i A **ii** B **iii** A′

iv A ∩ B **v** A ∪ B **vi** A ∩ B′

c Find the probability of each of the sets listed in part **b**.

What next?

Score		
0 – 3		Your knowledge of this topic is still developing. To improve look at Formative test: 2C-16; MyMaths: 1208 – 1210, 1262, 1264 and 1334
4 – 6		You are gaining a secure knowledge of this topic. To improve look at InvisiPen: 454, 461, 463 and 466
7 – 8		You have mastered this topic. Well done, you are ready to progress!

Answers

1 (Black, Black), (Black, Grey), (Black Brown) (Grey, Grey), (Grey, Brown), (Brown, Brown)

2 a

	1	2	3	4	5	6
1	0	1	2	3	4	5
2	1	0	1	2	3	4
3	2	1	0	1	2	3
4	3	2	1	0	1	2
5	4	3	2	1	0	1
6	5	4	3	2	1	0

b $\frac{2}{9}$

3 a

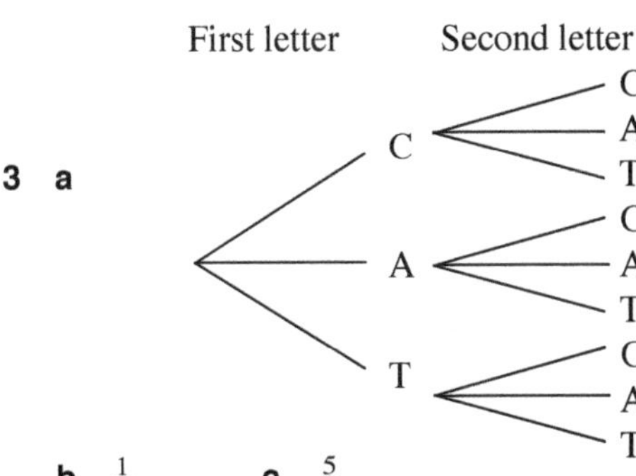

b $\frac{1}{3}$ **c** $\frac{5}{9}$

4 a Yes **b** No **c** No

5 a 0.41 **b** 148 women

6 a 0.4 **b** $\frac{1}{6}$ or 0.167

c No, although we did not get the expected results this does not prove it is unfair: the result of each throw is random and you won't necessarily get a six exactly $\frac{1}{6}$ of the time.

7 a Generate a random number, $R_\#$.
If $R_\# \le 0.6$ heads, otherwise tails.
Repeat 10 times.

b For the sample in **a**, count a success if number of heads > 5.
Generate many samples and estimate P ≈ number of success ÷ number of samples.

8 a

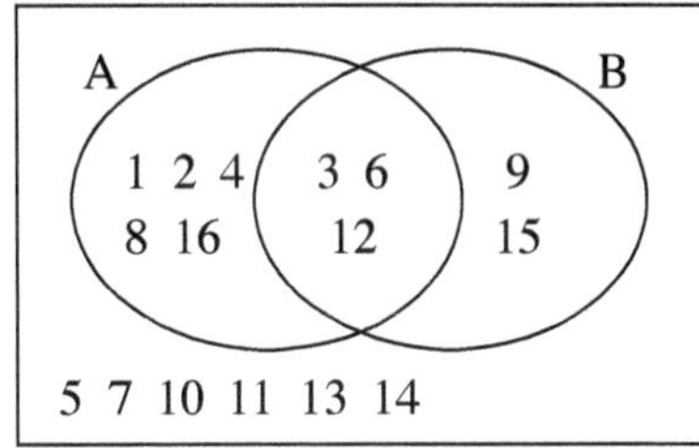

b i A = {1, 2, 3, 4, 6, 8, 12, 16}

ii B = {3, 6, 9, 12, 15}

iii A′ = {5, 7, 9, 10, 11, 13, 14, 15}

iv A ∩ B = {3, 6, 12}

v A ∪ B = {1, 2, 3, 4, 6, 8, 9, 12, 15, 16}

vi A ∩ B′ = {1, 2, 4, 8, 16}

c i $P(A) = \frac{8}{16} = \frac{1}{2}$ **ii** $P(B) = \frac{5}{16}$

iii $P(A') = \frac{8}{16} = \frac{1}{2}$ **iv** $P(A \cap B) = \frac{3}{16}$

v $P(A \cup B) = \frac{10}{16} = \frac{5}{8}$ **vi** $P(A \cap B') = \frac{5}{16}$

16 MyPractice

16a

1 A spinner with 3 equal sections coloured red, green and white is spun twice.
- **a** List all the possible outcomes.
- **b** In how many of these do you get a red and a green?
- **c** In how many of these do you not get a white?

2 Two fair dice are thrown.
- **a** Construct a sample space diagram which shows the product of the scores showing on the two dice.
- **b** What is the probability that the product is at least 20?

3 A lunch menu includes 3 starters, 4 main courses and 2 desserts.
How many different menu combinations are there for someone who can eat anything on the menu?

16b

4 A bag contains one black, one white and one purple ball which are identical except for their colours. A ball is taken out, its colour noted and then replaced before a second ball is taken out.
- **a** Draw a tree diagram to show the possibilities of the colours of the two balls.
- **b** **i** What is the probability that the two balls are a black and a white?
  ii What is the probability that the two balls are the same colour?

16c

5 A white and a black dice are thrown together and the events A to D are defined as
- A the sum of the scores is even
- B the white and the black dice show different scores
- C the total score is less than 3
- D the difference between the scores is not more than 1.

Explain why these pairs of events are mutually exclusive or not
i A and B **ii** B and D **iii** B and C

6 The faces of a regular tetrahedron are labelled 1–4 and those of a regular octahedron 1–8. They are both rolled and the number on the bottom face is counted.
- **a** List all possible outcomes.
- **b** Use your list to calculate the probabilities that
  i both show prime numbers **ii** only one shows a prime number.
- **c** Without looking at your list, what is the probability that neither shows a prime number?

16d

7 Jorge is making stakes which should be about 1.3 m long.
The lengths of a number of stakes he has made are listed below.
1.27, 1.24, 1.27, 1.31, 1.30, 1.26, 1.25, 1.29, 1.32, 1.26, 1.28
1.31, 1.25, 1.27, 1.26, 1.35, 1.26, 1.24, 1.27, 1.27, 1.25, 1.27
- **a** Estimate the probability that one of his stakes is longer than 1.3 m.
- **b** Explain how a better estimate of this probability could be made.

8 How could you estimate the following probabilities?
- **a** A vowel chosen at random in French is an `a'.
- **b** The National Lottery has a single jackpot winner in the next draw.
- **c** Seeing at least 1 six when 3 dice are thrown together.

16e

9 A trainee in a bank is surprised at how often transactions he sees start with the digit 1. He does a quick tally of 100 transactions.

first digit	1	2	3	4	5	6	7	8	9
frequency	33	19	14	10	6	5	3	4	6

Do you think 1 to 9 are equally likely to occur as the first digit of transactions?

16f

10 An otherwise fair dice is biased so that 5 and 6 are both three times as likely to occur as the digits 1–4.
- **a** What are the individual probabilities of obtaining the numbers 1–6?
- **b** Use a calculator to simulate rolling such a dice three times. Write down the rules which you use and your results.
- **c** Repeat your simulation nine more times and use the results to estimate the average sum of the three scores.
- **d** How could you improve the accuracy of your estimate?

16g

11 Rufus is investigating his classmates. He counts the number of students with red hair (R), freckles (F), both or neither. The Venn diagram shows his results.
- **a** **i** On a copy of the diagram, shade the region R · F.
  ii Find P(R · F).
- **b** **i** On a second copy of the diagram, shade the region R′ · F.
  ii Find P(R′ · F).

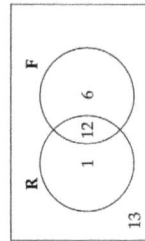

R F
1 12 6
13

Question commentary

Questions 1 and **2** – Probability answers are best given as fractions. Make sure students are systematic in processing information.

Question 3 – Encourage students to arrive at an answer without generating a complete list.

Question 4 – Ask students to compare this with a tree diagram showing the ball not being replaced.

Question 5 – Allow students to discuss in pairs.

Question 6 – Suggest students draw a sample space to help calculate answers.

Question 9 – Point out that larger transactions are generally less common than smaller ones.

Question 10 – The probabilities are out of ten, so can easily be given as decimals

Question 11 – Tell students that each question is asking for intersection, which are shown as '.' in question.

Answers

1 a RR, RG, RW, GR, GG, GW, WR, WG, WW

b 2 **c** 4

2 a

×	1	2	3	4	5	6
1	1	2	3	4	5	6
2	2	4	6	8	10	12
3	3	6	9	12	15	18
4	4	8	12	16	20	24
5	5	10	15	20	25	30
6	6	12	18	24	30	36

b 8/36 = 2/9

3 3 × 4 × 2 = 24 menu choices

4 a Tree diagram showing nine possible outcomes: BB, BW, BP, WB, WW, WP, PB, PW, PP

b i 2/9 **ii** 3/9 = 1/3

5 a i For example 1 and 3 (different numbers which are either both even or both odd)

ii 1 and 2, 2 and 3, 3 and 4, 4 and 5 or 5 and 6 (either way round).

iii C needs a total score <3 which means both dice must show a 1, so B cannot happen.

6 a

	1	2	3	4	5	6	7	8
1	1, 1	2, 1	3, 1	4, 1	5, 1	6, 1	7, 1	8, 1
2	1, 2	2, 2	3, 2	4, 2	5, 2	6, 2	7, 2	8, 2
3	1, 3	2, 3	3, 3	4, 3	5, 3	6, 3	7, 3	8, 3
4	1, 4	2, 4	3, 4	4, 4	5, 4	6, 4	7, 4	8, 4

b i 8/32 = 1/4 (Primes are 2, 3, 5 and 7 so there are 4 in every other row.)

ii 16/32 = 1/2

c 1 – (1/2 + 1/4) = 1/4

7 a 4/22 = 2/11

b By taking a larger sample on which to base the estimate

8 a Count the relative frequency of the letter a amongst vowels in a typical piece of French text.

b Looking at the data (available on the internet) on how many times there has been a single jackpot. For a particular draw - once it is known whether it is a rollover, you could improve the estimates (in rollovers more people enter so the chance of a single winner is lower).

c You could run an experiment or a simulation a number of times. Or calculate: 6 × 6 × 6 possibilities, 5 × 5 × 5 contain no six, so P = (216 – 125)/216 = 1 – $(5/6)^3$ = 91/216.

9 No, if equal likely each first digit would occur ~11 times, whereas low digits occur more often.

10 a P(1) = P(2) = P(3) = P(4) = 1/10, P(5) = P(6) = 3/10

b Students' answers

Score 1 if tenths digit is 1, likewise 2, 3, 4; score 5 if 5, 6 or 7, score 6 if 8, 9 or 0

c Expectation 129/10

d By taking more trials your estimate is more likely to be close to the true average.

11 a i Region $R \cap F$ shaded (overlap of R and F)

ii 12/32 = 3/8

b i Region $R' \cap F$ shaded (circle F but not the overlap with R)

ii 6/32 = 3/16

Related lessons		Resources	
Multiplication	11a	Divide decimals by whole numbers	(1008)
Division	11b	Multiply decimals by whole numbers	(1010)
Scale drawings	12d	Scale drawing	(1117)
Direct proportion	15c	Proportion	(1037)
		Examples of food packaging with 'free range', 'fair trade' or 'organic' labels	

Simplification

Concentrate on just the outside area in task **1**. In task **2**, encourage students to work together to find possible areas before proceeding to plan the layout.

Tasks **3** and **4** involve proportion and could be simplified by reducing the number of parts or changing some of the values.

Extension

Allowing students to assume that caged and free-range hens lay the same amount of eggs per day and that farmers would be able to sell all the eggs they produced regardless of type, students could explore each of the free-range farms and calculate the number of caged hens the farmer could keep to make more profit than they do selling their eggs as free-range.

Links

Students could look at the various rules for other produce labelled as 'free-range', 'fair trade' or 'organic'. Lots of information on this and other ethical foodstuffs can be found on the internet. An example can be found at http://www.co-operativefood.co.uk/food-ethics/ and a quick search in Google will throw up lots of other examples. Students could also keep a diary of their eating to record when they eat products that are labelled as ethical.

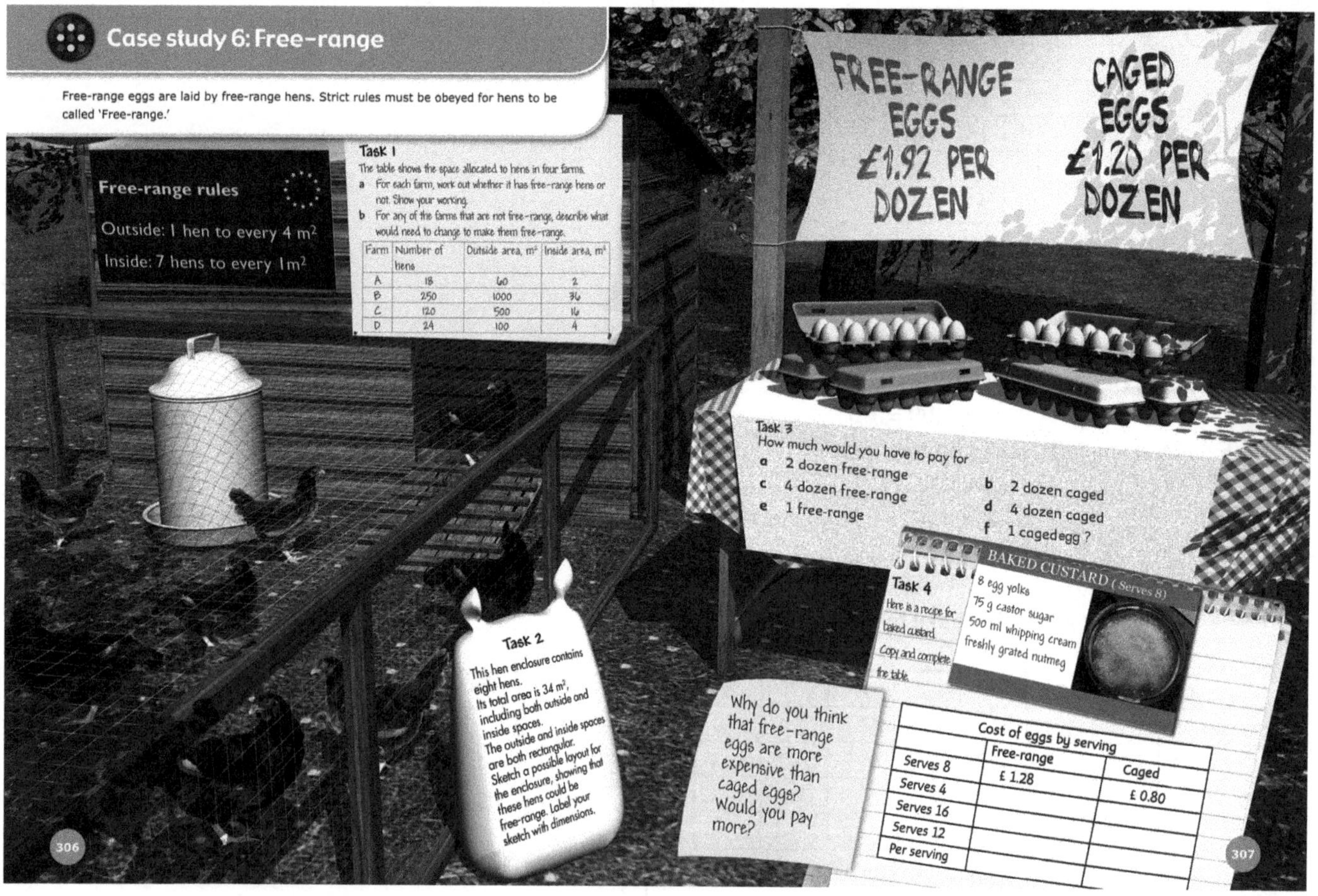

Case study 6: Free-range

Free-range eggs are laid by free-range hens. Strict rules must be obeyed for hens to be called 'Free-range.'

Free-range rules

Outside: 1 hen to every 4 m^2

Inside: 7 hens to every 1 m^2

Task 1

The table shows the space allocated to hens in four farms.

a For each farm, work out whether it has free-range hens or not. Show your working.

b For any of the farms that are not free-range, describe what would need to change to make them free-range.

Farm	Number of hens	Outside area, m^2	Inside area, m^2
A	18	60	2
B	250	1000	36
C	120	500	16
D	24	100	4

Task 2

This hen enclosure contains eight hens.
Its total area is 34 m^2, including both outside and inside spaces.
The outside and inside spaces are both rectangular.
Sketch a possible layout for the enclosure, showing that these hens could be free-range. Label your sketch with dimensions.

FREE-RANGE EGGS £1.92 PER DOZEN

CAGED EGGS £1.20 PER DOZEN

Task 3

How much would you have to pay for

a 2 dozen free-range

b 2 dozen caged

c 4 dozen free-range

d 4 dozen caged

e 1 free-range

f 1 caged egg ?

Task 4

Here is a recipe for baked custard. Copy and complete the table.

BAKED CUSTARD (Serves 8)

8 egg yolks
75 g castor sugar
500 ml whipping cream
freshly grated nutmeg

Why do you think that free-range eggs are more expensive than caged eggs? Would you pay more?

Cost of eggs by serving	Free-range	Caged
Serves 8	£ 1.28	£ 0.80
Serves 4		
Serves 16		
Serves 12		
Per serving		

306

307

Teaching notes

Many students are interested in animal welfare and how animals farmed for produce are kept. Mathematics can be used to explore some of these issues by considering the extra cost of free-range eggs versus eggs from caged hens. Not only can students explore the legislation that enables a farmer to label their eggs as free-range, they can compare costs and discuss the reasons why people may choose to pay more for free-range eggs.
Ask students whether they have heard of free-range eggs and what their understanding of the term is. Explain that there are rules in place to determine whether a farmer can sell their eggs as free-range.

Task 1

Ask students how big they think 4 m^2 is. Consider the size of the classroom to get a feel for relative size. Look at farms A to D. Discuss with the students how to decide whether they are free-range. Make sure they take account of both the outside and inside dimensions.

Task 2

Look at the farm in the picture and the dimensions given on the feed bag. Ask students to plan with a partner a possible layout of the farm pen so they can consider the hens to be free-range.

Task 3

Now look at the costs of the different types of eggs. Ask students to find the answers to questions **a** to **f**. Discuss the different strategies used.

Task 4

Ask students to spend a few minutes looking at the baked custard recipe with a partner. How would you calculate the cost of the eggs for the different amounts of the pudding? Share ideas then ask students to complete the recipe card.

Answers

1 **a** A: No; B: Yes; C: No; D: Yes

b A: Outside area to 72 m^2, inside to 2.57 m^2

C: Inside area to 17.14 m^2

2 Check students' drawings

3 **a** £3.84

b £2.40

c £7.68

d £4.80

e 16 pence

f 10 pence

4 64 pence/40 pence

£2.56/£1.60

£1.92/£1.20

16 pence/10 pence

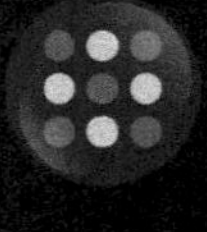

MyAssessment 4

These questions will test you on your knowledge of the topics in chapters 13 to 16.
They give you practice in the questions that you may see in your GCSE exams.
There are 75 marks in total.

1 For each of these sequences
- **i** find the next two terms (3 marks)
- **ii** find the position-to-term rule. (3 marks)

a 4, 7, 10, 13, … **b** 19, 14, 9, 4, … **c** -1, 6, 13, 20, …

2 For each of these geometric sequences
- **i** find the next two terms (3 marks)
- **ii** find the position-to-term rule. (6 marks)

a -8, 4, -2, 1, … **b** 0.06, 0.12, 0.24, 0.48, … **c** 125, 50, 20, 8, …

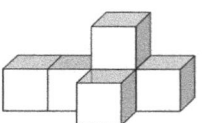

3 The diagram shows the construction of a 3D shape made from six cubes. On grid paper
- **a** draw a plan view (2 marks)
- **b** draw a front elevation view (2 marks)
- **c** draw a side elevation view (from the right hand side). (2 marks)

4 For these two prisms calculate the
- **i** surface area (5 marks)
- **ii** volume (4 marks)

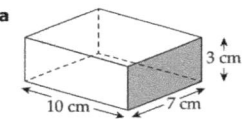

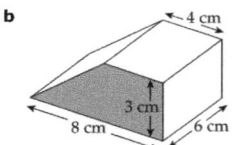

a

b

5 Many food items are sold in tins. For the example shown
- **a** work out the surface area of the tin (3 marks)
- **b** calculate the volume of the tin. (2 marks)

Use $\pi = 3.14$

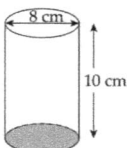

6 Ordinary brass is an alloy of copper and zinc in the ratio 7 : 3 while cartridge brass has a ratio of 13 : 7.
- **a** Which brass has the greater proportion of copper? (3 marks)
- **b** If 10 kg of copper is used to make cartridge brass how much zinc is required? Show your working. (2 marks)

7 Workmen are making a lean concrete mixture of cement, sand and aggregates in the ratio 1 : 3 : 6. They use 2 bags (50 kg) of sand.
- **a** How much cement do they need for the mixture? (2 marks)
- **b** How much concrete do they make altogether (in kilograms)? (3 marks)
- **c** They now mix a new batch of richer concrete in the ratio 6 : 5 : 8. For this they use 2 bags of cement (50 kg).
  - **i** How much sand do they use? (2 marks)
  - **ii** How much aggregate do they need? (2 marks)
  - **iii** How much concrete is made altogether? (2 marks)

8 A photographic image, 8 cm by 6 cm is being enlarged in the ratio of 6 : 5.
- **a** What are the dimensions of the new image? (2 marks)
- **b** What is the scale factor of enlargement? (2 marks)

9 A six-sided dice is thrown and a 2p coin is tossed at the same time.
- **a** What are such events called? (1 mark)
- **b** List all of the possible outcomes in a sample space diagram. (3 marks)
- **c** What is the probability of getting (4, head)? (1 marks)
- **d** Calculate the probability of getting (odd number, tail). (2 marks)

10 Three events are associated with the outcome of rolling an ordinary dice.

A a prime number **B** a multiple of 6 **C** a factor of 8

Which pairs of events are mutually exclusive? (3 marks)

11 An ordinary six-sided dice is rolled 100 times and the scores noted in a frequency table.

Score	1	2	3	4	5	6	Total
Frequency	18	15	12	21	18	16	100

- **a** Determine the experimental probability of obtaining a four. (1 mark)
- **b** How does this compare with the theoretical probability of obtaining a four? (1 mark)
- **c** How could you improve the experimental probabilities? (1 mark)
- **d** How many 'fours' might you expect if you threw the dice 500 times? (1 mark)

12 Consider the sets A and C defined in question **10**.

For the following combined sets **a** $A \cup C$ **b** $A' \cap C'$
- **i** draw a Venn diagram and shade the region containing the set (4 marks)
- **ii** calculate the probability of the set. (2 marks)

MyMaths.co.uk

Mark scheme

Questions 1 – 6 marks

a i 1 16, 19 **ii** 1 $3n + 1$
b i 1 -1, -6 **ii** 1 $-5n + 24$ or $24 - 5n$
c i 1 27, 34 **ii** 1 $7n - 8$

Questions 2 – 9 marks

a i 1 -0.5, 0.25
ii 2 Multiply previous term by -0.5
b i 1 0.96, 1.92
ii 2 Multiply previous term by 2
c i 1 3.2, 1.28
ii 2 Multiply previous term by 0.4 (or divide previous term by 2.5)

Questions 3 – 6 marks

a 2

b 2

c 2

Questions 4 – 9 marks

a i 2 242 cm^2
ii 3 210 cm^2
b i 2 156 cm^3
ii 2 108 cm^3

Questions 5 – 5 marks

a 3 351.9 cm^2 (accept 352 cm^2)
b 2 502.4 cm^3 (accept 502 cm^3)

Questions 6 – 5 marks

a 3 Ordinary brass 70% copper
Cartridge brass 65% copper
b 2 70/13 kg = 5.4 kg of Zn

Questions 7 – 11 marks

a 2 $\frac{2}{3}$ bag or 0.67 bag or 16.7 kg cement
b 3 $6\frac{2}{3}$ bags or 166.7 kg concrete
c i 2 $1\frac{2}{3}$ bags or 41.7 kg sand
ii 2 $2\frac{2}{3}$ bags or 66.7 kg aggregate
iii 2 $6\frac{1}{3}$ bags or 158.3 kg concrete

Questions 8 – 2 marks

a 2 9.6 cm by 7.2 cm
b s.f. = 1.2

Questions 9 – 6 marks

a 1 independent
b 3 (1,H), (2,H), (3,H), (4,H), (5,H), (6,H)
(1,T), (2,T), (3,T), (4,T), (5,T), (6,T)
c 1 1/12 or 8.3%
d 2 3/12 or ¼ or 25%

Questions 10 – 3 marks

A and B are mutually exclusive.
2, 3 and 5 are the outcomes that are prime numbers. (A)
6 is the only outcome that is a multiple of 6. (B)
A and C are not mutually exclusive. 2 is common to both sets.
B and C are mutually exclusive.
6 is the only outcome that is a multiple of 6. (B)
1, 2 and 4 are the outcomes that are factors of 8. (C)

Questions 11 – 4 marks

a 1 21/100 or 21%
b 1 16.7%
c 1 Roll the dice more times
d 1 Between 80 and 85 (accept 75-90)

Questions 12 – 6 marks

$\Omega = \{1, 2, 3, 4, 5, 6\}$
$A = \{2, 3, 5\}$; $C = \{1, 2, 4\}$

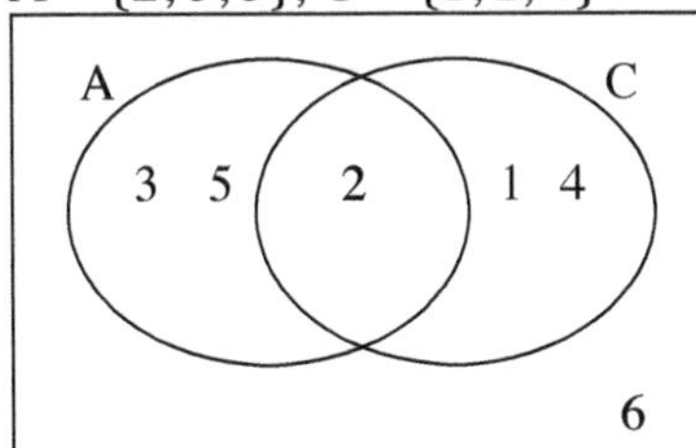

a i 2 Students' Venn diagrams as above with area **inside** circles A and C shaded
ii 1 $P(A \cup C) = \frac{5}{6}$
b i 2 Students' Venn diagrams as above with area **outside** circles A and C shaded
ii 1 $P(A' \cap C') = \frac{1}{6}$

Learning outcomes	
DF2 Select and use appropriate calculation strategies to solve increasingly complex problems	(L7)
DF3 Use algebra to generalise the structure of arithmetic, including to formulate mathematical relationships	(L7)
DF5 Move freely between different numerical, algebraic, graphical and diagrammatic representations (for example, equivalent fractions, fractions and decimals, and equations and graphs)	(L7)
DF7 Use language and properties precisely to analyse numbers, algebraic expressions, 2D and 3D shapes, probability and statistics	(L7)
RM2 Extend and formalise their knowledge of ratio and proportion in working with measures and geometry, and in formulating proportional relations algebraically	(L7)
RM6 Interpret when the structure of a numerical problem requires additive, multiplicative or proportional reasoning	(L7)
RM7 Explore what can and cannot be inferred in statistical and probabilistic settings, and begin to express their arguments formally	(L7)
SP1 Develop their mathematical knowledge, in part through solving problems and evaluating the outcomes, including multi-step problems	(L7)
SP2 Develop their use of formal mathematical knowledge to interpret and solve problems, including in financial mathematics	(L7)
SP4 Select appropriate concepts, methods and techniques to apply to unfamiliar and non-routine problems	(L7)

Introduction	Prior knowledge
The chapter consists of a sequence of five spreads based on the theme of a school trip to France. This allows questions to cover a wide range of topics taken from algebra, statistics, geometry and number. The questions are word-based and often do not directly indicate what type of mathematics is involved. Therefore students will need to work to identify the relevant mathematics and in several instances which of a variety of methods to apply before commencing. This approach is rather different from the previous topic based spreads and students may require additional support in this aspect of functional maths.	The chapter covers many topics; lessons which contain directly related material include • 1f • 2a, c, e • 4e • 5a • 8d, e, f • 9a • 10e • 11g • 12d, f • 14c, d • 15a

Using mathematics

The student book start of chapter suggests three areas of everyday life where aspects of the ability to apply mathematical ideas prove highly valuable.

Fluency: If you run a small business you need to be able to do your accounts. Are you making a profit? Is the money you make from sales bigger than all your overheads – wages, rent, materials…? People often use spreadsheet type programs to help them to do their accounts. However, should you trust what they say? It helps if you have a 'feel' for what the right answer should be and if you can quickly do simpler versions of the calculations yourself as checks.

Mathematical reasoning: Sometimes finding the answer to a mathematical problem is the easy part. The hardest part can be convincing other people that your solution is the right one. One way to help persuade other people is by choosing the best graph to show your results. You also need to be able to back up your results with carefully reasoned explanations.

Problem solving: Controlling a robot is surprisingly complex. It requires breaking down into smaller tasks in order to be manageable. Each of these smaller tasks might need skills from several different areas of mathematics. To control a robot's movements you will need to use geometry, coordinates and algebra to represent instructions.

Topic scheme

Teaching time = 5 lessons/2 weeks

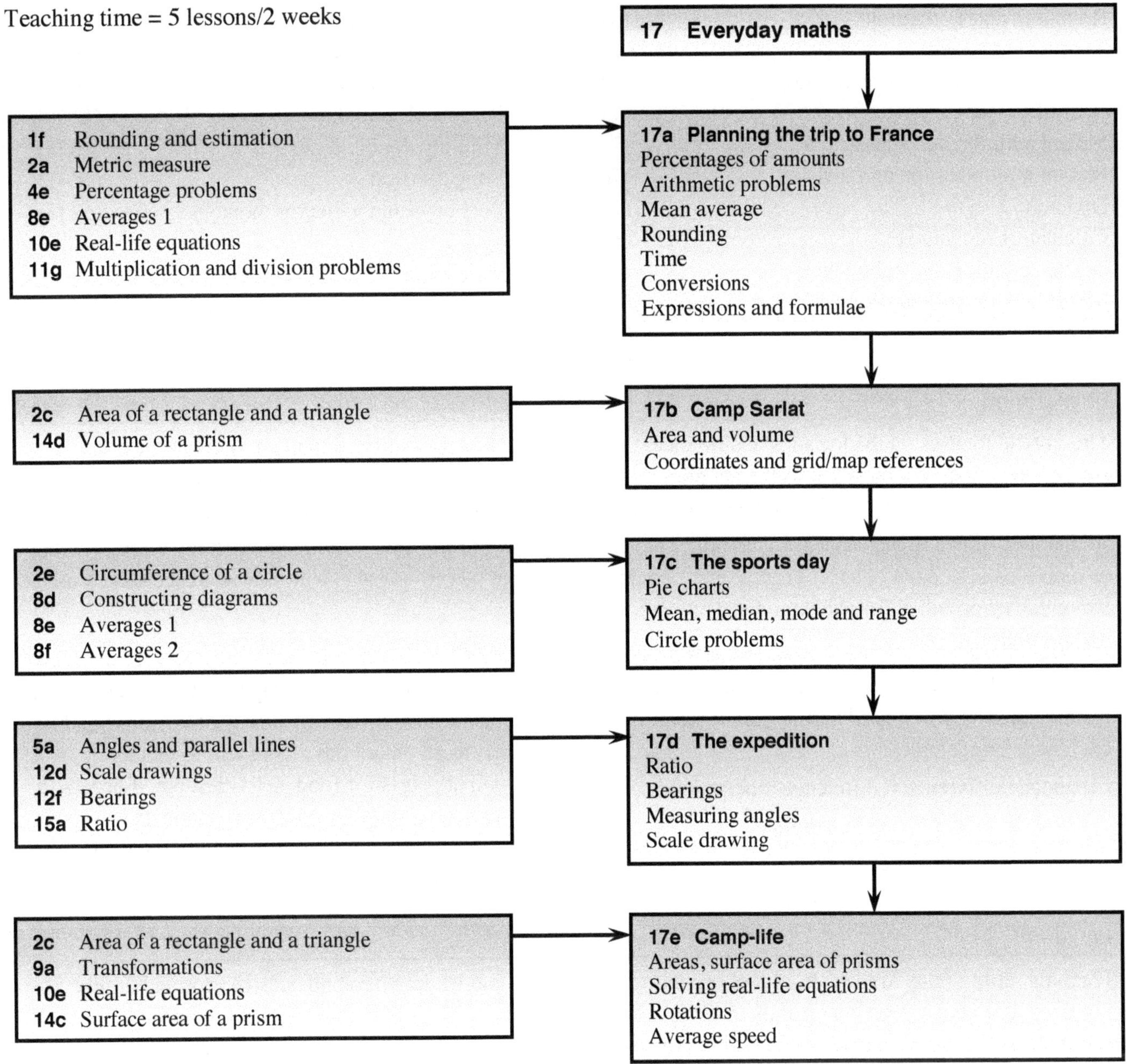

17 Everyday maths
1f Rounding and estimation
2a Metric measure
4e Percentage problems
8e Averages 1
10e Real-life equations
11g Multiplication and division problems
17a Planning the trip to France
Percentages of amounts
Arithmetic problems
Mean average
Rounding
Time
Conversions
Expressions and formulae
2c Area of a rectangle and a triangle
14d Volume of a prism
17b Camp Sarlat
Area and volume
Coordinates and grid/map references
2e Circumference of a circle
8d Constructing diagrams
8e Averages 1
8f Averages 2
17c The sports day
Pie charts
Mean, median, mode and range
Circle problems
5a Angles and parallel lines
12d Scale drawings
12f Bearings
15a Ratio
17d The expedition
Ratio
Bearings
Measuring angles
Scale drawing
2c Area of a rectangle and a triangle
9a Transformations
10e Real-life equations
14c Surface area of a prism
17e Camp-life
Areas, surface area of prisms
Solving real-life equations
Rotations
Average speed

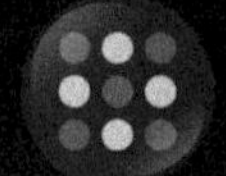

17a Planning the trip to France

Related lessons		Resources	
Rounding and estimation	1f	Rounding decimals	(1004)
Imperial measures	2b	Metric conversion	(1061)
Fractions, decimals and percentages	4f	Converting measures	(1091)
Real-life graphs	6f	Rules and formulae	(1158)
Mental addition and subtraction	7c	Multiply double digits	(1025)
Mental multiplication and division	7d	Long division	(1041)
Division	11b	Best buys and value for money	(1243)
Calculators in context	11d	Calculators	
Written addition and subtraction	11f	Travel brochures	
Multiplication and division problems	11g		
Direct proportion	15c		
Comparing proportions	15e		

Background

This spread focuses on the logistics and finances of the trip and largely exercises number skills. Issues surrounding costs, deposits and exchange rates may be familiar to some students from family holidays and this knowledge can be used to both enliven discussion and provide a source of illustrative examples.

As the first spread in the chapter it is important to establish how the students should approach the work, whether as individuals, as pairs or small groups, etc., should they work at their own pace, will they be expected to start straightaway or will an introduction be given, etc.

Simplification

Provide students with a reminder of some of the mathematics they will need during the problem solving exercise. For example

$$\text{percentage difference} = \frac{\text{difference} \times \text{percentage}}{\text{original}}$$

$$\text{speed} = \frac{\text{distance}}{\text{time}}$$

Extension

Provide students with a holiday brochure and ask them to calculate an approximate cost for two adults and two children to go on holiday. Ask them to include approximate costs for food, activities, etc. If access to the internet is available, encourage students to investigate total costs of flights including insurance and all surcharges, etc.

Links

Planning a trip of any kind takes a lot of organisation and links can be drawn to both school trips and family holidays. It is also a good opportunity to discuss with students the idea of planning any kind of expenditure such as saving to buy a new games console, shopping on the high street and working out if you have enough money to buy your food and drink in the local café.

Teaching notes

Invite pairs of students to imagine that they are a teacher planning a school trip and ask them to suggest what they need to consider. Focus on the costs involved: how should they calculate deposits, deal with exchange rates, etc. The student book can be used as a prompt. The subsequent discussion should concentrate on generic approaches, what is required and a suitable method, rather than specific details.

Supply students with some example calculations and ask them to explain how they would complete them. Total cost £3782, 20 students: cost per student, 15% deposit, £435 to be paid in Euros at £1= €1.28. Ask how they decide whether to use mental, written or calculator methods: can they give two pros and two cons for each method? Also ask how they would go about checking their answers (against an approximation, using an inverse operation, is it reasonable, is it to an appropriate degree of accuracy?)

Ask students if they can supply some handy hints for doing calculations, especial using mental methods. These can be collected on the board as a reminder for students as they work through the spread.

Exercise commentary

Question 1 – Encourage students to make a rough estimate before they do an exact calculation. Do their totals look about right? Encourage students to check their calculations at least twice.

Question 2 – Does it matter if you use the cost of the whole trip or the student's individual cost to find the percentage difference? What will the figure tell you? Encourage students to write down the calculation they are using. If the train is 15% more expensive than the coach, then is the coach 15% cheaper than the train?

Question 3 – Can proportion or ratio be used here to work out value for money? Why is it awkward to compare the total cost per student? Suggest using the unitary method.

Question 4 – What part of the timetable do you need to begin by looking at? Is there more than one option? Why do some trains have very long journey times? Can you foresee any problems in the timings, for example, long delays? (Three and a half hours in London in the middle of the night!)

Question 5 – When totalling the time, encourage students to show how they are summing the hours and minutes. What time is it in the UK when you arrive at Sarlat? Do you include the waiting time in your answer?

Question 6 – When converting units, ensure that the result feels right. Note that kilometres are a bit shorter than miles.

Question 7 – Will you include the waiting time in your speed calculation?

Question 8 – The handling charge must be worked out in pounds before converting the total to Euros in order to compare costs.

Answers

1 **a** **i** Coach: £9676 Train: £11 200
ii Coach: £194 Train: £224
b The train is the more expensive by £30.
2 16%
3 Coach: £38.70 per day Train: £37.33 per day
4 The 23:00 from Birmingham arrives at St. Pancras at 01:02 and the 04:30 from St. Pancras to arrive at Sarlat at 16:50.
5 17:00 hours
6 1492 km or 933 miles
7 88 km/h or 55 mph
8 £1550 + 8% = €1975.32 so paying in euro will be cheaper

17b Camp Sarlat

Related lessons		Resources	
Area of a rectangle and a triangle	2c	Area of a triangle	(1129)
Area of a parallelogram and trapezium	2d	Area of rectangles	(1084)
Graphs of linear functions	6a	Coordinates 2	(1093)
		Local area map	
		Small name cards	

Background

This spread takes up the theme of the school trip and arriving at the camp where they have to organise the accommodation and familiarise themselves with the campsite. The mathematics involves areas of rectangles and compound shapes, arithmetic with decimals, the use of six-figure coordinates (with direct cross-curricular links to geography) and logical reasoning.

Simplification	Extension
For question **1**, provide integer dimensions and possibly draw in the squares to allow the link between multiplication and counting squares to be reinforced. For question **2**, consider providing students with five counters, these could be labelled with the students names to allow them to be arranged to solve the problem.	Ask students to write their own logic puzzle, similar to that in question **2**. How should you begin designing the problem? How can you make sure you give enough information to solve the problem? Try the problem on a partner.

Links

Working out areas from plans forms a link to design subjects and to architecture and town planning in the real world. Work on maps, coordinates and grid references links directly to geography and navigation in the wider sense.

Teaching notes

The first question involves the multiplication and division of decimals. It will be useful revision to ask students to explain how to do this and how to check their answer. Test their understanding by asking them to calculate the area of a rectangular tent. Ask how they think this is related to how many people the tent will comfortably sleep. Is the ground area the only thing that needs to be considered? What about the tent's shape?

Question **2** is likely to be new to the students in the context of mathematics. It may help to provide a similar example and ask students to provide a 'method' for solving the puzzle and for verifying any solution.

Questions **3** to **6** involve interpreting a map and finding locations. Using a local area map, ask students to specify the positions of local landmarks. Can they do this is such a way that they don't refer to other locations on the map? This may be familiar from geography and the method used in the questions is easily tied in with the use of coordinates in mathematics. The map is also a scale drawing and students could be asked to think about how they could calculate real-life distances based on either the local area or campsite maps. One way to approach this is by asking students to say how they would go about creating an accurate map of the school. This could be a teamwork activity.

Exercise commentary

Question 1 – What shapes can you split the tent up into? How do you find the area of a triangle? Is there a way to find a missing length when you know the area without using trial-and-improvement? Consider looking at an arrow diagram to show how area is calculated for a rectangle.

Question 2 – Encourage students to look at all the information to begin with. Which piece is immediately useful? Can students rule out certain answers using the available information? Drawing a sketch may well help solve the problem.

Question 3 – Six-figure grid references are more commonly used in geography rather than maths. What tends to be used in maths to describe position? (Coordinates and bearings)

Questions 4 – Encourage students to be as accurate as possible, using a ruler to mentally subdivide the specific grid into ten equal parts. Is it necessary to draw in the subdivided grid lines?

Questions 5 – What assumption will you have to make about Ronnie's walk? (That he walks in a straight line.)

Answers

1 **a** 1·5 m **b** 4·9 m^2 **c** 3·25 m

2 A: John, B: Pete, C: Magnus, D: Cherry, E: Kadeja

3 **a** **i** J **ii** O **iii** R

b **i** Sports Hall **ii** Office **iii** Shop

4 **a** Bin a 084, 408 Bin b 101, 405

Bin c 111, 396 Bin d 117, 394

Bin e 132, 416

b Tap w 088, 399 Tap x 110, 399

Tap y 116, 404 Tap z 134, 404

5 Tent J

6 **a** 180 m^3 (180 000 litres)

b **i** 750 min **ii** 12.5 hours

c 10:30 am

Related lessons		Resources	
Circumference of a circle	2e	Circumference of a circle	(1088)
Constructing diagrams	8d	Reading pie charts	(1206)
Averages 1	8e	Drawing pie charts	(1207)
Averages 2	8f	Mean and mode	(1200)
Interpreting statistical diagrams	8g	Large copies of question 2 table	
Comparing distributions	8j		
Written addition and subtraction	11f		

Background

The sports day theme can be made even more real for the students if data from sports competitions in which they are involved can be used as illustrations or to replace numeric values in the questions.

A large range of mathematics is encountered in this spread broadly on the theme of statistics, including: interpreting and drawing pie charts, reading data and finding summary statistics, solving 'algebraic' problems, calculating perimeters of shapes involving circles.

Simplification

Provide students with a reminder of some of the mathematics they will need during the spread. For example,

$$\text{angle in pie chart} = \frac{\text{number in single group} \times 360^\circ}{\text{number in all groups}}$$

$$\text{circumference of circle} = \pi \times \text{diameter}$$

definitions of range, mode, median and mean.

Extension

Look again at question **7**. Can students work out the area of one running track? Encourage the use of a diagram to help support their answer. (403 m^2 to 3 sf using the pi button (or 3.14) and full calculator displays. Rounding during the intermediate steps may lead to the solution 402 m^2)

Links

Sports and the results from sports may be of interest to a large number of students who regularly follow a local football team or athletics events. A league table from the newspaper could be used to provide a contrast to that given in question **2**, while results from events at the Olympics could be analysed in discussion with other questions.

Check out http://espn.go.com/olympics/summer/2012/results for a full list of all results from London 2012.

Teaching notes

Given the breadth of knowledge being tested here it will be most useful to focus attention on those areas which are likely to cause the students most difficulty, rather than try to address all potential issues.

A majority of the class is likely to be familiar with scoring in football. Using results from the school or an international competition will allow several of the issues associated with question **2** to be discussed. In particular, cover how to interpret the results in the summary table.

Put students into groups and pose a question similar to **5**. Ask students for their ideas on how to go about solving it; did they get it right? How do they know? Several approaches are possible and it will be instructive to get students to compare their relative merits.

In question **7**, students are asked to calculate the `stagger' on a running track, is this something a mathematician should become involved in? How accurate do the distances need to be measured if times are measured to one hundredth of a second? (Assume sprinters run at 10 m/s) Distances need to be measured to at least 10 cm accuracy!

Exercise commentary

Question 1 – What fraction of the circle is taken up by each of the sports? Encourage students to measure the angle as carefully as possible. What methods do students have for finding a fraction of 48? How would you cope with a fraction answer?

Question 2 – What fraction are taking part in each of the sports? What information needs to be put on a pie chart? Encourage students to show both the name of the activity, and the number taking part.

Question 3 – The terms goals 'for' and 'against' may need explaining. Which data entries are the most useful when finding the missing values? What checks can students make against the other data values? For example, is the number of points gained correct?

Question 4 – Do you need to use both the table and scoreboard? Is the mean or mode a better estimate in this case?

Question 5 – What information does the centre target immediately give you? Can you make up any equations for the other two targets? How are the other two targets different? Can you assume the scores are integers? What is the highest/lowest score that gold/ blue could be? Encourage students to check any solution for all targets.

Question 6 –What do the two ends of the track form? What value should you take for pi? Ask students to draw a sketch showing the values used in their proposed solution.

Question 7 – Encourage students to adapt their sketch to show the effect of including an extra lane: each new lane increases the diameter by 2 m.

Answers

1 **a** Football 195° → 26 players
b Table Tennis 30° → 4 players
c Archery 75° → 10 players
d Athletics 60° → 8 players

2 Students' pie charts with following sectors

Football	150°
Table Tennis	90°
Archery	45°
Athletics	75°

3

Round 1	Row 1, Superstars	4
	Row 3, High 5	2
Round 2	Row 3, Champions	0
	Row 4, Cheetahs	7

4 **a** 9 goals
b 2 goals
c 39 ÷ 10 = 3.9 goals

5 **a** **i** 6 **ii** 2 **iii** 9
b 69 ÷ 3 = 23 points

6 **a** 251 m
b $y = 74$ m

7 **a** **i** 406.3 m **ii** 412.6 m
b They stagger the start for races which involve using curves.

Related lessons		Resources	
Angles and parallel lines	5a	Measuring angles	(1081)
Mental addition and subtraction	7c	Angle sums	(1082)
Averages 2	8f	Position and turning	(1231)
Scale drawings	12d	Mean and mode	(1200)
Written addition and subtraction	11f	Map scales	(1103)
Bearings	12f	Scale drawing	(1117)
Direct proportion	15c	Bearings	(1086)
		Proportion	(1037)
		Protractor	
		Ruler	
		OS maps	

Background

Students who are involved in the Duke of Edinburgh award scheme, Boy Scouts, Girl Guides, Woodcraft Folk, Combined Cadet Force, etc. may have direct experience of going on expeditions. Sailors and orienteerers may also have knowledge of navigation. These students' experiences of how mathematics can be applied should be used to enliven and inform classroom discussion.

The mathematics in this spread is broadly on the theme of geometry and includes giving compass bearings, measuring angles and measuring distances on scale drawings, as well as averages, time scales and finding proportions. There are direct links to the geography syllabus.

Simplification	Extension
For question **1**, consider making the weight of the students all multiples of 6 or possibly 3 to make calculation easier. For question **2**, ask students to identify with an arc the bearings they are intending to measure. Check with the teacher that they are in the correct position before measuring them.	Draw a polygon by joining the following vertices. Cliffs - Sarlat Camp – A – B – C – D – E – F – G – Cliffs. Find an approximation for the area. What shapes can you approximate with? For example, triangles FDE and ABG and trapeziums FCBG and AG 'cliffs' 'camp'.

Links

Route finding and planning can link into many different aspects of real life from walking to the shops to driving to a destination far away. Curriculum links to geography are very clear to see and other scenarios can be envisaged where map reading and calculating with angles is necessary in real life.

http://www.ordnancesurvey.co.uk/ is a good place to start exploring maps and the principles of mapping.

A link to history is provided by question **3**.

Teaching notes

In question **1c**, the mean can be thought of as a 'balance point' for the distribution of students' weights. This provides a means of checking the answer: The sum of the differences between individual students' weights and the mean should be zero. This provides a more formal definition of 'it should be in the middle'.

Question **2** has obvious links to geography with directions being specified by three-figure bearings, whilst in question **4**, angles are measured in degrees. Why are different approaches used?

A further option is to show how locations can be 'triangulated': what place is on a bearing 045° as seen from point A and 030° as seen from point B? (Castle/chateau) Can students provide their own examples, perhaps using a different base-line that requires larger angles to be measured? This could even be used as a challenge: can students produce an accurate scale drawing given the line AB and pairs of bearings for other locations? Distance can then be measured with a ruler and converted into a real-life distance using a scale; this skill is required for question **6**.

The first part of question **3** is likely to cause trouble due to the lack of a year zero – which some students might not appreciate. This is most easily clarified using small values and a number line.

Exercise commentary

Question 1 – How can the ration 6 : 1 be converted so that it changes into the persons weight? What can be done to both sides of a ratio so that it remains in the same proportions? Consider alternative ways of looking at the question. For example, for every 6 kg you weigh, you can carry 1kg. How many 6 kg make up each person?

Question 2 – Students may need reminding of the method for measuring bearings. Is it possible for students to work it out themselves from the example given in the question? How can a 180 degree angle measurer be used to measure reflex angles?

Question 3 – It might be helpful to look at the sketch of a timeline to establish that this is similar to negative numbers.

Question 4 – The terms acute, obtuse and reflex may need recapping. Encourage students to measure as accurately as possible. Ask students to consider if their answer is reasonable, have they read the angle measurer in the correct direction?

Question 5 – Suggest drawing the section MNOP out separately and labelling the angles. What angle rule is this? Extend each line to create corresponding and vertically opposite angles if need be to illustrate that OP and MN are parallel.

Question 6 – If 1 cm represents 1 m and you want answers accurate to 0.1 m, how accurately do you have to measure the lines with your ruler?

Answers

1 **a** Bart 6 kg; Gabby 7 kg; Martia 9 kg; Rick 8 kg; Jules 12 kg; Helina 6 kg
b 42 kg
c Rick

2

Section	3 fig bearing	Distance (m)
A to B	065°	330
B to C	018°	240
C to D	126°	360
D to E	354°	480
E to F	247°	340
F to G	236°	260

3 **a** 2150 + current year.
(For example, if now 2014: 2150 + 2014 = 4164)
b 122 years

4 **a** **i** 49° **ii** 64° **iii** 71°
b **i** 123° **ii** 97° **iii** 133°
c **i** 360° – 79° = 281°
ii 360° – 49° = 311°
iii 360° – 108° = 252°

5 Alternate angles are equal: $\angle$ MNO = $\angle$ NOP = 49°

6 **a** 5.8 m **b** 3.2 m **c** 4.1 m **d** 4.3 m
e 6.1 m

Related lessons		Resources	
Area of a rectangle and a triangle	2c	Area of rectangles	(1084)
Graphs of implicit functions	6e	Area of a triangle	(1129)
Real-life graphs	6f	Rotating shapes	(1115)
Transformations	9a	Rotation symmetry	(1116)
Calculators in context	11d	Symmetry	(1230)
Surface area of a prism	14c	Graph paper	
		Tracing paper	
		Calculator	

Background

The spread has a loose focus on incidents that occur in the life of Miss Perry and the students. It allows a breadth of mathematics to be covered including: finding areas, applying algebra, rotations, using systematic approaches to problem solving and the speed-distance-time relationship.

An aspect of camp life is giving awards for various types of achievement. This could be mirrored in this final spread with, for example, bronze, silver and gold awards being given to students in recognition of their 'effort', 'achievement' and 'support to others'. This ties in with a suggestion for an **extension** activity.

Simplification	Extension
For question **1**, consider giving students the net for the tent and asking them to add the dimensions onto the net. For question **2**, provide students with the 3 times table up to 3×20 and the 7 times table up to 7×10. For question **5**, consider altering the wind speed slightly from 10 m.p.h. to 42 m.p.h. This gives a journey time of 6.25 hours which is more easily seen to be 6 hours and 15 minutes.	Suppose that in question **2** you were told information such that $3A + B = 50$ and $A + 7C = 50$. How many sets of integer solutions can you find? $(A, B, C) = (15, 5, 5)$ or $(8, 26, 6)$ or $(1, 47, 7)$ Students will need to use a systematic way of listing the possibilities. Consider putting the results in a table.

Links

There are lots of problem-solving type questions and puzzles similar to the ones here that can be provided to students as 'end-of-term' activities, enrichment puzzles and maths club activities.

Some examples of number puzzles can be found at http://www.mathsisfun.com/puzzles/number-puzzles-index.html and a quick google search will certainly turn up more puzzles from other strands of mathematics.

Teaching notes

Question **1** involves finding areas. It may be instructive to ask students to explain where the formula for the area of a triangle comes from. Can they use this argument to simplify calculating the area of the two end triangles?

Question **2** should be tackled using algebra. Supply two similar simultaneous equations, for example $4A + 3B = 25$ and $A + 7B = 25$, and ask students to explain how they would solve these equations. Also ask how they could check that their answer is correct.

Question **3** may prove confusing to students given the apparent diagonal axes. It will be useful to get students to explain their methods for how to rotate a shape, drawn on a grid, through a right-angle. Do they get the same result if the same problem were posed but with the axes in a different orientation? In fact, are axes required at all? Would it make a difference if you turned the book through 45°?

Question **4**, requires students to work systematically through the possible combination of weights. Ask students to explain their methods for listing and testing the various possibilities

Question **5** involves the speed–distance–time relationship in a new form. This can be left for students to reason through what is required using common sense and experience or a simple example could be discussed to demonstrate how they should proceed.

Exercise commentary

Question 1 – Students may find it useful to draw the net of the tent and a 3D sketch showing the hidden lines. Which measurements are not needed for the calculation of the area of the triangle? Encourage students to write down their workings. What if you need a decimal number of cans of 'Seal It?

Question 2 – Ask students to suggest certain possible solutions that give the correct mathematical value and seem sensible in practice. Do you think B is smaller than A? Why? Are the diagrams drawn to scale?

Question 3 – When performing a rotation what resource could you use? (Tracing paper) What sort of triangle is the sandwich? How can you find the number of full turns from the total angle if it's over 360°?

Question 4 – To begin consider two weights, how many combinations are there? (Ten to check) And three weights? (Also ten) Does it make a difference where the weights are placed on the slide?

Question 5 – Students may need reminding of the formula for speed–distance–time. What is the effect of a head wind? How can a decimal number of hours be converted in minutes? Look at the effective use of the calculator when converting 4.583333 hr to hr and min.

Answers

1 **a** **i** 18 m^2 **ii** 3·9 m^2
b 18 m^2 + 3·9 m^2 + 3·9 m^2 = 25·8 m^2
c 6 cans

2 Carrier A holds 15 litres
Carrier B holds 5 litres

3 Students' drawings of
a Rotation through 90° clockwise
b Rotation through 270° clockwise
c 1890° = $5\frac{1}{4}$ revolutions so the same as **a**

4 8·5 kg + 9·5 kg + 19 kg

5 4 hours 35 min